£17-50

Medieval Pottery in Britain AD 900-160

Medieval Pottery in Britain AD 900-1600

Michael R. McCarthy and Catherine M. Brooks

LEICESTER UNIVERSITY PRESS   1988

First published in 1988 by Leicester University Press
Copyright © Leicester University Press 1988

Designed by Douglas Martin
Filmset in Linotron 202 Ehrhardt by Alan Sutton Publishing Ltd, Gloucester
Printed and bound in Great Britain by the Bath Press, Avon

British Library Cataloguing in Publication Data

McCarthy, Michael R. (Michael Robin)
Medieval Pottery in Britain, AD 900–1600.
1. Great Britain. Pottery, AD 900–1600
I.Title   II. Brooks, Catherine M. (Catherine Margery)
738.3'0941

ISBN 0-7185-1254-5
ISBN 0-7185-1271-5 (pbk)

In Memoriam G.E.B. and E.E. McC.

Contents

Illustrations

Acknowledgments

Preparing a book of this kind is only possible with the help, advice and support of a great many people and institutions. We wish to thank in particular Richard Coleman-Smith, Dr Chris Dyer, John Hurst, Jean Le Patourel, Steve Moorhouse and Professor Philip Rahtz, all of whom have read and commented upon one or more chapters of this book. We may not always have agreed with their comments, and we take full responsibility for what we have written, but there is no doubt that the book has benefited from their advice.

We are also extremely grateful to a large number of individuals for being so kind as to give up their time, and in some cases to provide copies of unpublished reports or theses in order to assist us; they are Lauren Adams Gilmour, Evelyn Baker, Kath Barclay, Lucy Bown, Duncan Brown, Georgie Brine, David Caldwell, Charlotte Cane, Martin Carver, Glyn Coppack, Eoin Cox, Steve Cracknell, Amanda Crowdy, Carol Cunningham, Sue Davies, Piers Dixon, Les Douch, Alec Down, Jon and Maureen Fairbrother, Mike Farley, Peter and Nita Farmer, Cynthia Gaskell Brown, Colvin and Moira Greig, Derek Hall, Adrian Havercroft, John Hawkes, Hilary Healey, Felix Holling, Nicholas Holmes, Keith Jarvis, Sarah Jennings, Philip Jones, Jeremy Knight, John Lewis, Norman MacAskill, Arthur MacGregor, Nigel Macpherson-Grant, Ailsa Mainman, Charlotte Matthews, Phil Mayes, Maureen Mellor, Trevor Miles, Bill Milligan, Sue Mills, Charlie Murray, Denis Mynard, Colm O'Brien, Clive Partridge, Terry Pearson, Mike Ponsford, Andrew Rogerson, Janet Rutter, Deborah Sawday, Steve Sell, Keith Scott, Ron Shoesmith, Mike Stokes, Jeff Taylor, Keith Wade, Gareth Watkins, Rosemary Woodland, Peter Yeoman, Jane Young.

The following institutions have also been of particular help in affording access to their collections and in the provision of photographic material: The Ashmolean Museum, Oxford, The Bodleian Library, The British Library, The British Museum, Carlisle Museum and Art Gallery, The Grosvenor Museum, Chester, The Royal Institution of Cornwall, The Herbert Art Gallery and Museum, Coventry, Derby City Museums, Guildford Museum, Oxfordshire County Museum, Woodstock, Salisbury Museum, The National Museum of Wales, The York Archaeological Trust, The Yorkshire Museum.

We would like to thank the following for providing both financial support and other invaluable resources: Carlisle City Council, The British Academy and The Society for Medieval Archaeology. The Leverhulme Trust awarded M.R. McCarthy a Research Fellowship to facilitate much of the writing of this work, and The York Archaeological Trust generously allowed C.M. Brooks to take three months' paid sabbatical leave.

One of our greatest debts of gratitude is to Helen Humphreys, who is responsible for the artwork, and without whom this work could not even have been contemplated.

Finally we must mention the cats who have helped in clearing up (and making) endless waste paper balls.

M.R.McC.
C.M.B.

Introduction

For over fifty years, the pottery of Anglo-Saxon and medieval Britain has been studied and reported on in the journals of local and national archaeological societies. For a very long time many of the most important advances were made by a distinguished quartet, the late Dr Gerald Dunning, Professor E.M. Jope, Mr John Hurst and Mrs H.E. Jean Le Patourel, all of whose work underlies not just the field of pottery studies but the discipline of medieval archaeology as a whole. These four scholars not only established the basic descriptive framework which is an essential first step in the development of any discipline, but they went further and attempted to place pottery in its context, relating it to the buildings in which it was used, to the people who created it and to wider issues of regional and international exchange.

From the 1960s the pace of research into medieval archaeology began to quicken, especially with the growth of city centre renewal schemes; these afforded unparalleled opportunities for investigating the origins and development of many towns. One result of these new opportunities was the increase in the number of professional field teams employing specialists to deal with the growing mountains of pottery. It soon became apparent that researchers were methodologically ill-equipped for the task of processing large quantities of pottery from complex multi-period urban projects. In 1975 the Medieval Pottery Research Group was founded, and almost immediately began work on producing the *Guidelines for the Processing and Publication of Medieval Pottery from Excavations* (Blake and Davey 1983), a document supported by the Department of the Environment and which provided a set of recommendations for those actively working on pottery.

It seems surprising that after all this activity, books on the subject are so few. One of the earliest to appear was Jewitt's *Ceramic Art of Great Britain*, published in 1878 and intended as a history of pottery from prehistoric times to the present day. Much of this work was understandably concerned with developments from the seventeenth to the nineteenth centuries, and it still remains an invaluable source for the period. Other works followed, notably Solon's *The Art of the Old English Potter* in 1885, but from the archaeological standpoint, Rackham's *Medieval English Pottery*, first appearing in 1948 and revised and updated by Hurst in 1972, was for a long time the only general reference work available. In 1974, Vera Evison, Henry Hodges and John Hurst produced *Medieval Pottery from Excavations*, a *Festschrift* dedicated to Gerald Dunning. This consisted of a collection of essays by ten leading scholars on aspects of ceramics between the Anglo-Saxon period and the seventeenth century, together with Dunning's formidable bibliography. Later books have included Haslam's *Medieval Pottery* (1978), a useful thumbnail sketch, Barton's *Medieval Sussex Pottery* (1979), and Grant's study of North Devon wares (1983). For a more comprehensive review of the way in which the study of medieval ceramics has developed, the reader is referred to Moorhouse's paper on the Medieval Pottery Research Group (1983c).

This book is aimed at archaeologists, historians and all students whose work may impinge upon or involve studying pottery between the late Saxon and the Tudor period. It has two broad objectives. Firstly, Part One (Chapters 1–3) considers aspects of ceramic technology and highlights some of the ways in which pottery can throw light upon matters of social or economic concern to students of the Middle Ages. We have deliberately omitted the manufacture of the technologically more advanced tin-glazed earthenware in the late 16th century. Whilst being based primarily upon archaeological data. Part One also draws attention to the potential of written sources and ethnographic material. Secondly, Part Two (Chapters 4–6) is an attempt to present a picture of the present state of knowledge in the form of a select gazetteer of sites and their main pottery types. This is based upon a series of visits made to museums, archaeological units and individual researchers as well as on published and unpublished reports.

In preparing a book like this, we are acutely aware that we are writing at a time when major changes are taking place in the directions of archaeological thinking. In Britain, these changes were heralded by the publication in 1968 of the late Dr David Clarke's *Analytical Archaeology* and the subsequent revolution brought about by the adherents of the so-called 'New Archaeology'. It is one of the archaeological tragedies of the last twenty years or so that so much useful work has been written on both sides of the Atlantic in incomprehensible jargon; this has delayed the adoption by many archaeologists, including those specializing in Roman or medieval Britain, of alternative ways of thinking about their subjects.

This present work does not follow any particular theoretical school. It is very easy to disregard such trends as providing nothing new, or telling us what we already know in a different language, and to take comfort in established ideas. Yet we cannot be dismissive of current theoretical thought, if only because we are still not equipped to cope with the huge amounts of data being recovered. It is quite clear, for instance, that despite the important contributions by Moorhouse, as in the Sandal castle report (1983b), we are still a long way from using pottery in the way that prehistorians or anthropologists use their data in reconstructing patterns of social or economic behaviour. Indeed, it is a matter for concern that students of Saxon and medieval pottery in Britain are not exploiting the very fertile grounds for ideas present in the vast ethnographic literature on ceramics.

Pottery is important because, as Le Patourel has said, 'it is culture specific' (1979b: 86), and it is the commonest artifact known in medieval Britain. Furthermore, 'pots are not simply by-products of behaviour. They are actively involved in social strategies. The patterning evident in pottery burial and settlement is complementary to, and yet an effective part of patterns in the social domain' (Hodder 1982: 158). On a very broad scale, and of fundamental importance in British archaeology, is the ability to link ceramic trends to great events (Adams W.Y. 1979; Brooks R.L. 1982): the Roman and Norman Conquests, the Anglo-Saxon and Scandinavian incursions. At a different level are the questions related to the production of stereotypes (Foster 1966; Rice 1981), and the implications for industrial specialization and social structure. The Late Saxon period is a prime candidate for such a line of questioning. Equally important to the excavator is the question of the *nature* of the archaeological deposits in terms of depth, surviving organic fraction, floor and midden deposits, and how these factors may affect the way in which we view the ceramic component.

If we are to exploit these possibilities, we have to learn to think laterally and to get away from the conventional approach of description, dating, and the idea that if it is not local it must be traded. We must also be prepared to abandon the idea that, because pottery has been recovered during the course of an excavation, it is somehow invested with qualities and an importance which require every sherd to be counted, weighed and identified to form and fabric. This means that we have to pay particular attention to what it is we want from the pottery, and how the various presences and absences can be interpreted in the light of the small finds assemblages, the structural remains and so on. Within this very general research strategy, the study of fabrics and form have their place. Identification of fabrics or wares, that is to say the analysis of the clay body in terms of its texture, hardness, colour, mineral component and additives, is vitally important in enabling us to isolate production centres and suggest market areas. The application of scientific techniques such as petrological thin sectioning or heavy mineral analysis, for example, techniques pioneered in Britain by Dr David Peacock on prehistoric pots, has already demonstrated its potential for medieval studies through the work of Dr Richard Hodges and Dr Alan Vince.

Detailed studies of form and decoration such as those attempted in other countries (Shepard 1956; Plog 1980) or periods (Clarke D.L. 1970) have not been regarded as a priority by students of medieval pottery in Britain. There may well be scope for the use of mathematical models and computer-assisted programmes in the analysis of form and decoration, especially for describing the often vaguely defined 'traditions' and contributing to an explanation of culture change. A ceramic tradition is the repeated occurrence of specific traits in space and time as, for example, in the East Anglian Thetford ware or the southern Surrey White wares traditions. Here as in many other instances, a number of production sites, sometimes spread over considerable distances, seem to produce pottery very similar in both fabric and form. The use of sophisticated analytical techniques now readily available could be used to see whether patterning apparent to the intuitive eye can be substantiated by a different and more rigorous means of scrutiny.

If we can place traditions on a sounder basis, we must then ask the more difficult question of what they represent. In 1963 Professor Jope attempted such a study, but concluded that the distribution of his ceramic traditions could not be correlated with those represented by other aspects of medieval society. This conclusion is not dissimilar to that arrived at by the study of African tribes in Kenya (Hodder 1979), and warns us that in the definition of ceramic traditions we should be alert to the work of both anthropologists and archaeologists working in other parts of the world.

The aspects of form and decoration that have received the most attention are those regarded as chronologically sensitive. Pot rims lend themselves to elaboration in both a decorative and functional sense, and these are usually seized upon as providing the dates so avidly sought by excavators. This is quite understandable, but many reports are still being written where, despite the warnings of Hurst (1962–3) over twenty-five years ago, the provision of dates seems to be the sole reason for work on the pottery. Dating archaeological deposits is clearly very important, and the increase in urban excavations since the mid-1960s has resulted in the recovery of a number of long stratified sequences, parts of which can sometimes be attributed with confidence to documented events, as in the case of the Norwich fire of 1507. In other cases dendrochronology (for example at Coppergate, York), coin sequences (Flaxengate, Lincoln) or a combination of dating techniques (the London waterfront sites) help to provide an absolute chronology.

These sites, and others where the deposits are only relatively dated, will come to be seen as regional yardsticks against which the majority of excavations with small assemblages and shorter stratigraphic sequences can be assessed. Indeed it is often precisely those excavations, where the quantities are limited and the conditions for preservation not conducive to the survival of the organic fraction, that raise questions about the role of ceramics in society. Tackling problems of how much pottery was in use, where it has all gone, whether it was used inside or outside the buildings, and how the assemblage compares with those from neighbouring sites, is likely to be much more informative about medieval peasant society than a brief discussion on dating and bare lists of fabrics. The emphasis, in other words, should be on explanation.

Rackham wrote in 1948:

> The definitive archaeological treatise [on medieval pottery], on historical lines, has yet to be written, and would entail not only a harmonisation of all the

reports scattered over a period of more than a century through the transactions and proceedings of antiquarian societies, but also a close comparative study of specimens preserved in museums, large and small, and other depositories, over the length and breadth of the country. (1st edn: 3)

If such a task was difficult to contemplate then, it would be impossible today, as we are only too well aware. We hope, however, that the present work will provide an introduction to the study of medieval ceramics, and encourage researchers to consider pottery in its wider context, by making use of other disciplines where appropriate, in the search for explanations.

Part One

Chapter 1   Pottery Technology

Principles of manufacture

The raw materials essential for the production of pottery are clay, water and fuel; fillers and decorative materials may also be used. Pottery is the product achieved when clay is heated to a high enough temperature to drive off the water of crystallization, chemically locked up within the structure of the clay crystals, at between 450°C and 700°C. The clay goes through an irreversible process and its physical properties are changed; it becomes hard and water resistant, and its colour is probably altered, depending on the amount of oxidization or reduction. If the heating is continued, the temperature will rise until the clay particles begin to melt and coalesce; the material is then said to be vitrified. If this happens at a temperature above 1200°C the product is known as stoneware. Unvitrified pottery is known as earthenware.

Clays are formed from decomposed rocks, and their properties depend on the nature of the parent rock, chemical impurities, and the effects (in what are called secondary or sedimentary clays) of being transported and eventually deposited by wind, water or ice. The plasticity of a clay depends on the size of the clay particles, the finest clays being the most plastic (known as 'long' or 'fat' clays); these are typically secondary clays, the weathering processes reducing the size of the clay particles. Primary clays, found in their places of origin, are usually of low plasticity ('short' or 'lean' clays), and white to buff in colour (Rhodes 1957).

The workability of a clay depends on its plasticity and strength; it must take a shape fairly easily, stand up to the stress of stretching, and support its own weight, when shaped, without collapsing. It is common to improve the workability of clay as dug by treating it in various ways. Clay often contains non-plastic inclusions such as sand, shale and rock fragments which detract from its plasticity. While a certain proportion of non-plastic material adds strength to a clay by providing friction between the particles, and aids the drying process, an excess of such inclusions, particularly large ones, will make the clay hard to work. Unwanted inclusions can be removed by sieving when the clay is in a dry and powdered state, by picking out by hand, or by mixing the clay with water and allowing it to settle out, the heavier particles falling to the bottom first.

The strength of a clay is improved by bringing the clay particles closer together, which involves compression and removal of any air. This can be achieved by vigorous wedging or trampling, or the use of a pugmill. Ageing, by storing the clay in a damp state, has the same effect; water slowly penetrates between the clay particles and breaks them down into smaller particles, which become compressed under the weight of the stack of clay. This may follow an earlier stage of breaking down the clay by weathering using frost action. Ageing is often combined with souring, which involves the breakdown of organic matter in the clay by bacteriological action. The decomposition releases amino acids which flocculate the fine particles and create a colloidal gel; this improves the plasticity of the clay.

Before the clay is worked, non-plastic materials may also be added to those already present in the clay; these are known as fillers, grogs, openers or temper. Among these materials are quartz sand, ground shell, rock fragments, grog (fired clay or pottery, ground small), chaff, grass and dung. The amount added depends on the plasticity of the clay and the purpose for which it is required. Fillers improve the strength of clay, reduce plasticity and enable the clay to dry out quicker with less shrinkage both before and during firing. Clay used for making tiles, for example, is often coarse with a high proportion of sand or grog; the tile-making process does not require plasticity, and the high shrinkage rate which plasticity entails would here be a great disadvantage. Fillers are usually added as the potter does the final preparation of the clay prior to forming vessels, by wedging or kneading to compress the clay and expel air, which would otherwise cause the pot to shatter during firing.

Pottery vessels can be formed in a variety of ways. They can be shaped by hand, by pinching out of a lump of clay, or they may be built up by adding coils or rings of clay to a base, and smoothing them together. Sheets of clay can be rolled out and cut into slabs and joined together, or pressed into moulds. Vessels may also be thrown on a potter's wheel. A single pot may be constructed using one or more of these techniques. Another method is known as 'paddle and anvil'; this involves beating the outer surface of a vessel with a flat tool while supporting the inside with the hand or a smooth shaped 'anvil' of stone or wood; it can be used to enlarge and thin out a pot built by hand-modelling or pinching out of a lump of clay, a coil- or ring-built pot, or a wheel-thrown vessel. In India, for example, pots that have first been thrown on the wheel are then further enlarged and shaped by beating with paddle and anvil (Fig. 1). Hand-made vessels can also be thinned and pulled up by drawing up with a rib, scraping it upwards over the outer surface while again supporting the wall with a hand on the inside.

The way in which a pot has been formed, however, may be obliterated to a greater or lesser extent by the final finishing of the vessel. Surfaces may be wiped and scraped, for example, and walls and bases thinned down by paring. To the basic vessel shape may be added features such as feet, spouts and handles. These can be made by hand shaping, by moulding or by wheel

Fig. 1   Use of paddle and anvil technique in India.
1, beater. 2, anvils. 3, potter enlarging the pot. 4, 5, baked clay and wooden bases for
beating. 6, potter beating on a baked clay base. 7–10, stages in the formation of a
pot: 7, as removed from the wheel; 8–10, changing shape of the same pot as it is
beaten. (After Saraswati and Behura 1966)

throwing. They are then attached to the pot, which may have been allowed to
dry out slightly and harden. Once attached, they are usually bonded to the body
of the pot by smoothing on to it. Attachment may be by luting with water or slip;
a stronger join may be made by pressing the vessel wall out into the clay of the
addition, or by forming a clay dowel on the inner face of the feature to be
attached and pushing it through the vessel wall.

Decoration may be added when the vessel is being made, during drying or
before firing. There are many ways to decorate a pot, most involving fairly
simple equipment. The surface may be incised, combed or impressed;

impressions may be made with the fingers, or with an implement such as a stick or bone, a roulette wheel or a stamp. Strips, pellets or pads of clay may be added to the vessel, as may free-standing ornament; these clay additions may also be incised, combed or impressed. Other forms of decoration involve the elaboration of techniques for finishing the surface of a vessel, such as burnishing and slipping. Burnishing is done by rubbing the leather-hard surface of a pot with a tool such as a smooth pebble or bone to produce a shiny surface by compression of the clay particles; this gives an attractive shiny finish and a much less porous surface. Slip is a mixture of fine clay and water which may be added by dipping, painting or wiping the surface of a pot to give a smooth finish and conceal any protruding inclusions in the clay; if the slip is made from a clay of a different colour to the pot, the contrasting colours may become a decorative feature. Patterns scratched or incised through a contrasting slip are known as sgraffito decoration.

Some types of decoration may also have a functional aspect; thumbed applied strips, for example, may be used to strengthen a vessel at a particularly weak point. Glaze, however, is used primarily as decoration on medieval pottery, and only occasionally has a functional aspect. The only glaze known to medieval potters in Britain was lead glaze, which is a glass formed by the reaction of lead oxide and silica, either the silica naturally present in the clay body or silica added in the form of quartz sand or ground calcined flint. Glaze may be formed by adding dry materials from which the glaze modifier, lead oxide, is to be derived, directly to the surface of the vessel; it may also be applied as a suspension of fine particles in water, with or without an adhesive. Either of the two lead oxides, litharge or red lead, may be used, or white lead (basic lead carbonate) or galena (lead sulphide ore). The raw materials that form the glaze can also be fused (fritted) in a crucible to form a glass or frit which is then pulverized, mixed with water and applied to the pot. If the raw glaze is applied as a powder, it results in a blotchy appearance with a number of small glaze-filled craters where larger lumps of the material have etched into the body of the pot. A smoother, better quality glaze results from its application in suspension.

The colour of the finished glaze depends on the colour of the clay at the surface of the pot, with which it has reacted, or the addition of oxides to the glaze itself. When fired in an oxidizing atmosphere, that is one with a surplus of oxygen, a clay high in iron will turn red, and one low in iron will be white or pale buff. When fired in a reducing atmosphere, that is one with much carbon monoxide and little or no oxygen, a clay high in iron will turn black or dark grey, and one low in iron will be pale grey. Organic matter within the clay will remain as carbon as there is no oxygen to burn it out, which will also darken the colour of the pot. A lead glaze on an oxidized surface will vary from pale yellow in the case of low iron clays to amber or brown with high iron clays. On a reduced surface it will vary from pale yellowish-green on a low iron clay to dark olive green on a high iron clay.

The decorative effect of a lead glaze can be enhanced by the use of colourants to achieve more than one colour on the same pot. The most common colourants used by medieval potters were copper, which gives a rich apple-green to dark green colour, and iron to give reddish-brown or brown. Copper could be added in the form of copper or brass filings ground down, or as copper oxide. Iron could be added as ground iron oxide, iron ore or as high iron clay.

Before a pot can be fired, it must be thoroughly dried to prevent water in the clay turning to steam in the kiln and shattering the pot. Drying must be slow and even or cracking will occur as the drier parts, which have lost most water, are subject to greater shrinkage. Temperature, atmospheric humidity and movement of air past the pot are factors affecting the rate of drying. The presence of non-plastic inclusions in the clay can speed the drying process by enabling the water to migrate to the surface to evaporate; as the gaps between the clay particles close, it becomes increasingly difficult for the remaining water to migrate. When this water, known as the water of plasticity, has dried out, the clay particles have contact with each other and generate friction, and the pot is known as 'leather hard'. It still contains a small amount of water in the pores, but it cannot easily be reshaped to any great extent.

The earliest stage of firing involves a slow and gradual rise in temperature to drive off the remaining water in the pores of the clay; the water may be turned into steam and shatter the pot if the rise in temperature is too sharp. This period of firing is known as water smoking. The temperature is then raised to drive off the water of crystallization, chemically bound within the clay structure; the ceramic change takes place between 450°C and 700°C. Here again the temperature must be controlled or steam will be generated. Finally the temperature is raised to the 'maturing point' of the ware, that is the temperature at which it produces the densest structure without sintering or vitrifying, below the melting point of the body. The 'maturing point' of a glaze, however, is slightly above its melting point, to allow it to melt and run together.

Pottery may be fired in an open hearth, a bonfire, or a 'clamp' kiln which is little more than a bonfire. Greater control of firing conditions can be achieved with a kiln structure, however. After the firing, the pottery must be cooled slowly, as too-rapid cooling, or the impact of cold air, may cause the pots to split or flake; this is known as dunting. If this happens the pots join the mass of wasters, or defective pottery, which characterize the rubbish heaps of potteries. Shattering of pots through generation of steam has already been noted; this also occurs if the clay has been poorly wedged, and air pockets remain within the clay to expand on heating. Warping of pots within the kiln may occur if there is uneven distribution of heat within the kiln, and there may be sagging if the pots are fired above their maturing point and so allowed partly to melt.

The manufacture of medieval pottery

A. RAW MATERIALS

A limited amount of evidence is obtainable from pottery production sites regarding the raw materials. Occasionally dumps of potting clay have been identified which may be compared with local sources of clay. Sometimes there is direct evidence for glazing materials, as at Chilvers Coton, Nuneaton, and the kinds of fuel used in the kilns.

More evidence can be obtained from studying the pottery products themselves. Scientific techniques such as thin section, heavy mineral and neutron activation analyses, by identifying the kind of clay used and the nature of the inclusions, whether naturally present in the clay or deliberately added, can be used to suggest provenances for the raw materials. In some cases sources can be identified precisely by these techniques, for example the origin of syenite inclusions in Potters Marston ware, which could be pinned down to an outcrop less than a mile from the production centre at Potters Marston, Leicestershire (Vince 1984c: 38–9). For the mass of medieval pottery with predominantly quartz sand inclusions, however, such detailed provenancing is not possible. Identification of fillers can in some instances be misleading when it comes to provenance studies; an early pottery type at Worcester has been found to be tempered with Inferior Oolite from the Cotswolds, but the pots were probably not made there. They are thought to be the products of local Worcester potters using stone chippings and waste from construction work being carried out in Inferior Oolite at Worcester cathedral during the eleventh and twelfth centuries (Morris 1980 a and b).

Historical documents which mention potters are often concerned with the rentals they are paying for the right to extract clay and take fuel. At Longbridge Deverill in Wiltshire, for example, the thirteenth-century potters were tenants of holdings of four acres or less. If they made pots for a full year, they were to pay 7d, if for half a year, 3½d, and this payment may have been for the wood they took as fuel. In addition to this, the potters had to pay 4d for clay if they took it from the lord's land, and 2d if they took it from their own (Le Patourel 1968: 105). Taking clay from the lord's land meant in practice taking it from moor, waste or common. There are indications that some clay-pits were originally on the peasants' crofts, but the better clay on many crofts must have been worked out at a fairly early date and alternative sources would have become necessary.

There was an increased use during the fourteenth and fifteenth centuries of clay-pits in the open fields. At West Cowick, Yorkshire, when the cost of a licence rose sharply in the second half of the fourteenth century, the increase is associated with a new formula specifying that the payment was for clay and sand taken in the moor, whereas previously there had been a simple licence to dig clay, implying perhaps that this had been done on the potters' own lands. If the crofts were worked out and taking clay on the common was forbidden, as at Harlow, or expensive, the potters' options were to buy clay or take it from their own strips in the common fields, and examples of both are known. At Heworth, Co. Durham, clay pits in the common fields had to be filled in when the field lay fallow in order not to present a hazard to grazing animals. At Toynton All Saints, Lincolnshire, Juliana Tagg in 1364 rented two crofts from the lord for a fixed number of years in order to dig and sell clay for making pottery to whomever she pleased. Occasionally there is evidence for the size of clay-pits. Harlow clay-pits were of two kinds, 'wells' four feet square, and long narrow ditches from two to four feet wide and up to four perches long. At Toynton, pits of up to twenty feet square are recorded (*ibid.*: 114).

The hazards represented by open clay-pits, which were easily flooded, have been noted, and complaints were frequently made against potters in manorial and burgess courts for not filling in pits. Sometimes the roads themselves were dug up for clay; at Burslem in 1549 Richard Daniel came before the courts for digging in 'the King's Way', and in 1533 the Wakefield Burgess Court ordered that 'the Cuppers from henceforth shall get no clay within eight yeards of the hye waye side' (Brears 1971: 84). Successive Yorkshire potters appear to have taken little notice of such strictures, for at the West Riding Quarter Sessions of 1680–1 the potters were accused of 'digging and getting of clay [on the common] for making pipes, potts, and other earthenwares, and making pitts and holes near ye hye waye to the danger of travellers' (*ibid.*: 87). Similarly, post-medieval potters in the Verwood area were frequently arraigned before the manor court in Cranbourne for failing to fill up their abandoned clay pits and for damaging and obstructing the highway between Cranbourne and Fordingbridge (Young 1979: 110). In some places these dangerous clay-pits may in fact have been fenced off from the fields, as has been suggested for the area west of Nuneaton and Chilvers Coton where clay-pits are generally sited along possibly medieval hedgelines (Gooder 1984: 8).

Ethnographic studies can be useful in shedding light on the interpretation of archaeological data. Ethnographic information on obtaining raw materials for pottery-making has to be treated cautiously, however, as for the most part it is derived from societies which have different attitudes to rights over mineral and plant resources, rentals and taxes to those prevalent in medieval Britain. Nevertheless, it is interesting to note that the preferred territory of exploitation for clay and tempering materials is 1km or less (Arnold 1985). It seems that potters are willing to travel up to one day's distance for clay. Of a sample of 111 societies, the distance to the clay source ranged from less than 1km to 50km, with the preferred territory of exploitation occurring at 1km. Some 33 per cent of the distances travelled were 1km or less, and 84 per cent of the distances were 7km or less. For a sample of thirty-one societies for which data concerning distances to temper resources were available, distances from less than 1km to 25km have been recorded, with the majority of the sample, 52 per cent, obtaining their temper at 1km or less, and 97 per cent obtaining it at 9km or less (*ibid.*: fig. 2.5). The distances which potters are prepared to travel to paint, slip and glaze resources, on the other hand, are much greater; quantities of these materials per pot are also much smaller. Of a sample of thirty-six communities, 36 per cent obtained their slips and paints at a distance of less than 10km, and this range is probably the preferred territory of exploitation; 57 per cent obtained their slips at 30km or less. Some, however, travelled up to 880km to acquire such materials (*ibid.*: fig. 2.6).

Such statistics compare fairly well with those we can assume for medieval Britain from the limited archaeological and historical evidence. The dramatic drop in modern communities whose potters travel more than 1km to clay and temper sources suggests that costs increase rapidly after 1km and that at greater distances exploitation of clay and temper resources becomes increasingly less economic (*ibid.*: 54–5). In the case of the few groups who do travel long distances to clay and temper, most use transport, either animal- or engine-powered, and this probably reflects the modification of the original economic system in existence when pottery-making began. This modification often occurs when local supplies of the raw materials are exhausted.

The evidence of post-medieval country potteries in Britain suggests that clay for general purposes was not carted for more than four or five kilometres, but clay for a particular purpose, such as making slip, would be carted much further. In the early 1840s, for example, a potter working at the Bishop Waltham potteries had to take his waggon over 43km to Farnham Park to obtain a supply of white clay for slipping the interiors of his milk pans (Brears 1971: 87).

B.   CLAY PREPARATION

Little evidence has been recovered from kiln sites for the preparation of clay. At Olney Hyde, Buckinghamshire, a large paved clay-pit was probably used to store and settle clay before it was taken away for final working. Small stone-lined pits were also found at the site, and are also known from Lyveden; these may have been used for sedimentation or storage of clay. The sixteenth-century complex at Bourne, Lincolnshire, had a large pit, interpreted as a clay puddling pit, in an open-ended structure attached to the potter's workshop (Moorhouse 1981: 104).

Study of the medieval potter's products shows that there was a wide range of levels of preparation of clay; this was probably determined by the characteristics of the clay as dug, the products to be made, the method of manufacture and the competence of the worker. Thin-section analysis can reveal how well mixed a clay was, as well as what kind of inclusions were added and in what frequency, although sometimes it is difficult to be sure which inclusions are added and which are naturally present in the clay. Generally speaking, there is more variety in the earlier part of the medieval period than in the later, with great contrasts between the coarse flint- and quartz-tempered hand-made scratch-marked wares of southern England, the relatively soft shell-tempered wares in East Anglia and the south and east Midlands, and the well-fired competently-thrown Stamford fabrics with very fine quartz sand grains. By the late Middle Ages, when wheel-throwing is almost universal, the majority of fabrics have quartz sand as their main inclusions. Bricks and tiles are, as might be expected, generally much coarser than pottery fabrics.

Sometimes clays of differing composition were used in the same pot; there are wares in which clay with more frequent and coarser inclusions than that used for jug bodies was used to make their handles. Handles are thicker than jug walls, and their longer drying time would have been cut by the use of the coarser fabric mixture.

There is little historical evidence for clay preparation by potters, probably because their craft was so lowly that they did not achieve guild status until the late medieval period, and so had no written records. The records of the fifteenth-century potters' guild in Bergen op Zoom, Netherlands (Weijs *et al.* 1970), which give details of the craft down to the sizes of clay balls required to make specific pots, have no equivalent in this country. Some classes of medieval pottery, however, do appear to be standardized in size (for example, the small jugs from Cheam), and this may indicate the use of similar prescribed measurements in preparing the balls of clay for the thrower.

Tilers, on the other hand, became subject to municipal regulations and acquired guild status at an earlier date. In 1468 the tilers of London successfully petitioned for their restoration to the status of a craft with leave to elect wardens, on the ground that tiles were being made so badly that they only lasted three or four years instead of forty or fifty. They laid down that

> the clay thereof shulde be diged and caste at Mighelmasse and soo lye open to Cristmas thanne next folowing, and thanne to be turned and caste agen wherby the marle and chalke shulde breke out like as chalkestones and cloddes liying in the frost are woned to doo. And thanne in the March thanne next ensuyng thereof shulde be made tyles goode and profitable like as it have been of olde tyme. (Salzman 1923: 176)

These representations were evidently borne in mind when it was considered necessary in 1477 to pass an Act of Parliament to regulate the manufacture of tiles (*ibid.*: 176). By this Act it was provided that the clay to be used should be dug, or cast, by 1 November, that it should be stirred and turned before the beginning of February, and not made into tiles before March, so as to ensure its being properly seasoned. Care was to be taken to avoid any admixture of chalk, marl or stones. Some medieval potters no doubt equally appreciated the value of weathering their clay over the winter months, and the importance of removing stones, particularly calcareous ones. If these are not removed, they decompose during firing to produce pockets of quicklime within the clay, which will absorb water from the air, expand and so cause flaking of the pot.

References to filler or temper are few, one example being that of the West Cowick potters already mentioned who had to pay for clay and sand, quartz sand being the main filler in the Humber wares they made. Grog as a filler is also occasionally mentioned, its qualities being particularly appreciated for the manufacture of industrial pottery such as crucibles which had to withstand high temperatures. Eraclius, in the late twelfth- or thirteenth-century collection of recipes known as *De coloribus et artibus Romanorum*, describes the making of grog for tempering potting clay:

> Take some potter's clay as strong as you can find. Put it either in a kiln with other pots where it will bake with a slow fire, or in another kiln until it is quite red. When it has cooled put it in a pot and pound it until it is quite pulverized. Then take some water and add it to this powder; pour all of this into another pot and let it stand for a day. After this throw away the water, take the residue, mix it with clay which is free of sand in the proportion of two parts to three for the very strong clay mentioned above. Pound the lot with a pestle. You can then make any sort of pot you like. (de Boüard 1974: 68–9).

Theophilus in his *De diversis artibus*, written in the twelfth century, describes the making of crucibles using grog as a filler:

> Take fragments of old crucibles that have previously been used for melting copper or brass and crush them into tiny pieces on a stone. Then take clay from which earthenware pots are made. . . Take any small pot and fill it twice with the raw clay and three times with the burnt clay. . . Put them together into a large pot and pour warm water over them; then knead them vigorously with hammers and with your hands until the mixture is completely tenacious (1979: 142–3)

Much of the ethnographic evidence suggests that potting clay is used almost straight after collection, after perhaps a few days. In the Mediterranean world and Middle East, clay often arrives at the workplace in a dry state, and the lumps must be beaten out with a simple wooden implement. After this it is sieved, and then placed into a tank of water and left for a few days. It is then kneaded on a clean surface and the filler added (e.g. Whitehouse 1984: 15–16). In India, clay is usually dried in the sun and then pulverized and sieved to remove impurities; after this it may be further cleaned by a process of sedimentation if it contains large amounts of impurities. A third method of cleaning clay can be used when the clay is dug out in large wet clods; the potter slices the clods with a sickle to detect and remove unwanted inclusions (Saraswati and Behura 1966: 41–3). Some potters allow the wet clay to sour for about eight to ten days until it starts to stink; then it is churned and sifted, the clay paste is slowly dried and kneaded by hand and foot (*ibid.*: 43). Ash, sand, sawdust and animal dung are commonly used as temper, the mixing usually being done when the materials are dry. The clay mixture is then allowed to absorb water for some time, and then kneaded using a small quantity of sand or ash to prevent it sticking to the mixing surface (*ibid.*: 43–7). In some areas, different kinds of temper are used in the preparation of the clay for different parts of a vessel (e.g. deBoer and Lathrap 1979: 116–21).

Climatic conditions in Britain are obviously very different to those in most places where the ethnographic evidence has been gathered, and so are the problems of processing potting clay. A greater understanding of how medieval potters may have prepared their clay can perhaps be gained from 'ethnographic' descriptions of post-medieval country potters in Britain, who inherited the medieval tradition. The Staffordshire potters of the late seventeenth century, for instance, prepared their clay in fairly simple fashion by soaking, beating and picking out impurities:

> They prepare the clay by steeping it in water in a square pit, till it be of a due consistence; then they bring it to their beating board, where with a long spatula they beat it till it be well mix't; then being first made into great squarish rolls, it is brought to the wageing board, where it is slit into flat thin pieces with a wire, and the least stones or gravel pick't out of it; This being done, they wage it, i.e. knead or mould it like bread, and make it into round balls proportionable to their work, and then 'tis brought to the wheel... (Plot 1686: 123)

At the Verwood potteries, Dorset, in the late nineteenth century, the raw lumps of clay were soaked in water in a shallow pit in the corner of the pottery building for about three days, then spread on a sand-coated brick floor. Here it was worked by treading with bare feet, and stones and other impurities removed. The sand was thus incorporated into the body of the clay. The treader used one stick to steady himself, and another with a nail in the end as a tool for cutting the clay into strips which were then rolled up. This process of sanding, treading and rolling was carried out three times, after which the clay was passed through a hand-turned pugmill. It was then weighed into balls of various sizes, according to the types of pots required (Young 1979: 111). Despite the introduction of the mechanical pugmill from the early eighteenth century, trampling clay with the feet seems to have been fairly widespread. Some potters, such as the Buckley workers, used bare feet while others in northern England wore heavy clogs. This process was often carried out after blunging the clay (breaking it down in water by mechanical means), removing the stones and impurities, and restoring the liquid clay to a thick, workable consistency by evaporation (Brears 1971: 88–92).

C. FORMING THE VESSEL

The evidence for manufacturing techniques from kiln sites is fairly scanty. Potters' equipment has only occasionally been recognized. Socketed stones found at Limpsfield, Surrey, for example, may have been the bases for the pivots of potters' wheels, although they might equally have had other functions such as door pivot stones; a similar stone was recovered from the kiln site at Olney Hyde, Buckinghamshire. Most of the evidence for potters' tools comes from Lyveden, Northamptonshire, where several types were found in and around the potters' workshops. A number of knives from Lyveden are thought to have been used in the pottery-making process rather than for domestic purposes, and worked antler tines were probably used for piercing the bung holes in cisterns and also for stabbing the backs of thick strap handles. A large number of sheep's tibiae and metapodials were perhaps used as templates for forming rim profiles, and bone was made into tools to decorate the pottery.

Some buildings have been identified as workshops, for example at Lyveden, Olney Hyde, Laverstock and Bourne (Moorhouse 1981). Some of these may have been rather slight structures, and open-sided workshops may be a possibility in some cases, as depicted in Agricola's sixteenth-century work *De re metallica* where a potter is making industrial pottery for use in iron working (Fig. 11 No. 4; Salzman 1923: 166).

The best evidence for methods of manufacture comes from the pottery itself, although in many cases finishing techniques can remove all signs of the preliminary shaping processes. While many examples of hand-made pots show signs of their coil or ring construction in the fracture, either as clearly visible lines where the coils or rings have not been smoothed well together or by the alignment of inclusions to form a pattern of wavy lines, wheel-thrown vessels are usually distinguished by characteristic rilling marks on the interior and regular alignment of inclusions (Fig. 2). The distinctions are not always clear-cut, however. Some vessels are considered to have been hand-made and then finished, by wiping, trimming or other means, while being turned round on some kind of turntable or device rotated by hand. When competently done, this can leave a finished product which resembles a wheel-thrown vessel. Pottery workers are not always in agreement about techniques of manufacture in some instances because of these difficulties.

Of the hand-made medieval pottery, not all is necessarily constructed by building up coils or rings of clay. The round-based cooking pots of scratch-marked type, for example, may well have been made by the paddle and anvil technique. The shape naturally produced by this technique is round-based. Such beating out will align the particles and inclusions within the clay so that they lie parallel to the surfaces, and obliterate any traces of coils or rings; this can be seen by visual examination of sherds, by thin-section analysis or by radiography (Rye 1977). The lack of visible coils has led to the suggestion that the Laverstock round-based cooking pots, for example, were made on a slow wheel (Musty *et al.* 1969: 101), but this possibility now seems less likely to be the only one, in view of the ethnographic evidence.

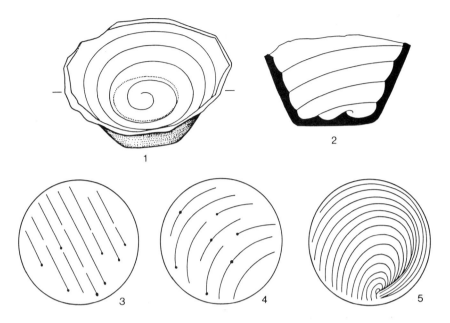

Fig. 2   Markings on wheel-thrown pots.
1, 2, spiral grooves and ridges on the interior of the base.
3–5, cutting-off marks on flat bases: 3, straight parallel lines indicate the vessel was stationary; 4, curved parallel marks indicate the vessel was rotating slowly; 5, spiral pattern indicates the vessel was rotating rapidly. (After Rye 1981)

In a wheel-thrown pot, the pressures on the clay are different from those involved in hand-forming, and these can also be seen in radiographs (Fig. 3). The inclusions always orient themselves at right angles to the direction of the force applied to the clay, which varies according to manufacturing technique. The presence of rilling, or fine horizontal grooves and ridges caused by the coarser particles in the clay and irregularities of the potter's hands, is often an indication of wheel-throwing, although pots finished by hand-rotation ('wheel-finished') may also show something of the same effect.

Slab-forming could be used for vessels such as dripping dishes. Moulding may also have been used in the manufacture of some medieval pots; certainly the technique was known in making crucibles, for example. Theophilus instructs the reader to 'take a round piece of wood and cut it to the size that you want the crucible to have [inside]. . . Shape a crucible upon this and, after it has been shaped, coat it at once with dry ashes and so put it close to the fire until it is dried' (1979: 143).

Some pots were piece-formed or made using more than one technique, for example some of the Northampton ware from St Peter's Street, Northampton,

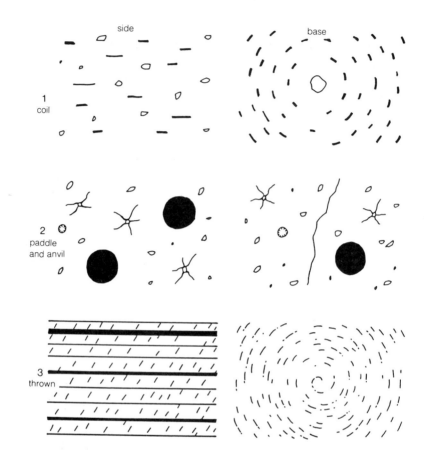

Fig. 3 Schematic appearance of radiographs of pots made in different ways.
1, coil-built. 2, paddle and anvil made. 3, wheel-thrown. (After Rye 1977)

which had hand-built bases, probably coiled, and wheel-thrown upper parts
(McCarthy 1979: 226). Some at least of the round-based Laverstock cooking
pots had their rims made from an extra ring of clay added after the main shape
had been completed, for example. The same method of rim manufacture has
been suggested for sand-tempered coil-built cooking pots of the eleventh and
twelfth centuries in east Yorkshire and north Lincolnshire (Hayfield 1980: 31).
Examples of bases being made separately and added to vessels are also known,
as for example in the Late Saxon shelly ware made in the Silver Street kiln,
Lincoln (Gilmour *et al.* forthcoming) and in the case of jugs in north
Lincolnshire (Hayfield 1980: 34–5).

The final stage in shaping the body of the vessel was forming the rim and
finishing the base. Rims were sometimes shaped by the use of simple templates,
as has been suggested at Lyveden for example; the standardized rim forms of

Saxo-Norman wheel-thrown cooking pots may also have been made using templates. Otherwise they were simply formed by the potter's fingers as the pot was rotated, either by hand or on a wheel. The vessel was then cut from the wheel with a needle, string or wire, or removed from the surface on which it had been formed. Although some vessels were left with flat bases, many were given convex or 'sagging' bases, thus obliterating the 'cheese-wire' marks typical of removal from the potter's wheel. This may have been achieved by pushing the base out from inside, or by trimming the outside and perhaps also shaving clay away from the inside (Fig. 4). Trimming the outside could also be done on the wheel, by inverting the vessel when dry, securing it with clay and shaving it while rotating. This served to trim the thickness of the base to something closer to the thickness of the walls, thus ensuring more even drying.

The function of the convex base is not fully understood. It had the effect of making the angle between wall and base more obtuse and so reducing stress at this point which can cause cracking during drying and firing; the base shrinks

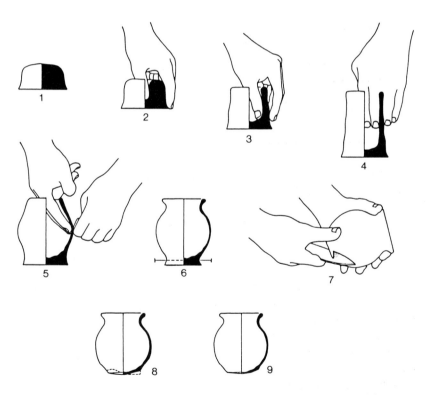

Fig. 4 Stages in the throwing and finishing of a pot with sagging base. (After van der Leeuw 1975)

most in a horizontal direction, the wall in a vertical direction. Flat-based pots were made successfully, however, so this shape was not essential to prevent cracking. It might be argued that this shape of base would be well suited to a cooking pot as the more even thickness and obtuse angle between wall and base might withstand the heat of the cooking fire better, and the greater surface area of the base might be more efficient in transmitting heat for cooking. This would not, however, explain the widespread popularity of convex bases on non-culinary vessels such as pitchers and jugs. From the twentieth-century point of view, it seems that the sagging base must have been a disadvantage as it would have made pots unstable when standing on a flat surface. Although in some instances small feet were added for stability, as in the case of tripod pitchers in southern England, or the tripod pipkins of the late Middle Ages, the majority of pots have no stabilizing devices. The thumbing around the bases of many thirteenth- and fourteenth-century jugs seems in most cases to have added little stability and was more of a decorative feature. Sagging bases occur on both hand-made and wheel-made vessels, and may simply reflect cultural prefer- ence. It should be remembered, however, that many vessels, particularly kitchen wares, were used in areas with earth floors which were not completely flat, or on hearths or trivets where a flat base was not a particular advantage.

Features such as handles and spouts were usually added to the vessel when it had dried to leather hardness, or was firm enough not to distort when being handled. The simplest, and commonest, form of spout is the pinched spout, found on jugs, pipkins and some cooking pots; it was made by pulling out the rim from inside with one finger while supporting the rim in position on the outside with two fingers. Tubular spouts were made either by throwing a small cylindrical shape, or by moulding clay round a forefinger or a stick or bone. This was then either smoothed on to the outside of the vessel when a hole had been made in the neck or shoulder, or passed through the hole and smoothed in inside and outside.

Handles could be made by throwing, pulling or rolling out, and also applied by smoothing on to the outside of the pot or carrying through a hole in the side (Fig. 5). Frequently a fillet of clay was added round the handle at its upper and lower junction with the pot and smoothed in to reinforce the join, as with London-type ware jugs (Pearce 1984: 19). Very often the junction of the lower end of the handle with the body is more clearly visible than that at the upper end, which being inside the rim or neck was more easily smoothed and obliterated. In some cases the potter pushed his fingers deep into the lower end of the handle from inside the jug, sometimes breaking through the vessel wall; this is seen in, for example, Mill Green ware (*ibid.*: 20–1) and Humber ware (Hayfield 1980: 33). Simply luting handles on to the outside of a vessel seems to be fairly rare, only occurring on small pots such as drinking jugs (Pearce 1984: 20) and Cistercian ware cups. That the methods of fixing handles were

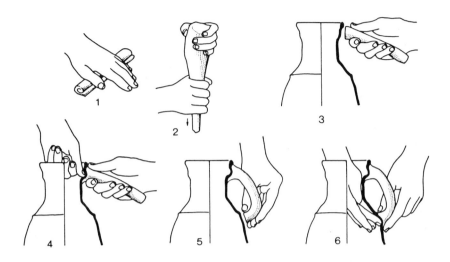

Fig. 5 Making and applying handles.
1, rolling clay into a handle. 2, 'pulling' or 'drawing' a handle. 3–6, applying a handle
to a jug. (After van der Leeuw 1975)

successful is shown by the fact that in most cases these joints were not the point
of weakness; jugs frequently broke in two parts, the neck, handle and part of the
shoulder being pulled away from the body of the jug (Hodges H. 1974: 38).

There is little historical evidence for construction techniques, but there are
occasional depictions of potters using wheels which give useful information;
these have been drawn together in a study by Rieth (1960). The potter's wheel
was invented in Mesopotamia in the fourth millennium BC, and knowledge of
this technology spread slowly to Egypt and the Mediterranean world. There
appear to have been two kinds of wheel construction in antiquity, the socketed
wheel which revolved on a wooden pivot fixed in the earth, and the pivoted
wheel which revolved in a socket set in the earth (*ibid.*: 75–6). These wheels
were turned by hand, either by the potter or an apprentice (Fig. 6 Nos. 1, 2),
although there are occasional examples of foot-turned wheels (Fig. 6 No. 3).
Classical Greek pottery was made on a socketed wheel turned by a boy,
presumably an apprentice (Fig. 6 No. 4), although for painting, the potter
would turn the wheel himself (Fig. 6 No. 5). Romano-British potters appear to
have used both slow hand-turned wheels and faster wheels pivoted on stones,
either hand-turned wheels little different from the Greek ones, or possibly
double wheels (kick wheels) (Peacock 1982: 55–7; Swan 1984: 50–1).

Slow hand-turned wheels ('turntables' or 'tournettes') of a simple nature
remained in use through the Middle Ages until the present day, both in areas
where fast wheels were not known, or where pottery-making remained on a

Fig. 6 Potters' wheels in the ancient world.
1–3, Egyptian. (1, after Childe 1954; 2, Rieth 1960; 3, Hodges 1970), 4–5, Greek.
(4, after Noble 1966; 5, *Encyclopedia Britannica*, 9th edn, 1876)

Fig. 7 Medieval and later turntables.
1, German, 15th cent. 2, Italian, 16th cent. 3, Pyrenean, 20th cent. 4, Portuguese,
20th cent. 5, Breton, 20th cent. (After Rieth 1960)

more domestic basis, and alongside faster wheels for specific purposes (Fig. 7).

Two kinds of fast wheel appear to have been used in the Middle Ages and have been depicted at various times (Rieth 1960). One is basically a cartwheel mounted horizontally on a pivot, the wheel being rotated by hand or with a stick (*tour à bâton*). The pot was thrown on a disc or small platform fixed to the centre or nave of the wheel. The earliest representations of this kind of wheel occur in French thirteenth-century manuscripts (Fig. 8 Nos. 1, 2). This type of wheel continued in use in post-medieval Europe until recent times (Fig. 8 No. 3; Fig. 9; Fig. 10), and can be seen in India today (Fig. 8 No. 4). Such a wheel has been inferred in the manufacture of fourteenth-century pottery at Haarlem (Van der

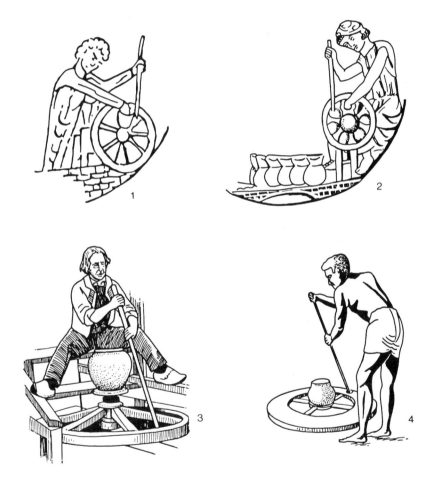

Fig. 8   Medieval and later potters' wheels: cartwheel type.
1, 2, French, 13th cent. 3, Breton, 20th cent. 4, Indian, 20th cent. (1, after Rieth 1960; 2, after Jope 1956; 3, after Scott 1954; 4, after Saraswati and Behura 1966)

Fig. 9   Potter's wheel, cartwheel type, from a drawing by Jan Luycken, 1694. (After van der Leeuw 1975)

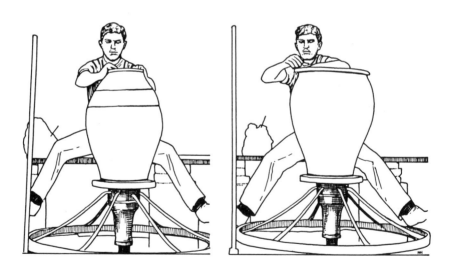

Fig. 10   Potter in Normandy working on a *tour à bâton*, late 19th/early 20th cent.; two stages in the manufacture of a large jar. (After Bavoux 1983)

Leeuw 1975); the wheel would have been heavy, being difficult to start and stop and turning relatively slowly, and this is considered to account for certain traits seen in this Low Countries pottery.

The other kind of medieval potter's wheel consisted of a lower wheel turned with the foot and an upper wheelhead for throwing the pot, the two wheels being connected by a series of struts (Rieth 1960). The earliest example of this wheel is seen on a mid-thirteenth-century carving in Reims Cathedral (Fig. 11 No. 1). It is frequently depicted in the fifteenth and sixteenth centuries (Fig. 11 Nos. 2–5), and also continued in use in the post-medieval period (Fig. 11 No. 6). One example is being used, unusually, by a woman potter (Fig. 11 No. 2); she is making a Rhenish stoneware jug. This illustration is interesting in that it shows a bone tool being used to produce emphasized rilling marks on the body of the vessel.

The kick wheel known to the modern potter, in which the wheel-head is

Fig. 11 Medieval and later potters' wheels: foot-propelled.
1, French, 13th cent. 2, 3, German, 15th cent. 4, German, 16th cent. 5, Polish, 16th cent. 6, Russian, 20th cent. (1, 3, 5, 6, after Rieth 1960; 2, after Jope 1956; 4, after Agricola's *De re metallica*, in Jope 1956)

joined to a heavy fly-wheel by a vertical iron shaft, does not appear to have been known during the Middle Ages. It is first depicted in the manufacture of fine maiolicas in Italy, by Picolpasso among others (Fig. 12), during the sixteenth century. There is no evidence, however, that this type of wheel was used in Britain until the post-medieval period; it may well have been introduced with the few continental potters who began to make tin-glazed earthenware here in the late sixteenth century, and who fall outside the scope of this book.

Ethnographic studies of pottery-making serve to remind the archaeologist of the variety of techniques that can be used in this process, and that a given vessel shape can be produced in a variety of ways. It has already been seen that round-based pots are a natural product of the paddle and anvil technique, for example, but similar-shaped vessels can be produced in other ways. The Mailu Island potters of New Guinea produce such vessels by coiling, beginning by laying the first part into a half coconut shell and then building it up above the rim of the shell. The vessel is thinned by scraping, and after some drying the coconut shell is removed from the base and the protruding bulge is beaten down with a flat stick to round off the base (Rye 1977: 206). Round-based pots can also be produced by a technique of throwing without a wheel. Mexican potters use a *molde*, or two ceramic saucer-shaped objects; the clay ball is placed in the upper saucer and this is balanced upon the other inverted saucer. The potter spins the upper saucer with his foot, using both hands to pull up and form the vessel, the weight of the clay itself providing much of the momentum

Fig. 12   Kick wheels, *c.* 1550. (After Picolpasso, 1934 edn)

for throwing. The end result is a round-based pot which has all the characteristics of a wheel-thrown vessel (Hodges H. 1964: 29).

Pots thrown on a true wheel can also be given rounded bases by shaving off surplus paste from the basal angle when the vessel is inverted on the wheel, one method suggested for the construction of medieval Arabic round-based jars (van der Leeuw 1975: fig. 12). They could also have been constructed by throwing the base first on a wheel, rings of clay being added, drawn up and closed together to form a dome. When this had dried a little, it was inverted and placed on a ring fastened to the wheel-head, and more clay was added to the upper part so that the shoulder and neck could be formed by throwing (Fig. 13). A similar result would have been achieved by throwing the neck and shoulder first, inverting it, adding more clay and then throwing a dome shape for the rounded base, closing the final small aperture at the top of the dome with the fingers and smoothing it over with a tool (van der Leeuw 1976: figs. 75–81). Indian potters, on the other hand, achieve round-based pots by paddle and anvil beating of wheel-thrown flat-based pots (Fig. 1), or by joining together two hemispherical bowls made by pressing clay over a convex mould, cutting out a hole for a neck to be added, and consolidating the joins by beating (Saraswati and Behura 1966: 55–64, 83–91).

This is not to suggest that English medieval potters producing round-based vessels were necessarily using any of these methods. Ethnoarchaeology instils an awareness of the many possible techniques, and helps to counter the archaeologist's twentieth-century prejudices.

The kind of tools used by potters today can shed light on those probably used by potters of the Middle Ages; among those published are examples from France (Peacock 1982: fig. 10), Iran (Whitehouse 1984: fig. 7) and India (Saraswati and Behura 1966: figs. 1:24–1:54). In general these tools are fairly simple, often of wood, bone or earthenware. An animal rib or flat piece of wood is often used in shaping the pot when throwing, and knives or points of iron or bone are used in decoration of the pot, for example. Templates for shaping pots while throwing were used by country potters in France; these were of metal, but originally they were of wood (Peacock 1982: fig. 10, nos. 2–4). A shaped piece of ceramic was used by the French potters to shape and compress the clay around the bottom of the vessel interior (*ibid.*: fig. 10, no. 1).

Experimental archaeology has seen little work on attempting to re-create medieval pots and understand the processes of their manufacture by this means. One exception is a recent study of the manufacture of jug handles, which considered and tested two probable methods (Pearce 1984). The project concerned jugs found in London, and the methods were rolling sausages of clay which could later be flattened if desired, and throwing a cylinder of clay which could be sliced into rings and then cut into lengths as required. Experiments were carried out using both techniques, but it was found that the end results

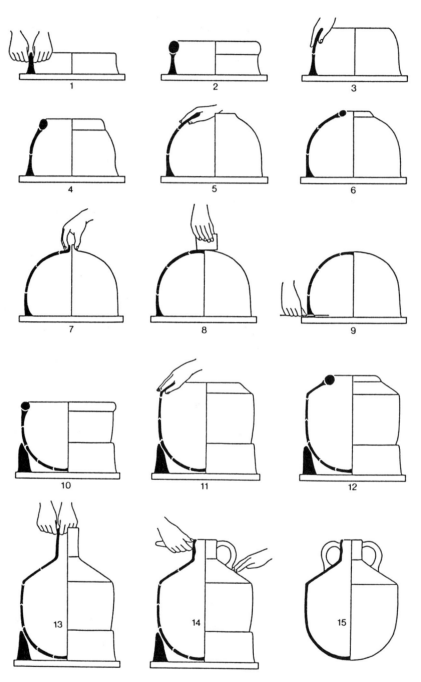

Fig. 13 Stages in wheel-throwing a jar with rounded base; the walls of the pot are built up by adding rings of clay. (After van der Leeuw 1976)

were very difficult to tell apart, although certain handle cross-sections are suggested as being inherently more likely to have been produced by throwing. Only by thin-section analysis to examine the orientation of inclusions could the two methods be distinguished. Such detailed studies are unfortunately rare.

D.   DECORATION

Potters' tools for decorating pottery have only occasionally been found; these are mainly stamps, in bone, earthenware or stone. Wood was probably also used for making tools, either for incising decoration or as stamps or roulette wheels, but these would not survive in archaeological contexts without exceptional conditions of preservation. Examples of such tools are a sheep's phalange with the end shaped into a grid stamp, from Lyveden, and a stamp of oolite from the Rye kilns in Sussex (Vidler 1936: 113). Earthenware stamps for the distinctive Cistercian ware rosettes have been found at Nuneaton and Wrenthorpe (Moorhouse 1981: 105–6). A few stamps are also known elsewhere; in the nineteenth century, three earthenware stamps depicting human heads were found at Lincoln, and a number of earthenware stamps were found in Nottingham. The Lincoln stamps (e.g. Fig. 14 No. 1) do not come from stratified levels, but are thought to be thirteenth to fourteenth century in date. The sherd of Lincoln ware stamped with a man's head (Fig. 14 No. 2) is

Fig. 14   1, Pottery mould for producing a face-mask, from Lincoln. (After Jope 1956)
2, Sherd of late medieval Lincoln ware with stamp-moulded face-mask, *c.* 15th cent. (After Adams L. 1978)

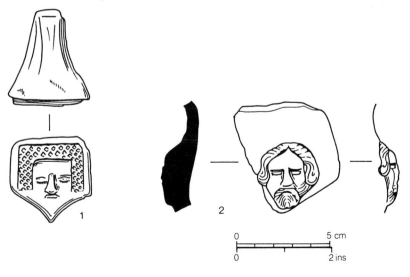

considered to be *c.* fifteenth century; the impression is slurred and suggestive of a degenerated mould. It seems that the Lincoln potters may have continued to use the same images for several generations, with fresh moulds being taken from time to time (Adams L. 1978).

The methods and motifs of medieval pottery decoration have been well studied. Impressed, incised and applied decorative techniques are widespread. Impressed decoration ranges from simple finger-tip impressions on the damp clay surface to pressing on shaped stamps or running a roulette wheel over the surface. Careful examination of rouletting found on pottery can lead to deductions about the size of the wheels involved; this was done at Winksley, Yorkshire, for example, where the impressions of certain damaged teeth were recognized in the rouletting. From the repeat distance of these impressions, the circumference of the wheel could be measured (Bellamy and Le Patourel 1970: n. 33). A certain type of impression, the stabbing often found on jug handles, was probably more functional than decorative, however, enabling the handles to dry out without cracking.

Incised decoration ranges from horizontal, vertical and sloping lines to the ornate zoomorphic and anthropomorphic designs of the Rye kiln products (Barton 1979). Multiple lines were produced by the use of a small toothed comb-like implement. Horizontal lines were made by simply holding a pointed implement or comb against the side of the pot while it rotated on the wheel; wavy lines could be achieved by moving the tool up and down while the pot turned.

Applied pellets, scales, strips and pads of clay are a particularly common form of decoration, the clay being either the same as the body of the vessel or of a different colour to achieve a bichrome effect. The arrangement of pellets and scales is usually random or in zones defined by strips. Applied and incised decoration are often combined; pads of clay can have stamped decoration, and applied strips may be thumbed or impressed. In some cases applied clay may be used to form low reliefs of animals, or occasionally human figures.

Anthropomorphic decoration often combines applied and incised decoration. On some vessels, such as the Mill Green ware miniature jugs, details of a face are added to the neck and clay arms are placed at the shoulder, and the whole pot becomes a person in the manner of the later Toby jugs. Other types of anthropomorphic vessel have figures added, incised, in low relief or defined by strips, as in Ham Green ware, or as freestanding ornament, as in the Scarborough ware knight jugs. In some cases only the head is represented, as in Scarborough ware and Grimston ware face-mask jugs. Jugs, chafing dishes and aquamaniles are the main forms to use anthropomorphic decoration, although it is also known on roof furniture and floor tiles.

Other forms of decoration involve surface treatment of pots. The simplest way to improve the surface appearance of a pot is to work it over with a damp cloth or with wet hands, which brings the finest clay particles to the surface. A slightly more complicated process is to coat the vessel with a slip, a creamy mixture of fine clay and water; this technique was often used to make a red-bodied vessel appear to be made of a white fabric by the application of white slip. The white slip was often applied by smearing on with the hands, at least in the case of white-slipped jugs found in the London area (Vince 1983: 330–1), and the practice of dipping pots into slip which is well known today did not become standard until the sixteenth century. A combination of white slip and incised decoration, or sgraffito, is sometimes found, as in Cambridge Sgraffito ware. Red slips as well as white were used in combination with lead glaze to produce polychrome effects, as on Mill Green ware. The use of slip for decoration was extended by slip painting, and in the later Middle Ages and post-medieval period by slip-trailing. Sometimes slip painting amounted simply to vertical stripes of slip, sometimes it took the form of scrolls and swirls. Both red and white slips were used in this way.

The use of glaze is for the most part a decorative surface treatment on medieval pottery. It first appears on the exterior of vessels, often just on the shoulder, and although some open vessel forms do have partial or overall internal glazing during the Middle Ages, it is not until the sixteenth and seventeenth centuries that this becomes widespread. Lead-based glazes are universal; relatively few analyses have been done on these glazes, however. On some wares, for example the splashed glaze wares of the twelfth and thirteenth centuries, it can be seen from the characteristic pitting that the glaze was added in dry powder form. Dipped glazes and glazes applied in a liquid, which become common as splashed glaze wares decline during the thirteenth century, are also known in the period before the splashed glaze wares, first appearing with the start of glazing in the Late Saxon period. Winchester ware is thought to have been dipped in glaze (Biddle and Barclay 1974: 140–1), and the glaze on Stamford ware is considered to have been applied in water or a thin slip (Kilmurry 1980: 69–77). Liquid glazes could be applied to the leather-hard pot by a brush or hand-smearing, which would account for the uneven thickness of some of the Stamford glazes. For the Stamford glazes, a mixture fritted with silica is not considered likely, but the actual form in which the lead was added is not known.

It is probable that some potters in the Middle Ages were using fritted glazes, as both methods of producing glaze were known. In the fifteenth century, potters at Chilvers Coton were possibly using a lead glazing frit. Two samples from a pit beside a hearth were submitted for analysis; the first sample consisted of mainly sand and basic lead carbonate (white lead), and the second of mainly lead and what was probably also basic lead carbonate. A lead ingot was also found in the same context. The first sample is suggested as being a lead glazing frit, and made a yellow glaze when fired at 950°C; the second probably represents the process of making white lead from metallic lead and vinegar (Clarke K.C. 1984). At the late thirteenth/early fourteenth century tile factory at Danbury, Essex, a hearth was found on which metallic lead had been melted in a pot and stirred until it was converted to lead oxide (Drury and Pratt 1975: 140). This lead oxide was probably used to glaze the tiles without being fritted with silica, since the Danbury glazes did not contain much sodium or iron, which would have been expected had the latter method been used. Such evidence has only rarely been found on production sites, however. At Hallgate, Doncaster, a shell-tempered vessel was found to have considerable accumulations of lead carbonate on its inside, and it is suggested that it was used to mix the glaze (Buckland *et al.* 1979: 12). Further details of the composition of the glaze and its method of application are not discussed in the report.

The form in which the lead was added to most medieval glazes is not known. Many writers have suggested the lead ore galena (lead sulphide), for example at Laverstock (Musty *et al.* 1969: 91) and Donyatt, where ore from the Mendips is a likelihood (Coleman-Smith and Pearson forthcoming). The process of lead smelting in the Middle Ages involved the sieving and discarding of all ore fragments under half an inch across, and these riddlings could have been ground to a fine powder by the potter with little effort. With the development of more efficient refining methods in the sixteenth century, small fragments could, for the first time, be smelted, and an industry grew up to sort and sieve the fine 'smitham' for the ore hearths (Blanchard 1981: 79). Though most of the 'smitham' was doubtless smelted, some was used by potters in post-medieval times at least. Outside lead mining areas, it is perhaps likely that scrap lead would be more readily available, and this could have been used to make lead oxide or white lead for glazing. Analysis of glazes can only show that lead and trace elements are present, but not the origin of the lead as ore or scrap metal.

Spectroscopic analysis of the surface of pots does not, unfortunately, reveal the presence of organic ingredients in slips or glazes, though historical evidence suggests that these may have been present. Analysis of the Laverstock glazes, however, suggested that a calcium compound of some kind may have been deliberately added, possibly to improve the adhesive quality of the glaze (Thomas and Musty 1961). The Laverstock glazes also had silver and tin as impurities, and both solder and pewter have been suggested as the sources for these, although the reason for this addition is not known; the darker brown colour of some strip decoration was shown to be due to enhanced concentrations of iron.

Some Stamford ware glazes have also been analysed, and the bright green colour of 'developed Stamford ware' was shown to be the result of adding copper to the glaze (Kilmurry 1980: 69–77). Low proportions of silica show that silica was not added to the glazes here but derived from the clay body. Brownish specks in some 'developed Stamford' glazes proved by analysis to be due to iron, although it is not clear if this was an intentional colourant here. Other trace elements in the glazes were present as lead impurities. The dark brown glazes of Cistercian wares are certainly due to iron, both in the body and the glaze. Analysis of a sherd from the production site at Silcoates, near Wrenthorpe, West Yorkshire, showed that the iron content of the glaze was similar to that in the body of the pot, implying that no extra iron was added to the glaze. A Cistercian ware sherd from Kirkstall, however, proved to have a higher iron content in the glaze than in the body, but the significance of this finding cannot be assessed from such a limited project (Brears 1967: 39).

With the exception of glazing, little of the available historical evidence deals with techniques of decoration. The collection of recipes known as *De coloribus et artibus Romanorum* by Eraclius includes several relating to pottery. One recipe for lead glaze is thought to have been set down by a northern French author in the late twelfth or thirteenth century (de Boüard 1974: 67–9). It describes how the surface of the pot is prepared by coating with a paste of wheat flour and water that has been boiled and cooled; for a yellow glaze, the pot is then to be sprinkled with powdered lead. To obtain a green glaze, the lead is melted in a pot and stirred until the oxide forms; copper or brass filings are mixed with the powdered lead oxide. The pot is then fired. The same text also describes the application of a slip to a pot, the slip being made by mixing with a sediment of powdered grog settled out in water.

The older recipes in Eraclius only mention painted decoration obtained by a combination of a colouring substance and powdered glass applied to the pot and then fired. Such decoration with translucent alkaline glazing was common in the Byzantine world, but not in western Europe, although there was some early experimentation with alkaline glaze in parts of the Carolingian empire (*ibid*.: 72–3).

Documentary evidence also supplies recipes for the manufacture of white lead (lead carbonate) from metallic lead, and this white lead may among other things have been used in glazing pottery, as has been suggested at Chilvers Coton, for example. The recipes involve hanging plates of lead above wine or vinegar in an earthen pot or a wooden vessel, sealing the pot and standing it in horse dung for some days or weeks until the white lead is formed (Moorhouse 1981: appendix 1c).

Descriptions of post-medieval and recent practices among country potters of western Europe provide probably the best 'ethnographic' parallels for medieval glazing. In nineteenth-century Normandy, for example, potters dipped their pots into a tub of flour and water paste before glazing them (de Boüard 1974: 73–4). This echoes the French recipe for glaze given in Eraclius quoted above. The country potters at Verwood, who used traditional methods well into the twentieth century, glazed their pots by converting metallic lead to lead oxide powder. This was either mixed with water to form a paste and applied with a paint brush to the leather-hard pots (Young 1979: 112), or mixed with barley meal and sprinkled on the pots which had first been dampened with urine (Algar *et al.* 1979: 16). A writer discussing industrial diseases in 1705 also described how potters glazed their wares with calcined lead, or lead oxide (quoted in Coleman-Smith and Pearson forthcoming).

Elsewhere, however, galena seems to have been widely used in post-medieval potteries. In 1821 a writer described a road:

> near Green Ore Farm on the Mendips, it is styled the Potters Road, from having been used by persons of that trade coming thither for the lead ore, which was required for glazing the inside of their vessels, the ore, we learn, needed merely to be pounded small, strained through a sieve, afterwards mixed with water to the consistency of paint, and laid on the inside of the vessels by a brush; when the clay was baked this became fused and formed a burnish or lacquer of a yellow hue. (quoted in Coleman-Smith and Pearson forthcoming)

Dr Plot, describing Staffordshire in 1686, mentions the use of lead ore: 'they lead [the vessels] with that sort of lead ore they call Smithum, which is the smallest ore of all, beaten into dust, finely sifted and strewed upon them; which gives them the gloss' (Plot 1686: 123). Powdered galena is insoluble in water, and so to be applied wet would have to be mixed with a clay slip. In north Devon galena was also used:

> At Fremington we still had the iron trough and pounders with which they pounded the lead ore a generation before. Both grandfather and John had seen this done, and they told how men got bellyache and called it colic, which was probably due to the dust from the lead. We had a mill made of heavy stones (such as a miller used for grinding flour) in which we ground glaze in the wet state. John took twelve dippers of slip made of clay from the river, containing iron nodules and of a sandy texture, to which he added twelve pounds of galena, ground to crystals, and half-pound of ground flint. This made a nice treacly brown glaze for pitchers and pans. (Holland 1958: 24–5)

For a better glaze, the Staffordshire potters used litharge or lead oxide:

> but when they have a mind to shew the utmost of their skill in giving their wares a fairer gloss than ordinary, they lead them then with lead calcined into powder, which they also sift fine and strew upon them as before, which not only gives them a higher gloss, but goes much further too in their work than lead-ore would have done. (Plot 1686: 123)

Lead oxide continued to be used for glazing into the twentieth century, for example at Verwood and at the Farnham potteries, where scrap lead was melted in a furnace and then stirred continuously until it was converted into lead oxide. This powder was then mixed with fine sand and sufficient water to form a stiff paste, and brushed directly on to the leather-hard pottery. A copper-green glaze was also produced at Farnham for the manufacture of art wares; powdered copper oxide produced by heating scrap copper in a furnace was added to the glaze mixture. The glaze thus produced was a rich, glossy dark green with an iridescence (Brears 1971: 75–6; 127–8).

Some experimental work has been done on glazes; French archaeologists have followed the method for lead glazing outlined in Eraclius, the glaze being coloured with copper oxide and applied in a flour paste to an unglazed medieval sherd. When fired at 920°C, it produced a light green glaze flecked with dark green, identical to medieval glazes (de Boüard 1974: 75). In this country, attempts have been made to replicate the Stamford ware glazes, and the most successful version was achieved by mixing white lead with water and applying this by brush to the Stamford clay tablets that were used for this experiment (Kilmurry 1980: 70). After firing to 1030°C, this produced a very glossy, slightly crazed pale yellow glaze. Here a fritted glaze was unsuccessful in copying the medieval glaze, but the effectiveness of a fritted glaze has been shown elsewhere, for example by the firing of a sand and lead carbonate mixture found in a pit at Chilvers Coton.

E. DRYING

Some drying buildings may have been fairly flimsy structures, possibly open-sided as in the depiction of a potter's workshop by Agricola (Fig. 11 No. 4), and so very difficult, if not impossible, to identify in archaeological terms. It has been suggested, for example, that Buildings 1–3 at Laverstock were storage buildings for pots, either before or after firing (Moorhouse 1981: 102); little remained to give any indication of the character of these buildings, however. At Limpsfield, Surrey, there is more definite evidence of drying arrangements. A Type 2 kiln (Musty 1974) was built into the western side of a structure which perhaps served to dry newly-made pots; immediately adjacent to the kiln was a chamber which might have been used to provide a final drying in warmth from the kiln. A possible pottery-drying oven has been excavated at Yardley Hastings, Northamptonshire (Moorhouse 1981: 102–5).

Occasionally evidence for the drying process has been noted on pottery. Pottery bases from the Thetford-type ware production site at Langhale, Norfolk, have grooves suggesting that they were dried upright on a wattle drying rack. One example appears to have been dried on a plank or similar flat surface with part of the base hanging over the edge (Wade 1976: 111). At Haarlem in Holland there is some evidence that vessels were stacked upside down to dry out, and sometimes one pot sagged under the weight of another. There was also, in Holland at least, a danger of mice nibbling holes in the side of the drying pot (van der Leeuw 1975: 84).

There is little documentary evidence for the drying process, although the importance of even drying to prevent cracking was undoubtedly recognized. A

French medieval author enjoins the potter, after slipping a pot, to 'put it in a place out of the way sheltered from draughts until it is quite dry' (de Boüard 1974: 69).

Much contemporary ethnographic literature concerns areas of the world where the problems of drying pottery are problems of slowing down the rate of drying rather than speeding it up. The comparatively cool and damp climate of northern Europe presents rather different problems. At the Verwood potteries, pots were dried outside in good weather, being brought into drying buildings at night or in bad weather. The drying buildings were heated by a stove, or turf or peat fires, during the winter (Young 1979: 112; Algar *et al.* 1979: 14). Dr Plot described the practice of the Staffordshire potters at the end of the seventeenth century: 'when the potter has wrought the clay either into hollow or flat ware, they are set abroad to dry in fine weather, but by the fire in foule, turning them as they see occasion' (Plot 1686: 123). Rooms with drying racks which could be heated have been described for the north Devon potteries and for recent potteries in Westmorland and Yorkshire (Brears 1971: 113–14). Drying pots in the winter at the Fremington pottery,

> we took a faggot of furze, divided it, laid it on the floor of the drying room and covered it with 'glows'. These were charred embers of furze and brambles obtained from the kiln fireplaces. We poured on water to prevent flaming and left it to simmer away till morning, when there would be a heap of ash. While it was undisturbed we could work over it. If more heat was required we had only to scrape away the ash to obtain a glowing mass of charcoal embers... The pots, on boards across the beams, needed attention every morning... When there was severe frost, and lots of pots about in the green state – that is, raw clay – we used what we called a devil... We would mix a pan of wet clay to a barrowload of small coal, tread it well and make it into balls the size and shape of a goose egg. These, placed in piles with a piece of sheet iron on top, on the draughty side, would make smoke and heat enough to keep off the frost which wet pots seem to attract (Holland 1958: 19–20).

F.   FIRING

Firing is the one aspect of the potter's technology for which much evidence survives, although even here the picture is incomplete as evidence for kiln superstructures is often not preserved. The excavation of so many pottery kilns in this country has enabled a typology of kiln forms to be constructed by John Musty (1974).

The simplest method of firing was in a 'clamp' kiln, which amounted to little more than a bonfire (Type 5 kiln; *ibid.*). This was either above ground, leaving only an area of fired earth or clay (Type 5b), or set in a shallow pit (Type 5a). Such kilns tended to be used for coarse unglazed wares, although experimental evidence suggests that glaze firings are possible in a clamp kiln, and at

Wrenthorpe in the sixteenth century, glazed wares were fired in saggars within a clamp. Most of the hand-made wares of the Saxon to early post-Conquest period were probably fired in clamps. Because the clamp kiln is in effect constructed from its own fuel, little remains to identify it for the archaeologist apart from an area of burning and perhaps wasters.

More readily recognizable are kilns constructed of more durable materials such as clay and stone, with one or more flues or fireplace areas. In the classical Mediterranean world, single-flue kilns, often with permanent clay domes, are commonly represented (Fig. 15). Romano-British pottery kilns have recently been the subject of a study by V.G. Swan (1984), and she has identified a number of types based on a simple updraught kiln which may have been in use shortly before the Roman Conquest. Romano-British kilns could have fairly elaborate structures for supporting the pots to be fired. Most were single-flued, but there were kilns with two opposed flues similar to medieval Type 2 kilns. As with other aspects of potting technology such as the potter's wheel, however,

Fig. 15   Greek kilns being fired, as depicted on votive plaques; 6th cent. BC.
1, stoking the kiln. 2, 3, potter climbing up to close vent hole for reduction firing. 4, potter using hooked stick to close vent hole, shielding his face from the heat with his hand. (After Noble 1966)

these kilns disappear from the archaeological record in this country for several centuries after the Romano-British period.

Musty defined four groups of medieval flued kilns: Type 1, single-flue kilns; Type 2, kilns with two opposing flues; Type 3, kilns with three or more flues, and Type 4, parallel-flue kilns (Fig. 16). Types 1 and 2, which are cut into the ground, are subdivided according to whether there is any internal structure or evidence for a raised floor. Type 1a lacks internal structure, whereas Type 1b has a raised oven floor, either without a central support or upheld by a pedestal or series of pedestals. Type 2a has no internal structure; Type 2b has a spine wall along the chamber, although the oven floor is not raised; and Type 2c has a central pedestal on which the pottery was stacked. Type 3 kilns are not subdivided, but do show some variation; these kilns are entirely above ground or slightly sunken. The most usual number of flues is five or six. Type 4 kilns were mostly used for firing bricks (Type 4c) and tiles (Type 4b), although some pottery-firing examples are known (Type 4a). The brick and tile kilns had a raised floor on which the items were stacked for firing.

Musty's work has shown that some general conclusions can be drawn concerning chronological and regional preferences for different kiln types (1974: 48–51; 1984). Type 1 kilns, which are the earliest flued medieval kilns, appearing in the pre-Conquest period, are mainly concentrated in eastern England. The kiln type does occur later in the medieval and post-medieval periods, but not in great numbers. Type 1 kilns may have been modelled on continental examples. Type 2 kilns are widespread in England, but with a southerly bias; they also occur, however, in Scotland and Ireland. They appear to have been introduced in the thirteenth century, and are probably a native invention. Type 3 kilns are mainly a Yorkshire and Midlands type, but are also known in Scotland. The earliest date from the later thirteenth century. At Chilvers Coton, there is a clear progression as Type 2a kilns are replaced by Type 3 kilns by the late thirteenth century; the earliest Type 3 kilns there are three-flued, and later ones have four and then five flues.

Excavated kilns usually lack evidence for their superstructure and loading arrangements. It is fairly rare, too, for the flue arches to survive intact as they did at Laverstock, for instance (Musty et al. 1969). At Langhale, Norfolk, a Thetford-type ware kiln was found with clay arches forming a floor for the firing chamber. The impressions of pot rims were found on these arches (Fig. 17), showing that the kiln had been loaded for the first time when the clay structure was still slightly soft, and indicating that no pre-firing had taken place (Wade 1976).

Fired daub fragments from the upper parts of kilns are sometimes found collapsed within the firing chambers of kilns. There is little evidence generally for domed superstructures, whether temporary or permanent, such as would be suggested by clay fragments with a double curvature. Clay domes have,

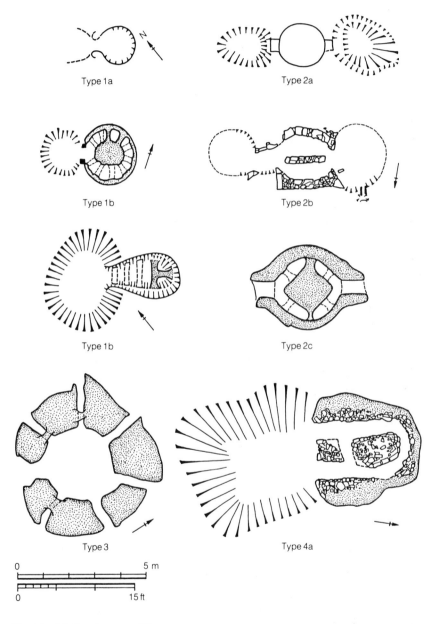

Fig. 16   Medieval pottery kiln types.
Type 1a, Ipswich. Type 1b, Torksey and Thetford. Type 2a, Laverstock. Type 2b, Ham Green. Type 3, West Cowick. Type 4a, Lyveden. (After Musty 1974)

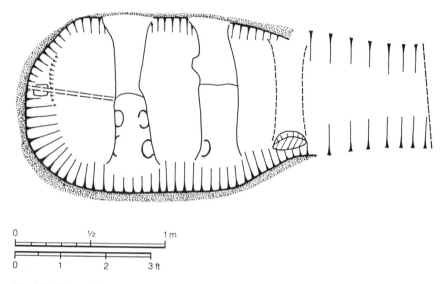

0   ½   1 m

0   1   2   3 ft

Fig. 17   Plan of Saxo-Norman kiln at Langhale, Norfolk, showing rim impressions on the clay arches. (After Wade 1976)

however, been inferred for the Type 1 kilns at Thetford, and a Type 2 kiln (no. 33) at Chilvers Coton, for example. It seems that temporary roofs of some kind were commonly used; whether temporary clay domes, rebuilt for each firing, were ever a reality has recently been seriously questioned (Bryant 1977: 109). Open-topped kilns capped with layers of suitable material such as sherds, tiles or turves have been suggested as a likelihood, as at Lyveden (Steane and Bryant 1975: 53).

Loading the kiln could be done through the flue, from the top, or, in the case of some large Type 3 kilns, through walk-in entrances. Some evidence for how pottery was stacked in the kiln comes from the pots themselves. Medieval glazed wares frequently show runs of glaze from base to rim, indicating that vessels were stacked upside down. The undersides of bases often have reduced grey areas where vessel rims have stood on them and prevented oxidization at that point. Glaze often ran over the rims of vessels, thereby sticking them to the pots beneath; when these were chipped apart, characteristic scars were left on rims and bases.

Occasionally kilns are found to contain some or all of the pots from the final firing if it had gone wrong. Laverstock Kiln 6, for example, was partly loaded with jugs which stood, upside down, directly on the oven floor. There was little sign of any propping to separate individual vessels. The flue arches had been blocked for cooling (Musty *et al.* 1969: 90). In other Laverstock kilns, attempts had been made at separation of pots with pieces of tile. Elsewhere, broken sherds (parting sherds) performed this function, for example at Colstoun, East Lothian (Brooks C.M. 1978–80: 383–5). At Upper Heaton, small lumps or wedges of clay were used (Manby 1965: 100).

Some kiln sites which have no fire-bars or raised floors have produced props or stands in the form of roughly-made hollow-ware pots, which presumably served to raise vessels from the oven floor (Fig. 18 Nos. 1–7). At Colstoun, complete examples were found *in situ*, upside down with their rims set into the floor (Brooks and Haggarty 1976–7: 380). Presumably the lowest layer of pots was placed on these props to raise them above the areas of direct heat where wastage was most likely to occur. There was no evidence that the props in this instance were supporting any kind of kiln floor of tiles or kiln bars, but this possibility might exist at other sites where these props occur. Saggars were not used until the end of the medieval period (Fig. 18 Nos. 8–9, 11), although large cooking pots may possibly have served as such when more unusual or valuable items were being fired. Saggars seem to have been developed by the end of the fifteenth century, for they are found on sixteenth-century sites producing Cistercian wares, for example; these wares mostly took the form of small cups, which were fired in an upright, slightly tilted position within the saggar, to judge from the way their glaze formed and flowed. Rarer forms of kiln furniture include the small clay cones found sometimes on Cistercian ware production

Fig. 18   Kiln furniture: props, saggars and clay cone.
1, from Rhuddlan. (After Miles H. 1977)
2, 3, from Audlem. (After Webster and Dunning 1960)
4, 5, from Colstoun. (After Brooks C.M. 1978–80)
6–10, from Wrenthorpe (Potovens). (After Brears 1971)
11, from Fulmodeston. (After Wade-Martins 1983)

sites, which may have been used to support the glazed lids of posset pots (Fig. 18 No. 10).

The fuel used varied according to the locality; where the evidence survives, wood seems to be the commonest fuel, although furze, peat and coal were also used. Charcoals found in stokepits at Laverstock were of oak, willow, hazel and birch, and at Lyveden hawthorn and oak were identified (Musty 1974: 56). The sixteenth-century potters at Donyatt probably obtained their fuel from hedges rather than from woodland; species identified as charcoal include oak, ash, elm, willow and poplar (Rackham O. forthcoming). At Chilvers Coton, the sequence shows that the Type 2a kilns were fired with wood, but the succeeding Type 3 kilns were coal-fired, with the exception of the occasional early three-flued kiln such as Site 3 K15, which was wood-fired (Mayes and Scott 1984). Coal produced a much smaller flame than wood, and so coal-fired kilns required a greater number of fireplaces to maintain an even heat in the kiln (Musty 1984: 27). Likewise peat produces a smaller flame than wood, and multi-flued kilns found at West Cowick and Toynton All Saints may have been peat-fired.

Firing was a risky business and the potters often had little control over the firing temperatures, as is shown by studies of waster material from kiln sites, and the colour variations that can be found on a single pot. In view of this, more valuable items of pottery would have been placed in the most favourable spot within the kiln to minimize breakage, and less valuable pots would have been put in less favourable positions. Consequently, wasted pottery found on a production site cannot be taken as reflecting the proportions of different pottery types made there. Furthermore, on sites with a number of kilns, waste could well be dumped into disused kilns; finding pottery within a kiln is no guarantee that it was fired there.

The length of time kilns were in use is difficult to estimate. Many kilns show signs of repairs and re-linings, indicating considerable usage. At Laverstock it was suggested that the life of a kiln was five years, and at Potterton a span of ten years was postulated for a sixteenth-century Type 3 kiln (Musty 1974: 53), but many kilns may have survived for longer than this. The figure of five years at Laverstock is based on the assumption that one kiln replaced another, and that the potter fired a load once a week during the summer (Musty et al. 1969: 92–3). On the evidence given, though, it seems that a number of the kilns are contemporary or overlapping in time; furthermore, one firing per week during the summer months seems an overestimate, in view of the work and time involved in firing and the potter's necessary farming commitments at that season. Historical evidence implies that most medieval potters were part-time producers, being dependent on working the land for some of their livelihood, and so pottery production would have had to be fitted into the agricultural schedule. Consequently, five years is probably an underestimate of the lifespan of a Laverstock kiln.

Kilns are referred to in historical documents, and several different Latin words are used, but there is no way of knowing whether any of the names can be related to specific structural forms. There is some evidence that kilns were permanent structures, for example the rentals paid by potters such as those at Brill for their kilns (Le Patourel 1968: 115). The capacity of kilns is occasionally hinted at; there is some evidence that multi-flue kilns at Toynton All Saints, might have held about 500 pots (*ibid.*: 115–16). Type 2 kilns would presumably have held less; a figure of 25–30 jugs per load was suggested for Laverstock (Musty *et al.* 1969: 92–3).

Some tile kilns at least were housed inside buildings or structures of some kind, which would have allowed firing to take place in wet weather; at Moulsham in Essex in the fifteenth century the tenant covenanted to keep the workshops and kiln covered with tile (Drury 1981: 136, 139). This was not a universal practice, however, for at Wye in the fourteenth century there is evidence that poor weather prevented tile firings. Peter at Gate only hired four kilns because of a labour shortage and 'on account of the great quantity of rain in the autumn, which did not allow him to burn more kilns' (Salzman 1923: 179). Occasionally potters also built structures to protect their kilns; the thirteenth-century kiln at Limpsfield built into a structure has already been mentioned. In the early sixteenth century, potters at Donyatt, Somerset, built a circular structure around a Type 2 kiln (Fig. 19; Coleman-Smith and Pearson

Fig. 19 Kiln with roof structure at Donyatt, *c.* 1500–50. (After Coleman-Smith and Pearson forthcoming).

forthcoming), and this idea of protecting kilns became more widespread in the post-medieval period.

There is some information on the types and quantities of fuel used by potters. Wood, in the form of loppings or brushwood, is commonly referred to; the potters either bought it in the form of faggots or bundles, or obtained it by renting an area of woodland on an annual basis and taking what underwood they could. Large timber was usually too valuable to be used for burning in kilns. In the thirteenth century the Brill potters had their sons, or perhaps apprentices and hired labourers, go through the forest collecting loppings for their kilns. In the Laverstock area, documents record men with the 'potter' surname paying 4s annually for roods of brushwood (Le Patourel 1968: 116–17). in the fourteenth century, a thousand faggots were required for firing ten tile kilns at Wye in Kent (Salzman 1923: 177), although this was the annual amount, and so must have fuelled more than one firing of each kiln (*contra* Drury and Pratt 1975: 148). Faggots could vary in size, although from the fifteenth century attempts were made to standardize them (Rackham O. 1980: 142–3), and so the statistics for the Wye tile kilns cannot be properly quantified.

During the later medieval period, peat and coal became more commonly used than wood in some areas. The use of peat is well documented for the brick and tile industry, but also for pottery-making; at West Cowick and Toynton All Saints, payments for peats by potters are recorded (Le Patourel 1968: 118). Coal became cheaper as a fuel relative to wood, its labour costs being less, and so became more attractive to various fuel-burning industries (Rackham O. 1980: 153). Although in some parts of the country the areas of woodland may have become more restricted and brushwood harder to come by in the late Middle Ages (Le Patourel 1968: 118; Rackham O. 1980: 154), this trend was by no means universal, and the woodland-based industries such as pottery had a protective effect on woodland (*ibid.*: 153).

Ethnographic studies provide much evidence for pottery firing methods, especially for the practice of bonfire or clamp firing, which is often associated with the manufacture of hand-made pottery. Firings can be in pits or above ground, with fuel varying from grass, bark and wood to animal dung (Shepard 1956: 75–80). In India, vertical or horizontal spaces or 'fire channels' are left within the pottery stack to enable heat to circulate effectively, with fuel placed among the pots. Leaves, hay and straw are placed over the completed pile, and these are then usually coated with mud to prevent draughts of cold air (Fig. 20; Saraswati and Behura 1966: 101–12). Up to a thousand pots at a time can be fired.

Where built kilns are involved, the majority are of the updraught variety, with a raised floor separating the firing chamber from the fire, and a single stokehole, resembling medieval Type 1b kilns (Peacock 1982: 30–3). They may be square, rectangular or round in plan, and may have clay domes or simply a

Fig. 20   Clamp firing of pots in India.
1, covering the pots with straw. 2, the mud-plastered pile before firing. (After
Saraswati and Behura 1966)

temporary roof of sherds put in place for each firing. Many kilns used by
peasant potters today last decades rather than years, and an average kiln-life of
twenty to thirty years is likely (Bryant 1977: 120).

   The two kiln types used by the Spanish potters of Pereruela have been
described in detail (Peacock 1982: 20–1). The simpler type consists of a fairly
shallow circular pit up to two metres across, with the walls lined with stones and
a small flue arch on one side. One or two large jars are placed on the pit floor,
and the largest pots stacked above this, resting on the large jars and the stones
lining the pit wall. Smaller vessels are placed on top. The whole pile is then
blanketed with sherds, and wood is introduced through the flue and pushed
around the jars at the bottom. A kiln of this type, a fairly primitive Type 1a kiln,
is said to fire about seventy cooking pots. The other kiln type, the high kiln, is
an open rectangular stone tower about 1.5m square built on the ground surface.
It has a flue opening near the base, an internal perforated clay floor about half
way up, and a flight of stone steps to enable the kiln to be loaded from the top.
The firing load is covered with sherds; the capacity is between 150 and 200
vessels. It resembles a Type 1b kiln, and its advantages over the smaller kiln
type are greater capacity and less dependence on the variability of the winds.

   The larger of these Spanish kilns is typical of many to be found in the
contemporary Mediterranean world. Fig. 21 shows two Italian kilns of different
sizes; the smaller one (No. 1) is given a temporary roof of sherds at each firing,
whereas the larger kiln has a permanent roof, made of small pots and clay, and a
walk-in entrance. For firing, the doorway is temporarily walled up, leaving a gap
for gases to escape and for the potter to observe what is happening in the kiln
(Hampe and Winter 1965). In Fig. 22, a Cretan potter is seen beside the
loading doorway of a kiln similar to Fig. 20 No. 1; sherds for making a
temporary roof can be seen on top of the kiln wall.

   English country potteries such as those at Verwood used kilns similar in
many ways to those used in the medieval period, but on a much larger scale
consistent with the economic demands of a year-round full-time industry. The
Verwood kilns consisted of open-topped brick cylinders of 3–4.5m internal

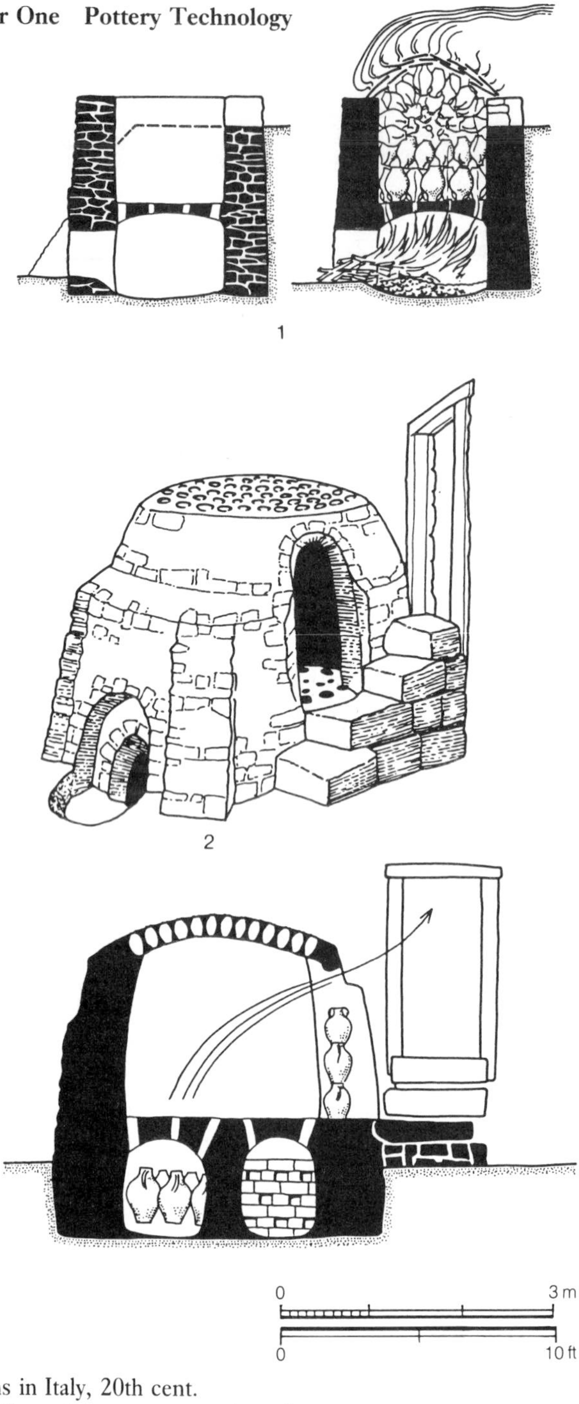

Fig. 21 Kilns in Italy, 20th cent.
1, small kiln, Santa Lucia; cross-sections showing kiln empty and during firing.
2, large kiln, Camerota; view and cross-section during firing, omitting main kiln load.
(After Hampe and Winter 1965)

Fig. 22   Potter beside his kiln at Margharites, Crete, 1984. (Photo C.M. Brooks)

diameter and 4.5m high, surrounded by mounds of earth and broken pottery. A single stoke-pit outside the mound led via a flue into a furnace chamber at the base of the oven. The pottery was stacked on a perforated floor supported on brick arches above the furnace chamber. Pottery was loaded from the working area at the top of the earth mound. No saggars were used, but parting sherds were employed to prevent glazed wares from sticking together. Large pots were stacked upside down, but mugs and small jugs were fired rim uppermost. When stacking was complete, layers of sherds were placed on top to act as a heat baffle and allow smoke and gases to escape.

The fuel used was wood, and the temperature was gradually increased over a period of three or four days. During the last day a final burst of intense heat was created to 'flash the glaze', and then the flue was sealed off and the kiln allowed to cool for three days before opening. During firing, a shed or shelter was erected at the mouth of the flue to provide protection from the weather, and temporary screens were set up on the earth mound to protect the top of the kiln from wind (Young 1979: 112–14; Algar *et al.* 1979: 18–9). The increase in size of these kilns from those of the medieval period added considerably to the whole length of firing, from loading to unloading.

The multi-flue kiln at the Fremington pottery was fired with coal for about a day and a half, and then furze was used to 'flash' the glaze.

> There must be no delay in getting the coal fire out, together with the firebars, clearing the firemouths in preparation for the flashing. . . We put the first faggot on end, the top sloping inward, then fed with wisps of furze spread over and gently pushed in. . . As soon as the firemouth began to heap up with embers grandfather gave the command 'Faggot and draw', which was passed round. Then we let the furze burn out, raked out the fire and poured just sufficient water over to put it out without soaking the 'glows'. After two stokings, the tests were taken out and examined with great expectations. It was a joy if they were brilliant, for then we could finish and get away quickly after claying up the firemouths. . . Three days later, we knew the result, and it was a recognized day's work for three men to empty the kiln and carry everything to its place in the chambers. (Holland 1958: 23–4)

Much work has been done on experimental pottery kiln firings; tile kilns have also been reconstructed and fired (e.g. Greene and Johnson 1978). In the Barton on Humber firings, two Type 2a open-topped kilns and a three-flued Type 3 kiln were built (Bryant 1977). During the pre-firing, large cracks developed which had to be repaired. The firings showed that it was essential to cover the pottery load with sherds and tiles before firing in order to maintain an even heat and reduce wastage. Useful evidence was obtained regarding the location of highest and lowest temperatures within the kilns. Both glazed and unglazed pottery was successfully fired. Firings of replica Romano-British kilns have shown that reduced grey wares can easily be produced by completely sealing the kiln during cooling, and although it is difficult to maintain the reducing conditions for long periods, it is easy to retain them for the length of time required to cool the pottery before it can be safely unloaded (Bryant 1970: 8–9). This has relevance not only to the production of Roman grey wares but also to the reduced wares of the Late Saxon period and later. Another experiment has shown that glazed wares can be successfully produced in a clamp kiln which consisted simply of a low circular mud wall on the ground within which the pottery and fuel were stacked (*Current Archaeology* 4, 1967: 97). Firings such as those at Barton on Humber and Leeds (Figs. 23, 24) also show the need for organization and the amount of space required for fuel and pots, and access areas, often heavily trampled, around the kilns.

Information about the quantities of fuel used and time taken for firing is available from these experiments, but care should be taken in applying these

Fig. 23 Leeds experimental kiln firings: upper left, Type 2 kiln based on Laverstock. Foreground, Type 1 kiln, based on Thetford, being loaded with pottery. Stacks of wood for firing the kilns can be seen. (Photo K. Stubbs, courtesy of P. Mayes)

Fig. 24 Leeds experimental kiln firings: multi-flued kiln, based on West Cowick, being loaded with pottery. The sacks in the background contain coal. (Photo K. Stubbs, courtesy of P. Mayes)

statistics to medieval kilns, which were fired by potters experienced in their use. The experimenters have found that accumulated experience leads to a more economical use of fuel (Musty 1974: 56). The time taken to reach maximum temperatures of *c.* 800°–1000°C seems to be between nine and twelve hours.

Technological and social considerations

The Sung period in China (AD 960–1279) is noted for the perfection of its ceramics, especially its high-fired stonewares and porcelain. A range of glaze colours was available to the Sung potters, and decorative brush painting was of an extremely high standard. In the same period, the Islamic world of the eastern Mediterranean was producing high quality decorated pottery with alkaline and lead glazes, including sgraffito wares and painted lustre wares. The contemporary pottery of north-western Europe was, by contrast, primitive, and British potters lagged behind their continental counterparts. They did not catch up until well into the post-medieval period, though it is not always clear why this should be so. Many of the major developments in British medieval pottery, such as wheel-throwing and glazing in the Late Saxon period, can be seen as resulting directly from imported ideas, objects or even craftsmen. Independent invention seems likely for some innovations, however, such as Type 2 kilns and sixteenth-century Cistercian ware.

After the early flowering of wheel-thrown ceramics in the Late Saxon period, when some potters seem to be making full use of the available technology, it seems that there was a period of stasis or decline in many areas. During much of the Middle Ages it seems that potters in Britain did not keep pace with technological developments, although many did improve their techniques of manufacturing and firing within a limited set of parameters. The labour of clay preparation, for example, appears to have remained rudimentary and unmechanized, although 'by the early fourteenth century Europe had made extraordinary progress towards substituting water- and wind-power for human labour in the basic industries' (White L. 1962: 88). Mills were used for a variety of purposes, including tanning, sawing, crushing ore, operating forge hammers and grinding pigments for paint. During the thirteenth century in England, mechanical fulling of cloth, using water power, was decisive in shifting the centre of textile manufacture from the south-east to the north-west (*ibid.*: 89). The mechanical preparation of clay for throwing is, however, first found in Italy in the sixteenth century (Hodges H. 1974: 36), and there is no evidence of such techniques being practised in Britain before the post-medieval period.

In the manufacture of pottery, there is no evidence for the modern type of kick wheel before the sixteenth century, again in Italy. The principle of the fly-wheel was known from an early date, however; it is mentioned in the late eleventh century. The spinning wheel, which existed in western Europe from the late thirteenth century, is a practical application of the fly-wheel principle (White L. 1962: 115). Neither of the two medieval types of potter's wheel make efficient use of momentum and the fly-wheel principle, however. It is possible that the kick wheel may have been introduced earlier than the date of its first representation, as is the case with certain other medieval inventions (Hodges H. 1973); this cannot, however, be proved at present. The finds of pivot stones on potting tenements are not helpful in defining the nature of the wheel used. At any rate, even when the kick wheel was available, it was not necessarily preferred; the primitive cartwheel survived into modern times in parts of western Europe. It has also been noted that traditions of hand-made pottery persisted until a surprisingly late date in parts of medieval Britain.

In firing pottery, also, medieval potters were slow to catch up with technological developments. There is no evidence, for instance, for the use of grates to improve the efficiency of kilns until the post-medieval period, although grates were used in metallurgy and alchemy (Dawson and Kent 1984: 14–15). There is little evidence either until the early post-medieval period of potters covering their kilns with roofed structures to enable firing to continue in bad weather.

This apparent conservatism among potters, manifested partly by their failure to reach the threshold of contemporary technological limitations, correlates with their lowly peasant status and minimal access to sources of capital for much of the Middle Ages. The question of cause and effect will be avoided here, to avoid circular arguments. It can be seen that the status of potters was for the most part very different from that of potters in China and the Middle East, where pottery was recognized as a craft, or sometimes an art, and patronage could come from the highest levels of society. An exception to this are some of the Late Saxon potters, who may also have had higher status and patronage (for example, the producers of high quality wares at Stamford and Winchester). The exploitation of technological developments such as animal, water and wind power fell to those who could afford it. Potters at the level of household industry and individual workshops (Peacock 1982: 8–9), supplying limited peasant markets, may have been both unwilling and unable to provide capital expenditure on technological improvements, particularly if they could see no immediate short-term advantage.

The conservatism of the market is seen in the range of items produced by potters, which often hardly varied over a number of generations. The peasant potters were mostly supplying the lower and middle ranks of society, and not competing for an aristocratic market; even when royal households in the post-Conquest period placed large orders for pottery, these vessels were probably for use mostly in the kitchens and by the lower echelons of the household. Vessels of other materials graced the highest tables. The situation

Fig. 25   Bronze aquamanile from Hexham, Northumberland; ht. 33 cm. (Reproduced by courtesy of the Trustees of the British Museum)

Fig. 26   Pottery aquamanile from Norfolk; ht. 21.3 cm. (Reproduced by courtesy of the Trustees of the British Museum)

has been described as a stalemate: 'because demand is limited, so the producer keeps within the limits of his market' (Hodges H. 1974: 37).

One of the main factors which did bring about changes in pottery forms and decoration was the desire to copy fashionable imported wares and metal wares, as well as other materials such as wood and leather. Potters could thus supply an already existing demand, particularly among people who aspired to more expensive items such as metal vessels but could not afford them. The influence of metal prototypes on vessels such as jugs, pipkins, skillets and chafing dishes can often be seen (Lewis 1978). Figs. 25 and 26 show a bronze aquamanile and a copy of such a vessel in pottery.

Some imported wares seem to have had more effect on the local production than others. The Rouen-type wares of north-western France, for example, had considerable influence on the London-type wares, and to a lesser extent on other types (Fig. 27). Saintonge polychrome decoration, on the other hand, which is very striking, seems not to have had any direct copies, perhaps through technological limitations, although the shapes of Saintonge jugs were imitated (Saintonge polychrome was itself probably the result of exotic inspiration, in this case that of Mediterranean maiolicas which would have been fairly well known in the south-west of France). Regional imports, too, could influence potters; Scarborough ware face-mask jugs, for instance, were copied by potters in north-east England and eastern Scotland.

Other factors influencing development in pottery technology, forms and decoration are less tangible. Social and economic variables doubtless played their parts; they would have affected, for example, what access a potter had to new ideas or materials, what kind of market was available for his goods, and

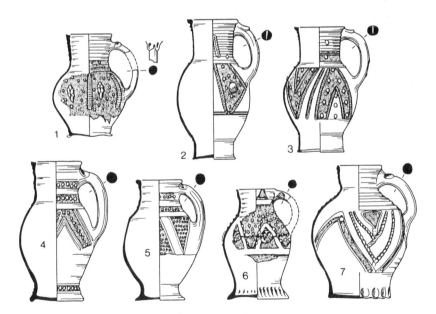

Fig. 27 Rouen ware jugs and English copies.
1–3, Rouen ware jugs from Southampton. (After Platt and Coleman-Smith 1975)
4–5, London-type ware jugs. (After Pearce *et al.* 1985)
6, south Somerset jug. (After Pearson 1984)
7, Grimston-type ware jug. (After Jennings 1981)

how much he had to earn from his craft in order to supplement the living from his sometimes small or marginal land holding. Little work has been done on theoretical aspects of innovation in medieval pottery, but a recent paper by Orton (1985) has considered the various factors involved and attempted to define some general principles relating to ceramic change.

Economic factors varied from area to area; dairying regions, for example, might have had a considerable demand for large shallow bowls suitable for cream separation. Regional markets, on the other hand, might have shown a preference for wooden vessels for this purpose; correlating pottery types with economic activities is not easy. Apart from the unknowable individual personality, regional fashion is perhaps the least understood factor influencing pottery development. In 1963 Jope described a number of regional pottery traits and traditions, and drew attention to the distribution of other cultural aspects such as place-names and sculpture styles, in an attempt to define regional cultures. From this preliminary survey, regional differences but no clear, integrated regional cultures emerged. A number of regional ceramic traditions have been studied and defined since that article was written, but Jope's lead in considering pottery with other cultural traits has not been followed up. His conclusion still holds good, that 'the distribution of pottery, peasant or industrial, is not to be simply correlated with the variants of rural economy, and has emphasized the many facets of medieval culture in Britain, the interplay of the material with the intangible, and their relation to the environment' (Jope 1963: 350).

Chapter 2   Production and Distribution

This chapter reviews the evidence for the production of pottery as well as for exchange and distribution mechanisms in Late Saxon and medieval Britain. The evidence varies in quality. In archaeological terms, the study of production sites has suffered by too great an emphasis on kilns rather than on the tenements and the settlements of which the tenements formed a part. On the other hand, the growth in excavations over the last twenty years has vastly increased the amount of pottery available for examination, from long stratified sequences and from sites varying from royal to peasant status. Historical sources are silent for production before the time of Domesday, although they are useful for wider social and economic issues. After the Norman Conquest, documentary sources are increasingly prolific, and while they contain only occasional references to potters, they are nonetheless an invaluable source of information about medieval society and the milieu within which the potters operated (Le Patourel 1968).

A considerable amount of attention has been devoted by anthropologists as well as archaeologists to the study of ceramics. Although pottery is only one of several materials used for containers, it has been widely employed by many societies today and in the past. Modes of production have featured in many studies, in terms of whether pottery was a full-time or part-time activity, whether vessels were made by men or women, the impact of ceramic manufacture on other domestic or livelihood pursuits, and whether production was geared to mass markets or for individual use (Arnold 1985; Foster 1966; Peacock 1982; Rice 1981; 1984; van der Leeuw 1984). Many of these studies are based upon the observation of contemporary situations and cannot strictly be used to extrapolate back to ancient societies. Even so, they provide an invaluable framework for thinking about how production could have been organized in the past. Peacock, for example, has defined four principal production modes (1982). At a very simple level is 'household production', a situation where each family might produce items of equipment as and when they needed them. Somewhat more advanced is 'household industry', in which certain families meet particular needs of their social group by supplying items of equipment. This represents a simple form of specialization in which the idea of selling products at a market first appears. 'Workshop industries' are much more sophisticated, and occur in societies with greater levels of social and economic organization. As the name implies, they are workshop-based and may well include several people, a degree of sub-division of labour and year-round manufacture geared towards selling at regular markets. Other modes of production may be organized by capitalist entrepreneurs on their estates or by the military, and are associated with more advanced societies.

In Britain during the first millennium AD several methods of producing pottery are apparent, ranging from the simple to very sophisticated. Within the Roman period the military were supplied, at least in the pre-Hadrianic period, by their own depots or works, an example of which has been excavated at Holt, Denbighshire, operated by the Twentieth Legion. Large-scale potteries are also known at Mancetter in Warwickshire, Alice Holt on the Surrey-Hampshire borders, the New Forest or Oxford, and the lower Nene Valley, though it is rarely clear under what aegis the potters were working. Such concerns were almost certainly run by specialist full-time craftsmen, assisted by others whose duties could have included digging clay, making balls for throwing, mixing the filler or transporting the finished goods to market. Smaller concerns, perhaps indicated by the proliferation of kilns in the upper Nene valley, Northamptonshire, were also in production, although run perhaps as family concerns by peasant farmers for whom potting was an alternative and additional occupation. At this level production may be defined as lying somewhere between the household industry and workshop mode.

The Romano-British potters possessed a relatively high level of technical competence, though their methods varied from the use of clamp firings and hand-forming to wheels and updraught kilns. The demand, as excavations testify, was considerable and the craftsmen, whatever their methods, clearly met the demand. Whilst in some situations we might expect that the advent of the faster and more efficient technique of wheel-throwing would reflect the presence of a greater market demand, other factors were clearly at work in Roman Britain as is demonstrated by Black Burnished Ware 1, a hand-made pottery type exported over most of the province throughout much of the period of Roman rule.

By the middle of the fifth century the Roman economy had collapsed, and with it many of the features sustaining the Roman system. The scale of pottery production declined dramatically after what Renfrew has called 'the crash' (1979). Some regions, such as parts of the west Midlands and the northern parts of England, ceased using pottery at all. Other areas, including parts of the east Midlands, where Late Saxon and medieval shelly ware traditions appear from recent work to have been deeply rooted in earlier times, may have continued using pottery. In pottery-using areas the nature of the demand changed during the Early Saxon period; the variety of domestic and table wares present in the fourth century were replaced by the simplest forms of plain, round-based vessels which presumably served many purposes.

The most noticeable difference, however, is in the introduction of highly decorated funerary wares used to accompany cremations. The methods used to make the pottery also changed. There is no evidence for the use of updraught kilns, and the assumption from the relatively soft surface textures is that much of the pottery was fired in bonfires. The use of wheel-throwing techniques also disappeared and was replaced with coiling, paddle and anvil, slab forming, and even possibly moulding (although evidence for the latter has yet to be demonstrated). We should also expect that organizational changes in the production of pottery would follow. Evidence for this is generally lacking, but studies of present day situations such as Balfet's work in the Maghreb (1966) or the application of catastrophe theory (Renfrew 1979; Rahtz 1982) suggest that a reversion to simple household production would not be surprising. Two strands of evidence are worth noting. Firstly, many of the stamped funerary wares such as those in the Illington and Lackford cemeteries or those in the Kettering area have been decorated with the same stamp, implying the presence of craftsmen supplying vessels on some sort of regional basis (Myres 1969). Secondly, plain domestic wares containing a mineral suite clearly derived from the Charnwood area of Leicestershire have been found along the length of the Nene valley, perhaps implying contact of some sort with the Leicester area (McCarthy 1977; 1979; Gryspeerdt 1981a). It is possible that a household-based industry may be invoked to explain such distributions.

Concomitant features of the collapse of the Romano-British socio-economic system are the absence of markets, competition and bureaucracy. New cultural influences are apparent in the pottery, and some of the forms as well as decorative motifs betray strong north German influences. The differences in the pottery between the late Roman period and the fifth–seventh centuries is so strong as to suggest that populations dispersed, thereby confirming the picture presented by excavations especially in urban areas. Furthermore, the advantages of ceramic cooking wares over other easily available materials are such, as Arnold (1985) has graphically demonstrated, that changes in both food production and diet are implied.

In the Middle Saxon period the historical and numismatic records show unmistakable signs of emerging kingdoms. These are characterized by such features as increased specialization, more co-operative effort and a re-distributive system under firm central control, as well as a coordination of religious, social and economic activities. Only to a very limited extent are these features reflected in the pottery of the period. The association of updraught kilns producing uniformly fired, hard grey sandy wares made on a turntable with the focal point of the kingdom of East Anglia may not be coincidental. The Ipswich ware potters not only produced a technically more advanced product than hitherto but extended the range of forms to include the occasional bowl and decorated pitcher. Such innovations perhaps spring from either higher status craftsmen who wish to confirm their existing pre-eminent position, or else from low status workers who have nothing to lose by experimentation (Arnold 1985). One potter experimented to the extent of replicating the face on the Sutton Hoo sceptre on one of his vessels (Smedley and Owles 1967). Elsewhere, at Canterbury, Mainman (1983) has shown how much better quality are the Middle Saxon Group 5 wares over their predecessors, whereas at Hamwih the local populace was supplied not only with local pottery but with a wide range of imported vessels (Hodges R. 1980). Whilst it is tempting to identify pottery with power at this date, it is worth recalling that in Mercia, one of the largest kingdoms, there is very little datable pottery. What can be identified bears no innovative features.

The pre-Conquest period

During the ninth and tenth centuries pottery is known from a number of 'leadership' sites such as Netherton, Goltho, Jarrow, Shaftesbury and Cheddar. Here too the correlation between pottery and influence can be suggested. It may indeed be the case, but as a blanket explanation it is unsatisfactory, for there are a number of rural sites, including those in the vicinity of St Neots in Huntingdonshire or Raunds in Northamptonshire, that have produced pottery in abundance. Moreover, virtually all the pottery is run-of-the-mill material and there is no evidence yet available for the production of high-class pottery vessels specifically associated with high-class sites. The kind of pottery being recovered from London or Winchester is no different in quality to that found elsewhere in the first half of the tenth century. Only at Winchester, and then not until about the beginning of Edgar's reign in the mid-tenth century, can we suggest a correlation between a high quality ceramic, in this case the fine, glazed Winchester ware followed by Tripod Pitcher ware, and the presence of the royal household.

From the late ninth and early tenth centuries we can also detect new strands in the social hierarchy with the development of urban-based communities. People who could be described as *burgware* or *portmenn*, that is inhabitants of a *burh*, constituted an increasingly important class exercising rights of justice and landlordship. With strong royal and ecclesiastical interest in the *burhs*, these people represent an elitist element who both supplied the market with a widening range of goods and helped create the demand for items drawn from further afield. One of the most eloquent testimonies to these exchanges are the coins of that period, which are the finest in Europe and which confirm the growing strength of royal authority across England as a whole. The coins are the products of craftsmen who must have operated as full-time moneyers in order to provide the millions needed to service the courts, the developing administrative machinery and the works put in hand by the king. The moneyers were one element in a growing group of people, including workers in leather, the metal trades, textile and wood-based crafts, whose living was substantially derived from their occupation rather than from agricultural pursuits.

Pottery production has its place in this milieu. The production of ceramics in the Bedford Street, formerly Pottergate, suburb of Norwich, attested by clay-pits, wasters, kilns and as yet slight structural evidence (Atkin *et al.* 1983), seems to represent a concentration of workers in one particular craft. The amount of industrial waste found here, together with the common occurrence of ceramics on domestic sites elsewhere in Norwich, suggests that pottery was in everyday usage and that we should consider the workshop as the most likely mode of production. Elsewhere, Vince (1985a) has argued on petrological grounds that the important Late Saxon Shelly wares in London were supplied from the Oxfordshire region, and also notes that Stafford-type ware has an equally extensive occurrence over the west Midlands. A similar phenomenon is noted in Wiltshire and Somerset. The wide distribution of these pottery types, combined with the efficiency of the wheel-throwing technique with which they were produced, is an additional argument in favour of a workshop mode of production, at least in the tenth century.

One of the more striking features of Late Saxon pottery distribution as it is currently understood is the strong bias towards urban production. Unfortunately, most of the sites identified consist only of a kiln or wasters. Apart from Norwich, several production centres are directly attested by more than one kiln, for example Stamford, Thetford, Ipswich, Torksey and Stafford, whilst at Lincoln the Silver Street kiln and wasters for Lincoln Gritty ware also point to the presence of several workshops. Other towns with single instances of kilns or wasters include Northampton, Leicester, Nottingham, Gloucester, Chichester and Exeter.

The picture of production in rural areas is less certain, as very few kilns have been found and the number of excavations on village or manorial sites with good pre-Conquest sequences is limited. Addyman has excavated a kiln and wasters at Michelmersh, Hampshire (Addyman *et al.* 1972), and has further suggested that burnt pits associated with wasters at St Neots, Huntingdonshire, may be connected with the production of St Neots ware (1973). The distribution of this type of pottery is very wide, extending from the region of the Wash south-west towards Oxford but with outliers well beyond. In view of this extensive distribution, the probability is that St Neots ware emanated from several production centres, some of which may have been rural whilst others may have been located near urban centres such as Northampton, Oxford and Bedford. In Herefordshire, Shropshire and Cheshire, no pottery attributable to the Late Saxon period is known outside the main urban centres although this picture may not be sustained by future work. Pottery dating from the early tenth century is known at Cheddar and Ilchester, whilst in Cornwall the distinctive 'bar lug' cooking pots, perhaps made at various locations, are thought to be tenth or eleventh century, although the dating evidence in many instances is very tenuous.

The relationship of the potting areas to settlement patterns in both pre- and post-Conquest times is imperfectly understood. At Norwich (Fig. 28), Stamford and Chichester production is known outside the *burh*, but at Lincoln, Stafford, Northampton and Gloucester potters seem to be working inside the

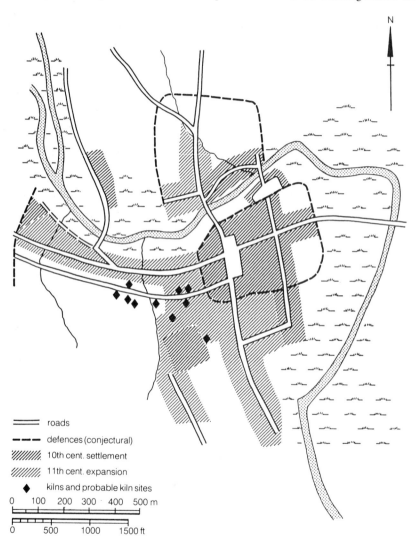

roads

defences (conjectural)

10th cent. settlement

11th cent. expansion

♦ kilns and probable kiln sites

0 100 200 300 400 500 m

0   500   1000   1500 ft

Fig. 28 Location of kilns and waster heaps attesting Thetford ware production at Norwich. (After Atkin *et al.* 1983)

burh; in the latter two instances the production areas are very close to the crossroads at the centre of the town. As already noted, evidence for the production areas is very scanty and is rarely represented by more than the occasional post-hole or pit. At Stafford a large open area excavation revealed three kilns on Tipping Street, but no evidence was found for the workshops, drying sheds, puddling pits or settling tanks needed during the manufacturing process.

At Thetford, Norfolk, several excavations have produced kilns, pits, gulleys and other features. Analysis of the earlier excavations there has been unable to confirm the identity of features which may be associated with potting, although it is clear that industrial activities tended to be located towards the periphery of the urban area (Rogerson and Dallas 1984). Knocker's work at Site 2 South revealed a multiplicity of activities, including ironworking, textile production as well as potting, juxtaposed without any real order. In the words of Rogerson and Dallas who have collated the records, this area was 'a slum' compared with that excavated by Davison (*ibid.*: 14). In the area investigated by Davison immediately adjacent to the defences, a potting tenement was defined by ditches with a centrally placed kiln in a yard. Around the kiln there were considerable trampled zones where the potters walked during the firing. No buildings were recognized but a pivot stone, tentatively identified as belonging to a potter's wheel, was found in a stone-packed post-hole, whilst a few feet away a large storage jar was sunk into the ground (Davison 1967). It is uncertain whether the areas excavated by Knocker and Davison represent different points in the development of the town, though Davison has suggested a phase of planned expansion in which some zoning of areas according to function might be discerned (*ibid.*: 194).

By contrast with the Middle Saxon period, the manufacturing techniques in use from the end of the ninth century show some variation across the country. Within the Danelaw, potters were using wheel-throwing techniques, as at Stamford, Norwich and Torksey, and a combination of throwing and coiling on the same vessels at the Northampton ware kilns. St Neots wares include both hand-made and wheel-thrown vessels. To some extent the methods adopted depended upon the form being made; thus a storage jar in St Neots ware from Northampton is hand-made, another in Stamford ware from Stamford Castle site is either coiled or slab-built, whilst a Torksey-type ware storage vessel from York is also probably hand-formed. In these instances the size of the vessel may have been the factor determining the technique used.

Similar variations exist on the frontier and beyond the Danelaw; at Exeter, Portchester and Michelmersh, for example, throwing techniques were in use. At Cheddar and Ilchester in Somerset hand-forming and throwing methods were employed in the tenth century. At Ilchester, vessels believed to be earlier than *c.* 930 are described as crude, hand-made pots with fingered surfaces, thereby contrasting with the wheel-thrown mid to late tenth-century Cheddar E type and other forms made on a turntable (Pearson T. 1982). Other hand-made wares can be identified at Cricklade, Christchurch, possibly Shaftesbury, Canterbury, Chichester and Southampton; the Cornish 'bar lug' and slightly later Sandy Lane wares are also hand-made. Variations exist, not surprisingly, in finishing techniques and methods of firing. Updraught kilns were in use in parts of the Danelaw but, as already pointed out, clamp firing may be assumed for some St Neots wares and, if Addyman was correct in the identification of pottery production at St Neots, pit firings were also taking place. Single-flued updraught kilns (Type 1) have been excavated at Grimston, Norfolk, Stamford, Exeter and Stafford, for example, and clamps revealed during work at Chichester.

It is not clear what, if anything, the distribution of different manufacturing or firing techniques means. There seems to be a larger number of updraught kilns and wheel-thrown vessels within the Danelaw or along the frontier than beyond, a feature noted in the early studies of Saxo-Norman pottery (Dunning et al. 1959; Hurst 1976). It may, therefore, seem reasonable to relate this to the Scandinavian invasions and settlement of the late ninth and early tenth centuries. For example, the production of the distinctive continental red-painted ware at Stamford and probably Northampton, both of which may well reflect the presence of immigrant potters coming over with or in the wake of the Scandinavian invaders, could be seen as reinforcing the connection between potting technology and the Scandinavian incursions. Furthermore, some forms appear to reflect foreign ideas; the large storage jars covered with decorated applied strips in Thetford ware have some similarity to Badorf *Reliefband* amphorae, and the same comparisons may be made with spouted pitchers and their continental counterparts.

To attribute the re-introduction of wheel-throwing in the ninth century just to Scandinavian 'influence' is not only too simple, however, but also confuses historical and archaeological evidence. There is almost certainly no relationship between manufacturing techniques and political divisions. Looked at from the pottery viewpoint, the examples quoted above may owe nothing at all to Scandinavian 'influence', whatever that may be, but result from either independent invention or straight copying by English potters of vessels brought over in the course of normal commercial contact. Again, just as specialists in Roman archaeology may at times focus too closely on the few historically recorded events, as in the case of Hadrian's Wall, so too must we beware of being mesmerized by the presence of the Danes. Quite apart from the fact that historians are not agreed on the impact and extent of Scandinavian settlement, the pattern of ceramic development and technical innovation, as pointed out earlier, is not confined to the Danelaw. In any case, the Danes did not themselves make pottery in their homelands at this period.

It can be shown that hand-forming and wheel-throwing, and clamp and updraught kiln firing, existed side by side in the Late Saxon period, a phenomenon also noted by ethnographers in contemporary societies. It can also be suggested that wheel-throwing is a potentially much faster and much more efficient method of producing pots than hand-forming techniques. The use of updraught kilns enables firing to take place in adverse weather conditions and to higher temperatures than bonfire or pit firings. We might, therefore, expect demand to play a part in determining the means of production; the greater the demand the more likely it is that the craftsmen will adopt techniques which enable him to keep up with it. Was this the case?

In Late Saxon England, the rapid development of urban communities certainly represented denser concentrations of demand, but it is by no means certain that the urban communities also indicate rising population levels. If it did, and if the increased numbers represented new households as opposed to the simple extension of existing households, then the demand for pots would also have increased. It is possible that this was the case, especially in those towns such as Winchester or York with strong royal and ecclesiastical associations, and therefore a greater degree of attraction, though there is no direct evidence as yet. Furthermore, as Boserup (1981) and Rice (1984) have indicated, where there are increases in population, there are inevitably stresses between the people and the resources needed to sustain them. Thus population increase compels society to adjust its production methods for the supply of food and equipment to the changed situation. One very obvious adjustment is that whereas in the mid-ninth century it appears that relatively little pottery was in use, in the mid-tenth century it had been widely adopted at all levels of society. From this time people had cooking pots, a range of bowls, storage jars, spouted pitchers and lamps to light their homes. They were, therefore, able to cook a wider range of foodstuffs than hitherto, an adjustment which surely has implications for both food supply as well as levels of health. When these adjustments were absorbed by society, the craftsmen were virtually guaranteed an outlet for their wares.

The response of the potters was variable, as can be seen by the use of different production methods at different times and in different places. For example, the peoples of Oxford, London and many Thames valley settlements in between seem to have been supplied by workshops using wheel-throwing techniques, probably located in Oxfordshire. Wide areas of the west Midlands from Chester to Hereford may have been supplied from the production centres identified at Stafford which also used wheel-throwing methods. At Chichester demand was met by the slower hand-forming techniques, whilst the producers of Northampton ware used a combination of a part-throwing and a part-coiling technique. In the eleventh century, areas formerly producing wheel-thrown pots reverted back to hand-forming methods, as can be seen for example in

London or Somerset. An even more dramatic example is the evidently very successful and widely exported clamp-fired, hand-made Black Burnished I industry of centuries earlier. Thus, the idea that manufacturing technique can be correlated with the strength of demand, an idea derived from ways of thinking induced by the industrial revolution, clearly does not apply in Late Saxon and Roman Britain.

Other factors must also have played their part. Amongst these are the questions of the extent to which the potters were full-time or part-time and the extent of their dependence upon potting for their livelihood, the role of men and women in the household, and the division of labour between the sexes. Social preference may also have contributed to the choice of technique adopted by the potter. Balfet (1984) observed in the Maghreb that wheel-thrown and turntable-made pots were on sale side by side in the markets. Not only were hand-made vessels considered more durable than the thrown pots but they commanded higher prices. Such factors are beyond the scope of archaeological enquiry and not recorded in historical sources, but as constraints operating on craftsmen of the time they are potentially at least as important as the sometimes somewhat nebulous 'influences' emanating from the Continent or the Danish invaders.

The post-Conquest period

During the eleventh and twelfth centuries great social, economic and political changes occurred; some of these might be expected to be reflected in the development of craft production. Changes in pottery can indeed be discerned; new forms were produced, some existing forms were made in very much larger sizes, the application of glazes and decoration was extended and there are indications of more production centres operating. The extent to which these changes can be attributed to the Norman Conquest is not easy to resolve. There are increasing archaeological indications to suggest that the picture in the Late Saxon period was not simply a matter of the introduction of cooking pots, bowls and the occasional spouted pitcher, all made by wheel-throwing. It appears to have been much more complex, with some production centres having shorter or longer lives than others, and forming and finishing techniques varying perhaps within a single production unit. The changes sometimes appear very suddenly in the stratigraphic record, but sometimes new types come in gradually and disappear just as slowly.

The Norman Conquest was by no means the only impetus for change. The settlement of a group of Danes, a local but devastating raid, or something as simple as the natural death of a potter may stimulate change. In Oxford, for example, a raid in 1009 may well have hastened the demise of the Shelly wares

(Mellor 1980a). This date is consistent with the evidence from London supplied by the same pottery, which disappears from the archaeological record at about that time (Vince 1985a). Close dating is necessary to establish links with even major historical events, and this can only rarely be demonstrated. Even when dates can be suggested, as for example with the apparent cessation of supplies of Torksey ware to Lincoln in the decade following the Conquest (Gilmour *et al.* forthcoming), we still cannot be certain that it was the direct or indirect actions of the Normans which resulted in the change. The same may be true at Exeter, where Bedford Garage ware drops out of the stratigraphic sequences after *c.* 1100 (Allan 1984). At Oxford, the local Early Medieval wares (AC) increase in popularity around the turn of the eleventh-twelfth centuries (Mellor 1980a), but it is possible that they were introduced before the Conquest, and their rise in importance may be due to factors other than the presence of the Normans.

The difficulties of dating archaeological sequences with great precision are such that the impact of the Conquest upon local production is impossible to assess. Yet we must not suppose that great events may not be reflected in the ceramic record, as Adams has demonstrated in Nubia for example (Adams W.Y. 1979). The very fact of the castle, cathedral and monastic building programmes is sufficient to show that new sets of demands and stresses were established in society. Amongst other things, these new buildings confirmed and enhanced the status of existing centres of population besides establishing new foci of power in other areas. They required a great deal of labour, besides a variety of craftsmen to supply, erect and adorn the new buildings. These were fertile grounds for innovation in which the multiplier effect would have come into operation. This is a mechanism whereby the proximity of related crafts encourages and stimulates specialization and innovation (Trigger 1972). It is also a means of explaining the rapid growth of crafts, including pottery, in many towns in the tenth century.

From the early twelfth century, the number of production centres seems to increase, and in rural parts of England such as parts of Herefordshire and Shropshire, where there is little prior evidence for the use of ceramic containers, sherds of pottery occur frequently in excavation and field survey. Other areas, such as parts of northern England, Scotland and Wales, were possibly aceramic from Roman times, although the truth of this assertion can only be tested with much more fieldwork. Even so, the evidence as it stands suggests that these areas began using pottery for the first time during the twelfth century. This development thus follows the Norman penetration and the creation of castles, boroughs and monasteries. Just as the urban communities of Late Saxon England created new pockets of demand, so the new elements in the pattern of northern and western settlements, combined with the presence of English and Norman settlers familiar with pottery from their homelands, provided the impetus for new crafts and realigned social and economic systems.

The chronology of these changes is difficult to establish because of the problems in dating pottery. At Hen Domen in Montgomeryshire, a motte and bailey castle associated with Roger of Montgomery, pottery is present, albeit in small quantities, certainly from the early twelfth century and possibly from the late eleventh (Barker and Higham 1982). Small quantities of possibly locally-produced pottery are known at Prudhoe, a castle in the Tyne valley. In the Scottish Borders, at the abbeys in Kelso and Jedburgh, Scottish White Gritty wares appear to be associated with levels attributed to the twelfth century.

One of the more striking changes from the twelfth century is the apparent increase in the number of production sites in rural locations. Production located within urban areas is still in evidence, as at Nottingham, Lostwithiel and possibly Northampton, and is known immediately outside the walls of Shrewsbury, Colchester and Chester. The number of production sites known or strongly suspected from the countryside, however, is now considerably greater. Rural production is attested from the heart of villages, as at Toynton All Saints (Fig. 29) and Potter Hanworth (Fig. 30), Lincolnshire, or Ashton and Audlem in Cheshire. At Brereton Park, Cheshire, the production site appears to be close to the ridge-and-furrow on the periphery of the village. At Stanion, Grimston, Boarstall (Fig. 31) and Olney Hyde, production sites are spread out along the village streets. One of the largest known concentrations of kilns in England is at Chilvers Coton, Nuneaton, but unfortunately there has been no analysis of the relationship of the kilns to the medieval topography.

These developments are clearly significant indicators of greatly expanded production. From the immediate post-Conquest period onwards in England, pottery vessels become standard items of equipment, from the richer south-eastern and Midland shires to the more remote uplands of Cornwall and Cumberland. In the Scottish burghs such as Aberdeen, Perth and St Andrews, ceramics become increasingly familiar from the twelfth century, although the nature of the earliest production units cannot yet be assessed. It remains to be demonstrated, however, that rural households in the Highlands and the Western and Northern Isles used pottery to any extent during the medieval period, although excavations at Breachacha Castle, Jarlshof and Kirkwall, for example, have produced evidence of coarse local hand-made pottery traditions supplementing pottery imported from mainland Scotland and further afield. A similar picture obtains in Wales, where pottery was used extensively in the towns, as in Cardiff and Carmarthen, as well as in the castles and monastic institutions. Again, it is not clear to what extent pottery was preferred to other materials by people in the remoter regions of central and west Wales.

Whilst this is not the place for a detailed explanation and examination of the chronology of these changes, their importance should not be underestimated. The adoption of pottery is a reflection of other changes taking place in society.

N

production site

wasters and probable
production sites

0   300 m

0   1000 ft

Fig. 29 Plan of Toynton All Saints and Toynton St Peter, Lincolnshire, locating
production sites and waster heaps. (After Healey 1984)

Fig. 30 Plan of Potter Hanworth, Lincolnshire, locating waster heaps.
(After Healey 1975)

Fig. 31 Plan of Boarstall, Buckinghamshire, locating kilns and
production sites. (After Farley 1982)

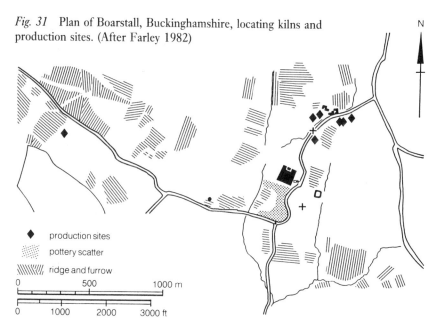

It was innovatory and required the modification of a range of routines, habits and tastes. In thirteenth-century St Andrews, for example, the presence of heavily sooted two-handled cooking pots of local manufacture establishes the use of such vessels on a regular basis for cooking; previously other materials must have been used. These might include metal cauldrons, although they are likely to have been confined to the wealthier segments of society. The peasantry may well have been restricted to baking and roasting, or cooking by other less effective means.

The result would have been limitations on the range of consumable foodstuffs, on diet, and possibly therefore on vitamin intake. A potential consequence of the adoption of ceramics for food preparation and cooking could well have been a healthier population. This is not to say that the adoption of ceramics *caused* a healthier population, but to suggest that it might have been one factor amongst others, including for example improved medical knowledge, a more effective means of distributing foodstuffs within society, and the development of trade links with the consequent acquisition of wider ranges of goods. Pottery can again provide a useful example. Most watching briefs and excavations in east coast Scottish towns produce very large quantities of fine glazed Scarborough ware vessels, many of which are jugs. They are also found in remote areas where there was no prior tradition of pouring from ceramic jugs, and as such reflect the increasing commercial ties with areas further south as well as the development of personal tastes in drinking habits. A similar phenomenon may be seen in the distribution of glazed and often decorated Ham Green ware jugs in south Wales and Ireland.

Clearly, then, the overall scale of production increased substantially, but attempts to define the levels of output in any one centre or region are impossible, given the absence of documented figures or large-scale excavations on well-dated production sites. The mode of production is equally difficult to define, but the order of magnitude probably lies somewhere closer to Peacock's household industry than his workshop mode. A feature of the latter is that some members of the workshop operated on a full-time basis, obtaining much of their livelihood in this way. 'Potter' names occur fairly frequently in medieval documentary sources, although as Le Patourel has warned (1979b), such appellations may refer to metal rather than earthenware potters.

Some villages had a number of potters; in Domesday Book, five potters are recorded at Harefield, Gloucestershire, for example, and at Crockerton, Wiltshire, thirteen potters paid rents in 1234. Clay rents were also paid by thirteen potters at Hanley, Worcestershire, in 1296. Some forty kilns have been excavated at Chilvers Coton, Nuneaton, spanning the thirteenth to sixteenth centuries; at Stanion, Northamptonshire, ten kilns are known in the village and others are suspected. This site lies only 6 km from Lyveden where potting is also attested. At Nottingham, twelve kilns inside and outside the defences have so far been located. Other substantial industries are known from Rye, Tyler Hill, Laverstock, Donyatt, Worcester, Docker Moor and Wrenthorpe, amongst many others. There are sufficient indications to suggest that potters' villages of the kind clearly present at Nuneaton were regular features of the landscape, and that many production sites known only from single examples of kilns or waster heaps are probably parts of larger concerns. The scale at which some of these industries were operating can sometimes be assessed.

Actual evidence for the workshops is scanty, although occasional pictorial representations in continental sources, such as the well-known views in Agricola's *De Re Metallica* (Fig. 11 No. 4) or in Picolpasso's *The Art of the Potter*, provide an impression of the thrower at his wheel with others digging clay or firing the kilns, a division of labour to be expected in an organized workshop. They appear not to be significantly different from country potteries in Britain, such as those at Verwood or Barnstaple, which continued to operate in a 'primitive' way until the present century.

Documentary references to potters' working areas are scarce, but one at Woodstock refers to Adam Beneyth's tenement with a kiln, garden, workshop, yard and two stalls. Archaeological evidence for workshops has been revealed by excavations at Olney Hyde and Lyveden. At the deserted village of Olney Hyde, Mynard excavated much of a thirteenth- to fourteenth-century potter's toft which contained a rectangular limestone-based structure, within which there were a number of post-holes, and a small stone-lined pit adjacent to another shallow pit used either for levigating clay or for water storage. This may be the workshop, abutting another building which could have been either the potter's living area or used for storage and drying. In the yard outside there were two raised cobbled zones, stone-lined gullies and a single-flued pottery kiln. On the opposite side of the workshop, a large pit with three steep sides and one very shallow side, possibly an entry for a cart, was interpreted as a clay-pit (Fig. 32). The toft appears to have been defined at the front by a stone-based wall adjacent to a road in a hollow way.

Excavations at Lyveden, a deserted village in Rockingham Forest, Northamptonshire, revealed evidence of pottery- and tile-making and iron working, set firmly within an agricultural community between the late twelfth to late fifteenth centuries. The possibility of earlier pottery-making extending back into the pre-Conquest period cannot be ruled out. One of the most informative excavations took place on Site D (Fig. 33), where three major industrial phases can be defined. Within the toft, a rectangular building, constructed initially of timber but rebuilt with stone walls, can be identified as a workshop. Much industrial waste was found trodden into the floors inside the building, which also had several hearths and pits, some containing clean clay. The distribution of features suggested to the excavator that one end of the workshop was for manufacture, as it contained pits with clean clay and tools

Fig. 32 Excavations at Olney Hyde, Buckinghamshire, showing clay-pit with access for carts. (Photo D. Mynard)

Fig. 33 Plans of Site D, Lyveden, Northamptonshire.
(a) workshop, storeshed and remnants of Kiln D2; mid to late 13th cent. (b) new layout in late 13th to early 14th cent. (After Bryant and Steane 1971)

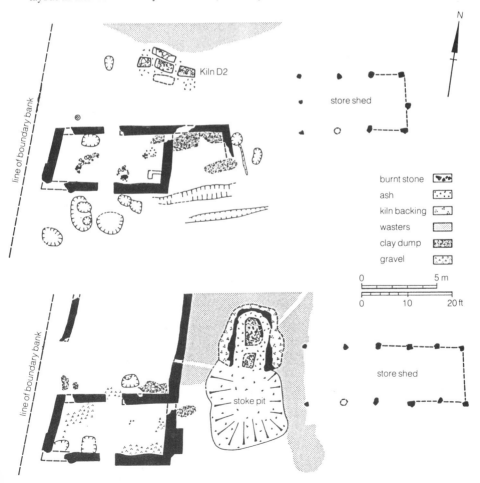

including iron knives, an antler stamp and whetstones; the other end with hearths may have been used for drying purposes (Bryant and Steane 1971).

The building contained two opposed doors in the centre of the long walls. The southern door gave access to the south yard which contained several deep pits, possibly clay-pits, in the early phase. The northern door opened into another yard which housed a Type 4a kiln in the first two major phases. To the east of the workshop a timber building based upon padstones was interpreted, not implausibly, as a store shed, although positive functional evidence was lacking. In the final phase, the kiln was moved from the north yard to a new site immediately adjacent to the store shed. In all phases, considerable quantities of industrial waste were located in and around the buildings and the kiln.

Excavations elsewhere in the village located further tofts with evidence of potting. The west end of Site J contained another Type 4a kiln and waster heap, a well, hard standing and various quarry pits. In the south-west corner large quantities of iron slag, coal, charcoal and fire-reddened stones indicate iron working. It is not clear whether the potting and iron working were being carried out at the same time. In most areas investigated at Lyveden, the industrial activity seems not to be associated with recognizable evidence of living quarters in the same toft, suggesting that these may have been purely working areas. The apparently organized nature of the layout is impressive, though not necessarily surprising, as is the amount of space (up to one third of an acre on Sites D and J) for all the activities and storage areas required by a working pottery.

For all the importance that attached to industrial activities at Lyveden, it should not be allowed to cloud our view of how the village functioned. All the evidence from medieval England stresses the importance of the land, and at Lyveden, as well as doubtless at Nuneaton, Mill Green and other places, farming was a major, if not the dominant, activity. At Lyveden this can be seen in the farming tools and equipment excavated, and on one toft, in the reversion to purely agricultural activity in the fourteenth–fifteenth centuries.

Although we have next to no evidence for the nature of production units in medieval communities in Britain, the documentary evidence for the period provides the context within which potters should be viewed. In the first place it should be said that the evidence referring to potters frequently identifies them as paying rents for clay or fuels, as litigants in the courts or with landholdings of very limited size (Le Patourel 1968). The nature of the documents or the circumstances of the case are usually sufficient to place the potters within the peasantry. Again, the infrequency with which potters appear to be recorded in the early fourteenth-century Lay Subsidy returns is probably a fair indication of the fact that they were too poor to be taxed (Gooder 1984; Streeten 1982). There will of course always be exceptions, including possibly several Shrewsbury potters, notably Robert and Peter le Potter in 1252 and 1281 respectively, and William, son of Peter le Potter, and Thomas of Boxstead of

Coleham, both in 1318–19, all of whom could have been earthenware potters and who were all members of the merchant guild. Before the fifteenth century the status of many potters may have been that of the unfree villein or cottar dependent upon the lord, but even freemen may not have had sufficient resources to enable them to rise above their servile counterparts.

During and after the fourteenth century, when many peasants were increasingly able to purchase their freedom and improve their standing in the community, and when written sources become more prolific, the evidence bearing upon potters is still tantalizingly thin. Few earthenware potters attained sufficiently high status to allow them to be admitted as freemen of their towns, and where occupational surnames do occur in this context one must be careful to allow for the possibility that they are metal potters rather than earth potters. In the York Freemens Rolls (Surtees Society, 1897), for example, Thomas de Brandesby is referred to in 1278. It is likely that Thomas was a metalworker as the York potters' guild in the fourteenth century comprised metalworkers (Le Patourel 1968). The possibly unusual difficulty with this reference is that potters at the village of Brandsby, north of York, are known from archaeological evidence to have been supplying York with a large proportion of glazed and decorated jugs at this time. Ricardus Beverlay is the first 'erthpotter' to be designated a freeman in York, in 1426, and there were several others in the fifteenth century.

Furthermore, the absence of examples of earthenware potters' guilds is not just a reflection of the largely rural nature of the craft's location, for as we have already seen, some potteries were located in urban areas, but it must mirror the very low status of the industry in England. Dyer (1982) has suggested that potting may have been regarded as drudgery to be given up as soon as possible. On the Continent, however, potters were much more organized, as at Bergen op Zoom, Netherlands, in the fifteenth century (Weijs *et al.* 1970), or in Florence and its satellite settlements in the fifteenth and sixteenth centuries (Blake 1978). Some potters in Tuscany had attained a social status approaching that of the artist during the Renaissance; one plate from Cafaggiolo dating to around 1520 shows the potter's painter and his two patrons, but nothing comparable seems to have occurred in Britain. There is some evidence that potters could achieve a degree of prosperity in a series of wills from Stock, Essex, dating from the sixteenth to the eighteenth centuries. In these, potters are seen to own fairly substantial properties, sometimes including more than one tenement (Cunningham and Drury 1985). Another example can be cited from Nuneaton, where the potter George Bayly was elected Constable of Nuneaton in 1506 and paid tax on £12 worth of goods, rather than the more normal 20 shillings, in the 1524–5 Lay Subsidy. As Gooder points out (1984), George Bayly may have been regarded as a substantial husbandman, and as such was probably atypical.

More commonly, villeins and potters in particular held less than twenty acres, or half to one quarter of a virgate (Le Patourel 1968). Postan's analysis (1972) of 104 manors recorded between the late twelfth and late thirteenth centuries in southern England showed as many as 33 percent of tenants holding 10–15 acres of arable, whilst nearly half had less than 10 acres. Dyer's work on twelfth- and thirteenth-century tenancies in the west Midlands has shown an equally low level of landholding (1980: 89). By the end of the thirteenth century, approximately one third of the population on the estates of the abbots of Glastonbury, Bury St Edmunds and Ramsey and the Prior of Christ Church, Canterbury, existed on holdings of less than 2.5 acres (Grigg 1980). Below the villein class, cottars, smallholders or landless peasants were even more numerous in some areas. The 1380–1 Poll Tax returns in East Anglian counties show that 50–70 percent of males were labourers or servants (Hilton 1975). Many of these families were existing on the very margins of subsistence and were especially sensitive to harvest failures, a point corroborated by the analysis of yields on the estates of the Bishop of Winchester (Postan 1973). Given that a 10–15 acre holding was in some areas sufficient to provide a family of five with around 2,000 calories each per day (Postan 1972), the economic condition of a substantial proportion of the peasantry, of whom the potters formed a part, was very low.

The impact of the famines, plagues and wars in the fourteenth century has been much discussed, with estimates of population losses varying from around 33 percent to 50 percent. There is, however, considerable diversity of evidence. Mate (1984) noted that demesne farming recovered quite quickly on some Canterbury estates after 1348, and pointed out that the difficulties experienced in the 1350s may have been due more to a run of dry summers. In Essex, analysis of tithing returns also points to a recovery immediately after the Black Death, but in addition confirms a general decline in the late fourteenth-century population levels (Poos 1985). Bridbury's work (1977) tends to confirm these trends, suggesting that land-labour relationships began to decline not so much from the middle as from the later fourteenth century, and continued at a low level for a prolonged period.

Although there is disagreement among historians about the point at which populations began to recover, recent research in Essex suggests that by the early sixteenth century the local population levels were still below half the level of two centuries earlier (Poos 1985). The significance of this for potters is that whereas before the fourteenth century, it might be suggested as a generalization that land was scarce and labour cheap, during the fifteenth century the pressures on land and food resources decreased. Although in the twelfth and thirteenth centuries peasants might be under-employed with too few resources to make ends meet, thus providing the impetus to seek alternative means of employment, in the late Middle Ages the situation for some could be reversed.

As Dyer suggests (1982), potting was hard work for little profit, and if the post-1349 reduced population levels resulted in more land becoming available, the temptation to abandon potting may have been too strong to resist. Even so, the presence of secondary occupations in late medieval and Tudor records suggests that many families found this an essential means of economic survival (Everitt 1967; Woodward 1981; Cunningham and Drury 1985: 87–8).

The basis of the production unit was probably the nuclear family of man, wife and children, though with the important additions of grandparents, whose presence may have been a normal feature of many households, as well as servants even in the poorer homes, and labourers (Hilton 1975; Dyer 1982). Within the peasant classes work could be done by either sex, and women followed the plough as readily as men. The division of labour on many manors is not always clear, though male names are frequently quoted for such tasks as haywards, carpenters and tilers, for instance. Where potters are recorded, they too are associated with male names though, as Gooder points out in her study of evidence from Nuneaton, there are several examples of female craftworkers (1984). There were four female carters and three female millers in the 1327 Lay Subsidy Rolls. In 1334 Edith the Smith, Alice le Pottere and Matilda le Tilere were recorded. In the Leicestershire Eyre of 1247, the name of Agnes la Pottere is recorded (PRO JUST/1/455 m12), and at Woodstock, Oxfordshire, Agnes Siber rented a kiln in 1279. A Christiana le Tornour appears as a wood turner in Nuneaton in 1373 (C. Morris, pers. comm.). Dr Morris has also drawn attention to husband and wife teams of coopers, smiths and turners in 1346 and 1329 respectively (1984). Gooder (1984) has pointed out that the relative scarcity of potters' names in documentary sources might suggest that many potters were women and not heads of the household.

A characteristic feature of peasant and primitive societies is the proliferation of small-scale similarly structured units, with little tendency to centralization, collusion or agglomeration (Nash 1966). The productive units, Nash suggests, are limited to the kind of people and capital they can muster. Tasks are apportioned with little regard to the effects on output, and the division of labour often follows the natural limits imposed by sex and age. The technological capabilities of the society and its productive output are also dictated by the nature of the workforce and the levels of investment (*ibid*). As Arnold notes (1985: 223), 'For the poor. . . the only commodities available for investment are time and labour, and any innovation that requires investment in anything other than these will not be successful.'

Such considerations must surely apply with regard to the technological levels of potters in medieval Britain. Certainly throughout the whole period covered by this book there were no significant technological advances or innovations in the British medieval pottery industry. The changes that were introduced, such as the use of lead glaze before the Conquest, and the use of wheel-throwing techniques or updraught kilns, were all similar to those either in use by other craftsmen or were introduced by immigrant potters. Blake has recently expressed the view that 'West European medieval ceramics do not have a place in the history of technology. The techniques re-acquired were already practised in other crafts, for example by woodturners and glassworkers. The early painting and glazing did not improve the use of the vessel and aesthetically were mere daubing' (1980: 4). Indeed it was not until the seventeenth and eighteenth centuries that English potters really began to introduce significant changes.

We have already seen how, in pre-Conquest England, the use of wheel-throwing as a technique combined with updraught kilns was a phenomenon limited in both time and space. For some types, such as the Gritty wares at York or Stamford ware, these methods continued into the twelfth century, but in areas such as Somerset or Sussex simpler methods persisted. It is quite striking how few examples of adequately dated twelfth-century kilns have been found, and how widespread is the use of hand-forming methods after the Norman Conquest (Hurst 1976: 342). The scarcity of kilns dating to this period after many years of excavation and fieldwork must now imply the use of bonfire or clamp firings, such as those identified at Blackborough End, Norfolk. Although many post-Conquest wares are relatively hard, their multi-coloured surfaces and cores support the idea that there was little control, and perhaps under-standing, of firing temperatures. Hand-forming methods such as coiling were normal practice, even for pots in use at major urban centres such as London, Winchester, Oxford, Leicester or Exeter.

The use of wheel-throwing techniques gradually becomes more apparent from the late twelfth and thirteenth centuries. London-type ware vessels, known from the late twelfth century on, are wheel-thrown, as are the thirteenth-century products of Rye, Nottingham, Grimston, Ham Green, Winksley, the Tees Valley, Colstoun, Perth and Aberdeen, for example. This is the period from which many of the excavated production sites, usually double-flued kilns, date. It is also the point at which the use of dipped treacly glazes and prolific decoration begins.

From this time onwards, pottery vessels are almost always made by wheel-throwing and fired under reasonably well-controlled conditions. From the fourteenth century in the Midlands, firing temperatures, formerly around 900–1000°C, were increased substantially with the manufacture of the almost vitrified Midland Purple wares. The adoption of multi-flued kilns at Nuneaton and in Yorkshire from the fourteenth century might be further testimony to the desire to achieve a specific hardness and colour range. Musty has suggested that the development of the multi-flued kilns was linked with the use of coal (Musty 1984), but it also enabled the potters to build larger kilns, and hence increase their output. Other technical improvements include the diminishing use of large amounts of tempering material, especially from the fifteenth century onwards, testimony to the care with which potters were selecting and preparing their clays and their ability to control firing conditions. The use of saggars is another minor advance. In all these cases the changes are but minor modifications to the existing technology, and even the introduction of tin glazing with its much more elaborate manufacturing procedures into Norwich from 1567 and London from 1571 had little impact for some considerable time.

Distribution and exchange

The study of international exchange has a long and distinguished history, in which the work of the late Gerald Dunning in medieval pottery studies is pre-eminent. Dunning's paper on trade relations between England and the Continent in the late Anglo-Saxon period (1956), in which he reviewed the archaeological evidence for trade across the North Sea, was a milestone. Whilst acknowledging the importance of schist whetstones, glass vessels and the like along with historical references, Dunning was principally concerned with pottery as an indicator of commercial contact; particular reference was made to discoveries in England of the Rhenish Badorf and Pingsdorf wares, glazed wares from the Dutch Limburg region, and the presence of glazed Stamford wares and other Saxo-Norman wares thought to have been modelled on continental prototypes. Other papers by Dunning explored the same theme, including later medieval finds of continental wares in Britain (1933) as well as discoveries of English wares at foreign sites (1968).

In England the possibilities of pottery acting as a means of defining regional cultures were propounded by Jope and Hurst in a series of articles. Basing his conclusions on a detailed examination of fabrics and form, Jope identified regional traits, especially in the Oxford and Cotswold areas (e.g. 1952: 61–76), and this was followed up with a more wide-ranging paper in which architectural style and building materials were considered (1963). Much of the early work of Hurst and Dunning on Late Saxon wares was summarized in a national overview in 1976, in which Hurst presented in graphic form the extent to which ideas about trade connections across the North Sea had been modified since 1955 (Hurst J.G. 1976: 288–90).

In the ten years that have elapsed since Hurst's major review, the picture has once again changed very substantially, as indeed he foresaw. This has come about largely as a result of the application of chemical and physical analyses to Saxon and medieval pottery, especially by Hodges and Vince. Hodges, for example, isolated Middle Saxon local wares from Rhenish and French imports occurring at a number of sites, most notably the port of Hamwih (Hodges R. 1980), whilst Vince, working in the same tradition as Jope, has defined manufacturing localities in southern and western England very much more precisely and satisfactorily than hitherto (1981). The really significant advances, however, lie in the approach to the subject. Whereas much of the early work of Hurst and Dunning was descriptive in character, as is essential in the early stages of any discipline (Sterud 1973), the newer work is oriented much more towards explanation (Hodges R. 1982; Vince 1981).

An important shortcoming in the earlier work was the failure to distinguish between different methods of distribution. The underlying assumption behind many of the discussions on imports is that they represent evidence for trade. Grierson's seminal paper was salutary in this regard; his work (1959), based securely in anthropology, classical literary sources as well as archaeology, showed the fallacy of such arguments by pointing to the numerous alternative explanations for the presence of imported goods. Possibilities such as personal gifts, dowries, payments, property carried around by itinerant pedlars or households and even political payments, to quote but a few examples, are as valid in explaining the existence of imported pottery as of exotic coins or articles made from precious metals.

Hurst acknowledged that distribution patterns will reflect the researcher's geographical areas of enquiry, but that if sufficient data are available they are capable of suggesting much more. As fabrics, for example, mirror the geology of the locality in which they are made, distribution patterns may thus define areas over which products of a specific type are dominant. Such patterns *may* be correlated with 'market' areas. Outliers of the distribution will be highlighted, and for these an alternative explanation to that of trade may be required. Distribution patterns may also point to the directions in which the pottery was moved and, perhaps, the extent to which communities located away from the major roads made use of pots from different sources (Hodder 1974). The numbers of pots reaching different centres may highlight the scale of production and popularity of vessel types, whilst the occurrence of unusual or elaborate forms may reflect upon the status of individuals in the community.

Similarly, the distribution of forms may define a specific aspect of trade, by reference to the typical contents of the pots, as for example amphorae in the Roman world which held commodities such as wine, olive oil and fish paste. In 1956 Dunning was able to speculate that discoveries of Badorf *Reliefband* amphorae mirrored the trade in Rhenish wine, and Hurst added that Pingsdorf pitchers and beakers were a by-product of this trade (Hurst J.G. 1976: 342). As an explanation of the occurrence of imported forms this is not implausible. It is an erroneous implication, however, that because trade in wine was the agency by which many amphorae were moved around in classical times, it was also the case in the Late Saxon period. The ceramic evidence for trade in the Roman world, discussed further below, is of an altogether different order of magnitude than is the case in the early Middle Ages.

We have already seen that the development of urban communities in the Late

Saxon period created new pockets of demand. One of the principal features of these communities was the possession of a market. Whilst means of protecting traders and vendors occur in the earliest law codes, specific references to markets as the places at which transactions must take place occur from the reign of Alfred onwards; at Worcester, for example, a late ninth-century document highlights the location and the economic importance of the market. The importance of *burhs* becomes clear from the proliferation of mints, the location of which was prescribed by the king and always located in what was officially regarded as a *burh*. Biddle (1976a) speculated that the number of *burhs* increased from around ten towns in the 880s to around fifty by 930, and that the number of mints grew from about 27 in the mid-ninth century to 40 between 973–5, and to 70 by the end of the tenth century. By 1066 there were nearly 100 mints in operation.

The boroughs varied in size and importance, but whilst all *burhs* had markets, not all markets achieved burghal status. Indeed some, such as Bampton in Oxfordshire, were very small. Some of these tiny markets were located outside the gates of monastic precincts or close to the manor of a local notable. The largest were relatively substantial and populous places by the standards of Late Saxon England. The best guide to size, apart from the acreage within the defences, is provided by Domesday Book, where it can be seen that Norwich, for example, had 1,320 burgesses and Thetford 943. If these figures are multiplied by a factor of 4 to account for dependents, they provide minimum population estimates of 5,280 and 3,772 respectively. Maxwell has suggested that York may have had a population of around 9,000 in 1066 (1962: 154–6), although here, as in many other places, especially in Yorkshire, the numbers had dropped substantially by the time the Domesday Survey was compiled.

Burgesses were regarded as quite distinct from non-urban dwellers, as a series of law codes from Edgar, Aethelred and Cnut make clear. It is also apparent that many must have obtained a livelihood that was based upon crafts or trading, as the acreage of arable land allocated to the town was often very low. At Norwich, for example, the burgesses held 180 acres of arable, whilst at Ipswich the 538 burgesses held just 40 acres (Tait 1936: 130). Indeed, over fifty years ago Tait drew attention to the likelihood of an abundance of urban employment, given the low acreages attached to the towns (*ibid.*: 71–4). Some indication of the economic base of these towns is provided by Domesday Book; at Gloucester it was iron working, in Cambridge textile manufacture, and at Dunwich fishing. Salt was a key commodity at Droitwich, whilst furs were important at Chester. Early in the eleventh century, the well-known Billings-gate Tolls refer to the presence in London of men and goods from Rouen, Flanders, Ponthieu, the Isle de France, Huy, Liège and Nivelles, and as the final clause puts it, 'women who deal in dairy produce. . .' (Robertson A.J. 1925: 71–3). This very informative document thus draws attention to the local as well as the international nature of the London market. Loyn makes a similar point by following Aelfric in distinguishing between merchants who deal in exotic goods, traders in agricultural surplus, and simple carriers of metal goods or salt (1962: 114).

One of the most comprehensive views of an Anglo-Norman town is provided by the surveys carried out for the king and bishop in Winchester in 1110 and 1148 respectively, although drawing on pre-Conquest material (Biddle 1976b). Even before these two surveys, known as the Winton Domesday, were produced, street names confirm the presence of butchers, shieldmakers and tanners in certain parts of the city by the end of the tenth century. This document has several important limitations in providing an assessment of trades and occupations, however, not the least of which is the failure to mention many of the craftsmen at the bottom of the social ladder. This factor may account for the absence of potters, who were too lowly to be of concern to the compilers. The 1148 Survey contains 48 occupational bynames which are divisible into cloth workers, leather workers, goldsmiths, metal workers, butchers, members of the brewing and victualling trades, building workers and merchants. A miscellaneous category comprises other service trades connected with brooms, tubs, furniture, floor coverings, needles and wood turning. The list of occupations is far from complete, but is a vivid reminder of the truly urban nature of some of the great towns of Late Saxon and Norman England. Whilst some of the smallest boroughs or markets may have differed little in appearance and occupational structure from some villages, towns such as Winchester, and by implication York, London, Norwich, Thetford, and Bristol, were able to support, and clearly needed the services of, large non-agricultural populations. In Winchester it can be shown that many of the trades were grouped, and the points of sale probably in the street close to where items were made. Thus markets specializing in specific foodstuffs might develop in those parts of the town convenient for the traders, whilst the main market along High Street may have performed the market function for a wide range of goods (*ibid.*: 459–60), including, no doubt, pottery.

Compared with the startlingly vivid picture which we have for Winchester, the evidence from archaeology for Anglo-Norman towns as centres of craft production, trade and distribution networks is very limited. At York, however, the archaeological potential of such an urban centre has been fully realized with excavations at Coppergate. Here the fortunate survival of the organic fraction has greatly enlarged our perspective on living conditions, as well as on the range of goods made and used on tenth- and eleventh-century urban tenements in a major urban context (Hall R.A. 1984). Other towns such as Lincoln, Northampton, Oxford, Southampton and Bristol also contribute to this picture, as many provide some evidence for craft production such as glass making, jewellery manufacture, bone working or smithing. At York we also have the astonishingly fortunate finds of coin dies and coin trial pieces (*ibid.*), arguably the most important single finds from excavations on Saxon and medieval sites in Britain. Evidence for long-distance trade is less convincing as far as the archaeological record is concerned. York, for example, has produced silks, coins and sea shells from the Middle and Far East and the Red Sea (*ibid.*), but these are such rare items that they cannot, on their own, be construed as evidence for long-distance trade. Indeed, many of these exotic items known from Britain would fit comfortably in a single traveller's baggage. Pottery imported from the Continent is rather more widely attested, and this may mirror trade patterns as Dunning and Hodges imply, although the evidence if quantified would barely stand statistical scrutiny.

There is no direct evidence for the methods by which potters distributed their wares in the Anglo-Norman period, apart from the hint in the story of Hereward the Wake (Hart 1974: 28–40). From this it seems likely that some potters may have travelled from village to village peddling their goods, but many probably took advantage of the local markets where they existed. Similar evidence exists for a slightly later period in the ballads of Robin Hood and the potter (Dobson and Taylor 1976). It is not inconceivable that the English and Danish armies also transported vessels in bulk, especially in the early days of settlement and campaigning at the end of the ninth and first quarter of the tenth century. The distribution patterns of Late Saxon pottery show a sufficient amount of variation to suggest that dispersal mechanisms may have differed from area to area. In Northampton and Exeter, for example, the local products seem to be confined to the town and the occasional site very close by. At Leicester the products of the Southgate Street kiln are known only from the kiln site despite numerous excavations in the city. The rarity of Derby ware, however, is almost certainly explicable in terms of the lack of excavation. It is possible that settlements in the south Cotswold area and the lower Severn valley had their own potteries whose products rarely travelled beyond the place for which they were made (Vince 1984b).

Some distributions cover wide areas, however. The Gloucester TF41a fabric made in the town centre has been recognized from the royal palace at Kingsholm in Gloucester as well as at Hereford, Worcester, and Winchcombe. The products of the Harefield kilns just north of Gloucester, possibly those referred to in Domesday Book, travelled to Hereford, Chepstow, Droitwich and Dublin (Vince 1984b). In the west Midlands, Stafford-type ware has been found from Chester and Tatton Park in the north to Hereford and Gloucester in the south and Dublin to the west (Vince 1985b). If all these vessels ultimately prove to be of Stafford origin, it is interesting to note that the range of forms present is usually much more restricted than at the production site. Petrological analysis by Vince has also shown that the Oxford Shelly ware production centre located in Oxfordshire also supplied London with Late Saxon Shelly wares in the late tenth and early eleventh centuries (1985a). Other wide distribution patterns occur with Thetford wares in East Anglia, St Neots wares in the east Midlands and Torksey wares in Lincolnshire. Thetford-type wares are known to have been made at several production centres including Thetford, Norwich, Ipswich, Grimston, Bircham and Langhale. It is possible that St Neots wares are also the product of multiple production sites, and Torksey-type ware may have been made near York (Brooks and Mainman 1984) as well in Lincolnshire.

One of the most detailed studies of a ceramic type is Kilmurry's work on Stamford ware (1980), the most widely distributed ware of all in Late Saxon and early post-Conquest Britain. Stamford vessels are heavily concentrated in Lincolnshire, but also spread out to Winchester, Canterbury, the Welsh Marches and Durham, and in the thirteenth century to Aberdeen and Perth. Kilmurry considers that, of the five possible modes of distribution proposed by Renfrew (1977: 9–10), the most appropriate for Stamford ware is that of selling through the market and distribution through middlemen (Kilmurry 1980: 172), and whilst these seem likely, no evidence is available beyond the distances and quantities of pottery involved. Some of the vessels could have been transported in the bags of travellers. There is certainly no evidence to suggest that production centres outside Stamford were producing Stamford ware.

Despite the impressive volume of evidence made available for Stamford ware, the way in which the data has been presented remains confusing and some re-working may be necessary in the future to bring out chronological and directional changes in the distribution. Distribution patterns emphasize the importance of Mercia in the early stages of production, for example, and the quantities of Stamford ware found in pre-Conquest levels at Lincoln, York and Northampton are probably sufficient to confirm trade as the dispersal mechanism. Similarly the very dense concentration in the Wash region, including the Lincolnshire coast and rivers draining into the Wash, suggests water transport as a possible means of distribution.

Despite the increasingly available amount of archaeological data for the late Saxon period, there has been no serious analysis to determine the nature of the exchange mechanisms operating. There have been many discussions in the archaeo-ethnographic literature, recently summarized by R. Hodges (1982: 13–20), assessing the role of markets and distribution patterns. From these it is clear that in order to further our understanding of the late Saxon economy and the role a study of the pottery may have in that process, we need to separate out and define more closely the distinction between local and long-distance trade, the nature of the markets and the range of distributive mechanisms. Renfrew has suggested, for example (1977: 9), that trading distances should be related to the size of social units and territories rather than mileage. From this it also follows that as trade involves considerable effort and organization in the movement of materials from place to place, the economic and social importance of trade will vary with the size, sophistication and location of the communities under consideration.

Hodges (1982: 15–16) has drawn attention to a useful tiered hierarchy of markets proposed by Skinner. At the lowest level, the minor or incipient markets, there is a simple interchange of peasant-produced goods. The next stage, the standard market, is the point at which surpluses generated at peasant level begin to flow more freely and imported goods cease to be distributed. The tier above, or central market, comprises those nodes on the major routeways with important wholesaling and regional functions. At the highest level, the regional markets possess major administrative functions in addition to a substantial redistributive role. Such a tiered system is attested in the Domesday Survey, where we can see from the numbers of burgesses present that towns such as York, and presumably London (the returns for which do not survive), must rank as the major regional and administrative markets, whilst places such as Ipswich, Northampton and Oxford acted as central markets. Tiering of this kind is also apparent in the middle of the tenth century in Aethelstan's Grately Decrees (Attenborough 1922).

Renfrew (1977: 9–10) has proposed a simple hierarchy of exchange mechanisms. At the lowest level the consumer obtains his pot from the home of the craftsman, and at the next level the producer peddles his wares around the homes of the consumers. Alternatively, the producer and consumer might exchange at a third place such as a market. Slightly more sophisticated is the idea of a middleman purchasing products from the craftsmen and arranging for the distribution. Finally, the potter might consign all his stock to some central body which gives him goods in exchange. The two lowest levels of distribution would require the survival of written sources, and it may be that Hereward exemplifies the itinerant pedlar. The use of the market and a middleman may be expected, although to demonstrate this would require the application of theoretical models such as the distance decay models proposed by Renfrew (1975). By such methods it may be possible, for example, to recognize the spheres of middleman operation within the core distribution area of Stamford ware, and to isolate potential markets at the lower levels of the hierarchy.

In post-Conquest times, and particularly from the thirteenth century, the increasingly plentiful supply of documents has long been exploited by economic historians concerned with trade, especially at the international level. Trade at a regional or local level has also received considerable attention. Hilton, for example, has discussed the nature of peasant society, markets and production in a series of papers mainly based upon work in the west Midlands (1975; 1985), and Everitt (1967) has focussed on markets in the fifteenth to seventeenth centuries, especially in the Midlands and in Kent. There have also been several studies of pottery distributions related to market areas. Jean Le Patourel, in a study of the kilns at Winksley, drew attention to the number of markets within a 32km radius of some major Yorkshire pottery production sites (Bellamy and Le Patourel 1970: 113–14). Allan has examined the redistribution of pottery by sea, especially imported stonewares, from Exeter to the ports of Dartmouth, Fowey, Plymouth, Falmouth, Helford, Penzance and Bristol (1984: 143–4).

Vince (1981) has compared the distribution of different wares through time in the south-west Midlands and parts of Wessex. He has shown that the number of the production sites and the size of their distribution areas varies considerably (Fig. 34). In the tenth century the relatively few kiln sites known appear to have spread their products over wide areas, in contrast to the eleventh century when there appears to be a proliferation in the number of producers but all marketing over very small areas. Vince has made the interesting point that whereas the early wares tend to be wheel-thrown, the eleventh-century pottery is largely hand-formed, and he has suggested that this is related to the size of the market areas. A slight increase in the number of kilns in the early to mid-twelfth century is followed by a decline, in which smaller numbers of production sites were in operation but marketing over wider areas from the late twelfth to the early thirteenth century. At this time there appears to be a greater number of sites making cooking pottery and fewer producers of table wares.

The possibility that some potters may have placed a greater emphasis on certain types of vessel has also been noted in East Anglia where the

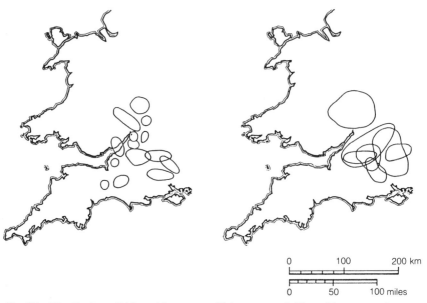

Fig. 34 Distribution of (a) cooking wares, 11th cent., and (b) cooking wares, late 13th-14th century, showing variations in number of production centres and size of market areas. (After Vince 1981)

Blackborough End potters, for example, made cooking pots and the Grimston craftsmen made glazed jugs; in Lincolnshire the Potter Hanworth workers seem to have concentrated on cooking pots and pancheons. In Yorkshire, the Staxton and Potter Brompton potters made coarse cooking wares, while the Scarborough craftsmen produced fine table wares. In general, however, specialization in one form to the virtual exclusion of all others is extremely difficult to demonstrate and probably unlikely. The explanation for the change in distribution patterns in the area of Vince's study is the increase in the number of markets, and therefore demand, especially from the late twelfth century; the growing specialization taking place in agriculture; and the consequent need for many to find additional means of support (Vince 1981: 319).

The number of markets increased very substantially in the twelfth and thirteenth centuries, and there can have been few pottery kilns not within easy distance of a market, whether it was urban or village-based, as Streeten has pointed out (1981). It is clear that many potters in lowland areas had equal access in terms of distance to more than one market in any one week. In upland regions, such as the Peak District in Derbyshire (Coates 1965: 104) and Northumberland, distances and terrain imposed their own constraints. The large number of outlets would certainly have stimulated demand not only for pottery, but for agricultural products and goods produced by other craftsmen.

It seems to be the case that the overall increase in the number of markets reflects the evidence for greater numbers of outlets. It might be expected, therefore, that during the late fourteenth and fifteenth centuries, when population levels were lower and markets declined in number, the number, size and distribution of production centres might show some variation. The decline in the markets is documented in Gloucestershire, Worcestershire and War-wickshire, for example, where there were 120 chartered markets by 1300 (Hilton 1985: 6), but only 62 between 1500 and 1640 (Everitt 1967). In Lancashire there were originally 135 chartered and prescribed markets, but by 1640 only 40 survived (*ibid.*); this is a process that seems to have begun in the late fourteenth century and continued into the sixteenth and is, moreover, a story that can be repeated from the south coast to the Scottish borders and into Wales. Accompanying this drop in the numbers of markets is a tendency towards market specialization and regionalization in agricultural practice, with local emphases on dairying, pig breeding or cereal crops, for example, becoming more pronounced (Thirsk 1967: 5).

In pottery there is appears to be a similar decline in the number of production centres in the fourteenth and fifteenth century, although by the later sixteenth century there are indications of an increase. Certainly, by the seventeenth century small country potteries are relatively numerous in some areas such as North Yorkshire, or the New Forest centred on Verwood. It is certainly the period which gives rise to the prolific North Devon industries and probably those on the Herefordshire-Welsh border.

The trends in pottery production from the fifteenth century exhibit both a movement towards some specialization, and a degree of standardization in form and fabric over wide areas, such as had not been seen since the days of the classic Midlands Saxo-Norman wares. These trends become more pronounced by the Tudor period. In Lancashire, Cumbria, across the Pennines into Northumberland, and into Scotland, for instance, the fine-textured late medieval reduced wares are ubiquitous from the fifteenth century on. Many Yorkshire and Midlands potteries, exemplified by the kilns at Wrenthorpe near Wakefield or Ticknall in Derbyshire, specialized in the mass production of the clearly very popular brown-glazed Cistercian drinking vessels, which develop into the equally popular Blackwares in the seventeenth century. The substantial white ware industries on the Hampshire-Surrey border also appear to have given particular emphasis to the production of fine wares for the table.

The later Middle Ages was thus a period of change. The earlier highly decorated wares gave way to much plainer vessels in most areas, whilst the normal and widespread practice of using pottery vessels for cooking, recognizable by sooting around the base and sides, is gradually superseded by the preference for metal pots, a trend beginning in some areas before the mid-fourteenth century. Potters made inroads into the wood turner's domain with the manufacture of ceramic drinking vessels, and in the seventeenth century, pottery plates, imitating pewter forms, began to edge out wooden boards and trenchers. New forms appear, with tripod pipkins becoming increasingly popular, and in some parts bowls not only increase overall as a percentage of the total assemblages but there appears to be a greater variety of bowl-dish shapes. Bung-hole cisterns are normal items of equipment found on all sites of the period, reflecting in many cases, no doubt, the developing habit of home brewing. Chafing dishes or food warmers, less common than cisterns and pipkins, are nonetheless frequent finds. A comparison between the products of kilns at Fulmodeston (Wade-Martins 1983) and Donyatt (Coleman-Smith and Pearson forthcoming) with those of two centuries earlier makes the point very clearly. Similar comparisons can be observed on domestic sites between the twelfth-thirteenth and the sixteenth centuries; the royal hunting lodges at Writtle and Hunsden are good examples.

Whilst the presence of markets and the size and number of production centres have considerable impact on the way in which pottery vessels are distributed, there were other means of circulating pottery that require consideration, as Moorhouse (1981) has so graphically demonstrated. Important factors here are the road and river systems, as these were the arteries along which pottery travelled. Hodder (1974) has shown how the relative proportion of wares on domestic sites varied in Roman times according to whether the settlement was located on a major routeway or some distance away. Pearson has also noted a similar phenomenon in Somerset, where the ceramic spectra of sites close to the River Parrett differ from those away from the river (pers. comm.). The late thirteenth- to sixteenth-century Humber wares from West Cowick, distributed in north and central Lincolnshire as well as the Pennine valleys, was doubtless moved along the Aire and Calder river systems (Moorhouse 1983a: 46). In many parts of the south-west, or indeed other coastal areas such as East Anglia, distribution patterns may well have been determined by proximity of the production sites to creeks. Seaborne movement of pottery almost certainly lies behind the distribution of wares in Devon and Cornwall (Allan 1984: fig. 144), and the presence of many Mill Green wares (Fig. 35) in

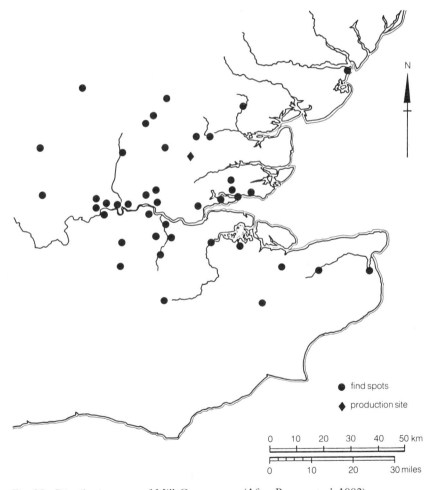

Fig. 35 Distribution map of Mill Green ware. (After Pearce *et al.* 1982)

north Kent may well be due to transhipment across the Thames estuary. Similarly, the presence of English goods in south-west Scotland during and after the reign of Edward I may be due in part to trading across the Solway Firth from the main regional centre at Carlisle.

Equally important factors affecting distribution patterns were administrative and tenurial links between widely separated properties held by the same person. A detailed study of the pottery from Sandal Castle enabled Moorhouse (1983a; 1983b) to identify some forty vessels from the Conisborough area in the thirteenth and fourteenth centuries, as well as at least 120 other pots from the Doncaster kilns. Also occurring at Sandal were vessels from West Sussex,

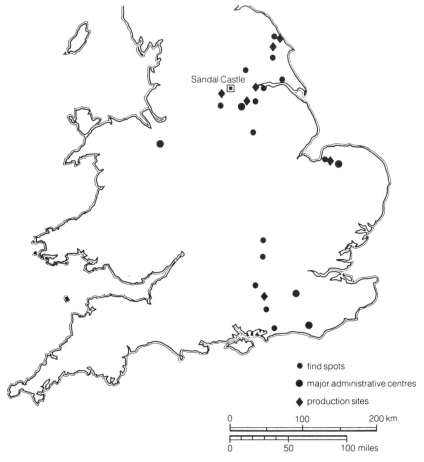

Fig. 36 Map locating main centres of the Warenne estates, showing identifiable sources of pottery found at Sandal Castle. (After Moorhouse 1983b)

Buckinghamshire and the Welsh Marches. The link between all these areas and Sandal is the distribution of holdings of the Warenne family (Fig. 36). The distances separating some of the sites inevitably leads to the suggestion that the pots travelled in the baggage of the family or officials moving between the holdings of a single estate. This conclusion stands as a corrective to the view that pottery found at some distance from its source is evidence of trade.

Another factor in the movement of goods over considerable distances is the supply of materials and men during military campaigns. This is well known in the Roman period, and has been documented especially for the campaigns of Edward I in Wales. Here the building of massive fortresses such as those at Conwy, Harlech and Caernarfon required craftsmen recruited from all over the kingdom, and materials supplied by many different areas. Expenditure on the castle and city walls at Conwy in 1286 included lead, iron, tin, steel, nails and ropes from Chester, Flint, Newcastle under Lyme and Boston (Colvin 1963: 349). Jugs found at Edward's castle of Beaumaris, Anglesey, probably came from the Ham Green kilns in Bristol (Dunning 1977a). Similarly, Edward I's Anglo-Scottish campaigns entailed the despatch of men from Carlisle into Scotland, as shown for example by the fifty-two men sent to Lochmaben in 1298 to erect a peel (Colvin 1963: 409). The bearded face-mask jug from Kirkcudbright may have originated in the Carlisle area, although detailed field-work combined with petrological analyses are required to test this assertion.

It is clear, then, that not all regional imports can be interpreted as items of trade, as there are several other means of distributing pottery. Indeed, in most cases identifiable in medieval Britain the evidence for pottery being moved as an item of trade in its own right is negligible. It is salutary to recall the position centuries earlier. Samian ware is known to have been manufactured on a truly industrial scale at the great Gaulish factories of La Graufesenque, Lezoux, Les Martres-de-Veyre and many other sites in East Gaul. In the Flavian period the output of La Graufesenque is known to have been hundreds of thousands a year, and it was exported to Britain by the shipload as the finds at Pudding Pan Rock and the Regis warehouse, London, illustrate (Marsh 1981: 221–4). Amphorae for trans-shipping olive oil, wines, sardines or fish-paste were made by the million, and they too, like Samian ware, are common finds on settlement sites. Their numbers in Britain are so colossal that by any statistical yardstick they can be regarded as unequivocal evidence of trade. It is true that the contrast between the Roman and medieval periods cannot and should not be pressed too far, yet the comparison is useful in illustrating the kind of evidence required before one can legitimately define trade in pottery vessels. Certainly, there is no example of pottery from the Late Saxon and medieval periods in Britain which remotely compares with the Roman period, at least in quantitative terms. Indeed, some regional and foreign imports are sufficiently scarce as to raise the possibility that other means of exchange, such as that based upon reciprocity or gifts, or movements of people or households, may have been responsible for the dispersal of pots considerable distances from their place of manufacture.

Without the kind of evidence adduced above, the case for trade must be made very carefully. It seems likely, for example, that the distribution of Ham Green products (Fig. 37), widely found in south Wales as well as in south and east Ireland, may be accounted for by trade, and there are documented examples of pots being imported into east coast ports such as King's Lynn and Hull from the Continent. The best archaeological evidence is unquestionably that of Scarborough ware, however. The potters at Scarborough, a relatively minor Yorkshire coastal town, produced glazed and decorated wares of exceptional quality, very largely it seems for the exporting market by sea: for whilst the products of this industry occur inland, in the Vale of York and at village sites for example, the numbers do not compare with the amounts imported through the ports of Newcastle upon Tyne, Perth or Aberdeen, as attested by many recent discoveries. Indeed, Scarborough ware is one of the most frequent non-local pottery finds along the north-east coast of England and the east coast of Scotland, ocurring as far north as the Northern Isles (Fig. 38), and it has also been recovered in some quantities from excavations in Norway.

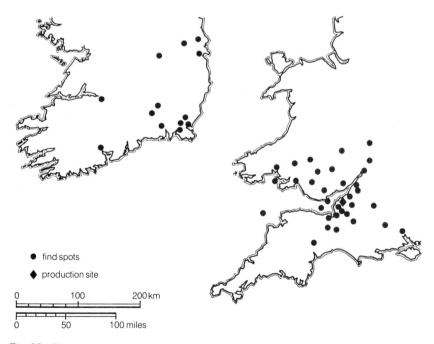

● find spots

♦ production site

0   100   200 km

0   50   100 miles

Fig. 37   Distribution of Ham Green ware. (After Ponsford 1983)

Fig. 38 Distribution of Scarborough ware. (After unpublished map by N. Farmer)

The entrepreneurial flair responsible for the remarkable distribution pattern has been attributed by P.G. and N.C. Farmer (1982), who have made a special study of this pottery, to the Cistercians, on whose land it is claimed the production centre was located. Although the interpretation of the written and the archaeological sources has been questioned (Pearson, Trevor 1982: 88), the idea that the Proctor of Cîteaux may have exploited the talents of the local craftsmen and had a hand in marketing their wares is not inherently unlikely given the Cistercians' talents for exploiting other resources of their estates such as sheep, lead or iron.

Chapter 3   Pottery and Society

The student of medieval Britain has a rich array of sources for the reconstruction of aspects of domestic life and to help identify possible functions for
the ceramic artifacts normally so prolific on excavations. In addition to
archaeology there are written records and illustrations in manuscripts and
paintings; these sources have been the subject of study by Stephen Moorhouse
in particular (1978).

The documentary evidence is very varied; there are, for example, references
to purchases of hundreds or even thousands of vessels for a particular occasion
such as Richard II's coronation banquet, word lists or dictionaries, culinary,
industrial and medical recipes, personal account books, household inventories,
menus and books of etiquette. Sculpture in wood and stone, paintings and
marginalia in manuscripts, show people using containers. They may be seated
at meals, preparing and serving food, or using vessels in a host of daily activities
unassociated with eating. Whilst the written and visual sources are good enough
to enable us to recognize the vessel form in many cases, they are often, however,
not detailed enough to enable pottery vessels to be distinguished from those of
leather, wood or metal. In addition, many of the table wares at the royal and
aristocratic feast scenes so often portrayed are obviously of metal, and in many
cases of precious metal (e.g. Fig. 39). Despite these limitations, such sources

Fig. 39   Feast scene; 14th cent. (After *Queen Mary's Psalter*, British Library MS.
Roy. 2.B.VII)

yield much information as to how pots may have been used, and close study of pottery from archaeological contexts may in some cases serve to confirm suggestions made from the historical evidence.

Non-ceramic vessels

Pottery containers formed only part of the total complement of household vessels, but the relative importance of items made in different materials is very hard to gauge from archaeological sources alone. Wood, leather and basketry containers, which are only preserved under exceptional archaeological circumstances, would have been widespread. Whilst wooden vessels are not uncommon, the kind of waterlogged deposits that may produce a range of goods on a reasonable scale are virtually restricted to sites such as the Viking age levels at York, medieval levels at Perth and the London waterfront infills.

In the medieval household, wooden vessels almost certainly occupied a position at least as important as that of pottery. It is quite plain from the archaeological record that pottery drinking vessels were not common before the fourteenth or fifteenth centuries in most parts of the country. There are, however, numerous medieval manuscript illustrations depicting people drinking

Fig. 40 Feast scene from the Bayeux Tapestry; 11th cent. (After Wilson D.M. 1985)

from small bowls, presumably of wood (e.g. Figs. 40 and 56), which closely resemble the wooden bowls sometimes found on excavations. Documentary sources confirm the presence of wooden drinking vessels; at Jarrow in 1395, for example, there were 'ij tankards de ligno', and iron-bound tankards, presumably stave-built, were recorded in 1294 (Baker 1921: 39, 69). 'Ashen cups' were replaced by pottery cups at the Inns of Court in London during the reign of Henry VIII (Matthews and Green 1970). Despite the competition of pottery cups, wooden ones were still common in the seventeenth century: a contemporary writer said that 'of drinking cups divers and sundry sorts we have, some of elme, some of box, some of maple, some of holly etc., mazers, broadmouth'd dishes, noggins, whiskins, piggins, cruizers, ale-bowls, wassell-bowls, court dishes, tankards, kannes, from a bottle to a pint, from a pint to a gill' (quoted in Baker 1921).

Wooden (or 'treen') trenchers and platters were widespread in the later medieval and early post-medieval periods (e.g. Fig. 41), replacing the bread trenchers of earlier times. Other items of wood which were common throughout the medieval period include boxes, barrels, chests, butter churns, pails, trays, troughs and cheese-presses. The larger items would mostly have

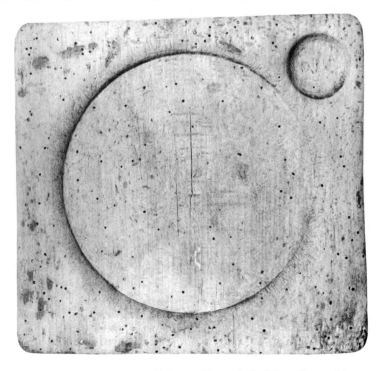

Fig. 41   Wooden trencher; 20.2 x 19.2 cm. (Photo Oxfordshire County Museum, Woodstock)

been of stave-built construction; jugs were also sometimes constructed by this method in the post-medieval period at least (Fig. 42).

Leather vessels appear to have been common, although they are rare archaeological finds. Moulded leather vessels are, however, known from very early times, a Saxon drinking-cup from Buxton being one pre-Conquest example (Waterer 1956: 169–70). Leather drinking vessels and jugs (blackjacks and bombards) survive from the post-medieval period, and were doubtless present in the Middle Ages. Dunning cites an example of a late thirteenth-century pottery jug with rows of notched decoration which may be imitating the stitched seams of a leather vessel (in Spillett *et al.* 1942: 60). Other leather containers included pouches, satchels and boxes, as for example a thirteenth-century chalice-box from Suffolk (Waterer 1956: fig. 138).

Probably the most common leather container was the bottle, flask or costrel (e.g. Fig. 43), known in England throughout the Middle Ages, and sometimes closely copied by the makers of pottery costrels (Dunning 1964: 132). In Aelfric's 'Colloquy' of *c.* 1000 the Saxon 'shoe-wright' enumerates his leather products, which include bottles and flasks (quoted in Baker 1921: 19). Guilds of bottlemakers, making bottles and other pots of leather, are known at London

Fig. 42 (left) Post-medieval wooden stave-built pitcher, ht. 35.5 cm. (Photo Oxfordshire County Museum, Woodstock)

Fig. 43 (right) Post-medieval leather costrel; ht. 23 cm. (Photo Oxfordshire County Museum, Woodstock)

and York from the late fourteenth and the fifteenth century (Baker 1921: 21, 31). The London guild was in decline by the late fifteenth century and during the reigns of Elizabeth and the Stuarts songs and rhymes refer to leather vessels in derogatory terms. A seventeenth-century writer noted that 'other bottles we have of leather, but they are most used among shepheards and harvest people of the countrey; small jacks wee have in many ale-houses, of the citie and suburbs, tip't with silver, besides the great blackjacks and bombards at the court' (quoted in Baker 1921: 53).

Horn, which rarely survives in archaeological contexts, was also used for making items such as drinking horns (Fig. 40) or moulded into shapes such as spoons and beakers. Like the Company of Bottlemakers, the London Company of Horners was impoverished by the late fifteenth century, presumably due to falling demand for their products, and in 1476 the two guilds amalgamated. This move did not halt their decline, and from 1564 the horners were petitioning to separate from the bottlers again (Baker 1921: 23–7).

Glass vessels appear to be uncommon, although they were more widely available by the later Middle Ages, especially in upper-class households. They are sometimes specifically mentioned in later medieval medical recipes (e.g. Dawson 1934: 156, 179). Glass urinals were commonly used by the medical profession to aid diagnosis of illness (Amis 1968). English glass technology before 1500 was greatly inferior to that on the Continent, however, and fine glass tablewares, which had to be imported, were costly. Vessel glass was little more than a crude sideline of the Weald glass industry before the mid-sixteenth century. By the end of the century, the situation had improved and the scale of vessel production increased; the migration of glass workers from the Weald and the spread of the industry to other parts of England ensured that glass vessels came into more common use (Hunter 1981: 149–50). Excavations attest to the frequent occurrence of glass drinking vessels and wine bottles after the turn of the sixteenth and seventeenth centuries.

Metal containers were of considerable importance, although their infrequency as site finds testifies to the fact that they could be repaired and re-used over a long period of time, and non-ferrous metal items could be melted down when they were worn out. Occasional fragments of metal vessels occur on sites of every social level, but from the fourteenth century onwards they become more frequent as site finds. Iron, copper alloy or brass pots must have been relatively expensive, however, as many were imported from the Continent; this applies particularly to those based on a copper alloy, as native sources of copper were not exploited before the reign of Elizabeth I (Goodall 1981). Written sources such as household inventories make it abundantly clear that metal cooking wares were well established throughout the social spectrum from the later fourteenth century onwards (Dyer 1982; Field R.K. 1965).

Many metal vessels, of iron, brass or bronze, were used for cooking, either as

Fig. 44 Man washing up in a tub, beside a fire with a cauldron; second quarter of 14th cent. (*Smithfield Decretals*, illuminated in England, MS. Roy. 10E.IV, fol. 144v; photo British Library)

cauldrons, with or without feet (e.g. Fig. 44), frying pans or handled pipkins. Vessels used at table, such as jugs, ewers, goblets, aquamaniles and chafing dishes, were made of base or precious metals, as were the church vessels associated with the mass. Plates of precious metal such as gold are shown in royal feast scenes in medieval manuscript illustrations, but the less exclusive pewter plates did not become widespread until the sixteenth century.

Pottery vessels and their uses

Over sixty-five vessel forms are archaeologically attested from Britain between the Late Saxon and Tudor periods. The numbers of the examples cited here refer to the pottery illustrations in Chapters 4–6. Only three forms are at all common up to the fourteenth century: the cooking pot, the bowl, pan or dish, and the jug or pitcher. From the mid-fourteenth century the emphases altered; cooking pots tended to diminish in importance whilst in some areas the use of ceramic pipkins increased. These changes may be equated with the increase in metal vessels. Other differences in the later Middle Ages included the increasing popularity of bowls as well as dripping dishes, cisterns, cups and jugs.

The uses of some ceramic forms, such as cups, candlesticks and colanders, may be largely self-evident, but as in the modern household, many vessels would have had more than one function, a fact which should not be overlooked. This complicates the archaeological interpretation of the relative proportions of different vessels occurring on a site. The actual functions of pots could even include some for which they were never intended. A number of fifteenth-century vessels were used to construct a drain at one of the Nuneaton kiln sites, the rim of each pot being set inside the broken base of its neighbour (Mayes and Scott 1984: pl. IVC). Another example is a London-type ware jug which was adapted for use as a lantern by cutting five circular holes at intervals round the body (Pearce *et al.* 1985: 47). The interior of the jug was blackened from the candle that would have been placed inside.

Pots could also be used as weapons. Moorhouse (1978) has drawn attention to court records of people attacking one another with pots, sometimes causing fatal injuries. In 1532 a Carmelite friar of Nottingham killed the prior of the Friary, following an argument, by hitting him on the head with 'a yerthyn potte' and causing a wound that penetrated his brain (*ibid.*: 17). The fourteenth-century Luttrell Psalter has an illustration of two combatants fighting with earthenware jugs (Fig. 45). Even the unfired clay could be used as a weapon on

Fig. 45   Fighting with earthenware jugs; 14th cent. (After *Luttrell Psalter*, East Anglian, British Library MS. Add. 42130, fol. 153, in Millar 1932.)

occasion; in the sixteenth century a tiler at Stoke killed a man by hurling 'a piece of clay from which he made a tile' (Redknap 1985: 75).

When a pot broke, it may have been mended; there are a number of examples of holes in pots being plugged with lead (for example, a London-type ware jug: Pearce *et al.* 1985: 47). If it could not be repaired, its useful life may not have been over. Pot sherds may have served as chicken-feeders or paint palettes, or they could be shaped and used as gaming counters. They may have made scoops for various household purposes; the Bible refers to 'a sherd to take fire from the hearth, or to take water withal out of the pit' (Isaiah 30: 14). Sherds were certainly used for medical and industrial purposes, with compounds being mixed or burnt on them (Moorhouse 1978: 12). One fifteenth-century medical recipe, for example, instructs the reader to 'take hempseed and rye, of each a drachm, and parch them in a sherd till they become black. . .' (Dawson W.R. 1934: 29).

It is also worth drawing attention to the rarity or even absence of certain items in earthenware during the Middle Ages, although it is difficult to suggest explanations for these gaps. The scarcity of lamps and inkwells in the high Middle Ages is noted below; presumably the need for these was met by craftsmen other than the potter. Items such as beads, toys, marbles, models of animals or everyday objects, and boards for board games are lacking in clay, and musical instruments such as bird whistles are very rare.

Similarly, fired clay sculptures or effigies are almost entirely absent, apart from occasional examples such as a fragment of a figurine or statue from Perth (N. MacAskill and D. Hall, pers. comm.). Representational art was not beyond the skills of workers in clay, however, as is shown by the interest in anthropomorphic decoration on both pottery and roof furniture during the high Middle Ages, and the figurines or salts in Cistercian ware of the sixteenth century (e.g. Lewis 1978: fig. 13).

A. VESSELS CONNECTED WITH FOOD AND DRINK

Much of the pottery from medieval domestic sites was involved with the storage, preparation and serving of food and drink. The generic term 'cooking pot' refers to a wide range of vessels, varying considerably in size from the small jar-like Late Saxon form with a capacity of around 3 to 5 pints (e.g. Nos. 156–7), to much larger cylindrical or globular vessels, frequently with convex or sagging bases, and often with capacities in the region of 1½–2½ gallons, for example twelfth/early thirteenth-century pots from York and Sandal Castle (Nos. 675–6, 799).

Although not all these vessels functioned as the name implies, there can be no doubt that some were used for cooking. Many have sooted bases, and analyses carried out on residues encrusted on to the internal surfaces of pots as well as on amino acids extracted from the pores of the fabric show that cooking or fermentation took place. Vessels discovered at Exeter, for example, contained amino acids, fatty acids and phosphates, indicating the presence of a meat stew, possibly based on chicken. In another instance it was possible to suggest a cereal gruel prepared with unsaturated vegetable oil, possibly linseed (Evans and Elbeih 1984). Samples from London-type cooking vessels were found to contain traces of meat, possibly cow or sheep, and in other instances milk products, possibly butter, cheese, cream or milk, could be identified (Pearce et al. 1985). Only limited experimentation has been carried out into the way fired clays are affected by different foodstuffs (e.g. Oetgen 1983–4), but clearly these lines of research are well worth pursuing.

Fig. 46 Domestic scene with cooking pot on trivet over fire; early 14th cent.
(Flemish Psalter, MS. Douce 6, fol. 22; photo Bodleian Library)

In some instances recipes specify that an 'earthen pot' or a 'new earthen pot'
is to be used, sometimes in preference to a metal pot, for cooking a particular
dish. The pot may have been placed directly onto the embers, on the hearth
next to the fire, or on a trivet over the fire, as can be seen on manuscript
illustrations (e.g. Fig. 46), although in some instances the pots thus depicted are
obviously of metal. Metal trivets or tripods are also mentioned in medieval
documents such as wills (Ferguson 1893). Occasionally, the need for separate
trivets was avoided by the manufacture of ceramic cauldrons with long legs, in
direct imitation of metal prototypes, but these are not at all common (e.g. Nos.
1344, 1803, 2201). The distinctive Cornish 'bar lug' cooking pots (Nos.
482–3), on the other hand, were obviously suitable for suspension over the fire.
Examining the patterns of sooting on ceramic cooking pots can help to
determine how they were used, and whether the fire was of wood, or of charcoal
which would only soot the part of the vessel in contact with it. This has been
done in the study of the Sandal Castle pottery (Moorhouse 1983b: 182–5).

Not all methods of cooking would leave sooting upon pots, however.
Methods of steaming food in pots within larger vessels, such as metal
cauldrons, would leave cooking pots unmarked; this technique can be seen in
Fig. 47. One medieval recipe describes how a sausage mixture was made and
stuffed into a long earthenware pitcher or jug, the mouth of which was then

Fig. 47   Preparing food and cooking in pots within metal cauldrons; 14th cent. (*Romance of Alexander*, MS. 264, fol. 170v; photo Bodleian Library)

covered with canvas. The pitcher was placed to simmer in a cauldron where meat was cooking, and was later removed and broken open to reveal the sausage. This was then basted with batter and roasted on a spit until golden (Austin 1888: 39).

When an earthenware pot was removed from the heat, care had to be taken lest it crack upon contact with a cold surface. One fifteenth-century recipe for stewed capons instructs the cook to place the pot 'upon a wispe of straw that hit toche not the cold grownde' (quoted in Moorhouse 1978: 6).

In addition to stewing or boiling up foods, cooking pots were also well suited to storage functions. Many cooking pots from archaeological contexts show no signs of sooting, for example, and if they were not used to cook by steaming, may well have been used for storage of food and other items. Some of the small Late Saxon cooking pots may have been used to store limited quantities of food, being the equivalent, perhaps, of the modern jam jar. Many of the larger post-Conquest cooking-pot-shaped vessels, such as the very large example from Eynsford, Kent, with a brimful capacity of around 13 gallons (No. 1214), could hardly have been used for any other purpose. Indeed, many of the moderately-sized pots with a capacity of 2 to 3 gallons would have been awkward to move around, especially when full. Storage vessels of more specialized shape are otherwise well known from Late Saxon contexts, such as those in Thetford ware with a capacity of 4 or 5 gallons or more (up to about 41 gallons in the case of No. 173), or the 11-gallon Chichester examples, although they are never very common.

Apart from 'cooking pots', other vessels were used for cooking; a pitcher used for steaming has been noted above. Late Saxon 'socketed' or 'spouted' bowls (e.g. Nos. 103–4), for example, may have been used for cooking, if the socket was indeed intended to take a wooden handle. A successor of this bowl type may be the pipkin, which appears in the twelfth/thirteenth century as a small cooking-pot shape with a pouring lip and a straight handle (e.g Nos. 761–2, 847–8). These vessels, which are much less common than cooking pots, would have been ideal for preparing food which was required in fairly small quantities and which needed frequent stirring while being heated, such as sauces. Small pipkins could also have served as ladles for use with large cauldrons, but many have sooting showing that they were used as cooking vessels in their own right. Some later examples of pipkins have three feet, in imitation of metal pipkins and cauldrons (e.g. Nos. 897, 1556); in manuscripts, however, it is not always easy to distinguish whether they are metal or ceramic. One example of a pipkin being used over a small fire in a bedroom can be seen in Fig. 48.

During the later Middle Ages, with the increasing frequency of metal vessels for cooking, there is in many areas a shift in emphasis away from cooking in large ceramic containers and towards the smaller pipkins. Low Countries tripod pipkins, with short legs and one or two loop handles, a shape presumably influenced by metal cauldrons, were widely imported into certain areas during the fourteenth and fifteenth centuries. These were copied by native potters in a number of places in the fifteenth and sixteenth centuries (e.g. Nos. 1661–2); in some instances, the close similarities to Low Countries wares can plausibly be explained by invoking immigrant potters, as at Exeter (Allan 1984).

Another major class of earthenware vessels includes pans, pancheons, dishes and bowls, the names of which are used indiscriminately in many pottery reports. Faced with sherd material, of course, the archaeologist may not be able to distinguish one from another, especially as they are morphologically closely related. Whilst there are slight indications in recipes that the terms might have meant different things (pans, for example, are almost invariably associated with frying and are sometimes specifically referred to as frying pans), in other cases the distinctions are blurred.

Frying was well known as a method of cooking, and for this purpose skillets or frying pans were used. Many were doubtless made of metal, but a reference to 'lytel erthen pannys' (Austin 1888: 54) shows that they could be made in pottery. Some of the pottery versions resemble spouted bowls or pipkins in some respects, but are very much broader and shallower, with the rim diameter being larger than the base diameter (e.g. Nos. 1149, 1197, 2200). Some skillets have straight solid handles, and occasionally feet (e.g. Nos. 785, 1954–5). In many cases recipes state that the pan should be greased; '. . .take a fayre panne with freyssche gres, and set over the fyre. . .' (ibid.: 43) is a typical instruction.

Dripping dishes or dripping pans (e.g. Nos. 1163, 1914–15), originally known as 'fish dishes' in the archaeological literature, were often used, as is suggested by manuscript illustrations (e.g. Fig. 49), beneath a spit to catch the

Fig. 48   Bedroom scene with woman heating food in a pipkin over a portable fire; 14th cent. (*Romance of Alexander*, MS. 264, fol. 2v; photo Bodleian Library)

Fig. 49 Boy turning spit over dripping dish; mid 15th cent. (After Flemish Hours, Pierpont Library MS. M917, fol. 101, in Henisch 1976: fig. 20)

juices of roasting meat; archaeological finds confirm their use beside rather than on the fire, as they are often sooted on one side only. Their possible use in poaching items such as fish cannot be precluded, however.

Dishes (or shallow bowls) are frequently associated with serving food at the table (*ibid.*: 42, 53; Fig. 55), but can be depicted in other circumstances such as in hand-washing (Fig. 53), or being washed up (Fig. 50). It seems likely that

Fig. 50 Washing the dishes; 15th cent. (After misericord, Rouen, in Kraus and Kraus 1975: fig. 18)

they were often made from wood, or metal in the case of wealthier households, but they could also be made from pottery (e.g. Nos. 368–9, 1864, 1866), although ceramic dishes are not common before the early post-medieval period.

Bowls (e.g. Nos. 59–60, 1024) were important for food preparation, particularly in dairying (for cream separation) and for making pastry or bread dough. Bowls were mixing vessels; 'put hit in a bolle, and medle [mix] hem well' (*ibid.*: 76). They were also used in connection with fairly liquid mixtures such as fish soup, egg whites in fritter making, and almond cream. Such functions clearly imply vessels with fairly high sides, such as the form often called a pancheon (e.g. Nos. 1843–4). In some areas, bowls have a hole perforated in the side for draining off a liquid (e.g. 'West Country dish', No. 405). Late Saxon spouted bowls resemble bowls used in more recent times for separating cream. The fact that there are references to 'a bolle of tre' or 'treen bolls' shows that the material out of which the vessels were made could vary, and this might be one factor which explains the regional variations in the occurrence of bowls in the archaeological record.

In some areas, Lincolnshire for example, bowls are found to have sooting on the exterior, indicating that they were used for heating and cooking; in some instances this may have been part of the process of separating cream from milk as clotted cream, but in other cases bowls may have been used as straight-forward cooking vessels. Bowls could also be used for washing clothes (Moorhouse 1981: 114). Only occasionally are small ceramic bowls found that might have served as drinking vessels, or perhaps bleeding bowls (e.g. Nos. 813, 1159–60, 1162).

Pitchers (e.g. Nos. 125–6, 395, 994, 1008) and their successors, jugs (e.g. Nos. 1351–3), constitute another important class of domestic ware, especially for the twelfth-thirteenth centuries. In the Late Saxon period, and indeed until well after the Norman Conquest, earthenware pitchers are either absent or uncommon. Their increasing popularity in the high Middle Ages may in part reflect the fashions in tableware fostered by the growth in the wine trade at that time, or may simply be due to changes in social customs.

A prime function of pitchers and jugs was to contain beverages to be served at table, although they also had other uses. In the field, thirsty harvesters could drink straight from the jug, thus obviating the necessity for separate cups (Fig. 51). Manorial accounts record that earthenware jugs were often purchased to hold milk in the dairy (Moorhouse 1978: 8–9), whilst large jugs were frequently used for fetching water to the kitchen, as is attested by the number of broken jugs found down wells on archaeological sites. Water for the bath was also

Fig. 51 Harvesters; early 14th cent. (After Franco-Flemish Hours, Baltimore Walters Art Gallery MS. 88, fol. 150, in Randall 1966: pl. XCVII, No. 469)

Fig. 52 Woman taking bath as servant pours water; 15th cent. (After misericord, Villefranche-de-Rouergue, in Kraus and Kraus 1975: fig. 109)

carried in jugs (Fig. 52), and pottery vessels which may have been jugs were bought for heating the water at stews or bath houses (Moorhouse 1981: 114). Metal ewers or jugs were used for washing the hands of guests at banquets (Fig. 53), and pottery jugs, particularly the more ornate ones, may have been used similarly. Large earthenware jugs, when full, must have been extremely heavy, and would have been best carried on the head or shoulder (Fig. 54).

Small jugs are often interpreted as drinking vessels, and many probably

Fig. 53 Washing of hands, from medieval manuscript. (After Jewitt 1878: fig. 282)

Fig. 54   (a) Woman carrying pottery jug of ewe's milk on her head; *c.* 1340. (After *Luttrell Psalter*, East Anglian, British Library MS. Add. 42130, fol. 163v. in Millar 1932)
(b) Men with tubular-spouted jugs; late 12th cent. (After Bodleian Library, English manuscript, MS. Gough, lit. 2, fol. 20r, in Haslam 1978: pl. 1)

served as such; but they could also be used for serving purposes. Fig. 55 shows a man pouring something, perhaps wine or sauces, into small bowls to be taken to the table. Similar small jugs were on occasion used as urinals and chamber pots (Fig. 57).

Another ceramic form that might be mentioned here is the costrel (e.g. Nos. 122, 1371, 1908), which like its leather counterpart (Fig. 43) was used as a portable liquid container. Bottles are also sometimes found in earthenware (e.g. Nos. 645, 1248, 1907), but are not common.

Cisterns (e.g. Nos. 1630–1, 1634, 1729) are basically large handled jars or jugs with a bung-hole near the base to allow fluid to be drawn off without contamination by sediment. They became common items among domestic

Fig. 55   Serving up food at a feast; *c.* 1340. (*Luttrell Psalter*, East Anglian, MS. Add. 42130, fol. 207v; photo British Library)

assemblages in many parts of the country during the fifteenth century. Their main function is assumed to be storing ale or beer, with wooden and copper alloy vessels perhaps being used for most of the mashing and fermentation processes (Evans and Carter 1985: 84); their increased occurrence probably reflects changing social habits with brewing on a more widespread basis. The flow of liquid from the bung-hole was controlled by wooden taps; these are referred to as 'spiggots' or 'forcets' in documentary sources, and were frequently purchased for use with 'alepots' or cisterns (Moorhouse 1978: 7–8). Cisterns could also, however, have functioned in more general ways as water containers in the kitchen.

In deposits attributed to the fire of 1507 at Pottergate, Norwich, large pottery cisterns with substantial internal traces of sediment occur in almost every pottery group (Evans and Carter 1985: 83). On the same site, samples of germinating barley and hop fruit were found. These finds tie in well with the documentary evidence, which indicates a gradual change in the area from ale to beer-brewing, as well as an increase in domestic brewing during the fifteenth century, to such an extent that the commercial brewers felt threatened (*ibid.*: 84).

Small bowls were the commonest drinking vessel for much of the Middle Ages (e.g. Figs. 40 and 56), and most were probably of wood as pottery bowls of

Fig. 56 Monks' cellarer helps himself to a drop whilst filling a jug; 14th cent. (After British Library MS. Sloane 2435, in Hartley and Elliot 1928: pl. 9(c))

this size are infrequent. Pottery cups were not in general use before the later Middle Ages. Imported stoneware drinking jugs from Siegburg and Langer-wehe were known in some parts of the country from the fourteenth century, and locally-made unglazed or sparsely glazed drinking jugs (e.g. Nos. 1659, 1692), probably influenced by these stonewares, are also found in some areas during the fourteenth and fifteenth centuries, for example in the region covered by the Humber ware tradition (Yorkshire and north Lincolnshire).

The later fifteenth and sixteenth centuries saw the development of more specialized drinking wares in the Tudor Green (e.g. Nos. 2165–7) and Cistercian ware (e.g. Nos. 1749–50, 1757–60) traditions, taking their place alongside imported stonewares. Some vessels, such as posset pots (e.g. Nos. 1746–8) and lobed bowls/cups (e.g. Nos. 1673, 2154), were probably intended to be communal rather than individual cups. In such lobed cups the free-standing internal figures would have been gradually revealed as the level of the liquid went down with drinking. Other drinking vessels with an entertainment value were devised, though they are not at all common; these include a Humber ware puzzle cup from York (No. 1660) and the Oxford puzzle jugs (e.g. Fig. 170; Cherry 1985: 15–16). They were used to provide a challenge to the unwary to drink from them without spilling, the secret of success lying in understanding the system of mouthpieces, hollow rims and handles. This idea was taken up again in a much bigger way in the post-medieval period. Similar trickery could be found in wooden drinking vessels, such as the Corpus Christi College mazer (*ibid.*: 16).

Some of the fragmentary pottery horns known could have been drinking horns rather than blowing horns, though if the tip of the horn is missing it is impossible to tell. A unique Kingston ware drinking horn with three feet, ornamented with a face-mask and a broken figure of a man with an erect penis (*ibid.*: 11–12), may be imitating a metal prototype.

A number of other pottery forms, some of which are very rare, are connected with food and drink. Storage jars have already been mentioned in the discussion of cooking pots, as in many instances the cooking pot shape performed both functions. There are, however, some specialized storage vessel forms from the Late Saxon period (e.g. Nos. 141–2, 173, and the 'ginger jar' type No. 219) onwards (e.g. No. 1270). The later medieval period saw a considerable increase in the production of storage jars (e.g. Nos. 1898–1900).

Lids, whether for cooking pots, storage jars or jugs, are rare in pottery until the late medieval–early post-medieval period (e.g. Nos. 662, 1922). Presumably lids were often of wood or stone (such as the stone lid mentioned in a medical recipe, p. 119); canvas or cloth is sometimes mentioned in recipes as being used to cover the mouths of cooking pots (pp. 105–6), and parchment could serve the same purpose. In cooking, lids were sometimes attached to the pot with a paste or thick batter of flour to seal in the ingredients: 'hele [cover] the potte with a close led, and stoppe hit aboute with dogh or bater, that no eier [air] come oute' (Austin 1888: 73).

In food preparation, recipes often call for a mortar to grind meats or spices, and although these were often of stone or metal, some ceramic examples are known (e.g. Fig. 60 No. 8; No. 1386; Fig. 226). Cheese presses are a rare find in earthenware (e.g. Nos. 96, 784), and colanders (copying Low Countries prototypes) are present in late medieval and early post-medieval pottery collections in some areas, East Anglia for example (e.g. Nos. 1939–40). Ceramic moulds (Fig. 59 No. 6) and stamps (Fig. 59 No. 5) for sweetmeats are very occasionally found. Culinary stamps were also made at Mill Green in the thirteenth and fourteenth centuries (Cunningham and Drury 1985: 80), although they were more commonly of wood.

Chafing dishes are another element of many late pottery groups (e.g. Fig. 60 No. 9; Nos. 1927–8); these are copies in earthenware of the metal chafing dishes owned by the wealthy. They held glowing charcoal to heat a dish resting on the rim projections. Their function could be either to heat food or keep it hot at the table, or to warm water for washing the hands. They provided a gentle method of heating, as in a sixteenth-century medical recipe: '. . .then strayne the jewse into a fayre vessell & sett on a chafyngdisshe with a softe fyre. . .' (Dawson 1934: 332). The term often used, chafer or 'chaffur', may at a slightly earlier period include some other vessel shape, however, or chafing dishes with no perforated holes between the bowl and the pedestal base or feet may have been used in a slightly different way. Some recipes refer to chafers themselves being used for cooking, with no mention of an upper dish (unless the upper vessel was taken to be part of the chafer, as in a modern fondue set): 'and then take a chaffur ful of fressh grece boyling; and then put thi honde in the batur and lete the bater ren thorgh thi fingers into the chaffur. . .' (Austin 1888: 93).

Less common vessels used at table include salts, often in the form of figurines (e.g. Brears 1968: fig. 1 nos. 18/a, 18/b; Lewis 1978: fig. 13) – ceramic equivalents of the elaborate metal salt-containers on the tables of the rich. There are also compartmented dishes or condiments (e.g. Nos. 646, 1157, 1196), which perhaps held spices. In connection with hand-washing at table, pottery aquamaniles or zoomorphic vessels (e.g. Nos. 651, 1119) were used in some households instead of ewers such as that depicted in Fig. 53. These vessels also were copies of metal originals (Figs. 25, 26).

B. OTHER DOMESTIC AND INDUSTRIAL VESSELS

Vessels such as cooking pots and small jugs could be used as urinals and chamber pots (e.g. Fig. 57), but a specialized form of pottery urinal is known from the late medieval period. This is a one-handled globular vessel with a small aperture, ideally suited for male use, and frequently (although not exclusively) found on monastic sites (e.g. Nos. 1627–9, 1653, 1825); its distribution appears to be mainly northern, from the Midlands up to Scotland. Ceramic chamber pots do occur, but are not common before the seventeenth century. For the aristocracy, however, urinals and chamber pots could be of pewter or even silver by Tudor times (Amis 1968).

Urine had many uses, in tanning and cloth-making for example. It was also

116

Fig. 57 Small jugs being used as urinals and stool pots; mid 14th cent. (After Franco-Flemish *Voeux du Paon*, Pierpont Morgan Library, William S. Glazier collection, MS. 24, fol. 103v and 27v, in Randall 1966: pl. LXXV, no. 361 and pl. CX, no. 532)

useful for diagnosing illness, when held up to the light in a glass urinal. Urine is mentioned as an ingredient, occasionally the sole one, in medical recipes: 'whoso dreadeth the palsy or the falling-evil, let him drink nine days his own urine, and he shall never have it' (Dawson 1934: 233). Urine was presumably collected and used in vessels such as the ubiquitous cooking pot: 'take two earthen pots each by itself; and let the woman make water in the one, and the man in the other; and put in each of them a quantity of wheat bran. . .' (*ibid.*: 171). Sometimes vessels from archaeological deposits have been found to contain white incrustations resulting from their use either as urinals or for storing urine for industrial purposes, for example several jugs at Humberston Abbey (Hayfield 1984a).

Some ceramic vessels are connected with heating and lighting; pottery lamps are quite well known from Saxo-Norman deposits in some parts of the country, but thereafter are fairly uncommon (e.g. Nos. 1367, 1369), although stone lamps continue to be used throughout the medieval period. These early lamps could be bowl-shaped or pedestalled, or have a pointed base ('spike' lamps) (e.g. Nos. 128–9, 151–3). Spike lamps are commonly depicted in manuscripts as being suspended from the ceiling (Fig. 58). So-called 'ring vases' (Nos. 131, 148, 1944) are probably also lamps. Candlesticks are not common until the later

Fig. 58 'The house of the Lord', 23rd Psalm; *c.* 1180–90. (After a copy of the Carolingian Utrecht Psalter made in Canterbury, MS. latin 8846, Bibliothèque Nationale, Paris)

medieval–early post-medieval period (Nos. 2183, 2275–6), and prior to that time candles were presumably put on metal spikes.

When vessels of cooking pot or bowl form are found with internal rather than external sooting, one explanation may be their use as fire pans, to carry hot embers about the house, to light portable braziers, or to contain the fire overnight (Moorhouse 1978: 13). Special perforated warming pots for carrying hot charcoal are known from the Tudor period (No. 1943), although such forms could also have been used as pomanders. An alternative way of dealing with a fire overnight and preventing sparks setting fire to the house was to cover it with a pottery curfew or 'couvre-feu' (e.g. Fig. 59 No. 4; Nos. 203, 896, 940–1). Objects similar to curfews, with a central chimney, have recently been identified as fish-smokers (Fig. 60 No. 1). Their function is thought to be to increase the smoke produced by the fire, although experimental work is needed to show how they would work.

There is a limited range of specialized pottery forms associated with horticulture. Watering pots for use in the garden are known from the Saxo-Norman period onwards, although they are never very common. Many are shaped like narrow-necked jars or bottles with a flat perforated base, and a small hole at the top which would be covered by the thumb to control the release of the water (e.g. Fig. 59 Nos. 2, 3; Nos. 1945–7). In the Tudor period, another type of earthenware watering pot, shaped like the modern watering can, was occasionally made. Watering pots may also have had subsidiary functions, such as sprinkling earthen floors to settle the dust in hot dry weather. In upper-class households, watering pots may have been of metal, but there are also medieval accounts which mention the purchase of earthen pots for watering plants (Moorhouse 1978: 9–10).

Although ceramic garden furniture has not hitherto been recognized from

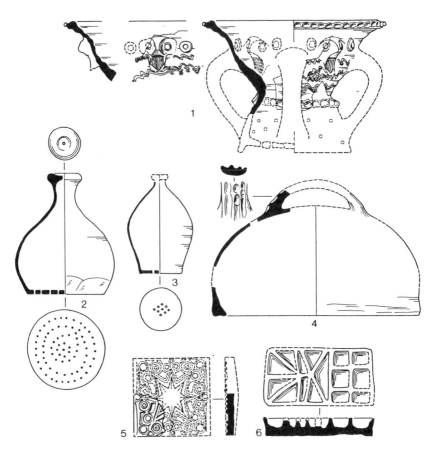

Fig. 59   1, Humber ware plant-holder from Beverley, Yorkshire. (After Moorhouse 1984)

2, 3, watering pots: 2, Late London-type ware; 3, London-type ware. (After Pearce *et al.* 1985)

4, curfew in scratch-marked ware, 13th–14th cent., from Netherton. (After Fairbrother 1984)

5, culinary stamp, *c.* early 16th cent., from Chelmsford. (After Cunningham and Drury 1985)

6, compartmented tray for small cakes or confections, *c.* 14th-15th cent., from Fenstanton, Cambridgeshire. (After Cunningham and Drury 1985) (Scale 1:8)

excavations before the post-medieval period, a recent article has pointed to the existence of a specific late medieval form of urn-shaped ornamental plant-holder in Yorkshire (Fig. 59 No. 1). All known examples apparently come from the production centre at West Cowick (Moorhouse 1984).

The products of the medieval herb garden played an important part in medieval medicine; medical recipes, like culinary ones, often refer to earthen pots or crocks as well as to metal pots. Although the shape of pot is not usually specified, most of the recipes involve boiling or soaking the ingredients, and so the common cooking pot form was probably often used. A pre-Conquest manuscript instructs one to 'seethe his [a badger's] brain in three sextarii of oil in a new crock, till that the third part be boiled away; bottle off, and preserve it' (Cockayne 1864–6, Vol. I: 239). Another recipe refers to keeping fennel in water for thirty days in a crock, 'one that is pitched on the outside', presumably to seal its porous surfaces (*ibid.*: 27).

Apart from heating the pot over a fire, it could also be used in an oven, as in a fifteenth-century recipe for gout ointment: 'take an owl, and pluck it clean; and open it clean, and salt it; and put it in a new pot, and cover it with a stone; and put it in an oven and let it stand till it be burnt; and then stamp it with boar's grease, and anoint the gout therewith' (Dawson 1934: 207). Other methods used include sinking the pot with its ingredients into the ground to keep it cold (*ibid.*: 141), or perforating the base of a pot and placing it on top of another set in the ground, as in a recipe for oils made from wood:

> [trees or branches] should be hewn into pieces, and put into a pot of which the bottom is drilled full of small holes; and another pot that is well glazed shall be put in the earth up to the rim-joint. Then shall the drilled pot be set above the other pot. And daub it well so that the ears [handles] of the one pot overlap the other pot. And daub it well about with clay. And make an easy fire about the upper pot, and then through the strength of the fire there will fall an oil out of the drilled pot into the pot that standeth in the earth (*ibid.*: 215).

Sometimes earthenware pots were filled with hot water infused with herbs, sealed, and used as a kind of hot water bottle (Moorhouse 1981: 117). Vessels with internal sooting may have been used for medicinal purposes rather than simply as domestic fire-pots; one fifteenth-century recipe begins: 'take heavy blue cloth and burn it in a red pot or upon a red tile-stone; and make powder thereof. . .' (*ibid.*: 175). Frying pans were also sometimes called for in medical recipes: 'take earthworms before they go into the earth in the morning, and fry them. . .' (*ibid.*: 155). Other vessels mentioned include jugs, basins, mortars, chafing dishes and colanders.

As with medical recipes, ordinary household vessels such as cooking pots may have been used for industrial purposes, although some items were specially made. Craftsmen's recipes, such as those for making white lead and vermilion, often specify the use of an earthen pot, sometimes with holes bored in it

(Moorhouse 1981: 117–18). More specialized industrial vessels include crucibles (e.g. No. 144), and Agricola's *De re metallica* shows a potter making vessels for use in metallurgy (Fig. 11 No. 4). Some ceramic mortars may also have had an industrial function, for example Fig. 60 No. 8 which was found on a kiln site. Other industrial forms connected with potting, such as kiln props and saggars, are described elsewhere (p. 45).

A major category of industrial pottery comprises vessels that were used in distilling. Distillation equipment of pottery and glass is now well known from the late medieval period, and the methods of distillation are fully described in literature of the sixteenth century (Moorhouse 1972b). In distillation, a liquid was boiled in a lower gourd-shaped vessel (cucurbit), or a flanged earthenware bowl known as a distilling-base (Fig. 60 Nos. 2, 6), and the vapour from this was condensed in an upper spouted vessel or alembic (Fig. 60 Nos. 3, 5). The condensate ran into a collecting channel and down the spout into a receiver (*ibid.*).

Distillation was used to make mineral acids with which to assay precious metals, and the earliest description of making a mineral acid dates from the fourteenth century, although it is not clear when the practice began. Distillation of alcohols seems to have been introduced at the same time as that of acids. The process is often associated with alchemy as well as metallurgy; at Sandal Castle, for instance, there were two alchemical workshops using industrial pottery, including distillation equipment, in the late medieval period (Moorhouse 1983b: 191–4).

A minor category of pottery usage comprises vessels associated with religion and superstition. Lamps, for example, were as necessary in the church as in the home; they may well have been made of earthenware as well as metal, particularly in poorer churches. Fig. 58 shows an example of a lamp very similar to the Saxo-Norman spike lamp form. Church vessels such as chalices, censers and candlesticks were presumably usually of metal, but occasionally cruets of earthenware are found (Fig. 63 Nos. 3, 4). These were used for mixing wine and water for the Mass, and most closely resemble pewter cruets (Dunning 1969b; Lewis 1968). Other pots found in churches include acoustic pots, or vessels such as jugs which were embedded in the walls of medieval churches (e.g. Tester 1956); this was done, it is thought, to improve the acoustic qualities of the building.

Ceramic inkwells might be expected to be a frequent find, particularly on monastic sites where copying of manuscripts was a common task, but in fact they are uncommon before the late medieval period. Examples such as that from Byland Abbey, Yorkshire, are rare exceptions (Dunning 1961).

In Scotland, burials are occasionally found to have been accompanied by pots; at Innerpeffray church in Perthshire, for example, pots were found with two burials which probably dated to the later sixteenth century (Robertson W.

Fig. 60 1, 'fish-smoker', *c.* 13th cent., from a fishery site at Short Ferry, Lincs. (After A.J. White 1984)
2–6, late medieval pottery distillation equipment: 2, distilling-base from Southampton; 3, alembic from London; 4, bottle-shaped vessel, possibly used as a cucurbit, from London; 5, 6, alembic and distilling-base from Nuneaton. (After Moorhouse 1972b)
7, ceramic horn from Bothwell Castle. (After Cruden 1951–2)
8, ceramic mortar from the 13th cent. kiln site at Colstoun, E. Lothian. (After Brooks C.M. 1978–80)
9, late 14th/early 15th cent. chafing dish with oak-leaf design and escutcheons bearing a schematic version of Bishop Despenser's arms, North Elmham. (After Rigold 1962–3)
10, 13th cent. jar stamped with alternate fleur-de-lys and arms of the Clare family, from Shotley, Suffolk. (After Owles 1973) (Scale 1:8)

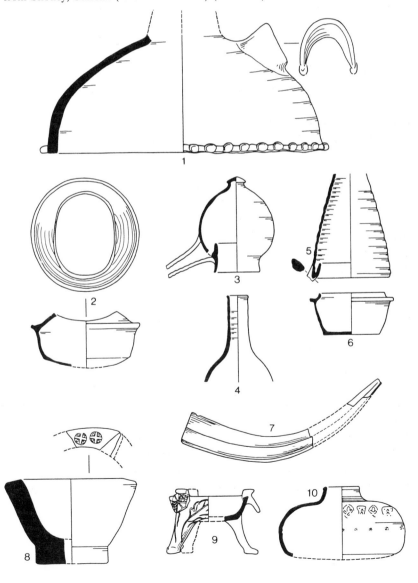

1974). The vessels were three two-handled jars (or ovoid bowls) (No. 1599), one of which may have contained something as it had been sealed with a wooden lid at the time of burial, and a shallow two-handled bowl or pan. These vessels are probably ordinary domestic wares of the period. It seems that this Scottish custom, which has been noted at other sites, is derived from French funeral practices, and is an indication of the close cultural links between France and Scotland in the Middle Ages (*ibid.*).

Apart from vessels accompanying inhumations, other examples of buried pots are known; some were found with coin hoards, but others, placed under medieval foundations, may have served to bring good luck or to ward off evil spirits (Moorhouse 1978: 12). They would thus be precursors of the seventeenth-century 'witch-bottles', or stoneware bellarmine bottles containing objects such as hair, iron nails, pins and personal items which were buried beneath hearths or thresholds in some parts of the country. Vessels with inscriptions or markings which may relate to magic or witchcraft are discussed below (pp. 131–4).

Among other miscellaneous items, very few ceramic musical instruments have been recognized. Horns in earthenware are known from various sites (e.g. Fig. 60 No. 7; Nos. 1060, 1941), but they are often fragmentary, so that it is not always clear whether they were used as blast-horns or as drinking horns. Blowing horns have, however, been recognized at the production site at Brill, along with a mouthpiece from a musical instrument. Natural horns were sometimes used for medical purposes, for example in administering clysters (e.g. Cockayne 1864–6, Vol. II: 261), and it is possible that some ceramic horns may have also served this purpose. Pottery bird whistles were made in France throughout the Middle Ages, and traded widely (Dunning 1968); some are found in Britain, but they do not appear to have been produced often, if at all, by British potters.

Money boxes are known, though usually as rare types, from most parts of the country (e.g. Nos. 1252, 1607, 1625). Another miscellaneous pottery type has been described as a 'chicken feeder' (Nos. 1942, 2090), but this interpretation is open to some doubt.

Regional differences in pottery

The impact of the adoption of ceramics on society has recently been reviewed (Arnold 1985), but has received no discussion with regard to Saxon and medieval Britain. Following Arnold, the proposition can be advanced that the acquisition of pottery in many parts of Britain between the late ninth and the late twelfth centuries could have had implications in the fields of diet and health. Where metal vessels are largely confined to aristocratic households, in humbler kitchens foods can be prepared and cooked in vessels made from wood, basketry, leather and stone. Ceramic cooking pots have a number of advantages, however. They can be left unattended for longer periods, sustain greater temperatures than vessels in some other materials, and be placed in direct contact with a fire. Pottery vessels will bear and retain sustained heat for prolonged periods, and this has the advantage of increasing the range of potential food resources. Many food plants such as brassicas, peas and beans, leeks and fruits, as well as cereals used for porridge, are rendered palatable and more digestible without loss of flavour by slow cooking. Indeed, there are references showing that ceramic vessels were preferred because they impart a better flavour to food than non-ceramic wares (Arnold 1985: 138; Wilson C.A. 1973: 199). A possible result of the adoption of pottery vessels may, therefore, have been an increase in the amount of boiled and stewed foods consumed. The range of potential foodstuffs was thereby widened, thus leading to a greater intake of certain vitamins; the general levels of health in the population might, therefore, be expected to improve.

The purpose of this proposition is to pose a question, rather than to provide an answer, concerning the possible dietary and health implications which may follow from the adoption of pottery as a food preparation and cooking medium. One of the problems is undoubtedly the paucity of the archaeological evidence for diet in the middle and lower ranks of society, especially between the late ninth and the mid twelfth century. Cereals and animals were clearly very important indeed, but much of the palaeobotanical evidence currently available for leafy foodstuffs is ambiguous; the range of edible plants is very wide and includes, for example, nettles, dock, sorrel and chickweed, but the number considered worth cultivating or even gathering from hedgerows and roadsides may have been very small given the quantities required for a single meal. Whilst we know from documentary sources that some greens and root vegetables were eaten, there is little indication that they ever formed part of a main crop before the Tudor period. When the seeds of edible plants are found in archaeological contexts, there is usually no certainty that they represent food plants rather than wild species. Similarly, studies of skeletal remains in Late Saxon and early medieval Britain are as yet too few to be able to define improvements in health. Such evidence as there is from medieval Britain points to a relatively low age at death, but much more work is required on rural as well as urban populations before this can be sustained.

The practice of using pottery for culinary purposes became widespread between the late ninth and the twelfth century, with the exception of parts of Wales and Scotland. Cooking pots are both ubiquitous and numerically the most important single vessel type; there are, however, regional and chronological differences in cooking pot shape. The narrow-based, jar-like forms of pre-Conquest cooking pots are widely distributed across the country from York to Gloucester, and differ from the more rounded bag-shaped vessels prevalent over wide areas of southern England from Dorset to Sussex. The Cornish 'bar lug' cooking pots, and their St Neots ware counterparts in the Midlands, are quite distinct from other kitchen wares and are especially well adapted to cooking large quantities and being suspended over a fire. Another variation can be seen in the aceramic parts of northern England, Scotland and Wales, where the absence of pottery before the twelfth century clearly shows that other means of preparing and serving food and drink prevailed. From the mid twelfth century, and in some parts from the mid eleventh century, cooking pots were made larger with capacities often in excess of 1½ gallons, compared with those made previously which were commonly in the 3–5 pint range. Many post-Conquest cooking pots also show more strongly developed variations in shape. This can be seen, for example, by comparing the cylindrical Oxfordshire-Cotswold forms with the broad but shallow so-called 'peat pots' in Staxton ware, or the more rounded Potters Marston vessels, distinctions first identified by Jope (1952; 1963). From the functional point of view, however, it seems likely that the differences between globular and straight-sided cooking pots or squared and everted rims was less important than capacity, the later vessels having two or three times the volume of those of the tenth/eleventh centuries.

Another major class of vessel is the pan, dish or bowl, terms which in many cases are probably interchangeable, as they clearly shared a number of common functions. Unlike cooking pots, bowls are not ubiquitous, and in both pre- and post-Conquest contexts show marked distributional differences. At Lincoln, Torksey and Stamford, bowls were the second most important culinary vessel (Gilmour *et al.* forthcoming; Barley 1981; Kilmurry 1980). The largest examples have a capacity in excess of 3 gallons, whilst the smaller bowls, some of which have sockets, are around the 2–6 pint range. By contrast, bowls appear to be much less common in parts of East Anglia. Excavations at Thetford and Langhale in Norfolk (Rogerson and Dallas 1984; Wade 1976) recovered very few bowls, although they were common at the Grimston Thetford-type ware production centre. Bowls are present in London in the tenth century, where they are described as dishes or frying pans (Vince 1985a), but are extremely rare between the eleventh and early thirteenth centuries. They are very common in the east Midlands, but are much less so in the west Midlands in the tenth-eleventh centuries except at the production site at Tipping Street, Stafford.

In the post-Conquest period, bowls occur rather more widely, although regional variations are still apparent. They are a common feature of the central Midlands area, for example, but totally absent in Devon and Cornwall and very rare in Cumbria. Current indications are that in Scotland pottery bowls never formed an important element in household equipment; they were present in a very minor capacity at the Colstoun production site, Perth, St Andrews, Aberdeen and Inverness, for example. A similar situation obtains in Wales, where excavations and field work have revealed cooking pots and jugs at Chepstow, Monmouthshire, Cardiff, Valle Crucis Abbey, Carmarthen, and St Dogmaels, Merioneth, amongst other sites; but, with the exception of the production site at Rhuddlan, bowls are virtually absent from medieval contexts. In the sixteenth century the north Devon industries at Barnstaple and Bideford were producing bowls as an important item in gravel tempered wares, which are attested all over the south-west as well as at several sites in south Wales including the production site identified at Trefaldu in Gwent, tentatively attributed to 1550–1650.

It is not clear what the distribution of bowls signifies. Although variations in the bowl form are apparent such as, for example, with the Late Saxon inturned rim or the socketed types, the basic form is especially well suited to bread making and various jobs connected with preparing meals, as has been seen above (p. 109–10). Bowls were vital items of equipment in the dairy where they were used for skimming milk and cheese-making, providing important items for the medieval diet. The distribution might, therefore, mirror regional and chronological variations in farming practice, stock rearing and pastoralism. On the other hand, bowls are so useful that their absence in pottery is unlikely to mean that they were not available, and in such cases the products of the wood turner probably substituted for those of the potter. It is too early yet to formulate any specific reasons why bowls should display both chronological and geographical differences, and certainly the study of medieval food production from historical sources is in many areas not sufficiently far advanced to enable this to be pursued.

Regional variations in other forms are also apparent. One of the most striking regional forms is the so-called 'West Country' dish, a shallow, flat-based vessel with slightly inward-sloping walls and a single hole perforated through the side near the base (e.g. No. 405). The form is known from wide areas of Wessex as well as in south Wales and the Malverns. In these areas the 'West Country dish' mostly occurs as a very occasional item, but in the Vale of Glamorgan large numbers have been recovered in what appears to be a local ware, 'Vale Fabric', from village sites such as Cosmeston and Barry village. Here the 'West Country dish' is the most prolific form, outstripping even cooking pots. The dates of these pots are not always easy to establish, but they are clearly twelfth century and later in south Wales and at many of the Wessex sites. At Lacock and Laverstock, Wiltshire, they were made in kilns datable to the mid to later thirteenth century, but there are few examples post-dating this. The relatively tight geographical and chronological distribution clearly points to a regional function with special emphasis in south Wales, but their usage, variously described as being in connection with cheese-making and bee-keeping, remains unknown.

Pitchers and jugs also show marked chronological and regional differences.

Spouted pitchers, essentially cooking pots with a tubular spout just below the rim and a short strap handle placed opposite, feature in a great many Late Saxon assemblages from Durham to Somerset though they are almost always numerically very minor elements. At Winchester and Stamford, spouted pitchers were partially covered with a clear lead glaze and, at Winchester, further elaborated with applied and rouletted decoration. It has been suggested that Winchester ware pitchers formed as much as 80 percent of the production (Biddle and Barclay 1974: 144), a situation which stands in contrast to Stamford ware where the well-known glazed pitchers may have actually formed a relatively small proportion of the production. Whilst some Winchester ware vessels have been found as far away as Bath, Somerset, the distribution as currently understood is strongly local and may owe something to the especially important royal associations with the town. This may also be the explanation for the early development of the large, glazed tripod pitchers which appear in Winchester early in the eleventh century, about a hundred years in advance of those known elsewhere.

From the mid-twelfth century pitchers and jugs become increasingly common on sites of all social status. As with cooking pots, twelfth- and thirteenth-century pitchers and jugs were invariably much larger than their Late Saxon counterparts, and also display minor variations of shape. Many production sites in Yorkshire, for example, made jugs with tubular spouts, whilst in Wessex and parts of the West Midlands three short feet were added to the base ('tripod pitchers'). Jugs occur in a very wide range of shapes, often glazed and sometimes highly decorated but frequently becoming less baggy from the thirteenth century. Apart from the small Humber ware drinking jugs, or those produced in the Surrey kilns, there is no suggestion that shape or surface treatment reflects different functions.

It can be suggested that whilst cooking pots and bowls were potentially multi-functional, many were used either for cooking or for food preparation. There is little in the variations in shape which would have affected their principal uses; the same can be said of jugs and pitchers. We have already noted how cooking pots become common items of equipment in England during the Late Saxon period, and that they seem to be ubiquitous over large parts of Scotland and Wales from the late twelfth century. Jugs, formerly rare on most sites, have by the late twelfth century become standard items on sites at all social levels, and from the fourteenth century onwards in some areas outstrip cooking pots as the most common form. The increasing use of metal cooking pots is probably responsible for much of the decline in ceramic ones, as is the growing inclination in some areas towards the use of Low Countries or locally-made pipkins. It might be asked, however, whether there are also implications here for the nature and availability of foods and drinks, and changing fashions in cookery.

Decoration and symbolism

Ceramic art offers a very wide range of possibilities to the potter wishing to make use of a variety of surface textures, slips, burnishing and glazing for decorative purposes. All have aesthetic value which can be combined in ornamental or symbolic fashion. Decoration is applied to the surface of pots, which are often curved in the horizontal as well as the vertical plane. Except in the case of carinations or where a cylinder is joined to a rounded shape, the curves tend to be continuous. Such factors place special demands on the potter wishing to go beyond a simple horizontal incised line, especially when complex plastic ornament is involved.

The surfaces to be decorated are usually those most prominent from the point of view of the onlooker, that is the shoulders, necks, rims and handles of hollow wares and the internal surfaces of flat wares. Breaks in the surface planes can impose constraints upon the type of motifs to be employed and the way they are disposed around the vessel; plastic ornament can be used to conceal the breaks in surface planes. On medieval jugs the space between the rim and the shoulder was sometimes filled with three-dimensional figures, most notably knights on horseback (e.g. Nos. 652–3, 656) but struts, arms and bearded face-masks (e.g. Nos. 647–8, 650) were also used to conceal the neck.

Several factors may have determined the motifs to be employed. These include the vessel's intended function, the availability of raw materials and the potter's perception of what kind of decoration will please or sell. Function is an important determinant, with table wares tending to be more elaborate than ordinary domestic vessels, although some cooking pots and bowls have surfaces with rouletted or incised decoration. Only occasionally, as at Exeter and in south Somerset, are cooking pots more elaborately treated, in this case with a profusion of combed lines all over. Applied strips on cooking pots and storage jars, however, can be interpreted simply as strengthening the vessels and providing a greater degree of purchase necessary when they were full and had to be moved. In the case of pre-Conquest storage jars with large numbers of applied and thumbed strips of clay, sometimes further elaborated with stamped decoration, the applied strips could also be skeuomorphic representations of basketry or rope containers. One of the most convincing such skeuomorphs, however, is the bottle or costrel imitating a 'picnic ware' leather hip flask in Winchester ware (No. 379). Apart from glazed Winchester and Stamford wares, which also have poor imitations of interlace on some vessels (e.g. No. 823), there is little evidence that potters in Late Saxon England exploited the possibilities of clay for decorative purposes.

Between the twelfth and fourteenth centuries potters took much more trouble to ensure that vessels for the table such as jugs and aquamaniles were pleasing to look at, by covering their shoulders, necks, rims and handles with glaze, and further enhancing the surfaces with a variety of apparently abstract or figural designs. On the one hand this is clearly related to the fact that enjoyment of food and drink can be enhanced by appreciation of artistic endeavour at the table, but it is also related to the greater availability of raw materials and the spread of glazing technology.

From this period, the great surge in building activity increased the demand for various metals used in the construction industry and also, from the reign of Henry III, the demand for polychrome floor tiles in which the decorative possibilities of using white and red firing clays together were exploited. Whilst one cannot point to a Romanesque or Gothic phase in ceramics, potters in the Middle Ages, as well as those in less developed countries at the present day, can be seen as working within the confines of their aesthetic background as well as the technological limits of their society. The more readily available metal ores, and the demand for greater figural expression in sculpture and painting on buildings which was increasingly evident from the twelfth century, formed part of the aesthetic and technological background for the post-Conquest potters. The impact on the production of table wares is self-evident.

There are three main characteristics of the decoration on medieval pottery: colour, abstract and figured ornament. The most striking and widespread is the use of lead glazes, sometimes clear but often using copper and iron-rich or iron-free clays, producing warm hues ranging from yellows, reds and browns to greens and white. The only colour missing from the primary and complementary range is blue. The glaze was usually applied to the upper half of vessels, sometimes liberally, sometimes sparingly, and sometimes to great effect. Applied or incised designs frequently embellish the surfaces in apparently random fashion, though in some cases simple or complex patterns, such as the slip-painted repeating arcs and lattices on jugs from Netherton, Hampshire (Nos. 1315–17), bear witness to the care and skill of the craftsmen.

Certain motifs recall features familiar from other aspects of daily life. In some cases applied strips with pellets resemble, as Le Patourel (1986) has suggested, ornamental ironwork on doors or chests, or rivets on vessels made of sheet metal. Applied stripwork is also used to depict brooches and buckles (e.g. Nos. 1260, 1265). Healey (1984: 76–8) has noted that some designs on Toynton jugs resemble heraldic motifs, and Jewitt long ago drew attention to the horseshoes and buckles on jugs found at Burley Hill (Fig. 61) being the same as the arms of the Earls of Derby, the de Ferrers family (1878: 79). The well-known York White ware seal jugs (e.g. Figs. 133, 134; No. 684) sometimes have seals with inscriptions which read 'SIGILLUM' and 'TOMAS ME FECIT'; Le Patourel (1979a: 87–8) has suggested that these may derive from seals of the de Quincy family in York, but other explanations are possible. Fig. 60 No. 10 shows a jar with the coat of arms of the Clares alternating with fleur-de-lys decoration. Such devices taken from heraldry may in many cases be purely

Fig. 61   Jug in Burley Hill ware with badge of the de Ferrers family, from Duffield; 13th/14th cent. (Photo Derby City Museum and Art Gallery)

decorative, a trend also observable in decorated floor tiles, although sometimes there is a close association between the household and the pots with these symbols. Fig. 60 No. 9, for example, is a 'bespoke piece'; this chafing dish with the Despenser coat of arms was recovered from Bishop Despenser's manor at North Elmham.

Religious symbols are only occasionally in evidence, such as the possible lamb and cross or *Agnus Dei* on a jug in St Albans-type ware found in St Albans. A jug from the Rye kilns has a haloed figure with the right arm raised in blessing (No. 1242). Crosses may also have religious significance, such as the incised cross crosslet on a jug possibly associated with the Dominican Friary in Cardiff (Fig. 231b; No. 1573), or the combed crosses on jugs from the Ashton kiln site, Cheshire (Fig. 222; No. 1519). An applied cross from Etton, North Humberside, looks like an imitation Knights Hospitaller's cross, whilst motifs such as the scallop shell are a reminder of pilgrim badges. We may be correct in attributing symbolic significance to some of these designs, but it should be remembered that many were simply part of the visual language of the period and can be found in non-religious contexts, and in many media besides pottery.

It is surprising to find that religious motifs and scenes are not more widely used on medieval pots, given the overwhelming importance of the church at all social levels. No representations of the nativity or the crucifixion, for example, are so far known on British medieval pots. The one possible Adam and Eve scene, on a jug from London, was originally interpreted as a bordello. It may in fact have secular rather than religious significance, possibly indicating that the owner of the jug was called Adam (Cherry 1985: 8–10).

Mythical beasts are excessively rare, and it is worthy of note that the dragon from Nash Hill, Lacock, Wiltshire (Nos. 1364–5), should be unique, given that such creatures were a favourite subject of metalworkers and sculptors from Anglo-Saxon times. Examples of other animals are not common, and when they do occur it is usually as an accessory, for example a horse with a knight.

A number of pottery vessels make use of phallic images (e.g. Fig. 62; Nos. 972, 1081), but there appears to be no evidence that phallic motifs had any amuletic significance in the Middle Ages. It is possible that these pots may have been based to some extent on bronze vessels known as aeolipiles or fire blowers, which were in the form of kneeling male figures with erect penises. Such a vessel was filled with water and placed beside the hearth, so that when it was heated, steam from the mouth would blow up the fire (Cherry 1985: 11–15). The appeal of such vessels which amused by their trickery is similar to the appeal of items such as puzzle jugs. The phallic imagery on pottery vessels may,

Fig. 62   Rim and tubular spout of jug with phallic decoration, from Oxford. (Photo Ashmolean Museum)

however, spring directly from the potter's (and customer's) bawdy sense of humour.

Pottery vessels sometimes have marks, letters or inscriptions, usually incised but sometimes applied (e.g. No. 808), which may have symbolic significance, although the precise meaning is usually unclear. Marks or letters that were incised before or after firing may indicate ownership, made either by the purchaser of the vessel, or by the potter to denote a pot or consignment of pots on order for a specific customer. Fig. 63 No. 1 has an arrow incised by the potter before firing; this may simply be a potter's mark or signature, in the manner of masons' marks, or may denote a particular client. Fig. 63 No. 2 also has symbols (only one shown here) which were incised on the body before firing.

In other cases, markings are made after firing, and these are presumably more likely to have been made by the purchaser or owner. Fig. 64 No. 4, a large cooking pot, has an inscription cut after firing; the upper line reads 'ADAM' and below it are less legible letters, 'VE(?)RM'. This may represent the name of the owner, Adam, with a surname, or it may possibly refer to Adam and Eve (Cherry 1985: 7). A rare documentary example of a pot being marked for a particular person can be found in a letter of John Paston II to Margaret Paston, written in 1479. He describes the condition of three pots of treacle from Genoa, bought in London: 'I send you. . . 3 pots of Genoa treacle. . . There is one pot that is marked under the bottom twice with these letters 'MP' for Margaret Paston, in which pot I have best trust. . .' (Davis 1971: 512–13).

Some markings on pots may have a less prosaic significance, however. A number of industrial vessels connected with alchemy at Sandal Castle, for example, bear symbols, presumably magical, that were incised before firing (Moorhouse 1981: 117; 1983b). Enigmatic stamped inscriptions found in the Midlands have been interpreted in terms of protection against witchcraft. Two examples of these inscriptions occur on jugs, Fig. 64 Nos. 2 and 3; the sequences of stamped letters appear to be random, but may represent the initials of words, presumably those of a protective formula (Dunning 1967). They might, on the other hand, be no more than an unintelligible sequence of letters, presumably for decorative effect (Cherry 1985: 6). A more comprehensible inscription is seen on a drinking jug from Lincolnshire (Fig. 64 No. 1), upon which 'Binedice' for 'Benedice' (with a reversed initial B) was incised before firing. This inscription may have a double meaning, and apart from being the first word of a Latin grace, it may by the alliteration of 'Benedice' and 'Benedict' allude to the story of St Benedict's escape from poisoned wine which he was offered (Dunning 1967).

Inscriptions are more common on vessels of bronze or precious metal than on pottery ones. Some name the person who ordered the pot to be made, for example, or record that the vessel was a gift from one person to another.

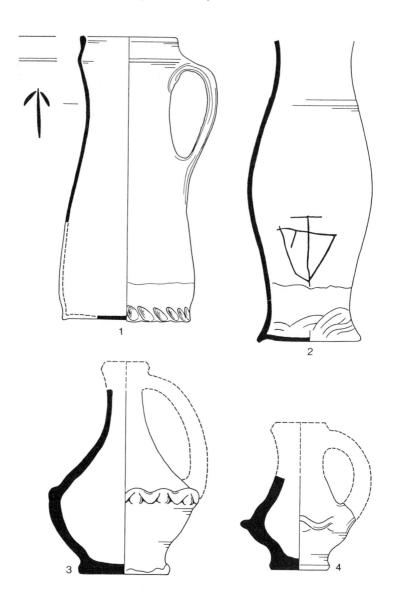

Fig. 63   1, Mill Green ware jug with 'maker's mark'. (After Pearce *et al.* 1982)
2, London-type ware baluster jug with 'maker's mark'. (After Pearce *et al.* 1985)
3, 4, 13th/14th cent. church cruets: 3, from the Dominican friary, Dunstable,
Bedfordshire; 4, from Weoley Castle, Warwickshire. (After Dunning 1969b; Lewis
1968) (Scale 1:4)

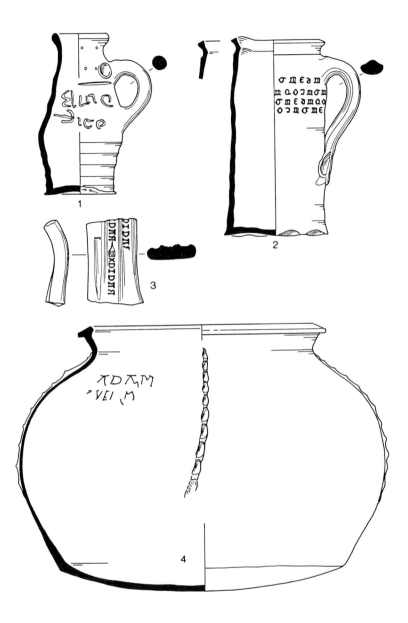

Fig. 64 1–3, 15th cent. vessels with lettering: 1, jug, probably for drinking, from Spilsby, Lincolnshire, inscribed 'Binedice'; 2, jug from Coventry with Lombardic lettering impressed by a roller-stamp; 3, jug handle from Abthorpe, Northamptonshire, with stamped letters. (After Dunning 1967)
4, large 13th/14th cent. cooking pot with inscription or 'owner's mark' from Norwich. (After Jennings 1981) (Scale 1:4)

Occasionally the inscription ends with a threat or curse against anyone stealing the pot. Cherry has, however, contrasted the scarcity of possible magical or amuletic devices on earthenware pots, and even on metal vessels, with their abundance in medieval jewellery (1985: 7–8).

Symbols are messages in code, which may be specific to a potter and/or his client, or generally understood within society. In medieval medicine, for example, red is associated with blood or the male principle, white with anaemia, yellow with the liver and green with fertility or the female principle. Perhaps the colours applied to some medieval pots represented these beliefs. It may be that the abstract designs of applied strips, wavy combed lines, or pads impressed with grid stamps are not just patterns but refer to folk beliefs or local superstitions, as can be demonstrated by ethnographic research on some American Indian or African pottery. Perhaps the knights modelled on some of the finest jugs commemorate particular tournaments or individuals renowned for their prowess at jousting. Some of the faces on anthropomorphic jugs may be portraits of real people. The ladies participating in a dance or carol on a Ham Green jug (Fig. 209; No. 1410) may represent a particular event. On the other hand, this decorative scheme may mean that the jug was related to a specific feast or feasts involving carols, and there are examples of vessels in other materials that were only used on certain occasions, such as Christmas (Cherry 1985: 17). Various interpretations of the decoration on medieval pottery are possible, but for the most part these must remain in the realm of speculation, for we have no means of confirming or refuting them. The potter's imagination, sense of humour and flair for design must be taken into account, however. One of the most impressive groups of decorative motifs is to be found on vessels from the kilns at Rye, Sussex, where fishes, shields, ships, a jousting scene, figures and a very wide variety of other incised and stamped devices occur (Figs. 192–3; Barton 1979). With the exception of the figure of a haloed saint or Christ, these all appear to be not so much symbolic as a record of the potter's high spirits.

Part Two

Introduction

Part Two describes and illustrates the major ceramic types from a wide range of sites in England, Scotland and Wales, dating for the most part to the period from the early tenth to the end of the sixteenth century. The sites chosen include both lordly and peasant establishments in rural and urban locations. It is intended as a select gazetteer, and does not attempt to provide comprehensive coverage for either the sites or the pottery types. It is not a corpus; indeed there is so much pottery from such a vast range of locations that it would probably be impossible to present a corpus, even if such a project were desirable.

On the whole, sites have been selected because they contain a useful stratified sequence, because the range of material present is in some way impressive or instructive, or else because the nature of the site itself has something to offer ceramic studies. The selection procedure does not, therefore, necessarily reflect the amount of work undertaken in the county, although this is sometimes the case. Many sites and reports, including some relatively well-known ones, have been omitted from this section. In some instances the omissions are because they add little to the picture already established, but in other cases, it must be said, they have been left out because the pottery reports are inadequate for our purposes. In addition, we have not accounted for the production of tin-glazed earthenware, made from 1568 by Jasper Andries and his compatriots in Norwich and London (Edwards R. 1974), because an assessment of this material is more appropriate to a study of post-Elizabethan pottery. English stonewares are regarded as being beyond the scope of this book, as the earliest patent for their manufacture is dated 1614 (*ibid*).

Part Two is divided into three main chapters, representing the early tenth to the mid-twelfth century, the mid-twelfth to the mid-fourteenth century, and the mid-fourteenth to the late sixteenth century. Each chapter is divided into counties, which are grouped into regions. This has been done for convenience and ease of compilation, although we are fully aware that these boundaries bear no relation in most cases to the areas covered by ceramic 'traditions'. The county boundaries are those of the old (pre-1974) divisions. We found these easier to use, especially with regard to the literature, and there is, we feel, a sense of historical reality behind such boundaries. A series of maps locating most of the places mentioned in the text within their county boundaries appears at the beginning of each region; where places are known only from documentary references, for example, it is not always possible to locate them. The maps have two symbols: diamonds indicate production sites, dots locate other sites mentioned in the text.

The entries for production sites include brief details of what is known about the site in structural terms; where no archaeological evidence exists, we have included references from documentary sources. On other sites, details of the structures associated with the pottery have been omitted for reasons of space. Pottery descriptions include references to the fabrics, forms and decoration of local wares, and highlight the quality of the dating evidence. We have occasionally drawn attention to both regional and continental imports, but this has not been our main concern; foreign imports have in any case been the subject of a recent appraisal (Davey and Hodges 1983). Our terminology tends to reflect the variety present in archaeological reports, though we have standardized the use of some terms, especially for form. Drawings are presented at one-eighth scale, and are intended to illustrate the range present at some of the sites described. Wherever possible we have used the most complete profiles, although of course there are many instances where sherd material is all that survives. Not all sites described are accompanied by illustrations, and not every variation in form is illustrated. If this detail is required, the reader is referred back to the original sources which are given at the head of each entry.

Chapter 4   Tenth to Mid-Twelfth Century

Northern England (Fig. 65)

Fig. 65   Northern England, location map
1 Jarrow, 2 Monkwearmouth, 3 Durham, 4 Hart, 5 Whitby, 6 Scarborough, 7 Bridlington, 8 Wharram Percy, 9 Beverley, 10 Hedon, 11 York, 12 Potterton, 13 Otley, 14 Sandal Castle, 15 Pontefract, 16 Doncaster, 17 Carlisle.

1. Co. Durham

a. *Monkwearmouth and Jarrow* (Hurst J.G. 1969)

Excavations in area of Saxon monastic sites.

Pottery of *c.* 9th century date includes wheel-thrown Fine Whitby-type ware; dating not clear, at Monkwearmouth occurs in foundation trench dated to immediately pre- or post-Conquest period, at Jarrow together with Ipswich and York-type wares in destruction level associated with 9th century Viking attack or later Scottish raids.

Saxo-Norman pottery of *c.* 850–1150 includes Thetford-type grey sandy ware and Stamford ware. The gritty ware designated 'York-type ware' includes bowl forms with flat rouletted rims, similar to those from the 12th century kiln at Newcastle.

b. *Durham* (Carver 1979): Fig. 66

Excavations within the town.

Durham-type ware – orange to pink quartz-tempered wheel-thrown fabric, generally similar to York ware; forms – mainly cooking pots, also storage vessels. Very occasional spots of glaze, which may be accidental or experimental. The main ware in later 10th-early 11th century.

Harsh gritty fabric with grey core, brown to red surfaces; forms include cooking pots spotted or splashed with green-yellow glaze. Main fabric in later 11th-mid 12th century.

Fine buff fabric, cooking pots spotted with glaze, appear in early/mid 12th century; probably fore-runners of the later square-rimmed cooking pots.

Fig. 66 CO. DURHAM
Durham: 1–2, 4, Durham-type ware, late 10th–early 11th cent. 3, 5–6, harsh gritty fabric, later 11th–mid 12th cent. (After Carver 1979)

c. *Hart* (Addis 1976)

Excavations at Hart Manor; little independent dating evidence.

Saxo-Norman wares include two shell-tempered sandy fabrics, micaceous gritty and sandy pink or red to grey fabrics; sandy grey Thetford-type ware; and a gritty 'pimply' ware similar to York ware. Date range *c.* late 10th-early 12th century on stylistic grounds.

2. Yorkshire, North Riding

a. *Whitby* (Hurst 1976): Fig. 67

Monastic site.

Fine Whitby ware – grey or black sandy micaceous fabric, wheel-thrown, but otherwise similar to hand-made Middle Saxon Whitby ware. Forms – cooking pots. Date range probably 9th century at Whitby itself, but Whitby-type ware could well continue later.

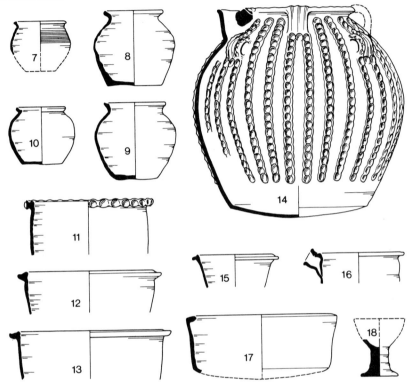

Fig. 67 YORKSHIRE, NORTH RIDING
Whitby: 7, Fine Whitby ware, Late Saxon. (After Hurst 1976)
York: 8–9, York ware, 9th–10th cent. 10–18, Torksey-type ware, 10th–11th cent. (After Holdsworth 1978; Brooks and Mainman 1984; York Archaeological Trust, unpublished material)

b. York (Holdsworth 1978; Brooks and Mainman 1984; A. Mainman pers. comm.): Fig. 67

Excavations at several urban sites, particularly Coppergate, have yielded Saxo-Norman sequences; Coppergate dated by coins, dendrochronology, archaeomagnetism.

York ware – hard wheel-thrown quartz-gritted fabric with protruding grits, light red to brown or grey; forms mostly cooking pots, usually flat-based, occasional lamps, pitchers. Little decoration. Source not known. Date range later 9th century (though it may begin earlier) – 10th century; dominant pottery type in early levels of Coppergate.

Torksey-type ware – wheel-thrown sandy fabric, often with 'sandwich' effect core;

colours mainly grey and grey/black, with some oxidization to reddish-brown. Forms resemble those from Torksey kilns; cooking pots, bowls with inturned and out-turned rims, socketed/spouted bowls, lamps, large storage pitchers. Decoration – some rouletting on shoulder or rim, thumbing on rims, thumbed applied strips on storage vessels. Source not known; apparently not Torksey, so perhaps more local production. Some partially wasted sherds found on Coppergate. Date range *c.* 10th-late 11th century, rare in early levels, taking over from York ware as dominant type in second half of 10th century.

Gritty ware ('Northern Gritty ware') – hard wheel-made quartz-gritted fabric, ranging from white to pink, buff or grey; forms – mainly cooking pots, usually with sagging bases, some bowls, occasional jugs with splashed glaze. Decoration rare; occasional diamond rouletting on cooking pots. Source not known; part of a widespread northern tradition. Date range *c.* later 11th-first half of 13th century. Fabric very similar to York ware, and may have developed out of the earlier tradition, although continuity at York itself not yet established.

Splashed wares – a group of wheel-made sandy fabrics, ranging from buff to red, with splashed yellowish-green to olive glazes. Forms – jugs, spouted pitchers, small cooking pots/pipkins, lamps; occasional decoration includes wavy combing and rouletting. Sources not known, though presumably fairly local. Date range *c.* late 11th-mid 13th century.

Minor types include early glazed wares, reddish gritty or smooth fabrics, sometimes thickly glazed, sometimes resembling 12th century splashed wares, from 10th century levels; source probably local. Also a late Saxon grey ware, 'd' ware, of unknown origin, in later 9th-10th century.

Regional imports include Stamford ware and small quantities of shelly wares; Stamford ware occurs in greatest quantities in the late 11th/early 12th century.

c. Scarborough (P. and N. Farmer pers. comm.)

Excavations within the medieval town.

Scarborough Gritty ware, white or buff to pinkish sandy fabric sometimes with splashed yellowish-green glaze, often applied in four vertical bands or zones. Forms – cooking pots and jugs. Source probably local, though not associated with any kilns. Date range *c.* late 11th-12th century.

3. Yorkshire, East Riding

a. Beverley (Hayfield 1985; Watkins forthcoming a; Watkins and Williams 1983): Fig. 68

(i) *Production site*

Wasters in Beverley 1 ware found at Grovehill Road (Albion House site), in suburb of medieval town; in sufficient quantity to suggest production.

(ii) *Pottery*

Several excavations within the town; dating based on coins, radiocarbon, historical associations.

10th century: Torksey-type ware (Hayfield's CB1 fabric), cooking pots and bowls. Also York Type A (York ware; = Hayfield's GB fabric) cooking pots, and York Type D ('d' ware at York) cooking pots. Minor types include Stamford ware and Shell Tempered ware.

11th/early 12th century: Beverley 1 ware, the fabric of the Grovehill Road wasters. Fabric similar to later Beverley 2 (Orangeware) but thinner, harder and grittier; splashed glazes. Forms mostly cooking pots, occasional jugs.

Also Torksey-type ware; and Reduced Chalky ware (Hayfield's CB2/3 fabrics), hand-made cooking pots and bowls, sandy reduced fabric with much chalk, probably local. York Lightly Gritted ware (= Gritty ware at York; Hayfield's GB fabric), cooking pots and bowls with rounded rims in pink quartz-gritted fabric, source unknown.

Minor types include Stamford ware, Shell Tempered ware, and Northern Gritty ware (white/buff quartz-gritted fabrics, cooking pots and bowls with squared rims).

b. Bridlington (Earnshaw and Watkins 1984)

Material from an excavation within the town; much of the pottery is not reliably stratified. No independent dating evidence.

Scarborough Gritty ware cooking pots and jugs present, from probably late 11th or early 12th century.

c. Hedon (Hayfield 1985): Fig. 68

Excavation within the medieval town; earliest occupation first half of 12th century.

Coarse sand-tempered fabrics, CH1–4, CH1 being the most common – hard heavily sand-tempered buff, brown and orange fabrics, sometimes reduced. Mostly coil-built with varying degrees of wheel-finishing. Forms – mostly cooking pots, some bowls and curfews; some thumbing of rims. Source – probably local; wares are in Staxton/Potter Brompton coarse sandy tradition. Date range: CH2, 4 – 12th century; CH1, 3 – 12th–14th centuries.

Fine sand-tempered fabrics, FH1, 4 and 5 – fine orange/red fabrics, sometimes reduced grey; forms – mainly jugs, with splashed olive or orange/yellow glazes. Mostly wheel-thrown but some coil-building noted. Source probably local. Date range 12th century.

Minor types include small quantities of Beverley-type Orangeware jugs (OB) and a possibly East Yorkshire Orangeware, OH.

d. Wharram Percy (Le Patourel 1979a)

Deserted medieval village site.

Most of Saxo-Norman pottery published so far is residual in later contexts. Torksey-type ware, grey sandy wheel-thrown fabric; cooking pots and bowls; possibly from Torksey, or York area. Date range *c.* 10th–11th century.

York ware – hard gritty wheel-thrown fabric; cooking pots; date range *c.* late 9th–11th century.

4. Yorkshire, West Riding

a. Doncaster (Hayfield 1984b; 1985): Fig. 69

(i) *Production site*

Market Place – pit-like feature with evidence of burning, containing wasters, interpreted as a clamp kiln. Situated within area of medieval town. Dated on pottery grounds to *c.* late 11th–first half of 12th century.

Fig. 68 YORKSHIRE, EAST RIDING
Beverley: 19, York Type A (York-type ware). 20, Torksey-type ware. 21–2, York
Lightly Gritted ware. 23, 25–6, Reduced Chalky ware. 24, 27, Beverley 1 ware. 19,
late 9th/10th cent.; 21–2, 24, 26–7, late 11th/early 12th cent.; 20, 23, 25, early/mid
12th cent. (After Hayfield 1985; Watkins forthcoming a; Watkins and Williams 1983)
Hedon: 28–9, 31, Fabric CH1. 30, Fabric CH2. 32, Fabric FH1. 33–4, Fabric FH5.
All early 12th cent. (After Hayfield 1985)

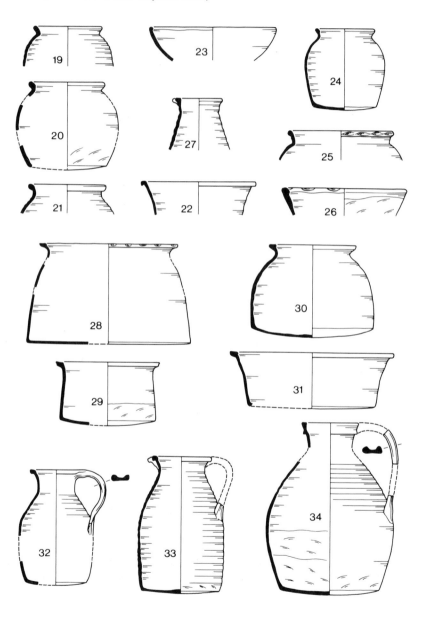

Fig. 69 YORKSHIRE, WEST RIDING
Doncaster: 35–7, Smooth Shelly ware (Fabric SD), 11th–early 12th cent. 38–9, Gritty
ware (Fabric GD), late 11th–early 12th cent. (After Hayfield 1985)

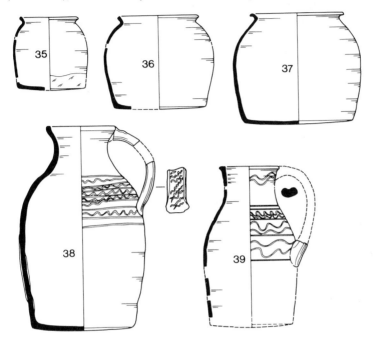

(ii) *Pottery*

Kiln products in Gritty ware (GD), orange or red quartz-gritted fabric with some
haematite and limestone inclusions, olive green to orange-brown splashed glaze; mostly
probably coil-built. Forms – cooking pots, jugs, pitchers. Decoration comprises crude
incised straight and wavy lines on jugs.

Other main fabrics present in town excavations:

Smooth Shelly ware (SD), hand-made and wheel-finished cooking pots; source
unknown, though forms similar to those found in Lincolnshire. Date range *c.* 11th-early
12th century.

Coarse Sandy ware (CD) – cooking pots, curfews; source unknown; 11th century.

b. Potterton (Mayes and Pirie 1966)

Production site

'Potertun' place-name recorded in Domesday Book in 11th century.

c. Sandal Castle (Moorhouse 1983b): Fig. 70

Castle site; excavations dated by finds and historical associations. Earliest deposits
date from *c.* 1106–1130. Sources of pottery types unknown; much probably local.

Type 1a – hard white wheel-thrown fabric with small angular inclusions, sometimes with light olive glaze. Forms – mainly cooking pots, also occasional jugs, bowls, cauldrons, pipkins. Date range *c.* 12th-early 13th century.

Type 2b – smooth light buff to pale pink wheel-thrown unglazed fabric. Forms – mainly cooking pots, few bowls and jugs. Date range *c.* 12th-early 13th century.

Type 3c – highly fired brown sandy wheel-thrown fabric with smooth surface. Forms – cooking pots. Date range *c.* 12th-early 13th century.

Type 4c, Pimply ware – light buff to brownish gritty wheel-thrown fabric with protruding grits, equivalent to Northern Gritty ware elsewhere. Forms – mainly cooking pots, few bowls. Date range *c.* 12th–mid 13th century.

Type 5d – pink to buff fine close-grained sandy wheel-thrown fabric with light pink core, unglazed. Forms – cooking pots. Date range 12th century.

Type 6e, Shelly ware – comprises several fabrics, forms – mainly cooking pots, occasional bowl. Present in small quantities from 12th–13th century.

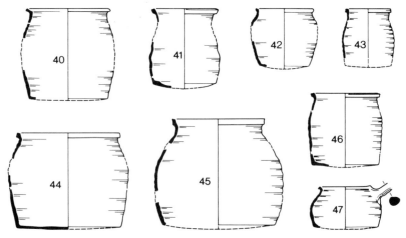

Fig. 70   YORKSHIRE, WEST RIDING
Sandal Castle: 40, 44, 47, Type 1a. 41, Type 3c. 42–3, 45, Pimply ware, Type 4c. 46, Type 2b. (After Moorhouse 1983b)

d. *Otley* (Le Patourel and Wood 1973)

Excavations at Archbishop of York's manor house.

Small quantities of wheel-thrown Saxo-Norman cooking pots, in fabric resembling that of Middle Saxon Otley-type ware; gritty grey sometimes micaceous fabric, presumably developing out of the earlier ware.

e. *Pontefract Priory* (Le Patourel 1965)

Monastic site, founded late 11th century.

Saxo-Norman wares present include shelly ware, gritty York-type ware and sandy grey wares. Transition from York-type ware to 12th century Northern Gritty ware thought to have taken place here by *c.* 1150.

5. Cumberland

a. Carlisle (unpublished material, Carlisle Archaeological Unit)

Annetwell Street, site very close to castle.

Several as yet undefined fabrics, varying from coarse micaceous wares with large quartzitic fragments to finer sandy wares. Fabrics are almost wholly reduced to dark and light greys, with some being wheel-thrown but others probably hand-made. Forms – cooking pots with narrow bases 8–9 cm diameter, walls sometimes have heavy internal rilling and everted rims. Some of rims are very simple, plain and flat-topped, others more sharply everted with internal thickening. Dates probably lie within the period from the 10th to mid 12th century, the simplest forms being typologically similar to other Saxo-Norman wares.

Eastern England (Fig. 71)

1. Lincolnshire

a. Lincoln (Gilmour *et al.* forthcoming; J. Young pers. comm.; Coppack 1973; 1980a): Figs. 72–3

(i) *Production sites*
Production indicated in Flaxengate/Silver Street area, in close proximity to glass- and metal-working industries, within early medieval town.

Silver Street – a succession of three clamp kilns, the first two simply hollows in the ground, the latest rectangular, *c.* 5m x 1.5m, sides lined with stones, open at one end but with no proper stokehole. Tips of clay, sand, shells nearby, also traces of other kilns and hearths. Silver Street kilns dated to early-mid 10th century.

Flaxengate – wasters of Lincoln Gritty ware (LG) from 1940s and 1970s excavations.

(ii) *Pottery*
Important sequence from 1970s Flaxengate excavation, chronology based largely on coins, archaeomagnetic dates. Lincoln Kiln-Type ware (LKT), the product of the Silver Street kilns, is regarded as industrially-produced, i.e. mass-produced to a considerable degree of uniformity and standardization. LKT is shell-tempered, partially oxidized orange to buff or light red-brown with grey core. Vessels mostly wheel-thrown, with some piece-forming, rims templated, competent manufacture. Forms – mostly cooking pots (84 percent of LKT found in 1970s Flaxengate excavation), with *c.* 14 percent bowls; small numbers of dishes, storage jars, spouted pitchers, pedestal lamps and small dishes and bowls for melting glass. Very occasional glaze spots, probably acquired accidentally. Decoration includes square and diamond rouletting on rims and shoulders, and thumbing on rims or applied strips.

At Flaxengate LKT fully developed by *c.* 870/80. LKT declined in quality of manufacture after mid 10th century; end date uncertain but production certainly ceased before Norman Conquest, probably mostly finished by *c.* 1000.

Fig. 71   Eastern England, location map
1 Barton on Humber, 2 Goltho, 3 Lincoln, 4 Torksey, 5 Stamford, 6 King's Lynn, 7 Grimston, 8 Bircham, 9 Castle Acre, 10 Thetford, 11 Fransham, 12 North Elmham, 13 Bunwell, 14 Norwich, 15 Langhale, 16 Great Yarmouth, 17 Ipswich, 18 Ely, 19 Cambridge.

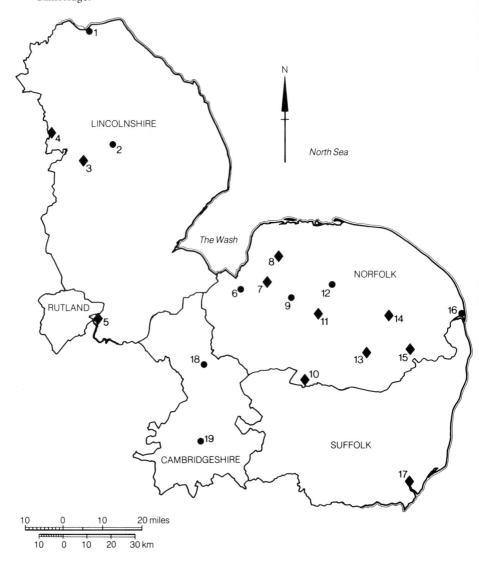

Lincoln industrially-produced shelly wares (LKT, Lincoln Early Shelly and Lincoln Saxo-Norman Shelly ware) accounted for 68 percent of all pottery from early medieval Flaxengate; LKT forms 94 percent of these. Distribution outside Lincoln uncertain, as has not previously been distinguished from other Lincoln shelly wares –

Fig. 72 LINCOLNSHIRE
Lincoln: 48–52, Lincoln Kiln-Type ware. 53–9, Lincoln Saxo-Norman Shelly ware.
60–5, Lincoln Fine Shelly ware. (After Gilmour *et al.* forthcoming)

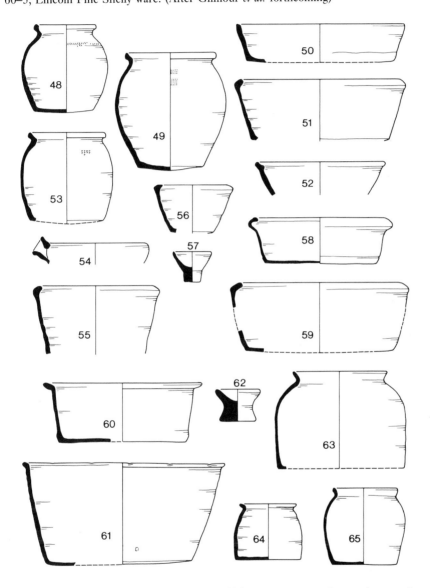

these noted at most Lincolnshire sites with 10th-century occupation, and some sites
further afield.

Lincoln Gritty ware (LG), mostly wheel-made, but not in any quantity – one main
fabric and several lesser ones. Local clay, large quartz sand inclusions giving a pimply
surface; often reduced to shades of grey. Forms mostly standardized cooking pots (86

Fig. 73 LINCOLNSHIRE
Lincoln: 66–71, Lincoln Gritty ware. 72–82, Lincoln Sandy ware. 83, Lincoln-type ware from Goltho, first half of 12th cent. (After Gilmour *et al.* forthcoming; Coppack 1973; Hayfield 1985).

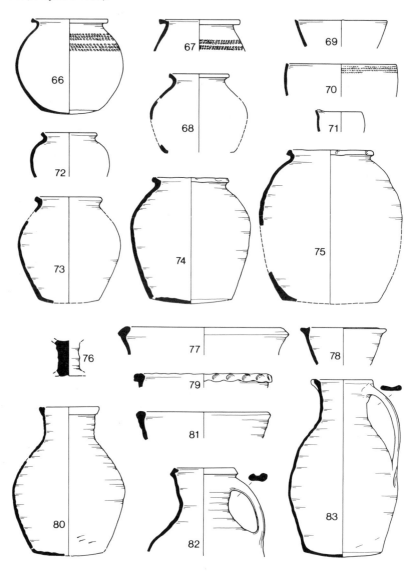

percent of LG vessels from 1970s Flaxengate excavation) with some bowls (8 percent); a few large storage containers and lamps. Decoration includes square and diamond rouletting. Numerically a minor ware; LG forms 4 percent of Lincoln industrially-produced sandy wares, which together account for only 6.5 percent of early medieval pottery from Flaxengate. LG present by *c.* 870/80; manufacture ceased between *c.* 900 and 930. LG is thought to have been produced by a continental potter.

Two industrially-produced shelly wares in much smaller quantities than LKT – Lincoln Early Shelly (LES) and Lincoln Saxo-Norman Shelly (LSNS), each comprising several fabrics. Clay from same source as LKT, inclusions mainly shell, some quartz and other materials. Colours from pink and grey to red and orange-brown, often with reduced core. Manufacturing techniques similar to LKT, but with some coil-building and wheel-finishing; many LSNS vessels carelessly finished. Some LSNS sherds have accidentally-acquired spots of lead glaze. LES – late 9th-mid 10th century; LSNS – late 9th-end of 10th century, though some fabrics continue until Conquest.

Two industrially-produced sandy wares, in smaller quantities than shelly wares – Lincoln Sandy (LS) and Lincoln Medieval Sandy ware (LMS). Clay similar to other local wares; both have quartz sand inclusions, but much finer than Lincoln Gritty. LS – usually reduced grey, but sometimes oxidized; some wheel-thrown but others wheel-finished, with coiling and piece-forming of bases. Late 9th-early 13th century; quality of workmanship deteriorates during 10th century; during 11th century shows strong Torksey ware influence. Some LS vessels lead-glazed in an experimental period in late 9th and early 10th centuries; copper colourant known. Otherwise glaze occurs on LS, mostly jugs, present in small quantities from *c.* 1060/70 onwards. A number of LS wasters present; possible nearby production. LMS – fabric similar to LS; glazed jugs, mostly mid 12th century on but one late 11th century example.

Lincoln Fine Shelly ware (LFS) – one fabric only, traditionally-made non-industrial ware. Soft fabric, mainly shell but also quartz and other inclusions, brownish surfaces and dark grey core. Vessels coil-built, grass-wiped and carelessly finished, although some wheel-finishing by later 11th century. Present in small quantities in 10th and early 11th centuries, increases dramatically in post-Conquest period, replacing industrially-produced shelly wares.

Forms for LES, LSNS, LS and LFS wares – restricted range and standardized sizes; *c.* 80–85 percent cooking pots, 10–15 percent bowls (LES had larger proportion of bowls and dishes). Rarer forms – socketed bowls, dishes, large storage vessels, lamps and pitchers; bowls for melting glass made in LSNS, LS. Decoration – square and diamond rouletting on shoulders and rims, some thumbing on rims and applied strips; criss-cross burnishing occasionally on early LS. Decoration on LFS rare; incised lines, finger- or nail-impressions, occasional stamps.

Pottery made elsewhere in Lincolnshire includes Torksey and Stamford wares, and in lesser quantities coiled and wheel-made shelly wares from unknown sources. Regional imports include Nottingham wares.

b. Torksey (Barley 1964; 1981): Fig. 74; see also Fig. 16 Type 1b

(i) *Production site*

Seven kilns found in presumed area of important late Saxon town. Kilns 1, 5, 6, 7 – Type 1b, central clay pedestals; 1 and 5 have evidence of firebars radiating outwards from pedestal to kiln wall, 6 and 7 destroyed to below firebar level. Kiln 4 – Type 1b, no pedestal but has unsupported firebar floor; Kiln 2 first thought to be 1a, but could resemble Kiln 4 although destroyed to below level of firebars. Kiln 3 – form unknown. Associated features include pits filled with raw clay, presumably potters' stores, and traces of a clay-walled building which probably housed one of the clay pits and was

Fig. 74 LINCOLNSHIRE
Torksey: 84–97, 99–105, Torksey ware, 10th–11th cent. 98, Torksey ware from
Lincoln. (After Gilmour *et al.* forthcoming; Barley 1964; 1981; Hurst J.G. 1976)

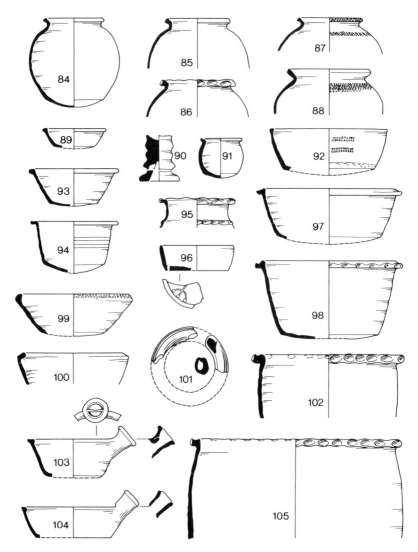

perhaps the workshop belonging to Kiln 5. Archaeomagnetic dating – Kiln 4 is 10th
century, Kilns 1 and 5 *c.* 1050–1150.

(ii) *Pottery*

Torksey ware – reduced grey sandy fabric with only minor variations; near-black
surface finish evidently intended but many vessels partially oxidized with reddish
surfaces or red sandwiched core. Local lias clay from east of Torksey, with wind-blown
sand (into which kilns are dug) as filler. Vessels probably coiled and wheel-finished, with

some being fully wheel-thrown; shaving and turning of sagging bases done with vessels inverted on wheel. Forms predominantly cooking pots (*c.* 70 percent of all identifiable vessels), with some bowls (27 percent); most bowl rims out-turned but some inturned. Rarer forms – socketed bowls, lamps, storage jars, spouted pitchers, cheese presses, watering pots and 'ring vases'. Decoration includes square, diamond, triangular rouletting on rims and shoulders, and thumbing on rims and applied strips. Cooking pot sizes very standardized, *c.* 5–7 pint capacity; slightly more variability with bowls, but two main sizes.

Little development in forms and fabric from earliest to latest production. Exact starting date not known; ware found elsewhere in Lincolnshire. but no firm evidence for pre-Viking (i.e. pre-late 9th century) production. General date range 10th–12th century.

c. Stamford (Kilmurry 1980; Mahany *et al.* 1982): Figs. 75–7

Fig. 75 LINCOLNSHIRE
Stamford: Stamford ware spouted pitcher from Oxford; ht 31.4 cm. (Reproduced by courtesy of the Trustees of the British Museum)

Fig. 76 LINCOLNSHIRE
Stamford: 106, Castle kiln product, red painted ware, late 9th cent. 107–9, Castle kiln products, late 9th cent. 112, 121–2, Wharf Road kiln products, late 10th–early 11th cent. 111, 114–18, 120, Stamford ware. 110, Stamford ware from Lincoln. 113, Stamford ware from Normanton, Lincs. 119, Stamford ware from Thetford. (After Dunning *et al.* 1959; Kilmurry 1980; Mahany *et al.* 1982).

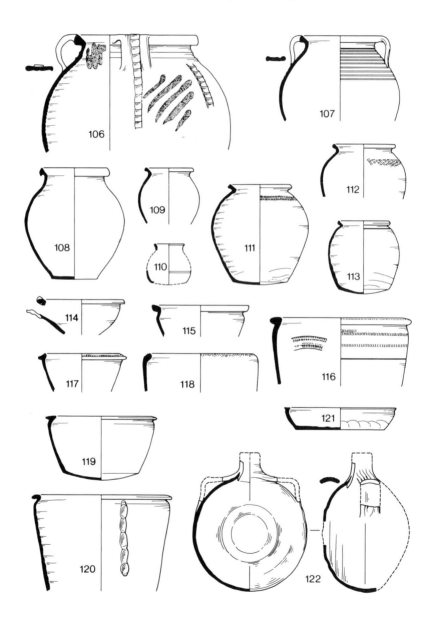

Fig. 77 LINCOLNSHIRE
Stamford: 123–4, 126, 129–30, 132–3, Stamford ware. 125, Stamford ware from
Goltho. 127, Stamford ware from Lincoln. 128, Stamford ware from Leicester. 131,
Stamford ware from Glaston, Rutland. (After Beresford 1975; Dunning *et al.* 1959;
Kilmurry 1980; Mahany *et al.* 1982).

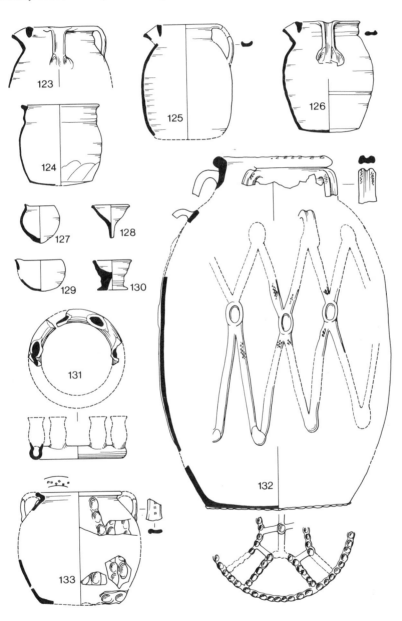

(i) *Production sites*

Several production sites just outside early medieval town, mostly to east except Castle site to south-west.

Castle site kiln complex – outside a fortified enclosure in area of later medieval castle. A long narrow Type 1a kiln with four phases; dimensions varying from 1.5–2.5 m x 0.75–1.0 m. May have been open-topped. Oak timber fuel. Kiln form compares with continental examples. Earlier pottery production indicated by a red-painted Stamford ware pot in a layer antedating the kiln. Wasters post-dating kiln on fabric grounds found in nearby Ditch B. Kiln dated archaeomagnetically to 850 ± 50; its products stylistically late 9th century. Ditch B wasters coin-dated to *c*. 890–925.

Wharf Road – circular Type 1b kiln, two baffle bars on kiln base, no other evidence for raised floor. Temporary roof suggested. Kiln form comparable to 9th or 10th century kiln at Duisburg, Germany. Archaeomagnetic date of *c*. 1020–60; pottery stylistically late 10th/early 11th century.

East Street – wasters from Pit 1, 20m from early 13th century kiln (1963 Stamford School kiln), dated stylistically to mid-late 11th century.

Greyfriars House, St Paul's Street – kiln discovered but inadequately recorded in 1911. Dome apparently still intact, suggesting a permanent structure. Stylistically, pottery dates to *c*. 1050–1150.

(ii) *Pottery*

Stamford ware, made at several sites in the town, comprises eight closely related fabrics (A-H), varying from very fine to sandy with very small quartz grains, made from local Upper Estuarine clays with low iron content. Colours white and buff to pink-orange or grey. Industrially-produced pottery, wheel-thrown from start of industry; kick-wheel suggested; some crucibles and large storage vessels hand-made. Extremely well-made pottery with thin even walls and symmetrical templated rims. Forms – cooking pots, bowls, jars and spouted pitchers common; other forms – pedestal, spike and ovoid lamps, socketed bowls, crucibles, large storage jars, ring-vases, watering pots, possibly bottles. Lead glaze known, though not common, in late 9th century, increasing thereafter; colour usually yellow to pale sage green; dipping and brushing known. Some early pots from Castle site kiln complex red-painted with iron-rich mixture. Decoration includes square, rectangular and diamond rouletting on rims and shoulders, thumbing on applied strips or rims, and occasional stamps.

Chronological variations in fabrics, forms and glazes have been well studied by Kilmurry. Industry thought to have been initiated by a continental potter, perhaps from northern France, on grounds of stylistic similarity (especially red paint and glaze). Stamford products, both cooking and table wares, very widely traded in England, particularly within Danelaw area; occasionally further afield. Trading pattern changes somewhat after Conquest, to more southerly and easterly concentration, although there is also a considerable increase in ware traded north to Flaxengate, Lincoln, from 1060/70.

d. Goltho (Beresford 1975; Coppack 1980b): Fig. 78

Deserted village and early manorial site. Shelly ware dominant in 11th and 12th centuries; much probably of Lincoln production. Other wares include Stamford, Torksey and Lincoln Sandy. Splashed glaze jugs in Lincoln and Nottingham fabrics present at Goltho Manor in first half of 12th century.

Fig. 78   LINCOLNSHIRE
Goltho: 134–7, shelly wares, 11th–early 12th cent. (After Beresford 1975; Hayfield 1985)
Barton on Humber: 138, Fabric C2. 139, Fabric G1. 140, Fabric F1. All *c.* first half of 12th cent. (After Hayfield 1985)

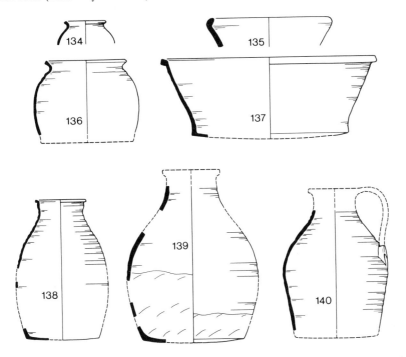

e. *Barton on Humber* (Hayfield 1985): Fig. 78

Sequences from several sites, chronology largely typological with some architectural dating for St Peter's Church site. Shelly wares predominate; wheel-finished from 9th century on; principal fabric S1 – forms *c.* 86 percent cooking pots, 13 percent bowls, few dishes. S1 replaced by shelly wares S3 (similar fabric to Potter Hanworth) and S4 by early 12th century. Lincoln Saxon Sandy-type and Torksey wares present from some time in 9th century to late 11th century; succeeded by N. Lincs. coarse sandy fabrics C1 and C2, forms mostly cooking pots, few bowls, coil-built and wheel-finished; C1 – *c.* 1000-early 12th century, C2 – early 12th century on. Glazed fabrics – G1, N. Lincs. white to orange gritty fabric, splashed olive glaze; cooking pots, jugs, bowls; late 11th/early 12th century. Fine orange-red sandy wares with splashed glaze, mostly jugs – F1, and O1 (Orangeware – possibly made locally); *c.* 1100 on.

2. Norfolk

a. *Thetford* (Davison 1967; Rogerson and Dallas 1984): Figs. 79–82; see also Fig. 16 Type 1b

Fig. 79   NORFOLK
Thetford: 141–54, Thetford ware. (After Rogerson and Dallas 1984)

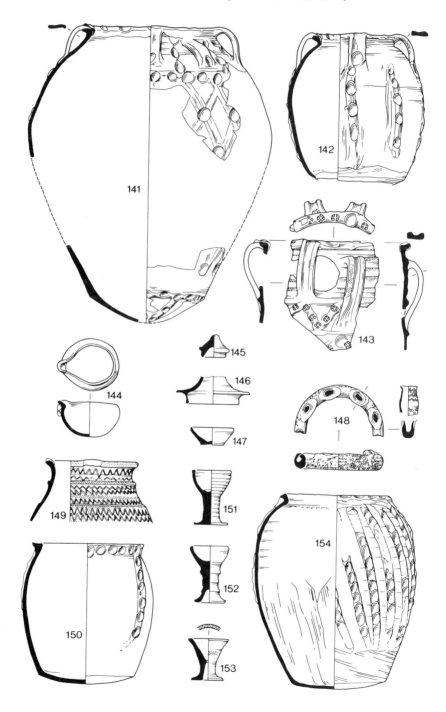

Fig. 80 NORFOLK
Thetford: 155–72, Thetford ware. (After Rogerson and Dallas 1984)

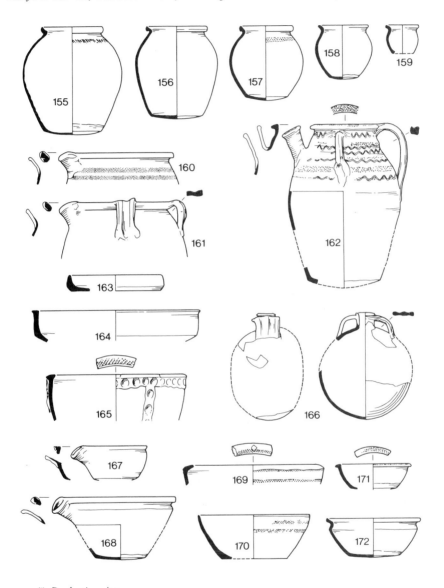

(i) *Production sites*

1948–59 excavations – a sequence of three kilns found in area of much industrial activity, within but towards edge of defended town. Kilns 2 and 3 fragmentary, kiln 1 was Type 1b kiln with arrangement of transverse and longitudinal clay arches forming raised floor, probably 11th century. Wasters from other kilns found in same area and on other sites nearby.

Fig. 81   NORFOLK
Thetford: 173, Thetford ware. (After Hurst J.G. 1976)

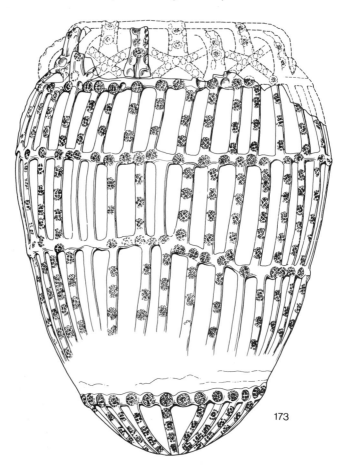

173

1964–66 excavations – kilns found in peripheral zone within town defences, divided by ditch from main part of town. Several Type 1b kilns, each with clay arches constructed on withy framework to support the pots. In two kilns the clay domes had collapsed, sealing stacked pots; loads of *c.* 25–50 pots suggested by excavator. Isolated stone-packed post-hole interpreted as possible pivot for potter's wheel, some 3m from large storage vessel sunk into the ground, possibly potter's water supply.

(ii) *Pottery*

Thetford ware from 1948–59 excavations – hard sandy fabric, wheel-thrown except for large storage vessels, usually reduced grey though sometimes surfaces partially oxidized to reddish or buff. In earliest levels, forms mainly cooking pots, some storage jars, pitchers, lamps, bowls, costrels and ring vases; sagging bases most common. Decoration comprises rouletting and applied thumbed strips. Later Thetford ware, 11th

Fig. 82   NORFOLK
Thetford: 174–6, 178–9, Late Thetford Smooth ware. 177, 180–1, Late Thetford Fine ware. 182–5, Early Medieval ware. All 11th–early 12th cent. (After Rogerson and Dallas 1984)

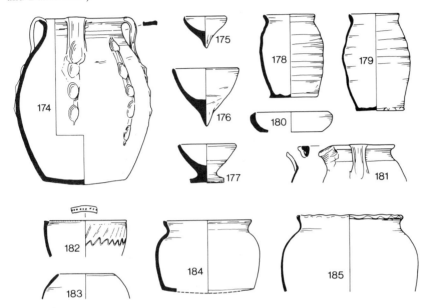

century, comprises a wider range of forms; plainer cooking pots, often with flat bases; lamps more frequent and varied in form; storage jars, large decorated jars and bowls, some costrels and ring vases. Other forms include crucibles, dishes, spouted bowls, lids.

Later Thetford ware includes very small proportions of two related finer fabrics. Smooth ware – mostly oxidized to buff or reddish, produced in kiln 1 and perhaps its predecessors; flat bases more common than sagging; undecorated apart from thumbed strips, some possible grey painted lines. Fine ware (may be a failed version of Smooth ware) – jars similar to Early Medieval ware, decoration confined to thumbed strips and a few wavy lines, though a few jars have rouletting; forms similar to those from the Langhale kiln.

Date range later 9th–early 12th century; initial date unknown, but perhaps industry results from changes caused by Danish settlement (from *c*. AD 869). Industry at Thetford may have been initiated by a continental potter. Fine ware and Smooth ware occur with Early Medieval ware and 11th century Stamford ware, and date to 11th–early 12th century. Thetford ware has wide distribution within the Danelaw area, although not traded in such quantities as Stamford ware; Thetford-type wares produced at a number of sites in East Anglia.

Other wares occurring at Thetford include small quantities of Stamford ware, St Neots-type ware and Early Medieval ware. Early Medieval ware – locally-produced coarse ware, black, grey, brown or reddish; main fabric is sandy, two minor fabrics with quartz grits and calcitic lumps. Forms include cooking pots, ginger jars, bowls; date range 11th–12th century.

b. *Grimston, Pott Row* (Clarke H. 1970; Clarke and Carter 1977): Fig. 83

(i) *Production sites*

One excavated Type 1a kiln, probably several other kilns in field between Pott Row and Grimston. Village site.

(ii) *Pottery*

Grimston Thetford-type ware – sandy fabric, poorer quality than true Thetford ware; grey reduced core, lighter grey to buff surfaces. Forms – mainly cooking pots, high proportion of bowls; also spouted pitchers, large storage vessels, some small bowls/ dishes, costrels/bottles, lids, curfews. Date range mainly mid 11th-mid 12th century. Present at Castle Acre in second half of 11th century but quantity greatly increases in early 12th century (Milligan 1982).

c. *Norwich* (Atkin *et al.* 1983; Jennings 1981): Figs. 84–5; see also Fig. 28

(i) *Production sites*

Thetford-type ware pottery industry in industrial suburb just outside supposed line of 10th/11th century defences, in Pottergate/Bedford Street/Lobster Lane area. In addition to the sites identified here, wasters (some associated with possible kiln lining material) have been recovered from a number of other sites in the area.

27 Bedford Street – Type 1b kiln with two chalk pedestals, but no evidence that these were supporting a floor. Archaeomagnetically dated to AD 1000 +60/−40. Traces of a second kiln.

5 Lobster Lane – Type 1a kiln; charcoal sample post-dating the use of the kiln radiocarbon dated to *c.* AD 1210–80.

2–4 Bedford Street – part of a kiln.

21 Bedford Steet – part of a kiln.

(ii) *Pottery*

Norwich Thetford-type ware – hard wheel-thrown grey sandy fabric. The only actual wasters known are of cooking pots and possibly some lamps, so production of other forms which occur in much smaller quantities, bowls, storage jars, pitchers, and 'ginger jars' in late Thetford-type ware, is not yet proved. Cooking pots typically flat-based, often with cheese-wire marks; sometimes decorated with square or diamond rouletting, or occasional incised wavy lines. The later cooking pots tend to have sagging bases. Jars and bowls sometimes decorated with applied thumbed strips.

Thetford-type ware industry probably lasts from late 10th century to mid-12th century.

Early Medieval wares cover the transition to medieval wares, *c.* 11th-early 12th century; sources unknown but presumably fairly local.

Early Medieval ware – hard sandy fabric like Thetford-type, usually partly or totally oxidized reddish or brown. Forms – cooking pots, 'ginger jars'; smaller vessels hand-made, larger ones wheel-thrown, with distinctive hand-finishing round neck. Decoration rare, mainly thumbing on rim edges or applied strips, stamps or incised lines. Co-exists with late Thetford-type ware.

Early Medieval Sandwich ware – dark grey fabric with some quartz and small white inclusions, margins often oxidized to red-brown under dark grey surfaces. Forms – mostly pitchers, few bowls.

Fig. 83 NORFOLK
Grimston: 187–90, 192–3, 195–9, 202, Thetford-type ware. 186, 191, 194, 200–1,
Grimston Thetford-type ware from King's Lynn. 203–4, Grimston Thetford-type
ware from Castle Acre. (After Clarke H. 1970; Clarke and Carter 1977; Milligan
1982)

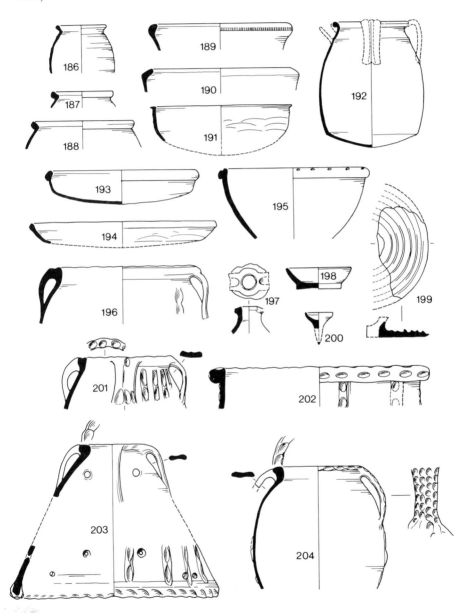

d. Langhale, Kirstead (Wade 1976): Fig. 84; see also Fig. 17

(i) *Production site*

Type 1b kiln, with two clay arches across oven pit to support pots; rim impressions found on arches. Fuel – alder, hazel, silver birch. Load of 100–120 vessels postulated. Kiln dated to 11th century on stratigraphic and typological grounds. Apparently an isolated kiln in a dispersed rural settlement; it has been suggested as being the work of an itinerant potter.

(ii) *Pottery*

Late Thetford-type ware, sandy, buff or grey with sandwiched core. Forms mainly cooking pots (92 percent), few bowls, pitchers, ginger jars; mostly flat-based. Decoration rare, limited to wavy incised lines, applied thumbed strips.

e. Bircham (Rogerson and Adams 1978): Fig. 84)

(i) *Production site*

Type 1b kiln similar to Langhale kiln, with two clay arches; dated on typological and circumstantial grounds to 10th or early 11th century. In centre of village; it has been suggested as being the work of an itinerant potter.

(ii) *Pottery*

Kiln producing Thetford-type ware, mostly hard grey wheel-thrown fabric, some softer oxidized sherds. Forms – mostly cooking pots, some with square rouletting; a few small bowls. Fabric differs from non-waster Thetford-type wares found elsewhere on site.

f. Bunwell, Mears Farm (Youngs et al. 1983, 197)

Production site

Thetford-type ware wasters found indicating production site.

g. Fransham (A. Rogerson pers. comm.)

Production site

Evidence of production of Thetford-type ware found; surface spread of wasters. Apparently isolated kiln(s) in scattered rural settlement.

h. King's Lynn (Clarke and Carter 1977)

Sequence constructed from results of a number of excavations within the town; chronology based on datable finds, coins, imported pottery.

Grimston Thetford-type ware found in earliest levels of mid 11th-12th century date.

An Early Medieval ware published as 'Grimston Software' but no evidence that it was produced at Grimston; soft fabric with chalk and quartz pebble inclusions, reduced grey with buff to grey-buff surfaces. Forms – cooking pots, jugs (sometimes with splashed glaze), and bowls/curfews. Dated on stratigraphic grounds to late 11th–c. mid 13th century.

Early Medieval grey sandy round-based cooking pots and bowls with wheel-finished rims also attributed to Grimston, but some may in fact be Blackborough End products. Dated late 11th–13th century.

Fig. 84 NORFOLK
Norwich: 205–19, Norwich Thetford-type ware, late 10th–early 12th cent. (After Jennings 1981)
Bircham: 220–5, kiln products, Thetford-type ware, late 10th/early 11th cent. (After Rogerson and Adams 1978)
Langhale: 226–8, kiln products, Thetford-type ware, 11th cent. (After Wade 1976)

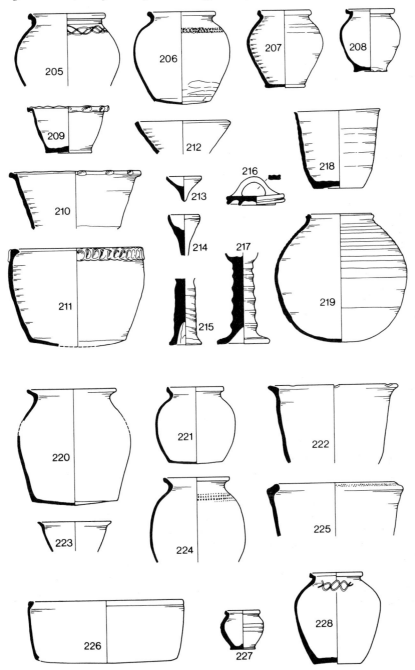

i. Castle Acre (Dallas 1980; Milligan 1982): Fig. 85

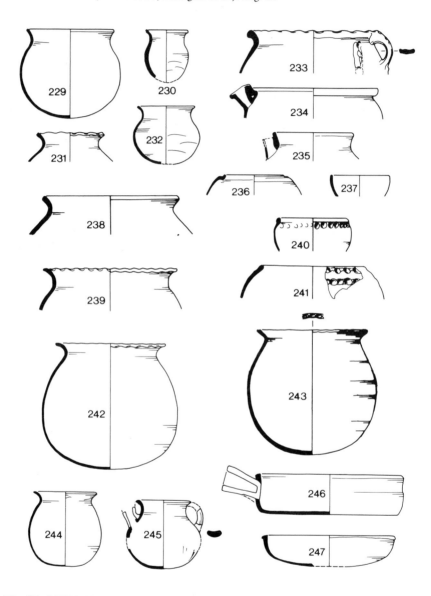

Fig. 85 NORFOLK
King's Lynn: 229–32, Early Medieval Grey Sandy wares, possibly from Grimston;
12th cent. (After Clarke and Carter 1977)
Norwich: 233–7, Early Medieval ware, 11th–12th cent. (After Jennings 1981)
Castle Acre: 238–47, Early Medieval ware, 11th–12th cent. (After Dallas 1980;
Milligan 1982).

Best sequence from Castle Acre castle; chronology based on historical, architectural and coin dates. Also sequence from priory.

Thetford-type ware present in earliest levels, mid-late 11th century, but very little in early 12th century. Grimston Thetford-type ware – present before *c.* 1085, but on small scale; increases in early 12th century.

Early Medieval wares – most common pottery type (77 percent of stratified assemblage at castle). Presumed local production, perhaps clamp-fired. Sandy fabrics, some similar to some Grimston Thetford-type fabrics; dark grey to black with some reddish-brown patches. Forms mainly thin-walled cooking pots, usually with rounded bases, and bowls; few spouted pitchers, skillets, 'ginger jars'. Rims often frilled. Present from earliest levels in second half of 11th century well into the second half of the 12th century.

j. Great Yarmouth (Mellor 1976): Fig. 86

Stratigraphic sequence dated by two C14 determinations and one coin.

Thetford-type ware, two fabrics (1 and 4), wheel-thrown grey sandy ware, some partially oxidized 'sandwich' cores. Forms – mainly cooking pots, also storage jars, spike lamps, lugged bowls; flat bases; applied strip decoration, no rouletting. Dated to *c.* 11th–mid 12th century.

Local Transitional ware (Fabric 2), wheel-thrown sandy fabric, usually reduced

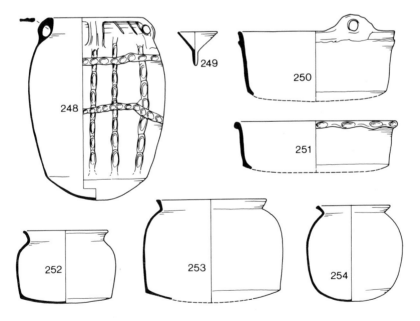

Fig. 86 NORFOLK
Great Yarmouth: 248–50, Thetford-type ware, 11th–early 12th cent. 251, Fabric 3. 252, Fabric 18. 253, Fabric 3/1. 254, Fabric 5. All 11th–early 13th cent. (After Mellor 1976)

grey. Forms – cooking pots, lamps (pedestal, cresset and cup types), ginger jars; flat bases. Decoration rare, includes thumbing, rouletting, shoulder bosses; *c.* 11th–early 12th century.

Early Medieval ware (Fabric 5), wheel-thrown sandy fabric, reddish brown to grey brown, becoming more consistently reduced grey by 12th century ('grey reduced ware'). Forms – cooking pots with sagging or occasionally rounded bases; decoration – occasional wavy lines. Dated to *c.* 11th–early 13th century.

Medieval coarse wares (Fabrics 3, 3/1, 8, 17, 18) – coarse sandy wares, sometimes with shell, calcite and flint inclusions, usually reddish brown with dark grey core, wheel-made but perhaps on slow wheel/turntable. Forms – cooking pots, bowls; sagging bases. Dated to 11th–13th centuries.

k. *North Elmham* (Wade 1980)

Village around Late Saxon cathedral precinct; chronology based on stratigraphic sequence, pottery and one C14 date.

Thetford-type ware dominant in late 9th-10th century, continues until *c.* mid 12th century. Early Medieval ware appears by *c.* 1000, current till *c.* mid 12th century.

Small quantities of St Neots-type and Stamford wares present.

3. Suffolk

a. *Ipswich* (Hurst J.G. 1957; 1964a; Owles 1976: 325; Smedley and Owles 1964; West 1964): Fig. 87; see also Fig. 16 Type 1a

(i) *Production sites*

Carr Street/Cox Lane area – within town defences on east side, a number of kilns (at least five), some at least of Type 1, producing Thetford-type ware; in area of earlier, Middle Saxon, Ipswich ware production. Kiln I of 1961 excavations dated archaeo-magnetically to *c.* 950–1000, and Kilns II and IV thought to be of similar date. Kiln III dated on pottery grounds to *c.* 1000–1050.

24 St Helens Street – just outside Saxon town defences, on east side, a Type 1a kiln; final load of over 30 Thetford ware pots.

(ii) *Pottery*

Ipswich Thetford ware – hard grey sandy wheel-thrown fabric; flat bases characteristic. Forms – mostly cooking pots, also spouted pitchers, storage jars, bowls, spouted bowls, lamps. Decoration includes rouletting on shoulders, thumbed strips on storage jars. Apparently develops out of earlier (7th-9th century) Ipswich ware – grey sandy thick-walled fabric, vessels made on a turntable and fired in kilns. Transition thought to occur *c.* third quarter of 9th century.

Early Medieval ware forms present, together with Thetford ware, in the 11th-century Kiln III.

St Neots ware also known from the town in the Saxo-Norman period.

4. Cambridgeshire

a. *Cambridge* (Hurst J.G. 1957; Addyman and Biddle 1965): Fig. 88

Saxo-Norman wares, mostly unstratified, from the town include Thetford-type ware cooking pots, spouted pitchers, bowls, large storage vessels. St Neots and Stamford wares also known.

Fig. 87 SUFFOLK
Ipswich: 255–66, Ipswich Thetford ware. (After Hurst J.G. 1964a; 1957; West 1964)

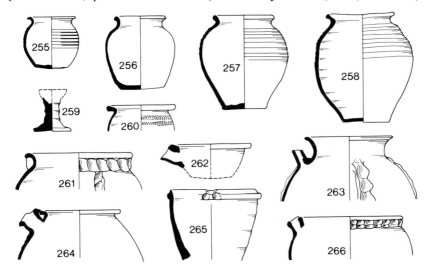

Fig. 88 CAMBRIDGESHIRE
Ely: 267, St Neots-type ware. 268, Thetford-type ware. (After Hurst J.G. 1957; 1976)
Cambridge: 269–72, Thetford-type ware (After Hurst J.G. 1957)

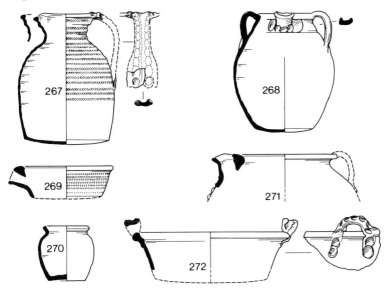

b. Ely (Hurst J.G. 1957): Fig. 88

Thetford-type and St Neots wares known.

North Midlands (Fig. 89)

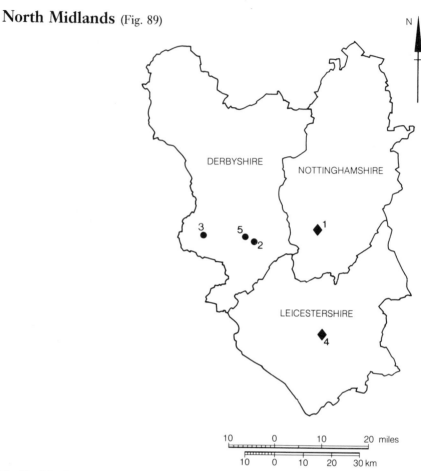

Fig. 89   North Midlands, location map
1 Nottingham, 2 Derby, 3 Barton Blount, 4 Leicester, 5 Little Chester.

1. Leicestershire

a. Leicester (Hebditch 1967–8; Woodland 1981)

(i) *Production site*

In Southgate Street a pit with burnt sides and a fill containing ash, granite lumps and wasters was interpreted as a kiln.

(ii) *Pottery*

Kiln products include hard, sandy, reduced wares; wheel-thrown cooking pots, a platter and two handle sherds possibly from storage jar. Dated to early 10th century from typology and coin associations at Northampton. Products of kiln as yet unknown from elsewhere in Leicester.

Deposits sealed below earliest Friary levels at Austin Friars includes wares potentially Late Saxon to early 12th century but evidence inconclusive.

2. Nottinghamshire

a. *Nottingham* (Coppack 1980b; Nailor 1984; Wildgoose 1961) 1961)

(i) *Production site*

In Halifax Place, within the pre-Conquest *burh*, a possible stoke-pit with roughly shaped fired clay lumps and wasters interpreted as belonging to a kiln.

(ii) *Pottery*

Kiln fabrics fairly smooth, with quartz inclusions and variations in hardness and colour. Cooking pots are wheel-thrown with some rouletting and incised lines. Bowls may be hand-made, as are storage vessels. Bowls sometimes rouletted on top of rim, and storage vessels have applied thumbed strips. Dated stratigraphically to pre-Conquest.

Upper fill of pre-Conquest *burh* ditch at Bridlesmith Gate contained splashed wares. Kiln not located but almost certainly local to Nottingham. Fabric – sandy, hard, oxidized wares with splashes of glaze; forms include pitchers, jugs, cooking pots, bowls, flasks and lamps.

3. Derbyshire

a. *Derby* (Coppack 1972; 1980b)

Excavations at Full Street produced three potentially pre-Conquest fabrics.

Brown Sandy ware or Derby ware, a quartzitic, brown-grey fabric; wheel-thrown cooking pots only known so far. Date tentatively attributed to pre-Conquest period on grounds of typology and similarity with Chester ware.

Grey Gritty wares and Orange Gritty wares, reduced and oxidized versions respectively of the same fabric; quartzitic with occasional grog, coarse sandy texture. Cooking pots are only form in reduced version but bowls and jugs appear in oxidized fabric. Types probably begin in early 12th century and continue through to the 14th.

b. *Little Chester* (Coppack 1980b)

Brown Sandy wares occur in association with recut ditch and bastion of Roman fort but considered to be 9th century or later and perhaps connected with a Danish re-fortification.

c. *Barton Blount* (Beresford 1975)

Excavations on deserted medieval village produced Chester ware as well as sherds of Derby ware, both assumed to be pre-Conquest. Coarse Sandy wares, the same as Derby Grey Gritty wares, also recovered.

South Midlands (Fig. 90)

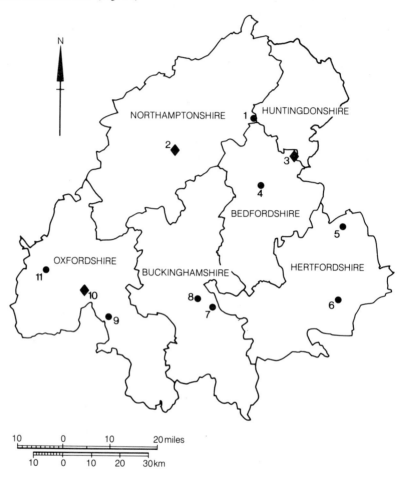

Fig. 90   South Midlands, location map
1 Raunds, 2 Northampton, 3 St Neots, 4 Bedford, 5 Therfield, 6 Hertford, 7 Weston Turville, 8 Walton, 9 Oxford, 10 Bladon, 11 Ascot Doilly.

1. Oxfordshire

a. Bladon

> *Production site*
> An *ollaria* or *potaria* yielded 10 shillings in Domesday Book.

b. Oxford (Jope 1952–3; Haldon and Mellor 1977; Mellor 1980 a and b; Radcliffe 1961–2): Fig. 91

Fig. 91 BUCKINGHAMSHIRE
Walton: 273–6, 11th cent. 277, 10th–11th cent. (After Farley 1976)
      OXFORDSHIRE
Oxford: 278, Late Saxon Sandy ware, mid 10th cent. 279–82, Abingdon-type wares, mid 10th cent. 289–91, 293, AC fabric, mid 11th to early 12th cent. 292, 294, late 11th to early 12th cent. 283–7, Oxfordshire Late Saxon Shelly wares from London, late 9th–10th cent. (After Haldon and Mellor 1977; Jope 1952–3; Vince 1985a)

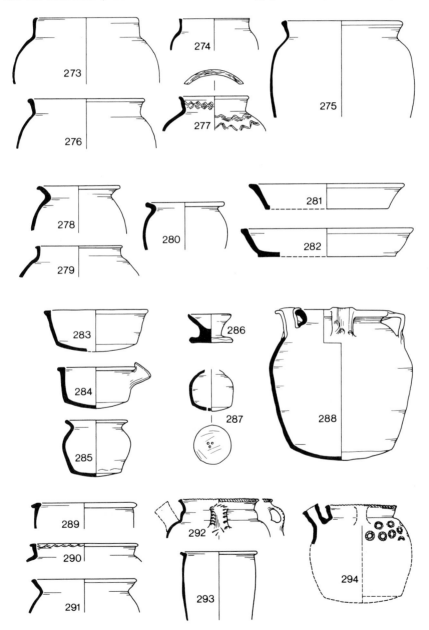

Excavations at St Aldates:

Phases 1–2, late 8th–mid 9th century: dominant fabric is B (Oxford Shelly ware), with coarse shelly limestone inclusions. Forms – hand-made cooking pots, simple shallow dishes and bowls. Rare examples of Oxford Late Saxon wheel-thrown cooking pots also recorded. At All Saints Church, B types associated with a radiocarbon determination of 993±77, extending the date range to the turn of the 10th–11th century. An Oxfordshire origin is suggested for the London Shelly wares which are petrologically very similar to the Oxford B wares (Vince 1985a).

Phase 3, 10th century: includes similar fabrics and forms but with addition of St Neots ware.

Phase 4, mid to late 10th century: major fabric continues to be B but St Neots ware increasingly important. First appearance of Oxford Early Medieval ware, oolitic tempering, hand-made cooking pots. Wider range fabrics present including two glazed sherds of uncertain origin. Subsequent work suggests that St Neots types take over from B wares from *c.* 1015–1020.

Phase 6a, late 11th century, following hiatus in early 11th century: ceramic spectrum changing with earliest domestic/industrial occupation on street frontage. Fabric B now superseded by four types of almost equal importance; these include St Neots ware, possibly in decline in Oxford, and Oxford Early Medieval ware, including coarse oolitic cooking pots and bowls. Other fabrics are very coarse flint-gritted cooking pots and the earliest appearance of Oxford Medieval ware, sandy fabric with wheel-thrown cooking pots and tripod pitcher forms.

Phase 6b, early 12th century: dominance of Oxford Early Medieval ware and increasing importance of the sandy Medieval wares, especially tripod pitchers.

Logic Lane excavation: pit groups produced one of largest collections of St Neots ware in Oxford – parts of 97 cooking pots, dishes and bowls.

Castle Mound excavation: motte erected *c.* 1070 sealed pits containing St Neots and Stamford wares but with Oxford Early Medieval wares as dominant type; hand-made straight-sided cooking pots with sagging bases and thumbed rims; some stamped sherds probably from stamped, spouted pitcher.

c. Ascot Doilly (Jope and Threlfall 1959)

Adulterine castle, built in reign of Stephen and demolished under Henry II, produced *c.* 100 vessels in Oxford Early Medieval ware including hand-made straight-sided cooking pots as main form, with some bowls, a 'West Country' dish and tripod pitchers. Cooking pots formed over 60 percent of total, bowls and tripod pitchers less than 10 percent each.

2. Northamptonshire

a. Northampton (Denham 1985; Gryspeerdt 1979; 1981a and b; Hunter 1979; McCarthy 1979; Williams J.H. 1974): Fig. 92

(i) *Production site*

At Horsemarket, very close to central crossroads of Late Saxon town, a bowl-shaped feature up to 0.5m deep with burnt sides and base excavated; function uncertain, but the association of wasters suggests it is a kiln.

Fig. 92   NORTHAMPTONSHIRE
Northampton: 295–306, Northampton ware, 10th cent. 307–315, St Neots ware, 10th–11th cent. 316, T1/2 fabric, 12th cent. (After Denham 1985; Gryspeerdt 1981a; McCarthy 1979; Williams J.H. 1974)

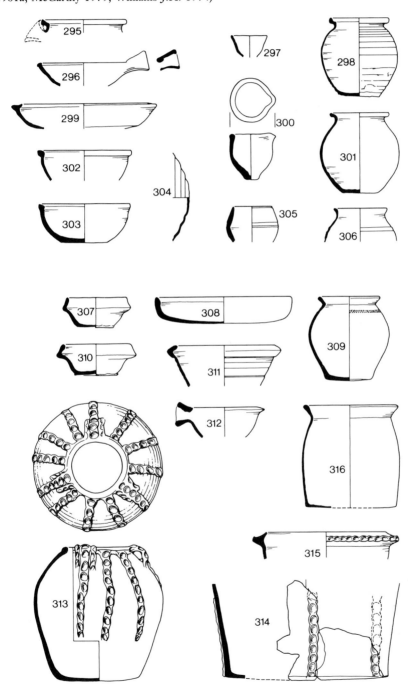

(ii) *Pottery*

Northampton ware kiln material – fabrics with predominantly quartzitic inclusions, with some ironstone; considerable colour variations and textural differences, not so apparent on sites elsewhere in town but typical of kiln waste. Usual colours are light grey. Clay source probably Upper Lias or Lower Estuarine, both available nearby. Forms at kiln site include wheel-thrown cooking pots and possible costrel; sites elsewhere in Northampton produced cooking pots (partly coiled and partly thrown), one spouted bowl, possible storage jar, lamps and crucibles. Decoration rare but includes rouletting and red painting, though latter not found at kiln site. Red-painted wares very similar to Beauvaisis and Stamford wares.

Other main local type is St Neots ware. Fabric contains abundant fossil shell and some quartz; soft to soapy textures and brown colours imply low firing temperatures. Forms are both hand-made and wheel-thrown, and are mainly cooking pots, bowls and dishes though spouted bowls, bar-lip cooking pots, storage jars and lamps are also attested. Decoration is rare and confined to rouletting and applied and thumbed strips. Four sub-divisions tentatively identified, based upon details of manufacturing methods.

Dating of Northampton and St Neots wares based on good stratigraphic sequences with coin associations. Former has *floruit c.* 900–975 whereas latter seems to be in continuous usage from *c.* 900 to 12th century after which the shelly tradition continues into 14th century.

b. Raunds (T. Pearson pers. comm.)

Very good stratified sequence of buildings with associated pottery from 6th century on. Late Saxon period dominated by St Neots ware (fabric as in Northampton), with cooking pots, bowls and dishes as main types. This site raises possibility that the local calcareous tradition originated as early as Early Saxon period.

3. Huntingdonshire

a. St Neots (Addyman 1965; 1969; 1973): Fig. 93

Production site

Production suggested on evidence of pits with heavily burnt sides and fill which included ash and charcoal layers; Pit 48 was 1.14m deep, Pit 49 0.76m deep. Wasters of cooking pots, bowls and dishes associated. Similar features recorded at Buckden. For description of St Neots wares see Northampton.

Numerous excavations on settlement sites in Ouse valley produced quantities of St Neots wares, with occasional associations of Stamford and Thetford types.

4. Buckinghamshire

a. Walton (Farley 1976): Fig. 91

Features attributed to 10th century contained mainly St Neots wares in typical fabrics and forms (see Northampton for description), but with a single sandy sherd with incised chevron decoration and 8-sectored stamp.

Features believed to be 11th century show increasing proportion of wares with limestone, quartz and flint filler. Forms are hand-made cooking pots with variation in size. Dated stratigraphically and by association with coin of 1102–4 in ditch.

Fig. 93 HUNTINGDONSHIRE
St Neots: 317, St Neots ware, 10th–11th cent. 318–20, St Neots ware from Little Paxton, 10th–11th cent. (After Addyman 1969; 1973)
      BEDFORDSHIRE
Bedford: 321–5, B4 fabric, 10th–11th cent. 326–35, B4 fabric, 12th cent. (After Baker *et al.* 1979)

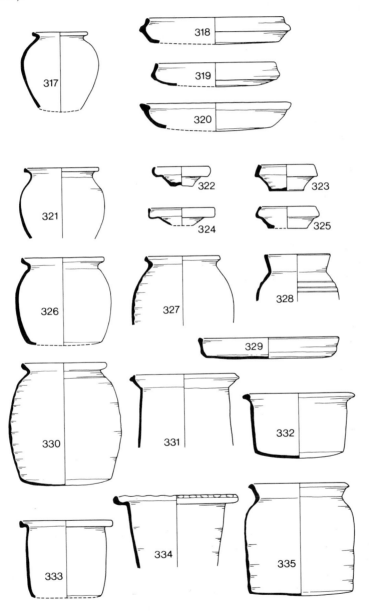

b. *Weston Turville* (P. Yeoman pers. comm.)

Motte excavation recovered flint-tempered and reduced cooking pots decorated with lattice decoration, and storage jars, in association with Stamford wares; dated to late 11th–early 12th century.

5. Hertfordshire

a. *Hertford* (C. Partridge pers. comm.)

Important sequence of timber buildings with pits in Railway Street. Main ceramic type is St Neots ware in similar range of forms to Bedford. In addition, some harsher shelly fabrics, possibly from different source to St Neots types.

The other major pre-Conquest ware is Early Medieval Sandy ware, tempered with quartz and some calcitic inclusions, not dissimilar to later production centre at Potters Green. Hand-made, possibly wheel-finished cooking pots; bowls, shallow and straight-sided forms, rare. Dating based upon stratigraphic sequence originating in early 10th century and continuing into post-Conquest period.

b. *Therfield* (Biddle 1964)

Pre-motte occupation contained St Neots types as well as two Early Medieval Sandy wares. Fabrics of latter were (i) hard, fine, sandy reduced and (ii) hard, smooth, quartzitic with some calcareous inclusions. These were perhaps the forerunners of Hertfordshire Grey ware tradition (see Fig. 96 for an example from London) but were less than 20 percent of totals.

Mid 12th century levels contained reduced grey sandy wares including cooking pots, bowls and pitchers, some with parallels at unpublished motte of South Mimms.

6. Bedfordshire

a. *Bedford* (Baker *et al.* 1979; E. Baker and G. Brine, pers. comm.): Fig. 93

B fabrics dominated by St Neots ware (B1–3) and similar to those at Northampton (see Northampton). Forms include cooking pots, bowls, lamps, storage jars and possibly jugs/pitchers. Decoration is rare and is confined to applied, thumbed strips, stabbing and rouletting. Dated stratigraphically to pre-Conquest period and by analogy with sites elsewhere.

Other versions of calcareous fabrics (B4) are coarser with less shell, more coarsely crushed and poorly mixed in clay. Forms include both thrown and coiled vessels. (B4) – mainly bowls; other minor forms include basket-handled vessels, lamps and candle-sticks.

The St Neots ware (B1) distribution is heaviest on northern side of river Great Ouse (the area supposed to contain Offa's *burh*), whilst in the area to the south of the river (occupied by Edward the Elder's *burh*) there is a greater concentration of coarser calcitic fabrics.

Group C fabrics – mainly quartzitic with varying amounts of grog, iron, flint and other inclusions. Forms – mostly wheel-thrown cooking pots finished on turntables, a variety of bowls, skillets and jugs. Decoration uncommon; includes combed lines, finger tipping on rims and some applied and thumbed strips. Dated stratigraphically to 11th century.

Overall picture is one of small-scale production centres firing in clamp kilns.

b. Chalgrave (E. Baker and G. Brine pers. comm.)

C fabrics dominant. Forms – mainly wheel- or turntable-finished cooking pots with a few small bowls. Finger tipping on the rims fairly common but otherwise decoration is rare.

South-East England (Fig. 94)

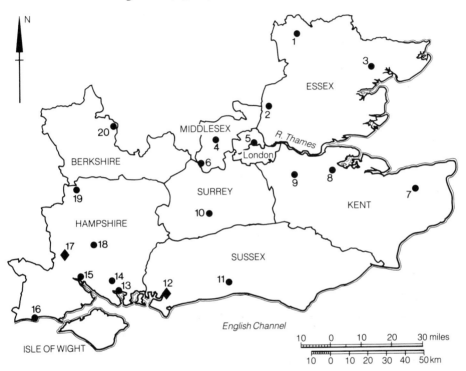

Fig. 94   South-East England, location map
1 Saffron Walden, 2 Waltham Abbey, 3 Colchester, 4 Northolt, 5 London, 6 Staines, 7 Canterbury, 8 Rochester, 9 Eynsford, 10 Abinger, 11 Bramber, 12 Chichester, 13 Portchester, 14 Wickham, 15 Southampton, 16 Christchurch, 17 Michelmersh, 18 Winchester, 19 Netherton, 20 Wallingford.

1. Essex

a. Colchester (Crummy 1981; Cunningham 1982a): Fig. 95

Several excavations within the town.
Thetford-type ware common in 10th-mid 11th centuries.
Fabric 13, Early Medieval ware, sandy grey fabrics with light red to brownish surfaces; sometimes dusted with powdered shell on the shoulders. Forms – mainly

Fig. 95　ESSEX

Colchester: 336–7, Thetford-type ware. 338–44, Early Medieval ware, late 11th–12th cent. (After Crummy 1981; Cunningham 1982a; Dunning 1962)

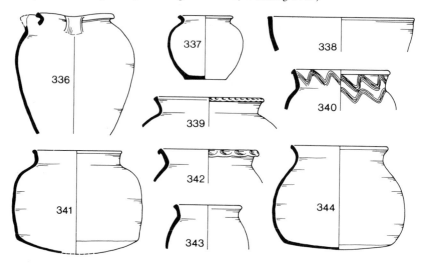

cooking pots, sometimes with thumbing on rim edges, occasional wavy combed decoration. Source probably local; kilns known at Middleborough from mid 12th century (see Chapter 5). Dated to *c.* 11th–12th century.

Fabric 12, sand- and shell-tempered ware, present in smaller quantities than Fabric 13; comprises 2 fabrics, soft and grey-black. Forms – mostly cooking pots; date *c.* 11th–12th century.

b. *Waltham Abbey* (Huggins 1972; 1973; 1976)

Excavations in area of medieval monastery.

Ware C – hand-made fabric with fine sand inclusions, brownish or black surfaces; mainly cooking pots. Date range *c.* 850–1060.

Ware D1 – St Neots-type wheel-made shelly ware, cooking pots and inturned bowls; date range *c.* 850–1200.

Ware D2 – coarse shelly fabrics, red, grey or black with shell, and later sand, added. Hand-made before Conquest, partially or fully wheel-thrown after Conquest. Forms – mainly cooking pots, some bowls in 12th century. Source presumably local; date range *c.* 850–1300.

Ware E1 – wheel-made sandy fabric with some coarse shell fragments, surfaces red with black core. Forms – mainly cooking pots. Date range *c.* 1060–1200.

c. *Saffron Walden* (Cunningham 1982b)

Excavations within the town.

St Neots ware cooking pots and bowls, and Thetford-type ware cooking pots and storage jars, found in Saxo-Norman levels. Local Early Medieval wares, mainly cooking pots, present; date range *c.* mid 10th-later 12th/early 13th century.

2. Middlesex

a. *Staines* (Jones 1984)

Late Saxon Shelly wares contain platelets of shell together with some ironstone, chaff and occasional quartz and organic fragments; hand-made cooking pots dissimilar to Oxford B wares and the London Shelly wares.

Chalk Tempered wares with rare additional inclusions, notably quartz, ironstone and flint; some possibly wheel-thrown and some hand-made cooking pots. Attributed to the 11th and 12th century by comparison with similar forms elsewhere.

At least three further calcareous fabrics, predominantly hand-made cooking pots.

Coarse flint-tempered wares with frequent quartz inclusions, hard, black and brown surfaces; hand-made cooking pots, some with scratch-marking. Dated by analogy and typology to 11th-12th centuries.

At least four Late Saxon and Early Medieval fabrics have been defined, mainly quartz inclusions but rare occurrences of flint, ironstone, chalk and shell. They appear to have been largely wheel-thrown, though some hand-made vessels also occur. The fabrics tend to be fairly long-lived; cooking pots are main form in 12th century, other forms such as curfews, jugs, bowls being included later.

b. *Northolt* (Hurst 1961)

Sequence of Late Saxon and early medieval fabrics (Groups e–h) including St Neots shelly wares, Thetford types and Developed St Neots wares. Some of the shelly wares (Group g in particular) are probably the same as London Late Saxon Shelly ware, especially some straight-sided bowls recognized by Hurst as anomalous within the normal St Neots tradition. The presence of true St Neots wares is demonstrable, and not surprising as it occurs in Hertfordshire, London and Staines.

Group h – Early Medieval; sandy, very hard, reduced grey ware often with semi-burnished surfaces; forms are cooking pots in large medieval shapes rather than the smaller Late Saxon forms, bowls and spouted bowls in straight-sided shapes similar to the largely 11th century London Early Medieval Sandy wares. Dated at Northolt to *c.* 1050–1150.

3. London

a. *City of London* (Vince 1984c; 1985a): Fig. 96

Shelly limestone-tempered wares: forms – thick wheel-thrown cooking pots, shallow bowls, socketed bowls, lamps, a watering pot and a hand-made storage jar. Large quantities known from several sites. Source possibly Oxfordshire, Oxford B wares are petrologically very similar; date range of the shelly wares in both Oxford and London is also comparable. In London the shelly wares are present in 9th century and appear to continue to the early 11th century. In Oxford, Mellor (1980 a and b) has suggested that a Danish raid in 1009, together with Danish settlers introducing St Neots wares, may have been factors in the demise of the B Shelly wares.

Early Medieval Sandy wares are characterized by abundant quartz grains and some calcareous inclusions. Forms – hand-made, thinner and cruder than the earlier shelly wares; cooking pots and shallow dishes; spouted pitchers and lamps possibly slightly later additions to the repertoire. The type is attributed to the late 10th and 11th century.

Fig. 96   LONDON and SURREY
London: 345–8, Early Medieval Sandy wares, late 10th–11th cent. 349, 351–2, Early Surrey wares, 11th–early 12th cent. 350, South Hertfordshire grey ware, 11th–early 12th cent. (After Vince 1985a)

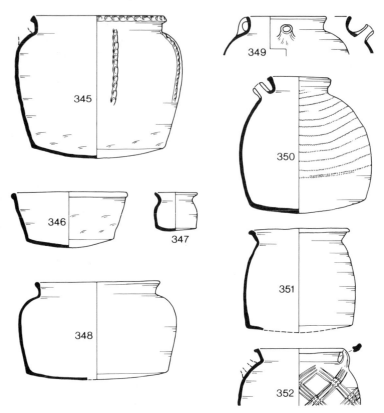

A variation in the sandy wares is Early Medieval Sand and Shell wares, in which quantities of shell have been added; forms include cooking pots and a spouted pitcher form resembling large cooking pot with small spout added to the shoulder.

The other major 11th century type is Early Surrey ware – white-firing clay with quartz and ironstone inclusions, possibly derived from the West Surrey Lower Greensand; dated to the late 11th and early 12th centuries. Forms include cylindrical cooking pots and spouted pitchers.

Also a number of less significant 11th century fabrics; some may be regional imports, the origins of others are less certain.

4. Surrey

a. *Abinger* (Dunning 1950b)

Coarse, sandy, harsh-textured grey ware; scratch-marked cooking pots with rounded bases and simple everted rims, directly comparable with Wessex forms. Attributed to *c.* 1100.

5. Kent

a. *Canterbury* (Wilson M. 1983; Frere 1954; Macpherson-Grant n.d.): Fig. 97

Sequence from urban sites based largely on stratigraphy and typology.

Late Saxon Sandy wares dominant from mid-9th/10th centuries; fabrics visually almost identical to medieval Tyler Hill wares, so possibly made in that area (this category includes Frere's Group I originally dated to *c.* 975–1025). Fabrics reduced but with increasing incidence of oxidization; hand-made but finished on a slow wheel from the later 9th century on. Forms – cooking pots, shallow cooking bowls, small dishes, spouted pitchers, lamps. Increased standardization of forms during 10th century. Decoration rare, some lattice burnishing on large pitchers probably copying imports. One small group of local Late Saxon pottery of *c.* 10th century date has splashes of glaze, but is almost certainly accidental rather than a deliberate glazing attempt.

Early Medieval Sandy wares (including Frere's Group II, *c.* 1050–1100, and Group III, *c.* 1080–1150) develop from earlier sandy wares. Hand-made, with increasing use of wheel-finishing; transition to fully wheel-thrown pottery probably *c.* 1150. Forms – cooking pots, dishes/pans, spouted pitchers; decoration limited; some thumbing on rims, and during the first half of the 12th century pitchers begin to be decorated with incised wavy lines. Cooking pots show marked increase in size from mid 11th century.

Shelly and sandy shelly wares, some possibly fairly local, some probably from North Kent coast, also present in smaller quantities, gradually increasing. Forms – cooking pots, large storage jars; decoration – thumbing on rims, thumbed applied strips on storage jars in 11th-12th centuries.

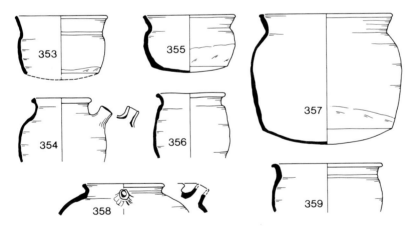

Fig. 97   KENT
Canterbury: 353, 358–9, reduced Late Saxon Sandy wares. 354–5, reduced Late Saxon Sandy wares, 11th cent. 356, shell-tempered grey-black ware, early 11th cent. 357, Group II Early Medieval Sandy ware, second half of 11th cent. (After Wilson M. 1983)

b. *Rochester* (Tester 1972; 1978)

Finds from several excavations in the town; for the most part, the pottery chronology is based on typology. Earliest dated levels are sealed beneath pre-1087/9 levels at Rochester Castle; both shelly and sandy wares present, from *c.* mid 11th century.

Shelly wares are predominant in 12th century; grey with red-brown to black surfaces, forms mostly cooking pots, some spouted pitchers. Grey sandy wares present in much smaller proportions; mostly cooking pots.

Two clay-lined pits used as clamp kilns for firing clay loom weights were found; these were dated on pottery grounds to *c.* 1100–1150. A pottery waster found in association indicates the possibility of pottery manufacture, perhaps on a domestic scale, although thin-section analysis of pottery from elsewhere in the city suggests that much was being brought from the Canterbury region (Streeten 1982).

c. *Eynsford Castle* (Rigold 1971; Rigold and Fleming 1973)

Sequence based on associated historical dates. Shell-gritted wares dominant from late 11th century; 3 main fabrics in early phases: (a) fine shell temper, hard compact fabric, dark red to black, becoming harder and thinner in early 12th century; (b) crude, possibly hand-made, fabric with fine shell and chalk filler, dark grey to brown, becoming smoother in early 12th century; (c) coarse shell filler, reduced with red oxidized surfaces, becoming commonest fabric by early 12th century. Forms – mainly cooking pots, occasional bowl/lamp.

Unglazed reduced sand tempered and partially shell-gritted wares present in very small quantities from earliest levels, late 11th century.

6. Sussex

a. *Chichester* (Down 1978; 1981): Fig. 98

(i) *Production sites*
Production known from two sites in the north-west quadrant of the town.

Tower Street – a Late Saxon clamp kiln and traces of others in the area found; daub fragments, perhaps from superstructure, and wasters. Pottery contemporary with that from Chapel Street.

Chapel Street – six Late Saxon clamp kilns excavated in area *c.* 100m from Tower Street site, archaeomagnetically dated to *c.*1030–50. These consisted of shallow scoops dug into earlier levels, with no flues; top levels had been ploughed away; one had traces of stone lining at the edge, and was clay-lined.

(ii) *Pottery*
Clamp kiln products of early Group 3 type, some wheel-made, others hand-made and wheel-finished.

Chichester pottery divided into three groups: Group 1, (B) and (C) – soft gritty fabrics, usually reduced black or grey but sometimes partially oxidized brownish-buff or red; hand-made, often finished on a slow wheel, particularly the later examples (C). Forms – mostly cooking pots, occasional larger jars with handles. Dated on typological grounds to *c.* 9th–early 10th century.

Group 2, (A) and (B) – soft gritty fabrics, with some organic tempering, chalk or shell, usually harder than Group 1 and with more oxidization. Some hand-made, most finished on a slow wheel. Forms – mostly cooking pots, some spouted pitchers, bowls, socketed bowls. Some stamp and 'stick end' decoration, and frilling of rims. Dated to *c.* 10th–11th century.

Fig. 98 SUSSEX
Chichester: 360–2, Chapel Street clamp kiln products, mid 11th cent. 363, 367,
Group 1(C), early 10th cent. 364–5, 368, 371–2, Group 2(B), 10th–11th cent. 366,
369–70, 373–4, Group 3, 11th–early 12th cent. (After Down 1978; 1981)

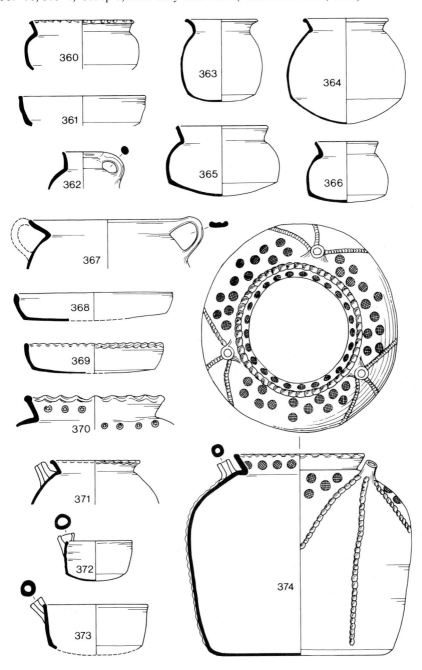

Group 3 – fabrics often heavily gritted with flint, and sometimes chalk inclusions. Oxidization more common. Forms – cooking pots, bowls, spouted bowls, spouted pitchers, large storage jars and triple-spouted vessels of unknown purpose, possibly for brewing. Decoration – stamps, applied thumbed strips, frilled rims common. Date *c.* 11th-early 12th cent.

b. Bramber Castle (Barton and Holden 1977).

Sequence based on finds and historical date for castle foundation; runs from late 11th century to 15th century, phases not closely datable. Sand and flint-tempered coarse wares, mainly cooking pots, predominate.

7. Hampshire

a. Michelmersh (Addyman *et al.* 1972): Fig. 99

(i) *Production site*
Small Type 1 kiln filled with wasters, stoke pit with ash and wasters. Site located on sand but close to several clay sources.

(ii) *Pottery*
Sandy fabrics with variations from fine to coarse and varied colours. Wheel-thrown cooking pots with finger impressions on rim and rilling comparable with Portchester ware. Spouted pitchers, often elaborately decorated with 8- and 4-sectored stamps in a variety of patterns, also applied strips, sometimes stamped. Other forms include shallow dishes and jugs or jars. Dated by analogy with stratified sherds at Winchester to 10th–11th centuries.

b. Portchester (Cunliffe 1970; 1976; 1977): Figs. 99–100

9th century fabrics contain coarse angular grits with some occasional chalk and crushed flint; hand-made cooking pots.

Portchester ware, kiln site uncertain but similarities with Michelmersh ware are clear. Fine lightly tempered fabric with some crushed flint. Forms – all wheel-thrown, including cooking pots with sagging bases and rilled bodies, sometimes decorated on top of rims and body with square-notched rouletting; other forms include shallow dishes. Attributed to 10th–11th centuries, but at Winchester it is known from deposits dated to 850–950 and thought to be residual thereafter.

Other fabrics are flint-gritted and include hand-made cooking pots and hollow-handled bowls.

The Early Medieval tradition is characterized by flint-gritted fabrics, some containing a proportion of sand. Four main types: glazed and unglazed tripod pitchers, cooking pots (including some described as cooking pots with short spouts) and dishes.

c. Southampton (pers. comm. D. Brown): Fig. 100

Flint-tempered fabrics attributed to 10th century, confirmed by a radiocarbon date centred on 930; bag-shaped coiled and wheel-finished cooking pots with occasional bowls, socketed bowls. Forms in a flint-free sandy fabric also include cooking pots and bowls. Wheel-thrown sandy wares, in the Michelmersh tradition but petrologically different, occur as spouted pitchers with stamped and applied strip decoration. Heavy

Fig. 99 HAMPSHIRE
Michelmersh: 375, kiln product. (After Addyman *et al.* 1972)
Netherton: 376–8, Fabrics S/N, U, I respectively, 9th–10th cent. (After Fairbrother 1984)
Winchester: 379–85, Winchester ware, 10th cent. (After Biddle and Barclay 1974)
Portchester: 386–9, Portchester ware, 10th–11th cent. (After Cunliffe 1970)
Christchurch: 390, quartzitic fabric, 11th–12th cent. (After Thomson *et al.* 1983)

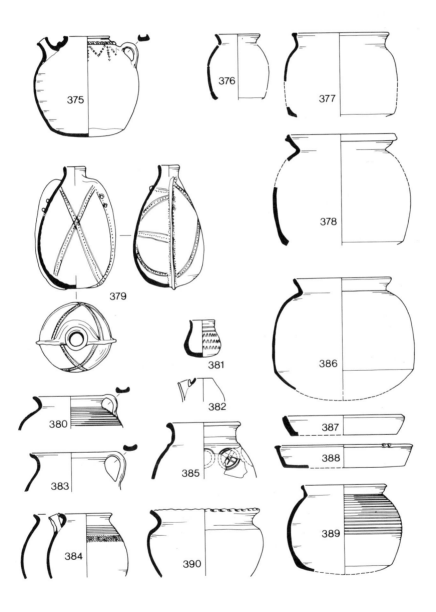

Fig. 100   HAMPSHIRE

Southampton: 391–3, Late Saxon wares, 10th–11th cent. 394–5, 397– 403, Saxo-Norman fabrics, 11th–12th cent. (After Platt and Coleman-Smith 1975)

Portchester: 396, post-Conquest fabrics, 12th cent. (After Cunliffe 1977)

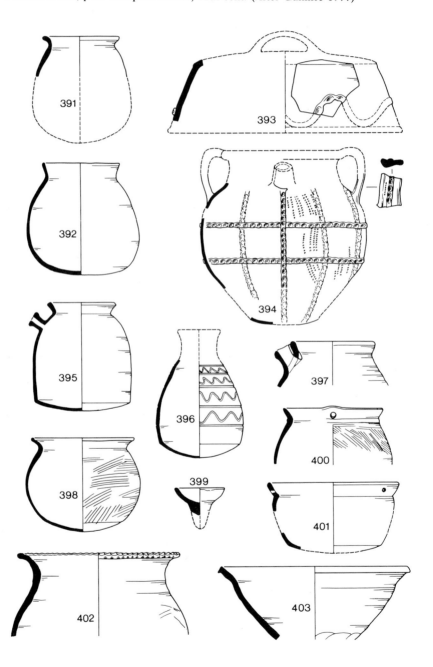

spouted pitchers in a chalk and flinty ware also occur, forming part of a tradition recognized at Chichester and Winchester.

In late 11th century, earlier types gave way to scratch-marked wares though bag-shaped cooking pot forms continue. Fabrics quartz- and flint-based; forms – hand-made cooking pots, often with thumb-impressed rims, also curfews and hand-made glazed tripod pitchers. The pronounced scratch-marking and fabrics continue into 13th century.

d. *Winchester* (Biddle and Barclay 1974; Hurst 1961; 1964a; K. Barclay and C. Matthews pers. comm.): Fig. 99

Long sequence major intra- and extra-mural excavations on sites varying in status up to aristocratic and royal. Much of material unpublished but sequence below from western suburbs not contradicted by that from intra-mural sites.

Late 9th-*c*. mid 10th century: four main fabrics recognized. Late Saxon Sandy ware, quartz-tempered, well levigated clay, hard, reduced surfaces. Forms mainly thick-walled cooking pots, wheel-finished if not thrown, sagging bases.

Dominant type – Chalk Tempered ware, oxidized and reduced, abundant chalk inclusions with minute amounts of flint and quartz; main form – cooking pots, with a few bowls; probably all coiled.

Other two fabrics are less common, with combinations of sand, chalk and flint inclusions; both fabrics include hand-made forms, of which cooking pots are most important.

Also occurring between AD 850–950 are small amounts of Michelmersh-type and Portchester wares. Fabrics of Michelmersh-type wares very similar to Late Saxon Sandy wares and may be from the same source; the Michelmersh-type wares differ from the products found at the kiln site in both the size and density of inclusions as well as in the more careless application of applied strips and stamps.

Mid-late 10th century; similar range of fabrics to previous phases but with slightly more Michelmersh-type ware and with addition of Winchester and Tripod Pitcher ware.

Winchester ware: quartz-based fabric with some calcitic inclusions, oxidized and part reduced, fired to about 1000°C. Many forms partly covered in dipped lead glaze, varying in colour from pale yellow to orange and olive green. Forms are wheel-thrown; main type – spouted pitchers, but also costrels, cups, bowls, lids, bifid-rim jars, handled jars, ?tripod pitchers, jugs and strainers. Decoration is common, including rouletting, incised lines, stamps, cordons and applied strips in a large number of combinations Winchester ware forms relatively low proportion of pottery in this phase, in which chalk-tempered and sand- and flint-gritted fabrics are dominant.

Late 10th–early 11th century: eight local coarse ware fabric groups, with variable amounts of of sand, chalk and flint temper, some of which can be shown to be regional imports. Forms are all very similar with hand-made cooking pots and bowls as main types, though there is a lamp and a perforated base, perhaps from a watering pot. Winchester ware present but thought to decrease in importance and be replaced by Tripod Pitcher ware. This has a quartz-based clay matrix with occasional flint and chalk inclusions and reduced or oxidized surfaces; variable green to amber glaze. Vessels hand-made and decorated with incised lines, rouletting, stabbing and thumbed applied strips.

Early 11th–late 12th century: characterized by presence of 'Developed Winchester ware', now termed '12th century glazed ware'. Quartzitic fabric with oxidized surfaces, glazed mottled yellow to green and decorated with applied strips. Hand-made jugs, forms comparable in some instances with baggy tripod pitcher shapes, others are in shapes reminiscent of post-Conquest jugs. Dating provided by absence in Old Minster deposits of late 11th century and presence in New Minster demolition levels of *c.* 1110. Current evidence suggests Tripod Pitcher ware continuing into later 12th century, whilst Developed Winchester ware may persist into 13th.

e. Wickham Glebe (C. Matthews pers. comm.)

Phase 1: sand- and flint-tempered ware, reduced and oxidized; forms – coil-built cooking pots and possible spouted pitchers. Flint-tempered fabrics make up most of remainder of Late Saxon pottery, with hand-made spouted pitchers and cooking pots. An important local import is Portchester ware, of which only cooking pots known from Wickham Glebe.

f. Netherton (Fairbrother 1984): Fig. 99

Early manorial site produced important stratified sequence of buildings with pottery.

Fabric S/N: flint, chalk and limestone inclusions, smooth soapy textures, multi-coloured; hand-made cooking pots and possible bowl attributed on stratigraphic grounds to 9th–mid 10th centuries.

Fabric U: quartz and flint tempering, relatively soft in early phases but harder later; hand-made cooking pots spanning period between 9th and 11th centuries.

Fabric I: mainly flint filler with occasional quartz, chalk and limestone, hard fabric with tendency to reduction. Hand-made but competently formed cooking pots, with some dishes and bowls. Dated to 11th century on basis of coin association with possibility, on evidence from Ludgershall, of continuing into first part of 12th century.

Eight fabrics dating to between the 9th and early 12th centuries known in flint-, chalk- and limestone-based fabrics. Mostly hand-made vessels of which cooking pots are dominant with occasional dishes. Earliest wheel-thrown ware (A14) is very minor element in early-mid 10th century; probably a regional import. Several of the flint-based fabrics also known in Newbury/Berkshire Downs region.

g. Christchurch (Davies 1983; Thomson, Barton and Jarvis 1983): Fig. 99

Fabric 4 – quartzitic with some limestone, rather coarse; Fabric 5 – similar but finer; forms in both fabrics probably hand-made, plain and scratch-marked cooking pots, glazed tripod pitchers.

8. Berkshire

a. Wallingford (Durham 1980; M. Mellor pers. comm.)

Excavations at St Martins Street recovered stratified sequence including St Neots-type wares which were dominant for a period. These dated at Oxford from mid–10th to mid 11th century by coin association and on stratigraphic grounds. Elsewhere, as at New Road and Wallingford Castle, earliest pottery comprises flint-filled, rosette-decorated hand-made wares which compare with mid–late 11th and 12th century finds at Oxford.

South-West England (Fig. 101)

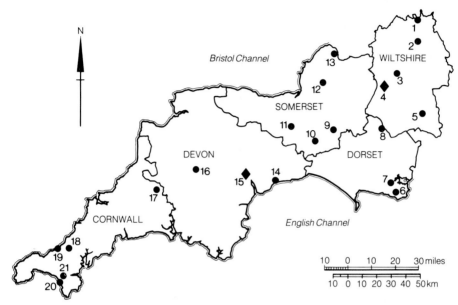

Fig. 101   South-West England, location map
1 Cricklade, 2 Great Somerford, 3 Potterne, 4 Westbury, 5 Old Sarum, 6 Corfe
Castle, 7 Wareham, 8 Shaftesbury, 9 Ilchester, 10 Castle Neroche, 11 Taunton, 12
Cheddar, 13 Bristol, 14 Honeyditches, 15 Exeter, 16 Okehampton, 17 Launceston,
18 Camborne, 19 Gwithian, 20 Gunwalloe, 21 Mawgan Porth.

1. Wiltshire

a. *Westbury and Potterne*

Production site
Clay payments referred to at Westbury in Domesday Book, and place-name hints at
Potterne.

b. *Cricklade* (Jope 1972)

Flint-tempered fabrics, grey to black. Forms hand-made, some possibly from clay
lump, others possibly coiled; mainly cooking pots, some pitchers decorated with
8-sectored stamps. Dated by association with *burh* defences and assumed to be
Alfredian.

c. *Old Sarum* (Musty and Rahtz 1964; Stone and Charlton 1935): Fig. 102

Fabrics include water-worn grits, brown buff colours; forms hand-made, mainly
scratch-marked cooking pots with round bases, some glazed tripod pitchers, 'West
Country dishes', possible crucible. Dated to early 12th century by analogy with Oxford
region and association with coin of William I.

Fig. 102 WILTSHIRE

Great Somerford: 404–5, calcareous fabrics, 12th cent. (After Thompson 1970)
Old Sarum: 406–10, sandy fabrics, 12th century. (After Musty and Rahtz 1964)
          DORSET
Wareham: 411–14, Fabric A, 11th–12th cent. 415, Fabric B, 11th– 12th cent. 416,
Fabric C, 11th–12th cent. (After Hinton and Hodges 1977)
Shaftesbury: 417–18, sandy fabrics, late Saxon. (After Keen 1977)

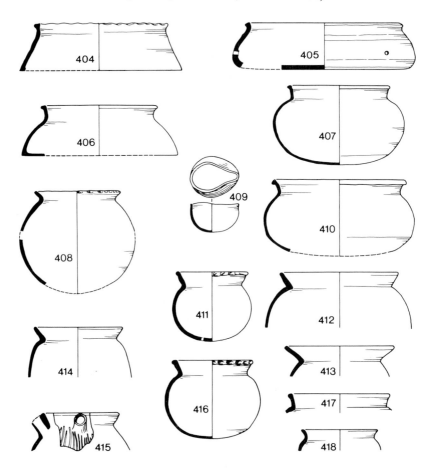

d. *Great Somerford* (Thompson 1970): Fig. 102

Calcareous, brown grey fabrics; hand-made cooking pots and 'West Country dishes'.

2. Dorset

a. *Wareham* (Hinton and Hodges 1977): Fig. 102

Fabric A: large flint fragments and quartz inclusions; presence of garnet suggests a source on Isle of Purbeck; very hard, reduced and oxidized. Forms include cooking pots and pitchers.

Fabric B: fabrics and forms similar but pitchers have rilled bodies.

Fabric C: fabrics very sandy with large quartz grains; presence of tourmaline suggests source on Wareham heathlands; very hard, reduced and oxidized. Forms include cooking pots, bowls, crucibles, storage vessels, plain spouted pitchers, tripod pitchers decorated with wavy lines.

Dates based on stratigraphy; Fabric A probably out of production by early 12th century; Fabric C became main medieval type and probably established by late 11th century, after which repertoire of forms expanded considerably.

b. *Shaftesbury* (Keen 1977): Fig. 102

Fabrics soft, quartzitic, reduced and oxidized. Forms include hand-made cooking pots with wheel-finished rims. Some sherds stamped but these not necessarily local. Dated typologically to Late Saxon period.

c. *Corfe Castle* (R.C.H.M. 1960; Renn 1960): Fig. 103

Fabrics as Wareham A and C. Forms include cooking pots, small bowls, large storage jar. Dating by association with construction and early occupation of building in west bailey attributed to late 11th century. In contexts assumed to belong to mid 12th century, tripod pitchers, shallow dishes and pedestalled lamps occur.

3. Somerset

a. *Ilchester* (Pearson 1982): Figs. 104–5

Group 12 fabrics: quartzitic, fine gritty and flinty; some soapy and some harsh textures, mainly reduced. Forms – hand-made cooking pots dated to pre-930.

Fabric 13: fabrics mainly limestone-gritted (same as Cheddar E). Wheel-thrown forms include globular cooking pots dated to 930–1000.

Fabric 14: varied, limestone- and quartz-based, mainly reduced with slightly soapy texture. Forms – hand-made cooking pots, and poorer versions of Fabric 13 forms with some evidence of wheel-turning; dated to 11th century.

Fabric 16: fabrics quartz- and flint-based; coarse-textured surfaces tend to be earlier and finer surfaces later; fairly soft, both oxidized and reduced. Forms – coiled and wheel-turned cooking pots, storage jars, occasional bowls, crucibles and spouted pitchers. Storage jars and spouted pitchers can be heavily combed and stabbed on sides, neck and rim; former also have unusual pierced upright lugs. Cooking pots are plain. Dated to 11th century and continuing as one of main medieval types.

b. *Taunton* (Pearson 1984): Figs. 104–5

Five pre-Conquest fabrics (including Cheddar E), mainly limestone and quartz temper but one had burnt out organic filler. Forms all hand-made with signs of wheel-turning; mostly cooking pots but one spouted pitcher and possible lamp known. Dated on basis of stratigraphy.

Five late 11th-early 12th century fabrics, similar to pre-Conquest wares; forms

Fig. 103   DORSET
Corfe Castle: 419–24, flint and quartzitic fabrics, 11th–12th cent. 425–6, quartzitic fabrics, 12th cent. (After R.C.H.M. 1960)

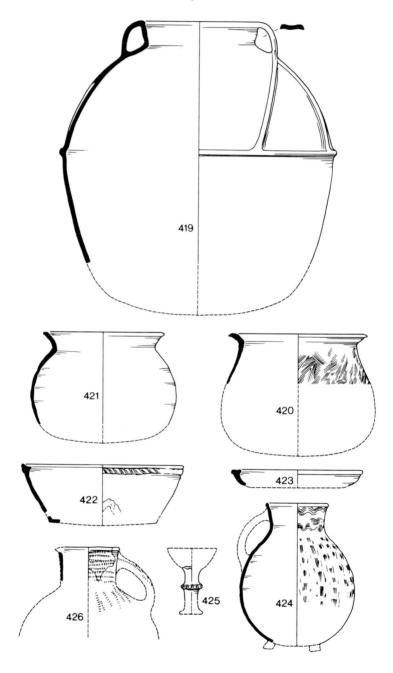

Fig. 104 SOMERSET
Castle Neroche: 427–8, 436, Standard fabric, late 11th cent. (After Davison 1972)
Ilchester: 429–31, Type B, 11th–12th cent. 435, Type H, 12th cent. (After Pearson T. 1982)
Taunton: 432–4, Types 241, 42, 224 respectively, 11th–12th cent. 437–8, Type 222, early 12th cent. (After Pearson 1984)

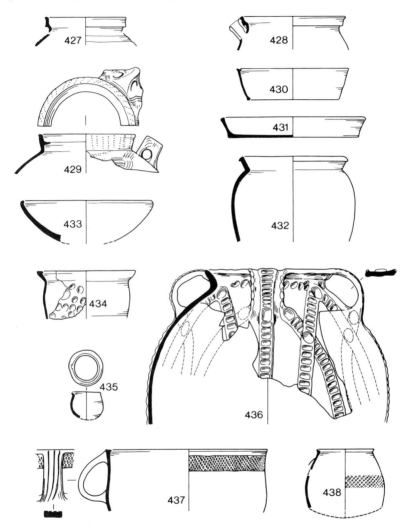

include hand-made sagging-based cooking pots, pitchers, a platter and thin-walled storage jars.

Eight early 12th century predominantly limestone- or quartz-based wares. Hand-made forms, with wheel-turned cooking pots decorated with combing; straight-sided bowls, pitchers, handled cooking pots, a platter and rouletted beaker.

Fig. 105 SOMERSET
Cheddar: 439–40, E fabric, 10th cent. (After Rahtz 1974)
Ilchester: 441, Type A, mid to late 10th cent. (After Pearson T. 1982)
Taunton: 442, Type 41, 10th cent. (After Pearson 1984)
Bristol: 443–9, 451–2, all calcareous fabrics. 443–7, 11th cent.; 448, 12th cent.;
451–2, 11th cent. (After Rahtz 1974; Watts and Rahtz 1985)
Glastonbury: 449–50, quartzitic fabrics, 11th cent. (After Rahtz 1974)
Beckery: 453, harsh sandy fabric, 11th cent. (After Rahtz 1974)

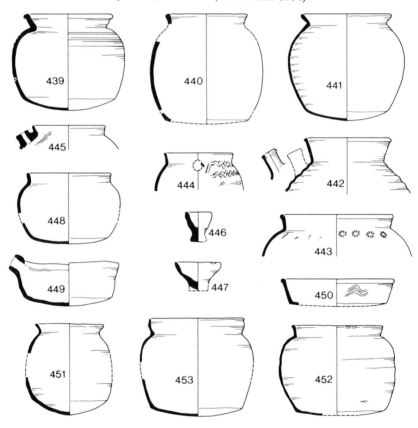

c. *Cheddar* (Rahtz 1974; 1979): Fig. 105

Very important sequence on royal palace site dated stratigraphically and by coin association to 9th–11th century; Wedmore hoard of *c.* 1040 in spouted bowl similar to Cheddar C or CC.

Six fabrics defined, some sub-divided but all essentially limestone-tempered and of Mendips area origin; textures smooth to coarse with some leaching of filler. Forms include wheel-thrown cooking pots (Cheddar E); the other main form comprises lamps (Cheddar B) and possible storage-jar (Cheddar G). Comparable pottery at Glastonbury and Beckery (Fig. 105).

d. Castle Neroche (Davison 1972): Fig. 104

Standard fabrics fine, slightly micaceous clay with quartz and chert; harsh brown-yellow surfaces. Thin sections suggest local clay source. Forms are wheel-thrown cooking pots with elaborate collar and sagging base, storage jars with multiple strap handles and rare spouted pitchers. Date based upon stratigraphy of rampart but also typological affinities of ring work and pottery with those of north-west France. Davison suggests immigrant potter operating c. 1060–80.

e. Bristol (Ponsford 1974; 1979; Watts and Rahtz 1985): Fig. 105

Bristol Castle excavations:

Type 1: shell- and quartz-tempered, shell often leached out, grey; hand-made cooking pots with upright rims and sagging bases. Possibly Cotswold product.

Type 2: limestone- and quartz-tempered, surfaces partly oxidized; everted rim cooking pots. Possibly local or Mendip product.

Type 3: basically quartzitic but some calcareous inclusions; forms are cooking pots.

Sequence dated to pre-1070 as it is sealed below castle bank; 3 pre-castle periods recognized but no differences observed in the ceramic sequence. Date range c. 1000–1070.

Motte ditch contained large group of pottery, of which those labelled fabrics AA-AG dated to 1080–1150. Fabrics essentially quartz-based with small calcareous inclusions and occasionally haematite or mica; colour and hardness variations. Forms – hand-made cooking pots finished on turntable, occasional bowls. Decoration combed wavy lines. One type (115) occurs in heavy limestone-tempered ware with some shell and quartz; hand-made, plain, turntable-finished; possible successor to pre-Conquest wares and datable to 1070–1200.

Second group of fabrics labelled AH-AP, limestone-tempered and some with quartz; variations in amount of filler, colour and hardness. Hand-made cooking pots splashed with glaze; tripod pitchers with thin green glaze and some applied strips, well known as the so-called 'Selsley Common' type, with date range from 1080–1250.

Mary Le Port – sequence of pre-Conquest wares similar to the Castle but also including spouted pitchers with stamped dimples and rosettes as well as cooking pots with upright and everted rims and full-bodied profiles.

4. Devon

a. Exeter (Allan 1984; Fox and Dunning 1957): Figs. 106–7

(i) *Production site*

Bedford Garage site located within north-east corner of medieval defences. Type 1b kiln, raised perforated kiln floor, no pedestal.

(ii) *Pottery*

Kiln fabric – quartz, chert and sandstone filler added to clay matrix, probably from local source; very hard, fully oxidized. Wheel-thrown cooking pots, including one that is perforated and known as 'solder' pot, possibly a brazier; bowls, storage jars, lamps and possible jug also known. Occasional patches and dribbles of glaze on many vessels. Originally dated to 14th century but now firmly established stratigraphically and by coin association as pre-Conquest; terminal dates from late 10th or early 11th century to c.

Fig. 106   DEVON

Exeter: 454–6, 459–60, Bedford Garage kiln material, 10th–11th cent. 457, Fabric 20, 10th cent. 458, Fabric 20, 11th–12th cent. 461–72, Fabric 20, 12th cent. (After Allan 1984; Fox and Dunning 1957)

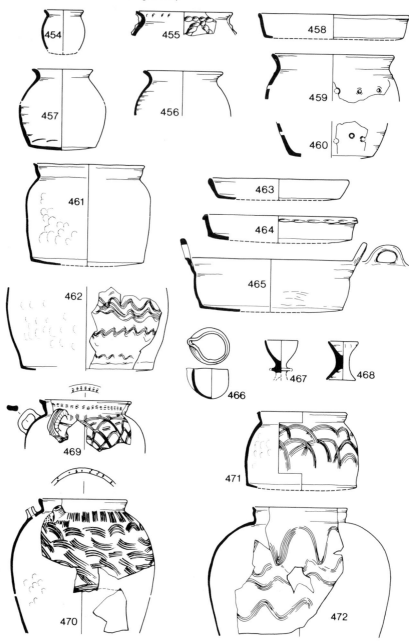

Fig. 107 DEVON
Honeyditches: 473–4, quartzitic fabrics, 12th cent. (After Miles H. 1976)
CORNWALL
Gwithian area: 475–7, Sandy Lane Style 1 fabric, 11th–12th cent. 478, Sandy Lane
Style 2 fabric, 11th–12th cent. 479, gritty fabric 'bar-lug', 10th–11th cent. (After
Thomas A.C. 1964)
Gunwalloe: 480–1, grass-marked pottery, pre-Conquest. (After Thomas A.C. 1963)
Hellesvean: 482, 'bar-lug', 10th–11th cent. (After Dunning *et al.* 1959)
Mawgan Porth: 483, 'bar-lug', 10th–11th cent. (After Hutchinson 1979)

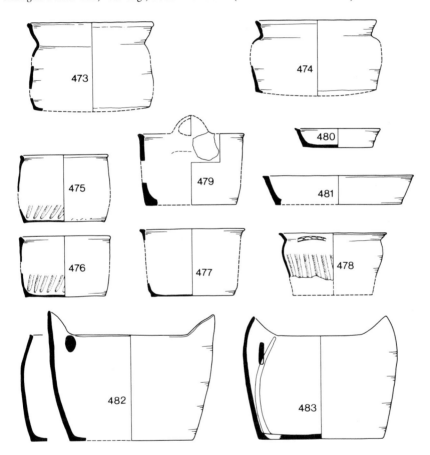

1100 but no later. Products of this kiln not known to have formed more than 17 percent
of assemblages in Exeter.

Other wares include Fabric 20, a rough fabric tempered with quartz and flint,
oxidized and reduced. Forms – hand-made, possibly coiled; mainly cooking pots, some
storage jars. Dated stratigraphically to 11th century; fabric in use by *c.* 1020 but
continues to 14th century. Widely distributed within Devon and possibly made in south
Somerset.

b. Okehampton Castle (Allan and Perry 1982)

Fabric 2, the same as Exeter Fabric 20, present in earliest levels.

c. Honeyditches (Miles H. 1976): Fig. 106

Late 11th-early 12th century group on Roman bath house site. Fabrics basically quartz- and flint-tempered; forms – hand-made cooking pots. Dated on typological grounds.

5. Cornwall

a. Gwithian (Hutchinson 1979; Thomas A.C. 1963; 1964; 1968): Fig. 107

Main Cornish types are grass-marked, with varied mineralogy reflecting very local manufacture in different places; often thin, soft wares in shades of brown, probably clamp-fired. Grass-marking on underside of bases is probably result of wet clay vessels adhering to grass-covered slabs on which vessels left to dry until leather hard. Source of grass possibly coastal dunes. Forms include platters and jars.

'Bar lug' forms are flat-based straight-sided vessels, round at base but oval at rim, and with distinctive upright lugs and internal bars which probably assisted in suspending pots over fire, with lugs protecting thongs from fire.

Sandy Lane Style 1: hand-made, probably coiled, straight-sided, flat-based cooking pots with flat-topped rims and characteristic vertical fingering on sides.

Sandy Lane Style 2: hand-made, possibly wheel-turned, cooking pots with more globular bodies, everted rims and sagging bases.

Dating rests on stratigraphic sequence and association with Mediterranean imports. Grass-marked wares found in Layer B, 7th–9th century, and in Layer C. 'Bar lugs' suggested as *c.* 850 to 1100 but no later at Launceston (T. Miles pers. comm.). Sandy Lane styles dated typologically and by association with 12th century buildings at chapel of Fentonian, Camborne and at St Helens, Scilly.

Many other sites, such as Gunwalloe, Hellesvean, Mawgan Porth (Fig. 107), Crane Godrevy, also produced similar wares to Gwithian.

West Midlands (Fig. 108)

1. Herefordshire

a. Hereford (Vince 1985b): Fig. 109

Fabric A7a: fine oxidized red-brown fabric, quartz inclusions with white mica; clay probably not levigated but larger inclusions removed. Forms include wheel-thrown pitchers with patchy yellow glaze. Local type dated 11th–12th century.

Fabric B–B1: mainly reduced fabric with large igneous inclusions, quartz, sandstone and other metamorphic rocks. Source – slopes of Malvern Hills. Hand-made cylindrical cooking pots, dated early 12th century and later.

Other wares are regional imports of which G–G1, Stafford-type ware, accounts for most of 10th century and 75 percent of 11th century pottery.

Fig. 108 West Midlands, location map
1 Chester, 2 Stafford, 3 Warwick, 4 Worcester, 5 Hereford, 6 Harefield, 7 Winchcombe, 8 Gloucester, 9 Cirencester.

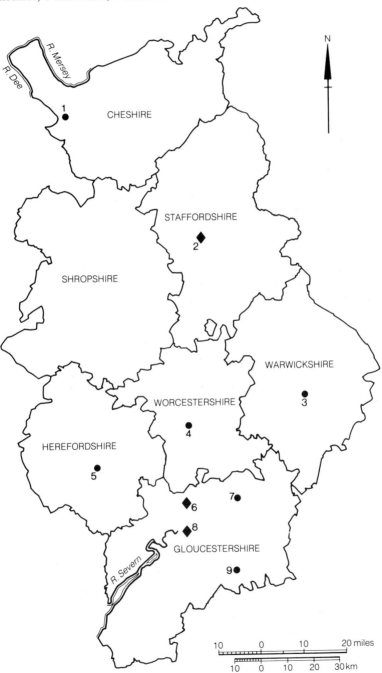

2. Worcestershire

a. *Worcester* (Morris 1980a and b): Fig. 109

Very little evidence of local production during 10th and early 11th centuries. Much of pottery comprises regional imports, including wares from Oxford (24 percent), Stamford (20 percent), Gloucester (29 percent), a general West Midlands source (22 percent), St. Neots (3 percent) and Northampton (1 percent). Forms in use mainly cooking pots, but a few glazed Stamford wares.

From late 11th century pattern changes, with predominantly local production of oolitic Cotswold wares accounting for over 75 percent of material. Local production of quartz-tempered wares starts around same time. Forms show increase in size of cooking pots, though the smaller late Saxon types continue as an important element for a while. Dating based on stratigraphic sequences in Worcester and the regional imports.

3. Gloucestershire

a. *Gloucester* (Vince 1979b): Fig. 109

(i) *Production site*

At Westgate Street, in centre of medieval town, a pit containing wasters was found; daub with wood impresssions may be kiln lining.

(ii) *Pottery*

Fabric TF41a: inclusions mainly limestone with some quartz; oxidized brown and reduced black wares; source possibly sandy clays on terraces north of town. Hand-made forms, possibly shaped from a lump, as well as some completely wheel-thrown vessels; no chronological difference apparent. Forms – only cooking pots, apart from some hand-made saucer-shaped crucibles used in glass working. Dating based on stratigraphy at Gloucester and Hereford.

Other wares include Fabric TF41b, tempered with oolitic limestone and quartz; harder than TF41a but also in varied colours. Hand-made forms include club-rimmed cylindrical-bodied cooking pots (first defined by Jope 1952 as a Cotswold type) and some tubular-spouted pitchers. This ware is main 11th century Gloucester type, forming 99 percent of assemblages. Dated by association with a coin of William I, and present in Abbey context attributed to *c.* 1107–1114. Dated at Hereford to late 11th-early 12th centuries. Source of fabric possibly clays around Harefield to north of town.

b. *Harefield*

Five potters paying 44d. recorded in Domesday Book.

Fig. 109 GLOUCESTERSHIRE
Gloucester: 484–91, kiln products (TF41a), 10th–11th cent. 492, Fabric TF41b, 11th cent. (After Vince 1979b)
WORCESTERSHIRE
Worcester: 493–5, Cotswold type, 10th–12th cent. 496, Gloucester type, 10th cent. (After Morris 1980a)

Malvern: 499–500, Malvernian ware from Worcester, 12th cent. (After Barton 1968; Morris 1980a and b)

HEREFORDSHIRE

Hereford: 497–8, fabrics D1, B1, 10th–11th cent. (After Vince 1985b)

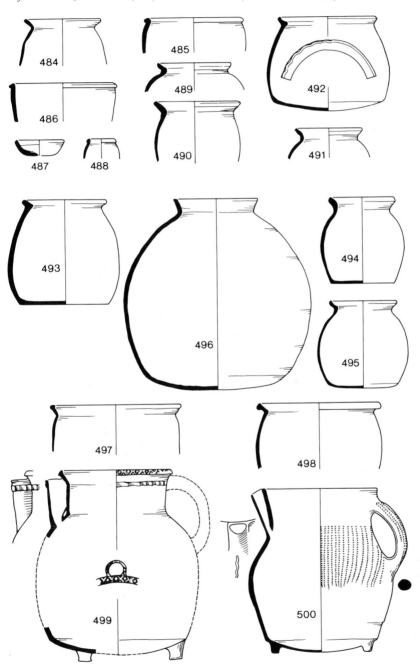

c. Winchcombe (Vince 1984b)

Limestone-tempered club-rimmed cooking pots with straight sides known from Late Saxon pits.

d. Lower Severn Valley (Vince 1984b)

It is possible that limestone-tempered wares, forms similar to those at Gloucester, found at Frocester, Wotton under Edge and Hillesley were made locally.

e. Cirencester (Vince 1982)

Fabric 202: limestone-gritted, both soft and hard; hand-made cooking pots, 'West Country' dishes, pitchers, flat-based dish and possible jug dated to mid 12th century at St John's Hospital.

4. Staffordshire

a. Stafford (Cane and Carver 1983): Fig. 110

(i) Production sites

Two Type 1 kilns and wasters known from Tipping Street, outside probable south-

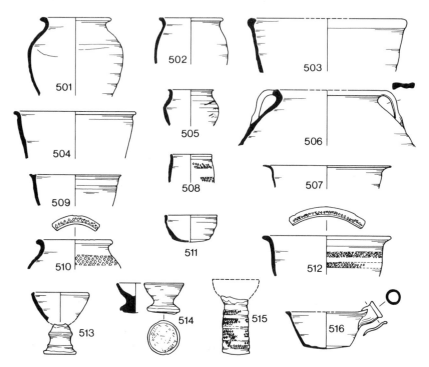

Fig. 110　STAFFORDSHIRE
Stafford: 501–16, kiln products, 10th cent. (After Cane and Carver 1983)

east corner of *burh* defences. Another Type 1 kiln known from Eastgate Street, outside likely line of defences. Quantities of wasters discovered at Clark Street, a marshy area beyond the *burh*, possibly used as infilling.

(ii) *Pottery*

Stafford ware fabrics are hard and quartz-tempered, oxidized red-brown though some reduced sherds present; firing temperatures estimated at around 950°C. Forms, all wheel-thrown, include plain and rouletted cooking pots, sometimes with applied and thumbed strips decorated with circular stamps, deep bowls, spouted pitchers, storage jars, plain and rouletted lamps, crucibles, bottles and a pitcher. Greatest range of forms is at Tipping Street; few other sites in Stafford or elsewhere in West Midlands produce so many. *Floruit* dated on stratigraphic grounds and by archaeomagnetism to 10th century.

5. Cheshire

a. *Chester* (Rutter 1985): Fig. 111

'Chester ware' is very similar to contemporary pottery made at Stafford, but a source there has not been confirmed for it.

Four variations of fabric identified; all essentially quartzitic with some sandstone, feldspar and mica; oxidized red-brown and fired to around 1000°C. Forms are wheel-thrown (confirmed by study of particle and void orientation), though cooking pots show signs of hand finishing. Cooking pots have rims similar to French forms; often impressed with bands of lattice decoration – 13 designs in single and multiple bands known. Bowls also rouletted occasionally on rims. Other forms include lamps, spouted pitchers and storage jars. Dated to late 10th century with coin hoard of *c.* 970 in Chester ware pot, but recent work suggests that production might have commenced perhaps in first half of 10th century, continuing into 11th century.

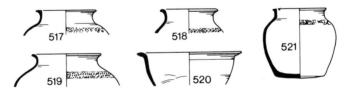

Fig. 111 CHESHIRE
Chester: 517–21, Chester ware, 10th–11th cent. (After Carrington 1977)

6. Warwickshire

a. *Warwick* (Mytum unpublished)

Three major fabrics recognized, of which St Neots ware almost certainly has status of regional import. Local wares include a shelly ware with sand inclusions, partly oxidized, and a fully oxidized quartz-based fabric. Forms include cooking pots and bowls in shelly fabrics but only straight-sided cooking pots in sandy wares. Stratigraphic sequences suggest that shelly wares disappear towards the end of the 11th century, succeeded by the quartzitic fabrics which were associated with coins of Cnut and Edward the Confessor.

Wales (Fig. 112)

N

ANGLESEY

FLINTSHIRE

R. Dee

3

CAERNARVONSHIRE

DENBIGHSHIRE

MERIONETHSHIRE

MONTGOMERYSHIRE

1

Cardigan Bay

RADNORSHIRE

CARDIGANSHIRE

PEMBROKESHIRE

CARMARTHENSHIRE

BRECKNOCKSHIRE

MONMOUTHSHIRE

GLAMORGANSHIRE

2

R. Severn

10   0   10   20   30 miles

10   0   10   20   30   40   50 km

Bristol Channel

Fig. 112   Wales, location map
1 Hen Domen, 2 Chepstow, 3 Rhuddlan.

1. Montgomeryshire

a. Hen Domen (Barker 1970; Barker and Higham 1982)

Motte and bailey castle; pottery has clear affinities with sherds known from field survey in the county as well as wider areas of West Midlands.

Group 2 fabrics contain sedimentary rocks, source probably fluvio-glacial gravels but impossible to localize. Forms are hand-made, straight-sided cooking pots, also known at Hereford, Worcester, Shrewsbury and Richards Castle. Dated at Hen Domen to periods 1 and 2 – late 11th and early 12th centuries.

2. Flintshire

a. *Rhuddlan* (J. Knight, pers. comm.)

Late Saxon wares similar to 'Chester ware' recovered.

3. Monmouthshire

a. *Chepstow* (Vince forthcoming)

Fabrics Kc and Kd contain limestone, sandstone, quartz and mica, probably derived from Severn valley carboniferous limestone deposits; some soft and some hard sherds with brown to red oxidized surfaces. Forms all hand-made, some wheel-finished; mainly sagging-based cooking pots, some decorated with 'wheel' stamps. Attributed to late 11th and early 12th centuries, accounting for nearly 70 percent of assemblages. Identical vessels occur at Bristol, which is most likely source, and Dublin.

Chapter 5   Mid-Twelfth to Mid-Fourteenth Century

Scotland (Fig. 113)

1. Shetland

a. Jarlshof (Hamilton 1956): Fig. 114

Viking and medieval farming settlement, dated by small finds.

Earliest Viking settlement aceramic; pottery first used in the 12th century (or possibly slightly earlier). Fabrics coarse and gritty, hand-made (ring-building); grass backing often used in manufacture. Most common form is small straight-sided or barrel-shaped pot with slightly everted rim. Also bowls, and vessels squared at the rim, but with circular bases. The latter form is influenced by four-sided steatite pots which appear in the 12th century; the pottery form lasts possibly into the 14th century.

Wheel-made grey sand-tempered ware with glaze splashes, presumably imported from mainland Scotland, found in the medieval farmstead of late 13th-early 14th century date.

2. Orkney

a. Kirkwall (MacAskill 1982b): Fig. 114

Several sites within the medieval town; much of pottery is redeposited, dated by typology.

Grass-tempered ware – sandy micaceous fabric with abundant quartz grits and grass temper, pink-brown with reduced grey core and/or internal surfaces, probably locally made. Forms mostly cooking pots, with one jug; mostly hand-made, although a few sherds show evidence of wheel-finishing or possibly wheel-throwing. Some vessels have roughly incised groove decoration. Probably medieval or earlier in date, although similar hand-made pottery, Craggan ware, made as late as 19th century in Hebrides and West Highlands.

Scottish White Gritty ware jugs, probably imported from mainland Scotland, in 13th–14th centuries.

Scottish Red Sandy wares – reddish or buff sandy fabrics, sometimes partly reduced, green to yellow-green glaze; forms mostly jugs; one has face-mask handle. Similar to local wares in Inverness, Perth and Aberdeen; probably imported from mainland Scotland, in 13th-14th centuries.

3. Caithness

a. Freswick (Batey *et al.* 1984; Curle 1939)

Grass-tempered ware – poor quality fabrics with heavy organic tempering; forms have rounded bases and simple everted rims. Dating uncertain, based on imported wares; thought to be 11th–13th century.

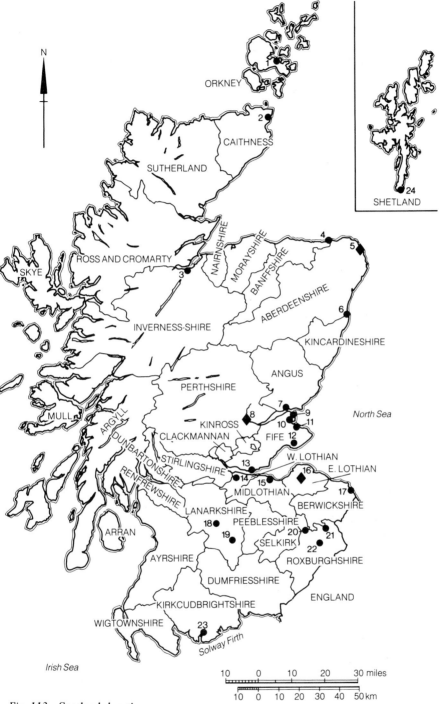

Fig. 113 Scotland, location map
1 Kirkwall, 2 Freswick, 3 Inverness, 4 Cullykhan, 5 Rattray, 6 Aberdeen, 7 Dundee,
8 Perth, 9 Tentsmuir, 10 Leuchars, 11 St Andrews, 12 Balchrystie, 13 Inverkeithing,
14 Linlithgow, 15 Edinburgh, 16 Colstoun, 17 Eyemouth, 18 Lesmahagow, 19
Roberton, 20 Melrose, 21 Kelso, 22 Jedburgh, 23 Kirkcudbright, 24 Jarlshof.

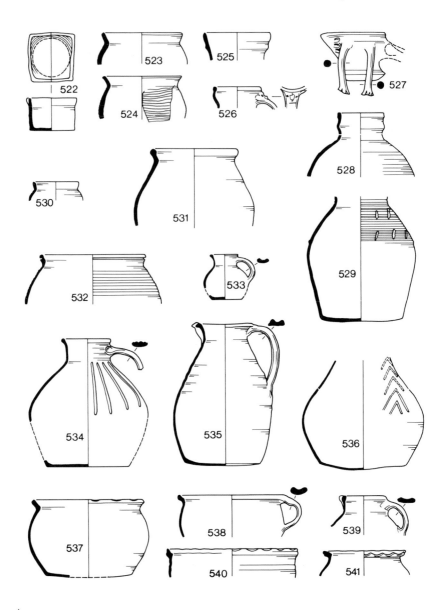

Fig. 114   SHETLAND
Jarlshof: 522, 12th–13th cent. (After Hamilton 1956)
          ORKNEY
Kirkwall: 523–4, Grass-tempered ware, probably medieval. 525, Scottish White
Gritty ware, 13th–14th cent. 526, Scottish Red Sandy ware, 13th–14th cent. (After
MacAskill 1982b)
          INVERNESS-SHIRE
Inverness: 527–9, Fabric Group A, early–mid 14th cent. (After MacAskill 1982a)

BANFFSHIRE

Cullykhan: 530, gritty fabric, c. later 12th cent. (After unpublished drawing by M.K. Greig)

ANGUS

Dundee: 531, White Gritty ware, 13th–14th cent. (After Laing 1973)

PERTHSHIRE

Perth: 532, Scottish East Coast White Gritty ware, c. 1300; 533–4, Perth Local ware, late 13th/early 14th cent. 535, Perth Local-type ware from Aberdeen (After Laing 1973; Murray J.C. 1982; Thoms 1982)

FIFE

Inverkeithing: 536–41, Scottish East Coast White Gritty ware, 13th–14th cent. (After MacAskill 1983)

4. Inverness-shire

a. *Inverness* (MacAskill 1982a): Fig. 114

Occupation site close to the castle but probably peripheral to the main medieval settlement. Dated by finds.

Fabric Group A – fabrics sandy with some mica, mostly fairly soft, usually orange or buff but sometimes reduced grey; yellow-green to orange-brown glaze. Identifiable forms all wheel-thrown jugs, mostly plain, but occasionally with dummy handles in imitation of English forms. Probably of local origin. It appears in the first half of the 14th century and becomes the predominant type, although a few sherds of late 13th/early 14th century date may also be local.

Fabric Group B – Scottish East Coast Gritty ware; off-white to pale brown hard fabric with quartz grits protruding. Forms – cooking pots and jugs, the jugs having splashy yellow-green glaze. Present in small quantities from beginning of sequence in 13th century to mid 14th century. Presumably a regional import.

Imports include Scarborough and Yorkshire wares and other probable English types.

5. Banffshire

a. *Cullykhan* (J.C. and M.K. Greig pers. comm.): Fig. 114

Medieval building, predecessor of later medieval castle, built on promontory; dated by coin and rich small finds to later 12th century.

Main ware is a hard reddish gritty fabric, often reduced or with grey core. Vessels wheel-finished, some may be fully wheel-thrown. Forms mainly cooking pots of rounded shape, with simple everted rims. Source presumably fairly local.

6. Aberdeenshire

a. *Rattray* (Brooks and Haggarty 1976–7; Murray and Murray 1986)

Production site

Finds of kiln props indicate a possible kiln site at this medieval burgh. Trial excavations have not so far confirmed this possibility, although much of the pottery found is thought to be local. Imports include large quantities of Scarborough ware.

b. Aberdeen (Murray J.C. 1982): Figs. 115–16

Several sites within the medieval town; dated mainly by associated finds.

Fabrics 1–8 – red fabrics, mostly wholly or partly oxidized, containing varying amounts of quartz sand, mica and some granite fragments; glaze varies from orange to green. Probably of very local origin. Forms are mainly cooking pots and jugs, also pipkins, cooking bowls, dishes, urinals, and beaker-like vessels usually with a cream slip and sometimes glazed. Many jugs plain but some decorated; decoration includes thumb impressions, stamps, applied strips, incised lines and anthropomorphic motifs. Bearded face-mask jugs made in imitation of Scarborough ware. Local fabrics present from earliest occupation, in late 12th/early 13th century, but in small quantities; becomes very common from late 13th/early 14th century.

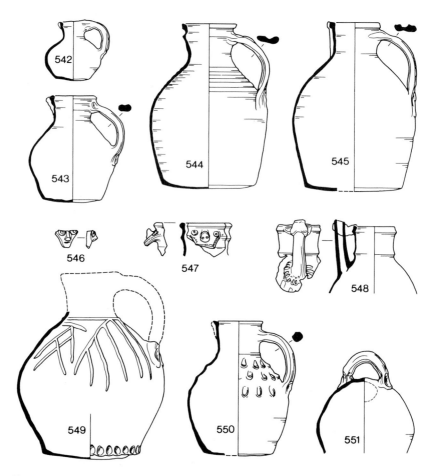

Fig. 115   ABERDEENSHIRE
Aberdeen: 542–51, Aberdeen Local Fabrics 3, 5, 6 and 7, 13th–mid 14th cent. (After Murray J.C. 1982)

Fig. 116 ABERDEENSHIRE
Aberdeen: 552–62, Scottish East Coast Gritty wares, Fabrics 12, 13 and 15. 553, 556, 560, late 12th–early 13th cent.; 552, 554–5, 557–9, 561–2, mid 13–early 14th cent. 563–73, Aberdeen Local Fabrics 2, 3, 5, 6, 7. 563, late 12th cent.; 564–73, 13th–early 14th cent. (After J.C. Murray 1982)

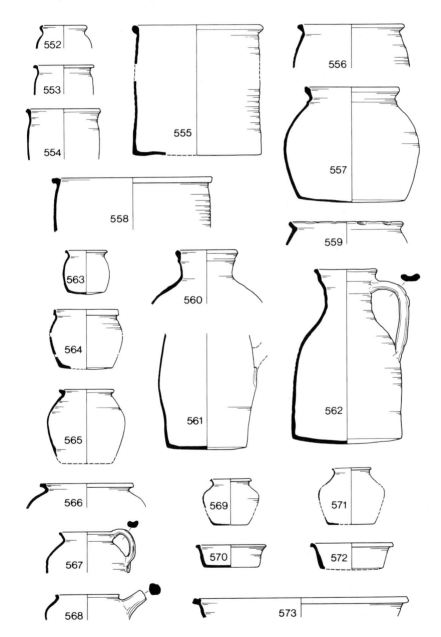

Fig. 117 PERTHSHIRE
Perth: jug in Perth Local fabric. Ht. 29cm (Photo: Scottish Urban Archaeological Trust)

Fabrics 12–16 – Scottish East Coast Gritty wares, usually off-white, sometimes reddish or grey; quartz-gritted. Forms – cooking pots, straight-sided or rounded, and yellowish- or green-glazed jugs. Source not known. These wares dominant in later 12th–later 13th century levels, declining in late 13th-14th century.

English imports include much Scarborough ware, also Yorkshire wares, Developed Stamford ware, probable East Anglian wares and South English shelly wares.

7. Perthshire

a. Perth (Haggarty and Thoms 1982; N. MacAskill and D. Hall pers. comm.; Scott and Blanchard 1983; Stevenson and Henshall 1956–7): Figs. 114, 117

(i) *Production site*

Production suggested by finds of pottery, daub and possible wasters, and a nearby 'Potterhill' place name, at Kinnoull, just across the river Tay from Perth, though the existence of a kiln there has yet to be proved.

(ii) *Pottery*

Perth Local (formerly 'Kinnoull') ware, which comprises 4 sub groups, is a fine sandy grey-brown to pink-buff micaceous fabric, sometimes with a white slip; glaze is yellow to olive-green. Forms – cooking pots and jugs. Decoration of jugs includes applied strips, scales, pellets, stamped pads and face-masks; some jugs have tubular spouts. Early Perth Local occurs in earliest excavated levels, of later 12th century, in small quantities, together with continental and English imports. Main local industry starts early 13th century; ware is dominant in Perth deposits of 13th-14th century date.

Scottish East Coast White Gritty ware, white quartz-tempered fabric, glaze yellow to pale green, present in small quantities from earliest levels on, including straight-sided cooking pots in contexts of 12th century date (Haggarty 1984: 397). Forms – mainly cooking pots and jugs. Decoration includes applied strips and scales, and incised grooves.

Imports include much Scarborough ware.

8. Angus

a. *Dundee* (Laing 1970–1): Fig. 114

Unstratified 13th–14th century pottery from midden deposits. White gritty wares common, jugs and cooking pots. Fine white sandy ware jugs also present, and possible waster sherds of these may indicate local production. Imports include Scarborough ware.

9. Fife

a. *Leuchars/Tentsmuir Forest area* (Laing 1966–7)

Production sites

East Coast White Gritty wares found in fieldwalking over this area, including some possible wasters, suggestive of possible production sites.

b. *Balchrystie* (Webster and Cherry 1974: 221)

Production site

East Coast White Gritty wares and daub, some sherds possible wasters, found in fieldwalking, suggestive of a possible production site.

c. *St Andrews* (N. MacAskill and D. Hall, pers. comm.)

Several excavations within the medieval town.

Wheel-made White Gritty wares predominate; forms – cooking pots, distinct regional shape being globular with two strap handles; also globular jugs. Decoration includes applied brown strips and pellets, and occasional anthropomorphic motifs. Date range from late 12th century–*c.* mid 15th century.

d. *Inverkeithing* (MacAskill 1983): Fig. 114

Several sites within the medieval town.

Scottish East Coast Gritty ware, hard off-white to brown or grey-brown quartz-gritted fabric, predominates. Green or yellow-green splashy glaze. Forms – cooking pots, jugs. Decoration includes wavy combing, applied strips and scales, bearded face-masks. Source probably local; dated 13th-14th century.

Scottish Medieval Sandy wares, red-orange to buff sandy fabrics, similar to local fabrics in Perth, Aberdeen and Inverness, occur in small quantities.

10. West Lothian

a. *Linlithgow* (Laing 1966–7; 1968–9)

Excavations at Linlithgow Palace, and stray finds.

13th/14th century levels include off-white or pink gritty wares, similar to Scottish East Coast Gritty ware; forms – cooking pots and jugs. Some Colstoun-type ware present.

11. Midlothian

a. *Edinburgh* (Thoms 1975–6; N. Holmes pers. comm.)

Several sites excavated within the medieval town.

White Gritty wares, hard quartz-gritted fabrics, dominate in 13th-14th centuries. Forms – mainly cooking pots and jugs; straight-sided cooking pots are attributed to late 12th/early 13th centuries. Sources – probably Colstoun and Fife, though it is possible that there was a more local production site.

12. East Lothian

a. *Colstoun* (Brooks C.M. 1978–80): Fig. 118; see also Fig. 18 Nos. 4–5; Fig. 60 No. 8

(i) *Production site*

Three kilns excavated, two Type 2 kilns dated by pottery typology to 13th century, one Type 3 kiln of probable 14th century date. Kiln props and parting sherds associated with the kilns. Further (unexcavated) kilns located by geophysical survey.

(ii) *Pottery*

Wheel-thrown white to buff hard fabrics, with quartz gritting ranging from very fine to coarse, in East Coast Gritty tradition. Glaze yellow to olive green, occasionally copper green. Forms – mainly cooking pots, straight-sided or globular, and jugs, sometimes with bridge or tubular spouts; some bowls, handled cooking pots, pipkins and jars. One example of a ceramic mortar, built into the wall of a kiln after breaking, perhaps connected with the potting process, e.g. glaze preparation. Decoration of cooking pots confined to thumbing of rims. Jug decoration includes applied brown or self-coloured strips, scales and stamped pads, incised wavy lines, rouletting, 'raspberry' and 'wheatear' stamps and anthropomorphic motifs, including bearded face-masks imitating Scarborough ware, applied arms, and face-masks on bridge spouts.

13. Berwickshire

a. *Eyemouth* (Crowdy 1986)

Several urban sites, including a midden deposit, excavated within the town; some coin-dating.

Scottish White Gritty ware dominant, from earliest deposits of later 12th century on; cooking pots predominate over jugs.

Fig. 118   EAST LOTHIAN
Colstoun: 574–96, kiln products, 13th cent. (After Brooks C.M. 1978–80)

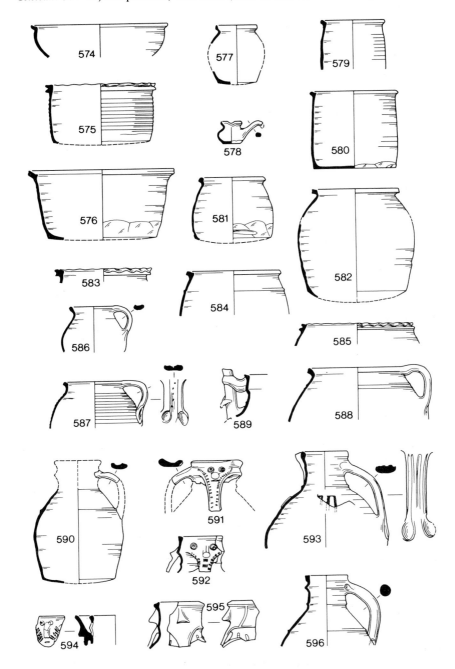

14. Lanarkshire

a. *Lesmahagow Priory* (Hall D. 1982)

Fabrics A1 and B1 comprise most of the 13th–14th century pottery; both quartz-tempered, micaceous fabrics with some grog; A1 – grey, B1 – brown or red. Wheel-thrown forms, mainly jugs, with splashed glaze; some cooking pots. Decoration includes incised wavy lines, applied strips.

Fabric D – light grey micaceous quartz-gritted fabric, very similar to East Coast White Gritty wares; probably regional imports.

b. *Roberton* (Haggarty and Tabraham 1982)

Motte site. Only small quantities of pottery; much in white gritty ware typical of S.E. Scotland, some sherds in a local Clyde valley fabric with shale inclusions. Forms – mainly jugs, one watering pot. Dated typologically to 13th/14th century.

15. Kirkcudbrightshire

a. *Kirkcudbright Castle* (Dunning *et al.* 1957–8): Fig. 119

Occupation of site dated on historical grounds to *c.* 1288–1308; castle garrisoned by the English.

Pottery unstratified; much in a powdery fine orange or grey fabric, probably made from local clays; two wasters or near-wasters noted. Wheel-thrown, with orange-brown or olive to deep brown/blackish glaze. Forms – mostly jugs. Decoration includes dot-and-circle stamps, rouletting, applied brown strips.

Probable regional or English imports include several jugs with anthropomorphic decoration, one a bearded face-mask jug.

16. Roxburghshire

a. *Kelso Abbey* (Cox 1984; Haggarty 1984; Tabraham 1984): Fig. 119

Excavations dated mainly by historical associations and architectural evidence. Main pottery group from Phase 1 pits, date range *c.* second or third quarter of 12th century.

Fabric 1, white to grey hard quartz-gritted fabric, most common in Phase 1; source probably local. A series of other minor gritty fabrics are also probably local, made of a similar carbonaceous clay (Fabrics 2–5, 10 and 12). Glazes yellow to green. Forms mainly straight-sided cooking pots, also jugs. Decoration rare; incised lines, wedge-shaped rouletting.

b. *Melrose Abbey* (Cruden 1952–3): Fig. 119

Large group of unstratified pottery, dated only by typology, but useful for the range of forms. Fabrics not defined. 13th–14th century wares include jugs similar to Colstoun types, with vertical applied brown strips.

c. *Jedburgh Abbey* (Cruden 1955–6; E. Cox. pers. comm.)

Fig. 119   ROXBURGHSHIRE
Kelso Abbey: 597, 599–603, Fabric 1. 598, Fabric 4. 604, Fabric 3. 605, Fabric 5.
12th cent. (After Tabraham 1984)
Melrose Abbey: 606, 13th–14th cent. jug. (After Cruden 1952–3)
             KIRKCUDBRIGHTSHIRE
Kirkcudbright Castle: 606a, local fabric, late 13th–early 14th cent. (After Dunning *et al.* 1957–8)

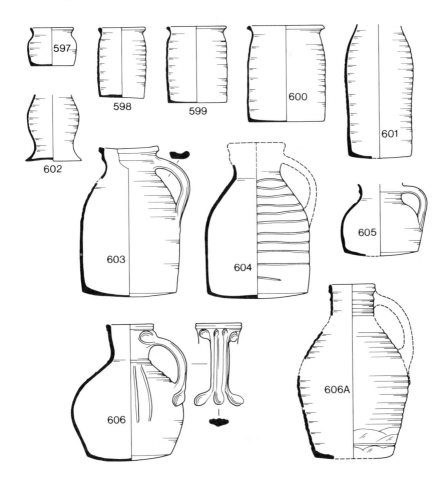

Much unstratified medieval and late medieval collected from abbey; recent excavations have yielded early pottery sequence.

White Gritty ware straight-sided cooking pots, similar to the 12th century types at Kelso Abbey, are preceded here by red gritty wares, of unknown date but similar to products of the Newcastle 12th century kiln.

Northern England (Fig. 120)

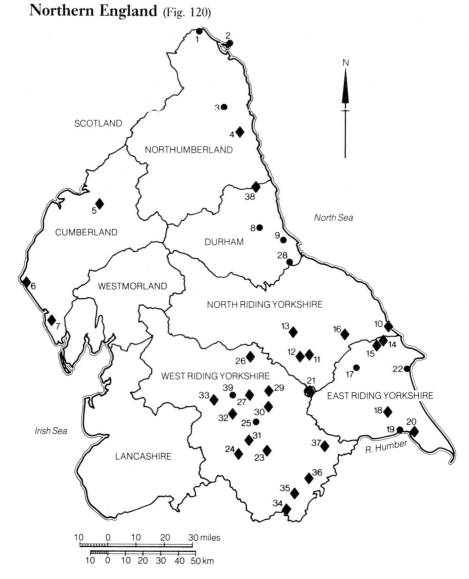

Fig. 120   Northern England, location map
1 Berwick upon Tweed, 2 Lindisfarne, 3 Edlingham, 4 Eshott, 5 Carlisle, 6 St Bees,
7 Waberthwaite, 8 Durham, 9 Hart, 10 Scarborough, 11 Brandsby, 12 Crayke, 13
Thirlby, 14 Staxton, 15 Potter Brompton, 16 Pickering, 17 Wharram Percy, 18
Beverley, 19 Hull, 20 Hedon, 21 York, 22 Bridlington, 23 Sandal Castle, 24 Upper
Heaton, 25 Kirkstall Abbey, 26 Winksley, 27 Follifoot, 28 Yarm, 29 Knaresborough,
30 Thorner, 31 Potter Newton, 32 Baildon, 33 Brunthwaite, 34 Rawmarsh, 35
Conisborough, 36 Doncaster, 37 Cowick, 38 Newcastle, 39 Otley.

1. Cumbria

a. Carlisle (Jarrett and Edwards 1964; Jope and Hodges 1955; Taylor forthcoming): Figs. 121–3

(i) *Production site*

Castle Street – wasters associated with burning thought to be possible production site. Occasional potter names could be metal rather than earthenware potters.

(ii) *Pottery*

Castle Street wasters in hard, sandy grey wares; wheel-thrown glazed jugs.

Major urban excavated sequences in the Lanes and at Blackfriars Street.

Main early wares – hard, gritty fabrics with oxidized surfaces. Sand possibly deliberately added, but igneous inclusions and feldspar naturally occurring in clay. Forms mainly cooking pots with slightly rounded profiles, flat and sagging bases. Bowls and spouted pitchers uncommon. Large baggy jugs with splashed glaze. Dated to 12th–early 13th century on stratigraphic grounds.

Small number of sherds in quartz-based fabric, petrologically different to gritty wares above, occur as everted or flared rim cooking pots. These potentially earlier, perhaps first half 12th century.

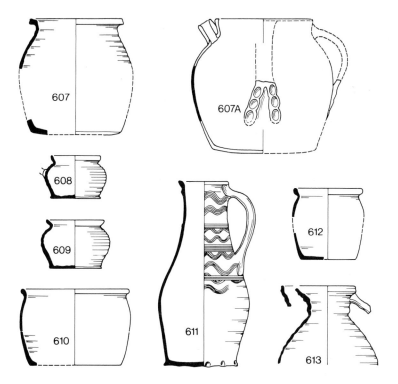

Fig. 121 CUMBERLAND

Carlisle: 607–13, gritty wares, 12th–14th cent. (After Jope and Hodges 1955; Taylor forthcoming)

Fig. 122   CUMBERLAND
Carlisle: Gritty ware, ht. 30.3cm., 13th cent. (Photo: Carlisle Museum and Art Gallery)

Fig. 123   CUMBERLAND
Carlisle: sandy reduced ware, ht. 30.6cm., 13th–14th cent. (Photo: Carlisle Museum and Art Gallery)

Later fabrics essentially sandy in slightly oxidized or grey fabrics; glazed wheel-thrown jugs, usually plain but with some combed wavy lines; some anthropomorphic bearded jugs; 13th–14th century.

b. *Waberthwaite* (Cherry 1984)

Production site
Large number of wasters recovered from sides of stream.

c. *St Bees*

Production site
Unpublished documentary reference to the king having pots made for him at St Bees in 1307.

2. Lancashire

a. *Ellel parish* (White A.J. 1977)

Production site

13th century references to personal and place names suggest the presence of earthenware potters.

3. Northumberland

a. *Newcastle upon Tyne* (Ellison 1981; Dodds and O'Brien 1984; C. O'Brien and L. Bown, pers. comm.): Fig. 124

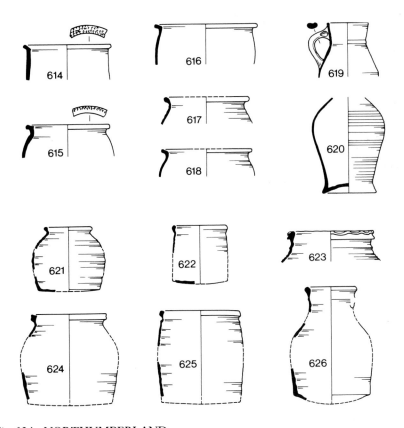

Fig. 124 NORTHUMBERLAND
Newcastle: 614–16, Dog Bank/Broad Garth kiln products, *c.* mid 12th century. 617, Oxidized Gritty ware, late 13th/early 14th cent. 618–19, Buff/White ware, 13th–14th cent. 620, Reduced Greenware, Type 2, first half of 13th cent. (After Ellison 1981; unpublished drawings by P. Irving).
Berwick upon Tweed: 621–4, Type 2. 625–6, Type 1. All late 12th–late 13th/early 14th cent. (After Moorhouse 1982)

(i) *Production site*

At Dog Bank/Broad Garth, on edge of medieval town, possibly on original river bank, wood-fired kiln excavated; two flues, though not directly opposed to each other as is usual in Type 2 kilns; central pedestal. Archaeomagnetically dated to *c.* mid 12th century.

(ii) *Pottery*

Kiln products gritty oxidized white to pinkish-buff fabric in Northern Gritty tradition, unglazed; forms mainly cooking pots, some bowls; some decorated with rouletting on the rim.

Other main fabric types, from Castle ditch where sequence starts first half of 13th century:

Oxidized Gritty wares, quartz-gritted orange/buff fabrics, usually with dark grey core; forms – mainly cooking pots, few jugs with splashed green glaze. Source unknown, probably local; date range 13th century.

Reduced Greenwares, Types 1 and 2 – black or dark grey gritty green-glazed fabrics, sometimes with whitish or buff surfaces, very similar to Oxidized Gritty wares but reduced. Type 3 – mid to light grey ware, moderately or sparsely quartz-gritted, green-glazed, sometimes with whitish or buff surfaces. Forms – mainly jugs; date range – 13th–early 14th century.

Buff/White wares – off-white or pale grey to pink fabrics, with black inclusions, probably iron, and quartz grits, ranging from fairly soft to vitrified. Some jugs have light red slip; glaze varies from yellow to green, or purplish on vitrified examples. Forms – mainly cooking pots, jugs, few large storage vessels; little decoration. Source unknown, probably local; some of the vitrified examples are near-wasters, and examples of wasters are known from elsewhere in the town. Date range 13th–14th century, dominant type in early-mid 14th century, residual from early 15th century.

Regional imports include much Scarborough ware.

b. Eshott (Dixon 1981)

(i) *Production site*

Remains of a kiln, probably a clamp kiln, and two clay-pits, in area of a medieval village; kiln archaeomagnetically dated to *c.* mid-late 12th century.

(ii) *Pottery*

Orange gritty and sandy wares, often with dark grey core; forms – unglazed cooking pots, splashed-glazed rod-handled jugs, some bowls. Decoration includes stamps, rouletting and combing.

c. Berwick upon Tweed (Moorhouse 1982): Fig. 124

Stratified sequence from Oil Mill Lane site within the medieval town, dated by pottery.

Main local fabrics:

Type 1 – hard-fired light brown to pink pimply fabric with grey core, smooth surfaces, light olive glaze. Forms – mainly jugs, occasional cooking pots. Decoration rare, includes self-coloured applied pellets and vertical strips, brown vertical strips, one face-mask. Source probably local. Date range *c.* late 12th–late 13th/early 14th century.

Type 2 – dull white to buff lumpy unglazed fabric, forms mainly cooking pots. Probably local. Date range *c.* late 12th–late 13th/early 14th century.

Imports include much Scarborough ware, also other Yorkshire types and Grimston-type ware.

d. Lindisfarne (Bown 1985)

Excavation of a small area within Holy Island village; some disturbance of the stratigraphy, and much of the medieval pottery is residual.

Fabric 3, Tweed Valley ware, common. Very pale buff quartz-tempered wheel-thrown fabric with powdery external surfaces produced by a thin brushed-on slip. Mostly cooking pots, rounded and straight-sided; occasional jug and dish. Source unknown; probably part of the Scottish White Gritty ware tradition. Date range *c.* late 12th–13th century.

Fabrics 8a and 8b, Colstoun-type ware, fairly common. Pink-buff to laminated streaky quartz-tempered fabrics, glazed jugs and unglazed cooking pots. Source not known; date probably 13th century.

Pottery types of lesser importance: Fabric 5, Kelso-type pottery, white quartz-gritted cooking pots similar to those from Kelso Abbey; Fabric 7, possibly local to the Tweed Valley, cooking pots in buff to pinkish-white fabric with abundant fine quartz inclusions; Fabrics 9a and 9b, Buff White ware cooking pots and jugs in fabric similar to that at Newcastle, late 13th–early 14th century. Regional imports include much Scarborough ware.

e. Edlingham Castle (Bown forthcoming)

Excavations at castle; earliest pottery of *c.* early 13th century date.

Several local gritty fabrics from a similar boulder clay source predominate in the earlier levels; oxidized light reddish brown, yellow or green glazes. A1 – early 13th–15th century; A2, A7, A8 – late 13th–early 16th century. Forms – cooking pots, jugs, jars, dripping dishes; decoration includes zones of white slip and brown iron staining. Some wasters in A2 fabric.

Minor wares, possibly local, include A6, buff fabric with quartz inclusions, olive glaze; forms – jugs, jars; date range 13th century.

Regional types include Reduced Greenwares, B9; Type 1 – gritty dark grey fabric, sometimes oxidized, olive green glaze. Forms – jugs, large storage vessels, cisterns; equivalent to Type 4 Greenware at Newcastle. Date range *c.* late 13th/early 14th century–16th century.

Minor regional fabrics include white or buff gritty and sandy fabrics (B2 and B3), occasional yellow or green glaze splashes; forms mainly cooking pots; date range 13th–15th century. Also B8, fine brownish pink micaceous fabric with green or yellow/orange glaze; forms – mainly jugs; probably related to Reduced Greenware Types 1 and 2 but oxidized; date range *c.* late 13th–16th century.

4. Co. Durham

a. Durham (Addis 1980; Carver 1974): Fig. 125

Type 16, buff quartz-gritted fabrics, sometimes with splashed glazes; forms mainly cooking pots, jugs. Date range *c.* 13th–early 14th century.

Types 13, 14, 15 – pink gritty fabrics with quartz inclusions, reduced grey core; forms – cooking pots, jugs. Present in 13th century but full date range not known.

Fig. 125   CO. DURHAM
Durham: 627, Type 14. 628, Type 17. 629, Type 16. All mid 13th cent. (After Addis 1980)
Hart Manor: 630–4, Ware 7(ii), later 12th–early 13th cent. 635, Ware 7(i), later 12th–early 14th cent. 636, Ware 9, *c.* 13th cent. 637–9, Hartlepool-type ware, late 13th–14th cent. 640, Ware 8(iii), *c.* 13th cent. (After Addis 1976)

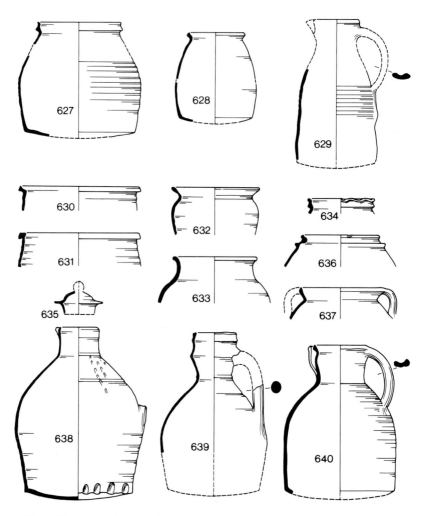

Type 17, white-gritted oxidized fabric, with quartz inclusions; forms include jugs and cooking pots. Present in 13th century but full date range not known.

Type 11, green-glazed reduced wares – dark grey to buff or red smooth or sandy fabrics, olive glaze. Forms mainly jugs and cisterns, also dripping dishes. Little decoration apart from some thumbing and incising, though some stamped decoration and applied brown strips found on 14th century jugs. Date range *c.* 1300–1550.

b. Hart (Addis 1976): Fig. 125

Ware 7, buff gritty/sandy ware, with three fabric sub-groups, (i)–(iii); forms – mainly cooking pots, also green-glazed jugs, often with copper colourant in the glaze, lids. Decoration includes applied brown scales, comb-stabbing. Source unknown, perhaps local. Date range mainly *c.* later 12th–early 14th century.

Ware 8, pink gritty ware, with 2 fabric subgroups, (i) and (ii); Ware 8(iii) is a glazed version of 8(i). Forms – mainly cooking pots, some jugs. Source unknown, perhaps local. Date range mainly *c.* later 12th–early 14th century.

Ware 9, pinkish orange sandy ware; forms include cooking pots.

Ware 14, Hartlepool-type ware – oxidized fine orange ware, surfaces often daubed with patches of red slip; glaze usually yellow with brown striations or patches over red-slipped areas, occasional use of copper colourant, particularly on applied scales. Forms – mainly jugs, single-handled (though large three-handled jugs known from Hartlepool), also two-handled cooking pots/jars. Decoration mainly applied copper-green scales, occasional face-masks. Within the 'Tees Valley ware' tradition (Barrett 1985; Patterson 1985). Date range mainly late 13th–early 15th century, though some present in earlier 13th century.

Regional imports include Scarborough ware.

5. Yorkshire, North Riding

a. Scarborough (Rutter J.C. 1961; Farmer 1979; Farmer and Farmer 1982): Figs. 126–8; see also Fig. 38

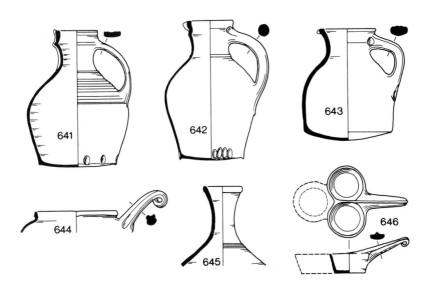

Fig. 126 YORKSHIRE, NORTH RIDING
Scarborough: 641–3, Scarborough ware. 644, Scarborough ware from Aberdeen. 645–6, Scarborough ware from Rievaulx Abbey. All 13th–14th cent. (After Drummond forthcoming; Murray J.C. 1982; Rutter J.G. 1961)

Fig. 127 YORKSHIRE, NORTH RIDING
Scarborough: 647, Scarborough ware from Dartford. 648, Scarborough ware from Bruges. 649, Scarborough ware from Richmond. 650, Scarborough ware from Nottingham. 651, Scarborough ware from Seaford. All 13th–14th cent. (After Coppack 1980b; Dunning 1968; 1973)

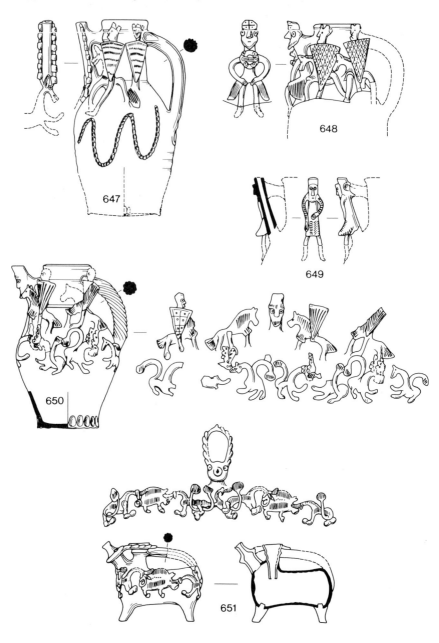

Fig. 128   YORKSHIRE, NORTH RIDING
Scarborough: 652, 656, 672, Scarborough ware from King's Lynn. 653–4, 660–2,
Scarborough ware from Aberdeen. 655, Scarborough ware from Groningen. 657–8,
Scarborough ware from York. 659, Scarborough ware from Flixton. All 13th–14th
cent. (After Brewster 1952; Brooks C.M. 1987; Clarke and Carter 1977; Dunning
1968; Murray J.C. 1982; York Archaeological Trust, unpublished material)

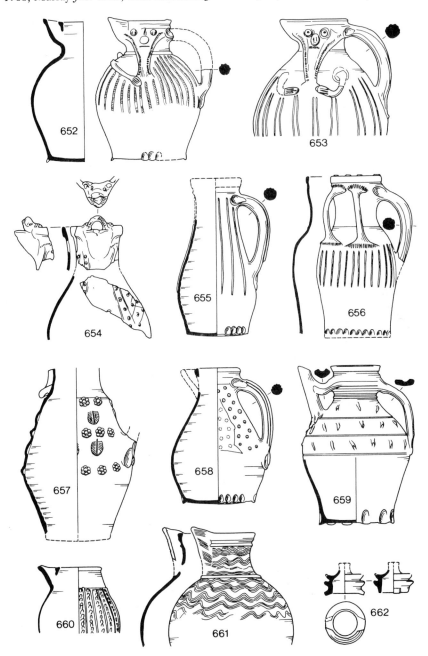

(i) *Production site*

Several kilns (*c.* 9) found in Castle Road area, just within the gate of the medieval town, in 19th century and more recently; also pits probably connected with clay preparation. Kilns dated on stratigraphic and pottery grounds to *c.* mid 12th–mid 14th century. Some kilns at least appear to have been of Type 1; latest kilns appear to have had brick superstructures. Coal was used, but not as the sole fuel.

(ii) *Pottery*

Kiln products all high-quality glazed wares; coarse ware cooking pots for town supplied by Staxton/Potter Brompton kilns.

Phase I – soft sandy pinkish-red fabric; Phase II – hard smooth pinkish-buff to off-white fabric with sandy inclusions. Glaze on both fabrics usually thick glossy even mid to dark green with copper colourant; sometimes yellow glaze in combination with brown pellet decoration. Phase I clay sometimes used for decorative details on Phase II vessels. Phase I fabric dated to *c.* mid or later 12th–early 13th century; Phase II fabric to *c.* early 13th–mid 14th century. Forms – mainly jugs, with pinched, bridge or tubular spouts, also lids, aquamaniles, bowls, bottles, pipkins, condiment dishes, lamps. Decoration includes applied strips, scales and pellets, stamped pushed-out bosses, anthropomorphic and zoomorphic motifs such as bearded face-masks, animals modelled in relief and free-standing modelled knights, sometimes mounted, on 'knight jugs'.

Scarborough ware was exported widely, particularly along the eastern seaboard and across the North Sea.

b. *Thirlby* (Ellis *et al.* n.d.): Fig. 129

(i) *Production site*

Traces of four kilns found; small squares of baked clay used as parting sherds during firing. Dated on pottery typology to *c.* early/mid 13th century.

(ii) *Pottery*

White or buff to pink wheel-thrown sandy fabric; forms – mainly cooking pots, very thin-walled, some jugs of 'splashed ware' form with flared necks, vertical runs or 'stripes' of yellow glaze. Decoration restricted to thumbing of cooking pot rims; one jug has horizontal incised lines and wavy combing.

c. *Brandsby* (Le Patourel 1979a; Webster and Cherry 1972: 208; 1973: 185; Wilson and Moorhouse 1971: 178): Figs. 129–30

(i) *Production site*

Waster tips from a series of superimposed kilns, at western end of village; industry dated on typological grounds to mid 13th–mid 14th century. Documentary evidence for pottery industry from 14th–16th centuries (Le Patourel 1968: 124).

(ii) *Pottery*

Pale buff or pinkish lightly gritted wheel-thrown fabric with small quartz inclusions, glaze light to mid green with dark green copper speckles. Forms – mainly jugs, including baluster jugs, also cooking pots, bowls, condiment dishes. Decoration includes rouletting, combing, applied strips and pellets, stamps, occasional anthropomorphic ornament and seal motifs similar to those on York Glazed ware, but with stag on field of pellets.

d. *Crayke* (K. Adams pers. comm.)

Fig. 129 YORKSHIRE, NORTH RIDING
Thirlby: 663–5, Thirlby ware from Rievaulx Abbey, *c.* 13th cent. (After Drummond forthcoming)
Brandsby: 666–7, Brandsby ware from Wharram Percy. 668–74, Brandsby-type ware from York. All mid 13th–14th cent. (After Brooks C.M. 1987; Holdsworth 1978; Le Patourel 1972; 1979a)

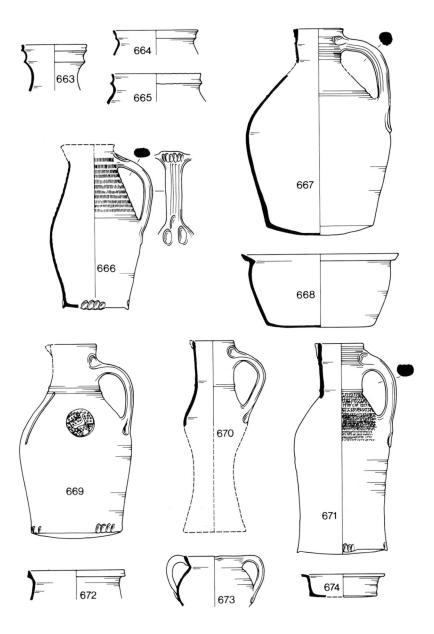

Fig. 130 YORKSHIRE, NORTH RIDING
Brandsby: Brandsby-type ware baluster jug from York, late 13th–early 14th cent.; ht. 40 cm. (Photo: Yorkshire Museum)

(i) *Production site*
Wasters of 13th–14th century type found.
(ii) *Pottery*
Red sandy fabric, sometimes buff, varying from lightly gritted to gritty in texture; forms – cooking pots, jugs.

e. *Pickering* (Hayes 1978)

Production site
Documentary reference to a potter in 1301.

f. *Skelton* (Le Patourel 1968: 113)

Production site
Documentary reference to a potter in 1301.

g. *York* (Brooks C.M. 1987; Holdsworth 1978): Figs. 131–4

Fig. 131 YORKSHIRE, NORTH RIDING
York: 675–7, Gritty ware, 12th–early 13th cent. 678–81, Splashed ware, 12th–early 13th cent. 682–5, 687–9, York Glazed ware, 13th cent. 686, York Glazed ware from Lincoln, 13th cent. (After Coppack 1973; Holdsworth 1978; Le Patourel 1972; York Archaeological Trust, unpublished material)

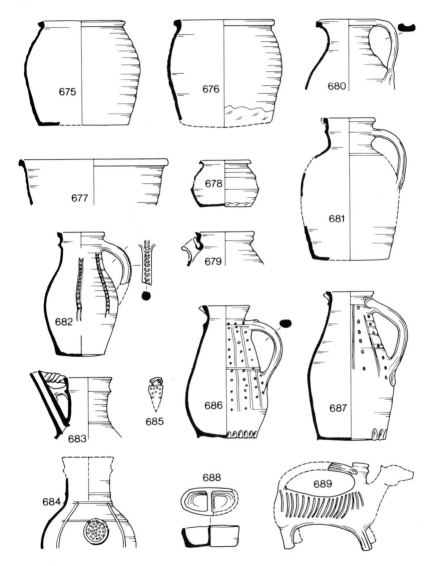

(i) *Production site*
Part of possible pottery kiln excavated (Le Patourel 1979a: 88)
(ii) *Pottery*
Pottery from possible kiln apparently of developed splashed ware type.

Fig. 132   YORKSHIRE, NORTH RIDING
York: Splashed ware jug, 12th cent.; ht. 27.5 cm. (Photo Yorkshire Museum)

Medieval sequences from several sites. Gritty and splashed wares continue into first half of 13th century, probably becoming residual after that.

York Glazed ware ('York White ware') – usually white or off-white sandy wheel-thrown fabric, sometimes with buff surfaces, glaze mid-green with dark green copper speckles, dark green or yellow; some jugs are bichrome, having yellow glaze on one side and green on the other. Forms – mostly jugs, some with tubular spouts, some lids, cooking pots, condiment dishes, aquamaniles. Many jugs are highly decorated; decoration includes vertical combing, often combined with applied brown or green pellets on yellow glaze, scales, strips, occasional zoomorphic and anthropomorphic motifs (including knight jugs). Most distinctive decoration is applied clay pads stamped with seals, sometimes consisting of an infill of pellets or strips and pellets, sometimes of heraldic motifs, e.g. bird, animal or complex scene, and often has traces of an inscription, e.g. 'sigillum', and 'Tomas me fecit', lettering sometimes being reversed; seals are considered to be versions of the de Quincy arms (Le Patourel 1979a: 88), and are present from the early 13th century on. Some jugs have 'wings' or 'ears' at the top of rod handles, in imitation of Rouen ware. Source unknown; probably fairly local, but white-firing clays are not known within the city itself. Date range *c.* late 12th–13th century.

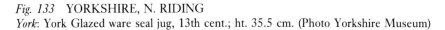

Fig. 133   YORKSHIRE, N. RIDING
York: York Glazed ware seal jug, 13th cent.; ht. 35.5 cm. (Photo Yorkshire Museum)

Brandsby-type ware, buff to pink wheel-thrown fabric with fine quartz inclusions, glaze pale to mid green with darker copper speckles. Forms – mainly jugs, also bowls, cooking pots, condiment dishes. Decoration includes rouletting, combing, applied strips and pellets, stamps, and occasional seal stamps similar to those on York glazed ware, with stag motif; vessels tend to be much less ornate than York glazed ware. Much probably comes from the known source at Brandsby, but not all features can be matched there. Date range begins *c.* mid 13th century, becomes dominant pottery type in late 13th–14th century, probably ending by late 14th century.

Humber ware, fine or sandy red to reddish brown wheel-thrown fabric, often reduced dark grey internally, olive green glaze often with brown margins. Forms mainly

Fig. 134   YORKSHIRE, NORTH RIDING

York: detail of seal on York Glazed ware seal jug, 13th cent. (Photo Yorkshire Museum)

jugs, cooking pots, drinking jugs. Decoration usually confined to horizontal grooves on jug shoulders, occasional stamped motifs and anthropomorphic ornament. Source – probably most comes from West Cowick. Date range from later 13th century on, in small quantities until later 14th century.

Other wares occurring in very small quantities are light-coloured and reddish sandy fabrics of unknown origin; some may be regional imports.

h. Yarm (Barrett 1985; Patterson 1985)

Two sites within the town.

Predominant medieval type is Tees Valley ware (a tradition which includes Hartlepool-type ware), comprising several related fabrics, wares 1–5. Most common is Tees Valley ware 1, oxidized pink to red-orange gritty fabric with fairly smooth surfaces, often with darker pink slip; thick greenish-brown or pale green to orange-brown and yellow-brown glaze, often speckled or striped. Ware 2 is finer, often with copper colourant in the glaze; products include jugs with face-masks; this may be from a more specialized production centre, or late in the Tees Valley ware sequence. Forms include jugs, cooking pots, jars, bowls. Decoration includes applied pellets, combing, incised wavy lines, thumbing of cooking pot rims. Source not known; possibly fairly local. Date range from *c.* later 12th century on.

Other minor wares include a partially-reduced grey to orange sandy ware with grey or black core, reduced green glaze, present from later 12th century on.

6. Yorkshire, East Riding

a. Staxton (Brewster 1958; Le Patourel 1979a): Fig. 135

(i) *Production site*
Four 'pit-kilns' excavated.

(ii) *Pottery*
Buff or grey to red coarse sandy fabric with occasional limestone inclusions, often with grey core; usually wheel-thrown but some hand-made (although it has recently been suggested that most are coil-built and wheel-finished – Hayfield 1980: 31). Forms – mainly cooking pots, shallow broad-based cooking pots ('peat pots'), bowls, also pipkins, lids, curfews. Decoration restricted to thumbing on rims, applied thumbed strips, occasional wavy incised lines. Date range probably *c.* 12th-mid 15th century.

b. Potter Brompton (Brewster 1958)

(i) *Production site*
Five 'pit-kilns', using peat as fuel, excavated at Potter Hill Farm. 'Potter' prefix first occurs in 1285, though there is indirect evidence for potting *c.* 1250 (Earnshaw and Watkins 1984: 35).

(ii) *Pottery*
Reddish coarse sandy fabric in Staxton ware tradition; for forms, see Staxton. Date range probably *c.* 12th–mid 15th century.

c. Beverley (Hayfield 1985; Watkins forthcoming a; Watkins and Williams 1983): Figs. 135–6

(i) *Production site*
'Potter' street names present between 13th and 16th centuries, all in eastern suburb of the town in an area where brick and tile makers were also established. Beverley 2 (Orangeware) wasters reported to have been found in the eastern suburbs off Grovehill Road, near the find spot of the Beverley 1 wasters.

(ii) *Pottery*
Beverley 1 ware in later 12th century comprises cooking pots and jugs; jugs sometimes decorated with horizontal wavy combing. Transition from Beverley 1 in late 12th century to Beverley 2, Orangeware (Hayfield's OB fabric), which becomes dominant ware – fine sandy orange fabric with suspension glazes, olive green to brownish, or sometimes with copper added. Forms mainly jugs, also curfews, pipkins, bowls, dripping dishes, cisterns. Decoration includes applied strips and pellets from late 12th century on, 'raspberry' and 'wheatear' stamps on pushed-out bosses in late 13th/early 14th century. Fabric and decorative techniques very similar to Low Countries highly decorated wares.

Reduced Chalky ware and small quantities of York Lightly Gritted and Northern

Fig. 135   YORKSHIRE, EAST RIDING

Staxton: 690, Staxton ware. 691–7, Staxton ware from Wharram Percy. (After Brewster 1952; Le Patourel 1979a).

Beverley: 698–701, Beverley 1 ware, mid to late 12th cent. 702–3 Beverley type 2 Orangeware from Hull, later 13th cent. (After Hayfield 1985; Watkins and Williams 1983; Watkins forthcoming b)

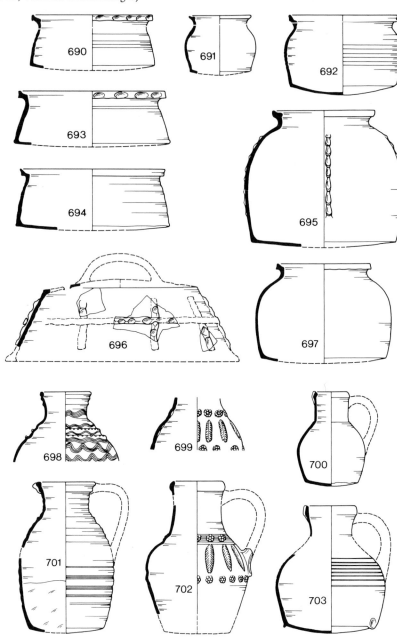

Fig. 136 YORKSHIRE, EAST RIDING
Beverley: 704–13, Beverley type 2 Orangeware from Hull, late 13th–mid 14th cent.
(After Watkins forthcoming b)

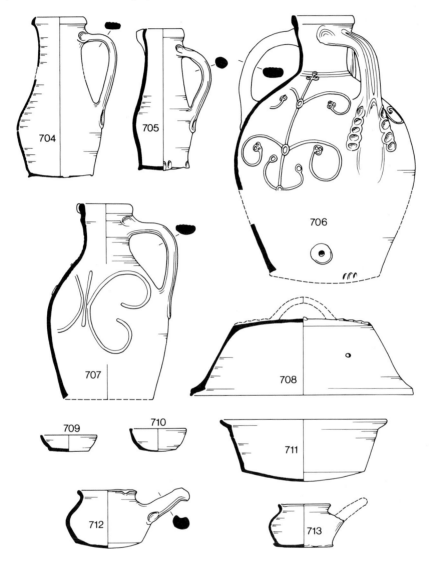

Gritty wares continue to end of 12th century; replaced by Staxton/Potter Brompton wares in 13th century. Humber ware present in small quantities from later 13th century.

d. Hedon (Hayfield and Slater 1984): Figs. 137–8

Fig. 137 YORKSHIRE, EAST RIDING
Hedon: 714–15, coarse sand-tempered fabric CH2, 716–21, coarse sand-tempered fabric CH1. 722, coarse sand-tempered fabric CH3; 723–4, fine sand-tempered fabric FH3. 725–6, fine sand-tempered fabric FH1. 727–30, fine sand-tempered fabric FH2. 714–15, 721, 725–9, second half of 12th cent.; 717–30, 722–4, 730, 13th–early 14th cent. (After Hayfield and Slater 1984)

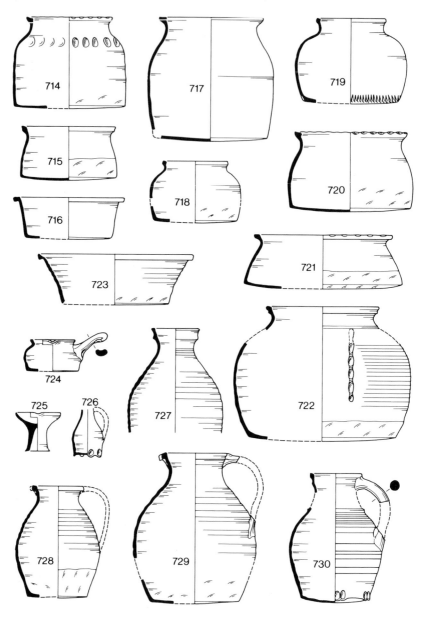

Fig. 138 YORKSHIRE, EAST RIDING
Hedon: 731–2, fine sand-tempered fabric FH2. 733–4, fine sand-tempered fabric
FH3. 735, Humber ware. 731–4, 13th cent.; 735, late 13th/early 14th cent. (After
Hayfield and Slater 1984)
Hull: 736–8, 740–1, Humber ware. 739, Heavily Gritted Humber ware. 736, 740–1,
later 13th cent.; 739, late 13th/early 14th cent.; 737–8, early/mid 14th cent. (After
Watkins forthcoming b)

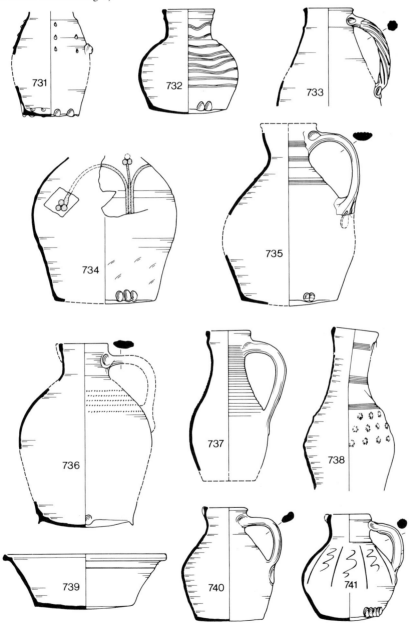

(i) *Production site*

A number of wasters and partly wasted sherds in CH1 and FH2 fabrics suggest local production. Potters mentioned in documents, working just outside the town; 13th century reference to land 'where the potters used to dwell', but continuation of potter place-names in this area suggests production may have continued here.

(ii) *Pottery*

Excavated area continued in occupation only until the later 14th century.

Coarse sand-tempered fabrics continue to 14th century. Forms now include a shallow broad-based cooking pot or 'peat pot'; occasional jugs are also made. Decoration restricted to shoulder thumbing, vertical thumbed strips, thumbing on rims.

Finely sand-tempered fabrics FH2, 3 and 5 continue to 14th century; wheel-thrown, with suspension glazes. Forms mostly jugs, also pipkins, bowls, lamps, cruets; one later 12th century round-based pipkin clearly copying imported continental 'Blue-grey' ladles. Decoration first occurs after *c.* 1150, but not common until 13th century; includes horizontal grooves, wavy combing, applied strip and scale decoration, occasional 'wheatear' and 'raspberry' stamps on pushed-out bosses, one example of a face-mask.

Humber wares present from the mid 13th century on, in increasing quantities.

e. *Hull* (Armstrong 1977; 1980; Hayfield 1985; Watkins forthcoming b): Fig. 138

Several sites within the town; earliest levels later 13th century, on historical grounds.

Orangeware – smooth orange wheel-thrown fabric, copper or olive green to orange-brown glazes. Forms mainly jugs, also pipkins, bowls, dripping pans, cisterns, curfews, jars, small bowls/cups, condiment dishes. Decoration common; includes applied self-coloured or white strips, brown pellets, pushed-out bosses with 'raspberry' and 'wheatear' stamps, and one possible example of a knight jug. Source probably Beverley. Fairly common from later 13th to mid 14th century, probably becoming residual during second half of 14th century.

Coarse sandy ware in Staxton/Potter Brompton tradition, but most vessels differ slightly in fabric; coarse sandy grey-buff, pinkish brown or orange fabric with grey core. Forms – cooking pots, bowls, curfews. Source unknown; mainly in late 13th–14th century levels.

Humber ware – hard fine sand-tempered orange to red fabric, often with reduced grey or black core and internal surfaces; a few examples more heavily gritted; glaze mostly olive green, though during 14th century a small proportion of Humber ware has copper colourant. Forms – mostly jugs; decoration usually limited to bands of horizontal grooving on shoulder and/or neck; less common are wavy combing, applied strips and pads, shoulder rouletting, ring-and-dot stamps, stamps on pushed-out bosses, anthropomorphic motifs. Source probably West Cowick. Present in small quantities from late 13th century, becoming most common pottery type during 14th century.

Regional imports include Brandsby and York White wares. Continental imports common.

f. *Bridlington* (Earnshaw and Watkins 1984)

Staxton/Potter Brompton ware, coarse sandy buff to brown fabrics; forms mostly cooking pots, bowls, 'peat pots', also curfews.

Scarborough Gritty ware, buff to white sandy cooking pots and jugs, present; presumably residual after early 13th century.

Scarborough ware, mostly Phase II, is the major fineware fabric.

Humber ware present, some Cowick-type, some with chalk inclusions not found in pottery from the known kiln sites.

Minor wares include Beverley Orangeware and Brandsby ware.

g. *Wharram Percy* (Le Patourel 1979a)

Pimply ware ('Northern Gritty ware') – off-white to buff quartz-gritted wheel-thrown fabric; forms – mainly cooking pots, also bowls. Source unknown. Common in 12th–early 13th century.

Splashed ware – a range of sandy wheel-thrown fabrics with splashed glaze; forms include spouted pitchers, jugs; source unknown. Date range *c.* 12th century.

Staxton ware – grey-brown to reddish coarse sandy fabric, usually wheel-thrown. Forms – cooking pots, 'peat pots', bowls, also pipkins, curfews. Decoration includes thumbing, especially on rims, combing, occasional thumbed strips. Sources – Staxton, Potter Brompton. Date range *c.* later 12th-mid 15th century.

Other fabrics include an early 13th century red ware possibly related to Doncaster Hallgate wares; York White wares, late 12th-13th century; Brandsby ware, mid 13th-mid 14th century; Scarborough ware, late 12th-14th century; Humber ware and Hambleton ware in small quantities from second half of 13th century.

7. Yorkshire, West Riding

a. *Doncaster* (Buckland *et al.* 1979; Hayfield 1985): Figs. 139–40

(i) *Production sites*

Hallgate – a kiln, probably of Type 2a, and traces of another probable kiln nearby, excavated together with three pits; just outside medieval town. Wasters incorporated in the kiln walls suggest earlier production on the site. Production in this area dated on pottery grounds to later 12th–end of 13th/early 14th century.

Cattle Market – wasters found; within medieval town, but in area probably marginal to main settlement. Date *c.* 14th century.

(ii) *Pottery*

Hallgate 'C' fabric (GD) – gritty orange to red fabric with haematite inclusions, often with dark grey to reddish-brown surfaces; very similar to earlier Market Place fabric. Suspension glazes. Forms – mostly cooking pots, some jugs, bowls, pipkins. Some wavy combing on cooking pot rims. Earliest of the Hallgate fabrics, apparently largely residual by time of main production of 'B' and 'A' wares; date range uncertain, *c.* later 12th century.

Hallgate 'B' fabric (WD) – white gritty fabric, often with buff surfaces, olive-green to yellow suspension glazes. Forms – mostly jugs, including tubular and bridge spouts, also cooking pots, bowls, pipkins, occasional aquamaniles. Jug decoration includes notched strips, combing, rouletting; cooking pot rims have thumbing and wavy combing. 'B' ware in production earlier than 'A' ware; probably later 12th century.

Hallgate 'A' fabric (FD) – hard orange or red wheel-thrown sandy fabric, sometimes reduced internally, more finely tempered than 'B' and 'C' wares. Olive to orange-brown suspension glazes. Forms – mostly jugs, with pinched, bridge or tubular

Fig. 139 YORKSHIRE, WEST RIDING
Doncaster: 742–6, Hallgate 'B' ware, *c.* second half of 12th cent. 747–51, Hallgate 'A' ware, 13th cent. (After Buckland *et al.* 1979; Hayfield 1985)

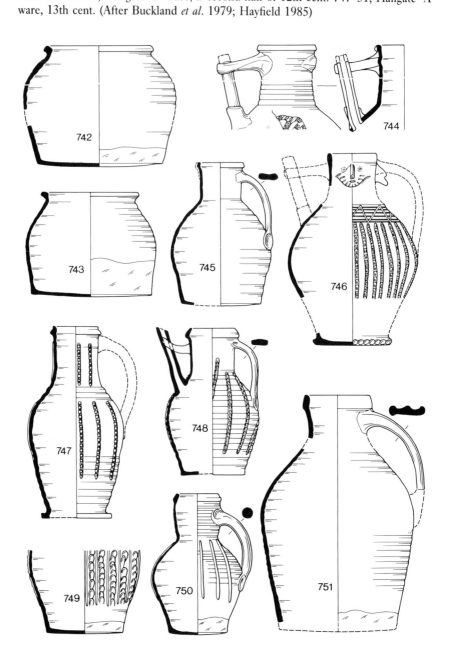

Fig. 140 YORKSHIRE, WEST RIDING
Doncaster: 752–5, 758–62, Hallgate 'A' ware, 13th cent. 756–7, FDC fabric (Cattle Market-type fabric), 13th cent. 763–4, Shelly ware SD1, 13th cent. (After Buckland *et al.* 1979; Hayfield 1985)

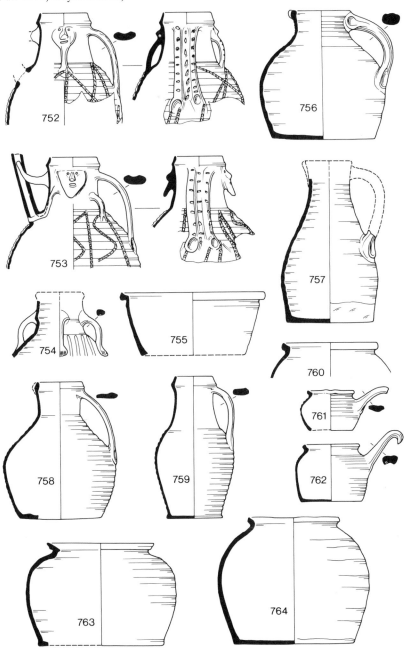

spouts, also cooking pots, bowls, pipkins, occasional cisterns, curfews, lamps. Decoration includes horizontal wavy combing, vertical applied comb-impressed strips, applied scales, and anthropomorphic ornament in the shape of face-mask jugs. Date range end of 12th-end of 13th century.

Cattle Market fabric (FDC) – red gritty fabric, similar to Hallgate 'C' (GD) though with no haematite grains; glaze often over an off-white slip. Forms – jugs, cooking pots, akin to Humber ware tradition. Date – on typological grounds, probably later than Hallgate, perhaps 14th century, although the fabric may occur earlier, in later 13th century, elsewhere in town.

Other main fabrics present in town excavations:

Harsh Shelly ware (SD1) cooking pots and occasional curfews present in 13th century.

Coal Measure fabrics, cream or white gritty fabrics, sometimes overfired to purplish, glaze yellow-green to orange or purple. Forms – cooking pots, bowls, jugs, pipkins. Sources – probably Firsby Hall, Rawmarsh. Date range – begins late 13th/early 14th century, or possibly slightly earlier.

b. *Winksley* (Bellamy and Le Patourel 1970; Le Patourel 1968: 123): Fig. 141

(i) *Production site*

Four kilns excavated, one of Type 2, the others multi-flued, and pits filled with wasters, daub and wedges of prepared potting clay. Dated on pottery grounds to *c.* mid 13th century. Documentary reference to potters in and just before 1233.

(ii) *Pottery*

Off-white to light buff hard thin sandy fabric, glaze olive green or greenish-yellow, occasionally brown or dark green. Forms – jugs, including some with tubular spouts, bowls, cooking pots, few aquamaniles. Decoration includes applied clay strips, pellets, scales, stamped pads, combing, simple and complex rouletting, and anthropomorphic motifs – knight jugs and face-jugs with beards. Rouletting considered to be in imitation of Low Countries decorated wares.

c. *Upper Heaton* (Manby 1965): Fig. 142

(i) *Production site*

Three Type 2 kilns excavated, together with waster heaps; probably brushwood-fired. Rural site, between hamlets of Upper Heaton and Colnebridge. 'Poter Heton' mentioned in 1314 document, referring either to Kirkheaton or Upper Heaton.

(ii) *Pottery*

Off-white to pink, light brown or light grey gritty fabric with rounded quartz and shale inclusions; some jugs are in a finer less gritty fabric; olive green glaze. Forms – mostly cooking pots, some jugs (a few with tubular spouts), bowls, pipkins, occasional dishes, skillets, cheese-presses, storage jars. Decoration includes occasional incised wavy lines, thumbed applied strips on cooking pots and jars. Jug decoration includes four broad vertical stripes of glaze; vertical stamped, rouletted or comb-stabbed strips, stamped pads, wavy combing; stamped decoration also found on one ornate skillet. Pottery dated on typological grounds to late 13th–early 14th century, but this dating may need to be revised as it is based on traditional chronology for introduction of features such as bridge and tubular spouts and pipkins, which now evidently begin much earlier, as at Doncaster Hallgate.

Fig. 141 YORKSHIRE, WEST RIDING
Winksley: 765–73, kiln products, 13th cent. (After Bellamy and Le Patourel 1970)

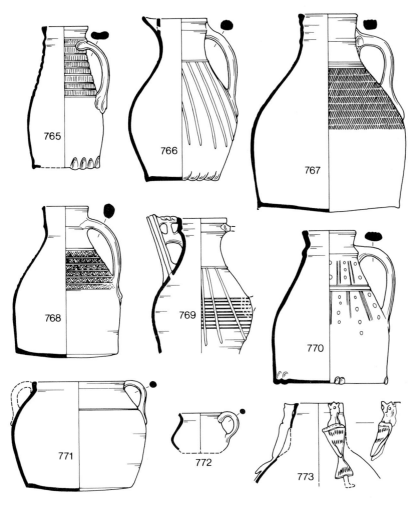

d. *West Cowick* (Le Patourel 1968; Wilson and Hurst 1964: 297); see Fig. 16 Type 3

(i) *Production site*

Documentary evidence of potters from 1320s on. Pottery wasters from many sites in the village; a series of superimposed kilns excavated adjacent to High Street. Lowest kiln disturbed; upper three were 6-flued Type 3 kilns, each rebuilt many times. Kilns dated from late 13th-late 15th century; archaeomagnetic date for one kiln, not the earliest one, of *c.* 1350 (Le Patourel 1979a: 92).

(ii) *Pottery*

Kilns producing Humber ware – red or orange fine sandy wheel-thrown fabric, often reduced grey internally, olive-green glaze (very occasionally with copper

Fig. 142 YORKSHIRE, WEST RIDING
Upper Heaton: 774–85, kiln products, late 13th–early 14th cent. (After Manby 1965)

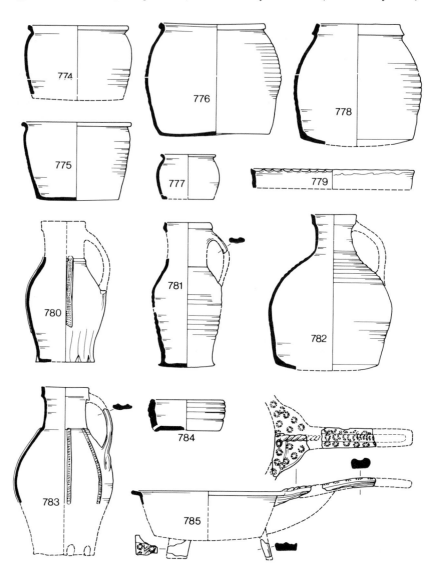

colourant). Forms include jugs, drinking jugs, cooking pots, bowls, cisterns, urinals, though date ranges of individual forms not known. Decoration on jugs from late 13th-14th century levels of kilns includes rouletting, 'raspberry' and fleur-de-lys stamps, anthropomorphic decoration and applied scroll and pellet work.

e. Potter Newton (Le Patourel 1968: 124)

Production site
'Potter' prefix recorded in 1285. Possible production of East Pennine Gritty ware (Le Patourel and Wood 1973: 137).

f. Thorner (Wilson and Hurst 1967: 318; Le Patourel 1968: 109; 1979a: 82)

Production site
Documentary evidence for potting. At least one pottery ceased in 1358 when clay payments lapsed; although 'Potter' and 'Potemen' surnames survived in the village for another century, it is not clear whether they practised potting. Probable production of Northern Gritty or Pimply ware in 13th century; remains of probable kiln and wasters found.

g. Conisbrough (Le Patourel 1968: 113, 115, 123)

Production site
Documentary evidence for potters from 1321 on.

h. Rawmarsh (Le Patourel 1968: 124)

Production site
Documentary evidence for potters from 13th-15th century.

i. Baildon (Wilson and Hurst 1965: 218; 1966: 218; Le Patourel 1967: 43; 1968: 124)

(i) *Production site*
Documentary evidence of production from 14th-16th century. Disturbed kiln (Kiln 3), probably of 13th/early 14th century date, found; pots stacked on gritstone slabs over a clay floor.
(ii) *Pottery*
Products in light gritty fabric, green or brown glaze; jugs and bowls; decoration includes incised wavy lines, stamps, thumbing.

j. Follifoot (Le Patourel 1967: 43; 1968: 124)

Production site
'Potters' prefix recorded in 1329. Wasters of 14th century type found, in same gritty fabric as 16th century kiln products.

k. Alverthorpe (Brears 1967: 3)

Production site
Potter mentioned in document of 1297, at village near later production centre of Wrenthorpe (Potovens).

l. Brunthwaite (Wilson and Hurst 1966: 218; Le Patourel 1967: 43)

Production site
Daub, kiln debris and much pottery found. Site producing East Pennine Gritty ware, probably in late 12th-early 13th century.

m. Other production sites (Le Patourel 1968: 126)

Other sites in the West Riding for which there is documentary evidence for production, of unspecified medieval date: Altofts, Askwith, Bramham, Bretton, Ecclesfield, Long Marston, Loversall, Oulton, Pontefract, Ripley, Roundhay, Ryther, Silsden, Tankersley, Thorpe, Wetherby.

n. Sandal Castle (Moorhouse 1983b; Brears 1967. 3): Fig. 143

(i) *Production site*

Pottery production at and near Sandal indicated by documentary references to potters or place-names: 'Le Kilngrenes' at Sandal in 1314, 'Le Pottargrenedales' in Liversedge township in the 13th century, and a potter in 1218/19 at Emley township.

(ii) *Pottery*

Pottery types 1a, 2b, 3c, 4c Pimply ware, 6e Shelly ware, continue into 13th century. Other main fabrics:

Type 7c, Northern Gritty ware – red to brown thick-bodied wheel-thrown fabric with large protruding angular inclusions, grey core, olive green glaze. Forms – mainly cooking pots, jugs, also curfews, few bowls. Decoration includes white applied clay strips and discs, combined with dot-and-ring stamps and comb impressions, vertical combing. Date range *c.* mid 12th-15th century; this is the main coarse ware until early 15th century.

Type 14i – white to light pink lumpy wheel-thrown fabric with medium to large inclusions protruding, sometimes with light grey core; light apple-green glaze sometimes mottled with iron spots. Forms – mainly jugs, occasional dripping dishes. Decoration – vertical rouletted or comb-stabbed strips, red or self-coloured applied decoration, thumbed strips, pellets. Date range *c.* mid 12th-mid 13th century.

Type 10f, Hallgate-type ware – sandy reddish-brown fabric, brown to olive green glaze. Forms – jugs, pipkins. Decoration – vertical comb-stabbed self-coloured applied strips; occasional self-coloured pellets. Source – probably Hallgate, Doncaster, or a production centre in the same tradition. Date range *c.* mid 12th-13th century.

Humber ware, Types 25f, 27f, 29f – fine-grained sandy red or grey fabric, olive green glaze. Forms – mainly jugs, drinking jugs. Source – probably some at least from West Cowick. Occurs in small quantities from *c.* mid 13th century on.

Regional imports include Staxton ware, York Fine ware (= York White ware), Yorkshire Red ware (= Beverley Orangeware); also occasional vessels from Oxfordshire, West Sussex and Grimston, probably brought in by peripatetic manorial household.

o. Knaresborough (Le Patourel 1966a; 1968: 110; Waterman 1953)

(i) *Production site*

Evidence for potters working in Knaresborough Forest.

(ii) *Pottery*

Pottery from limited excavations at Knaresborough Castle.

Northern Gritty ware, cooking pots and some bowls, common in 12th-early 13th century.

Fabric 1 – local gritty red or buff fabric, often with grey core, yellowish-green glaze. Forms – cooking pots, jugs; decoration includes rouletting, applied brown strips. Present in a late 13th/early 14th century group.

Fig. 143 YORKSHIRE, WEST RIDING
Sandal Castle: 786, Type 1a. 787–90, Type 2b. 791–5, Pimply ware. 796–9, Northern
Gritty ware. 800, Type 14i. 790–2, 794, 799, 12th–early 13th cent.; 787–9, 793,
795–8 *c.* mid 13th cent.; 786, 800, late 13th–14th cent. (After Moorhouse 1983b)

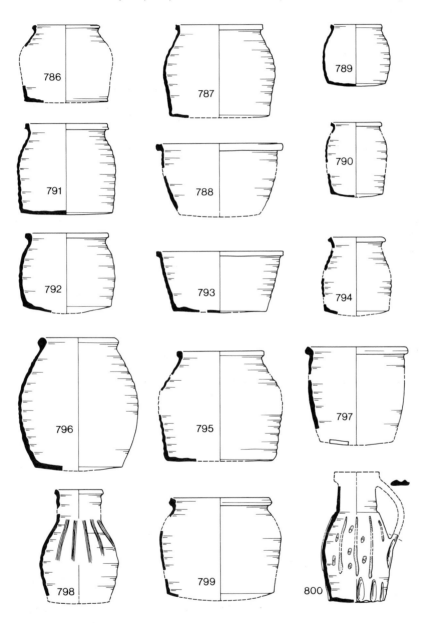

Humber ware – jugs and cooking pots present in late 13th/early 14th century group; some at least probably from West Cowick.

p. *Otley* (Le Patourel and Wood 1973)

Manor house little used after early 14th century.

Northern Gritty, or Pimply, ware found in 12th–13th century – buff, pink or light grey fabric with quartz grits protruding from the surface.

East Pennine Gritty ware – pink gritty fabric, light brownish-green glaze, occasionally over a white slip. Forms – cooking pots, jugs; decoration includes wavy combing, applied brown strips and scales. Most common fabric in 13th century. Source – probably Potter Newton.

Humber ware – present in small quantities in later 13th/early 14th century.

q. *Kirkstall Abbey* (Le Patourel 1967)

Monastic site, probably dating from *c.* mid 12th century on.

Pimply ware (Northern Gritty ware), buff gritty fabric, forms mainly cooking pots, occasional bowls, jugs; dominant in later 12th century, continuing in 13th century.

East Pennine Gritty ware (Ware A), becomes dominant fabric. Derives from Pimply ware; source probably Potter Newton. Forms include jugs, cisterns. Continues to 16th century.

Humber ware (Ware B); source – some probably from West Cowick.

Eastern England (Fig. 144)

1. Lincolnshire

a. *Lincoln* (Adams 1977; Chapman *et al.* 1975; Coppack 1973; 1980b): Fig. 145; see also Fig. 14

(i) *Production sites*

St Mary Le Wigford – kiln and wasters found in 19th century in medieval suburb south of city.

Lindum Hill Road – medieval street on east side of city known as 'Poteregate' by 1200; wasters known from this area.

Bailgate – feature found in 19th century at corner of Eastgate and Bailgate may possibly have been a kiln, though none of the surviving pottery can substantiate this.

(ii) *Pottery*

Shelly wares, hand-made and wheel-finished, mainly cooking pots – Lincoln Fine Shelly ware continues from earlier period; Lincolnshire Early Medieval Shelly ware, present in 11th century, becomes common by later 12th century. These wares replaced during 13th century by Potter Hanworth products.

Sandy wares probably made in Lincoln – Lincoln Sandy ware (LS) continues to early 13th century, mainly as splashed glaze jugs (Lincoln Splashed Glaze ware). Lincoln Medieval Sandy ware (LMS), or Lincoln ware, becomes commoner from mid-12th century, replacing LS in 13th century; sandy fabric, usually reduced, but with surfaces

Fig. 144 Eastern England, location map
1 Thornholme Priory, 2 Yaddlethorpe, 3 Nettleham, 4 Goltho, 5 Lincoln, 6 Potter
Hanworth, 7 Toynton All Saints, 8 Boston, 9 Bourne, 10 Stamford, 11 King's Lynn,
12 Grimston, 13 Castle Acre, 14 Blackborough End, 15 North Elmham, 16 Barton
Bendish, 17 Fransham, 18 Norwich, 19 Woodbastwick, 20 Potter Heigham, 21 Great
Yarmouth, 22 Gislingham, 23 Walberswick, 24 Ipswich, 25 Hollesley, 26 Debenham,
27 Denny Abbey, 28 Waterbeach Abbey, 29 Thornton Curtis, 30 East Runton.

Fig. 145 LINCOLNSHIRE

Lincoln: 801, Lincoln Splashed Glaze ware. 802–3, 805–10, 812–13, Lincoln ware.
804, 811, Lincoln-type ware from Nettleham. 814, Lincoln-type ware from Goltho.
801–3, later 12th cent.; 807, later 13th cent.; 805, 812, 814, 13th/14th cent.; 804,
806, 808–11, 813, first half of 14th cent. (After Adams L. 1977; Beresford 1975;
Chapman *et al.* 1975; Coppack 1980b; Healey 1975; Russell and Moorhouse 1971a)

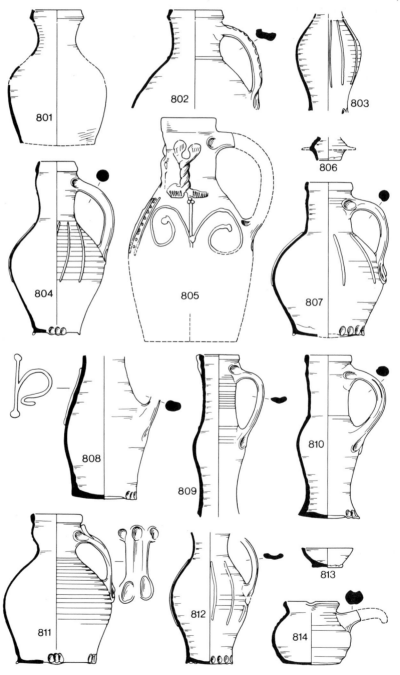

often oxidized to orange-buff or grey-brown. Forms – mainly glazed jugs (influenced by imported Nottingham wares from 12th century on), also pipkins, few lids, pedestal lamps, dripping dishes; occasional knight jugs, aquamaniles. Glaze usually has copper colourant; jug decoration – applied strips and scales, often stained brown, motifs such as horse-shoes, pellets in triangles, occasional stamps on pads. Anthropomorphic decoration, e.g. faces of the same type as stamps found at St Mary le Wigford, rare. Highly decorated wares thought to be *c.* mid 13th-mid 14th century.

b. *Stamford* (Kilmurry 1980; Mahany *et al.* 1982): Figs. 146–7

(i) *Production sites*

Pottery production continued mostly in area to east of early medieval town.

59 Scotgate – small group of pottery, not well stratified, possible production group; dated stylistically to mid-late 12th century. Outside town defences to north-west.

'The Pantiles', St Paul's Street – numerous wasters from pit on site adjacent to the earlier Greyfriars House kiln; dated stylistically to mid-12th century. Outside town defences to east.

1963 Stamford School (Elm Street) kiln – Type 1b kiln, firebar floor supported on clay pedestals. Archaeomagnetically dated to *c.* 1200; pottery stylistically early 13th century.

1874 Stamford School kiln – *c.* 100m west of 1963 School kiln; apparently similar in form to 1963 kiln, with firebar floor on four clay pedestals. Pottery stylistically dated to *c.* 1170–1250. School kilns just within north-eastern corner of 12th–13th century defences.

(ii) *Pottery*

Stamford ware continued to be produced; certain changes in fabrics, forms and decoration in early-mid 12th century. New fabric and glaze with copper green speckles ('developed Stamford ware') and new forms, e.g. jugs, some with tubular spouts, supplement earlier types by *c.* 1150. Jugs more highly decorated in late 12th-early 13th century, and replace spouted pitchers as tableware. Rarer new forms – pedestalled dishes, lids for jugs; bottles, possibly present earlier, more numerous. Decoration – on cooking pots, rouletting ends by mid 12th century; bowls often have thumbing on rims; tablewares, incised wavy lines, combing on handles and strips applied in patterns or as interlace.

Stamford ware production declined in quantity from the late 12th century, ended by *c.* 1250, perhaps in face of increased competition from rural potteries in second half of 12th and 13th century. Proportion of non-Stamford wares in Stamford, very low previously, increases; Lyveden, Nottingham and Bourne products become common.

c. *Potter Hanworth* (Healey 1974; 1975): Fig. 148; see also Fig. 30

Production sites

Numerous unstratified pottery finds in village indicate a slightly sandy shelly ware production of mainly cooking pots and bowls, also pipkins and occasional jugs, in 13th and 14th centuries. Vessels unglazed; coil-building and wheel-throwing known. 'Potter' element first occurs in 1327.

d. *Bourne* (Healey 1969; 1975; Kerr n.d.; Webster and Cherry 1974: 220): Fig. 148

Fig. 146 LINCOLNSHIRE
Stamford: 816, 821, 823–4, Stamford ware. 819–20, 825–8, Stamford ware from
1963 Stamford School kiln, early 13th cent. 822, Stamford ware from 'The Pantiles'
production site, mid 12th cent. 815, Stamford ware from Alstoe Mount, Burley,
Rutland. 817–18, 829, Stamford ware from Castle Acre, Norfolk. (After Dunning *et
al.* 1959; Kilmurry 1980; Mahany *et al.* 1982; Milligan 1982)

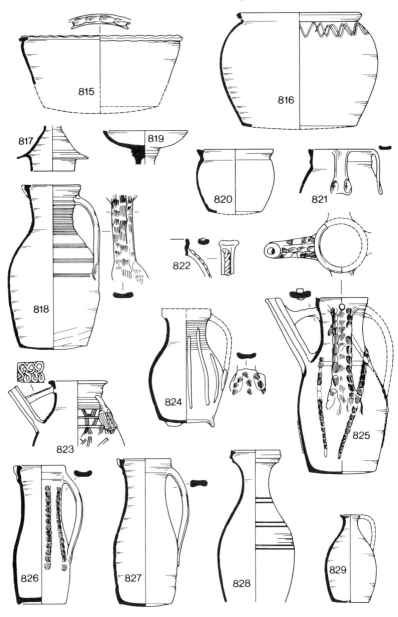

Fig. 147 LINCOLNSHIRE
Stamford: 'Developed Stamford ware' jug, 1963 Stamford School (Elm St) kiln, early
13th cent; ht. 31.4 cm. (Reproduced by courtesy of the Trustees of the British
Museum)

Fig. 148 LINCOLNSHIRE
Potter Hanworth: 831, 834–6, Potter Hanworth ware. 830, 832, Potter Hanworth-type
ware from Lincolnshire. 833, 837, Potter Hanworth-type ware from Lincoln. All
13th–14th cent. (After Adams L. 1977; Coppack 1980b; Healey 1974; 1975)
Bourne: 839, 842–3, Bourne A ware. 838, Bourne A ware from Stamford. 840–1,
Bourne B ware, *c.* 13th–14th cent. (After Healey 1975; Mahany *et al.* 1982)

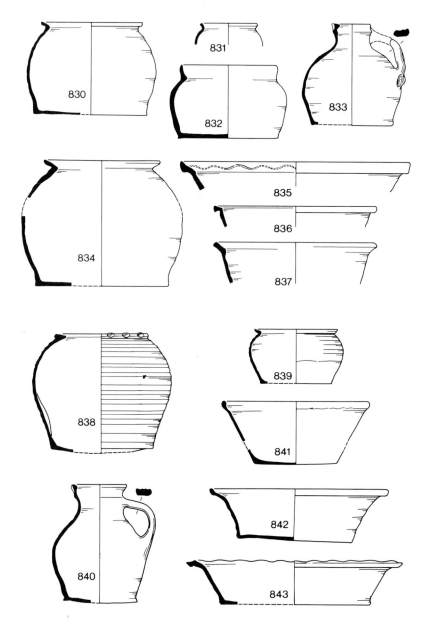

(i) *Production sites*

Eastgate – on eastern outskirts of town, two Type 3 kilns, each with four flues and four triangular clay pedestals in the firing chamber; destroyed to below level of possible raised floor. Kilns built on thick layers of pottery providing hard standing, so earlier production implied. Other features include large backfilled clay-extraction pits. Kilns dated on typological grounds to *c.* 14th century. Industry probably starts 13th century; one of principal streets documented as 'Potter Street' by 1330.

(ii) *Pottery*

Bourne A ware – sparsely gritted with sand and calcitic inclusions; mostly grey, some partially oxidized buff or brown; olive green glaze with no added copper, some brown strip decoration on 13th century examples. Forms – mostly cooking pots, also jugs, jars, bowls, pipkins.

Bourne B ware – coarser sandier fabric, usually oxidized to buff, red or brown; internally-glazed pancheons or bowls common, also cooking pots, jars, pipkins, curfews, drain pipes and decorated ridge tiles.

e. Toynton All Saints (Healey 1975; 1984; Wilson and Hurst J.G. 1958: 325; 1960: 163; Wilson and Hurst D.G. 1962–3: 348; 1964: 296; 1965: 217; 1966: 217): Figs. 149–50; see also Fig. 29

(i) *Production sites*

Waster material found on a number of sites in and near village, and kilns recorded as being bulldozed. Two kilns of this period excavated, Kilns 1 ('The Roses') and 3 – five-flued Type 3 kilns. Kiln 1 archaeomagnetically dated 1275–1300; Kiln 3 of similar date. Coin of 1302–10 from infill of Kiln 1 flue, post-dating use of kiln. Village known as 'Potter Toynton' in 14th century.

(ii) *Pottery*

Toynton ware – sandy fabric of local Jurassic clay, red to buff surfaces, often with grey core; olive green glaze with no added copper. Forms – high proportion of jugs, also pancheons, cooking pots, drinking jugs, pipkins and dishes. Larger jugs often decorated, with brown slip-trailed decoration. Stylized motifs include pellets, scrolls, crosses, horse-shoes, fleur-de-lys, 'ladders' and 'roofs'; no figural elements. Large-scale production; decorated Toynton jugs traded widely through the county.

f. Thornton Curtis (Hayfield 1985)

Production site

Humber ware (H2) wasters known from the parish, possibly indicating production. Date range of H2: 13th–16th century.

g. Yaddlethorpe (Hayfield 1985)

Production site

Documentary reference to potter in 1338 contracted to supply pots to a man from Appleby, perhaps buying pottery for Thornholme Priory, Appleby.

h. Bishop's Palace, Nettleham (Moorhouse 1971a)

Shelly ware cooking pots and bowls, Lincoln-type ware jugs in medieval deposits, including a well group dated stylistically to the first half of the 14th century.

Fig. 149 LINCOLNSHIRE
Toynton All Saints: 845–8, 850–3, Toynton ware from Kiln 1. 844, 849, 854, Toynton ware from Kiln 3. All *c.* late 13th cent. (After Healey 1975)

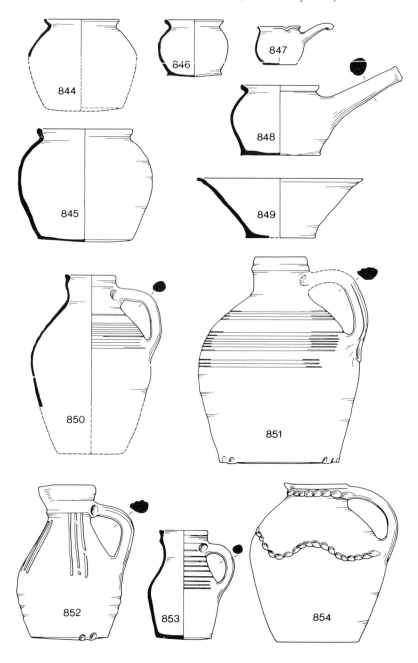

Fig. 150 LINCOLNSHIRE
Toynton All Saints: 855–8, 860–1, Toynton ware from Kiln 1, *c.* late 13th cent. 859,
Toynton ware from Oslo. (After Dunning 1968; Healey 1975)

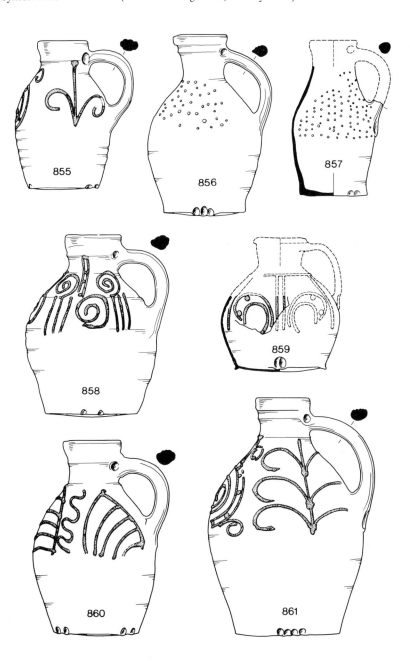

i. Goltho (Beresford 1975; Coppack 1980b): Fig. 151

Shelly wares commonest until these die out after mid 14th century; forms – cooking pots, bowls, pancheons, lamps, curfews. Probably much from Potter Hanworth in 13th and 14th centuries.

Splashed ware jugs at Goltho Manor in first half of 12th century; not found in peasant houses till late 12th/early 13th century. Lincoln ware replaced splashed wares *c.* mid 13th century; jugs, also cooking pots, bowls, pipkins. Toynton ware jugs and cooking pots present.

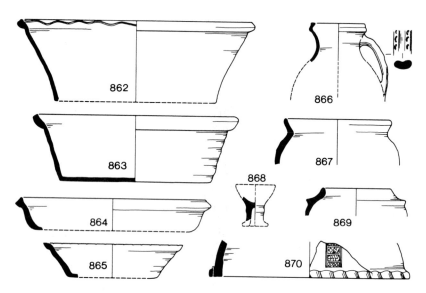

Fig. 151 LINCOLNSHIRE
Goltho: 862–5, 867–70, Shelly wares. 866, Developed Splashed ware. (After Beresford 1975)

j. Thornholme Priory, Appleby (Hayfield 1985): Figs. 152–4

Chronology of excavated sequence based on historical dates, architectural details and coins. Dominant fabrics Orangeware (O1) and medium sandy fabric (M1), both probably of North Lincolnshire origin.

O1 – oxidized orange fine sandy wheel-thrown ware, glaze usually copper green, sometimes orange-yellow; splashed glazes replaced by ordinary suspension glazes by *c.* 1150. Forms mainly jugs, some pipkins. Decorated jugs by *c.* 1150, peak of decoration late 12th/early 13th century; wavy combing, applied decoration either brown or sometimes in white iron-free clay – vertical strips (sometimes notched), scales and pellets. Some jugs have one side copper-green glazed, other side plain yellow glazed; 'relief-moulded' wheatear and raspberry stamps in imitation of Humber wares by early 13th century. O1 finishes by *c.* 1300.

Fig. 152 LINCOLNSHIRE
Thornholme Priory: 871–81, Orangeware O1. 882–4, medium sandy Fabric M1.
872–3, 875–8, 881, second half of 12th cent.; 871, 874, 879–80, 883–4, early 13th
cent.; 882, early 14th cent. (After Hayfield 1985)

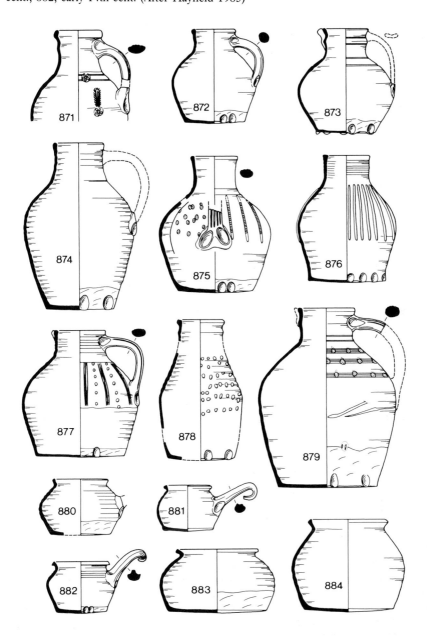

Fig. 153 LINCOLNSHIRE

Thornholme Priory: 885–97, medium sandy Fabric M1. 886, 889, 893, 895–6, early 13th cent.; 885, 887–8, 890–2, mid–late 13th cent.; 894, 897, early 14th cent. (After Hayfield 1985)

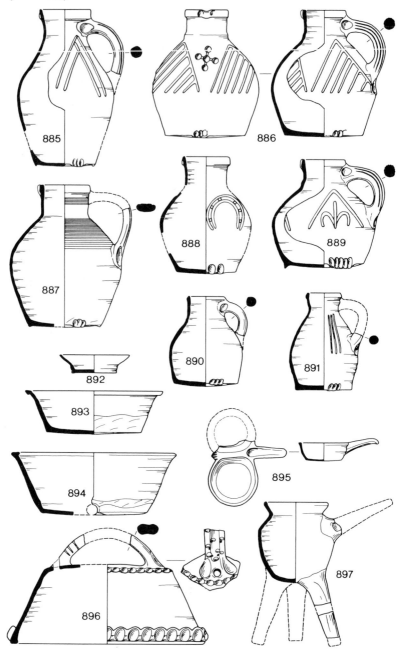

Fig. 154 LINCOLNSHIRE
Thornholme Priory: 898–900, medium sandy Fabric M1. 901–2, Humber ware H1.
903–4, Humber ware H2. 898–9, 901–3, early 13th cent.; 900, 904, early 14th cent.
(After Hayfield 1985)

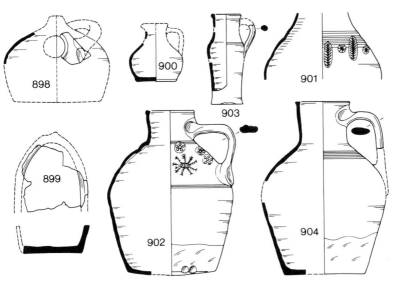

M1 – medium sandy fabric, buff or orange with olive-green glaze; appears in late
12th century, increases in 13th; dominant fabric by mid 14th century. Forms – jugs,
cooking pots; occasionally curfews, bowls, condiments, urinals, dripping dishes,
cauldrons. Some wheel-thrown, some coil-built and wheel-finished. Decoration –
applied brown vertical strips and scales; horse-shoe, 'roof' and fleur-de-lys motifs in
imitation of Lincoln/Toynton wares. Anthropomorphic decoration rare, but includes
bearded face-masks.

Humber ware H1 – smooth textured early Humber ware, transitional from
Orangeware; wheel-thrown orange to red fabric, sometimes reduced grey, with olive
glaze. Forms – mostly jugs, also cooking pots, dripping dishes, pipkins, bowls, drinking
jugs, lids, cisterns, urinals. Decoration includes stamped pushed-out bosses, wheatear
and raspberry motifs most common though whorls and other stamps known. Source not
known. Date range early-late 13th century.

Humber ware H2 – wheel-thrown orange to red sandy fabric, sometimes reduced
grey internally, olive glaze. Forms – mostly jugs, also cooking pots, drinking jugs.
dripping dishes, pipkins, tripod pipkins, bowls, cups, lobed cups, cisterns, urinals.
Decoration rare, includes bands of horizontal incised lines, relief-moulded wheatear and
raspberry designs, also applied strips, often thumbed. Source – possibly Thornton
Curtis, where wasters are known. Date range 13th-16th century.

Minor wares – few shelly cooking pots and bowls; fine sandy North Lincolnshire
jug fabric F1 finishes by end of 12th century; Lincoln-type and Toynton-type wares.

k. *Dominican Friary, Boston* (Moorhouse 1972a)

Chronology based on jettons, imported pottery and historical dates. Shelly ware cooking pots found in late 13th and early 14th century, disappearing after *c.* 1350. Tablewares mainly in Lincoln, Nottingham and Toynton fabrics, as well as continental imports.

2. Norfolk

a. Grimston, Pott Row (Clarke and Carter 1977): Figs. 155–7; see also Fig. 27 No. 7

(i) *Production sites*
Much waster material known from field-walking.
(ii) *Pottery*
Grimston ware – reduced grey sandy fabric, surfaces often lighter grey or buff; olive green glazes with no copper colourant. Forms – mainly glazed jugs, some cooking pots and bowls. Highly decorated jugs have applied decoration, often iron-washed brown strips, pellets and scales; anthropomorphic face-mask jugs, usually with short beards, most distinctive and widely distributed form. Knight jugs and aquamaniles also known. Date range later 12th–16th century, with highly decorated wares dated typologically to mid 13th–mid 14th century.

b. Blackborough End, Middleton (Rogerson and Ashley 1985)

(i) *Production site*
Evidence for clamp or bonfire production of pottery indicated by superimposed layers of burning and large quantities of discoloured or distorted sherds.
(ii) *Pottery*
Pottery in Early Medieval ware tradition – fabric contains mainly profuse sub-rounded quartz grains, rare iron ore, grog/clay and calcitic inclusions; varies from soft to hard, grey to reddish brown and red. Rims are wheel-thrown or wheel-finished, bodies and bases are hand-made; vessels are luted together at the shoulder. Forms mainly round-based cooking pots, small proportion of bowls, one handle (possibly from a pitcher). Dated to *c.* mid 12th–later 13th century, mainly by its presence or absence in dated contexts elsewhere in the area. The rise of this cooking pot industry perhaps related to the Grimston potters changing over to glazed jug production.

c. Potter Heigham (Clarke 1953–7)

Production site
'Potter' element first appears 1182. Pottery, including wasters, said to date to 12th–15th century, found at Pot Hills.

d. Woodbastwick (Wilson and D.G. Hurst 1961: 337)

Production site
12th–13th century pottery production site, known from surface collections.

e. Fransham (A. Rogerson, pers. comm.)

Production site
Three separate waster scatters; cooking pots and bowls in Early Medieval ware, probably hand-made, of 12th–13th century date.

Fig. 155   NORFOLK
Grimston: 909–13, Grimston ware from King's Lynn. 905–8, 914–18, Grimston-type ware from Norwich, 13th–14th cent. (After Clarke and Carter 1977; Jennings 1981)

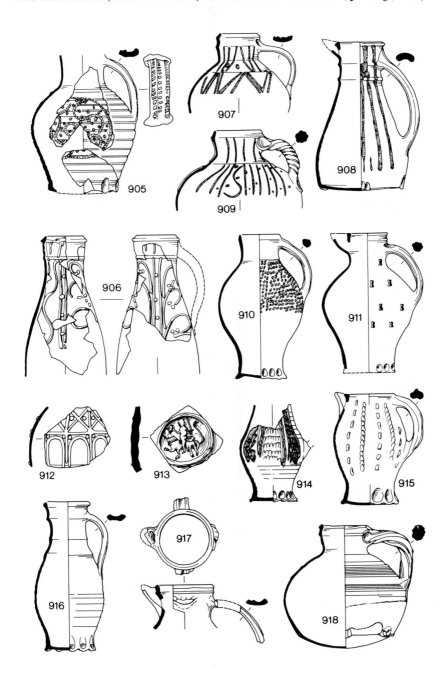

Fig. 156   NORFOLK

Grimston: 923–4, Grimston ware from King's Lynn. 919, 922, Grimston-type ware from Norwich. 920, Grimston ware from Cambridge. 921, Grimston ware from Oslo. 13th–14th cent. (After Clarke and Carter 1977; Dunning 1968; Jennings 1981)
Norwich: 925–33, Local Medieval Unglazed wares. 925–9, 11th–13th cent.; 930–3, 13th–14th cent. (After Jennings 1981)

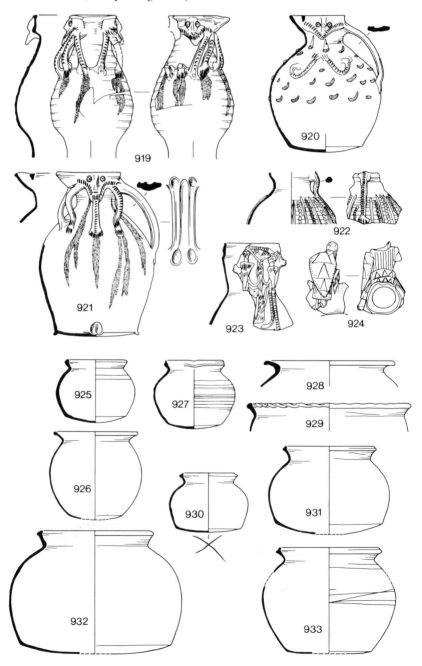

Fig. 157 NORFOLK
Grimston: Grimston ware face-mask jug from Cambridge, late 13th–early 14th cent.;
ht. 27.6 cm. (Reproduced by courtesy of the Trustees of the British Museum)

f. Barton Bendish (A. Rogerson pers. comm.)

Production site
Wasters known from site in centre of village, grey sandy fabric, mainly wheel-made
bowls, dated to *c.* 14th century; also glazed undecorated jugs in oxidized fabric.

g. East Runton (Davey N. 1939–41; A. Rogerson and S. Jennings pers.comm.)

13th–14th century pottery, originally published as kiln material, has recently been
reassessed and discounted as evidence of a production site.

h. Norwich (Jennings 1981): Figs. 156, 158; see also Fig. 64 No. 4

No production sites known after decline of Thetford-type ware industry; in first
half of 13th century, there is a reference to a 'Potteres Pit' in village of Eaton, 3 km
south-west of Norwich (Atkin *et al.* 1983: 65).

Fig. 158   NORFOLK
Norwich: 934–41, Local Medieval Unglazed wares. (After Jennings 1981)
King's Lynn: 942–5, 'Grimston Software', 12th–mid 13th cent. (After Clarke and Carter 1977)

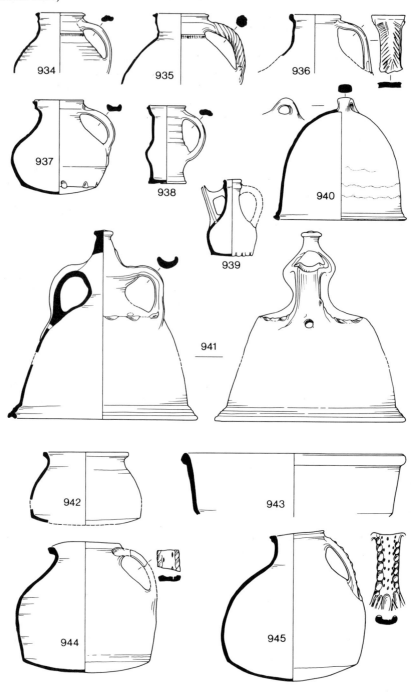

Local Medieval Unglazed ware – slightly sandy hard wheel-made fabric, similar to that of Early Medieval ware, usually reduced but sometimes partly oxidized reddish brown or buff. Forms – mainly cooking pots, also bowls, curfews, unglazed jugs. Decoration of jugs common, rouletting or plain, thumbed or rouletted applied strips. Ware replaces Thetford-type in 12th century, continues till 15th century; jugs probably mostly later 13th/early 14th century. Source unknown, but possibly Potter Heigham or Woodbastwick.

Grimston-type ware – nearly all the glazed medieval jugs are in this fabric. Decoration includes brown applied pellets and strips, applied iron-free pale clay stylized flowers, also rouletting, incised lines, applied thumbed strips; face-mask jugs. Decorated wares mainly 13th–mid 14th century. Most probably from Grimston as no other sources are known.

i. *Great Yarmouth* (Mellor 1976; Rye and Hurst 1968)

Early Medieval Grey Reduced ware dominant fabric in late 12th/early 13th century group; also medieval coarse wares, continuing from earlier period. By *c.* late 13th/early 14th century, Grey Reduced ware replaced by other grey coarse ware fabrics for cooking pots and bowls; glazed jugs and occasional cauldrons in local oxidized ware. Glazed jugs also in Grimston-type and Scarborough wares.

j. *Castle Acre* (Dallas 1980; Milligan 1982)

Early Medieval wares continued through the second half of the 12th century, and perhaps into the early 13th century. Local sandy grey and brown wares – cooking pots; one complete unglazed sand-tempered jug in later 12th century context. Grimston ware, first appearing in second half of 12th century (although not highly decorated at this time), becomes dominant tableware in 13th/14th centuries.

k. *North Elmham* (Wade 1980)

Thetford-type and Early Medieval wares replaced by medieval wares in later 12th century; Sandy Medieval Coarse ware cooking pots and bowls, mostly undecorated; Grimston-type glazed wares.

l. *King's Lynn* (Clarke and Carter 1977; A. Rogerson pers. comm.): Fig. 158

So-called 'Grimston Software' continues to *c.* mid 13th century. Grey sandy cooking pots and bowls attributed to Grimston, but now thought to be from other sources, continue; rounded bases gradually replaced by sagging bases.

Much Grimston ware, mainly glazed jugs, including highly decorated vessels, and aquamaniles; also some internally-glazed bowls.

Regional imports include Stamford and shelly wares in the first half of the period, Scarborough ware in the second half.

3. Suffolk

a. *Ipswich* (Youngs *et al.* 1983: 204)

Production site
Fore Street – Type 2 kiln excavated, traces of other kilns; production of 13th-14th century decorated glazed pottery.

b. *Walberswick* (Wilson and Hurst D.G. 1970: 205)

Production site
Possible production of medieval pottery deduced from surface finds.

c. *Hollesley* (Webster and Cherry 1972: 207; Wilson and Moorhouse 1971: 177)

Production site
Poplar Farm – hollows with ash and wasters; forms – jugs, cooking pots, storage jars, pancheons, curfews and dishes; green or orange glazes; jugs decorated with white slip. Documentary evidence for pottery production in later 13th century.

d. *Gislingham* (Wilson and Hurst J.G. 1959: 325)

Production site
Sherds from two apparent clamp kilns at Ivy House Farm; no dating known.

e. *Debenham* (Owles 1970): Fig. 159

Moated farmstead, probably occupied from *c.* 12th–early 14th century. Pottery mostly unglazed coarse ware cooking pots, bowls, jars; three main types:
Ware C – buff harsh gritty fabric; some vessels decorated with thumb impressions on body. Probably of 12th century date. Commonest pottery type on the site.
Ware B – smooth grey slightly micaceous fabric; date perhaps *c.* mid 13th century.
Ware A – dark rough shelly fabric; date perhaps *c.* late 13th/early 14th century.
Very few glazed jugs, probably non-local; one is similar to a glazed jug found in Ipswich, another probably from London area.

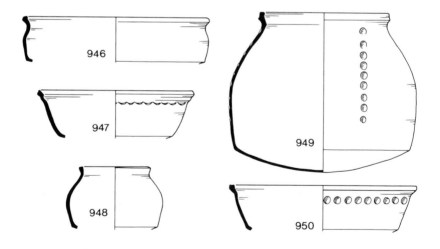

Fig. 159 SUFFOLK
Debenham: 946, Ware A, *c.* late 13th/early 14th cent. 947–8, Ware B, *c.* mid 13th cent. 949–50, Ware C, *c.* 12th cent. (After Owles 1970)

4. Cambridgeshire

a. Waterbeach Abbey (Hurst J.G. 1966)

Excavation at monastic site, only occupation historically dated to 1293–1359.

Coarse wares comprise brown shelly sandy fabric, brown sandy fabric with grey core, and grey sandy wares sometimes with sandwich-effect core. Forms – mainly cooking pots, also jugs, bowls, storage jars. Decoration includes occasional thumbing on cooking pot shoulders, applied thumbed strips on storage jars.

Non-local jugs include Hedingham, Lyveden and Grimston wares.

b. Denny Abbey (Coppack 1980a)

Excavation at monastic site, founded in 1159.

Shell-Tempered ware – hand-made fabric, dark grey or orange-brown with grey-buff core, with sparse fine fossil-shell inclusions. Forms – mainly cooking pots, also bowls.

Brown Gritty ware – brown to orange-brown hard finely sand-tempered wheel-thrown fabric with grey core, some angular white inclusions. Forms include cooking pots, jugs with yellow-green splashed glaze.

Light Grey Sandy ware – fine slightly sandy grey fabric. Forms – jugs, cooking pots; cooking pots sometimes decorated with bands of incised horizontal grooves.

Smooth Red ware (= Hedingham ware) – very fine, slightly sandy, orange to red fabric, mottled green glaze. Forms mainly jugs; applied and stamped decoration. Date range of this and above three wares *c.* second half of 12th–14th century.

Orange Sandy ware – hard sandy orange to red fabric, often with grey core, occasionally with thin clear lead glaze. Forms – jugs, bowls; decoration is rare, and confined to painted white slip or sgraffito. Equivalent to Red Sandy ware at Waltham Abbey, Essex. Source not known, but part of distinctive regional tradition. Date range *c.* second half of 14th–16th century.

North Midlands (Fig. 160)

1. Leicestershire

a. Potters Marston (Haynes 1952; Sawday forthcoming; Woodland and Sawday, pers. comm.): Fig. 161

(i) *Production site*

Village with the potter name element first recorded in 13th century and depopulated in 15th. Type 2 kiln excavated; stone-walled oven contained pots on the floor mixed in with soot, wasters, wattle and daub, slates with nail holes.

(ii) *Pottery*

Pots made from local iron-rich boulder clays containing syenite, the source of which has been identified at Croft, 1km from the kiln site. Vessel colours mainly red-yellows, incompletely oxidized. Forms include coiled (or possibly slabbed in some cases) cooking pots, storage jars, spouted pitchers, and lamps, some of which may be clamp fired; also coiled, glazed and highly decorated jugs. Wide-mouthed bowls,

Fig. 160   North Midlands, location map
1 Nottingham, 2 Burley Hill, 3 Duffield, 4 Derby, 5 Leicester, 6 Potters Marston.

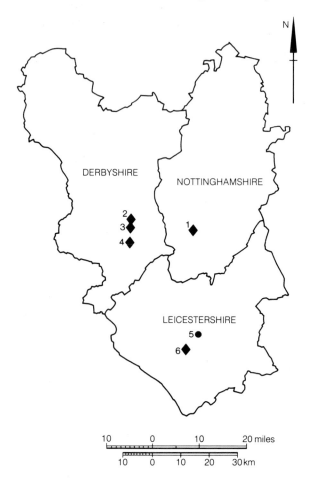

dripping pans, curfews, shallow dishes, a possible costrel, urinals and glazed crested ridge tiles appear during the 13th century. Originally dated typologically to 13th century, but more recent work in Leicester suggests Potters Marston ware production from *c.* 1150 if not earlier, continuing into 14th century.

b. Leicester (Woodland 1981): Fig. 161

Major excavations in domestic areas of Austin Friars founded in 1250s.

Periods 2–3, 13th and 14th centuries: Potters Marston and Nuneaton products dominant; Potters Marston ware the most common coarse ware in Leicester in earlier part of period. Main vessel types were jugs but cooking pots and bowls were well represented. Other forms included urinals, flasks and dripping pans.

Fig. 161 LEICESTERSHIRE
Potters Marston: 953–5, Potters Marston ware. 951–2, Potters Marston ware from Leicester, 12th–13th cent. (After Haynes 1952; Woodland 1981)
Leicester: 956–60, fabrics Pii, Pv, Pviii and Pix, possibly Nuneaton-type wares 13th–14th cent. (After Woodland 1981)

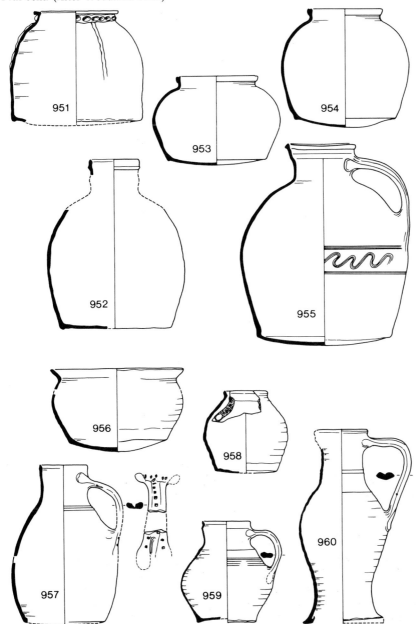

2. Nottinghamshire

a. Nottingham (Carter 1971; Coppack 1978; 1980b; Parker 1932; Ponsford 1971): Figs. 162–3

(i) *Production sites*

Pottery kilns attested at Parliament Street, between George and Thurland Streets, St Paul's Church, Clinton Street, Glasshouse Street, Broad Street, St Anne's Street. At least twelve kilns known, from 19th and early 20th century discoveries, several being within the northern defences of the town, and some such as those at St Anne's Street immediately outside walls.

(ii) *Pottery*

Main types derived from study of waster material and groups known from Moot Hall Caves, Houndsgate, Goosegate, Bridlesmithgate Caves, Castlegate and Park Row.

Splashed wares: fine sharp sand inclusions, probably derived from local Bunter sandstone; hard, fully oxidized. Forms include coiled pitchers, jugs, flasks, cooking pots, bowls, pipkins and a lamp. Pitchers and jugs splashed with clear lead glaze initially but copper added later. Made at St Anne's Street kilns. Dates from pre-Conquest times to 13th century.

Shelly wares: hard brown fabric, filler consisting of fossil shell and quartz sand; hand-made cooking pots and bowls attributable to 13th–15th century and similar to Lincolnshire Shelly wares.

Cream Sandy wares: tempered with quartz sand, fired very hard; colour range cream to orange. Wheel-thrown thin-walled jugs, cooking pots and bowls. Jugs decorated with face masks and iron-rich strips below the glaze. The earliest known wheel-thrown pottery in Nottingham; made in the St Anne's Street kilns. Dated to 13th century on typological grounds.

Pink Sandy wares: fully oxidized hard fabric with quartz sand filler. Wheel-thrown jugs, the only known form, are highly decorated with twisted and combed applied strips and rouletting. Made at St Anne's Street kilns, perhaps over a short period.

Off-white wares: heavy sand tempering in pale grey to off-white fabrics; wheel-thrown glazed jugs, including knight jugs and aquamaniles known.

Orange Sandy wares: hard fine sandy wares, often oxidized but the poorly finished jugs are reduced internally. Other forms include cooking pots and bowls. Made at several kilns incuding St Anne's Street, Clinton Street, and Parliament Street. This type continues in the later medieval period, and resembles the products of the Keighton kilns.

3. Derbyshire.

a. Burley Hill (Coppack 1980b; Hughes 1957; Jewitt 1878): Fig. 164; see also Fig. 61

(i) *Production site*

In parish of Duffield, north of Derby, kilns excavated by Jewitt; re-excavation in 1957 confirmed presence of wasters and kilns fired with coal.

(ii) *Pottery*

Hard pink sandy wares. Wide range of forms; highly decorated jugs bearing a variety of motifs, including applied buckles and horseshoes, possibly the arms of the de Ferrers family, pads, leaves, faces, strips and other motifs with glaze, are one of principal elements. Other forms include plain jugs, bowls, pipkins, drinking jugs, possibly

Fig. 162 NOTTINGHAMSHIRE
Nottingham: 961, 965–8, Splashed Glaze ware, late 12th–early 13th cent. 962–3, 971, Orange Sandy ware, 13th cent. 964, 969–70, Cream Sandy ware, 13th cent. 972, Off-white Sandy ware, mid 13th cent. 973, Pink Sandy ware, mid 13th cent. (After Coppack 1980b)

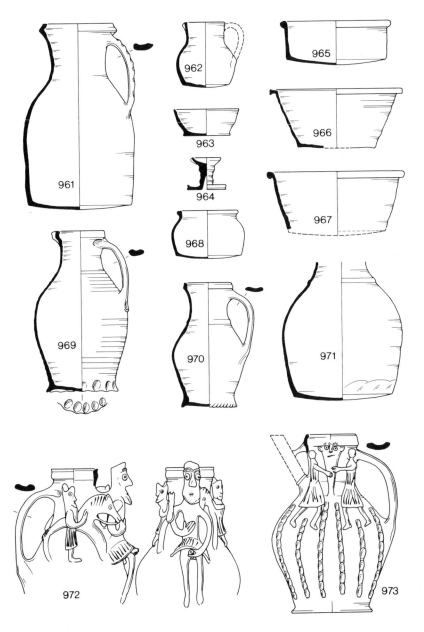

Fig. 163   NOTTINGHAMSHIRE
Nottingham: 974, Pink Sandy ware from Blythe Priory, 13th cent. 975, Off-white Sandy ware, 13th–14th cent. 976, Splashed Glaze ware, 13th cent. 977–84, Orange Sandy ware, 13th–14th cent. (After Coppack 1980b)

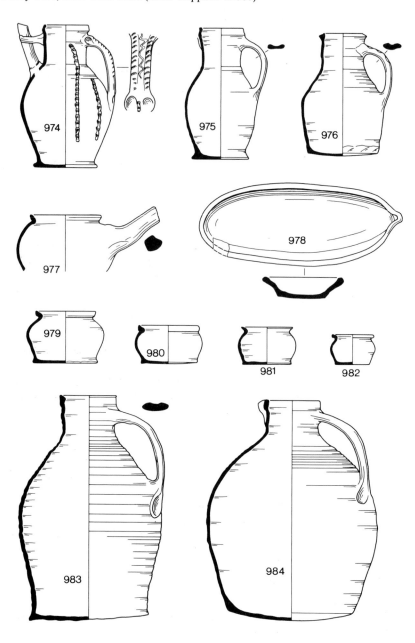

Fig. 164 DERBYSHIRE
Burley Hill: 985–91, Burley Hill ware from Derby, 13th–14th cent. (After Coppack 1980b)

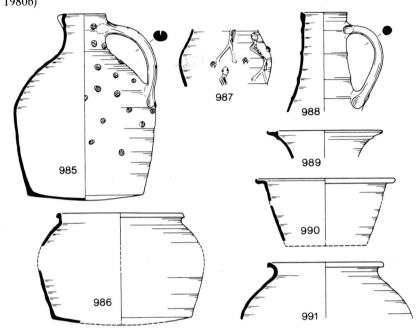

cauldrons and cooking pots. Dating is by reference to the de Ferrers family. If the horseshoe motifs are the arms of Ferrers, a likely date for those jugs is 13th century as the family were deprived of the earldom in 1278. The production site may, however, have had a much longer life.

Coppack notes that Burley Hill wares and purple wares are very similar in fabric and that wasters from production site show noticeable proportion of overfired vessels, a tendency which could have become deliberate.

b. *Duffield* (Wilson and Hurst D.G. 1967: 316)

(i) *Production site*
Type 1b kiln excavated close to the castle; firebars and wasters also recovered.
(ii) *Pottery*
Hard, sandy/gritty fabric; fairly coarse and buff-pink in colour. Unglazed, probably hand-made, cylindrical cooking pots with roughly combed surfaces, bowls with some horizontal combed decoration, and unglazed jugs on which the necks were separately applied. Dated by analogy with other sites to 12th–13th century.

c. *Derby* (Coppack 1972; 1980b; Le Patourel 1968)

(i) *Production site*
A reference in 1323 mentions land held by a potter; there is as yet no archaeological evidence for production in Derby.

(ii) *Pottery*

In addition to Burley Hill ware and other vessels from Duffield which may equate broadly with Coppack's grey and orange gritty wares, three other types can be defined:

Limestone-tempered ware with some sand, in varied colours; forms include cooking pots and bowls.

Splashed glazed ware in a hard, sandy fabric with tendency to oxidization; surfaces covered with patchy splashed glaze; forms – jugs, with some cooking pots.

Cream sandy ware, a hard quartz-tempered fabric in off-white to cream colours and with painted-on glaze. Mainly jugs but some cooking pots and bowls occur.

Group D14 at Full Street excavations one of earliest to contain intentionally-produced purple wares; these present in fabrics otherwise identical to Burley Hill wares and in medieval globular jug forms. This group attributed to early 13th century though subsequent work may suggest a revision.

The dating of many Derbyshire types is insecure and rests on typological comparisons with material in Nottingham and Lincoln.

d. *Bentley and Wigwell* (Le Patourel 1968)

Production sites
Land held by potters in 1247 and late 13th century respectively.

South Midlands (Fig. 165)

1. Oxfordshire

a. *Oxford* (Haldon and Mellor 1977; Mellor 1980b; 1985a and b): Figs. 166–70

Large number of excavations and watching briefs carried out in medieval town. The range of local types has been apparent for many years but the post-Conquest sequences only placed on firm stratigraphic footing latterly, most notably at St Aldates and The Hamel; also other sites such as the Dominican Friary.

St Aldates: Phase 7, *c.* 1150–75: oolitic Oxford Early Medieval wares – hand-made cooking pots and bowls, equally dominant with Oxford Medieval wares, sandy cooking pots and tripod pitchers. Similar wares also present at Ascot Doilly.

Phase 8, late 12th to mid–13th century: very large group with sandy Oxford Medieval wares absolutely dominant and superseding earlier limestone and flint-gritted fabrics. Main deposit is a midden containing tripod pitchers, cooking pots, bowls, dishes, a lid, a skillet and a double shelled lamp, with some French and Rhenish imports. Earliest appearance of Oxford Late Medieval wares, very similar to if not actually the products of the Brill-Boarstall industry.

Phase 9, attributed to 1250–1325 though more recent work at The Hamel suggests a re-dating of this phase to *c.* 1250–1265: increasing importance of Oxford Late medieval wares. Main forms are all wheel-thrown and include cooking pots, jugs, a possible lamp, a bottle and a chafing dish; a high proportion of highly decorated pottery.

Phase 10, originally attributed to 1325–1400 but The Hamel sequence now suggests starting date from 1260s–1270s: Oxford Late Medieval wares dominant; forms include bowls, cooking pots, jugs, skillets and a baking dish but marginally less highly decorated pottery than previous phase.

Fig. 165 South Midlands, location map
1 Lyveden, 2 Stanion, 3 Faxton, 4 Wythemail, 5 Northampton, 6 Potterspury, 7
Olney Hyde, 8 Harrold, 9 Bedford, 10 Eaton Socon, 11 Ellington, 12 Wintringham,
13 Ashwell, 14 Standon, 15 Great Munden, 16 Chandlers Cross, 17 Hatfield, 18 St
Albans, 19 Potters Crouch, 20 Barnet, 21 Denham, 22 Great Missenden, 23
Aylesbury, 24 Brill, 25 Boarstall, 26 Oxford, 27 Nettleden, 28 Pottersheath.

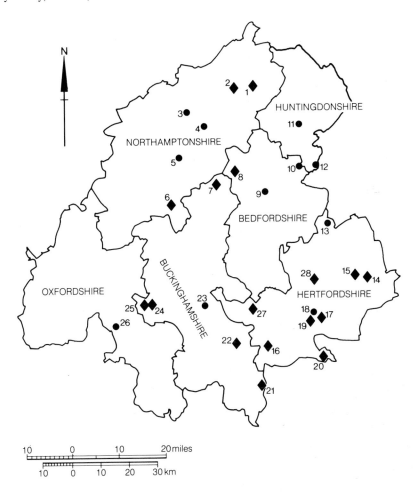

The Hamel: site consists of part of a western suburb with tenements linked by
documentary sources to named individuals. Two 12th century phases of ditches and
gullies reflect demise of oolitic wares and rise of Oxford Sandy ware tradition. Forms are
mainly cooking pots and pitchers in ratio of 5:1. By *c.* 1200 there seems to be a greater
variety of cooking ware and more regional imports.

Early to mid-13th century: the site was built up; parts of three tenements excavated,
two attributed to a tanner and a carpenter contained 14 fabrics, including regional

Fig. 166   OXFORDSHIRE
Oxford: 992–5, St John's College, local wares, late 12th cent. 996, 999–1000, Fabric
AC, late 12th–early 13th cent. 997–8, 1002–4, Oxford Medieval ware. 1001, 1005–7,
local wares. (After Bruce-Mitford 1939; Haldon and Mellor 1977; Jope *et al.* 1950;
Mellor 1980b)

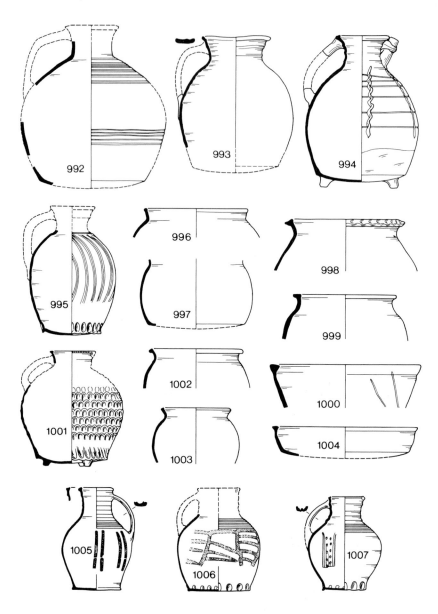

Fig. 167 OXFORDSHIRE
Oxford: 1008, Oxford fabric, 12th cent. (After Jope and Threlfall 1959)
Ascot Doilly: 1009–11, calcareous fabric, 12th cent. 1012, quartzitic fabric, 12th cent.
(After Jope and Threlfall 1959)

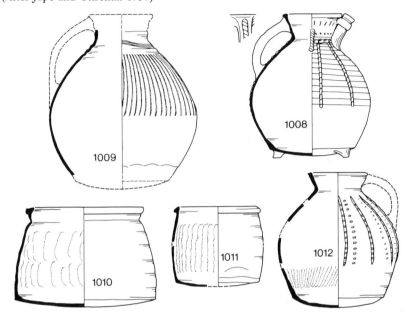

Fig. 168 OXFORDSHIRE
Oxford: cooking pot, 12th–13th cent.; ht. 21.2 cm. (Photo: Ashmolean Museum)

Fig. 169   (left) OXFORDSHIRE
Oxford: tripod pitcher from Radcliffe Square, 12th cent.; ht. 29.8 cm. (Photo: Ashmolean Museum)

Fig. 170   (right) OXFORDSHIRE
Oxford: puzzle jug from St Aldates, 13th cent.; ht. 35.5 cm. (Photo: Ashmolean Museum)

imports. Forms are cooking pots, bowls, decorated jugs and a lamp, but nothing in finds or in nature of ceramic spectra to indicate occupations or status.

By the mid-13th century, the southern tenement had been rebuilt by a wealthy citizen as a stone-based ground-floor hall. Pottery from the limited area exposed no different to that of other tenements which, a little later, were occupied by a tanner, quarryman and cooper. These latter contained a wide range of fine, highly decorated jugs, bowls/porringers, lamps and bottles, as well as normal domestic forms. Continuing ascendancy of Oxford Late Medieval wares (Fabrics AM, AW) of Brill-Boarstall facies.

Cooking wares occur in coarser flint-gritted fabrics from quite different source, possibly further south. Probably the vogue for highly decorated wares was over by 1300, though some deposits from turn of 13th-14th century could have been removed in antiquity. Wasters were found in one of northern tenements, and an Alexander le Poter is known to have leased land in the vicinity in 1316–20. However, the wasters could represent seconds and there is no documented connection between Alexander and the properties excavated.

Dominican Friary: *terminus post quem* in 1245. Dating of Oxford Late Medieval wares, Fabrics AM and AW, broadly matches that at The Hamel; Brill-Boarstall wares well established by 1250. Main forms jugs and pitchers; clearly the Dominicans, despite their Rules, used the most elaborate vessels including decorated baluster jugs and the elaborate puzzle jugs (Fig. 170).

2. Northamptonshire

a. Stanion (Bellamy 1983; Pearson 1983 and pers. comm.): Fig. 172

(i) Production site
Ten kilns known and others suspected along main street of nucleated village, located in Rockingham Forest. Complex geological background based on Inferior Oolite of Jurassic system is reflected in fabrics; essentially oolitic but some with ironstone. Earliest kilns (not located) possibly clamps. Secondary phase includes Type 4a kilns similar to, though not identical to, Lyveden kilns.

(ii) Pottery
Earliest wares – soft, poorly mixed clays; coil-built, wheel-finished cooking pots, bowls, dishes, jugs with some rouletting.

Secondary phase wares – harder, better mixed clays fired to higher temperatures; some coiled and some wheel-thrown vessels. Sequence at Raunds suggests sub-divisions in this phase in which throwing technique appears late, possibly at end of 13th or early 14th century.

Third phase – use of more refined clays and widespread use of wheel-throwing.

Technical competence at Stanion ranges from very good to very poor. Some vessels very porous with very badly finished surfaces. Cooking pots seem to be made to specific capacities with forms produced with aid of templates. One jug shows signs of having been marked out in zones before decoration applied. Several clays used sometimes on same vessel, as with an aquamanile with head in white firing clay and body in iron-rich clay; use of two clays is a feature of Stanion but not apparently of Lyveden. Other products include crested ridge-tiles and glazed floor-tiles.

b. Lyveden (Bryant and Steane 1969; 1971; Steane 1967; Steane and Bryant 1975): Figs. 171–2

(i) Production sites
Deserted village in Rockingham Forest, four miles east of Stanion, based on similar but not identical geological formation. Place name recorded as 'Lyvedene Pottere' in 1285 and 'Potteres Livedene' in 1312.

Excavations between 1965 and 1973 revealed layout of several tenements including those of potters:

Site B – building with walls using kiln-bricks and dump of clean clay outside, possibly used for potting.

Fig. 171 NORTHAMPTONSHIRE
Lyveden: 1013–22, kiln products, 13th cent. (After Webster A. 1975)

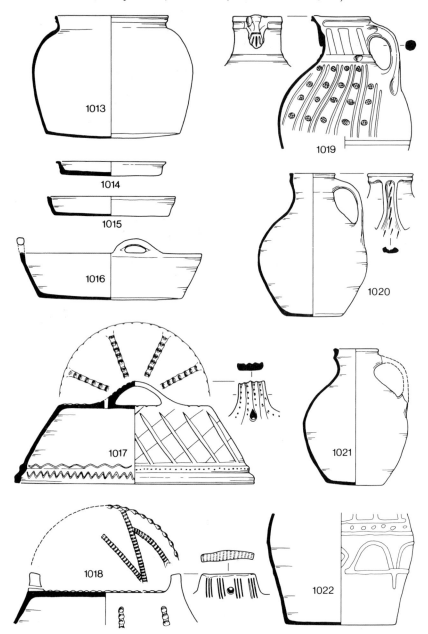

Fig. 172 NORTHAMPTONSHIRE
Lyveden: 1023–4, kiln products, 13th–14th cent. (After A. Webster 1975)

Stanion: 1025–7, kiln products, 13th–14th cent. (After Bellamy 1983)
Lyveden/Stanion: 1028–9, 1036, Lyveden/Stanion ware from Northampton, 13th–14th
cent. 1030–1, 1035, Lyveden/Stanion ware from Ellington, 13th cent. 1032–4,
Lyveden/Stanion ware from Wythemail, 13th–14th cent. (After McCarthy 1979;
Mynard 1969a; Tebbutt *et al.* 1971; Williams D.W. 1983)

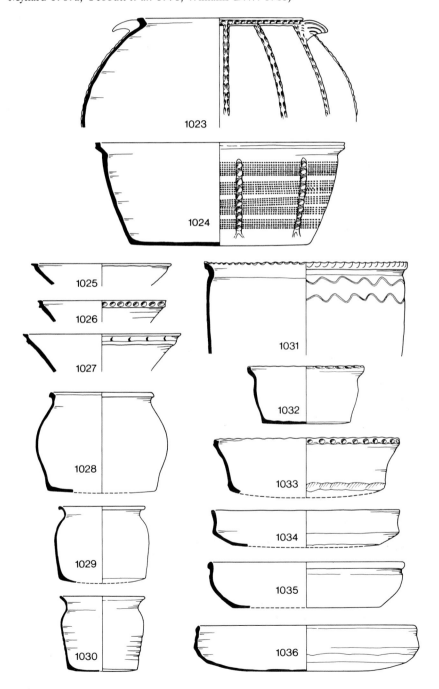

Site C – possible base of clamp kiln.

Site D – (see Fig. 33) sequence in three main phases set within toft of about one third of an acre. Earliest phase: timber-built 'workshop' with much industrial waste on floors; six small pits, four filled with clean clay; south yard had palimpsest of pits filled with clean clay and industrial waste; north yard contained Type 4a kiln and adjacent waster heap. At eastern edge of excavation feature including surfaces interpreted as a 'hut' of uncertain function.

Secondary phase: overlying timber 'workshop' there was a stone-built 'workshop', a building 7.3m long x 3.3m wide with two opposed doors and an eastern extension; the latter could be part of primary stone workshop. Within the 'workshop' there were four hearths and a number of pits, some stone-lined, containing clean clay and industrial waste. South yard had fewer pits than previously. East yard contained three-bay timber building based on pads, interpreted as a 'store-shed' but function must be regarded as uncertain. North yard continued to house Type 4a kiln, though re-orientated through 180°.

Tertiary phase – 'workshop' building continued but without the extension and with signs of burning and pits inside. In north-east corner of 'workshop' there was half a circular limestone slab with central hole, possibly either potter's wheel pivot or door pivot, but position of stone implies re-use as building material in wall. Distribution of pits and hearths within building suggested to excavator that west end of 'workshop' used for manufacture and east end used for drying vessels before firing. Tools found in west half included iron knives, six-sectored antler stamp and whetstones. South yard apparently devoid of features except one pit, but east yard 'store-shed' extended and abutted waste heap. The wasters surrounded a new Type 4a kiln, partly reconstructed on at least four occasions. North yard enclosed by stone walls.

Dating and general comments: coin of *c.* 1250 below wall of 'store-shed', but otherwise dates difficult and rely largely on relative sequence and typological considerations of pottery. Position of workshop remained constant but uses of surrounding yards indicate slight modifications to working practices. If the pits in the earliest phase were quarries for clay, their abandonment suggests that clay was brought in from outside toft subsequently. The identification of yard areas, 'store-shed' and minor structural elements is very difficult although common sense dictates the necessity for store areas. This site is currently the best evidence from medieval Britain of a potter's working area, but the reports are not without difficulties and should be used with care.

Site G – stratigraphic sequence less well developed than at Site D: toft area about one third of an acre. Toft encloses Type 4a kiln with waster heap on two sides; eight stone-lined pits, some containing clean clay. Three pits had two cooking pots and a bowl inserted into top of fill. A well was found backfilled with waste and a circular stone platform was associated with fragmentary walls. There were seven quarry pits for clay and or stone. Date attributed to mid 13th/early 14th century.

Site J – area bisected into eastern and western halves by fragmentary linear boundary feature. The report identifies two tofts, each about one third of an acre. East toft: earliest phase contained rectangular stone building about 11m long x 4m wide, partially paved, with large amounts of industrial waste trodden into floor; building interpreted, possibly correctly, as a potter's 'workshop'. External areas included several stone-lined pits and a drain, badly plough-damaged. South side was defined by substantial stone-based wall and metalled road. West toft: remains of feature believed to be Type 4a kiln, a waster heap associated with circular stone-surfaced hard standing, a well and four quarry pits. In south-west corner a rectangular stone surface was associated with a great deal of charcoal, fire-reddened stones, coal and iron slag. No iron-smelting hearths recognized but area was probably related to iron working or smithing. Date of both tofts attributed to 13th–14th century.

(ii) *Pottery*
Products of Lyveden and Stanion kilns very closely related but it is now becoming possible to distinguish the fabrics because of the slightly different geological backgrounds. Forms at Lyveden include cooking pots, bowls and jugs in various sizes. Bowls sometimes thumbed on rims and one is elaborately rouletted. Jugs decorated with applied strips, stamped pads and very rare anthropomorphic motifs. Also produced were side-handled bowls, curfews, shallow dishes, cisterns and roof-tiles.

c. *Potterspury* (Jope 1950; Mynard 1970)

Production site
Potter element in place name first recorded in 1287.

d. *Northampton* (Gryspeerdt 1978; 1979; McCarthy 1979): Fig. 172

St Neots types continue from previous period, but manufactured differently and fired harder. Forms mainly cylindrical cooking pots early on, but with globular forms more important in 13th century; bowls less common than hitherto. Some jugs, initially unglazed; later jugs are partially glazed as Lyveden-Stanion products appear. Likely sources of calcareous wares are Olney Hyde, Harrold and Lyveden-Stanion. Potterspury ware first appears in St Peter's Street sequence and at Marefair in 13th century but quantities are insignificant. Dates of sites largely stratigraphically derived, combined with typological considerations and presence of regional imports.

e. *Faxton* (Butler 1969 and pers. comm.)

Six tofts excavated in deserted village. Lyveden-Stanion wares main types; cooking pots, some jugs and bowls present. There seems to be a general correspondence between ratio of fine to coarse wares with architectural style and presence of other finds. Tofts 6–9 produced few glazed wares and regional imports or any other finds and the buildings appear to be very small cottages. Tofts 29 and 53 more pretentious architecturally, associated with a wider range of metalwork, abundant coins and jettons and pottery, including larger number of glazed wares and regional imports.

f. *Wythemail* (Mynard 1969a): Fig. 172

Multi-period toft in deserted village produced short stratigraphic sequence. Local calcareous wares of Olney Hyde and Lyveden-Stanion type dominant early on, with cooking pots and bowls with some jugs. Subsequently calcareous wares remain dominant, but the fine sandy Potterspury types increase in quantity, suggesting a date not earlier than 14th century.

3. Huntingdonshire

a. *Ellington* (Tebbutt *et al.* 1971): Fig. 172

Earliest phase (pre-moat timber building) includes Stamford products and some post-Conquest calcareous types, with Lyveden-Stanion wares and other Early Medieval quartz-based fabrics. Lyveden wares include coiled, oxidized and reduced cooking pots and bowls as well at least twenty coiled but highly decorated jugs with applied pads, strips and stamps. Early Medieval Sandy wares quartzitic, varying degrees of harshness; forms include cooking pots bowls and jugs.

In subsequent phase, attributed to the moated platform, Lyveden ware continues as major local product but more regional imports present. No independent dating for site; dating dependent upon typological considerations.

b. *Wintringham* (Beresford 1977)

Moated platform on which ceramic sequence begins in 12th century with local calcitic wares and Stamford products. In later phases, which show increasing elaboration of building complex, pottery shows greater diversification with Brill-Boarstall, Coventry, Grimston and Potterspury wares occurring alongside the main local types, mostly Lyveden-Stanion products. In addition to regional imports, continental imports and finds reflect high status of site.

c. *Eaton Socon* (Addyman 1965)

Norman castle with limited sequence including post-Conquest calcareous wares, Stamford ware and local sandy fabrics. Forms include hand-made cooking pots and an unglazed jug from castle bank.

4. Buckinghamshire

a. *Olney Hyde* (Mynard 1984): Fig. 173

(i) *Production sites*

At least fourteen kilns identified at deserted village in Salcey Forest. Part of one tenement, defined by road on one side, excavated. Toft includes clay-pits, buildings, cobbled areas and two kilns. One clay-pit excavated, 8m x 6m x 1.5m deep with three steep sides and one gradually sloping side, possibly a drive-in entrance for cart (Fig. 32). A possible workshop, at least 14m x 8m, with stone walls, earthen floors and three pits less than 0.5m deep lined with limestone slabs. Pivot-stone set in floor may be part of potter's wheel, or door-pivot, though location makes this less likely. A second stone building without internal features may have been domestic. External surfaces of cobbles and limestone perhaps for fuel stacks. Two Type 1b kilns had stone-lined ovens with firebars; one stoke-hole was revetted in stone.

(ii) *Pottery*

Fabric A heavily filled with limestone, mostly oxidized, fairly smooth. Forms – wheel-thrown cooking pots, bowls and jugs with occasional pipkins, storage jars and dripping pans. Source of this fabric, probably made at sites 12–13, was located by geophysical means 270m to south-east of excavated tenement.

Fabric B contains less limestone and some quartz, coarser texture, mostly oxidized. Forms – wheel-thrown cooking pots, some with bifid rims, jugs, bowls with side and basket handles, lamps, curfews, bottles, pipkins, lids, money boxes, mortar, chimney pots, crested and knobbed ridge-tiles.

Decoration is rare in both fabrics and neither is glazed. Techniques include rouletting, stabbing, some thumbing and one crude anthropomorphic motif.

Fabric A attributed typologically to 13th century and Fabric B to 14th century.

Fig. 173 BUCKINGHAMSHIRE
Olney Hyde: 1037–43, 1046–51, B ware, 13th cent. 1044–5, A ware, 13th cent. (After Mynard 1984)

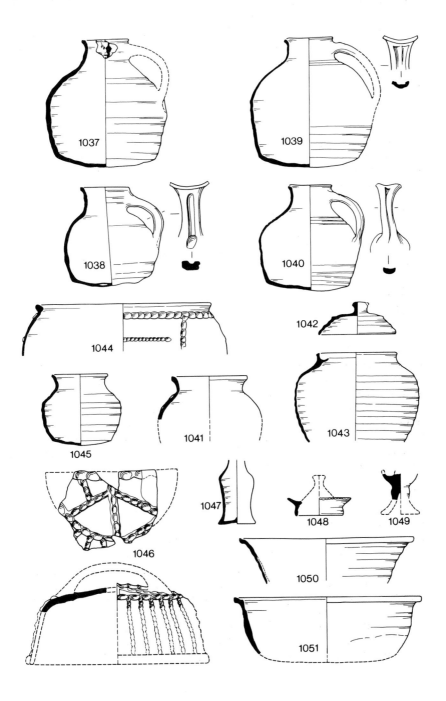

b. Boarstall (Farley 1982)

(i) *Production sites*

Potter names referred to at Brill in a Boarstall cartulary *c.*1210–20 and Hundred Rolls of 1254 mention 'furnaces' in Brill which are thought refer to also to Boarstall. At least nine kilns tentatively identified by field work, most concentrated around Manor Farm at north end of village but one close to centre and one apparently isolated to west. Kilns seem to be located in or close to ridge and furrow (Fig. 31). Local clays almost certainly exploited; extensive pits occur in both Brill and Boarstall villages and clay payments are recorded. Fuel probably obtained from local woods which are part of Forest of Bernwood, and potters occasionally summonsed for taking wood.

(ii) *Pottery*

Sandy fabrics with some mica, fairly smooth with reduced surfaces and oxidized core. Wheel-thrown jugs dominate, lesser forms include jars, costrels, dripping pans, bottles, cisterns and bowls but few cooking pots. Jugs are lead-glazed with copper added, and decorated with applied strips which are sometimes rouletted, aligned vertically or in swirls; some have grid-stamps. Decorated floor-tile production also seems likely. Date suggested by Ivens as mid 14th century but Farley, following sequence at Oxford, has indicated that a 13th century date would be more acceptable, terminating in early 14th century.

c. Brill (Ivens 1981; 1982; Jope and Ivens 1981): Figs. 174–5

(i) *Production sites*

Six Type 2c kilns and large numbers of wasters. One kiln dated archaeomagnetically to 1300–25.

(ii) *Pottery*

Earliest fabrics very mixed with varying amounts of quartz, limestone, flint, chert; fairly soft and largely oxidized wares. Forms probably hand-made with possible wheel-finishing; cooking pots with thin internal wash of glaze. Early stratigraphic dating for this material at kiln site seems possible when compared with material from west country.

Other medieval fabrics defined as 'standard' and 'fine jug' wares; inclusions basically fine quartz, slightly sandy textured with oxidized surfaces. Harsher fabrics referred to as 'cooking pot' ware tend to correlate with more heavily-filled wares; forms cooking pots, pans, bowls, skillets and pipkins. Jugs one of the dominant forms, glazed with copper additives and somewhat restrained decoration as at Boarstall. Motifs include rouletted applied strips, some incised lines, painted lines and rilling. Jugs occur in a variety of shapes from biconical, globular to baluster. Other rare forms include costrels, small bowls, blowing horns, a mouthpiece from a musical instrument.

d. Great Missenden, Potter Row (Ashworth 1983)

(i) *Production site*

Potter name occurs in 1234–7 in Missenden Abbey cartulary and may refer to Potter Row which otherwise not recorded until 1311. Wasters found close to street frontage.

(ii) *Pottery*

Quartz-tempered fabrics displaying variations in colour and hardness. Forms include cooking pots, glazed jugs, bowls and lids.

Fig. 174 BUCKINGHAMSHIRE
Brill: 1052–4, 1059, 1064, standard jug fabric, 13th cent. 1055–8, 1060–3, 1065–6, cooking pot fabric, 13th cent. (After Ivens 1982)

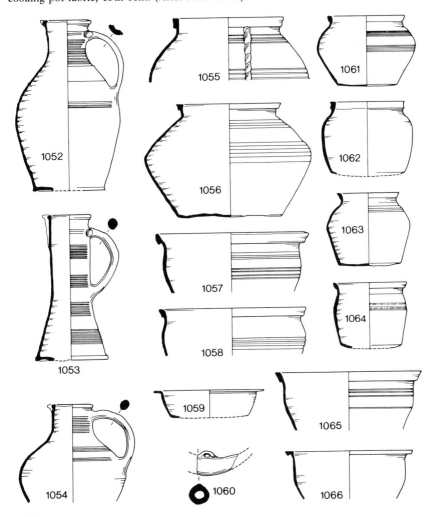

e. Denham (M. Farley pers. comm.)

(i) *Production site*

Parts of four Type 2b kilns excavated, with clay-pits and minor structural features.

(ii) *Pottery*

Very large quantity of pottery recovered; mainly dark grey sandy fabrics, harsh surfaces; forms include cooking pots with scored surfaces as well as glazed jugs, bowls and possibly lamps. Dated archaeomagnetically to 1250±20. Similar vessels with scored surfaces are attested elsewhere in the Chilterns, e.g. Fulmer (Fig. 295), and are sometimes known as M40 ware.

Fig. 175   BUCKINGHAMSHIRE

Brill: 1067, early fabric, early–mid 13th cent. (After Jope and Ivens 1981)
Aylesbury: 1068–70, 1072–6, Group III fabrics, late 13th–early 14th cent. 1071, Group I fabric, 13th cent. (After Yeoman 1983)

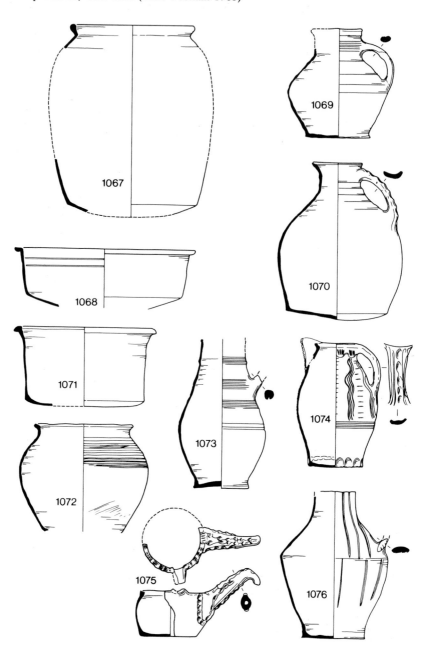

f. Aylesbury (Farley 1974; Yeoman 1983): Figs. 175–6

Excavations at George Street produced pit groups, of which one associated with coin hoard of 1258–81; work at Bourbon Street also included pre-Brill pit groups.

Three main fabrics, including shelly St Neots types with hand-made and wheel-thrown cooking pots, bowls. Flint-tempered fabrics occur: hand-made cooking pots, bowls and jugs. Sandy wares of Brill-Boarstall facies are mainly glazed jugs but also include cooking pots, bowls, curfews and a pipkin/saucepan with side spout and elaborately thumbed handle.

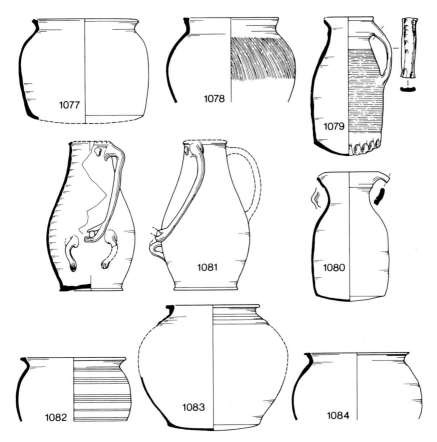

Fig. 176 BUCKINGHAMSHIRE
Aylesbury: 1077, 1079 quartzitic, 1080, calcareous fabrics, 12th cent. (After Farley 1974)
Fulmer: 1078, sandy fabric, 12th–13th cent. (After Farley 1982)
        HUNTINGDONSHIRE
Wintringham: 1081, possibly Brill ware, 13th–14th cent. (After Dunning 1977a)
        BEDFORDSHIRE
Bedford: 1082–4, Fabric C3, 12th–13th cent. (After Baker *et al.* 1979)

5. Hertfordshire

a. Various sites (Renn 1964; C. Partridge pers. comm.): Fig. 177

  (i) *Production sites*
    At least nine separate production sites attested by either place-names (e.g. Pottersheath, Potterscrouch) or by wasters, including in some instances kiln furniture,

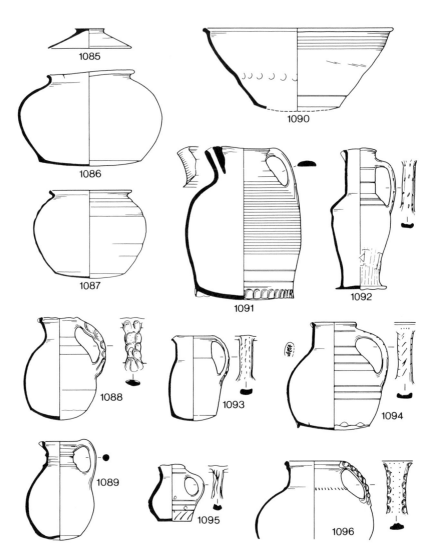

Fig. 177   HERTFORDSHIRE
Misc. sites: 1085–95, Hertfordshire grey wares, 12th–14th cent. 1096, Hertfordshire grey ware from Bedford. (After Linger and Kennett 1972 ; Renn 1964)

and excavation (Elstree, Arkely Barnet, Potters Green, Standon, Hatfield). One Type 2b kiln excavated at Nettleden and another kiln excavated at Chandlers Cross.

(ii) *Pottery*

Fabrics in all cases quartz-based, sometimes with addition of flint. Textures vary from smooth to harsh but colours of products predominantly reduced greys to black; known as Hertfordshire Grey wares. Forms wheel-thrown, especially after 14th century, and include cooking pots, deep bowls, glazed and unglazed jugs, cisterns and possible storage jars.

b. Ashwell (Hurst and Hurst 1967)

Range of pottery includes post-Conquest calcareous wares of general St Neots types, but otherwise cooking pots and jugs typical of Hertfordshire Grey ware tradition with some regional imports from Brill-Boarstall.

c. St Albans (A. Havercroft pers. comm.)

Excavations within the medieval town have produced quantities of medieval pottery, mostly in the typical Hertfordshire Grey ware tradition, but as yet no good stratigraphic sequences.

6. Bedfordshire

a. Harrold (Hall D.N. 1971)

(i) *Production site*

Kiln of uncertain type in village centre; daub may possibly be from superstructure but no kiln furniture; evidence tenuous.

(ii) *Pottery*

Calcareous, coarse, oxidized and reduced fabrics; unglazed jugs, cooking pots and bowls similar to products of kilns at Olney Hyde.

b. Bedford (Baker 1979; E. Baker pers. comm.): Figs. 176–7

All fabrics local to Bedford area are sandy with quartz, some grog, flint and occasional other minerals. Textures vary from harsh and pimply to smooth; surfaces often reduced or partly reduced. Forms, all wheel-thrown, include cooking pots, bowls in several sizes, unglazed jugs.

Two of main types are Fabrics C3 and C5, covering period 12th-14th century and probably manufactured in or close to Bedford. Products so far only known from the town. An important component is the unglazed jug decorated with applied thumbed strips and combing in criss-cross or horizontal bands, and elaborately thumbed handles.

c. Grove Priory (E. Baker pers. comm.)

Local sandy wares comparable to those at Bedford include unglazed jugs decorated with applied and thumbed strips, and wavy lines; also cooking pots and bowls. Glazed wares, as at Bedford, are regional imports from neighbouring counties.

South-East England (Fig. 178)

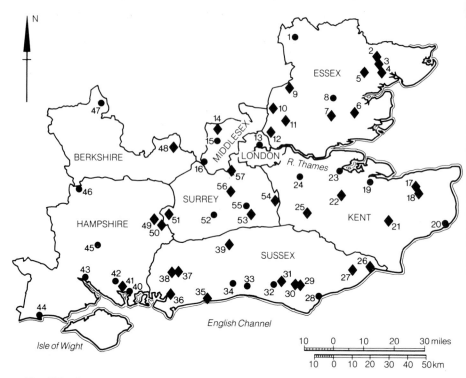

Fig. 178   South-East England, location map
1 Saffron Walden, 2 Great Horkesley, 3 Mile End, 4 Colchester, 5 Sible
Hedingham, 6 Danbury, 7 Mill Green, 8 Writtle, 9 Harlow, 10 Waltham Abbey, 11
Navestock, 12 Chingford, 13 London, 14 Pinner, 15 Northolt, 16 Staines, 17 Tyler
Hill, 18 Canterbury, 19 Ospringe, 20 Dover, 21 Ashford, 22 Maidstone, 23
Rochester, 24 Eynsford, 25 Leigh, 26 Rye, 27 Brede, 28 Pevensey, 29 Michelham,
30 Upper Dicker, 31 Ringmer, 32 Lewes, 33 Hangleton, 34 Bramber, 35 Binsted,
36 Chichester, 37 Graffham, 38 Heyshott, 39 Horsham, 40 Portchester, 41
Boarhunt, 42 Wickham, 43 Southampton, 44 Christchurch, 45 Winchester, 46
Netherton, 47 Seacourt, 48 Maidenhead, 49 Bentley, 50 Alice Holt, 51 Farnham, 52
Abinger, 53 Earlswood, 54 Limpsfield, 55 Reigate, 56 Ashtead, 57 Kingston upon
Thames.

1. Essex

a. *Colchester* (Cunningham 1982a; 1984): Fig. 179

(i) *Production site*

Middleborough – at least seven, perhaps nine, small Type 1b kilns, each with a
central tongue attached to the rear wall; situated outside north gate of town. Kilns dated
on pottery grounds to mid 12th-early 13th century.

Fig. 179 ESSEX
Colchester: 1097–1102, Middleborough kiln products, mid 12th–early 13th cent.
1103–5, Fabric 20, 13th–14th cent. 1106–7, Colchester ware, late 13th–14th cent.
(After Cunningham 1982a; 1984).
Mile End: 1108–11, Fabric A, late 12th–early 13th cent. (After Drury and Petchey
1975)

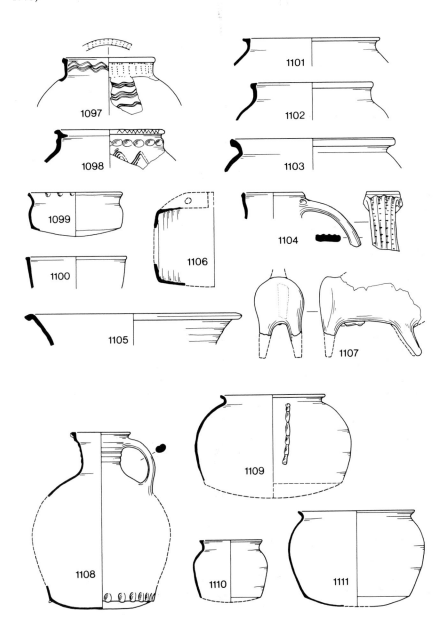

(ii) *Pottery*

Middleborough products – Fabric 13, Early Medieval ware, sand-tempered unglazed coarse ware varying from light red to grey, but mostly grey; some vessels with limited and superficial shell inclusions. Mostly wheel-made. Forms – mostly cooking pots, some hand-made bowls, a few pitchers, large bucket-shaped vessels, possibly curfews. Decoration includes burnishing, combing, thumbed applied strips, thumbed rims. Date range mid 12th-early 13th century.

Other fabrics from elsewhere in the town include Colchester ware – hard orange wheel-made sandy fabric with grey core, usually with overall white or cream slip and copper-flecked green glaze. Cooking pots often have white slip and plain glaze around the inside of the rim. Forms include cooking pots, costrels, aquamaniles, louvers. Source probably local, as fabric is identical to later Colchester slip-painted ware, in which wasters are known. Date range *c.* later 13th century on.

Fabric 20 – coarse grey wares; forms – cooking pots, jugs, bowls, few dripping dishes. Date range 13th-14th century.

b. Mile End (Drury and Petchey 1975): Fig. 179

(i) *Production site*

Pits filled with kiln debris; kilns not located.

(ii) *Pottery*

Essex sandy grey wares; Fabric A most common.

Fabric A – grey to red-brown or orange sandy fabric, red-brown core; intended appearance was probably grey.

Fabric B – red-brown or grey fabric, sandier than Fabric A.

Fabric C – similar to Fabric A; colour ranges from black through grey and orange-brown to red-brown.

Forms – mainly unglazed cooking pots; also jugs, bowls. Decoration includes applied thumbed strips, finger impressions on vessel body, wavy lines on top of rim or shoulder. Date range probably end of 12th century-mid/late 13th century.

c. Great Horkesley (Drury and Petchey 1975)

(i) *Production site*

Much kiln debris and wasters found.

(ii) *Pottery*

Essex sandy grey ware. Fabric D – sandy grey fabric; forms include cooking pots and jugs, a few jugs with overall cream slip or painted cream slip lines under a green glaze; some cisterns. Date range probably 14th century, perhaps earlier rather than later in that century.

d. Sible Hedingham/Southey Green and Halstead area (Webster and Cherry 1972: 205; 1973: 184; 1974: 220; Wilson and Hurst J.G. 1958: 211; 1959: 325; Wilson and Hurst, D.G. 1965: 216–17): Fig. 180

(i) *Production sites*

A number of kilns, some at least of Type 2, known at Hole Farm and Starling's hill, and in the Halstead area to the south and east. Reference to potter at Halstead in 1229, and documentary evidence for Sible Hedingham and Halstead pottery industry from 13th to 19th centuries (Le Patourel 1968: 123–4).

Fig. 180 ESSEX
Mile End: 1112–13, 1116, Fabric A, late 12th–early 13th cent. 1114–15, Fabric C,
13th cent. 1117, Fabric B, late 12th–early 13th cent. (After Drury and Petchey 1975)
Sible Hedingham: 1118–19, Hedingham ware from Colchester, *c.* 13th cent. (After
Cunningham *et al.* 1983)

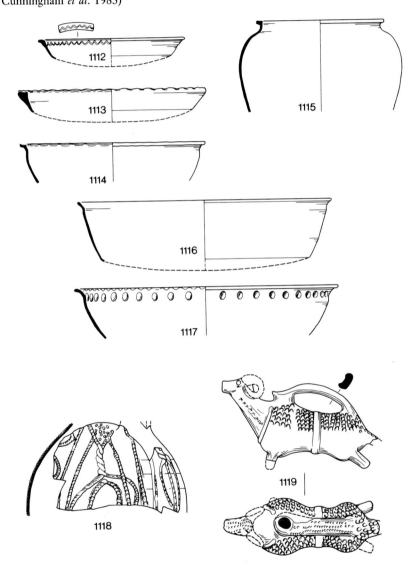

(ii) *Pottery*
Hedingham ware – fine micaceous slightly sandy light orange or pink buff fabric,
usually associated with decorated glazed jugs, also aquamaniles; decoration includes
polychrome effects achieved with slips and copper glaze colourant, some white slip

painting, applied scales, strips and pellets, stamped pellets, bearded face masks. Date range *c*. late 12th century on, declining by late 13th century.

Sible Hedingham products also include unglazed grey coarse wares, from later 12th century on. Forms include cooking pots, storage jars, jugs, large shallow bowls (some with a small hole perforated just below the rim), occasional lamp.

e. Mill Green, Ingatestone (Pearce *et al.* 1982; Sellers 1970): Figs. 181–2; see also Fig. 35; Fig. 63 No. 1

(i) Production sites
Kiln dumps excavated at several sites. Documentary reference to potters in 1275.
(ii) Pottery
Mill Green ware (formerly known as 'West Kent ware') – sandy red slightly micaceous fabric, often with grey core, varying from very fine to coarse sandy in texture. Forms include cooking pots (some in Essex grey wares), jugs (conical, rounded, squat and baluster), bowls; some pipkins, dishes, jars, culinary stamps, plates/lids and cups. Decoration includes slip painting, simple combed sgraffito, and polychrome patterns (in imitation of London-type ware Rouen copies) on baluster jugs using white, red and copper-green slips as paint and as applied blobs and strips. Occasional scale decoration and anthropomorphic motifs, including face-on-front miniature jugs. Cooking pots sometimes have applied thumbed strips, and often have a thin green glaze on the inside of the base. Fine glazed ware jugs traded to London; date range there later 13th-early 14th century, but pottery production at Mill Green probably continues after that.

f. Chingford (Le Patourel 1968: 123)

Production site
Documentary evidence for potter in 1222.

g. Navestock (Le Patourel 1968: 123)

Production site
Documentary evidence for potter in 1222.

h. Harlow (Le Patourel 1968: 124; Newton and Bibbings 1958)

Production site
Documentary evidence for pottery manufacture from 13th–19th centuries. Earliest reference is probably 1254.

i. Danbury (Drury and Pratt 1975; Eddy and Priddy 1981: 45): Fig. 183

(i) Production site
Danbury was a centre of small-scale brick, tile and pottery manufacture from the late 13th century onwards (for tile production, see Drury and Pratt 1975). Some documentary references to potters (C.M. Cunningham, pers. comm.).
(ii) Pottery
Main fabrics from excavation of tile factory, all of late 13th-early 14th century date range:
Fabrics A and B – sand and grit-tempered fabrics; A is a hard grey fabric, B is a soft

Fig. 181 ESSEX
Mill Green: 1120–7, 1129–31, Mill Green ware from London, later 13th–early 14th
cent. 1128, Mill Green ware, Colchester and Essex Museum (After Pearce *et al.*
1982)

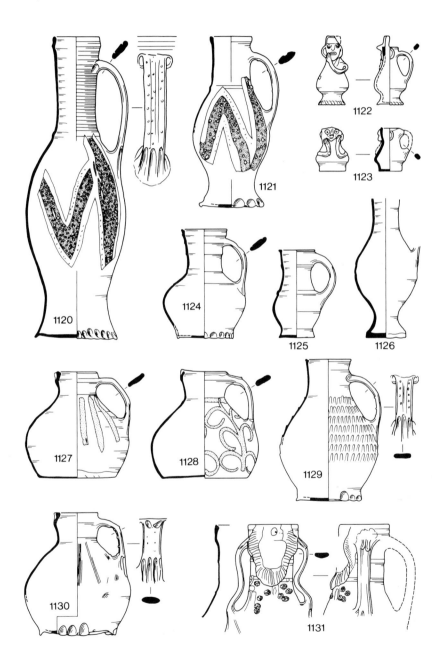

Fig. 182   ESSEX
Mill Green: 1132–7, 1139, Mill Green ware from London, later 13th–early 14th cent.
1138, Mill Green ware, Colchester and Essex Museum. (After Pearce *et al.* 1982)

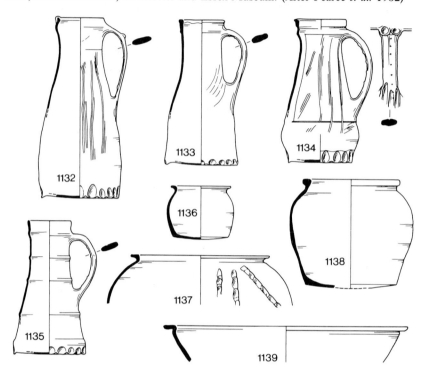

grey-brown or orange fabric, the two being identical apart from firing conditions. Mainly cooking pots, some jugs, occasional pipkin.

Fabric C – fairly hard orange fabric, slightly sand-tempered with occasional large grains; white slipped or slip-decorated and glazed. Forms mostly jugs, few cooking pots, bowls.

Fabric G – very hard grey fabric with some sand and grit inclusions, dull orange or grey surfaces. Forms – jugs, slipped or slip-decorated and glazed.

Fabric H – a group of very hard, finely made fabrics, orange through dull red to grey. Forms – jugs, white-slipped with mottled green glaze, some decorated with rows of iron-rich dots. Some examples may be highly-fired versions of Fabric A.

j. Waltham Abbey (Huggins 1972; 1973; 1976): Fig. 183

(i) *Production site*
'Potteryshylle' mentioned in 1312; a later kiln known near Potkiln Shaw, but dating not given (Renn 1964: 11).

(ii) *Pottery*
No archaeological evidence for production of particular wares.

Fig. 183 ESSEX
Danbury: 1140–2, Fabric A. 1143–4, Fabric B. Late 13th–early 14th cent. (After Drury and Pratt 1975)
Waltham Abbey: 1145, 1147, Ware J2. 1146, Ware G. 1148–9, Ware H. 13th–14th cent. (After Huggins 1972; 1976)

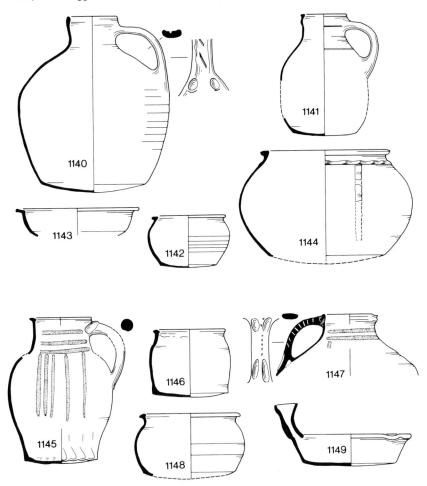

Shelly wares D1 and E1 continue to *c*. 1200; Shelly ware D2 to *c*. 1300.

Ware E2 – rough sandy wheel-thrown ware with brown or grey surfaces; forms mainly cooking pots. Date range *c*. 1150–1250.

Wares F and G – coarse sand-tempered wheel-made wares, grey or grey/black, sometimes partially oxidized to red. Forms mainly cooking pots, some bowls, pitchers. Decoration includes incised wavy lines, thumbing on rims and applied thumbed strips. Source probably not local, perhaps Hertfordshire or Middlesex. Date range *c*. 1150–1250.

Ware H – red sandy ware, forms mainly cooking pots, also skillets, bowls. Date range *c.* 1200–1500.

Ware J2 – Essex-type red sandy ware; forms – cooking pots, jugs. Decoration includes white slip-painted lines, or overall white slip; green or brownish-green glaze. Source probably local. Date range *c.* 1250–1500.

k. Saffron Walden (Cunningham 1982b)

Local Early Medieval wares continue to *c.* late 12th/early 13th century. Some Hedingham ware in 13th and 14th centuries, and hard pimply grey and orange wares.

l. Writtle (Rahtz 1969a)

Excavation of a moated site, dated by coins and documentary evidence.

13th and 14th century pottery includes small quantities of shelly wares in early 13th century, and Mill Green-type and Hedingham-type wares; also orange and grey ware cooking pots.

2. Middlesex

a. Pinner (Sheppard 1977)

(i) *Production site*
Kiln, possibly Type 1b, partly excavated.
(ii) *Pottery*
Hard reduced grey sand-tempered ware; forms – mainly cooking pots, some with applied and thumbed strips, bowls and jugs. Fabric resembles Northolt Group k.

b. Northolt (Hurst J.G. 1961)

Group i – Developed Early Medieval ware: quartz-tempered, hard reduced grey ware, harsh textured. Forms possibly hand-made cooking pots and bowls. Attributed to *c.* 1100–1200.

Group j – Rough Medieval ware: very gritty harsh-textured light grey to off-white fabric. Forms – possibly wheel-thrown cooking pots, occasional bowls and curfew. Dated to 1150–1250.

Group k – Hard Medieval Grey ware: very gritty, flint identified in report, but if the source is Pinner (see above) the filler may be quartz sand; hard, grey harsh-textured surfaces; forms – cooking pots, bowls being exceptionally rare. Dated to 1225–1325.

c. Staines (P. Jones pers. comm.)

Some local production possible, though most vessels the products of Hertfordshire Grey ware tradition, Surrey kilns, Denham and Maidenhead. Local wares may include fabrics with crushed ironstone and quartz tempering; forms are wheel-thrown cooking pots and some spouted bowls. Dates attributed to the late 12th and early 13th centuries.

3. London

a. City of London (Pearce *et al.* 1985; Vince 1985a): Figs. 184–5; see also Fig. 27 Nos. 4–5; Fig. 59 No. 2; Fig. 63 No. 2

Fig. 184   LONDON
London: 1150–65, London-type ware, 13th–14th cent. (After Pearce *et al.* 1985)

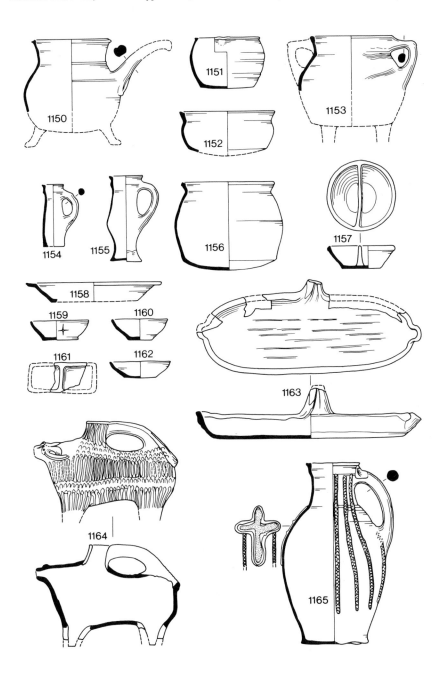

Fig. 185   LONDON
London: 1166–74, London-type ware, 13th–14th cent. (After Pearce *et al.* 1985)

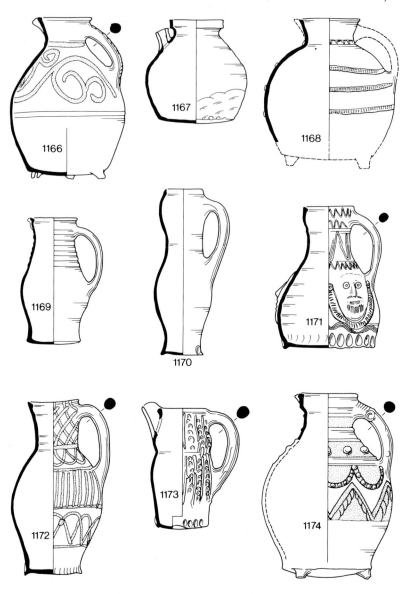

Large number of excavations, main sequences based upon waterfront sites where pottery is associated with small finds, coins and dendrochronological dates dating to between the mid–12th and mid–15th centuries. Whilst there is a broad measure of agreement between the various methods of dating which appears to provide an accurate chronology, it remains the case that the deposits are dumps, whose origins within the City are not known. Some of the material incorporated in the dumps may therefore result from the clearance of deposits significantly earlier than the dates provided by the waterfront timbers or other artifacts. Even so, there appears to be a degree of consistency in the ceramic spectra between the eleven waterfront sites studied, suggesting that the general trends outlined by Vince are probably correct.

Mid 12th to mid 13th century: main sites Swan Lane, Seal House and Billingsgate Lorry Park. Important changes took place from the mid–12th century. Three main coarse wares and four major glazed wares have been defined; of these, Sandy-Shelly ware, Coarse London-type ware and London-type ware are petrologically very similar to the clays of the London area and may originate very close to the City. they are currently the earliest wares known to have been made in London. All are wheel-thrown; Sandy-Shelly ware consists of cooking pots, bowls and large cauldrons amongst other forms.

The fabrics of London-type wares are sandy with quartz and occasional sandstone, iron ore and shell fragments; at least six variants, suggesting more than one source in the immediate vicinity of the City. Colour is usually a dull reddish brown; vessels fired at between 600° and 800°C but not higher, as organic inclusions are still present in carbonized form within the clay. 13th century wares were fired at slightly higher temperatures. Glazes were dusted on to the surface, with copper added in some cases. Wide range of forms, including tripod pitchers and many varieties of jug, spouted pitchers, aquamaniles, miniature jugs, cooking pots, bowls, dishes, dripping pans, occasional chafing dishes, pipkins.

Elaborate decoration, with the use of white slip-painted lines, pellets, horizontal lines of scales, dimples and incised lines occurring on mid to late 12th century splashed-glaze tripod pitchers and rounded jugs. From the early 13th century local copies of imported Rouen wares, resembling them in the use of slipped bands in two colours giving a polychromatic appearance as well as in the shape of the jugs and disposition form the basis of decorative elements. Some of the basic features of these designs form the basis of decoration applied to jugs in the mid 13th century. Other decorative schemes imitate northern French vessels, especially in the use of vertical lines of applied slips sometimes accompanied by rouletting. Highly decorated jugs also occur with a wider range of techniques and motifs including foliate, curvilinear, anthropomorphic and zoomorphic representation. Although decorated jugs continue to be used, and presumably made, throughout the century, the proportion of decorated wares noticeably decreases from around 1250; from about this time potteries in Hertfordshire and Surrey, especially Kingston, begin supplying the London market.

Late 13th to mid 14th century; main sites Trig Lane, Swan Lane and Ludgate Hill. Shelly-Sandy wares cease production and only the London-type ware continues as the locally-made pottery. Plain jugs predominate, though other forms, including drinking jugs, bottles and cauldrons, also appear. Much of London's need for pottery increasingly being met from external sources, notably Kingston and Mill Green, probably by riverine trade: other pottery from the Hampshire-Surrey borders (known as Coarse Border ware) and from South Hertfordshire was probably brought in overland.

4. Surrey

a. Ashtead (Frere 1941)

(i) *Production site*

Possible kiln marked by quantities of ash and charcoal as well as wasters.

(ii) *Pottery*

Coarse gritty pink-grey wares; forms include cooking pots with applied and thumbed strips, bowls, socketed bowls, pipkins and glazed jugs decorated with white slip and some applied strips. Plain unglazed floor and roof tiles also manufactured.

b. Earlswood, Bushfield Shaw (Turner 1974): Fig. 187

(i) *Production site*

Type 1b kiln constructed partly of roof tiles excavated together with wasters. Nearest source of clays for the white slip are the Reading Beds at Cheam.

(ii) *Pottery*

Sandy orange-pink fabrics. Main products include cooking pots, bowls and decorated jugs. Some cooking pots have applied and thumbed strips. Jugs frequently covered with white slip and a green or clear lead glaze; many have painted bands of white slip arranged horizontally or in a criss-cross pattern, often combined with sgraffito curvilinear motifs. Anthropomorphic decoration in the form of faces on bridge spouts also occurs.

c. Limpsfield (Jope 1956; Prendergast 1974)

(i) *Production site*

Stone structure enclosing irregular area approximately 8m long and containing post-holes, four pivot-stones and lumps of raw clay. Interpretation of this stone structure not clear from the published plan but there are two integral features, namely a small rectangular room and a twin-flued pottery kiln. It seems likely that this is a potter's working area with kiln and adjacent drying room. Other kilns suspected from wasters at Watts Hill, Scearn Bank, and attested at Lakestreet Green.

(ii) *Pottery*

Generally hard, quartz-tempered, sometimes very sandy, light grey to light brown though other variations do occur. Forms – mainly cooking pots, jugs and dishes, with rare cisterns and possibly storage jars. Decoration includes incised and combed wavy lines, applied strips, some white slipped lines, but little glazing apparent.

d. Farnham (Cole and Timby 1982)

(i) *Production site*

Kiln excavated close to castle. Report identifies structure as Type 2 but site plan suggests a multi-flued structure with at least three stoke areas. Additional kilns suspected in immediate vicinity from discoveries of wasters. A Nicholas Pother, possibly a potter, recorded as holding land in the borough in 1244.

(ii) *Pottery*

Surrey White-ware is a generic term which embraces the products of a large number of kilns, including at this period Farnham and Kingston upon Thames; Surrey white wares are not always attributable to source (e.g. Fig. 186). The tradition becomes more widespread after 1350, with the addition of the production centres at Cheam, Farnborough and Southwark.

Products of Farnham kiln essentially quartz-tempered, fairly coarse. At least two

Fig. 186 SURREY
Jug in Surrey White ware; ht. 34.2 cm. (Photo: Guildford Museum)

clay sources exploited, (i) the Reading Beds in Farnham Park and (ii) Gault clays within half a mile of production site. Forms are wheel-thrown and include cooking pots, bowls, dishes, frying pans, jugs, occasional cisterns and possibly curfews. Decoration is limited but yellowish and green glazes occur on jugs. Dated typologically to 13th–14th century.

e. Kingston upon Thames (Hinton and Nelson 1980; Orton 1982): Fig. 187

(i) *Production site*
Part of kiln of uncertain form excavated together with quantity of wasters on eastern edge of medieval town in Eden Street.

Documentary references to royal orders or payments to the bailiffs at Kingston for the supply of 1000 pitchers to be sent to the king's butler in Westminster in 1264. Further requests were made in the same decade for quantities varying from 500 to 1000 pitchers. Other references concern a John le Poter at Surbiton in 1296 and Alicia Poter amongst the Kingston entries of the 1332 Lay Subsidy Rolls.

Fig. 187 SURREY

Reigate: 1175–9, local calcareous and sandy, late 12th–13th cent. wares. (After Williams D.W. 1983)

Kingston-upon-Thames: 1180–2, kiln products, late 13th–early 14th cent. 1185–8, Kingston-type ware from London, mid 13th–early 14th cent. (After Hinton and Nelson 1980; Vince 1985a)

Earlswood: 1183–4, kiln products, late 13th–early 14th cent. (After Turner 1974)

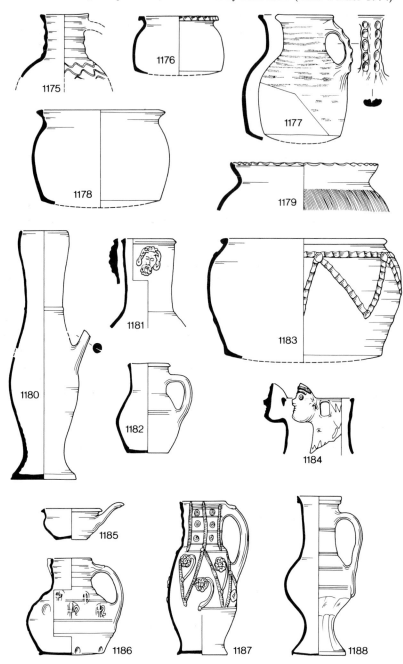

(ii) *Pottery*

Hard with some quartzite and ironstone, off-white colours with variations through grey to orange-pink. Coarser and sandier than Cheam products, though difficult to distinguish by eye. Wheel-thrown but poorly finished, partially glazed on external surfaces. Forms include biconical, barrel-shaped, baluster and conical jugs, cooking pots, dishes, bowls, crucibles, lobed cups. Decoration includes anthropomorphic motifs, amongst which are crowned stamped heads.

Dating dependent upon stratigraphic sequences elsewhere, e.g. that at Trig Lane, London. At this site, Orton argued that the cumulative evidence of coins, dendrochronology and other finds supported a date for the arrival of Kingston wares in London from *c.* 1250.

f. Farnborough (F. Holling pers. comm.)

Production site

Possible early production centre excavated datable to early 14th century.

g. Alice Holt, Frithend and Bentley (Barton and Brears 1976; Lyne and Jefferies 1974)

(i) *Production sites*

Documentary references to land held by Hugo the Crokkere and by his son Peter the Crockere in the late 13th and early 14th century. Further references in connection with East Worldham church mention 'ye dykers croft, ye potteris crofts and ye carpenterrs crofts'. A Stephen the Crockere held 20½ acres of land in the vicinity in 1331 and 1344. Other potters include William the Potter of La Fryth, Roger the Potter of Hawkely and Richard the Potter of Broxhead in 1257. Kiln attested at Bentley but details not known.

(ii) *Pottery*

Sherds from two locations at Frithend are essentially sandy, some being coarse and with chaff impressions; colours range through oranges, browns and greys. Forms include cooking pots with very simple everted rims and scratch-marked surfaces as well as more developed forms, jugs, some decorated with 'wheel stamps', bowls, cisterns and skillets. Pottery dated typologically to 13th–14th century but no later, as it seems likely that the Alice Holt industry may have been overtaken by development of Surrey White wares.

Bentley wares probably calcitic, partly oxidized fabrics. Forms known to include cooking pots, skillets, a curfew, handled bowls, tripod pitchers and highly decorated jugs, some with faces below bridge spouts. Site dated by analogy with Sussex material, with which it shares a number of common features.

h. Abinger (Dunning 1950b)

Coarse-textured sandy grey wares with fairly smooth but pitted surfaces; forms include cooking pots and a bowl. Ascribed to mid 12th century.

Sandy grey wares with occasional flint inclusions; cooking pots, bowls and decorated jugs. Regarded as 13th century.

i. Reigate, Bell Street (Williams D.W. 1983): Fig. 187

Early Reduced ware – coarse, sandy, grey and brown fabric; cooking pots with simple everted rims and decorated with occasional finger tipping on rims.

Red Brown-Surfaced Grey ware – cooking pots with finger tipped rims and combed wavy lines. Jugs, partly oxidized, some plain unglazed, some glazed and decorated with applied strips, rouletting or anthropomorphic motifs.

Black-Surfaced Grey Sandy ware – includes cooking pots, some with applied and thumbed strips, and jugs. Fabric akin to Hertfordshire grey ware but has not been confirmed as a regional import.

Cream-slipped ware – probably Earlswood products, though clearly akin to Mill Green ware and that formerly known as West Kent ware; decorated with a cream slip below glaze, and curvilinear sgraffito motifs.

j. Other sites

Numerous small-scale excavations in Reigate and elsewhere in Surrey provide a general picture of both shelly and scratch-marked wares in the 12th–early 13th century being supplanted by a grey sandy ware tradition, to which the products of the Earlswood kilns provided a finer alternative.

5. Kent

a. Tyler Hill (Bennett and Macpherson-Grant 1980; Macpherson-Grant 1978; n.d.; Spillett et al. 1942; Tatton-Brown and Macpherson-Grant 1983): Figs. 188–9

(i) Production sites

A number of kiln sites are suspected from the location of large quantities of pottery wasters around Tyler Hill, although the only kilns excavated seem to have been mainly concerned with tile production.

(ii) Pottery

Tyler Hill ware – sandy micaceous fabric, utilizing the London Clays, often grey with orange red or buff surfaces, olive-green glaze. Increasing tendency to partial or complete oxidization from mid 12th century onwards. Earliest production attested so far is near Brittancourt Farm; wares dated by their occurrence in Canterbury groups to *c.* 1150–75; forms include pitchers with collared rims and square rouletting, showing continental influence; probably copying products of the Pound Lane pottery in Canterbury. 13th–14th century Tyler Hill forms include cooking pots, large cooking pots/storage jars, jugs, bowls, skillets, dripping dishes, aquamaniles, candlesticks, curfews, money-boxes, chimney pots. Highly decorated period from *c.* 1250–1325; decoration includes straight and wavy incised lines and combing, impressed and applied decoration, anthropomorphic and zoomorphic motifs, and pale slip painting, either as horizontal or vertical lines, lattice, or simple geometric patterns. One jug has a slip-painted letter H. Cooking pots and storage jars often have thumbed vertical strips.

Tyler Hill supplied much of Canterbury's pottery as well as many other places in east Kent.

b. Ashford (Grove and Warhurst 1952)

(i) Production site

Potters Corner – pottery finds, including many wasters, indicate the presence of a kiln of 13th century date.

Fig. 188 KENT
Tyler Hill: 1189–93, kiln products, 13th–14th cent. 1194–6, Tyler Hill ware from
Dover. 1197–1201, Tyler Hill ware from Canterbury. (After Mynard 1969c; Spillett
et al. 1942; Wilson M. 1983)

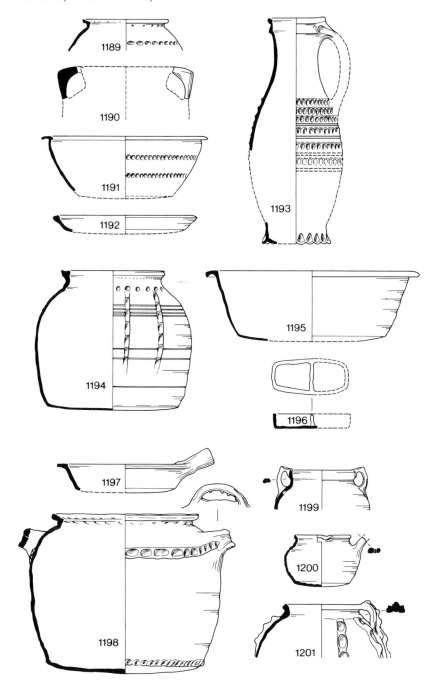

Fig. 189   KENT
Tyler Hill: 1202–7, 1209–13, Tyler Hill ware from Canterbury. 1208, Tyler Hill ware from Ospringe, 13th–14th cent. (After Smith 1979; Wilson M. 1983)

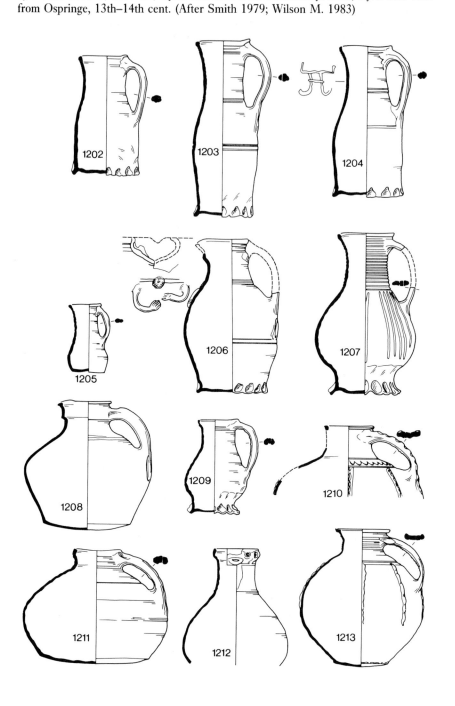

(ii) *Pottery*

Fabric is hard, sandy with some shell and flint inclusions (Rigold 1964: 61), pinkish-buff to red, often with grey core. Forms include cooking pots, bowls, jugs; decoration includes vertical applied thumbed strips on cooking pots, thumbing on the body of cooking pots and bowls, wavy or zigzag incised lines on bowls and jugs, and stabbing on jug handles.

c. Maidstone (Grove 1967)

Production site

Week Street – pottery, kiln props and what was thought to be a pottery kiln found in 1921.

d. Coteham (Le Patourel 1968)

Production site

Documentary evidence for potters in 1275.

e. Canterbury (Macpherson-Grant 1978; n.d; Wilson M. 1983)

Production site

Pound Lane – wasters and a small type 1b kiln with a central spine excavated, with the possibility of another kiln nearby. Site close to Canterbury's West Gate. kiln dated on basis of pottery and historical evidence to *c.* 1150–75.

(ii) *Pottery*

Pound Lane kiln products in a sandy ware, more competently made and generally harder than the normal 12th century pottery. Forms – distinctive plain and glazed spouted pitchers decorated with neat diamond or triangular rouletting, cooking pots, and large storage jars. Collared rims are characteristic. Some pitcher bases have single or grouped thumbed feet; few appear to have had handles. Some large cooking pots have thumbed rims, probably reflecting local influence. This ware is so far unknown outside the kiln site, though a few examples have been recovered from the Almonry Chapel within the Cathedral precinct. The technical expertise, rouletting and rim forms suggest strong connections with northern France – kiln and pottery may be products of an immigrant French potter, working for a limited market, perhaps supplying high quality goods to the Cathedral authorities and/or an immigrant French population.

Local wares – sandy wares continue, now definitely seen to be produced in the Tyler Hill area. From *c.* 1150–1250 a sub-group of this ware, comprising only cooking pots and pans, has crushed shell sprinkled on the surfaces in imitation of shelly wares. Continental influence seen in the rouletting and rim forms of pitchers. Transition from spouted pitchers without handles to jugs occurs between *c.* 1175–1200; glazing present from *c.* mid 12th century. Tyler Hill wares dominate in 13th and 14th centuries.

Shelly wares continue, but decline and disappear during the 13th century. Sandy shelly wares survive well into 13th century, with fabrics becoming harder and shell inclusions more sparse.

Regional imports include London-type ware, Mill Green-type ware and Surrey wares.

f. Rochester (Tester 1968; 1970; 1972; 1978; 1979): Fig. 190

Shelly wares continue into 13th century, perhaps through till early 14th century; forms – mainly cooking pots, some spouted pitchers, which may have incised wavy line decoration, in 12th-early 13th century. Some unglazed jugs in shelly ware in 13th century.

Grey sandy wares also present in small quantities; forms – mainly cooking pots; some jugs, mostly unglazed, in 13th–14th centuries; jugs may be decorated with wavy combing.

Regional imports include Mill Green-type jugs (formerly known as 'West Kent ware') and east Surrey wares.

g. *Ospringe* (Thorn 1979)

Excavations at Hospital of St Mary (Maison Dieu), hospital with royal patronage, founded *c.* 1234. Sequence dated by historical associations, coins, pottery imports.

Shelly wares dominant in early-mid 13th century; decline and disappear from *c.* 1260. Fabric 17, a red fabric, has no sand inclusions; Fabric 20 has coarse sand as well as shell. Forms – mostly cooking pots, few bowls.

Tyler Hill wares dominant from *c.* mid 13th century; mainly jugs, cooking pots, one condiment dish.

Other wares include Mill Green-type ware, Surrey wares and fine sandy fabrics of uncertain origin. West Kent grey ware conspicuous by its absence.

h. *Dover* (Cook *et al.* 1969)

Sequence from Dover Castle dated largely by historical associations.

Group (i), later 12th/early 13th century – hard sandy coarse ware dominant, dark grey but some with orange-brown patches; mostly cooking pots, some jugs. Also some less harsh shell-tempered coarse ware, reduced but sometimes with orange-brown surfaces.

Group (ii), mid-later 13th century – grey shelly ware cooking pots, occasional lamps; sandy grey ware with orange-brown surfaces, and sandy ware with sparse shell filler, both similar to Tyler Hill wares but perhaps local, as there seems to be continuity with earlier coarse wares; forms – cooking pots and large cooking pots/storage jars with vertical thumbed strip decoration, some jugs.

Group (iii), late 13th-early 14th century – probably local 'Tyler Hill type' coarse wares predominate; forms – cooking pots, large cooking pots/storage jars with vertical, and sometimes horizontal, thumbed strips; bowls with some internal glaze, condiments, and jugs with patchy olive or orange glaze. Some jugs have separately-applied bases. Jug decoration includes crude painted vertical or oblique white slip lines. The 'Tyler Hill type' wares are very similar to true Tyler Hill products, and although it may be likely that much of the coarse ware was locally produced, the fabric evolving from group (i) coarse wares, many or most of the jugs may be from Tyler Hill itself, as has been suggested for jugs from elsewhere in the town (Rix and Dunning 1955).

i. *Eynsford Castle* (Rigold 1971; Rigold and Fleming 1973): Fig. 190

Fig. 190   KENT
Eynsford Castle: 1214–15, 1218, Shell-gritted wares, *c.* later 12th–early 13th cent. 1216, shelly-sandy ware SSg, early 14th cent. 1217, shelly-sandy ware SSa or b, early 14th cent. (After Rigold and Fleming 1973)

Leigh: 1219–22, partially shell-gritted coarse wares, late 13th–early 14th cent. (After Parfitt 1976)

Rochester: 1223–4, Shelly wares. 1225, unglazed grey sandy ware. 1224, late 12th–early 13th cent.; 1223, 1225, 13th cent. (After Tester 1970; 1972)

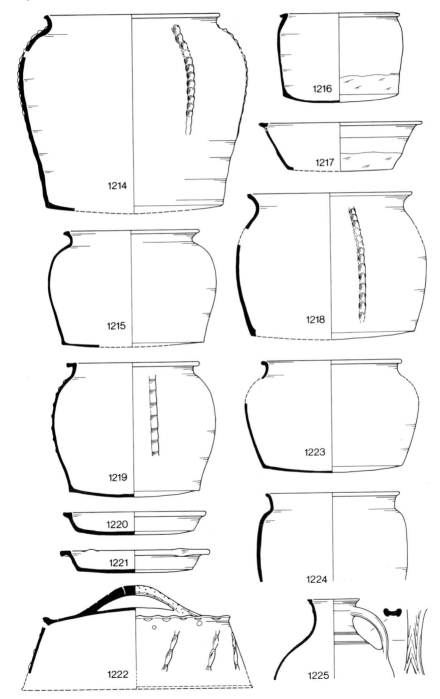

Shell-gritted ware, derived from (c) fabric of earlier period, dominant, but declining during 13th century; ceases by early 14th century, by time of deposits associated with the dismantling of the castle. Surfaces vary from light red to buff brown, with grey core. Forms – mostly cooking pots, some large cooking pots/storage jars with vertical thumbed strips, bowls, dripping dishes, occasional pedestal lamps, jugs.

Reduced sand-tempered and partially shell-gritted wares – rare until 13th century, then increase, becoming dominant by early 14th century. Five main fabrics, usually grey to black in colour; proportion of sandy wares STa and STb to shelly-sandy wares SSa, SSb and SSg increases through time as full shell-gritted wares decline. Source for these wares not known; some similar to east Surrey fabrics, e.g. Limpsfield, but they may well originate in north-west Kent. Forms – mainly cooking pots, also large cooking pots/storage jars, bowls, dripping dishes, unglazed jugs, occasional curfews. Jugs may have combed decoration, either horizontal straight or wavy, or lattice, and usually have slashed or stabbed strap handles. SSg vessels have rough surfaces with regular latitudinal striations, a London-Middlesex feature.

Small quantities of other grey sandy fabrics, probably non-local, cooking pots and unglazed jugs, also present in 13th century.

Glazed wares, non-local, present only in small quantities during 13th–early 14th century; some from Surrey, others from London area.

j. Leigh (Parfitt 1976): Fig. 190

Buildings within a moated enclosure at Moat Farm, occupation dated to late 13th-early 14th century by comparison with Eynsford pottery.

Mostly coarse unglazed partially shell-gritted grey wares, with medium to light shell gritting, surfaces from pink to grey; forms – cooking pots, cooking pots/storage jars, some with vertical thumbed strips, bowls, dishes, jugs; occasional cisterns, curfews, skillets. Jugs usually have stabbing on handles, sometimes have incised wavy or straight horizontal grooves or combing, or incised chevron decoration.

Glazed wares, mostly jugs, are of non-local origin; mainly from London area, some from Surrey; three bowls with internal glaze may be of Tyler Hill type.

6. Sussex

a. Chichester (Down and Rule 1970; 1974; Down 1978; 1981): Fig. 191

(i) Production sites

Documentary references to potters in 13th century.

Orchard Street – just outside medieval town wall to north. Type 2 kiln with three longitudinal internal walls to support floor of kiln bars; superstructure evidently composed of clay reinforced with tile wasters. Kiln dated on pottery grounds to 13th century. Kiln built over pit containing wasters, implying earlier production on site. Two other sites on Orchard Street with areas of burnt clay may also have been production sites.

Southgate – on east side of Southgate, just outside town wall to south, traces of three kilns found. One Type 1b kiln excavated, dated on pottery grounds to 13th century. Other medieval kilns known to west of Southgate.

Eastgate, Adcock's site – just inside town wall on east side. Part of a possible kiln and wasters dated on pottery grounds to c. 13th/14th century. The kiln may have been operated by the Black Friars for their own domestic requirements.

Fig. 191 SUSSEX
Chichester: 1226–32, Orchard Street kiln products, 13th cent. 1223–4, Southgate kiln products, 13th cent. 1235–6, Eastgate, Adcock's kiln products, 13th/14th cent. 1237–8, West Sussex ware, 14th cent. (After Barton 1974; Down 1978; Down and Rule 1970)

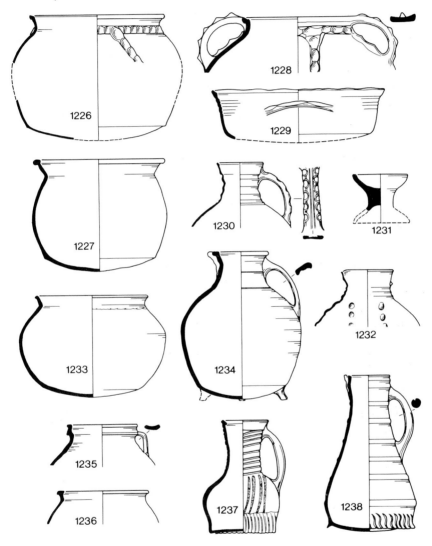

West Street – a medieval kiln or clamp known, from site within the town wall.
(ii) *Pottery*
Orchard Street – mostly oxidized red/buff, the fabric varies from untempered and red sand-tempered to heavily flint-gritted. Forms – glazed tripod pitchers, glaze varying

from orange to olive green, some decorated with raised bosses or horizontal combing; few jugs; cooking pots, some with applied thumbed strips; bowls, storage jars, lids, mortars, chimney pots and roof tiles.

Southgate – sandy or flint-gritted fabric, buff to reddish, sometimes reduced grey. Glaze pale to dark olive green or brown. Forms – tripod pitchers (one with internal glaze), cooking pots, bowls and roof tiles; pottery types similar to Orchard Street, of 13th century date.

Eastgate, Adcock's kiln – fabric mostly oxidized reddish buff, tempered with sand or flint; forms mostly cooking pots, some jugs.

Other wares present in the town include, by the early 14th century at least, glazed jugs of West Sussex type.

b. *Rye* (Barton 1979; Vidler 1933; 1936): Figs. 192–3

(i) *Production sites*

Five kilns of Type 4a (Sussex type) found at Spitalfield, probably in vicinity of the Hospital of St Bartholomew of Rye. Main period of production dated on stylistic grounds to *c.* 1275–1375. Documentary evidence for potters in 13th and 14th centuries.

(ii) *Pottery*

Products in sandy red fabric, mostly oxidized, glaze varying from yellow or brown to copper-green; jugs usually white-slipped inside the neck. Barton has divided the pottery products into two main phases, with manufacture of bowls, curfews and chimney pots going back to *c.* 1200.

Phase 1 forms – jugs, cooking pots, dripping dishes, bowls, curfews, bottles, skillets and money boxes. Chimney pots and inlaid floor tiles were also produced. Decoration of jugs includes incised motifs and scenes, various kinds of stamps and occasional 'face on front' anthropomorphic decoration. The incised decoration includes human figures, animals, fish, ships, letters of the alphabet and patterned shields; sometimes contrasting slip is used to colour shields. Phase 1 dated by Barton on stylistic grounds to *c.* 1275–1375; it overlaps with the second production phase.

c. *Binsted* (Barton 1979; Wilson and Hurst D.G. 1967: 316–18): Fig. 194

(i) *Production site*

Two pottery kilns and a tile kiln excavated. The earliest pottery kiln was a Type 2 kiln similar to that at Orchard Street, Chichester; it was superseded by a tile kiln. Constructed at a slightly later date, but running in parallel with the tile kiln, was an unusual pottery kiln resembling a Type 4a but with two subsidiary side flues. There is no absolute chronology for these kilns; the earliest kiln dates perhaps to the late 13th/early 14th century. Barton suggests that the later pottery kiln dates to the later 14th or possibly early 15th century.

There is documentary evidence for a tiler and a potter in the 1330s.

(ii) *Pottery*

Earliest kiln associated with coarse red sandy cooking pots.

Later kiln – fabrics vary from buff to red, mainly sandy but some with flint inclusions, which do occur naturally in the clay (Streeten 1980: 108). Forms – cooking pots, bowls, jugs of West Sussex type. Only a general 14th–early 15th century date range can be given to this jug type (Barton 1979). Decoration on jugs includes horizontal grooves on the neck, vertical combing, iron-rich black slip stripes; glaze olive or

Fig. 192   SUSSEX
Rye: 1239–47, Phase 1 kiln products. (After Barton 1979; Vidler 1933; 1936)

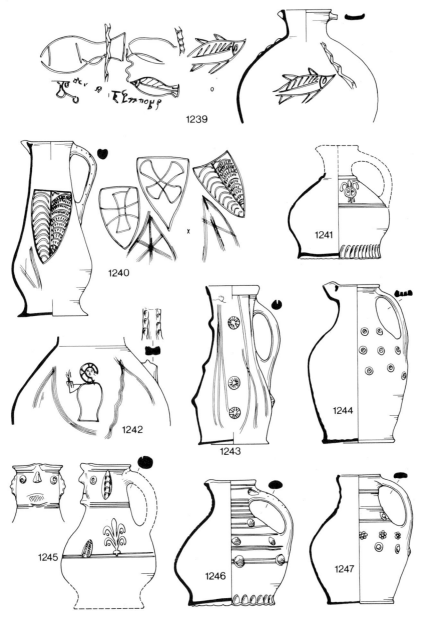

copper-green. Occasional applied 'buckle' and anthropomorphic decoration, this probably being early in the sequence.

Fig. 193 SUSSEX
Rye: 1248–54, Phase 1 kiln products. (After Barton 1979; Vidler 1933)

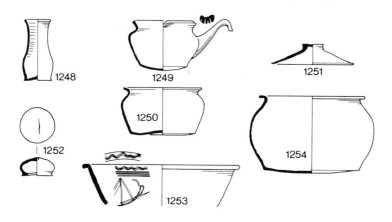

d. Graffham/East Lavington area (Aldsworth and Down 1976; Down 1978: 359 note 2; Streeten 1980)

Production site
    Wasters from several sites indicate pottery industry from *c.* late 13th century on. Buff-coloured fabric similar to Binsted but generally coarser. The material includes face jugs. Documentary reference to potters in 1341.

e. Abbots Wood, Upper Dicker (Barton 1979)

Production site
    Two areas of wasters known; products include coarse ware cooking pots and chimney pots.

f. Ringmer (Barton 1979)

Production site
    Two kilns discovered in late 19th century, probably late medieval; much earlier waste material spread over three fields with potting names. Products include cooking pots and face-on-front jugs.

g. Brede (Streeten 1980)

Production site
    Wasters indicate pottery production.

h. Heyshott (Webster and Cherry 1973: 185)

Production site
    Type 1b kiln excavated, associated with West Sussex ware of mid 13th century date.

Fig. 194 SUSSEX
Binsted: 1257–8, 1261–3, kiln products, *c.* later 14th–15th cent. 1255–6, Binsted-type ware from Chichester. 1259, 1265, Binsted-type ware from Bramber Castle. 1260, Binsted-type ware from Pulborough. 1264, Binsted-type ware from Selbourne Priory, Hampshire. (After Barton 1979; Barton and Holden 1977)
Horsham: 1266–9, West Sussex ware, *c.* 14th–early 15th cent. (After Barton 1979)

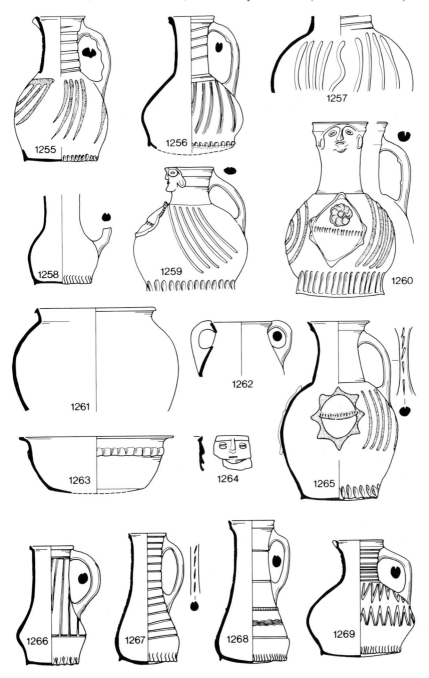

i. Horsham (Barton 1979): Fig. 194

A group of West Sussex ware jugs, of slightly different character to the Binsted types, reported as having come from a kiln in West Street, but there are no wasters among the collection so production is not yet proved. Decoration includes horizontal grooving over whole of jug body, vertical grooving and combing, wavy horizontal combing and black slip stripes; *c.* 14th–early 15th century.

Two West Sussex ware jugs in the Barbican House Museum, Lewes, are labelled as having come from a kiln at Lower Beeding, near Horsham, but there is no more definite evidence of production there.

j. Lewes (Barton 1979; Freke 1975; 1976): Fig. 195

Coarse flint-gritted wares, fabrics with grey-brown to orange-brown surfaces and reduced core, recovered from late 12th-13th century levels in excavations. Forms include cooking pots, storage jars, bowls. Flint-gritted wares also known in Saxo-Norman forms. Coarse sandy red wares, including cooking pots, glazed and unglazed jugs, probably begin during 13th century.

k. Hangleton (Hurst and Hurst 1964; Smith and Hurst 1963): Fig. 195

Deserted village; occupation in area excavated dated to *c.* 1150–1450 on pottery grounds. Pottery mostly coarse ware, cooking pots and some jars and bowls; some fabrics, including wares (c) and (d), with flint inclusions, others with shell or sand, colours varying from red and buff to dark grey; fabrics become finer through time. Some jugs, glazed and unglazed, from 13th century; local jugs in gritty grey or brown wares, plain globular forms with slashing on strap handles, and some olive glaze.

l. Bramber Castle (Barton and Holden 1977): Fig. 195

Tripod pitchers in coarse sandy buff fabric, sometimes with flint or chalk inclusions, with olive glaze, in late 12th century. Soft red-ware jugs, pale-slipped with copper-green glaze, appear from 13th century. Also occasional unglazed jugs, in hard red sandy fabric, or in coarse reduced sand- and flint-tempered wares. West Sussex wares, fine buff fabric, mostly jugs but some cooking pots, present by *c.* early 14th century. Some jugs also in sparse-glazed hard fabrics.

Red/black sandy ware cooking pots, in thin hard fabrics, oxidized or reduced, common in 13th and 14th centuries.

m. Pevensey (Dulley 1967): Fig. 195

Excavations in the town yielded a 12th-14th century building sequence. Most of pottery in local flint-gritted coarse ware, fabrics with brown surfaces and grey core, varying from Ware (a), very gritty, and Ware (b), gritty, to Ware (c), sparsely-gritted sandy. Mostly hand-made, the necks and rims being wheel-finished. Fine tablewares represented by continental imports, Rye and Hastings wares and West Sussex ware.

A possibility of local pottery production is hinted at by a mention of a Reginald le Potere in 1292.

n. Michelham Priory (Barton and Holden 1967): Fig. 195

Fig. 195 SUSSEX

Lewes: 1270–3, coarse flint-gritted wares, late 12th–13th cent. (After Freke 1976)
Hangleton: 1274, coarse ware (c). 1275, coarse ware (d). Early–mid 13th cent. (After Smith and Hurst 1963)
Bramber Castle: 1276, black sandy ware, late 13th–early 14th cent. 1277, unglazed hard red sandy ware, late 13th cent. (After Barton and Holden 1977)
Pevensey: 1278–80, Ware b, *c.* 13th–early 14th cent. (After Dulley 1967)
Michelham Priory: 1281, grey calcitic ware, early 14th cent. 1282, flint- and calcite-gritted coarse ware, early 14th cent. (After Barton and Holden 1967)

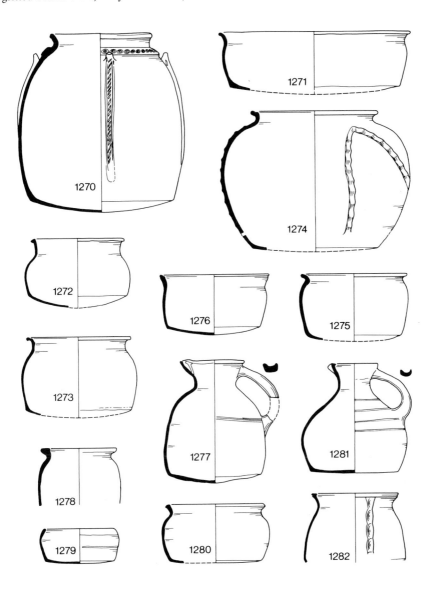

A group dated to *c.* early 14th century on pottery grounds included flint- and calcite-gritted coarse ware cooking pots, varying from red to black. Glazed grey ware jugs with some calcite are possibly from the local production site at Abbots Wood. These were associated with Rye wares, and continental imports dated to *c.* 1300.

7. Hampshire

a. *Boarhunt, Jack-o-Tooles Row* (Whinney 1981)

(i) *Production site*

Waster dump including damaged and distorted pottery, kiln furniture, excavated. Source of clay thought to be London Clays.

(ii) *Pottery*

Four main fabrics identified, all basically quartzitic, but some flint and calcitic inclusions present, and fired in oxidizing atmosphere. Forms include wheel-thrown glazed pitchers and jugs, some decorated with faces as well as applied strips and pellets; cooking pots, curfews, skillets, roof tiles, ridge tiles and chimney pots. Dated by stratigraphic associations at Winchester, Southampton and Portsmouth to 13th–14th century.

b. *Bentley* (Barton and Brears 1976)

This site is included under Alice Holt, Surrey.

c. *Portchester* (Cunliffe 1977; Dunning 1977c): Figs. 196–7

12th–14th centuries characterized as Early Developed and Late Medieval Traditions; fabrics generally tempered with flint and sand early on and fine sand later. 12th century pottery hand-made, 14th century pottery wheel-thrown. Cooking pots in simple baggy forms, bowls, pitchers and jugs. Curfews include one with two handles and green external glaze. Pipkins and costrels appear in the 14th century.

d. *Southampton* (D. H. Brown 1986 and pers. comm.; Platt and Coleman-Smith 1975): Fig. 196

Possible production centre evidenced by wasters in High Street of a richly green glazed white ware imitating French types.

Local coarse wares in quartz- and often flint-tempered fairly coarse fabrics; flint more usual in larger vessels. Local fine wares have quartz, flint, chalk and some organic tempering. Coarse wares dominated by hand-made scratch-marked vessels, mainly cooking pots, which continue to end of 13th century in similar simple baggy forms to those prevailing earlier. In later 13th and early 14th century, forms retain globular shape but are wheel-made with folded rims, with flatter bases; they lose the surface texturing, and some have finger tipping on shoulders. At Madison Street, on castle site, cooking pots of this form used in an industrial context had resinous substances identified as pitch on both surfaces; site dated to *c.* 1270. Tripod pitchers represent the early glazed form in coarse quartzitic fabrics; they are hand-made and poorly glazed. Many of jugs and highly decorated forms which become a feature of local assemblages from *c.* 1250 are imported from Sussex or from Wiltshire. West Sussex ware jugs are also found at nearby Havant (Fig. 197).

Locally-produced red sandy wares from an unknown source include squat, tripod and baluster jugs, curfews, distilling equipment, dishes, lids, pipkin, shelled lamps, dripping pans, divided bowls, money boxes, and costrels.

Fig. 196 HAMPSHIRE

Portchester: 1283, sand- and flint-gritted ware, 12th cent. 1284, sandy ware with some flints, 14th cent. (After Cunliffe 1977)

Southampton: 1285, 1291–3, 1295–7, possible local wares, first half of 13th cent. 1286–90, 1294, source not identified, first half of 14th cent. (After Platt and Coleman-Smith 1975)

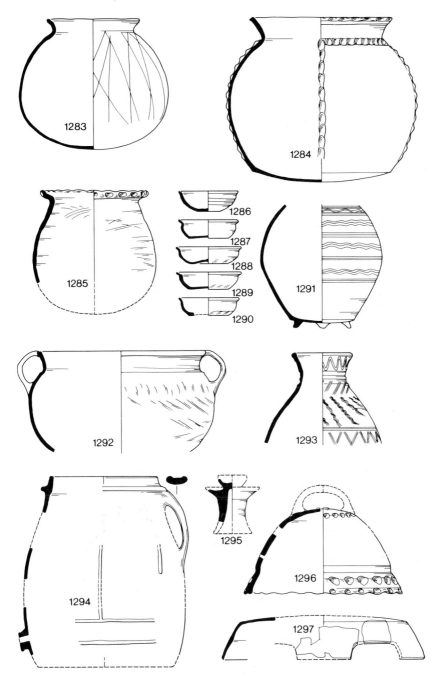

Fig. 197   HAMPSHIRE
Winchester: 1298–1302, 12th–14th cent. local wares. (After Collis 1978)
Portchester: 1303, early 14th cent. West Sussex ware. (After Cunliffe 1985)
Havant: 1304–6, West Sussex wares, 14th cent. (After Barton 1967b)

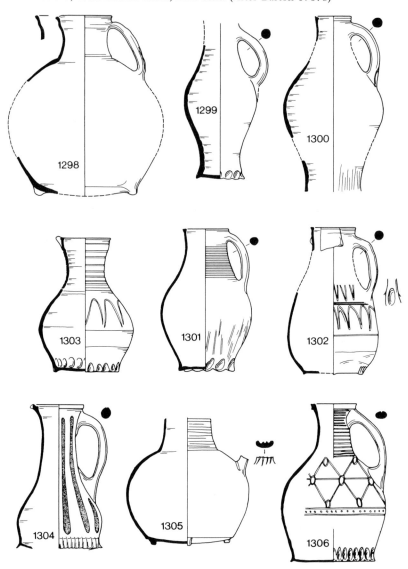

e. Winchester (Dunning 1964; Hurst J.G. 1964b; C. Matthews and K. Barclay pers. comm.): Fig. 197

Western suburbs dominated by fine sandy wares, possibly made in vicinity of Winchester, and replacing the chalk- and flint-filled wares of the previous period. Jugs an important element, with decorative schemes reminiscent of Chichester and Laverstock products, examples of which are known in Winchester.

f. Wickham Glebe (C. Matthews pers. comm.)

Phases 2–3, 14th century, contained two major local fabrics considered to be potential products of Jack-o-Tooles kiln, Boarhunt though jugs belong to general West Sussex type.

Fine sandy glazed wares in reduced and oxidized fabrics; forms are wheel-thrown jugs decorated with face on the front, combed, applied and incised decoration. Sand- and flint-tempered wares numerically dominant, and wheel-thrown cooking pots the principal form, though bowls and jugs also occur. Dating by association with French and Spanish imports and by analogy with material elsewhere, especially Southampton and West Sussex.

g. Netherton (Fairbrother 1984): Figs. 198–9; see also Fig. 59 No. 4

Fabrics are grouped into calcareous (Group 1) and sandy (Groups 2–3) wares.

Group 1 fabrics (A, AC, C, D, K, P) contain varied combinations of quartz with flint, chalk and limestone; they tend to be earlier – 12th to mid–13th century – than the Group 2 types. The forms in Group 1 are all hand-made and include cooking pots as major type, with bowls, dishes, curfews, socketed bowls, pans, storage jars, and occasional frying pans, cruets and jugs.

Group 2 fabrics (B, E, L, M, Q, T, V) are essentially fairly hard quartzitic fabrics, with a tendency to oxidization; late 12th–mid 14th century. Forms are wheel-thrown, and include jugs decorated with anthropomorphic motifs, as well as struts and elaborately-painted lines of white slip arranged in symmetrical patterns. Coarse wares include cooking pots in several sizes, deep and shallow bowls, curfews of different shapes, cisterns, dripping pans, pipkins, costrels and condiment dishes.

h. Christchurch (Davies 1983; Thomson et al. 1983): Fig. 200

Fabrics predominantly quartz-tempered with occasional flint, limestone or chalk inclusions; sometimes poorly fired and soft-textured, especially the earlier material. Later fabrics tend to be harder. Main forms – cooking pots, tripod pitchers, jugs, bowls and dishes. Source of local wares may be Poole area. Other local types include Dorset Red Painted wares, a sandy red-brown fabric used for wheel-thrown jugs decorated with vertical red painted lines. Dorset White wares occur in sandy fabrics and include both cooking pots and jugs. Dorset Red and White wares attributed to 13th-14th century.

8. Berkshire

a. Maidenhead (Pike 1965–6)

(i) Production site

Four Type 2c kilns excavated and seven others, also probably Type 2c, recorded. Fill of ovens, stoke pits and flues consists of charcoal, wasters and clay with wattle impressions.

(ii) Pottery

Flint- and sand-gritted, mainly oxidized, fabrics; forms include cooking pots, socketed bowls, dishes and pitchers. Some glaze on internal surfaces of bowls and dishes

Fig. 198   HAMPSHIRE
Netherton: 1307–8, Group 2 (Fabric B), mid 14th cent. 1309, 1314, Group 1 (Fabric A), late 13th–early 14th cent. 1310, Group 3 (Fabric G2), 13th cent. 1311, Group 1 (Fabric P), mid 12th cent. 1312, Group 1 (Fabric D), late 12th–early 13th cent. 1313, (Fabric A/C), late 13th cent. (After Fairbrother 1984)

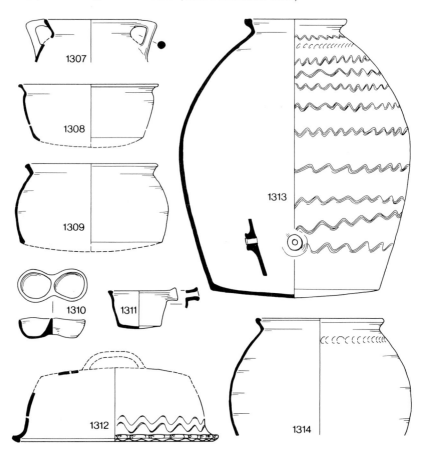

and external surface of jugs. Latter also decorated with white slip-painted lines, scrolls and loops as well as rouletting and finger tipping.

b. Seacourt (Biddle 1961–2)

Deserted medieval village at which large quantities of mostly unstratified pottery recovered. Fabrics and forms reflect Oxford, Brill and Cotswold types but with some from further east. Cooking pots dominant forms, but relatively large number of shallow pans or dishes, some with loop handles, and some jugs.

Fig. 199   HAMPSHIRE
Netherton: 1315, Group 2 (Fabric B), early 14th cent. 1316–17, Group 2 (Fabric B), late 13th–mid 14th cent. 1318–19, (Fabric M), mid 13th–mid 14th cent. 1320–1, Group 1 (Fabric AC), late 13th–early 14th cent. (After Fairbrother 1984)

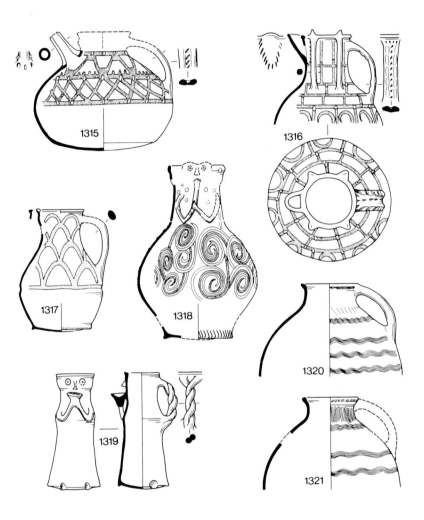

Fig. 200   HAMPSHIRE
Christchurch: 1322–33, 12th–14th cent. wares. (After Thomson *et al.* 1983)

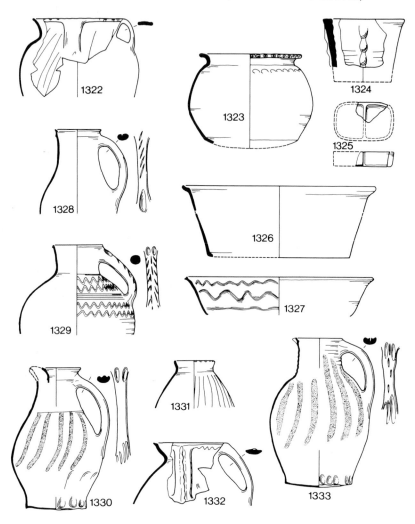

South-West England (Fig. 201)

1. Wiltshire

a. Crockerton (Le Patourel 1968)

Production site

Up to thirteen potters recorded paying clay rents in 1234.

Fig. 201   South-West England, location map
1 Minety, 2 Lyneham, 3 Nash Hill, Lacock, 4 Crockerton, 5 Old Sarum, 6
Laverstock, 7 Clarendon Forest, 8 Poole, 9 Wimborne Minster, 10 Wareham, 11
Corfe Castle, 12 Holworth, 13 West Stafford, 14 Dorchester, 15 Toller Porcorum,
16 Hermitage, 17 Sherborne, 18 Ilchester, 19 Bath, 20 Bristol, 21 Ham Green, 22
Donyatt, 23 Taunton, 24 Exeter, 25 Hound Tor, 26 Dinna Clerks and Hutholes, 27
Beere, 28 Okehampton, 29 Launceston, 30 Penhallow, 31 Tresmorn, 32 Treworld,
33 Lostwithiel.

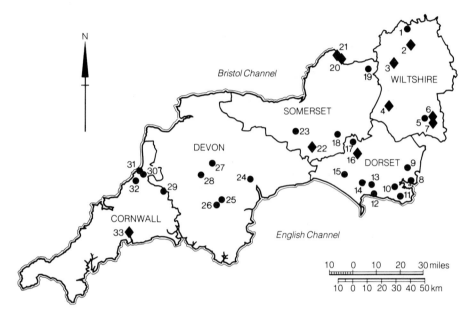

b. Lyneham (Annable 1958–60)

Production site
Wasters recorded.

c. Laverstock (Musty *et al.* 1969): Figs. 202–5; see also Fig. 16 Type 2a

(i) Production site

Site located close to entrance to Clarendon Palace. Eight Type 2a kilns excavated;
fuels used were oak, birch, beech, willow/poplar and hazel, probably derived from
Clarendon Forest. Site based on marl which was used for kiln construction. Three
buildings excavated; Building 1 had large post-hole in corner, suggested as bearing for
potter's wheel; chalk floor and a pit containing wasters. Building 2 contained large
central hearth. Seventeen pits excavated, function uncertain but possibly cess pits. Kiln
products were stacked directly on kiln floors.

(ii) Pottery

Clays used for pots derived from either Reading or London Clay beds; nearest
source 2½km distant. Inclusions in clay mostly natural, but some additives including

Fig. 202 WILTSHIRE
Laverstock: 1334–44, kiln products, 13th cent. (After Musty *et al.* 1969)

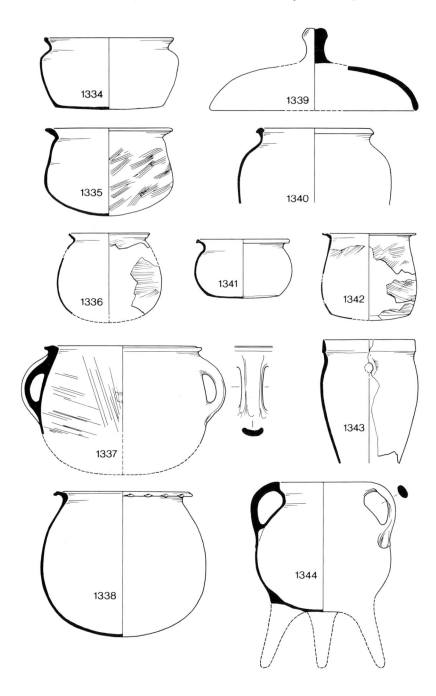

Fig. 203   WILTSHIRE
Laverstock: 1345–53, kiln products, 13th cent. (After Musty *et al.* 1969)

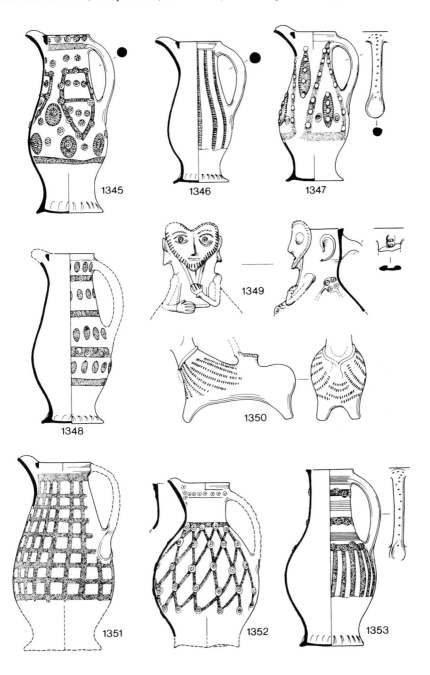

Fig. 204   WILTSHIRE
Laverstock: 1354–7, 1367–71, kiln products, 13th cent. (After Musty *et al.* 1969)
Lacock: 1358–66, kiln products, 13th cent. (After McCarthy 1974)

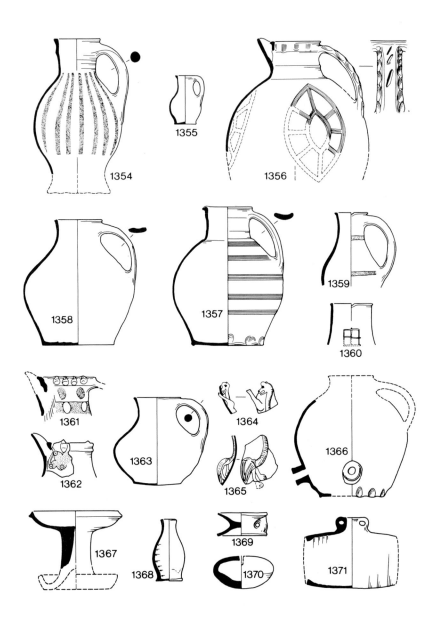

Fig. 205 WILTSHIRE
Lacock: 1372, 1374–8, kiln products, 13th cent. (After McCarthy 1974)
Laverstock: 1373, 1379–86, kiln products, 13th cent. (After Musty *et al.* 1969)

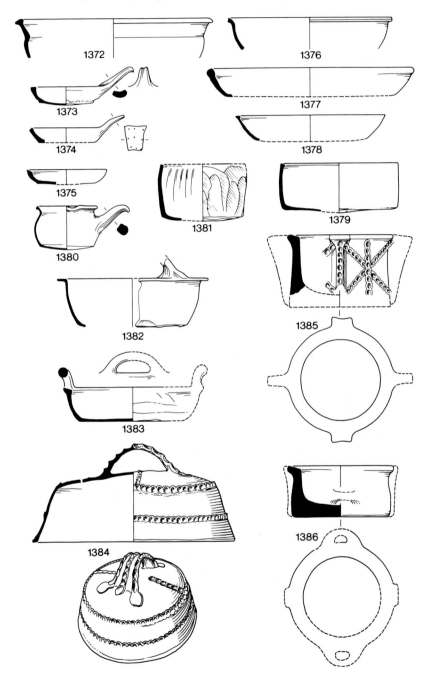

ironstone and flint. Glazes lead-based with tin additives. Main product – highly decorated jugs with polychrome decoration and variety of motifs, amongst which the anthropomorphic are notable. Hand-made, scratch-marked cooking pots were relatively important; less numerous types included 'West Country' dishes, cauldrons, pipkins, curfews, skillets, money boxes, aquamaniles, costrels, bottles, mortars and lids. Building materials also made, notably crested ridge tiles, chimney pots, louvers, finials and drainpipes. Archaeomagnetic date for Kiln 1 of 1230–75; other kilns in stratigraphic sequence. Pottery kilns thus broadly contemporary with Clarendon tile kiln, for which there is an archaeomagnetic date of 1239–52.

d. Clarendon Forest

Production site
Potter names recorded in 13th-early 14th century.

e. Nash Hill, Lacock (McCarthy 1974): Figs. 204–5

(i) *Production site*
Site located on hillside away from medieval village and abbey. Two Type 2a kilns in stratigraphic sequence with parts of two rectangular tile kilns. Potter names recorded in 1270 and 1280.

(ii) *Pottery*
Very sandy hard fabrics, some with a great deal of quartz sand but others containing less; mainly oxidized reds and browns. Forms include cooking pots, some possibly hand-made, but highly decorated wheel-thrown jugs also an important product. Variety of motifs and techniques present, including use of slip, anthropomorphic and zoomorphic designs. Amongst other forms are bowls, 'West Country' dishes, pipkins, skillets, alembics, tripod pitchers and lobed cups. Building materials include roof tiles, louvers, finials, chimney pots and inlaid floor tiles. Dating based on typological factors as well as tile designs, which extend date from later 13th century to 1300–25.

f. Minety area (Vince forthcoming): Fig. 206

Production sites
Potters' names recorded in Thornhill and Startley areas in north of county, close to Minety.

Pottery from Chepstow and Bristol in hard limestone-based oxidized wares, suggested on petrological grounds as possibly originating from Minety area. Forms include hand-made tripod pitchers decorated with applied strips and thin glaze.

g. Old Sarum (Musty and Rahtz 1964; Stone and Charlton 1935)

Sandy micaceous wares, hand-made cooking pots, bowls, pitchers, deep pans and lamps. Scratch-marking a normal feature of cooking pots. Very similar wares present at nearby Salisbury and deserted village of Gomeldon.

2. Dorset

a. Hermitage (Field N.H. 1966): Fig. 207

Fig. 206 WILTSHIRE
Minety: 1387–92, Minety-type calcareous wares from Selsley Common, 13th cent. 1393, Minety-type ware from Bristol, 13th cent. (After Dunning 1949; Watts and Rahtz 1985)

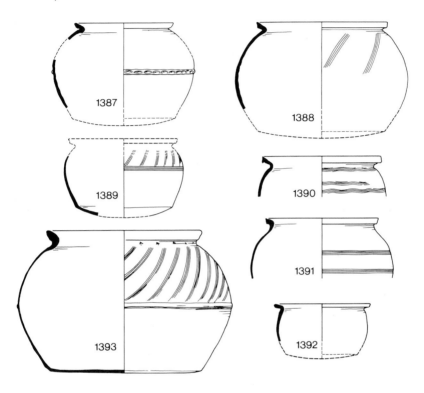

(i) *Production site*

Site located on main road between Dorchester and Sherborne close to Cerne Abbas. Kiln of possible Type 2 excavated; evidence difficult to interpret and could be a Type 1 kiln.

(ii) *Pottery*

Fabrics almost certainly based on Oxford Clays with quartz inclusions. Forms include cooking pots, bowls, glazed and decorated jugs, pans and a 'griddle' as well as crested ridge tiles. Attributed to 13th/15th century.

b. Holworth (Rahtz 1959)

Deserted medieval village with a range of quartz- and flint-gritted fabrics. Most pottery unglazed; cooking pots, some of which are scratch-marked, as well as bowls, skillets, lamps, a bung-hole pitcher and possibly plates. Glazed wares account for less than 5 percent of total pottery recovered, but include tubular spouted pitchers. Dated to 13th century.

Fig. 207   DORSET
Sherborne: 1394–9, Hermitage-type ware. 1398, flinty B ware.
1400–3, other local wares. (After Harrison and Williams 1979)
West Stafford: 1404–6, sandy wares, 12th cent. (After Draper 1976)

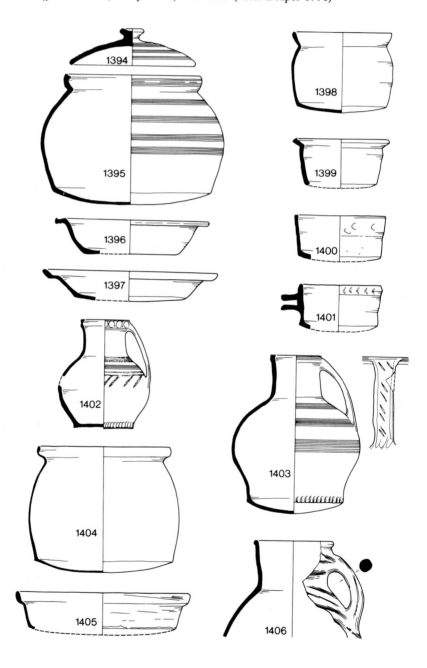

c. Poole (K. Jarvis pers. comm.)

Four fabrics defined visually, of which only Fabric 1 is petrologically distinctive, with quartz, flint and tourmaline suggesting a source in area south of Wareham or vicinity of Poole harbour. Forms include cooking pots, bowls, tripod pitchers and dishes, an assemblage comparable to material from Wimborne and Christchurch. Some of 12th–13th century forms hand-made, but from the 13th century two types of hand-made green-glazed jugs occur. One type, known as Red Painted ware, usually has vertical stripes under the glaze, whilst Applied Strip ware has applied iron rich strips. Local production of more ornate jugs suggested by sherds with scales and 'hand' and raspberry motifs. Range of forms widens in 13th–14th century to include skillets, curfews, lamps, pipkins, and cooking pots with bifid rims.

d. Wareham and Corfe Castle (Hinton and Hodges 1977; R.C.H.M. 1960; Renn 1960)

Main medieval fabric is Wareham C, probably the same as Poole 1. Forms, hand-made with use of turntable, include cooking pots, crucibles, flanged bowls, small bowls, lids, glazed and decorated jugs; some jugs have distinctive tubular spouts and others have French-type 'parrot beak' spouts.

e. Sherborne (Harrison and Williams 1979): Fig. 207

Two major fabrics identified, flinty (B) and sandy (E) wares; latter very similar to Hermitage products. Forms include cooking pots, lids, and glazed and decorated jugs not dissimilar to south Somerset types. Bowls have vertical sides and flared rims and, in some cases, hollow handles. 12th–15th centuries.

f. Other sites (e.g. Davies 1983; Thomson et al. 1983): Fig. 207

Range of fabrics and forms at Poole and Holworth similar to those at Wimborne, West Stafford, Christchurch, Dorchester, Toller Porcorum.

3. Somerset

a. Ham Green, Pill (Barton 1963; 1967a; M. Ponsford, pers. comm.; Vince forthcoming): Figs. 208–9; see also Fig. 16 Type 2b; Fig. 37

(i) Production site

On outskirts of modern Bristol; Type 2b kiln excavated with encircling drainage ditch filled with wasters.

(ii) Pottery

Fabrics A and B defined; the former with high proportions of limestone and clay pellets and the latter large quantities of quartz. At kiln site fabrics very hard and reduced. However, at Chepstow petrological work has identified red-firing clays with similar mineral suites and lenses of vitrified clay, also believed to originate at Ham Green. All forms are hand-made (some possibly moulded – T. Pearson pers. comm.). Jugs are one of main forms, frequently decorated with variety of motifs, including anthropomorphic. Tripod pitchers also known in A fabric. Other forms include cooking pots, bowls, lamps, dripping trays and spindle whorls. These dated at Bristol Castle and Taunton to 1225–1300, but at Chepstow, where the forms also include a spouted

Fig. 208 SOMERSET
Ham Green: 1408–15, 1418–19, kiln products, 13th cent. 1407, Ham Green ware from Wedmore, 13th cent. 1417, Ham Green-type ware from Gloucester. (After Barton 1963; Hassall and Rhodes 1974; Ponsford 1979)
Redcliffe: 1416, Redcliffe ware from Camel, 14th cent. (After Ponsford 1979)

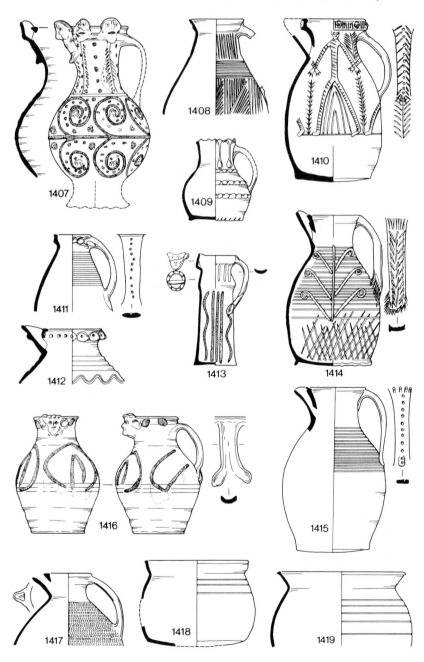

Fig. 209   SOMERSET
Ham Green: Ham Green ware jug from Cardiff; ht. 34.3 cm. (Photo: National
Museum of Wales)

pitcher, hand-made cooking pots and a shallow bowl in Ham Green red wares, they are
one of commonest types in 12th century contexts.

b. Bristol (Dawson *et al.* 1972; Ponsford 1979; Price 1979; Vince forthcoming; Wilson and Moorhouse 1971: 152): Fig. 208

(i) *Production sites*
St Peter's Church – dump of ashy soil, kiln furniture and wasters adjacent to walls
of church.
Redcliffe – ash, burnt clay and wasters in pits.
Several references to 'Crocker' surnames in various parishes in early 14th century.
(ii) *Pottery*
St Peter's Church – Fabric A, quartz-based with some possible slag, very hard,
off-white to pink-red; wheel-thrown jugs with iron-rich slip line decoration, and applied
and thumbed strips; cooking pots.
Fabric B, lime and limestone filler but no quartz, very hard, oxidized sherds;
wheel-thrown cooking pots.

Forms, fabric and decoration make these quite distinct from Ham Green ware. Attributed by excavator to 14th century or later.

Redcliffe – sandy fabric with some shale, ironstone grits; off-white, creamy and pink red fabrics; wheel-thrown jugs, some imitating French styles. Dated at Bristol Castle to 1300–50.

Close similarity between some St Peter's and Redcliffe fabrics. Other forms in Fabric Jb at Chepstow, equivalent to products of the two Bristol kilns, include wheel-thrown cooking pots, a bottle and a bowl, all with some internal glaze.

Other sites – Bristol Castle produced useful sequences in which Ham Green and Redcliffe wares are dominant local types.

c. Donyatt (Coleman-Smith and Pearson forthcoming): Fig. 210

(i) Production site

Rural location in Forest of Neroche. Site 1, interpreted as a clamp kiln, consists of a burnt oval depression c. 1.6m x 1.1m x 0.1m deep; two opposed areas of ash indicate possible flues.

Site 2 consisted of waste material in a gulley.

(ii) Pottery

Site 1 fabrics consist of local clays to which flint, quartz and limestone have been added. Vessels coiled and finished on turntable; forms include cooking pots with distinctive everted rims, bowls. Wasters at Site 2 quartz-based and less harsh than Site 1. Forms are wheel-thrown; cooking pots with incised and thumbed decoration. Site 1 attributed to 13th century and Site 2 to 14th century.

d. Ilchester (Pearson 1982): Fig. 210

Group 18 (Type B) fabrics: quartz- and flint-tempered, harsh and multi-coloured. Hand-made cooking pots, storage jars, shallow pans, bowls and lamps; dated stratigraphically to 12th century.

Group 21 (Type G): quartz- and fossil shell-tempered fabrics, harsh with oxidized surfaces. Wheel-thrown glazed baluster and globular jugs dated stratigraphically to late 13th century. This group also includes flint-based reduced fabrics, amongst which are hand-made tripod pitchers with pulled and tubular spouts, attributed to late 12th and early 13th century on stratigraphic grounds, but could start earlier.

Group 22 (Type D-F): fine quartzitic wares with oxidized buff surfaces; wheel-thrown cooking pots and storage jars dated to late 13th century.

Group 24 (Type G23): fine, sandy, micaceous Donyatt wares, wheel-thrown jugs with white slip below patchy lead glaze; dated stratigraphically to 14th century.

e. Taunton (Pearson 1984): Fig. 210

Late 12th-early 13th century: 18 types assumed to be of local manufacture. Fabrics, hard and harsh-textured, have combinations of quartz, limestone and flint inclusions. Forms hand-made with wheel turning, especially on rims; cooking pots, bowls, spouted vessels, dishes and rare tripod pitchers.

Late 13th to 14th century: four types defined, with mainly quartz filler, hard and oxidized with buff surfaces; two hand-made and two wheel-thrown. Only forms are jugs, some highly decorated. Dates attributed partly on stratigraphic grounds, partly by analogy with other sites.

Fig. 210 SOMERSET
Donyatt: 1420, Site 2, 14th cent. 1421–3, Site 1, 13th cent. (After Coleman-Smith and Pearson forthcoming)
Taunton: 1424, Type 46, 12th–13th cent. 1426–7, Type 241, 12th–13th cent. (After Pearson 1984)
Ilchester: 1425, 1428–9, Group 18 (Type B), 12th–13th cent. (After Pearson T. 1982)

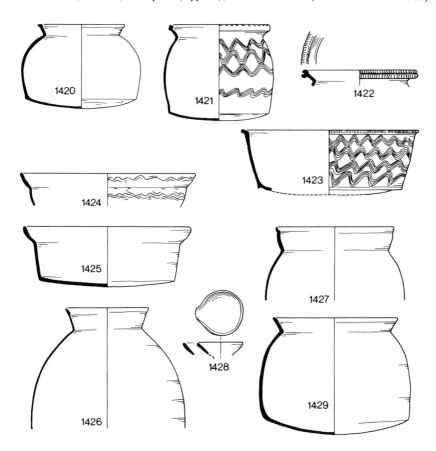

f. Bath (Vince 1979a)

Two main fabrics at Citizen House site, A limestone-tempered, and B sandy. Forms include cooking pots, 'West Country' dishes, handled bowls and tripod pitchers.

4. Devon

a. Exeter (Allan 1984): Figs. 211–13

Late Saxon and medieval pottery divided into ceramic horizons A–K on basis of stratigraphy, typology and associated imports. Major fabric is 20, which begins in

Fig. 211   DEVON
Exeter: 1430, Fabric 60, late 12th–13th cent. 1431–2, Fabric 62, late 12th–13th cent. 1433, Cornish jug, first half of 13th cent. 1434, 1437–9, Fabric 40, mid 13th–early 14th cent. 1435, Fabric 20, 12th cent. 1436, Fabric 45, 13th cent. 1440, Fabric 42, second half of 13th cent. (After Allan 1984)

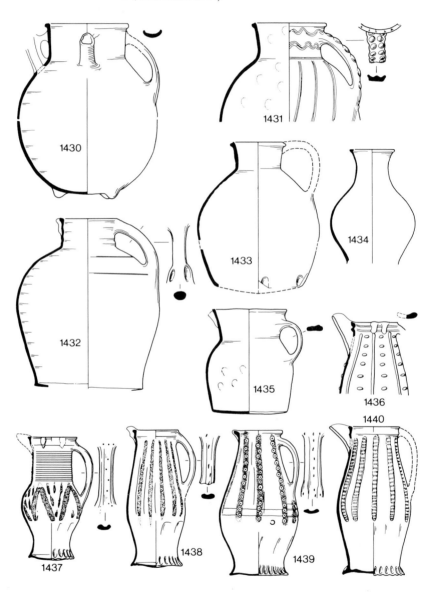

Fig. 212 DEVON
Exeter: 1441, Scratch-marked ware, 12th–13th cent. 1442–3, Fabric 20, mid 13th cent. 1444, Fabric 40 (After Allan 1984)
Beere: 1445–6, sandy micaceous fabrics, 12th–13th cent. (After Jope and Threlfall 1958)
Dinna Clerks: 1447–9, Fabric 1, late 13th cent. (After Beresford 1979)

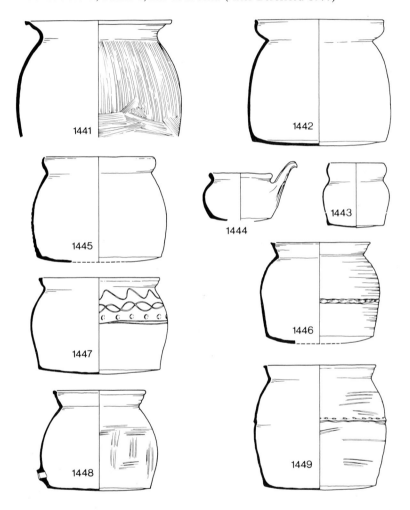

Saxo-Norman period and continues into 14th–15th century. Other important types: 40 and 42 – fine sandy, mainly oxidized to pink-reds, jugs; 14th century but continuing into 15th. 60 – hard light grey sandy fabric with some chert, mainly tripod pitchers; late 12th to early 13th century. 64 – large-grained quartz-tempered fabrics used for tubular spouted pitchers; 13th century. 62 – cream sandy fabric similar to Dorset White wares; 13th century. Ceramic horizons summarized below.

Fig. 213   DEVON
Dinna Clerks: 1450–1, quartzitic fabrics, late 13th cent. (After Beresford 1979)
Okehampton: 1452, Fabric 3, late 13th–early 14th cent. (After Allan and Perry 1982)
Exeter, Polsloe Priory: 1453, Fabric 40, early 14th cent. (After Allan 1984)
Beere: 1454, sandy micaceous fabrics, 12th–13th cent. (After Jope and Threlfall 1958)

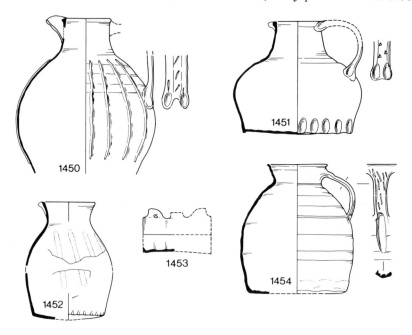

D – 12th century: larger cooking pots than hitherto with elaborate combed decoration, spouted vessels, occasional side-handled bowls, lamps, shallow dishes, storage jars.

E – late 12th-13th century: first appearance of glazed tripod pitchers.

F – early 13th century: combed cooking pots replaced by others with curved, almost S-shaped rims and some combed pitchers.

G – mid 13th century: minor changes in cooking pot forms; jugs in Fabric 40 appear with metallic and white painted strips.

H – late 13th-early 14th century: increasing importance of Fabric 40, with greater variety of decorative motifs, including anthropomorphic designs.

Polsoe Priory has very similar range to Exeter but with additional dating evidence in early 14th century levels.

b. Okehampton Castle (Allan and Perry 1982): Fig. 213

12th century – Fabric 2 (equivalent to Exeter 20) common, but none of typical Exeter combed cooking pots present.

Early 13th century – Fabric 1 dominant, micaceous cooking pots and patchily glazed jugs. In late 13th century these replaced by equivalent of Exeter 40 jugs, fine sandy oxidized wheel-thrown wares in North Devon/East Cornish fabric.

c. Hound Tor, Hutholes and Dinna Clerks (Beresford 1979): Figs. 212–13

Deserted villages on edge of Dartmoor; fabrics and forms comparable with those at Exeter and Okehampton. Mostly 13th century cooking pots with some cisterns, jugs rare.

d. Beere (Jope and Threlfall 1958): Figs. 212–13

Very coarse fabrics containing chert and black mica, fairly soft 'sandpapery' texture, fired to low temperatures. Hand-made but wheel-turned cooking pots with some finger tipping at rim and shoulder.

6. Cornwall

a. Lostwithiel (Miles T.J. 1976; 1979)

Production site

Documentary references to Alexander le Poter in *c.* 1200 and Odo le Pottere in 1337.

b. Penhallam and Tresmorn (Beresford 1971; 1974): Fig. 214

Manorial and deserted village sites respectively. Fabrics and forms compare closely with Beere, Devon. Similar material from Treworld and Trewortha. Uncertain whether pottery made at each village, or whether at one location and then sold. Probably clamp-fired.

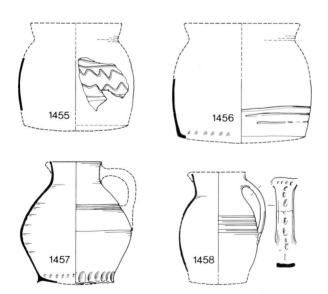

Fig. 214   CORNWALL
Penhallam: 1455–8, micaceous, possibly chert-filled fabrics, early 14th cent. (After Beresford 1974)

c. Launceston (T.J. Miles pers. comm.)

Excavations at castle, seat of Richard Earl of Cornwall. Sequences compare with Exeter and Okehampton, but despite high status of castle the only ceramic forms are cooking pots and jugs, with some cisterns.

West Midlands (Fig. 215)

1. Herefordshire

a. Hereford (Vince 1985b): Figs. 216–17

Group A wares contain naturally-occurring quartz with some mica and occasionally other sedimentary rocks; absence of large inclusions suggests that they may have been removed by hand and clay not levigated. Three possible sources: close to Hereford; the gravel areas of the rivers Lugg, Arrow or Teme; or the Forest of Dean. Forms include hand-made cooking pots and tripod pitchers, wheel-thrown jugs of various shapes, bowls, a baking tray and an aquamanile. Tripod pitchers and jugs commonly glazed and decorated with incised wavy lines, combing, rouletting, applied strips and, in one case, anthropomorphic motifs. Date range from 12th century through to 15th century on stratigraphic and typological basis.

Group B is Malvernian, with angular igneous inclusions derived from superficial deposits on sides of Malvern Hills. Subdivisions of fabrics can be recognized, seeming to indicate different production centres, which tends to be supported by distribution patterns. Possible sources are in Hereford/Breinton area, around Richards Castle in Shropshire, the Forest of Dean and Wye Valley, as well as Malvern Hills. Forms include hand-made cooking pots, curfews, 'West Country' dishes (not at Hereford itself), and globular glazed tripod pitchers and jugs.

2. Shropshire

a. Shrewsbury (Barker 1970; Carver 1983): Fig. 218

(i) *Production sites*

Documentary references to Robert and Peter le Potter, members of the merchant guild in 1252 and 1281 respectively. Juliana, widow of Peter le Potter, lived in Coleham, a suburb of Shrewsbury, and in 1313 was taxed on goods including *formule terr*, possibly clay or potter's equipment, valued at 7s. William, son of Peter le Potter, was a member of the merchant guild in 1318/19. Thomas of Boxstead of Coleham was also a member of the guild and taxed in same way as Juliana. As Boxstead is in Surrey, Thomas or his antecedents were presumably immigrants to Shrewsbury. Coleham appears to have been

Fig. 215   West Midlands, location map
1 Norton Priory, 2 Chester, 3 Eaton by Tarporley, 4 Ashton, 5 Audlem, 6 Nantwich, 7 Brereton Park, 8 Tunstall, 9 Sneyd Green, 10 Stafford, 11 Walsall, 12 Loppington, 13 Shrewsbury, 14 Richards Castle, 15 Breinton, 16 Hereford, 17 Malvern Hills, 18 Worcester, 19 Pershore, 20 Alcester, 21 Weoley Castle, 22 Nuneaton, 23 Potters

Harnall, 24 Stoke, 25 Coventry, 26 Brandon Castle, 27 Pottersfield Coppice, 28 Warwick, 29 Upton, 30 Gloucester, 31 Cirencester, 32 Selsley Common, 33 Bourton on the Water, 34 Brockworth, 35 Whittington.

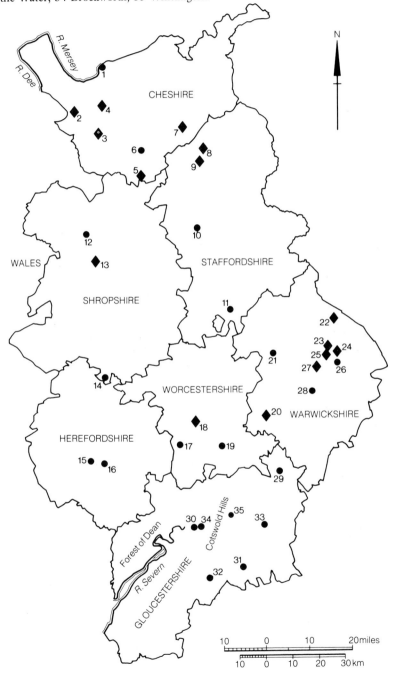

Fig. 216   HEREFORDSHIRE
Hereford: 1459–61, Fabric B1, 12th–13th cent. 1462–4, Fabric A2, 12th–13th cent.
1465–8, Fabric A76, 13th–14th cent. (After Vince 1985b)
       WORCESTERSHIRE
Worcester: 1469, 1472–3, Malvernian ware, 12th cent. (After Morris 1980a)
Malvern: 1470–1, Malvernian Chase ware from Gloucester, 13th–14th cent. (After
Hassall and Rhodes 1974)

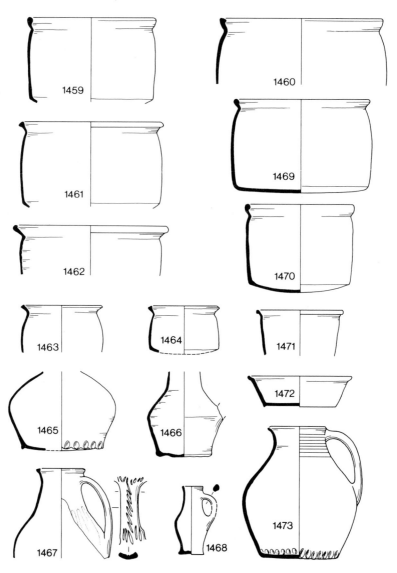

Fig. 217   WORCESTERSHIRE
Worcester: 1474–5, local sandy fabric, late 12th–early 13th cent. 1476–8, 1483, sandy fabric, mid 13th–mid 14th cent. 1479–82, sandy fabrics, 13th–14th cent. 1485, sandy fabric, 12th–14th cent. (After Barton 1968; Morris 1980a)
        HEREFORDSHIRE
Hereford: 1484, Worcester sandy fabric, 13th cent. (After Vince 1985b)

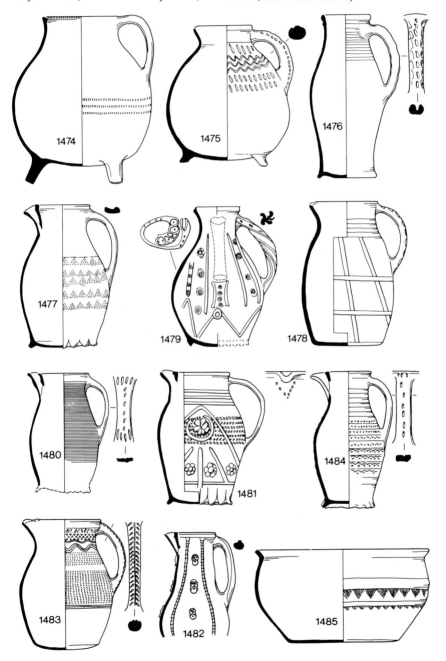

Fig. 218 SHROPSHIRE
Shrewsbury: 1486, sandy fabric. (After Barker 1970)
Loppington: 1487, fine sandy fabric. (After Barker 1970)
Richards Castle: 1488–90, fine sandy fabric. (After Barker 1970)

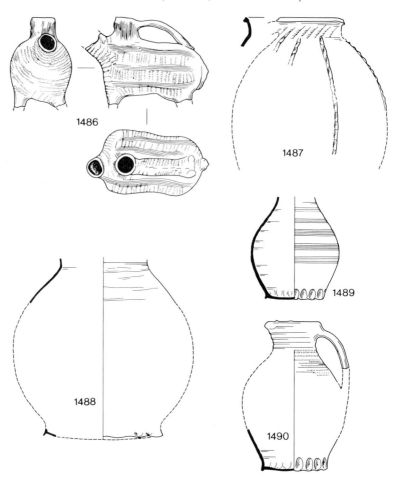

a potters' quarter outside the city walls and close to the abbey, but there is no archaeological confirmation as yet. It is possible that these potters were metal workers rather than earthenware craftsmen.

(ii) *Pottery*

Cooking pots appear similar to those from Hen Domen; tripod pitchers, highly decorated jugs and a fine aquamanile are similar to Worcester products, whilst some cooking pots, skillets, bowls and jugs resemble Malvernian wares.

b. Other sites (Barker 1970): Fig. 218

Excavations and fieldwork throughout the county, but especially at Loppington, Richards Castle, Haughmond Abbey and Brockhurst, have revealed a wide range of sandy fabrics, chiefly cooking pots and jugs, forms that have affinities with Shrewsbury, Hen Domen, Montgomeryshire, and Worcestershire vessels.

3. Worcestershire

a. Worcester (Barton 1968; Morris 1980a and b): Figs. 216–17, 219

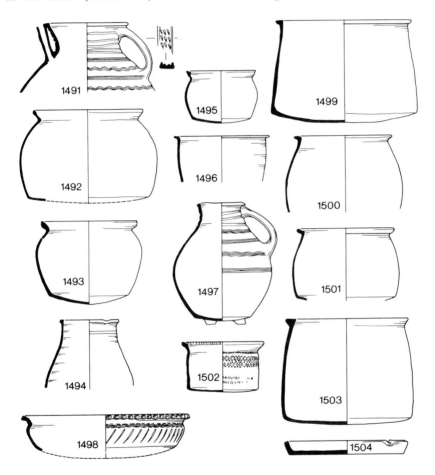

Fig. 219 GLOUCESTERSHIRE
Gloucester: 1491–2, 1500–1, 1504, Limestone-gritted ware, 12th–13th cent. (After Hassall and Rhodes 1974)
Upton: 1493–6, Limestone-gritted ware, 12th–13th cent. (After Rahtz 1969b)
Selsley Common: 1497–8, Limestone-gritted ware, 13th cent. (After Dunning 1949)
Bourton on the Water: 1499, Limestone-gritted ware, 12th cent. (After Jope 1952)
Cotswold Hills: 1502, Sandy fabric from Worcester, 12th–14th cent. 1503, Limestone-gritted ware from Worcester, 12th–13th cent. (After Morris 1980a)

(i) *Production site*

Potters named as Herbert, Osbert, Godfrey and John all paying clay rents in 1187 but there is no archaeological evidence for the industry.

(ii) *Pottery*

Three main fabrics identified in pottery from Worcester sites between 12th and 14th centuries: local ware is quartzitic with sandstone; igneous and micaceous wares from the Malvern area are well represented; calcareous wares from the Cotswolds. Worcester types include large cooking pots as well as glazed and decorated tripod pitchers. In the late 12th century, the Malverns was the principal source of glazed wares, contributing 87 percent. From the 13th century, Worcester continued supplying its own cooking pots and a greater proportion of jugs although the Malverns were still important. Wheel-thrown Worcester jugs are decorated with roller stamped designs, chevrons, applied strips, some anthropomorphic motifs, and the use of white slip on rims and green glazes. Barton originally suggested 13th century date for Worcester jugs but more recent work suggests that this should be extended into the 14th century. By this time the Malvernian wares were making greater inroads into the Worcester market.

b. Pershore (Vince 1977)

In late 12th–early 13th century, Malvernian fabrics with igneous inclusions appear; hand-made cooking pots, tripod pitchers and 'West Country' dishes. Worcester contributed quartzitic and sandstone fabrics as hand-made cooking pots and jugs, whilst a calcareous fabric with some quartz additives, hand-made cooking pots, may originate in the Avon valley.

4. Gloucestershire

a. Gloucester (Hassall and Rhodes 1974; Vince 1984a and b): Fig. 219

Fabrics calcareous with limestone fragments and oolites, in varied colours and textures ranging from harsh to smooth; source possibly north Wiltshire, Minety area. Forms include globular cooking pots similar to Selsley Common types, tripod pitchers with applied strips and combing, shallow dishes and 'West Country' dishes.

b. Cirencester (Vince 1982)

Fabric 200 main type: hard reduced oolitic ware, similar to Minety products; forms are hand-made cooking pots, tripod pitchers and jugs, dated stratigraphically and by analogy to 13th century.

c. Upton (Rahtz 1969b): Fig. 219

Deserted village in which limestone-tempered wares, possibly from Avon valley, are especially important. In later 12th–early 13th century cooking pots, jugs and bowls present, though in late 13th–early 14th century jugs and bowls seem to increase in popularity.

d. Selsley Common and other sites (Dunning 1949; Jope 1952): Figs. 206, 219

Many of regional characteristics of Cotswold wares, including calcareous fabrics, straight-sided and globular cooking pots as well as 'West Country' dishes, first defined by Jope and Dunning by reference to material from Selsley Common, interpreted as a temporary military encampment of the mid–13th century, as well as Brockworth, Bourton on the Water and Whittington. The fabrics and types are now well known from urban excavations at Bristol, Gloucester and Cirencester.

5. Staffordshire

a. *Sneyd Green and Tunstall* (Bemrose 1956–7)

Production sites
Type 3 kiln known at Sneyd Green, whilst at Tunstall William the potter and Robert the potter attested in 1348 and 1369 respectively.

b. *Stafford* (C. Cane pers. comm.)

Large quantities of pottery include, in 12th to mid 13th century, mainly quartz-based wares with voids, in medium to hard fabrics, often grey or slightly oxidized. Hand-made cooking pots with straight sides, flat bases. Jugs are hand-made, wheel-finished, in both reduced grey and oxidized orange quartzitic fabrics; glazed with rouletted and incised wavy line decoration. Associated with C14 dates of 1170 and 1260±60. White wares not in evidence in this group.

c. *Walsall* (Wrathmell and Wrathmell 1976–7)

Four main wares, all sandy; one of most important is hard, white-cream, fairly smooth ware; forms – wheel-finished glazed jugs and large cooking pots. Glazed jugs also occur in very sandy soft pink-white wares. Some jugs, decorated with red painted and wavy lines, matched at Weoley, Castle Bromwich and Tamworth. Cooking pots in coarse sandy grey-black or red wares. Source of some of pottery possibly in southern part of Cannock Chase; fabrics compare with others from Walsall, Tamworth, Weoley Castle and Wednesbury. Pottery attributed to 13th–14th century; site abandoned in 15th century.

6. Cheshire

a. *Chester* (J.A. Rutter pers. comm.)

Production site
Just outside east gate of town, wasters and small group of kiln furniture including separators; possibly indicating a production site.

b. *Audlem* (Webster and Dunning 1960): Fig. 220; see also Fig. 18 Nos. 2, 3

(i) *Production site*
Type 2a kiln excavated in centre of village.
(ii) *Pottery*
Pottery fabrics are quartz-based with some feldspar, mica, chert and iron ore. Some reduced wares, but mainly fully oxidized light red fabrics. Kiln material fairly soft, but this probably a result of weathering and the wasted nature of the pottery. Forms include cooking pots, some of which are relatively large, as well as large bowls, shallow dishes, pipkins and glazed jugs. Decoration is sparse but includes rouletting and

Fig. 220 CHESHIRE
Nantwich: 1505–8, sandy fabric, late 12th cent. (After McNeil 1983)
Audlem: 1509–18, kiln products, 13th–14th cent. (After Webster and Dunning 1960)

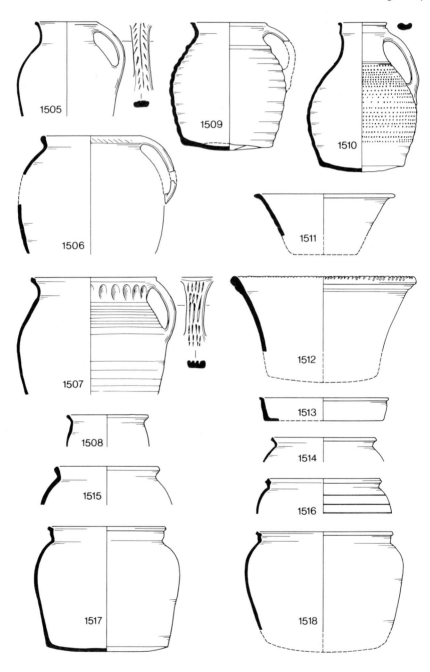

horseshoes and one anthropomorphic figure in applied strips. Dated typologically to 13th–14th century.

c. *Ashton* (Rutter 1977a): Figs. 221–2

(i) *Production site*
Type 3 kiln and wasters excavated.

(ii) *Pottery*
Fairly soft light red to red brown quartz-based fabric, with some feldspar, chert, iron ore, mica and occasional large sand grains. Forms include cooking pots, shallow dishes, and bowls; main product seems to be single- and double-handled jugs, often decorated with combed motifs, a range of stamps, applied strips and horseshoes. Clear glaze present on all forms. Dated to late 13th-early 14th century.

d. *Brereton Park* (J.A. Rutter pers. comm.)

(i) *Production site*
Located away from the nearest settlement on heavy clay soils. Wasters, separators and parts of two kilns known; site currently under excavation.

(ii) *Pottery*
Fabrics are quartzitic with feldspar, mica and iron ore present. Forms mainly jugs, many highly decorated; also cooking pots.

e. *Eaton by Tarporley* (J.A. Rutter pers. comm.)

(i) *Production site*
Located close to centre of nucleated village. Parts of kilns, kiln furniture and wasters.

(ii) *Pottery*
Fabrics are quartzitic with some feldspar and mica; forms include jugs, cisterns and other small vessels.

f. *Nantwich* (McNeil 1983): Fig. 220

Frequent types include fine-textured reduced sandy wares. Main forms are cooking pots, jugs and storage vessels. Jugs sometimes decorated with applied vertical wavy strips or more complex motifs.

g. *Norton Priory* (Greene and Noake 1977): Fig. 221

Group 1: quartzitic fabrics, hard and partly reduced; main form is cooking pot, possibly hand-made, dated to 12th century by association with early timber buildings.

Group 2 (Norton Priory Type ware): coarse and fine quartzitic fabrics. Characteristic form is jug with with horizontal rouletting. Source likely to be local to Norton Priory-Runcorn area. Dated stratigraphically to 13th–14th century.

7. Warwickshire

a. *Coventry area* (Redknap 1985; M. Stokes, pers. comm.): Figs. 223–4

(i) *Production sites*
At Cannon Park, Coventry, wasters attested; whilst at Pottersfield Coppice, Potters

Fig. 221 CHESHIRE
Ashton: 1519–28, kiln products, late 13th–early 14th cent. (After Rutter J.A. 1977a)
Norton Priory: 1529, coarse sandy ware, 13th–14th cent. 1530–1, fine sandy ware, 13th-14th cent. 1532–3, sandy fabric, 12th cent. (After Greene and Noake 1977)

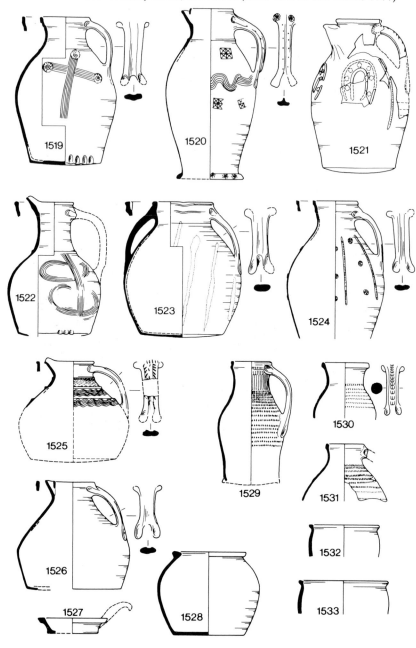

Fig. 222   CHESHIRE
Ashton: jug from kiln site; ht. 35.2 cm. (Photo: Grosvenor Museum, Chester)

Fig. 223 WARWICKSHIRE

Alcester: 1534–6, kiln products, 12th–13th cent. (After Cracknell and Jones forthcoming)

Coventry: 1537–8, Cannon Park wares. (After Redknap 1985)

Warwick: 1539–41, sandstone-tempered ware (F1). (After Mytum unpublished)

Weoley Castle: 1542–4, red painted wares, early 13th cent. (After Oswald 1962–3)

Fig. 224 WARWICKSHIRE
Coventry: 1545–56 local sandy wares of Cannon Park and Coventry type; 1545–9, 12th–13th cent.; 1550–1, 1556, mid 12th–mid 13th cent.; 1552–5, mid 12th–mid 13th cent. (After Redknap 1985)

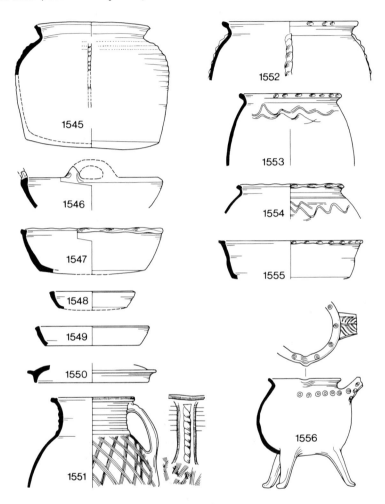

Harnall and Potters Green, place names attested in 13th and 14th centuries imply production centres. *Le Pottisrowe* street name in Coventry in 1310 may refer to potters' booths, perhaps for metal wares, rather than a manufacturing site.

(ii) *Pottery*

Cannon Park wasters in hard and soft gritty partially oxidized fabrics; forms are mainly wheel-thrown glazed jugs, sometimes with rouletted decoration. Minor forms – lamps, mortars and dripping pans. Dated by analogy with early Nuneaton wares to late 12th or early 13th century.

Coventry D ware, almost certainly of local manufacture, made from red Keuper Marls; reduced grey quartz-tempered fabric; major form is tubular spouted tripod pitcher with inlaid cable decoration on strap handle. Equally important are cooking pots, whilst minor elements are dripping pans, chafing dishes, bowls, curfews, a ceramic drinking horn, ladles and jugs.

b. Alcester (Cracknell and Jones forthcoming): Fig. 223

(i) Production site
Wasters and firebars excavated in area between burgage tenements and gate to Benedictine Priory.

(ii) Pottery
Principal fabric is hard coarse quartzitic ware with some mica and iron ore. Forms wheel-finished and possibly hand-made; large cooking pots, some glazed tripod pitchers (similar to Coventry D wares), small bowls, jugs and lids.

c. Nuneaton (Mayes and Scott 1984; M. Stokes, pers. comm.): Figs. 225–7

Fig. 225 WARWICKSHIRE
Nuneaton: Nuneaton ware 'eel' jug from Coventry, 13th cent.; ht. 38.5 cm. (Photo: Coventry City Council: Herbert Art Gallery and Museum)

Fig. 226 WARWICKSHIRE
Nuneaton: Ceramic mortar, probably Nuneaton ware, from Coventry. (Photo: Coventry City Council: Herbert Art Gallery and Museum)

Fig. 227 a and b WARWICKSHIRE
Nuneaton: Anthropomorphic 3-handled jug, possibly Nuneaton ware, from Coventry; ht. 45 cm. (Photo: Coventry City Council: Herbert Art Gallery and Museum)

(i) *Production sites*

Kilns, wasters and other features located in Nuneaton and adjacent villages. Production appears to be concentrated in Chilvers Coton (formerly Potters Coton) parish. Raw materials locally obtained, but geology is very complex with large number of alternating clay and coal seams; they include Red Marls of Keele Series, Etruria Marls and Keuper Marls. The abundant supplies of clay have been exploited since Roman times.

Numerous clay and marl pits in Nuneaton and adjacent parishes but few are datable. Many seem to be located along hedge lines, which has led to the suggestion that they were fenced off from fields let to pasture. Abundant supplies of water and fuel; the west part of Chilvers Coton is in the Forest of Arden. Potter names are attested from the early 13th century.

The report identifies 15 Type 2a kilns and 11 Type 3 kilns, but others have been discovered subsequently. Kilns, where not built on virgin land, were constructed on top of earlier kilns or into deposits of industrial waste. Products stacked on floors of firing chambers, but in one case, Kiln 30, perforated fragments of fired daub may indicate a raised floor. Little evidence for kiln superstructures recognized. Several kilns associated with drainage channels, one being constructed from a line of vessels with the bases knocked out, the purpose being presumably to keep ground water away from the stoke holes and the oven. Post-holes near some of the flues may represent windbreaks. It has been suggested that the Type 2a kilns were wood-fired, and Type 3 kilns fired with coal; Musty (1984) pointed out that the transition from twin- to multi-flued kilns could have been related to a change in the nature of the fuel being used. Recent experimental work, however, has highlighted the need for a grate if coal was the main fuel.

Excavations have focussed almost exclusively on the kilns, so that little information is available on the workshops, domestic quarters and ancillary structures. At Site 18 cart ruts, ditches and a stone-founded building were recorded. The building, *c.* 12m x *c.* 4m, was internally divided by a partition resting on pads. The relatively clean floor has a hearth and a pit containing raw glaze and white lead. An external ditch was partially filled with wasters. It seems likely that this was a potter's work area.

(ii) *Pottery*

Two main groups of fabrics identified, labelled A and B: essentially quartzitic with variations of mica, iron, shale and sandstone; mostly hard coarse-textured fabrics. A wares – white to pinkish-white in colour; B wares – light red to red. Forms from the Type 2a kilns included jugs, cooking pots, pipkins, bowls, dripping pans, bottles, cisterns, costrels, tripod pitchers, chafing dishes, a clay head, a cup, an aquamanile, a mortar, and a handled bowl. Type 3 kilns produced a much more restricted range of forms, only jugs, cooking pots, bowls, storage jars and pipkins.

Dates of the pottery are partly typological and partly stratigraphic. The Type 2 kilns were seen in places to underlie the three-flued kilns which were themselves overlaid by five-flued kilns.

d. Brandon Castle (Chatwin 1955)

Large collection of cooking pots, tripod pitchers and some highly decorated jugs from within the keep and western enclosure. Products almost certainly Coventry D wares for the most part. Close dating by reference to construction date early in 13th century and destruction in 1266.

e. *Warwick* (Mytum n.d.): Fig. 223

Local sandy oxidized wares in which sand probably derived from Bunter sandstone. Forms include cooking pots, occasional examples being oval in plan, and jugs. 12th–13th century vessels possibly hand-made, but later wares were wheel-thrown.

f. *Weoley Castle* (Oswald 1962–3): Fig. 223

Useful sequence associated with floors of timber-built kitchen. Fabrics 'gritty' and largely reduced. Characteristic forms are cylindrical or globular cooking pots, some of which have incised and red-painted lines over body and both sides of rim. Other forms are jugs and bowls. Dated stratigraphically to 13th century, on typological grounds and by association with coins of John and Henry III.

Wales (Fig. 228)

1. Glamorgan

a. *Cardiff, Bridgend and Llancarfan* (Evans 1983; Lewis 1964–6; 1970): Figs. 229, 231b

Personal and field names with *croc* element attested in 13th–14th centuries may attest presence of earthenware potters. Medieval pottery is known from a number of excavations and earlier discoveries in Cardiff but it not yet clear to what extent the material is of local manufacture rather than imported from other regions. See under Chepstow.

b. *Loughor* (Lewis and Vyner 1979; Vyner 1982)

Stratified sequence includes three groups of pottery potentially local:

Type 1 – large white calcitic inclusions, partly leached out, grey-buff surfaced plainware vessels. Probably 12th century.

Types 2, 3, 7 – quartz and limestone filler, hard, buff-grey, everted-rim cooking pots. Probably later 12th-13th century.

Type 4 – 'Vale Fabric', fine quartz tempering with orange-brown surfaced cooking pots. Possibly 12th–13th century.

c. *Cosmeston* (Price and Newman 1985; Sell 1984): Fig. 229

Stratified sequence from deserted village and manorial ('castle') site; material not yet studied in detail but main fabric consists of two variants of 'Vale Ware'.

Vale Fabric Type 1: lightly sanded ware with grey cores and oxidized orange-red surfaces, hard and relatively smooth-textured. Cooking pots and and glazed jugs, with some 'West Country' dishes.

Vale Fabric Type 2: similar fabric but consistently chocolate-coloured, softer and more friable. Cooking pots, possible storage jars; no glazed jugs. Most prolific form is the 'incurved' or 'West Country dish', with the characteristic single hole pierced in the vessel side. A variant also has a hole pierced in the base.

Fig. 228 Wales, location map

1 Rhuddlan, 2 Hen Domen, 3 Montgomery, 4 Chepstow, 5 Penhow, 6 Cosmeston, 7 Barry, 8 Llancarfan, 9 Cardiff, 10 Monnow valley, 11 Bridgend, 12 Llandough, 13 Llantrithyd, 14 Kenfig castle, 15 Loughor, 16 Carmarthen, 17 Cardigan, 18 Gwbert.

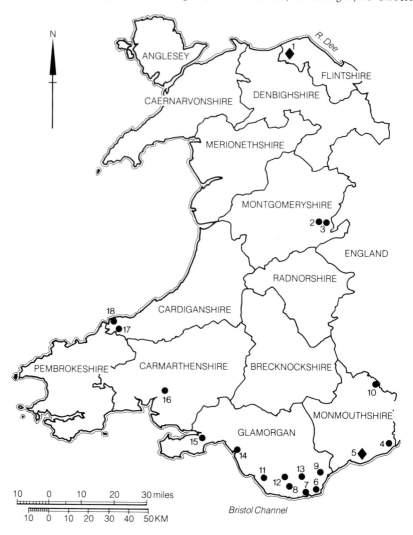

Fig. 229 GLAMORGAN

Llandough: 1557, Vale fabric. (After Vyner 1982)

Cosmeston: 1558–62, Vale fabric, 13th–14th cent. (After Price and Newman 1985)

Cardiff: 1572–4, possibly Bristol area fabrics, 13th–14th cent. (After Lewis 1964–6)

MONMOUTHSHIRE
Chepstow: 1563–4, Fabric Ha. 1565–7, Fabric Hg. (After Vince forthcoming)
Penhow: 1568–71, kiln products, 12th–14th cent. (After Wrathmell 1981)

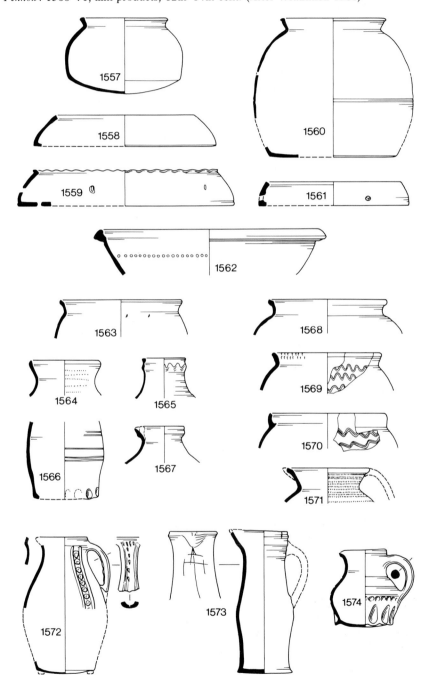

The distribution of Vale Fabric has suggested two possible production areas in south Glamorgan, perhaps to east and west of Barry respectively. Dated to 13th–14th century, on basis of coin evidence from Llantrithyd and Cosmeston, and stratigraphy at Loughor.

d. Llantrithyd (Webster 1977)

Ringwork producing large amounts of pottery, some associated with buildings but much unstratified. Fabrics essentially coarse, sandy wares in various colours; probably hand-made. Main forms are everted- or upright-rimmed cooking pots with occasional combed wavy lines or finger tipping. Pottery assumed to be of local manufacture but no petrological analysis. Primary date assumed to be c. 1100; coin hoard of c. 1125.

e. Barry Village (S. Sell pers. comm.)

Excavations at shrunken village site produced two main fabrics.

Fabric A: fine-grained limestone inclusions with some mica, quartz and iron ore; possibly from local lias deposits in vicinity of Barry; cooking pots only. Fabric B: fine-grained volcanic sandstone inclusions, possibly from either side of Bristol Channel; cooking pots, glazed jugs and 'incurved' or 'West Country' dishes. Similar to Vale Fabric Type 2, which is now recognized as the product of a local industry.

f. Kenfig Castle (Francis and Lewis 1984): Fig. 230

Collection of unstratified pottery. Several fabrics identified, the commonest being Fabric A: partially reduced hard quartzitic fabric with sandstone fragments, thin speckled green glaze. Forms – wheel-thrown jugs, decorated with horizontal grooves, applied strips and pellets, stamps. This fabric occurs throughout Glamorgan.

Other fabrics present include Ham Green ware. Among unglazed wares are small quantities of Vale Fabric, and other fabrics comparable with those from Loughor.

2. Monmouthshire

a. Penhow (Wrathmell 1981): Fig. 229

(i) *Production site*
Part of kiln oven with central spine located; fill included oak charcoal and wasters.
(ii) *Pottery*
Micaceous clays to which quartz seems to have been added; mostly reduced but some oxidized wares. Forms are hand-made; everted-rim cooking pots, some decorated with incised wavy lines and applied and thumbed strips, pitchers with rouletted decoration and short spouts. Two bifid-rim cooking pots may have been part of distilling equipment. Dated on stratigraphic grounds at Penhow castle, where it is attributed to 13th–early 14th century.

b. Monnow valley (Craster 1967; Knight 1982 and pers. comm.): Figs. 231a, 232

Distinctive local type only very rarely found outside Monnow valley; production centre not known but could be in Monmouth area. Fabric very fine, no visible inclusions; orange, light grey or dark bluish grey. Forms include heavy clumsy cooking pots, later superseded by infolded-rim cooking pots similar to those at Lydney. One of most

Fig. 230 GLAMORGAN
(left) Kenfig Castle: Jug in Fabric A; ht. 25 cm. *(right) Cardiff*: Jug, possibly Bristol area fabric (same vessel as 1573); ht. 30.4 cm. (Photos: National Museum of Wales)

Fig. 231 MONMOUTHSHIRE
Monnow valley: Monnow valley ware jug from Skenfrith castle; ht. 35.7 cm. (Photo: National Museum of Wales)

distinctive forms is baluster jug decorated with complex rouletting and green glaze. Attributed to 13th-14th century at Skenfrith and White castles, and occurring in phase 1 construction levels of 1223 at Montgomery.

c. *Chepstow* (Vince forthcoming): Fig. 229

Stratified sequences from The Priory, Nelson Street, and the monastic barn. Local pottery identified as well as regional imports, for which the Bristol connection is the most important. The local wares are broadly defined below as Group 1, and contain similar quantities of quartz, white mica and sandstone fragments; likely sources include the Forest of Dean and the Vale of Glamorgan, though some are similar to Hereford types.

Fabric Ha: hard oxidized hand-made ware; globular cooking pots, wheel-finished with rouletted decoration on the shoulder; unglazed pitchers are also hand-made, with globular bodies and rouletting or wavy line decoration. A variant of the fabric has glazed jugs. Source is likely to be close to Chepstow; dated to the late 12th and 13th century, with the glazed wares appearing in the late 13th century. A third variation of the fabric has hand-made cooking pots with infolded rims comparable to those found at Lydney.

Fabric Hb: hard reduced and oxidized wares, subdivided on basis of rim typology; forms are mainly hand-made cooking pots but one pitcher also recorded. Likely source – Forest of Dean or Wentwood; dating centred on late 12th-early 13th century, extending a little on either side; some occur in Period 1, early 12th century.

Fabric Hg: hard brown oxidized ware, probably from Vale of Glamorgan; wheel-thrown cooking pots and glazed jugs with horizontal grooves. Possible source in Cardiff area. Dated to 14th century.

Fabric Hh: soft to hard oxidized ware, probably from Vale of Glamorgan; hand-made glazed pitchers dating to the late 12th-early 13th century.

Other vessels known from very occasional examples in fabrics that could originate in Vale of Glamorgan, or are in other respects local to Chepstow area.

3. Carmarthenshire

a. *Carmarthen* (James 1982)

Various urban sites including Church Street, St John's Priory and the Castle produced some stratified material. Main types include Gwbert or Dyfed Gravel-tempered ware cooking pots, jugs, and one 'West Country dish' similar to those from Wessex and Burry Holms, where they were common.

Also present:

(1) Heavily gravel-tempered ware with quartzite and mica, grey to orange and buff; hand-made poorly-fired unglazed cooking pots.

(2) Coarse sand-tempered buff to orange thick-walled well-fired glazed jugs; one possible pan. Rouletted and applied decoration; some abstract, some crudely anthropo-morphic.

(3) Fine sand-tempered ware with some possible calcite inclusions, white to grey; hand-made glazed jugs.

4. Cardiganshire

a. *Gwbert* (Benson *et al.* 1978; James 1982; O'Mahoney 1985): Fig. 232

Fig. 232   FLINTSHIRE
Rhuddlan: 1575–8, kiln products, 13th cent. (After Miles H. 1977)
          CARDIGANSHIRE
Gwbert: 1579–83, 1585, local ware (After Benson *et al.* 1978)
Cardigan: 1584, Gwbert-type ware (After O'Mahoney 1985)
          MONTGOMERYSHIRE
Montgomery: 1586, Siltstone-tempered ware, early 13th cent. 1587, Fine grey ware, 13th cent. 1588, Monnow valley ware, 13th cent. (After Knight 1982)

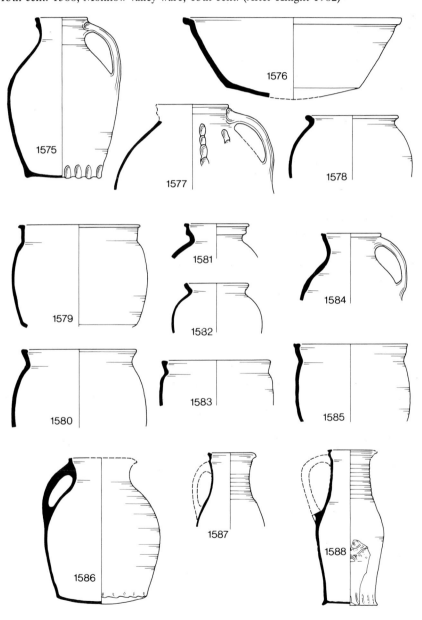

Relatively large pit group containing 35–40 vessels. Hard fabric, mainly oxidized orange, heavily tempered with quartz, some sandstone, and rare slate and siltstone. Forms possibly hand-made and wheel-finished; cooking pots with upright rims and slightly curved bodies. This is also known as Gwbert-type ware or Dyfed Gravel-tempered ware.

b. Cardigan (ibid.): Fig. 232

Gwbert-type wares at Cardigan and St Dogmaels include a tripod pitcher and jugs. Other forms, a compartmented dish, a tubular spouted jug and lid-seated vessels, also known. Kiln location not known. Date of Gwbert-type wares attributed to 13th century on basis of Ham Green associations.

5. Montgomeryshire

a. Montgomery (Knight 1982 and pers. comm.): Fig. 232

Well-documented castle, founded 1223, producing wide range of 'Marcher' wares and some foreign imports.

Siltstone-tempered ware: major type, grey fabric with grey siltstone inclusions, possibly from Severn valley; forms include tripod pitchers, glazed baluster jugs similar to Monnow valley products, cooking pots, handled skillets and slab-made baking trays. Dated stratigraphically and by association with architectural features; present in early 13th century, disappearing in 14th century.

Fine grey ware: also important in 13th century; fine sandy grey ware in which sand could be natural constituent of clay. Forms are plain glazed jugs and cooking pots.

Redwares: iron-rich fabrics with quartz sandstone, some micaceous but variants without. Forms include unglazed cooking pots and brown glazed jugs, some with white slip and chevron rouletting.

b. Hen Domen (Barker 1970; Barker and Higham 1982)

Group 2 pottery contains quartz, chert, igneous and some sedimentary inclusions, but source of clays uncertain. Main forms include cooking pots with many variations of rim types in 12th-13th century, possibly reflecting different kiln sources. Amongst other forms are tripod pitchers and highly decorated jugs.

6. Flintshire

a. Rhuddlan (Miles H. 1977): Fig. 232; see also Fig. 18 No. 1

(i) *Production site*
Kiln excavated just within Norman defences; oven consisted of circular pit 1.5m diameter x 0.5m deep, with two opposed rectangular projections. Fill of wasters and large lumps of clay.

(ii) *Pottery*
Hard sandy orange-buff fabrics; forms include globular cooking pots, some with glaze on upper part, and jugs with bridge spouts. Less common forms are bowls and an externally-glazed curfew. 13th century date (reign of Henry III).

Chapter 6   Mid-Fourteenth to Sixteenth Century

Scotland (Fig. 233)

1. Orkney

a. *Kirkwall* (MacAskill 1982b)

Post-medieval Reduced ware jugs present, in small quantities, from the 16th-18th centuries; presumably imported from mainland Scotland.

Large quantities of European imports.

2. Argyll

a. *Breachacha Castle, Coll* (Turner and Dunbar 1969–70): Fig. 234

Castle occupation dated on historical grounds to 15th century onwards.

Coarse hand-made pottery of Hebridean Craggan ware tradition, brown or brown-black fabrics with coarse sand or stone temper. Forms – small globular vessels, sometimes with stabbed decoration. Small dishes occur in finer hand-made red ware. Date range 16th-19th century.

Grey-brown ware, hard wheel-made fabric with olive-brown glaze, in Scottish Reduced ware tradition, appears in late 16th century; source presumably mainland Scotland.

Continental imports comprise much of post-medieval pottery.

3. Inverness-shire

a. *Inverness* (MacAskill 1982a): Fig. 234

Fabric Group A jugs continue through the 14th–mid 15th century or slightly later, fabrics becoming smoother through time.

Fabric Group AL, brown or grey sandy fabric in Scottish Reduced ware tradition, appears in small quantities in 15th century.

4. Aberdeenshire

a. *Aberdeen* (Murray 1982)

Aberdeen wares evidently continue into the late medieval period; buff to red and reduced grey micaceous fabrics appear to be local.

5. Perthshire

a. *Perth* (Scott and Blanchard 1983; N. MacAskill and D. Hall, pers. comm.)

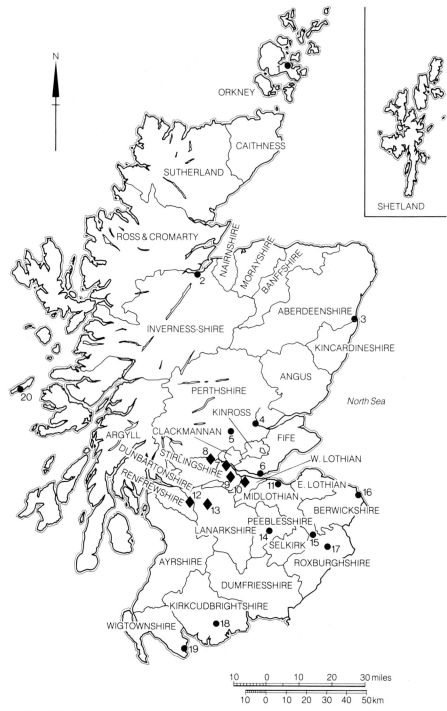

Fig. 233 Scotland, location map
1 Kirkwall, 2 Inverness, 3 Aberdeen, 4 Perth, 5 Innerpeffray, 6 Inverkeithing, 7 Throsk, 8 Stirling, 9 Stenhouse, 10 Linlithgow, 11 Edinburgh, 12 Hagg's Castle, 13 Bothwell Castle, 14 Lour, Stobo, 15 Melrose, 16 Eyemouth, 17 Jedburgh, 18 Threave Castle, 19 Cruggleton Castle, 20 Breachacha Castle, Coll.

Perth Local ware continues into late medieval period, with a much greater tendency to reduction, becoming a local version of Scottish Reduced Greenware. Forms mostly jugs; some bowls, dripping dishes, pipkins; cooking pots virtually absent. Jugs become plainer, though in 16th century some jug bases are thumbed or frilled in imitation of imported Rhenish stonewares.

East Coast White Gritty ware declines and probably disappears during 15th century.

b. Innerpeffray (Robertson W.N. 1974): Fig. 234

Several pots excavated within the Church of St Mary, apparently placed within graves; dated to c. 1508–1600 (or slightly later) on historical grounds.

Three vessels were of two-handled cooking-pot/jar form, one was a shallow pan or dish with two handles. The two-handled pots, fabric not described, had light green or brownish-green glaze and incised wavy line decoration; form characteristic of late medieval Scotland (Haggarty 1980).

6. Fife

a. Inverkeithing (MacAskill 1983)

East Coast Gritty wares current up to c. mid 15th century; cooking pots become rarer in proportion to jugs. Some jug sherds may be wasters, indicating possible local production.

Scottish Reduced Greenware present from 15th century on.

7. Stirlingshire

a. Stenhouse (Laing and Robertson 1969–70; Wilson and Hurst J.G. 1960: 165; *Discovery and Excavation in Scotland* 1959: 33–4; 1960: 37–8; 1961: 46; 1962: 45–6): Fig. 234

(i) *Production site*
A series of kilns, probably Type 2, excavated under rescue circumstances.
(ii) *Pottery*
Pottery not yet published; smooth, sometimes soft, reddish fabric. Much of the pottery appears to be late medieval in date; stylized face-mask decoration on some of the jugs is probably 15th century.

b. Throsk (Caldwell and Dean 1981; 1986)

(i) *Production site*
Large quantities of pottery, including wasters and kiln props, indicate production site of 17th century date, perhaps starting in the 16th century on the stylistic evidence of jugs with bases imitating continental stonewares. Documentary evidence in 17th and 18th centuries for potters or 'piggers', and for a pottery in the 16th century at St Ninians, in which parish Throsk lies.
(ii) *Pottery*
Very smooth fabrics, oxidized red or reduced grey, olive green to brown glazes; vessels thick-walled, often with extensive knife-trimming. Forms – mainly large jugs, a few with frilled bases in imitation of Rhenish stonewares; also skillets/pipkins with folded-back handles, bowls, storage jars, one-handled bowls/chamber-pots, dripping

dishes, money boxes ('pirlie pigs'), platters, lids, small ointment jars, candlesticks. Decoration restricted to rilling and incised wavy lines.

c. Stirling (Caldwell and Dean 1986: 107)

Production site
Documentary evidence for a 'pigmaker' or earthenware potter in 1521.

8. West Lothian

a. Linlithgow (Brooks *et al.* n.d.; Laing 1966–7; 1968–9)

(i) *Production site*
16th century documentary evidence for a clay potter.
(ii) *Pottery*
Excavations at Linlithgow Palace and within the town have yielded pottery of the period. Grey and orange fabrics replace earlier light-coloured fabrics during the 14th century. Reduced Greenware, hard smooth grey fabric with olive or green-brown glaze, predominates in late medieval levels, from *c.* mid 15th–18th century. An oxidized orange ware is also present. Forms – jugs, some with frilled bases imitating Rhenish stonewares, one- and two-handled cooking pots/jars, small drug jars, pipkins/skillets with folded-back handles, lids. Source unknown; some may be fairly local.

9. Midlothian

a. Edinburgh (Holmes 1975, and pers. comm.: Thoms 1975–6): Fig. 234

White Gritty wares appear to continue into the later 15th century, but are then replaced by reduced wares.

Reduced Greenware, smooth grey fabric, and an oxidized red version of the ware, dominate excavated groups from 16th century on; glazes olive green to brown. Forms – mostly jugs; also one-handled ovoid or globular bowl/cooking pot forms similar to vessels at Throsk, probably used at least sometimes as chamber pots (judging by their occurrence in an early 17th century group from a drain on the Tron Kirk site); money-boxes ('pirlie pigs'), pipkins/skillets with folded-back handles, small drug jars/inkwells.

10. Berwickshire

a. Eyemouth (Crowdy 1986)

Scottish White Gritty ware current well into 15th century; Reduced Green-glazed wares appear from *c.* 15th century on.

Fig. 234 ARGYLL
Breachacha Castle, Coll: 1589–92, hand-made Craggan-type pottery, 16th cent.
1593–4, hand-made red ware, 16th cent. (After Turner and Dunbar 1969–70)
    INVERNESS-SHIRE
Inverness: 1595–8, Fabric A, late 14th–mid 15th cent. (After MacAskill 1982a)
    PERTHSHIRE
Innerpeffray: 1599, late medieval ware, 16th cent. (After Robertson 1974)

STIRLINGSHIRE

Stenhouse: 1600–1, kiln products, probably 15th cent. (After Laing and Robertson 1969–70)

MIDLOTHIAN

Edinburgh: 1602–12, Reduced Greenware and oxidized red variants, 15th–17th cent. (After Holmes 1975; Thoms 1975–6)

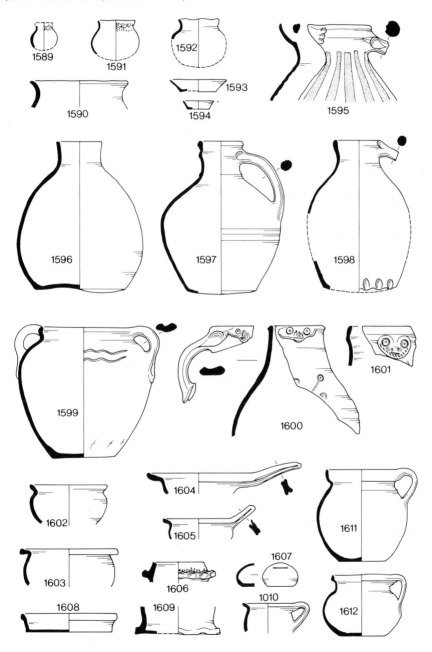

11. Renfrewshire

a. *Hagg's Castle, Pollokshields* (Webster and Cherry 1972: 210)

(i) *Production site*

Finds of wasters and place-name evidence ('Potterfield') suggest a production site of late 16th or early 17th century date.

(ii) *Pottery*

Reduced Green-glazed ware, dark grey fabric, sometimes oxidized red, with olive glaze; forms mostly jugs.

12. Lanarkshire

a. *Lanark* (Youngs *et al.* 1983: 225)

Production site

Wasters of 14th century date known from Castlegate, suggesting local production; former local street name, Potter's Wynd, may be relevant.

b. *Bothwell Castle* (Cruden 1951–2): Fig. 235; see also Fig. 60 No. 7

(i) *Production site*

Documentary references to 'the pottair of Bothuile' in 1501–4 (Cruden 1955–6: 68); the potter is assumed to be an earthenware potter.

(ii) *Pottery*

Collection of unstratified pottery, of medieval and late medieval date. Main fabric, presumably local, is red, slightly sandy, often with a reduced grey core, glaze olive to green-brown. Late medieval forms include jugs, sometimes with crudely-incised anthropomorphic decoration in 15th or early 16th century, three-handled jugs/storage jars, urinals, dripping dishes.

13. Peeblesshire

a. *Lour, Stobo* (Dunbar and Hay 1960–1; Laing and Talbot 1974: 44): Fig. 236

Tower-house and associated buildings of later medieval and post-medieval date.

Reduced Green-glazed jugs in smooth grey fabric with olive or brownish glaze, of 16th-17th century type: the main occupation of the building where they were found was dated to the early 17th-mid 18th century so they may in fact be of this period; they are, however, a long-lived and ubiquitous vessel form in Scotland.

14. Wigtownshire

a. *Cruggleton Castle* (Haggarty 1985)

Castle site; because of scarping, most of the material surviving on the site dates from the latest occupation in the 16th and 17th centuries.

Fabric 1, Reduced Green-glazed ware, hard smooth grey fabric with very fine quartz grains, dark olive-green glaze, is most common fabric. Forms – jugs. Date range from *c.* 15th century on.

Fabric 2, a friable micaceous fine red to brown fabric with red to dark red glaze, present in small quantities; possibly a Solway local type. Two other fabrics, 5 (Post-medieval Oxidized ware) and 12, are very similar.

Fig. 235 LANARKSHIRE
Bothwell Castle: 1613–19, late medieval forms, 14th–16th cent. (After Cruden 1951–2)

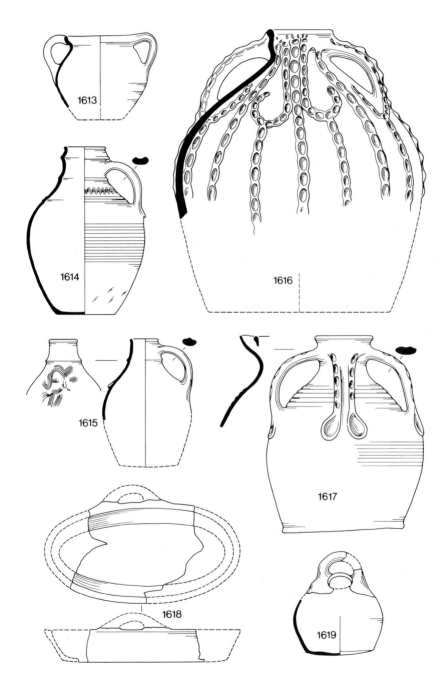

Fig. 236   PEEBLESSHIRE
Lour, Stobo: 1620–1, Reduced Greenware of 16th–18th cent. type. (After Dunbar and Hay 1960–1)
ROXBURGHSHIRE
Jedburgh Abbey: 1622, late medieval ware. (After Cruden 1955–6)
Melrose Abbey: 1623–9, late medieval wares, 14th–16th cent. (After Cruden 1952–3)

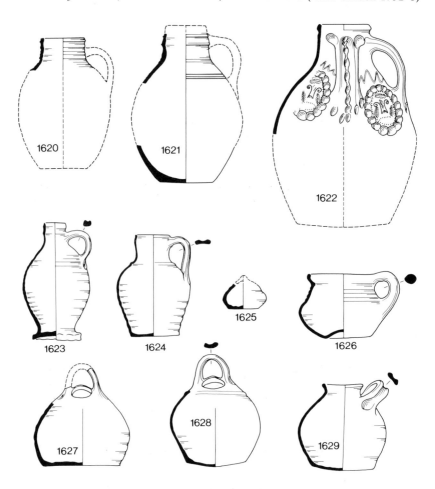

Scottish East Coast Gritty ware, off-white quartz-gritted fabric, represented by one sherd (in a context not dated but earlier than levels producing Fabric 1). Similar sherds found by fieldwalking in the vicinity of the castle.

15. Kirkcudbrightshire

a. *Threave Castle* (Haggarty 1981)

Castle site on an island in the river Dee, dated by historical and architectural evidence, dendrochronology and a few coins. Much of pottery recovered was unstratified. A number of wooden plates and bowls found in waterlogged deposits, dated to later 14th-mid 15th century. Pottery considered to be relatively sparse on the site, perhaps because of the use of wooden vessels, but this might also result from disposal of refuse in the river etc.

Fabric 1, main ware, soft wheel-thrown red or grey fabric with sub-angular quartz grits, glaze dark green/brown. Forms include large storage vessels, bowls, small dishes; later 14th-mid 15th century.

Reduced Green-glazed ware jugs occur in small quantities, in undated contexts but probably 17th century.

16. Roxburghshire

a. *Jedburgh Abbey* (Cruden 1955–6): Fig. 236

Unstratified pottery collection, includes typical late medieval form of three-handled jugs or jars, sometimes with crude anthropomorphic decoration.

b. *Melrose Abbey* (Cruden 1952–3): Fig. 236

Unstratified pottery collection, includes typical late medieval forms, including jugs (one with a frilled base imitating Rhenish stoneware), urinals and 'pirlie pig' moneyboxes.

Northern England (Fig. 237)

1. Lancashire

a. *Prescot* (Davey 1978)

Production sites
Documentary references to three clay potters who held property in the north-east corner of the town in 1577, 1579, 1584 and 1585. The references include Edward Glover who was awarded damages of 30 shillings in 1577 for 'an oven ffull of earthen pottes' and another 18 pence for two loads of turves. In 1579 he was awarded 8s 8d for 'half one oven of yearthen pottes'.

b. *Silverdale and Docker Moor* (Edwards 1977; White A.J. 1977)

Production sites
Waste material known from both places. Hard slightly sandy Reduced Greenwares known at Silverdale; forms include jars with applied and thumbed decoration around the rim and jugs, some possibly cisterns. These are very long-lived types known to be current in 15th century, present in pre-Dissolution deposits at Cockersand Abbey but continuing into post-medieval period.

2. Northumberland

a. *Newcastle upon Tyne* (Ellison 1981): Fig. 238

Fig. 237   Northern England, location map
1 Berwick, 2 Lindisfarne, 3 Edlingham, 4 Newcastle, 5 Durham, 6 Hart, 7 Yarm, 8
Osmotherley, 9 Helmsley, 10 Gilling East, 11 Yearsley, Soury Hill, 12 Coxwold, 13
Crayke, 14 Brandsby, 15 Stearsby, 16 Potter Hill, 17 Lastingham, 18 Newby, 19
Bridlington, 20 Little Kelk, 21 Beverley, 22 Hull, 23 Holme on Spalding Moor, 24
Staxton, 25 Potter Brompton, 26 Wharram Percy, 27 York, 28 Cowick, 29
Doncaster, 30 Firsby, 31 Rawmarsh, 32 Sandal Castle, 33 Wrenthorpe (Potovens), 34
Potterton, 35 Knaresborough, 36 Thorner, 37 Shadwell, 38 Kirkstall, 39 Follifoot,
40 Baildon, 41 Prescot, 42 Docker Moor, 43 Silverdale, 44 Carlisle.

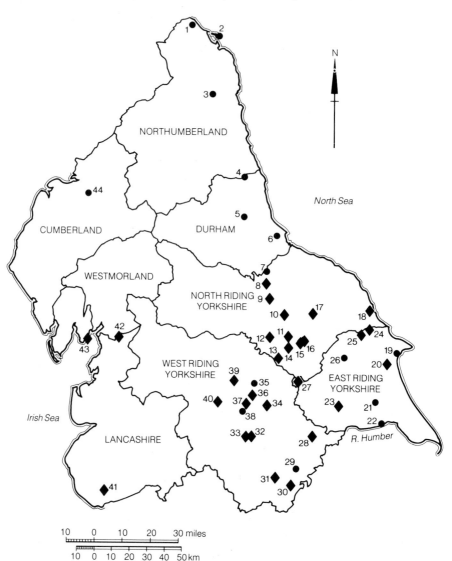

Fig. 238 NORTHUMBERLAND
Newcastle upon Tyne: 1630, 1632–3, Reduced Greenware Type 4, late 14th–early 15th
cent. 1631, 1634–9, Reduced Greenware Type 5, late 15th–16th cent. 1640,
Reduced Greenware Type 4, 15th–early 16th cent. 1641–6, Cistercian ware, mid–
late 16th cent. (After Ellison 1981)

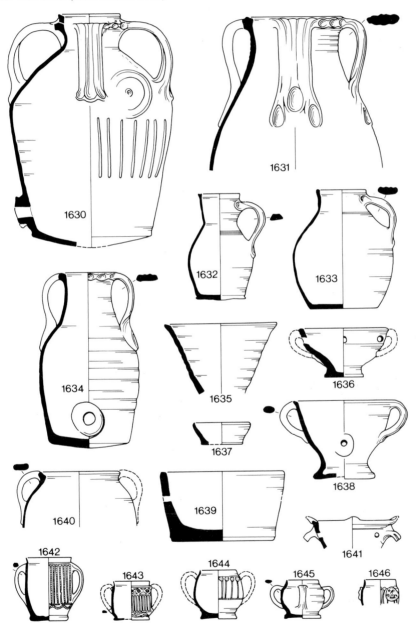

New types of Reduced Greenwares are dominant local pottery from later 14th century on, though by end of 16th century local wares have declined to small proportion of total pottery compared to imported Low Countries and Rhenish wares. Low Countries culinary wares largely replace local cooking pots by beginning of 15th century.

Reduced Greenware, Type 4 – smooth hard mid to dark grey ware with buff, light red or black surfaces, green glaze. Forms – mostly jugs, two- and three-handled cisterns, storage jars; occasional cooking pots, dripping dishes, bowls, chafing dishes, urinals, lids. Decoration includes applied strips, thumbing and incised wavy lines; occasional crude face-masks on body sherds. Source probably local. Date range mid 14th-early 16th century.

Reduced Greenware, Type 5 – smooth grey fabric with occasional quartz grits, green glaze; softer and paler than Type 4. Forms – mainly cisterns with two, three or four handles, also jugs, chafing dishes, storage jars, dripping dishes, bowls, cups, chamber pots, mortars, curfews/fish smokers. Less highly decorated than Type 4, apart from 'pie-crust' thumbing on rim or neck cordon. Source probably local; in late 15th/early 16th century many sherds show overlapping of Type 4 and Type 5 characteristics. Date range late 15th–late 16th century, becoming dominant type during 16th century.

Reduced Greenware, Type 6 – sandy buff fabric often partly reduced, olive green or pale orange glaze. Forms – cisterns. Occurs in small quantities; date range *c.* mid–late 16th century.

Cistercian ware occurs in late 15th and 16th century levels; some probably from Yorkshire, some perhaps more local, as characteristics differ from Yorkshire types. Cistercian wares decorated with applied white clay motifs dominant in second half of 16th century.

Blackware mugs, black-glazed red earthenware more common in 17th century, occurs in late 16th century; source unknown.

Regional imports include Surrey White wares, Midland Purple ware.

b. Berwick upon Tweed (Moorhouse 1982)

Major types include:

Type 19, thick fine sandy red fabric with grey core; fabric and glaze similar to earlier Type 1, and Types 1 and 19 are probably successive local coarseware traditions. Forms – mainly two-handled cooking pots/jars, some bowls, jugs, possible curfews. Date range *c.* 14th–15th century.

Types 21 and 22 – thick hard-fired pimply-surfaced fabric, Type 21 grey, Type 22 oxidized pink, with lime green or olive glaze; forms – jugs, occasionally with stamped pad decoration. Source unknown; date range *c.* later 14th-15th century.

Type 23 – thick-bodied fine sandy dark grey fabric, dark green glaze; forms – large globular jugs. Source unknown; date range *c.* later 14th-15th century.

c. Lindisfarne (Bown 1985)

Fabric 13, Reduced Greenware, similar to that from Newcastle, most common type from *c.* 15th–early 17th century. As at Newcastle, comprises several fabrics. Forms – cisterns, jugs, dishes, occasional skillet, possibly a chafing dish.

Fabric 14, Oxidized Greenware, common; large fabric group, usually red with dark reduced core or internal surfaces, heavily quartz-tempered and micaceous. Olive glaze.

Forms – cooking pots, jugs; also a chafing dish, possible storage jars, a small bowl. Probably a parallel tradition to Reduced Greenware.

Fabrics 15, 16 and 17, Scottish White Gritty wares, common. Quartz-tempered pale fabrics with light olive glaze, similar to those found on later medieval sites in the Forth-Tay region. Forms mostly jugs.

Fabric 24 common; rough light grey quartz-tempered fabric with olive glaze, forms mainly jugs. Provenance and date not certain.

Fabric 23 fairly common; grey gritty fabric, occasionally with oxidized pale brown surfaces, thick dark olive glaze. Possibly a reduced variant of the Scottish Gritty ware tradition. Source unknown; probably *c.* 15th century.

Minor late medieval fabrics include Fabric 4, possibly a development from Fabric 3, with heavier quartz tempering, forms mainly jugs; Cistercian ware; Fabric 44, Stenhouse and Throsk-type ware, smooth red fabric; Fabric 45, local post-medieval earthenware, light red finely gritted fabric with brown to dark green glaze.

d. *Edlingham Castle* (Bown forthcoming)

Local gritty fabrics A1, A2, A7, A8 continue through 14th and 15th centuries; also similar fabric A3 in *c.* later 14th-16th century. A2 probably continues into 16th century. Fine light red regional fabric B8 continues into 16th century.

Reduced Greenwares increase; dominant type from *c.* mid 14th century. Source not known. Types 2, 3, 4 and 5 – coarse gritty dark grey green-glazed fabrics, sometimes with oxidized surfaces. Type 6 – coarse sandy buff-brown fabric, green glaze. Forms include cisterns, storage jars, jugs, urinals, chafing dishes, bowls; decoration includes occasional rouletting, applied strips. Types 2 and 6 equivalent to Reduced Greenware Types 5 and 6 at Newcastle. Date of each fabric varies slightly; together they range from the mid 14th to the 16th century.

Minor regional types, white or buff gritty and sandy fabrics, continue into 15th century.

In late 16th century, with change of ownership of castle, most local and regional wares replaced by imported continental and southern English wares.

3. Co. Durham

a. *Durham* (Addis 1980; Carver 1974): Fig. 239

Various late medieval fabrics represented but full analyses not yet published. Green-glazed reduced wares, varying from smooth to sandy, form an important fabric group. Forms include jugs, cisterns, dripping dishes. Date range *c.* 1300–1550.

Cistercian ware cups present in 16th century levels; also hard brown-glazed red to reddish-brown fabrics.

b. *Hart* (Addis 1976)

Hartlepool-type ware common in later 14th/early 15th century.

Ware 16, smooth powdery grey fabric with olive green/brown glaze, common in late 14th and 15th century.

Ware 17, orange-buff smooth fabrics with reddish surfaces, smooth green glaze, common in 16th century.

Fig. 239   CO. DURHAM

Durham: 1647–8, Green-glazed Reduced wares, 15th cent. 1649, buff green-glazed fabric, 15th–16th cent. 1650, pale orange fabric, orange-green glaze, 15th–16th cent. 1651, hard green to brown glazed red fabric, 15th cent. 1652, hard slightly gritty buff fabric, second half of 14th cent. (After Carver 1974)

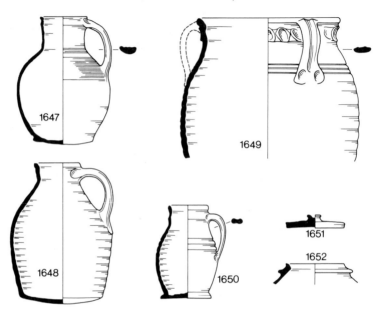

Minor fabrics include Ware 12, a highly fired sand-tempered fabric with purplish surfaces, a local variant of Midland Purple wares, in late medieval period.

4. Yorkshire, North Riding

a. York (Brooks, C.M. 1987; Holdsworth 1978): Figs. 240–3

(i) *Production site*

Documentary evidence for clay potters from 15th century (Le Patourel 1968: 112). Large quantities of wasters found at a site on Walmgate, probably from a nearby kiln.

(ii) *Pottery*

Wasters in Walmgate ware, a fine compact wheel-thrown red fabric with relatively large sparsely-distributed angular quartz grits; olive glaze, sometimes over a white slip, occasionally with small quantity of copper added. Forms – mainly jugs, including baluster shapes influenced by Brandsby-type ware, large jugs and drinking jugs similar to Humber ware, occasional storage jars. This ware forms only a small proportion of contemporary pottery from other sites in the city. Date range probably later 14th–15th century.

Humber ware becomes dominant fabric after decline and disappearance of Brandsby-type ware in later 14th century, until early 16th century; probably ends by second half of 16th century. Forms in 15th century include jugs, drinking jugs, cisterns,

Fig. 240 YORKSHIRE, NORTH RIDING
York: 1653–60, Humber ware, 14th–15th cent. 1661, Post-medieval Red Coarse
ware, 16th cent. 1662, Purple Glazed ware, 16th cent. 1663–70, Cistercian ware,
16th cent. (After Brears 1968; Brooks C.M. 1987; Holdsworth 1978; Le Patourel
1959; York Archaeological Trust, unpublished material)

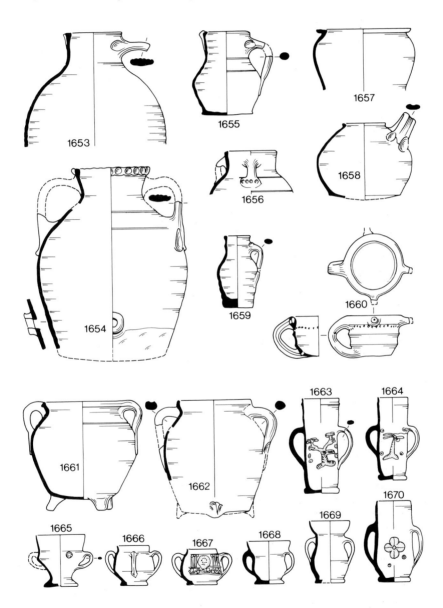

Fig. 241   (left) YORKSHIRE, NORTH RIDING
Humber ware urinal from York, 15th cent.; ht. 15 cm. (Photo: Yorkshire Museum)

Fig. 242   (right) YORKSHIRE, NORTH RIDING
Humber ware cistern from York, 15th cent.; ht. 40.5 cm. (Photo: York
Archaeological Trust)

cooking pots, bowls, urinals, flat-based lobed bowls/cups, and a puzzle cup. Decoration
mainly confined to thumbed applied strips on rims or necks of cisterns, horizontal
grooves on jug shoulders. Sources – probably mainly West Cowick and Holme upon
Spalding Moor.

Purple glazed ware – smooth to sandy red fabric, sometimes with grey reduced
internal surfaces, purplish-brown glaze; forms – cisterns, tripod pipkins, bowls, jugs,
plant holders. Evidently a later version of Humber ware; fabrics very similar, but forms
differ; source probably West Cowick. Date range *c.* late 15th–later 16th century.

Hambleton-type ware – buff, light grey or pink sandy wheel-thrown fabric, apple
green to dark green glaze, sometimes with darker copper speckles. Forms – cisterns,
jugs, flat-based lobed bowls/cups, chafing dishes, lids. Decoration includes wavy
combing, thumbed applied strips, dummy twisted handles; lobed bowls/cups often
decorated internally with stamps or free-standing modelled animal or human figures.
Source unknown; similar pottery found on a number of monastic sites in North Riding,
and fabric similar to Brandsby-type ware, so kiln(s) could be in that area. Date range *c.*
later 15th–later 16th century.

Cistercian ware, mainly cups and occasional chafing dishes, common in 16th
century; sources probably Wrenthorpe and Potterton.

Ryedale ware – fairly smooth wheel-thrown fabric, grey or wholly/partially oxidized
buff to reddish-buff, pitted glaze usually olive but sometimes yellow, often internal on
open vessel forms. Forms – bowls, jugs, chamber pots, tripod pipkins, cisterns, chafing

Fig. 243   YORKSHIRE, NORTH RIDING
York: 1671–4, Hambleton-type ware, later 15th–16th cent. 1675–81, Ryedale ware, later 16th–17th cent. (After Brooks C.M. 1987; Holdsworth 1978; Le Patourel 1959)
Yearsley, Soury Hill: 1682, kiln product, 16th cent. (After Brears 1968)

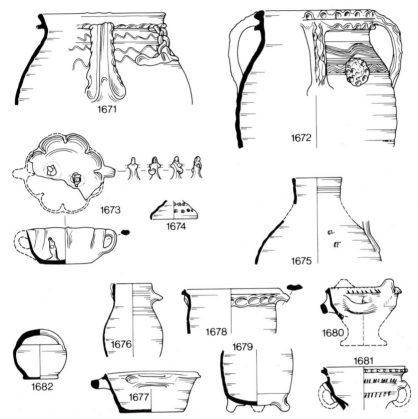

dishes, dripping dishes, lids. Decoration not common, apart from thumbed strips on cistern necks; wavy combing, occasional stamps. Sources – probably Stearsby and other kilns in that area. Date range – *c.* 16th–17th century, becoming dominant coarseware type by late 16th/early 16th century.

Post-medieval red wares – fine red fabrics, smooth glazes usually olive to brown, sometimes copper green; forms include bowls, jars, cisterns, dishes. Source unknown. Date range – most common in later 17th–19th century, but some present from 16th century.

b. Brandsby (Le Patourel 1968: 124)

Production site
Documentary evidence of pottery industry from 14th–16th century.

c. Newby (Rutter J.G. 1961: 53)

Production site
Kiln site producing pottery of *c.* 15th–16th century date.

d. *Skelton* (Le Patourel 1968: 124)

Production site
Documentary evidence for pottery industry from 14th-15th century.

e. *Yearsley, Soury Hill* (Brooke 1948–51): Fig. 243

Production site
Many wasters found; products, probably of 16th century date, include jugs, bowls, platters, cisterns, basket-handled bowls and a beaker.

f. *Crayke* (Sheppard T. 1939)

Production site
Kiln site of probable 16th century date.

g. *Stearsby and other sites* (Hayes 1978; Moorhouse 1971e: 14–15)

(i) *Production sites*
Evidence of pottery production from finds of wasters, bases of kilns or single-flued kilns, sometimes associated with place-name or documentary evidence, from a number of towns, villages or former villages: Coxwold, Gilling East, Grimstone, Helmsley, Lastingham, Osmotherley, Potter House, Stainsby and Stearsby. 'Potter Hill' in Pickering may also hint at pottery production.

(ii) *Pottery*
Pottery from these sites falls into the category of Ryedale ware: fine wheel-thrown sandy buff, orange-brown or grey fabric with pitted glaze, usually olive but sometimes yellow to brownish; open forms often glazed internally. Forms – cisterns, jugs, one-handled bowls, tripod pipkins, chafing dishes, storage jars, shallow bowls/platters. Decoration restricted mainly to applied thumbed strips under rims, occasional wavy combing, small stamps. Much of this pottery reached markets in Hull and York. Date range 16th–17th century.

h. *Yarm* (Patterson 1985)

Tees Valley ware continues into later medieval period, but is succeeded by Green Glazed ware as dominant type.

Green Glazed ware – hard partly reduced pink-grey to buff fabrics with few deliberate inclusions, olive green glaze; some later examples have copper green glaze. Forms mainly thick-walled large storage vessels, some at least probably cisterns, also bowls and dishes; little decoration apart from thumbed strips below rims.

Other late medieval wares include other partly reduced green-glazed fabrics and a fine red fabric with copper green glaze internally and externally.

5. Yorkshire, East Riding

a. *Staxton/Potter Brompton* (Brewster 1958)

Production sites
Production of coarse wares continued until *c.* mid 15th century. Forms include a

small proportion of crudely-glazed jugs, probably late in the sequence (Earnshaw and Watkins 1984: 40).

b. *Holme upon Spalding Moor* (Mayes and Hayfield 1980): Fig. 244

(i) *Production site*

Type 3 kiln with seven flues; associated kiln props; dated by pottery to late 15th/early 16th century. Probably other kilns in the area.

(ii) *Pottery*

Humber ware, red or orange-buff hard fabric with fine even sand tempering; some vessels reduced internally; olive to orange and brown glaze. Forms – cooking pots, jugs, drinking jugs, cisterns, also urinals, bowls, pipkins/cauldrons.

Fig. 244 YORKSHIRE, EAST RIDING
Holme upon Spalding Moor: 1683–92, kiln products, late 15th–early 16th cent. (After Mayes and Hayfield 1980)
Little Kelk: 1693–4, kiln products, *c.* 14th cent. (After Hayfield 1985)

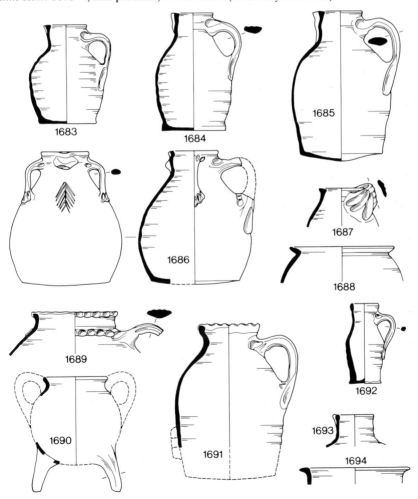

c. *Little Kelk* (Hayfield 1985): Fig. 244

(i) *Production site*
A pottery kiln excavated.
(ii) *Pottery*
Soft to hard orange-red slightly micaceous fabric with minimal sand-tempering, olive green glaze; fabric similar to Orangewares but thicker walls and cruder manufacture closer to Humber ware tradition. Forms – mostly jugs, also bowls, pipkins. Dated stylistically to *c.* 14th century.

d. *Beverley* (Hayfield 1985; Watkins and Williams 1983): Fig. 245

Orangeware – largely absent from Hull after mid 14th century, but it is not yet known whether production ceased at Beverley at that time, or whether manufacture continued a little longer, supplying the local market but not Hull.

Humber ware dominant during 15th and early 16th centuries. Cistercian ware present in 16th century. Occasional Hambleton-type wares.

e. *Hull* (Armstrong 1977; 1980; Watkins forthcoming b): Figs. 245–6

Humber ware dominant fabric, declining during 16th century. Wider range of vessels introduced during late medieval period; jugs, drinking jugs, urinals, small bowls, cooking pots, pipkins, jars, cisterns, condiment dishes, lids, lobed bowls/cups. A heavily-gritted Humber ware variant, mainly large bowls, occasional dripping pans, cooking pots, jugs and condiment dishes, found in small quantities. Sources – West Cowick, Holme upon Spalding Moor.

Purple Glazed Humber ware – fabric as Humber ware, with dark purplish-black glaze, often with a metallic sheen; glaze probably due to high firing temperatures, with no extra colourants. Forms mainly jugs, also cisterns, jars, dishes, urinals; combed wavy decoration common on jugs. Date range late 15th–16th century.

Green-Glazed Coarseware (Late Humber ware) – fine fabric, usually grey, with smooth olive glaze, often internal as well as external. Forms – jars, bowls, dishes; also urinals, cisterns, chafing dishes, cups. Part of a widespread tradition in Northern England, defined as Northern Reduced Greenware (Brears 1971: 17–18). Sources probably West Cowick and other sites. Fairly common from 16th to 19th century.

Ryedale ware, grey sandy fabric, sometimes oxidized buff or pinkish-buff, olive to yellowish pitted glaze. Forms – jugs, jars, cisterns, tripod pipkins, chafing dishes. Decoration usually restricted to thumbed strips below rims, occasional stamps. Sources – a number of kiln sites, Stearsby etc., in North Riding. Common in late 16th–17th century.

Cistercian ware present in 16th century.

f. *Bridlington* (Earnshaw and Watkins 1984)

Staxton/Potter Brompton ware continues to *c.* mid 15th century; includes some jugs, crudely glazed olive green, probably no earlier than late 14th century.

Humber wares continue, becoming more common; chalky fabric apparently declining as Cowick-type fabric increases, disappearing by 15th century.

Minor wares include Kelk Humber-type ware.

Fig. 245 YORKSHIRE, EAST RIDING
Beverley: 1695–7, Humber ware, later 15th–early 16th cent. 1698, Hambleton-type
ware, first half of 16th cent. 1699, post-medieval coarse ware, first half of 16th cent.
(After Hayfield 1985; Watkins and Williams 1983)
Hull: 1700–3, 1706, Humber ware; 1704–5, Heavily Gritted Humber ware. 1700–2,
1704–6, second half of 14th cent.; 1703, second half of 15th cent. (After Hayfield
1985; Watkins forthcoming b)

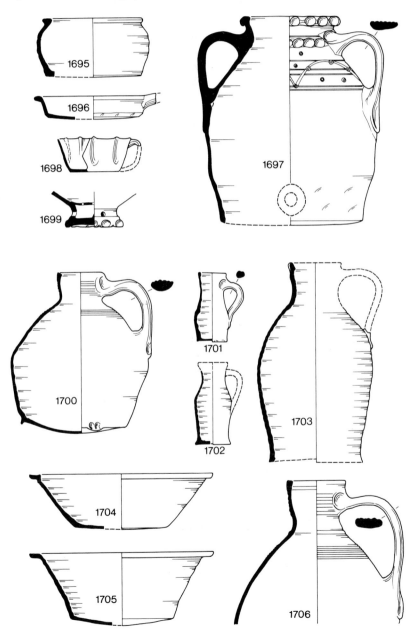

Fig. 246 YORKSHIRE, EAST RIDING
Hull: 1707–10, Humber ware, later 14th–first half of 16th cent. 1711, Purple Glazed Humber ware, late 15th–16th cent. 1712–14, Ryedale ware, later 16th–17th cent. (After Armstrong 1977; 1980; Watkins forthcoming b)

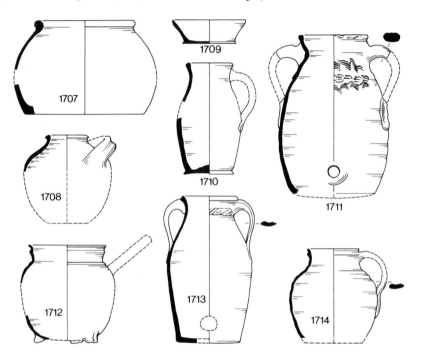

g. *Wharram Percy* (Le Patourel 1979a)

Staxton ware continues until *c.* mid 15th century.

Humber ware becomes more common during 14th and 15th centuries; sources probably West Cowick and Holme upon Spalding Moor.

Hambleton ware – grey, sometimes buff or white sandy fabric, glaze usually copper green. Forms – jugs, urinals, cisterns; some jugs have frilled bases copying Rhenish stonewares. Decoration includes horizontal grooved lines, stamps. Source unknown; type common in North Yorkshire. Becomes more common during 14th and especially 15th century.

Cistercian ware present in 16th century.

6. Yorkshire, West Riding

a. *West Cowick* (Hayfield 1985; Wilson and Hurst D.G. 1964: 297): Figs. 247–8; see also Fig. 59 No. 1

(i) *Production site*

Kilns excavated and documentary evidence (see Chapter 5). In late 14th century, evidence of use of peat by potters (Le Patourel 1968: 118, 124).

Fig. 247 YORKSHIRE, WEST RIDING
West Cowick: 1715–29, vessels from the King's Moat waster group, *c.* 14th–16th cent.
(After Hayfield 1985)

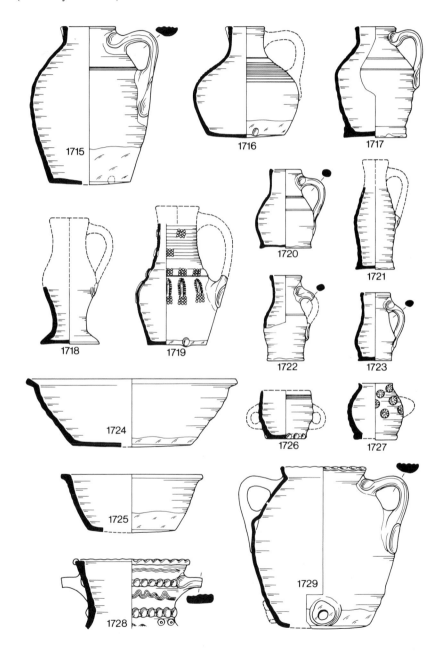

Fig. 248   YORKSHIRE, WEST RIDING
West Cowick: 1730–4, vessels from the King's Moat waster group, *c.* 14th–16th cent.
(After Hayfield 1985)
Firsby Hall: 1735–9, kiln products, *c.* 15th–early 16th cent. (After Hayfield 1985)
Doncaster: 1740–5, Coal Measure fabrics, *c.* 15th cent. (After Hayfield 1985)

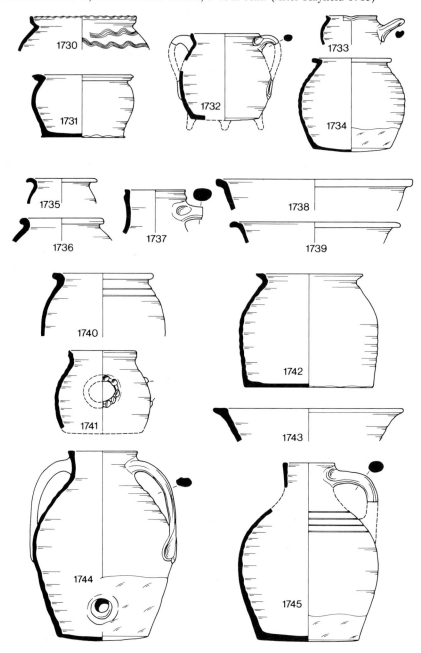

(ii) *Pottery*

Unstratified waster group from the King's Moat to the south of the village. Humber ware forms from this group include pipkins, dripping dishes, lids and cups as well as more usual Humber ware forms. Dating uncertain – moat dug in 1323; group dated to 15th-16th century, but tall-necked jugs with 'raspberry' and 'wheatear' stamps are more likely to be *c.* mid 14th century on stylistic grounds and by analogy with earliest finds at High Street kiln site, where level producing highly decorated pottery was archaeo-magnetically dated to *c.* 1350 (Le Patourel 1968: 110).

Later Humber ware is plainer, decoration restricted to incised grooves on shoulder, thumbed strips on necks, thumbed rims, wavy combing, occasional pads of cream clay in imitation of Cistercian ware. Among more unusual late Humber ware forms are plant-holders.

b. *Firsby Hall, Conisbrough Park* (Hayfield 1985): Fig. 248

(i) *Production site*

Four waster scatters known. Documentary evidence for a potter at Conisbrough in 1379 (Le Patourel 1968: 113).

(ii) *Pottery*

Coal Measure fabric – hard white or cream coarse sand-tempered fabric, sometimes dull reddish-purple with blistered surfaces; glaze yellow to green, or olive green to purple. Paler fabrics probably earlier than purple over-fired ones. Forms – cooking pots, bowls, jugs, cisterns, drinking mugs, lids, dripping dishes, curfews, urinals. Date range from later 13th/14th–16th century; purple wares not common until later 15th century.

c. *Rawmarsh* (Hayfield 1985; Le Patourel 1968: 124)

(i) *Production site*

Wasters found. Documentary evidence for potters from 13th-15th century.

(ii) *Pottery*

Coal Measure fabric (or 'East Pennine gritty ware' – Le Patourel 1967: 43); similar in fabric and forms to pottery from Firsby Hall.

d. *Thorner* (Le Patourel 1968: 118)

Production site

Documentary reference to a potter in late 14th century.

e. *Baildon* (Le Patourel 1967: 43; 1968: 124)

(i) *Production site*

Documentary evidence of production from 14th to 16th centuries. Two late medieval kilns known: Kiln 1, late 14th/early 15th century; Kiln 2, early 16th century. Both producing East Pennine Gritty ware.

(ii) *Pottery*

East Pennine Gritty ware – light-coloured hard gritty fabric with brown to green glaze; forms mainly jugs and bowls, the jugs often having a wavy combed line on the shoulder.

f. *Follifoot* (Le Patourel 1967: 43; Wilson and Hurst D.G. 1965: 218–19)

Production site

Multi-flued kiln dated to early 16th century. Pottery of East Pennine Gritty type, with dark brown glaze; forms mainly cisterns, jugs and bowls. Pots stacked on thin gritstone slabs overlying the clay floor.

g. *Shadwell* (Webster and Cherry 1978: 187)

(i) *Production site*

Three-flued kiln of late medieval date excavated.

(ii) *Pottery*

Products comprise heavily gritted jugs and bowls, usually partly glazed dark brown to green, and cooking pots; also a few lobed cups in finer fabric.

h. *Wrenthorpe (Potovens)* (Bartlett 1971; Brears 1967; Woodrow 1971): Fig. 249; see also Fig. 18 Nos. 6–10

(i) *Production sites*

'Potovens' place-name dates from at least 1650 if not earlier; references to 'cuppers' in 16th century legal documents (see p. 15). A number of kilns excavated in and around Potovens (now Wrenthorpe) village, and nearby Silcoates, on the edge of the Wakefield Outwood. Production dates from 15th–18th centuries; extent of waster deposits indicates large-scale production. Kilns wood- and coal-fired; saggars and sometimes kiln props used. Either Type 3 kilns with six flues, or clamp kilns in which saggars with pots were stacked on a clay floor or raised floor of kiln props and covered with clay and sherds. Parting sherds were put beneath cups to prevent them sticking to the saggars; small cones of clay were used to support lids during firing. A baked clay stamp used to impress decoration on clay pads was also found.

(ii) *Pottery*

Cistercian ware – smooth red wheel-thrown fabric with dark brown glaze. Forms mainly cups and posset pots, also chafing dishes, costrels, small jugs. Decoration consists of applied white clay, either as notched strips or pads, often with stamped or incised decoration; motifs include stylized floral or stag's head designs. Occasionally 'reversed Cistercian' ware occurs, in cream fabric with pale yellow to pale greenish glaze. Date range late 15th-16th century.

Small proportion of coarse wares also produced; forms – cisterns, storage jars, pipkins, cooking pots. Plates produced by late 16th-early 17th century.

i. *Potterton* (Le Patourel 1966b; Mayes and Pirie 1966): Fig. 249

(i) *Production site*

Six-flued kiln, coal-fired, excavated; pottery fired in saggars, used upside-down; one kiln prop found. Small clay cones also used. 16th century.

(ii) *Pottery*

Cistercian ware – fabric and forms similar to Wrenthorpe. Coarse wares also made; forms include bowls and two-handled jars or cisterns.

j. *Doncaster* (Hayfield 1985): Fig. 248

Coal Measure fabrics continue; dominant in late medieval period, into 16th century. Forms now include jugs, cooking pots, bowls, urinals, cisterns. Cistercian wares present in 16th century.

Fig. 249 YORKSHIRE, WEST RIDING
Wrenthorpe: 1746–61, kiln products, Cistercian ware, 16th cent. 1762–4, kiln products, coarse ware, 16th cent. (After Brears 1967; 1971; Woodrow 1971)
Potterton: 1765–77, kiln products, Cistercian ware, 16th cent. (After Le Patourel 1966b)

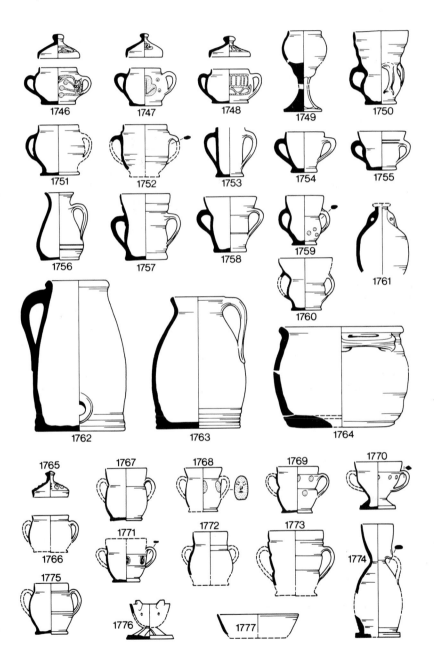

k. Sandal Castle (Brears 1983; Moorhouse 1983b): Figs. 250–2

Type 7c Northern Gritty continues, declining and disappearing during 15th century. Humber ware types 25f, 27f, 29f, 32f continue; Humber ware becomes more common, range of forms increases to include cooking pots, cisterns, lobed cups, industrial vessels.

Other main fabrics:

Type 40c Late Medieval Gritty ware – hard fired pink to brown gritty fabric with smooth surfaces, buff or light grey core, lime green or purplish glaze. Forms – jugs, cisterns, bowls, pipkins, two-handled cooking pots/jars, occasional chafing dishes. Source unknown; part of the Rawmarsh ceramic tradition, similar in fabric and forms to Rawmarsh products. Date range mainly 15th–16th century, though may start a little earlier; replaces Type 7c Northern Gritty ware as main coarseware during early 15th century.

Type 47u – brick red coarse sandy fabric with brown to light purple surfaces, orange to purple glaze. Forms – mainly jugs, cisterns, bowls; also cauldrons, pipkins, cooking pots, two-handled cooking pots, puzzle jugs, watering pots, frying pans. Decoration includes applied crosses with ring-and-dot stamps, applied discs and strips, incised wavy lines and other motifs, crude anthropomorphic ornament. Date range mainly 15th–16th century, some possibly earlier.

Type 42t 'Midland Purple' – hard coarse sandy grey or brown to purple fabric, dark purple glaze. Forms – mainly cooking pots, also jugs, cisterns, occasional curfew. Source unknown; probably a local version of Midland Purple ware. Date range mainly early-mid 15th century.

Type 60 Cistercian ware – mainly cups, occasional figurine or salt; main sources Wrenthorpe, Potterton. Date range late 15th-16th century.

Type 45t – industrial pottery, hard dull red sandy fabric; forms include bowls, jars, cucurbits, probably connected with alchemy. Date range mainly 15th century.

Type 61 Blackware – similar fabric to Cistercian ware but darker glaze and different forms: cups, costrels. Date range late 15th-16th century and later.

Type 59 Yellow ware – fine smooth cream fabric with yellow glaze. Earlier forms are reversed Cistercian wares, later ones anticipate 17th century Yellow wares. Forms include cups, bowls, chamber pots, joined bowls/condiment dishes, candlesticks, chafing dishes. Source probably Potovens area. Date range late 15th–16th century and later.

Imports include Type 48v Tudor Green ware, from Farnham area, Surrey, in 15th century.

l. Kirkstall Abbey (Le Patourel 1967)

East Pennine Gritty ware (Ware A) continues until Dissolution in 16th century. Humber ware continues. Cistercian and Midland Purple-type wares present.

m. Knaresborough (Le Patourel 1966a)

Early 15th century group – Fabric 1, local gritty ware, and Humber ware continue. East Pennine Gritty ware, forms include cisterns, jugs, cooking pots, present; source perhaps local.

Fig. 250   YORKSHIRE, WEST RIDING
Sandal Castle: 1778, Type 7c Northern Gritty ware, early 15th cent. 1779–87, Type
40c Late Medieval Gritty ware, 15th–16th cent. 1788–91, Humber ware, 15th cent.
(After Moorhouse 1983b)

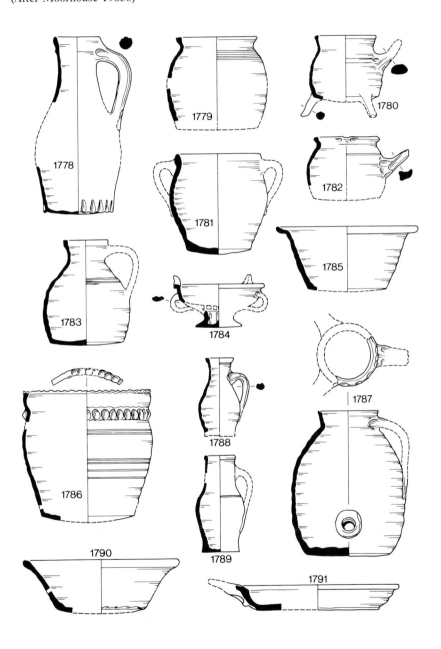

Fig. 251 YORKSHIRE, WEST RIDING
Sandal Castle: 1792–5, Humber ware, 15th cent. 1796–1805, Type 47u. 1796–7, 1803–4, 15th cent. 1798–1802, 1805, 16th cent. (After Moorhouse 1983b)

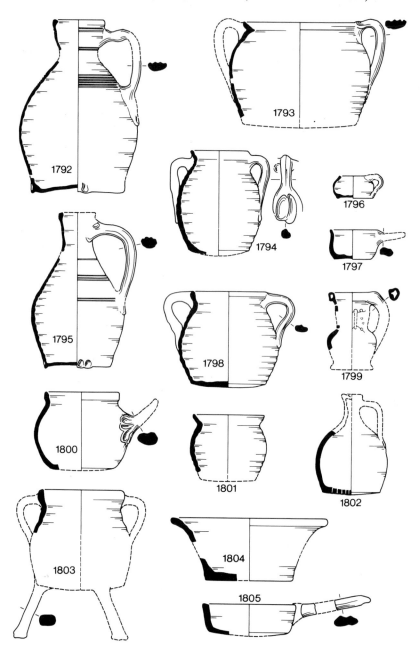

Fig. 252 YORKSHIRE, WEST RIDING
Sandal Castle: 1806–11, Type 47u; 1806–7, 1809–11, 15th cent. 1808, 16th cent.
1812, Type 61 Blackware, 16th cent. 1813–14, Type 59 Yellow ware, 16th cent.
1815, Type 42t 'Midland Purple' ware, 15th cent. (After Moorhouse 1983b)

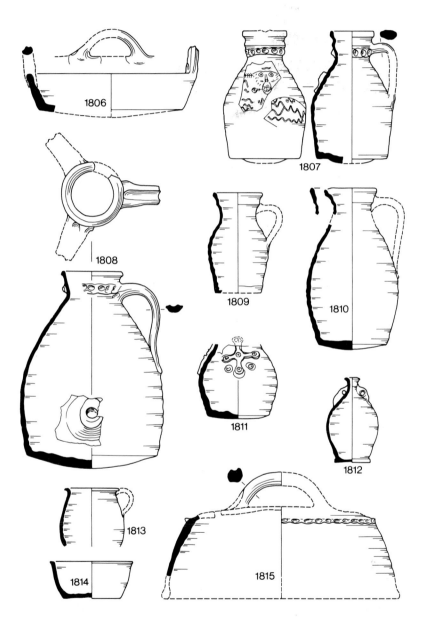

Eastern England (Fig. 253)

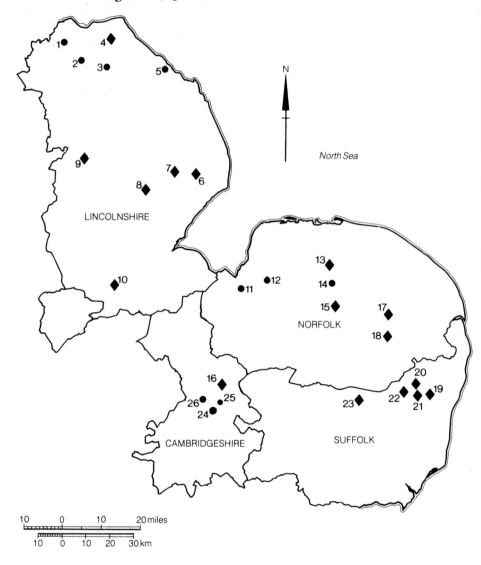

Fig. 253   Eastern England, location map
1 Thornholme Priory, 2 Broughton, 3 Somerby, 4 Thornton Curtis, 5 Humberston,
6 Toynton All Saints, 7 Old Bolingbroke, 8 Kirkstead, 9 Lincoln, 10 Bourne, 11
King's Lynn, 12 Grimston, 13 Fulmodeston, 14 North Elmham, 15 East Dereham,
16 Ely, 17 Norwich, 18 Saxlingham Nethergate, 19 Wissett, 20 Mendham, 21
Metfield, 22 Weybread, 23 Hinderclay, 24 Cambridge, 25 Denny Abbey, 26
Haddenham.

1. Lincolnshire

a. Lincoln (Chapman *et al.* 1975; Coppack 1980b): Fig. 254; see also Fig. 14

(i) *Production sites*

Documentary references to potters in 15th and 16th centuries.

(ii) *Pottery*

Lincoln Medieval Sandy ware declines, becoming less decorated, ends perhaps in 15th century. Shelly wares probably end by 15th century. Toynton/Bolingbroke ware and Humber ware become important; some Cistercian and Midland Purple wares in 16th century; these supplemented at end of period by glazed post-medieval red earthenwares.

b. Bourne (Healey 1969; 1975; Kerr n.d.): Fig. 255

(i) *Production site*

Eastgate, on eastern outskirts of town – three-flued Type 3 kiln with associated waster heaps, house, workshop and outhouse with clay puddling pit (see Moorhouse 1981: fig. 88). Kiln dated to *c.* 16th century by pottery. Workshop probably destroyed by fire; documentary evidence that much of Potter Street and Eastgate destroyed by fire, due to 'carelessness at the Potteries', in 1637.

(ii) *Pottery*

Products of kiln in Bourne D ware – smooth fine-textured pale red oxidized fabric, some small calcitic inclusions, usually with thin white slip beneath glaze; glaze mottled varying from light green to yellow and brown, sometimes with copper speckles. Forms – storage jars, bung-hole cisterns, jugs, pancheons, bowls, dishes, bottles, pipkins, chafing dishes. Little decoration. Bourne D ware not closely dated; *c.* 1450–1637.

c. Toynton All Saints (Healey 1975): Figs. 255–6

(i) *Production sites*

Kiln 2, five-flued brick-built Type 3 kiln, archaeomagnetically dated to 1475–1525; other possible kiln sites may belong to this period.

(ii) *Pottery*

Toynton/Bolingbroke ware – pottery produced here and Old Bolingbroke (and at other sites) is of very similar character, and potters from Toynton may have moved to Old Bolingbroke. Hard sandy fabric, pale orange to buff external surfaces, core and interior often reduced on closed forms; olive green to brownish glaze. Forms – pancheons, cisterns, jugs, drinking jugs, dishes, pipkins and chafing dishes. Little decoration apart from thumbed strips on some cisterns. Ware not closely dated but common in Lincolnshire in 15th and 16th centuries; produced into early 18th century at Old Bolingbroke, and at 17th century kiln at Boston.

d. Old Bolingbroke (Coppack 1976; Healey 1975; Whitwell 1966): Figs. 255–6

(i) *Production sites*

Two waster pits and part of a Type 3 kiln similar to Toynton kiln 2 excavated. Other kilns known from fieldwalking, indicating a large-scale industry. Production thought to date from mid 15th century to early 18th century.

(ii) *Pottery*

Toynton/Bolingbroke ware – see Toynton All Saints. This ware dominant in 16th

Fig. 254   LINCOLNSHIRE
Lincoln: 1816–26, Lincoln ware. 1816–22, 1826, 14th–15th cent.; 1823–5, 16th cent.
(After Chapman *et al.* 1975; Coppack 1973; 1980; White 1976)
Somerby: 1827–8, Coarse Sandy Shelly ware, 14th or 15th cent. 1829, Humber ware,
14th or 15th cent. (After Mynard 1969b)

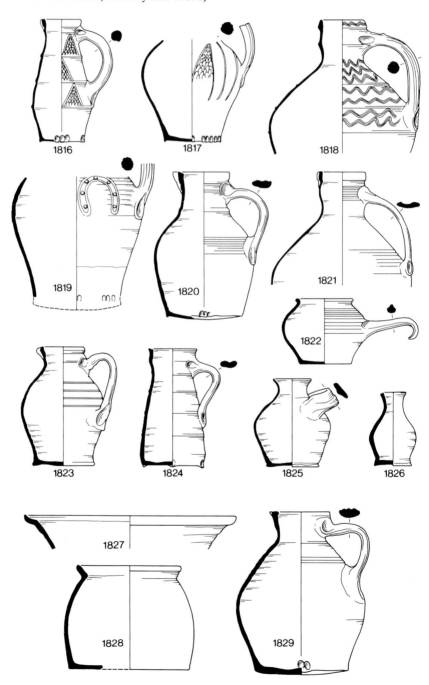

Fig. 255 LINCOLNSHIRE
Bourne: 1830–5, 1837, Bourne D ware, *c.* 16th cent. 1836, Bourne D ware from
Lincoln, early 16th cent. (After Coppack 1980b; Healey 1975)
Old Bolingbroke: 1838–9, kiln products from Old Bolingbroke. 1841–3, 1845,
Bolingbroke ware from Old Bolingbroke Castle. (After Coppack 1976; Whitwell
1966)
Toynton All Saints: 1844, kiln product from Kiln 2. 1840, Toynton-type ware from
Goltho. (After Beresford 1975; Healey 1975)

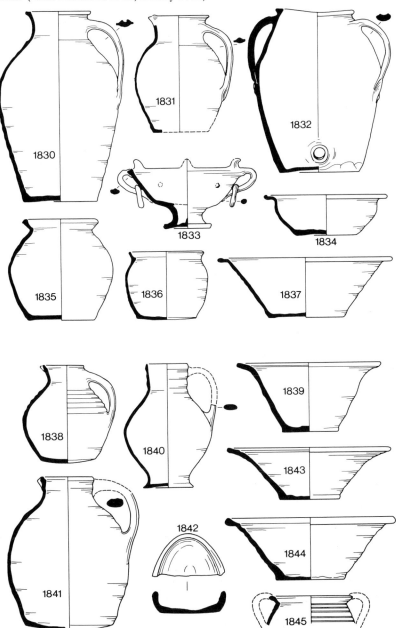

Fig. 256   LINCOLNSHIRE
Toynton All Saints: 1846, kiln product from Kiln 2. (After Healey 1975)
Old Bolingbroke: 1847–8, kiln products from Old Bolingbroke. 1850, Bolingbroke
ware from Old Bolingbroke Castle. (After Coppack 1976; Whitwell 1966)
Coningsby: 1849, Toynton/Bolingbroke ware. (After Healey 1975)

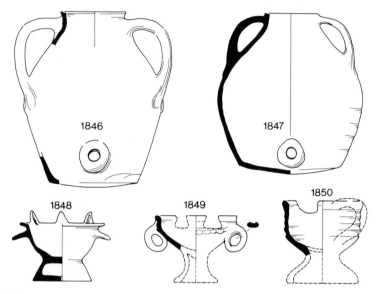

and 17th century groups excavated at Old Bolingbroke castle – groups dated by typology,
imported pottery and occasional coins.

e. *Coningsby* (Healey 1975): Fig. 256

Production site
Toynton/Bolingbroke ware wasters found.

f. *Kirkstead* (Healey 1975)

Production site
Toynton/Bolingbroke ware wasters found.

g. *Thornton Curtis* (Hayfield 1985)
Production site
Humber ware (H2) wasters known from the parish, possibly indicating production.
Date range of H2, 13th–16th century.

h. *Thornholme Priory, Appleby* (Hayfield 1985): Figs. 257–8

Dominant fabric M1 medium sandy ware, coil-built, wheel-finished; wide range of
forms; pancheons and curfews become more common. Vessels much plainer after mid
14th century. M1 jugs no longer copy Lincoln/Toynton styles but Humber wares. M1
continues in 15th and probably early 16th century; terminal date not known.

Fig. 257 LINCOLNSHIRE
Thornholme Priory: 1851–66, M1 medium sandy ware. 1851–6, 1859–64, 14th cent.;
1857–8, 1866, 15th cent.; 1865, early 16th cent. (After Hayfield 1985)

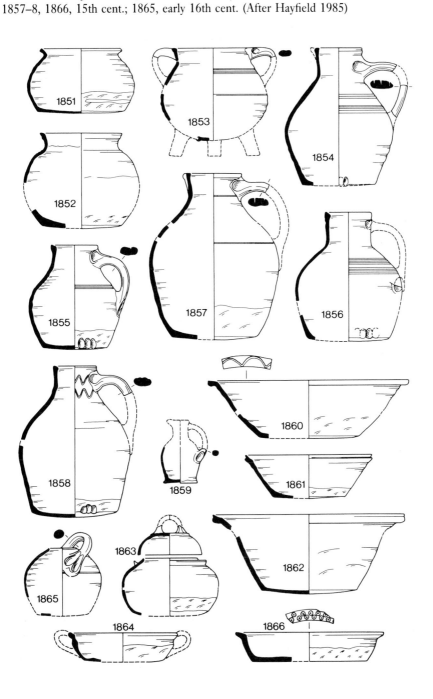

Fig. 258   LINCOLNSHIRE

Thornholme Priory: 1867–9, M1 medium sandy ware. 1870–4, Humber wares. 1867–8, 1871–2, 14th cent.; 1869–70, 1873–4, 15th cent. (After Hayfield 1985)
Humberston Abbey: 1875–7, Humber ware, second quarter of 16th cent. (After Hayfield 1984a)

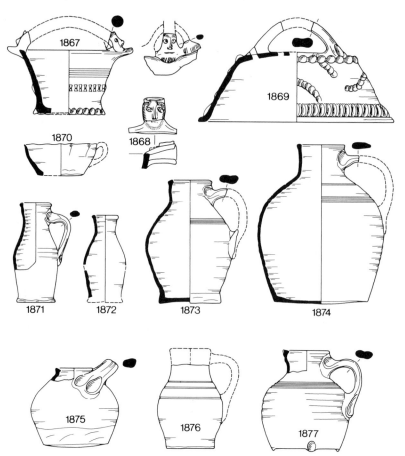

Humber wares, wheel-thrown, outnumber M1 vessels by mid 15th century, dominant from then on; elsewhere in North Lincolnshire Humber wares dominant by mid 14th century. Hard red fine sandy fabric, often reduced internally, olive glaze; forms – mainly jugs, cisterns, drinking jugs, urinals; little decoration apart from thumbed strips on cisterns and horizontal grooving on jug/cistern shoulders.

Minor wares – shelly fabrics, never common at Thornholme, probably finished before 15th century; Toynton/Bolingbroke-type ware; Coal Measures fabric, probably from Firsby, Yorkshire; Cistercian wares in 16th century, and some Humber ware copies of Cistercian ware.

i. Humberston Abbey (Hayfield 1984a): Fig. 258

Large group of complete or near-complete vessels recovered from *rere dorter* drain; Humber ware and Toynton/Bolingbroke fabrics, jugs, cisterns and urinals. Group dated to second quarter of 16th century.

j. *Somerby* (Hayfield 1985; Mynard 1969b): Fig. 254

Deserted village site; Gulley 6 yielded a group of Coarse Sandy Shelly ware cooking pots and bowls, and Humber-type ware jugs, whose stratigraphic association may be presumed although not well recorded. Typologically dated to 14th or 15th century. The continuation of shelly wares into the late medieval period is paralleled by an unstratified group from Broughton, North Lincolnshire (Moorhouse 1974b).

2. Norfolk

a. *Grimston* (Clarke and Carter 1977; Wilson and Moorhouse 1971: 176): Fig.259

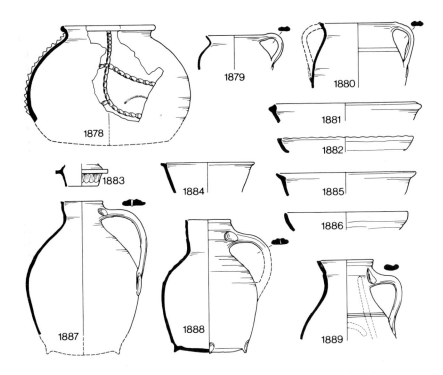

Fig. 259 NORFOLK
Grimston: 1878–81, 1884–5, 1887–9, Grimston ware from King's Lynn; 1889 has painted glaze decoration. 1888, late medieval; 1881, 14th cent., 1884–5; later 14th–15th cent.; 1878, 15th–16th cent.; 1879–80, 1887, 1889, 16th cent. 1882–3, 1886, Grimston-type ware from Norwich, late medieval. (After Clarke and Carter 1977; Jennings 1981)

(i) *Production site*

Floor of a four-flued kiln and late medieval features found; kiln presumably late medieval; it is suggested that pottery production continued here until 1500.

(ii) *Pottery*

Late medieval production of Grimston ware: fabric and glaze similar to earlier Grimston ware with increasing tendency for glaze to be applied more thickly and extensively, including internal glaze. Main forms – jugs, plainer than previously, though some have glaze painted on in curves and stripes; storage jars, internally-glazed bowls; also handled cooking pots and glazed pipkins.

b. *Fulmodeston* (Wade-Martins 1983): Figs. 260–3; see also Fig. 18 No. 11

(i) *Production site*

Two waster groups found, Group 1 being typologically earlier than Group 2; both dated typologically to 16th century.

(ii) *Pottery*

Red sandy fabric, glaze mostly brown to olive-green (with some tankards of Group 2 being glazed dark green to blackish); vessels often glazed internally as well as externally. Wide range of forms – jugs, storage jars, tripod pipkins and skillets, pancheons, bowls, chafing dishes, costrels, bottles, dripping dishes, cisterns, curfews, colanders, watering pots, warming pots/pomanders, tankards, chamber pots; rare forms include a horn, 'ring vase' and 'chicken-feeder'. The Group 2 material included saggar fragments. Decoration was confined to some thumbing and wavy lines, and stamping on the 'ring vase'.

c. *East Dereham* (A. Rogerson pers. comm.)

Production site

Production site, 16th-17th century, known near town.

d. *Saxlingham Nethergate* (A. Rogerson pers. comm.)

Production site

Surface scatter of wasters in Late Medieval and Transitional (LMT) ware (see Norwich).

e. *King's Lynn* (Clarke and Carter 1977): Fig. 265

(i) *Production site*

126 Norfolk Street – small group of tile wasters and cooking pot in the same fabric; documentary evidence in late 16th century for manufacture of tiles at least in this area.

(ii) *Pottery*

Norfolk Street products in NS ware, fairly common elsewhere in town; soft fine off-white to pink fabric, copper-green or yellow-brown glaze. Forms – cooking pots, chamber pots, jars, pipkins, lids, colanders, chafing dishes. Date range late 16th–18th century.

Red wares – fairly soft, slightly sandy red fabric, glaze varying from light to dark brown; a small sub-group (West Norfolk Bichrome) has brown glaze internally, copper green glaze externally. Forms – tripod pipkins, handled cooking pots, jars, chamber pots, lids, dripping dishes. Date range late 16th–18th century.

Fig. 260   NORFOLK
Fulmodeston: 1890–5, 1900, kiln products, Group 1, 16th cent. 1896–9, 1901–2, kiln products, Group 2, 16th cent. (After Wade-Martins 1983)

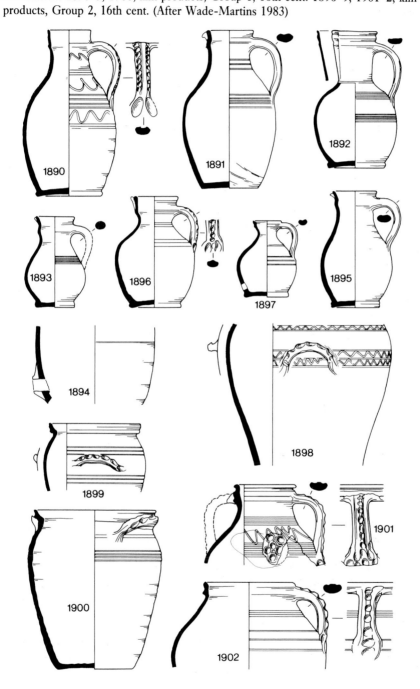

Fig. 261   NORFOLK
Fulmodeston: 1903–8, 1913–16, kiln products, Group 1, 16th cent. 1909–12, kiln products, Group 2, 16th cent. (After Wade-Martins 1983)

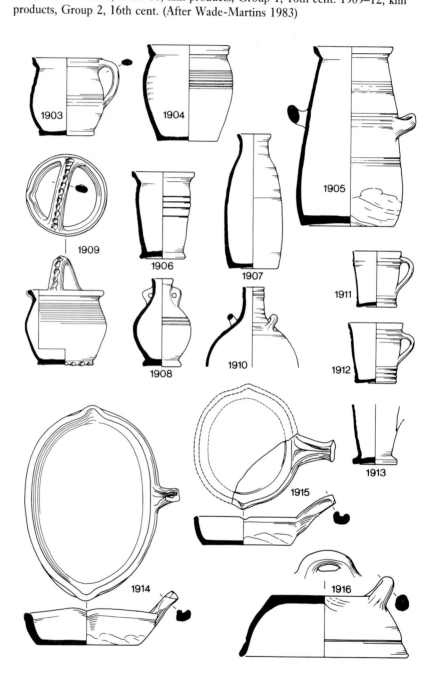

Fig. 262 NORFOLK
Fulmodeston: 1917–18, 1926–7, 1930–4, kiln products, Group 1, 16th cent. 1919–25, 1928–9, 1935–8, kiln products, Group 2, 16th cent. (After Wade-Martins 1983)

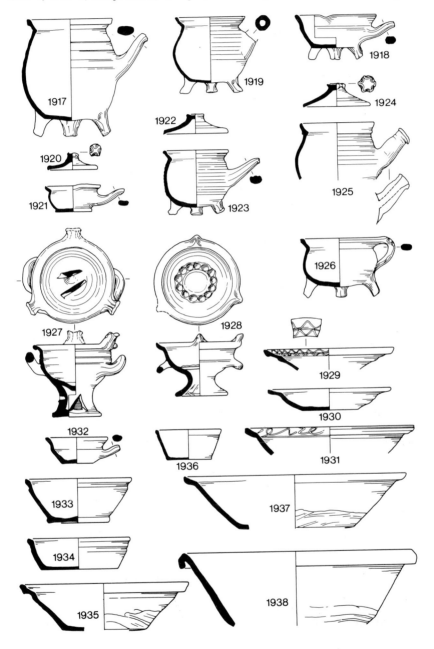

Fig. 263 NORFOLK
Fulmodeston: 1939, 1943, 1947, kiln products, Group 1, 16th cent. 1940–2, 1944–6,
kiln products, Group 2, 16th cent. (After Wade-Martins 1983)

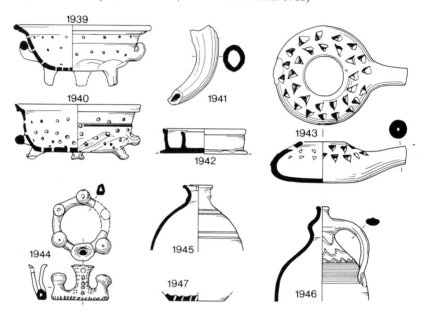

Other wares include late Grimston ware and black-glazed Cistercian-type ware
cups, possibly from Ely; regional imports include Bourne D-type ware. Few good 16th
century pottery groups excavated.

f. Norwich (Evans and Carter 1985; Jennings 1981): Figs. 264–5

At Pottergate, excavation of several tenements revealed deposits burnt in a fire
attributed to 1507, and in which the ceramic assemblages should be representative of the
range of vessels in domestic use. Commonest forms were storage vessels in various sizes,
including cisterns; many of cisterns contained traces of sediments, and had been used
for storing ale or beer. Most of pottery in LMT ware but some in late Grimston-type
ware. Numerous pottery drinking vessels found, mainly in Rhenish stoneware but a few
in Cistercian-type blackware, perhaps from north Cambridgeshire; Tudor Green and
Surrey White wares absent, though found elsewhere in the city. A few local bowls, dishes
and jugs found. Cooking vessels sparsely represented; local LMT pipkins are conspi-
cuously absent, though two imported Low Countries pipkins and a few LMT frying pans
are present. It is suggested that most cooking was done in metal vessels.

Late medieval/early post-medieval wares present in Norwich:

Grimston-type ware continues in 14th and 15th centuries.

Late Medieval and Transitional ware (LMT) – hard slightly sandy compact fabric,
usually oxidized orange to brown, sometimes reduced or with grey core; glaze yellow to
olive green, sometimes copper green; open forms often glazed internally. Forms include
jugs, pancheons, cisterns, storage jars, bowls, cauldrons, frying pans, pipkins, lids; in

Fig. 264   NORFOLK
Norwich: 1948–65, LMT ware, mid 15th–16th cent. (After Jennings 1981)

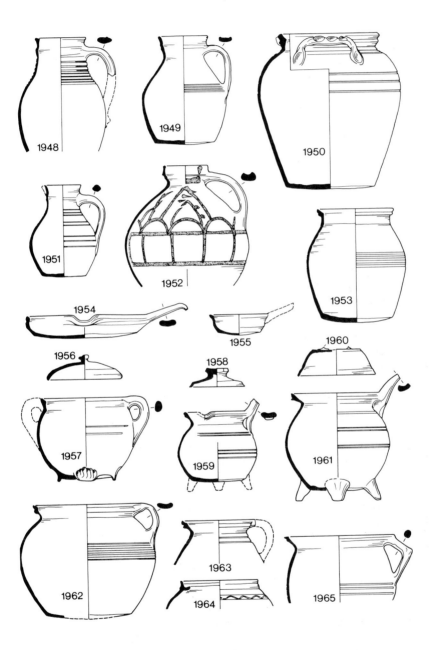

Fig. 265 NORFOLK

Norwich: 1966–79, LMT ware, mid 15th–16th cent. 1980–92, Early Post-Medieval Local ware, 16th–early 17th cent. (After Jennings 1981)

King's Lynn: 1993, NS ware. 1994–5, Cistercian-type ware ware. 1996, Red ware. All *c.* 16th cent. (After Clarke and Carter 1977)

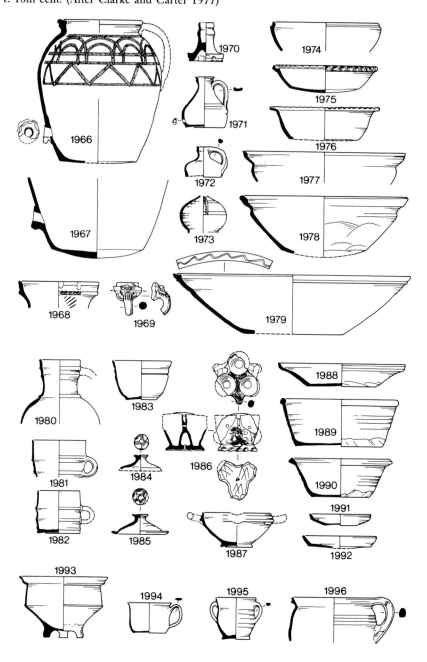

16th century also chafing dishes, drinking vessels, money boxes. Decoration includes brown iron oxide slip in elaborate arcaded designs on jugs and cisterns, thumbing on bowl rims, incised wavy lines, pinched faces on chafing dish handles. Several LMT vessels found set in church floors as acoustic pots. Date range mid 15th–later 16th century; presumed local production; some forms show continental influence.

Early Post-medieval Local wares – fine orange fabric, copper-green glaze; forms – bowls, jugs, jars, cordoned mugs, lids; decoration rare. Many forms continental in origin. Presumed 16th–early 17th century local production.

Glazed Red Earthenware (GRE) – slightly sandy orange, red or brownish fabric, usually oxidized; glaze usually orange to brown, occasionally has copper added. Forms – dishes, bowls, pancheons, storage jars, pipkins, lamps, dripping dishes, lids, colanders, chafing dishes; few jugs, no drinking vessels. Dominant post-medieval pottery type, showing Dutch influence; dates from first half of 16th century to 18th century; detailed dating of vessel types not known.

Iron-glazed ware – orange to grey fabric, glaze dense black to streaky thin brown or greenish-black. Forms – mostly two-handled cups or tankards. Dating – early 16th–17th century. Source – some possibly from Fulmodeston, and Wroxham, a site producing 17th-century GRE wares and blackware.

West Norfolk Bichrome – present in small quantities; late 16th–17th century. Forms – pipkins, jars, bowls, mugs copying German stonewares.

g. *North Elmham* (Rigold 1962–3; Wade 1980)

In 14th/15th century Grimston-type glazed jugs and internally-glazed bowls and handled jars important.

'Despenser' ware – yellow-glazed ware, in two fabrics, type 1 fine pale buff sandy, type 2 red fabric with pale buff slip and sgraffito decoration. Associated with late 14th/early 15th century manor house of Bishop Despenser. Forms include pipkins, cauldrons, chafing dishes (one with sgraffito decoration of a schematic version of Despenser's arms – see Fig. 60 No. 9), lids and probable cisterns.

3. Suffolk

a. *Hinderclay* (Wilson and Hurst J.G. 1959: 325; 1960: 164; Wilson and Hurst D.G. 1964: 297)

Production site
Wasters and kiln fragments indicate one, possibly two, kilns; pottery of 15th century date.

b. *Metfield, Docking hall* (Martin *et al.* 1984: 324)

Production site
Kiln, dated to *c.* 1480–1520.

c. *Wissett* (Balkwill 1980: 150)

Production site
Late medieval wasters and kiln debris; products include large jugs, dishes and frilly-based mugs, resembling vessels from Hinderclay.

d. *Weybread* (Owles 1973: 213–14)

(i) *Production site*
Kiln waste; several kiln sites known.
(ii) *Pottery*
Sandy light orange green-glazed fabric; forms – cisterns, jugs, bowls/dishes; also cups, chafing dishes. Date range late 15th-early 16th century.

e. *Mendham* (Martin *et al.* 1985: 47–8)

Production site
Evidence of kilns in four areas producing LMT ware (see Norwich); green-glazed or unglazed. Forms include pancheons, skillets; some pots decorated with iron oxide strips. Similar to pottery from Metfield and Weybread. Date range *c.* mid 15th-16th century.

Two sites producing similar but possibly slightly later wares – dark green-glazed, black-glazed and unglazed fabrics. Forms – pancheons, jugs.

4. Cambridgeshire

a. *Ely* (Clarke and Carter 1977: 262)

Production site
Production of Cistercian-type and blackware cups and tygs known.

b. *Cambridge* (Addyman and Biddle 1965; Bushnell and Hurst 1952; Dunning 1950a): Fig. 266

Mostly unstratified material. Cambridge Sgraffito ware – hard red ware, partly covered by a buff slip through which designs are incised; clear yellowish glaze, sometimes flecked with green. Forms – mainly jugs; source unknown, but may be fairly local. Date range *c.* 14th–15th century.

c. *Denny Abbey* (Coppack 1980a): Fig. 266

No 15th century groups published. Orange Sandy ware continues; mainly bowls, cooking pots, jugs, also chafing dishes, bottles/cruets, dripping dishes, pipkins, cisterns, alembics, cucurbits. Decoration includes sgraffito, and impressed rosette motifs on chafing dish rims. Very common in 16th-century groups.

Grey Sandy ware – hard grey or black sand-tempered ware; forms – cooking pots, bowls, jugs. Occurs in 16th century groups.

Probable regional imports include Cistercian ware.

d. *Haddenham, Hinton Hall* (Brooks C.M. forthcoming)

Late medieval and Tudor wares include quartz-tempered pottery in hard red wares; forms – wheel-thrown jugs, bowls, pancheons. Source uncertain but some possibly from Essex, whilst other very smooth-textured wares, some with sgraffito, may be from Bourne, Lincolnshire. Cistercian wares also present.

Fig. 266 CAMBRIDGESHIRE
Cambridge: 1997–2000, Cambridge Sgraffito ware, *c.* 14th–15th cent. (After Addyman
and Biddle 1965; Bushnell and Hurst 1952; Dunning 1950a)
Denny Abbey: 2001–6, Orange Sandy ware, 16th cent. (After Coppack 1980a)

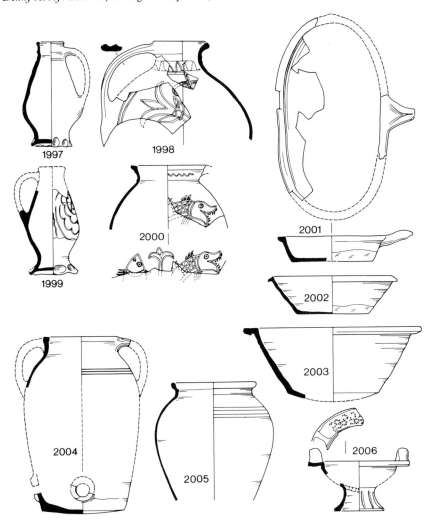

North Midlands (Fig. 267)

1. Leicestershire

a. Leicester (Woodland 1981): Fig. 268

Fig. 267 North Midlands, location map
1 Nottingham, 2 Keighton, 3 Brackenfield, 4 Derby, 5 Ticknall, 6 Leicester

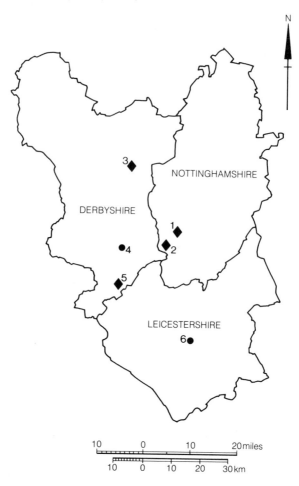

Major rebuilding on Austin Friars site in mid 14th century; levels dated by slight documentary sources and presence of early Midland Purple types. Some increase in range of vessels towards end of 14th century. Possible midden deposits in Period 4b contain jugs, cisterns, urinals; a Period 5a drain contains distilling equipment and crucibles, suggesting use of area for drinking and/or alchemy.

Contents of 15th-century drain (Period 7a) – cisterns, jugs, cups and urinals, as well as Tudor Green and large amounts of Cistercian ware. Arrival of Cistercian ware attributed to *c.* 1450 but there seems no good evidence for this date, which should possibly be closer to 1500. Periods 9a and 10, 16th century: large number of Cistercian wares – cups, jugs, posset pots, chafing dishes and a candlestick. First example of Midland Yellow ware occurs in pre-Dissolution levels; it increases in popularity with Cistercian ware and blackwares in Period 10.

Fig. 268 LEICESTERSHIRE
Leicester: 2007–17, Cistercian ware, 16th cent. 2018–21, 2023–7, Midland Purple ware, late 14th–15th cent. 2022, unattributed fabric (Pviii), late medieval. (After Woodland 1981)

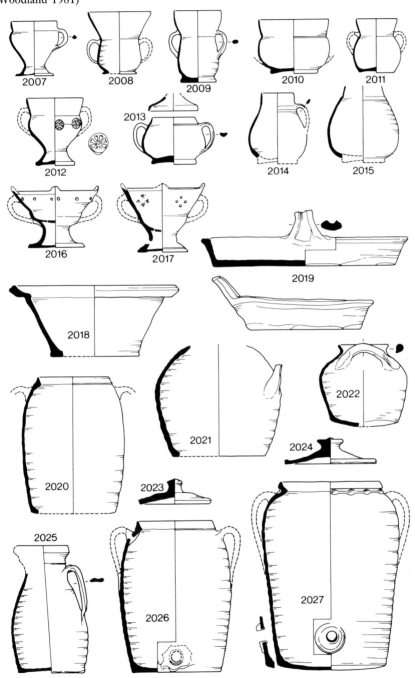

2. Nottinghamshire

a. Nottingham (Brears 1971; Coppack 1980b): Fig. 269

(i) Production sites

Kilns at Clinton Street believed to be late medieval and purple ware wasters from Parliament Street likely to be similar date. Charles Morley of Barker Gate taken to court in 1629 for 'diginge a clay pite in the fields wch is a hindrance to the burgesses Common, and danger overthroinge mens' cattell'.

(ii) Pottery

Main type is purple ware, possibly derived from Orange Sandy ware, the ubiquitous mid-13th to 14th century type. Fabric has fine sand tempering, glazes purple-black; very hard to partial vitrification; forms are wheel-thrown jugs, skillets and two-handled cisterns. Very few useful late medieval groups.

b. Keighton (Coppack 1968; 1980b)

(i) Production site

Village deserted at uncertain time in Middle Ages. Kilns excavated rapidly in 1950s thought to be for manufacture of decorated floor tiles, but presence of considerable pottery waster deposits also implies pottery production although no kilns identified.

(ii) Pottery

Fine sandy hard orange fabrics; wheel-thrown forms are pancheons, jugs and bowls. The decorated floor tiles are in style of Malvern School and are dated 1457–8.

3. Derbyshire

a. Ticknall (Brears 1971)

Production site

Excavations in 19th century in grounds of Calke Abbey uncovered extensive remains of potteries dating to 16th century. Fabrics include Midland Purple ware as well as Midland Yellow and Cistercian wares. Potteries continued to operate throughout 17th century and finally terminated in late 19th century.

b. Derby (Coppack 1972; 1980b): Fig. 269

Full Street excavations produced series of groups containing purple wares and Cistercian products. Earliest change from medieval to late medieval types attributed to late 15th century, but there is no reliable dating.

c. Brackenfield (Webster and Cherry 1973: 184)

(i) Production site

Two Type 2 kilns excavated; accumulation of ash and clay deposits hinted at multiple firings in one of the kilns; cylindrical kiln props present.

(ii) Pottery

Buff to white fabrics; forms – glazed jugs and bowls, the latter decorated with rouletting and applied motifs; unglazed cooking pots; glazed crested ridge and roof tiles. Dated to *c.* 1400.

Fig. 269 NOTTINGHAMSHIRE
Nottingham: 2028–35, Orange Sandy ware, 15th cent. 2036–7, Purple ware, 15th cent. (After Coppack 1980b)
     DERBYSHIRE
Derby: 2038, 2040–3, Purple ware, 14th–16th cent. 2039, Cistercian ware, 16th cent. (After Coppack 1980b)

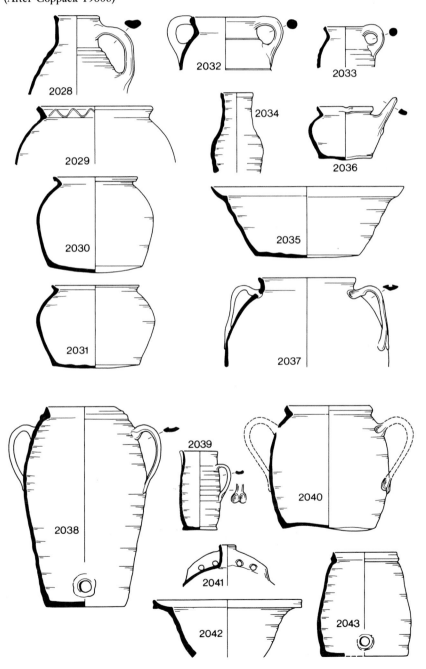

d. Potters Somersal (Le Patourel 1968)

Production site
Documentary reference to place-name.

South Midlands (Fig. 270)

1. Oxfordshire

a. Swyncombe (Mellor 1983)

Production site
Kilns located by magnetometer survey but unexcavated. Products made from local iron-rich and iron-free clays. Forms include 'bifid' rim cooking pots, bowls, jugs and cisterns.

b. Nettlebed (Stebbings *et al.* 1980)

Production sites
Potter name attested in 1442; place name, Crocker End (*crocca* – pot; *aern* – house), perhaps the house where pots were made, documented in 1417. The name 'Pottys' recorded in manor of Bensington (Benson) in 15th and 16th century. There is a will of William Butler, potter of Nettlebed in 1560. Brick and tile works in the Nettlebed and Crocker End area from the 14th century. There is abundant evidence of brickmakers and tilers between the 17th and 20th centuries.

c. Oxford (Mellor 1980b; 1985b): Fig. 271

The Hamel – northern tenements between the mid 13th and late 15th centuries show many minor structural modifications but no significant differences in pottery. Oxford Late Medieval wares (e.g. Fabrics AM, AW, ZZ) continue to dominate.

Southern tenement probably continues to be occupied by relatively wealthy citizen, as implied by finds of window glass, plaster and numerous coins; wider range of ceramic types than neighbouring properties, including continental imports. Pottery includes jugs, bottles, cups, cisterns and lobed cups. By the 16th century Cistercian wares are important, with some Hampshire-Surrey borders products.

Cornmarket and Queen Street – Oxford Late Medieval wares (Fabrics AM, ZZ) important. Fine series of money boxes in Brill and Surrey White wares in 16th century.

2. Northamptonshire

a. Stanion (Bellamy 1983; T. Pearson pers. comm.): Fig. 272

Production site
Kilns of uncertain type associated with hard red and orange-brown wares with very few inclusions. Wheel-thrown forms include cisterns, jars, jugs and dishes; late medieval.

b. Lyveden (Steane and Bryant 1975): Fig. 272

Fig. 270 South Midlands, location map
1 Stanion, 2 Lyveden, 3 Northampton, 4 Potterspury, 5 Paulerspury, 6 Yardley Hastings, 7 Yardley Gobion, 8 Bedford, 9 Everton, 10 St Neots, 11 Sawtry, 12 Flitwick, 13 Standon, 14 Gt Munden, 15 High Cross, 16 Hunsden, 17 Hertford, 18 Hatfield, 19 Potters Crouch, 20 St Albans, 21 Manor of the More, 22 Gt Brickhill, 23 Brill, 24 Oxford, 25 Bensington, 26 Swyncombe, 27 Crocker End, 28 Nettlebed.

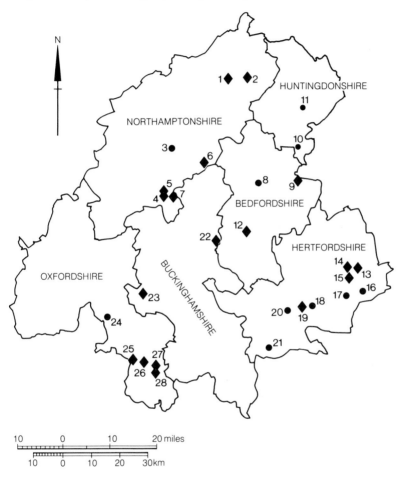

(i) *Production sites*

Potter names in late 14th and early 15th century include John Weston, Thomas Pottere and William Warde, who held three acres for 8s for digging clay for water pots in 1403. A William Crestmaker also mentioned.

Site E: excavation of damaged Type 1b kiln associated with flat roof tile wasters in stoke pit.

Site J: tofts of previous period converted to domestic/farming usage. In late 15th century and early 16th century industrial activity re-established in west toft. Rectangular

Fig. 271   OXFORDSHIRE
Oxford: 2044, Fabric AM, 13th–15th cent. 2045–7, Fabric ZZ, 16th cent. 2048–9, late medieval fabrics (After Jope 1950; Mellor 1980b)

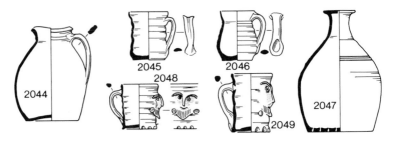

tile kiln of standard type located, as well as a building with projections at both ends, one projection possibly housing a clay dump.

(ii) *Pottery*

Pottery in hard quartz sand-tempered fabric oxidized orange to red-browns; forms – wheel-thrown cooking pots, jugs, bowls, cisterns and dripping pans. Dated by association with Tudor Green and Cistercian ware and by analogy with sites elsewhere.

c. *Potterspury* (Jope 1950; Mayes 1968; Moore 1974; Mynard 1969a; 1970): Fig. 273

(i) *Production sites*

Pottery production in Potterspury and neighbouring villages of Paulerspury, Yardley Gobion and Yardley Hastings. Documentary sources for 17th century industry only, though occasional potters' names recorded earlier. Type 1b kilns excavated along High Street, Potterspury, dated archaeomagnetically to mid–late 14th century; also at Yardley Gobion. At Yardley Hastings, a possible stone-lined drying oven over 2.5m x 0.8m x 0.4m deep; fill included pottery, kiln furniture, ash and charcoal.

(ii) *Pottery*

Hard fabric, smooth to slightly sandy, reddish yellow and buff with reduced cores; forms – wheel-thrown cooking pots, bowls, jugs, some chafing dishes, ring costrels, lids, dripping dishes, cisterns and ridge tiles.

d. *Northampton* (Gryspeerdt 1978; 1979; McCarthy 1979; McCarthy and Williams 1978): Fig. 273

(i) *Production site*

Potters Hill and Potters Field place names in northern part of urban area may indicate both selling and manufacture of pottery in late medieval period.

(ii) *Pottery*

Most important sequence – St Peter's Street; local calcareous wares, mainly of Lyveden-Stanion type, clearly continue into late 14th if not early 15th century; associated with coins of Edward III and Richard II.

Potterspury wares a very minor element in 14th century; become more important in 15th century, when Tudor Green and Midland Purple wares also appear. Forms – mainly cooking pots, bowls and jugs; these properties on what may have been an unimportant street on the edge of the medieval town also had wide range of other

Fig. 272 NORTHAMPTONSHIRE
Lyveden: 2050–55, hard sandy (type D) wares, 15th cent. (After Webster A. 1975)
Stanion: 2056–9, kiln products, 15th cent. (After Bellamy 1983)

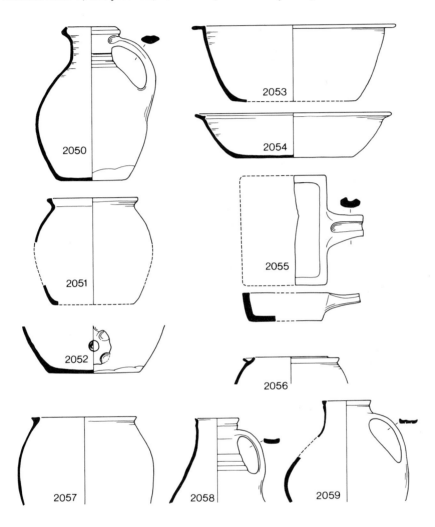

Potterspury types, including cups, lobed cups, cisterns, bottles, lids, chafing dishes, dripping pans and costrels. The general trend is confirmed at Marefair and Greyfriars sites.

Late 15th–16th century – Potterspury and Cistercian wares important; associated with Raeren stoneware. The succeeding phase, late 16th–early 17th century, includes Midland Black and Yellow wares, but none of the Potterspury slip-trailed wares current in the mid-17th century.

Fig. 273 NORTHAMPTONSHIRE
Potterspury: 2060–72, Potterspury ware from Northampton, 14th–15th cent. (After Gryspeerdt 1979; McCarthy 1979; Mynard 1970)
Northampton: 2073–6, Midland Black ware, 16th–early 17th cent. 2077, Midland Yellow ware, 16th cent. (After McCarthy 1979)

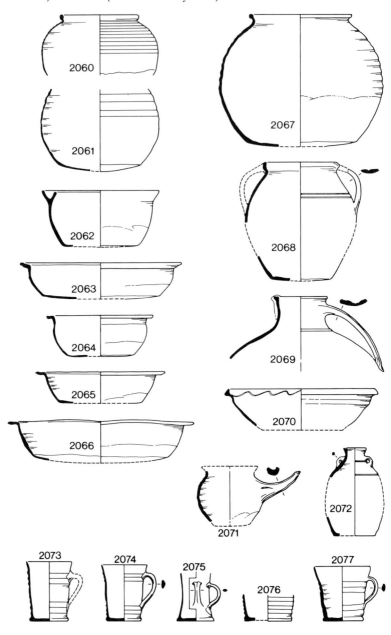

3. Huntingdonshire

a. St Neots and Sawtry (Addyman and Marjoram 1972; Moorhouse 1971b; 1974a): Fig. 274

At St Neots fishpond, local types include Late Medieval Reduced ware, hard heavily quartz-tempered reduced grey wares: one of main forms is the flanged bowl; less common are cooking pots, cisterns, jugs, shallow bowls, chafing dishes and possible cucurbits. Dated at Sawtry to late medieval period; confirmed at Northampton, Lyveden and by association with coin hoard dated 1503 at Hartford.

Other forms present include oxidized deep bowls, cooking pots, pipkins, jugs, cisterns and a possible chicken-feeder.

4. Buckinghamshire

a. Brill (Farley 1979 and pers. comm; Ivens 1981; 1982; Yeoman 1984–5)

(i) Production sites

Manufacture of pottery probably continuous from 13th to mid-19th century. Potters recorded in Temple Street in 1580. Type 4 kilns and saggars attributed to early 17th and possibly late 16th century

Further kilns located in Temple Street. Period 1 includes Kiln 1, described as a clamp but seems to have Type 2 characteristics, though clamps located nearby. Overlying and incorporating part of earlier structures was a rectangular brick-built kiln, associated with ash spreads and wasters. Post-holes at one end may be for temporary covering during loading or firing. Kiln reconstructed as of typical tile kiln form.

(ii) Pottery

Wasters from rectangular kiln consisted of three times as many pots as tiles. Forms – large jugs, cisterns, delicate bowls and saggars in which Cistercian wares were fired; also flat roof and crested ridge tiles. Dated to c. 1500 but could be slightly later. Late 16th and early 17th century kilns produced similar forms with addition of chafing dishes, costrels, jars and chamber pots.

b. Great Brickhill (D. Mynard pers. comm.)

Production site

Large number of wasters known from Jack Ironcaps Lane. Very sandy hard reduced grey wares; bowls a major form, with some cooking pots, jugs and cisterns. Very similar to Late Medieval Reduced Grey wares as defined by Moorhouse (1974a).

5. Hertfordshire

a. High Cross, Standon and Potters Green, Great Munden (C. Partridge, pers. comm; Renn 1964)

Production sites

Production likely at both places from late 14th century into 17th century.

b. Potterscrouch (Renn 1964)

Production site

'Le Potterscrouch next the way leading from St Albans to Langley' recorded in

1346–7; 'Potters', a field name attested in 1349–50; 'Pottershegge' in 1465 and other similar names in 1491–2 and 1597.

c. Hatfield, Wildhill, Woodside (Renn 1964)

Production sites

Potter names recorded from 14th century. Tolls on potters' wares charged at Highgate in 1377; 'Potwellgrove' documented in 1482; Tudor kilns at Pigbournes Lane, where 'baking plates' and wasters are recorded. Inventory of William Potter in 1612 refers to a 'working wheel and a walking stock and lumber belonging to his trade'.

d. St Albans (A. Havercroft pers. comm.)

St Albans-type ware or Late Medieval Hertfordshire Grey ware – fine slightly sandy orange-pink fabric; wheel-thrown forms, mainly jugs, sometimes highly decorated – one with a lamb and cross, possibly the *Agnus Dei*, also stamped bosses with rosettes, fleur-de-lys, horseshoes and flowers. Several sizes of bowls present, cisterns, some cooking pots, drinking jugs, a urinal and slab-made dripping trays. Dated stratigraphically and by association with dated deposits in London to 1340–1450. This type is petrologically distinct from but visually very similar to Brill-Boarstall wares.

From mid-15th century, St Albans was supplied from outside the area, though Hatfield and Woodside, where 17th century production is attested, are possible sources of blackwares. Cistercian wares known from early 16th century, but no useful assemblages found.

e. Hertford (C. Partridge pers. comm.)

Grey wares continue into 16th century, though not apparently from the Potters Green kilns. Glazed Red Earthenwares present in 16th century.

f. Hunsden House (C. Partridge pers. comm.)

Royal hunting lodge from reign of Henry VII to Elizabeth. Sealed and stratified garderobe deposits datable from *c.* 1530 to before 1630. Local types – wide range of forms in glazed red earthenwares, including straight-sided tankards, pipkins, chafing dishes, chamber pots, tripod bowls; also German and French stonewares, Dutch and Italian maiolicas and Spanish wares, glass and textiles.

g. The Manor of the More (Biddle et al. 1959)

Sequence of late medieval pottery, comprising largely Hertfordshire Grey wares and some oxidized fabrics, continuing into 15th century. Forms are jugs, 'bifid' rimmed cooking pots; bowls in glazed red earthenwares of 16th–17th century form. Tudor Green and Cistercian wares present in early 15th and early 16th century levels respectively.

Fig. 274 BEDFORDSHIRE
Flitwick: 2078–83, kiln products, 15th cent. (After Mynard *et al.* 1983)
Bedford: 2094–5, Fabric C14, 14th–15th cent. 2096–7, Fabric E1, 16th–17th cent. (After Baker *et al.* 1979)

HUNTINGDONSHIRE

Sawtry: 2084, Late Medieval Reduced ware, 15th cent. (After Moorhouse 1971b)
St Neots: 2085–90, Late Medieval Reduced and Oxidized wares. 2091–3, Cistercian
ware, 16th cent. (After Addyman and Marjoram 1972)

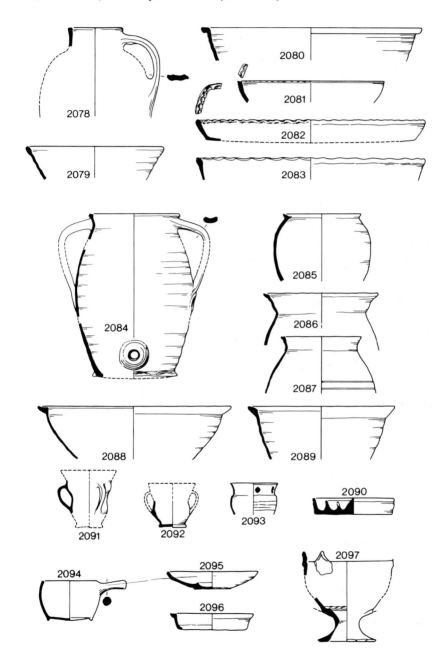

6. Bedfordshire

a. *Everton* (Hassall 1976)

(i) *Production site*
Village at junction of Oxford Clays and Greensands which are possible sources of clay and tempering material. Wasters and kiln bars known from four locations within village. Roman and post-medieval kilns also known locally.

(ii) *Pottery*
Seven fabrics defined: all quartz-based; various other inclusions such as limestone, flint, white mica and grog. Surfaces mainly rough-textured, predominantly reduced. Forms are wheel-thrown, and include cooking pots, several bowl forms, and unglazed jugs. Attributed to 14th-15th century on typological grounds.

b. *Flitwick* (E. Baker pers. comm.; Mynard et al. 1983): Fig. 274

(i) *Production site*
Village on Lower Greensand; nearest clay source over 1km north. Clay pits recorded in adjacent parish of Ampthill in 1468. Wasters found in village.

(ii) *Pottery*
Fabrics all hard quartzitic wares, mostly reduced. Forms probably all thrown; six bowl shapes are dominant types; also unglazed jugs. Cooking pots, dripping pans and cisterns less important. Dated by analogy with other Late Medieval Reduced wares to period 1375–1500.

c. *Bedford* (Baker et al. 1979): Fig. 274

Group E fabrics similar to those at Everton, Flitwick and Great Brickhill, but other sources nearer to Bedford are possible. Fabric E1 is a hard, reduced gritty ware dated to the 15th–17th centuries. Fabric C14, also a local ware, is quartzitic and micaceous and attributed to the 14th–15th centuries. All forms are wheel-thrown; bowls especially important, with jugs, cisterns, chafing dishes, jars amd a possible colander also present. Between the 16th and 18th centuries Bedford was supplied almost entirely by Potterspury and Paulerspury, Northants.

d. *Grove Priory* (E. Baker pers. comm.)

Group E wares from Flitwick, Great Brickhill and possibly other sources dominant. Forms mostly reduced bowls, cooking pots, jugs and cisterns. In post-medieval period, Brill wares dominant.

South-East England (Fig. 275)

1. Essex

a. *Sible Hedingham and Halstead* (Le Patourel 1968: 124)

Production sites
Documentary evidence for pottery production up to the 19th century.

Fig. 275   South-East England, location map
1 Colchester, 2 Sible Hedingham, 3 Halstead, 4 Chelmsford, 5 Writtle, 6 Woodham
Ferrers, 7 Stock, 8 Mill Green, 9 Harlow, 10 Waltham Abbey, 11 Canterbury, 12
Tyler Hill, 13 Ospringe, 14 Hareplain, 15 Rye, 16 Winchelsea, 17 Hastings, 18
Boreham Street, 19 Ringmer, 20 Lower Parrock, 21 Bramber, 22 Binsted, 23
Graffham, 24 Chichester, 25 Knighton, 26 Portchester, 27 Wickham Glebe, 28
Winchester, 29 Southampton, 30 Christchurch, 31 Basing House, 32 Farnham, 33
Farnborough, 34 Hawley, 35 Ash, 36 Pirbright, 37 Nonsuch, 38 Cheam, 39
Kingston upon Thames, 40 Southwark, 41 London.

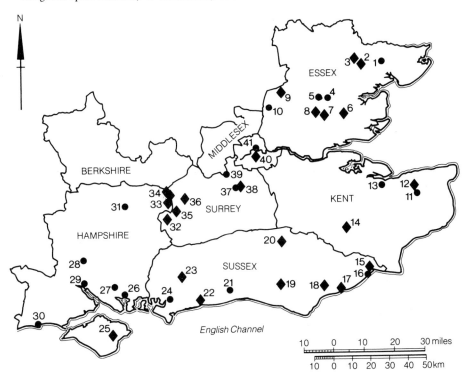

b. *Mill Green, Ingatestone* (Pearce *et al.* 1982; Sellers 1970)

Production site

Mill Green ware, although ceasing to be traded to London by *c.* mid 14th century,
probably continued in production to end of 14th or into 15th century, with coarse ware
forms such as cisterns, dripping dishes, cauldrons and skillets.

c. *Stock* (Cunningham and Drury 1985)

Production site

Documentary references to potters from late 15th century on. Wasters from area in
smooth red earthenwares, mostly of 17th and 18th century date – forms mainly jars,

platters, bowls, with some jugs, lids, cisterns, skillets, dripping dishes, costrels and chafing dishes; also black-glazed mugs of 16th century date.

d. Harlow (Le Patourel 1968: 124; Newton and Bibbings 1958)

Production site

Documentary references to pottery production from 13th–17th centuries, in area just south of Harlow: Foster Street, Potter Street and Latton Street. Blackwares and 'Metropolitan' slipwares made here in 17th century, though production of blackwares may have begun earlier.

e. South Woodham Ferrers (Couchman 1979: 67–9)

Production site

Early 15th century documentary references to potters. Wasters found; sandy orange slightly micaceous fabric. White or cream slip decoration, especially on jug necks and handles; brown or green glaze. Forms – cooking pots, jugs. Date range probably late 14th-early 15th century.

f. Colchester (Cunningham 1982a): Fig. 276

(i) *Production site*

Local production suggested by finds of wasters in Colchester Slip-painted ware, one from the castle area, one from Magdalen Street immediately outside town wall.

(ii) *Pottery*

Colchester ware continues into late medieval period; hard red sandy fabric, finer and plainer than previously. Forms now include chafing dishes with anthropomorphic decoration in later 14th/early 15th century.

Colchester Slip-painted ware – a later variant of Colchester ware; wasters known, so probably of local production. Forms include jugs, cisterns, storage jars; some watering pots, cooking pots. Decoration different from earlier Colchester ware; overall white or cream slip replaced by white slip-painted decoration, including dashes on the tops of rims; glaze becomes rare, though a few jugs have bibs or splashes of glaze; copper no longer added to glaze. Date range *c.* later 15th–16th century.

Colchester ware and Colchester Slip-painted ware form part of large fabric group, Fabric 21 – hard sandy orange or light brown fabrics, often with a grey core. Forms include jugs, storage jars, cisterns, watering pots, skillets, dripping dishes. Mostly of late medieval and early post-medieval date; predominant type until mid 16th century.

Fabric 40 – smooth red earthenware of post-medieval type; forms include jugs, storage jars, bowls, dishes, chafing dishes. From later 16th century on.

g. Chelmsford (Cunningham and Drury 1985): Figs. 277–8; see also Fig. 59 No. 5

Essex Grey wares and Mill Green ware die out by end of 14th century.

Fabric 21 – hard coarse red sandy ware with pimply surfaces, similar to Colchester ware, replace earlier wares; forms mainly jugs, bowls, cisterns; also jars, pipkins, chafing dishes, costrels, dripping dishes, cups. Glaze becomes more sparse, often just a bib below the neck; vessels plainer except for some painted white slip and sgraffito

Fig. 276 ESSEX
Colchester: 2098–2102, Colchester Slip-painted ware, late 15th–16th cent. 2103,
Colchester ware, late 14th–early 15th cent. 2104–7, 2112, Fabric 21, late 15th–16th
cent. 2108–11, Fabric 40, late 16th–17th cent. (After Cunningham 1982a)
Waltham Abbey: 2113–18, Ware M, 16th cent. (After Huggins 1972; 1976)

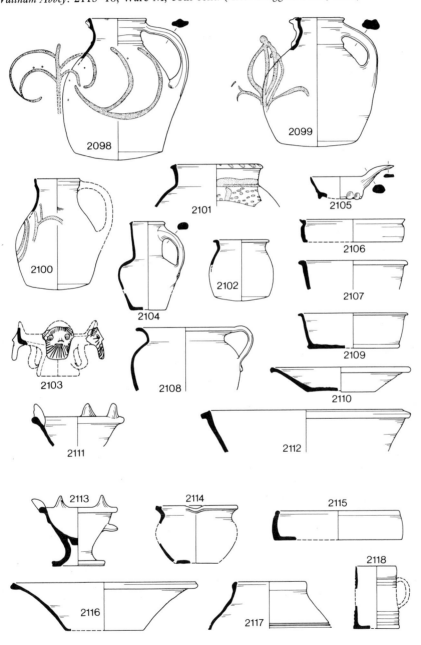

Fig. 277   ESSEX
Chelmsford: 2119–23, Fabric 21, 15th–16th cent. 2124–37, Fabric 40, 15th–late 16th/early 17th cent. (After Cunningham and Drury 1985)

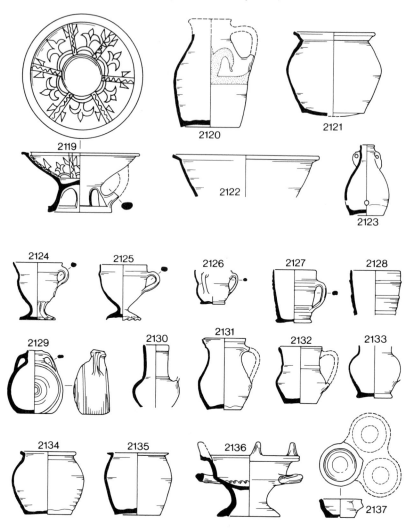

decoration. Occurs mostly in 15th-mid 16th century levels; source unknown but probably much comes from Stock/Ingatestone area.

Fabric 40 – smooth red earthenware with very fine sand inclusions (though some larger vessels are coarser); many vessels completely unglazed; some jugs have only a bib of glaze below the pouring lip, but by later 16th century many vessels have plain lead glaze internally or throughout. Forms – mostly bowls, jugs, cisterns; also dripping dishes, jars/cooking pots, chafing dishes, cups, lids, condiments, costrels. Mostly

Fig. 278 ESSEX
Chelmsford: 2138–47, Fabric 40, 15th–16th cent. (After Cunningham and Drury 1985)

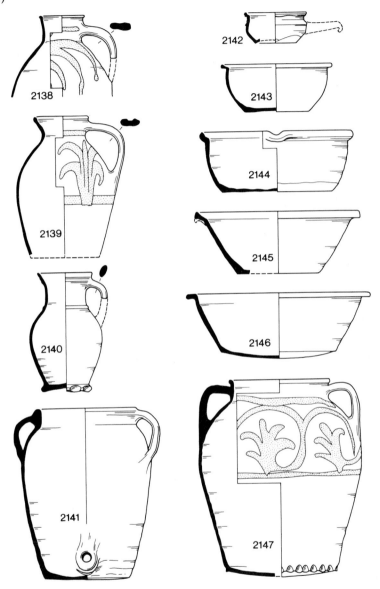

undecorated; slip painted decoration rare, usually on unglazed vessels, and not after 16th century. Date range – begins late 15th century, becomes dominant in 16th century. Source probably Stock for most of this material.

Metropolitan slipware, in Fabric 40 but distinguished by white or cream slip-trailed decoration under a clear glaze, appears on jars or jugs in the late 16th century, although dishes in this ware do not appear until the second half of the 17th century. Source probably Harlow, although some slipware known to have been produced at Stock.

Black-glazed cups and mugs, in Fabric 40, appear in second half of 16th century, becoming common in 17th century; sources probably Stock and perhaps Harlow.

Tudor Green tableware (Fabric 41) common, mostly in late 15th century contexts; Surrey White ware (Fabric 42) common in late 15th and 16th century.

Other ceramic artifacts include culinary stamps with geometric designs, from 16th–17th century contexts, perhaps for use in making pastries and confections.

h. Waltham Abbey (Huggins 1972; 1973; 1976): Fig. 276

Wares H and J2 continue to c. 1500.

Ware K – pinkish-buff fabric with green mottled glaze; date range c. 1450–1600.

Ware L – rough hard sandy grey ware; forms include jugs, sometimes decorated with white painted bands, and cooking pots. Date range c. 1450–1540.

Ware M – fine red brown-glazed ware; forms – jugs, pipkins, skillets, storage vessels, cooking pots, bowls, cisterns, chafing dishes. Date range c. 1500–1640.

i. Writtle (Rahtz 1969a)

Slip-painted grey and red ware jugs, and sgraffito-decorated jugs similar to Cambridge Sgraffito ware, present in later medieval period. Orange and grey ware cooking pots continue during 14th century. Site sequence ends by early 16th century.

2. London

a. City of London (Pearce et al. 1985): see Fig. 59 No. 2

Late London-type ware – fabrics petrologically similar to though finer than the earlier London-type wares, which appear to continue until the mid 14th century. The forms are wheel-thrown, and include rounded and barrel-shaped jugs with a 'bib' of glaze, similar to if not imitating Cheam forms, cisterns, pipkins, flanged and handled bowls, watering pots. Stratigraphic sequences suggest a break in production of London-type wares between the earlier products and the Late London-type wares, sherds of which are dated to mid 15th century at Trig Lane.

Apart from Late London-type ware, and less common red sandy Late London Slipped Wares, in green-glazed 'bifid' rimmed cooking pots and dripping dishes, London was supplied by potteries outside, notably Cheam and the Hampshire-Surrey borders, from the mid 14th century.

b. London, West End (Haslam 1975)

Large group of Tudor pottery from a cess pit at Arundel House, The Strand. Vessels, probably products of Hampshire-Surrey borders, include white ware chafing dishes, costrels, skillets, bowls, jugs, dishes, pedestalled and handled cups. Red ware forms include chafing dishes, jugs including some with tubular spouts, bowls, chamber pots, condiment dishes, pipkins and plates. Probably mid–to late 16th century, as several forms can be matched at Farnborough, but the range of forms may represent vessels in production in first half of century.

c. *London, Moorfields* (Edwards 1974)

Production site

Documentary references to potter Richard Dyer, citizen of the City of London, who in 1571 was licensed to make earthen furnaces, earthen fire-pots and earthen ovens which were transportable. Dyer acquired his skill and knowledge in Spain where he was a servant to a potter. Dyer was granted his licence because his fire pots and furnaces were recognized as innovatory and saving in fuel.

d. *London, Lambeth* (Edwards 1974)

(i) *Production sites*

Documentary sources refer to .Robert Moody, a potter in Lambeth whose dangerous and defective kiln was ordered to be removed. Other sources mention Peter Wilbert in 1576, an alien potter whose name occurs in a list above another name which may be Jasper Andries, the tin-glazed earthenware potter. There is no evidence that Wilbert or his immediate potter descendants made tin-glazed wares.

Wasters excavated at Salamanca Place.

(ii) *Pottery*

Salamanca Place pottery – coarse red fabrics with brown and green glazes. Forms – 'milk pans', pipkins, jugs, large storage vessels, 'industrial vessels'.

e. *London, Greenwich and Woolwich* (Edwards 1974)

Production sites

Several potters are documented in Greenwich from the 1540s. They are mostly aliens, and include a Peter Coper, or Coter, who was a servant of an English potter, John Capelwood. Despite being a servant, Coper was assessed very highly at £18 in the Lay Subsidy. The foreign potting community was important, and may have depended on the royal palace of Greenwich as an outlet. The earliest pottery site is that of Thomas Fern in 1583.

f. *Other sites* (Green and Curnow 1963)

Major unpublished collection from the former palace of Whitehall at The Treasury, Downing Street, where rubbish pits dated 1531–2 contained over 1,000 vessels, including wide range of English coarse wares as well as many foreign imports.

3. Surrey

a. *Kingston upon Thames* (Hinton and Nelson 1980): Fig. 279

(i) *Production site*

Wasters discovered in High Street, sealed below a brick oven provisionally dated to 16th century; no trace of kilns located in narrow trench.

(ii) *Pottery*

Reddish brown fabrics with only limited sand content, made from high-iron clays (compared with earlier Kingston wares which were almost iron-free). Hard slightly sandy-textured sherds, with glaze inside and outside on pipkins and some bowls but sparsely applied on other forms. Wheel-thrown jugs and pitchers predominate, with pipkins, bowls, dishes, jars, costrels, chafing dishes, watering pots and distilling apparatus. Decoration rare, but includes applied rosettes and one sgraffito pigeon on the base of a bowl. Dated to late 15th and early 16th century by analogy with Cheam products and association with Tudor Green and Raeren stonewares.

Kingston White wares made from non-local clays and possibly, therefore, imported; all local clays are iron-rich. Forms poorly finished; wheel-thrown biconical, rounded, barrel and baluster jugs, cooking pots, dishes, bowls and lobed cups. Dated to 14th century.

b. Cheam (Marshall 1924; 1941; Orton 1982;): Figs. 280–1

(i) *Production sites*

Type 2d kiln with split pedestal excavated in High Street. Internal dimensions 3m x 2.6m, the largest late medieval kiln known in the region. A kiln of similar dimensions was excavated at Parkside, Cheam, in 1923.

(ii) *Pottery*

White ware, part of the Surrey White ware tradition – slightly sandy whitish fabric, probable clay source the Reading Beds. Forms entirely wheel-thrown though poorly finished; 'bibs' of glaze on front of jugs. Main forms – barrel and biconical jugs, cooking pots, lids, pitchers, jars, dishes; minor forms include straight-sided dishes, condiments, cups, saucepans, skillets and chafing dishes. Dated to *c.* 1350, continuing throughout much of 15th century on evidence of London Trig Lane sequence.

Red ware – light red sandy fabric with quartz filler. Wheel-thrown forms include pitchers, pipkins, jars in more than one size, lids, costrels, lamps, jugs, straight-sided dishes, skillets, chafing dishes, small dishes, dripping pans, mugs, watering pots. Dated to late 15th and 16th century.

c. Southwark, Bankside (Dennis and Hinton 1983)

Production site

Waster dump close to Thames foreshore. Hard white fabric with quartz filler, in Surrey White ware tradition, smooth internally but coarser externally. Forms include biconical, barrel-shaped, conical and baluster jugs, dishes, bowls, cooking pots, crucibles, lobed cups and a probable candlestick. Fabrics are indistinguishable by eye from Cheam products.

d. Surrey-Hampshire borders (Brears 1971; Holling 1971; 1974; 1977; 1984; pers. comm.; Hurst D.G. 1970: 183; Moorhouse 1970; 1971c; 1971d; 1979; Rackham B. 1952; Vince 1985a): Figs. 279–80

(i) *Production sites*

Reference in a letter from Sir Julius Caesar in 1594 to the white clays of Farnham Park being the source of clays used for the drinking vessels in the Temple during the 16th century.

Fig. 279 SURREY

Kingston upon Thames: 2148–9, Kingston White ware from London, 2nd half of 14th cent. 2155–9, Kingston Red ware, late 15th–early 16th cent. (After Hinton and Nelson 1985; Vince 1985a)

Surrey-Hampshire borders: 2150–4, Coarse Border ware from London, mid 14th–mid 15th cent. (After Vince 1985a)

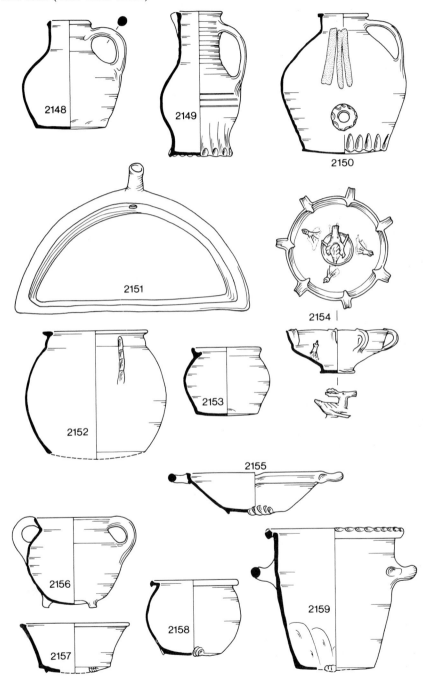

Fig. 280 SURREY
Cheam: 2160–3, kiln products, late 15th cent. (After Orton 1977)
Surrey-Hampshire borders: 2164–76, Tudor Green ware from Guildford, 16th cent.
(After Holling 1977; 1984)
Farnborough Hill: 2177–86, kiln products, late 16th cent. (After Holling 1971).

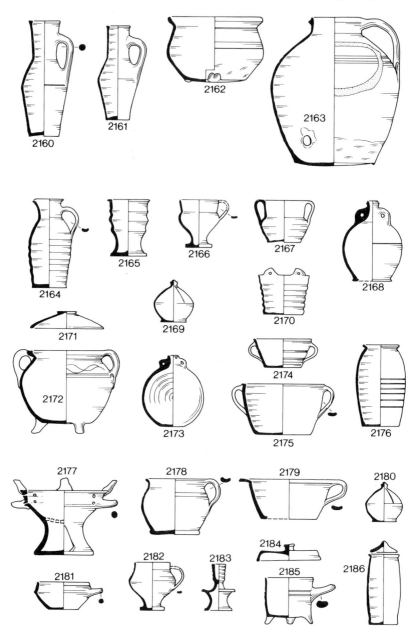

Fig. 281 SURREY
Cheam: Cheam jug; ht. 36cm. (Reproduced by courtesy of the Trustees of the British Museum)

Ash – wasters dated to the 13th-17th centuries known from several locations.

Cove – wasters dated to 16th–17th centuries.

Farnborough Hill – at least four kilns located; large quantities of wasters dated to 15th and late 16th centuries. Kiln 1 – possible Type 2a kiln with brick floor. Kiln 2 poorly constructed with very insubstantial walls, possibly Type 2; pedestal was hollow with pots collapsed in centre; dated archaeomagnetically to 1560–75. Kiln 3 – Type 2a; Kiln 4, 'horse-shoe shaped' with a single flue, may be Type 1. Probable date range for Kilns 1–3 *c.* 1550–80. Kiln 4 thought to be late 15th century.

Hawley and Pirbright – kiln of uncertain type excavated; wasters, and some documentary references to pottery manufacture in 17th century.

(ii) *Pottery*

Exclusively white wares, in Surrey White ware tradition, until the 16th century. Late 15th century production also known as Tudor Green – fine off-white to creamy white fabric with lead-based glaze containing copper; glaze frequently present internally and externally. Forms present at Farnborough are all wheel-thrown, including tall jugs, round-bodied jugs, straight-sided bowls, and cups of various types including lobed cups, two-handled, corrugated and pedestalled forms.

Tudor Green is a long-lived tradition; earliest examples in London, in a group of *c.* 1380 at Trig Lane (though not in groups at the same site dated to *c.* 1360), and in the first quarter of the 15th century at Coventry, the Manor of the More and Winchester. Although lobed cups are known from the Cheam kilns, no other production centre has been identified earlier than Kiln 4 at Farnborough, possibly *c.* 1490–1500.

Early 16th century production sites not found at Farnborough, but deposits at Farnham, Overton (Hampshire) and Basing House, together with an early 16th century group at Guildford, suggest the continuation of a restricted industry. A few late medieval forms were retained, including jugs, bowls, costrels and money boxes, whilst new types of cup and skillet appeared, with other forms such as plates and dishes. By about 1550 a fully re-established industry was producing a wide range, including hollow-handled pipkins, cups with horizontal handles, plates, jars, jugs, chamber pots, chafing dishes, candlesticks and a variety of bowls. Green no longer the predominant glaze colour; a significant proportion of the output was red ware. Further changes also apparent in the 17th century; the forms excavated at Hawley and Ash are markedly different from those at Farnborough.

In addition to the fine wares, coarser sandier quartz-tempered glazed fabrics, known as Coarse Border wares, were made; forms – rounded jugs, cisterns, large flanged-rim bowls, skillets, cooking pots with flat-topped rims and 'bifid' rims, dripping dishes and lobed cups. Coarse Border wares appear in 13th century Trig Lane assemblages, but become a significant element from the mid 14th century to the mid 15th century. Terminal date uncertain but may be *c.* 1500.

e. Nonsuch (Biddle 1961)

Large-scale, mostly unpublished, excavations on Henry VIII's palace at Nonsuch produced very large quantities of pottery, including Hampshire-Surrey borders products, though many are 17th century.

4. Kent

a. Tyler Hill (Bennett and Macpherson-Grant 1980; Macpherson-Grant n.d.; Tatton-Brown and Macpherson-Grant 1983)

(i) *Production site*
Pottery, floor and roof tiles, chimney pots and drain pipes known to have been made in area until at least the beginning of the 16th century; roof tiles made until the 19th century.

(ii) *Pottery*
Jugs generally become plainer from *c.* mid 14th century, and fabrics are harder; flat bases more common but sagging bases continue to end of production. Cisterns probably made from *c.* mid 14th century; full range of forms not yet published. Glazes in 15th century often purple-brown with a metallic lustre, probably influenced by continental stonewares. The Late Medieval fine red earthenwares found at Canterbury from the late 15th to *c.* mid 16th century may well have been made in the Tyler Hill area.

b. *Hareplain* (Kelly 1972)

(i) *Production site*
Type 2 kiln, probably belonging to the first quarter of the 16th century; dated by pottery typology, imported pottery and a series of rather scattered archaeomagnetic measurements.

(ii) *Pottery*
Fabric is hard, fairly fine with small sand inclusions, orange-red, sometimes with a grey core, surfaces varying from pinkish buff through reddish brown to purple-grey. Mostly unglazed, except for patchy glaze on bowls, dishes, and costrels, and very rarely on the interior of jug bases. Forms – mainly large jugs, bung-hole cisterns, bowls, dishes, lid-seated cooking pots, also small jugs with frilled bases imitating Raeren stoneware, lids; rare forms include costrels and a distilling base.

c. *Canterbury* (Macpherson-Grant n.d.; Wilson C.A. 1983)

Late Tyler Hill wares common. Transition to Late Medieval fine red earthenwares taking place from late 15th century. Main regional imports Surrey and Tudor Green wares.

d. *Ospringe* (Thorn 1979)

Tyler Hill wares dominant in later medieval period; present in 16th century Dissolution deposits, but may well be residual by that time. Fine sandy wares and hard red earthenwares of post-medieval type characterize 16th century; also continental imports.

5. Sussex

a. *Rye* (Barton 1979; Vidler 1933; 1936): Fig. 282

(i) *Production sites*
Kilns excavated (see Chapter 5).

(ii) *Pottery*
Second main pottery production phase overlaps with earlier phase; dated by Barton on typological grounds to *c.* 1350–1500.

Forms – jugs, plainer than previously, bung-hole pitchers/cisterns, globular pitchers/jugs, cups, bowls, skillets, tripod pipkins, cauldrons, curfews. Decoration includes non-representational incised patterns and painted slip decoration. Some vessels are white-slipped with brown-black iron-rich slip painting, others have white slip-painting under a plain glaze. Jugs often have pinched spouts imitating south-west French 'parrot's beak' spouts.

b. *Hastings* (Barton 1979): Fig. 283

(i) *Production sites*
Field at Bohemia, Hastings – seven kilns located in 19th century.

(ii) *Pottery*
Surviving wasters in fine sandy fabric, varying from grey or buff to pink and brick-red; olive glaze. Forms – jugs, cooking pots, shallow bowls, skillets, chimney pots. Decoration includes horizontal grooving, wavy lines or combing, and slashing or

Fig. 282   SUSSEX
Rye: 2187–2203, kiln products, later 14th–15th cent. (After Barton 1979; Vidler 1933; 1936)

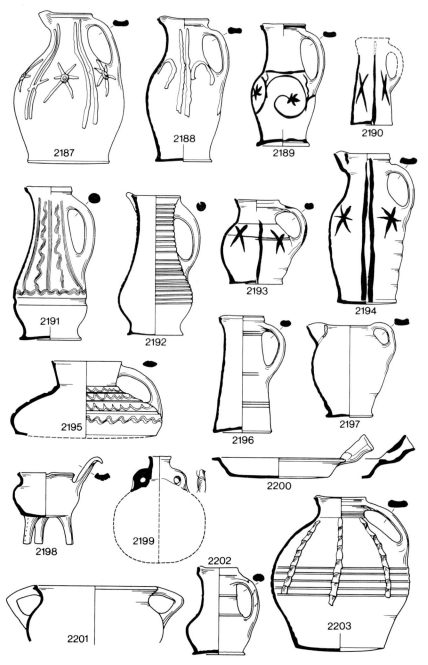

Fig. 283   SUSSEX
Hastings: 2204–6, kiln products, *c.* 14th cent. (After Barton 1979)
Lower Parrock: 2207–18, kiln products, 16th cent. (After Freke 1979)

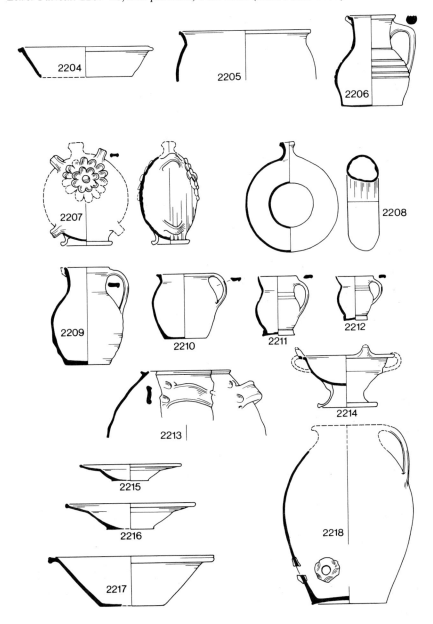

combing of handles. Extant pottery dated on typological grounds to *c.* 14th century. Other pottery reported from site in 19th century sounds like Rye types, but as this material does not survive it is impossible to say whether it was from Rye or local products copying Rye wares.

c. Binsted (Barton 1979)

(i) *Production site*
The later of the two pottery kilns is an unusual variant of a Type 4a kiln with two subsidiary side flues, dated by Barton on pottery grounds to the later 14th and possibly early 15th century. Possibly other kilns in the area.
(ii) *Pottery*
Later Binsted forms include West Sussex ware jugs, skillets, cisterns, double-handled cooking pots and small partially-glazed lid-seated cooking pots; decoration includes white slip-painting.

d. Boreham Street (Barton 1979; Barton and Holden 1977)

Production site
Type 2 kiln excavated, producing slip-painted pottery (Black and White Painted ware) in late 15th–early 16th century.

e. Ringmer (Barton 1979)

Production site
Two kilns discovered in late 19th century, both Type 4a, of brick construction. From brick size, Kiln A is probably 15th-16th century in date; Kiln B is probably slightly earlier.

f. Graffham/East Lavington area (Aldsworth and Down 1976; Down 1978: 363)

Production sites
Wasters from sites in this area span the 14th-17th centuries; products include Black and White Painted wares.

g. Lower Parrock (Freke 1979): Fig. 283

(i) *Production site*
A Type 1a kiln with two phases excavated outside village, in area of iron-working industry. Kiln possibly had a permanent superstructure. First kiln phase archaeomagnetically dated to *c.* 1520–45. Historical and pottery evidence strongly suggests that this kiln may be the work of an immigrant French potter.
(ii) *Pottery*
Hard-fired smooth red fabric, sometimes with grey surfaces, with quartz and siltstone inclusions; some examples have more quartz and a harsher surface texture. Forms – jugs, cooking pots, storage jars, cisterns, pipkins, platters, bowls/pancheons, chafing dishes, costrels, bottles, watering pots, cups, candlesticks. Decoration restricted to occasional incised straight or wavy lines, and moulded decoration on costrels.

h. Chichester (Barton 1974; 1979; Down 1978): Fig. 284

Fig. 284   SUSSEX
Winchelsea: 2219–22, Winchelsea Black ware, *c.* 14th cent. (After Barton 1979)
Chichester: 2223, Late West Sussex ware, *c.* 14th–15th cent. 2224–31, Black and
White Painted ware, 15th–16th cent. (After Barton 1979; Barton in Down 1974;
Down 1978)

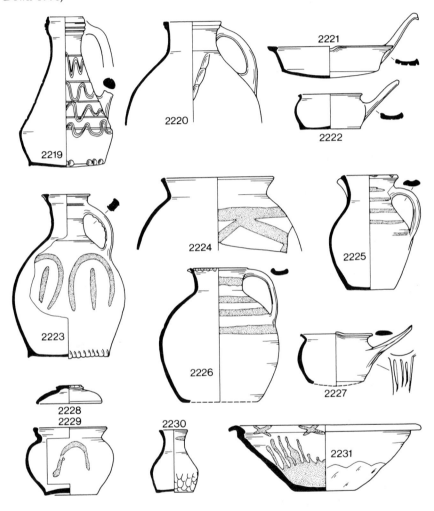

West Sussex ware jugs common *c.* 14th-15th century. Late West Sussex ware often
decorated with painted white slip under green glaze.

Black and White Painted ware very common from mid-15th to 16th century – fine
grey slightly sandy fabric, usually oxidized buff with a final reduction so that the exterior
surface is black, enhancing the painted white slip decoration. Forms – cooking pots,
cisterns, jugs, bowls, lids, dishes, jars, pipkins, watering pots, condiments, dripping

dishes, costrels. Some open forms glazed on interior of base, exterior usually only partially glazed. Source – much probably from Graffham area.

i. Bramber Castle (Barton and Holden 1977)

14th century levels contain much red/black sand tempered coarse ware and West Sussex ware jugs, just overlapping with the introduction of Black and White Painted wares in the 15th century.

j. Winchelsea (Barton 1979): Fig. 284

Winchelsea Black ware, of unknown source but possibly local, from town. Fabric buff/red, with dark reduced surfaces; forms include jugs, skillets and pipkins. Probably of 14th century date.

6. Hampshire

a. Knighton, Isle of Wight (Dunning 1969a; Fennelly 1969; Mynard and Barton 1969): Fig. 285

(i) *Production site*
Type 2 kiln, reconstructed at least once; filled with wasters.
(ii) *Pottery*
Fine sandy hard fabric; wasters mostly fully reduced but some show variations in colour. Forms wheel-thrown but poorly finished, glazes haphazardly applied and poor in quality. Forms – mainly cisterns and large bowls; also small jugs, handled cooking pots, handled cups, dripping dishes and costrels. Ridge tiles, flat roof tiles and floor tiles were also made. Dated to 15th century.

b. Portchester (Cunliffe 1977; 1985)

Pottery defined in terms of Late Medieval Tradition (1300–1400), Ultimate Medieval Tradition (1400–1470) and Painted Ware Tradition (1470-1570). Small number of groups associated with dated buildings show presence of grey sandy wares with flint inclusions being superseded in late 14th century by hard grey and red quartz-based fabrics; range of forms increases, with costrels, curfews, dishes, dripping pans occurring in association with stonewares and Tudor Green forms.

c. Southampton (Brown 1986 and pers. comm.; Platt and Coleman-Smith 1975): Fig. 286

As at Portchester, earlier flint-gritted fabrics give way to harder grey and brick-red sandy wares, often with organic tempering materials, in late 14th-15th century. Forms all wheel-thrown, include plain pitchers and jugs with a 'bib' of glaze on the front, as well as pipkins, skillets, cisterns, handled jars, costrels, dripping pans, and chafing dishes, from production centres in Hampshire. By 1600 a harder-fired grey ware was increasing in popularity, with wheel-thrown cooking pots, jars, jugs, bowls and dishes.

d. Winchester (Cunliffe 1964): Fig. 285

Late medieval wares not well represented, but important groups published from

Fig. 285   HAMPSHIRE
Knighton: 2232–6, kiln products, 15th century (After Mynard and Barton 1969)
Winchester: 2237–43, Red wares, 16th cent. (After Hurst J.G. 1964b)

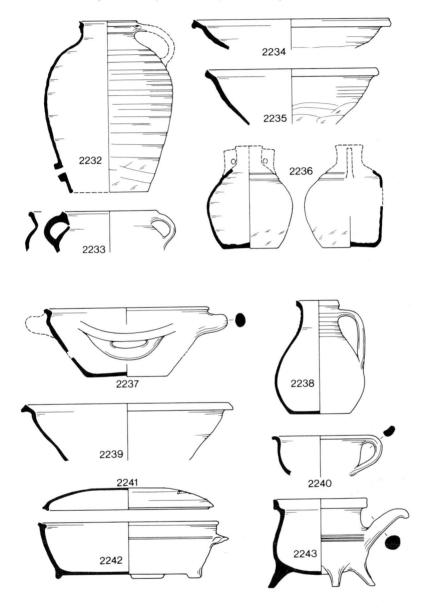

George Hotel and Kingdon's Workshop. Main types very similar to Southampton and
Wickham Glebe.

Fig. 286 HAMPSHIRE
Southampton: 2244–54, possible local fabrics, 16th cent. (After Platt and Coleman-Smith 1975)

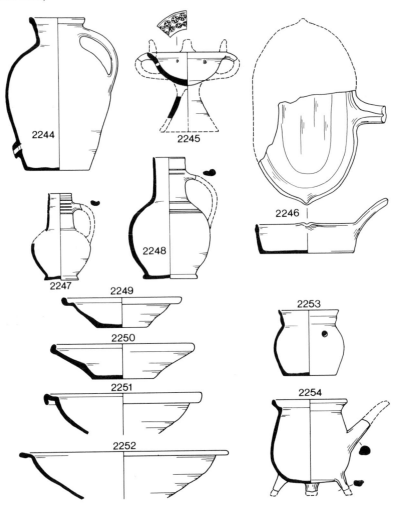

e. *Wickham Glebe* (C. Matthews pers. comm.)

Phase 4, dated to 15th century: coarse sand- and flint-tempered wares; wheel-thrown bowls and larger forms. Reduced and Oxidized Sandy wares; some partially-glazed cooking pots, bowls, chafing dishes, jugs and cisterns, some stylistically comparable to West Sussex types.

Whereas in earlier periods Wickham was supplied by local kiln at Boarhunt, by the 15th century vessels supplied by various external sources, some probably in the Sussex area, and the production centres on the Hampshire-Surrey borders.

f. Basing House (Moorhouse 1970)

Major Tudor country house dated to between 1540/50 and 1642/45, excavated at turn of century. Wide range of pottery published, including fine, white sandy wares, fine red wares and Tudor Green products.

Fine sandy white and buff wares, products of the Surrey kilns on the county boundary; wide range of forms including hollow-handled pipkins, candlesticks, chafing dishes, colanders, chamber pots, straight-sided jars, sweetmeat dishes, flasks, costrels, bowls, lids, cups in various forms, jugs, jars, platters, a tripod skillet.

Fine sandy red-pink ware, probably a local product: forms include jugs, some copying 16th and early 17th century stoneware forms, pipkins, chafing dishes, bowls, jars, cups and some slipwares.

Tudor Green wares in smooth, creamy-textured green-glazed fabrics, distinguished as an offshoot of the Surrey-Hampshire borders industries; forms occurring here include jugs, lids, cups, small bowls and condiment dishes. It is now accepted that the term 'Tudor Green' is misleading and is not distinct from the local white ware industry.

g. Farnborough

Pottery from this area of the Hampshire-Surrey borders is more conveniently discussed under Surrey.

h. Christchurch (Thomson et al. 1983; K. Jarvis pers. comm.): Fig. 287

Wessex Red, Wessex Black and Wessex Coarse sandy wares: hard quartz sand-tempered fabric which is reduced for Black wares and oxidized for Red wares. Wheel-thrown handled jars, cooking pots, bowls and dripping dishes. Dated typologically to late medieval period. Coarse wares possibly made in Verwood-Alderholt area.

South-West England (Fig. 288)

1. Wiltshire

a. Crockerton (Hurst D.G. 1968: 187–8)

(i) *Production site*
Type 1b kiln excavated; wide pedestal, firebars in position. Flue nearly 1m long and very large stoke pit.
(ii) *Pottery*
Red fabric with green-brown glaze; large pans, dripping dishes, jugs, and bowls in several sizes. Dated to late 16th century.

b. Minety (Musty 1973)

Production site
Site located on Oxford Clays in Forest of Braydon; possible clay pits near to point at which wasters excavated. Limestone-tempered fabric; forms mainly pans and jugs, also cisterns, pipkins, lids, shallow dishes, bowls, bottles and possibly ridge and oven tiles. Dated typologically to 14th–15th century.

Fig. 287   HAMPSHIRE

Christchurch: 2255–8, Fine sandy buff ware, 14th–15th cent. 2259, Fine sandy brown ware, 15th cent. 2260, Wessex Red Painted ware, mid 14th cent. 2261, fuming pot or pomander, sandy glazed ware, 15th cent. 2262, coarse sandy ware, 14th cent. 2263, Wessex Black ware, 15th–16th cent. 2264, Wessex Red ware, mid–late 15th cent. (After Thomson *et al.* 1983)

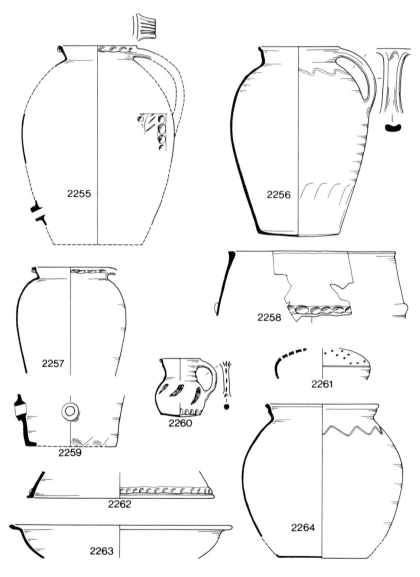

Fig. 288 South-West England, location map
1 Minety, 2 Crockerton, 3 Alderholt/Verwood, 4 Poole, 5 Holnest, 6 Bristol, 7 Chew
Valley, 8 Nether Stowey, 9 Taunton, 10 Wrangway, 11 Donyatt, 12 Exeter, 13
Plymouth, 14 Okehampton, 15 Barnstaple, 16 Bideford, 17 St Stephens, 18 St
Germans, 19 Lostwithiel, 20 Constantine, 21 Mawgan.

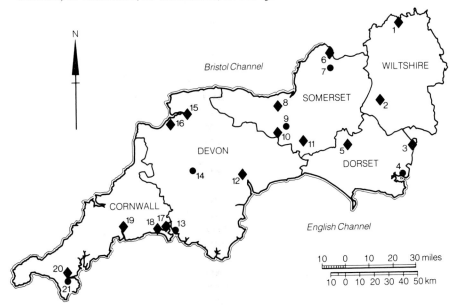

2. Dorset

a. Alderholt/Verwood area (Algar *et al.* 1979; Brown 1986; Young 1979)

Production sites

Alderholt – New Forest location near to Verwood, documentary references only.
Payments for clay digging in 1337. By 1500 clay obtained from Crendell Common 3km
distant, a source which lasted until 1742 when the clay was said to be worked out. Many
kilns known in Verwood area, especially between 17th and 20th century. At Southampton dumps in the motte ditch included Verwood types in contexts attributed to the
15th-16th century.

b. Holnest (Brears 1971)

Production site

Potters working in late 16th and early 17th century. A potter's will known from
1617.

c. Poole (K. Jarvis pers. comm.; Thomson *et al.* 1983)

Wessex Red, Wessex Black and Wessex Coarse sandy wares: hard quartz
sand-tempered fabric which is reduced for Black wares and oxidized for Red wares.
Wheel-thrown handled jars, cooking pots, bowls and dripping dishes. Late medieval

date; associations with continental imports give potential for closer dating. Coarse wares possibly made in Verwood-Alderholt area.

3. Somerset

a. *Donyatt* (Coleman-Smith and Pearson forthcoming): Figs. 289–91

(i) *Production sites*

These sites include some producing fabrics referred to as 'South Somerset wares' in Exeter and Plymouth reports (similar 'South Somerset wares' were also produced at Wrangway and Nether Stowey, Somerset). Sites located in forest of Neroche. At Site 3, excavated kiln had two opposed flues slightly below the level of oven floor; kiln superstructure possibly constructed from large clay coils. Post-holes around kiln reconstructed as an encircling open-sided roofed structure to protect kiln and potter from inclement weather (see Fig. 19). The flues have drains leading away, presumably to keep them clear of water. Pots probably stacked on floor and fired to maximum of 1100°C.

(ii) *Pottery*

Hard, smooth-textured quartzitic fabrics. Wheel-thrown globular and baluster jugs, double-spigoted cisterns, costrels, lobed cups, pedestal cups, bowls, chafing dishes, curfews, pancheons, frying pans, lids and cooking pots. Dated to late 15th–early 16th century.

b. *Bristol* (Ponsford 1979 and pers. comm.; Price 1979)

(i) *Production sites*

Documentary references to potters in the 15th century may refer to earthenware potters.

(ii) *Pottery*

Bristol Castle – fabrics of Redcliffe type (123, 126, 149) continue into 15th century; otherwise external sources, principally Minety and Malverns in later medieval period. From *c.* 1550 red wares imported from Donyatt and Nether Stowey in Somerset.

c. *Taunton* (Pearson 1984)

14 fabrics of late medieval date and 6 Tudor types, including Donyatt products. Some vessels possibly from Wrangway or Nether Stowey, but these difficult to distinguish from Donyatt.

Late medieval types mostly hard quartzitic fabrics with oxidized surfaces. Forms mostly wheel-thrown, and include cooking pots, bowls, baluster and globular jugs, cisterns, bottles and lids.

Tudor fabrics are similar but entirely wheel-thrown; greater range of forms, including pancheons, bowls, cooking pots, jugs in more than one size, bottles, cisterns, candlesticks, handled bowls, mugs (some copying Raeren forms), chafing dishes and condiments. Glazed jugs with applied iron-rich strips and pads or lines of white slip painted on below glaze. The baluster forms of jugs, together with some of the decorative techniques, recall 13th- and 14th-century types, yet are dated here to *c.* 1500–1550 by associated Raeren mugs, Spanish lustre wares and a Tudor jetton.

Fig. 289 SOMERSET
Donyatt: kiln products. 2265–6, 2269, late 14th–15th cent., 2267–8, 2270–6, 16th–early 17th cent. (After Coleman-Smith and Pearson forthcoming)

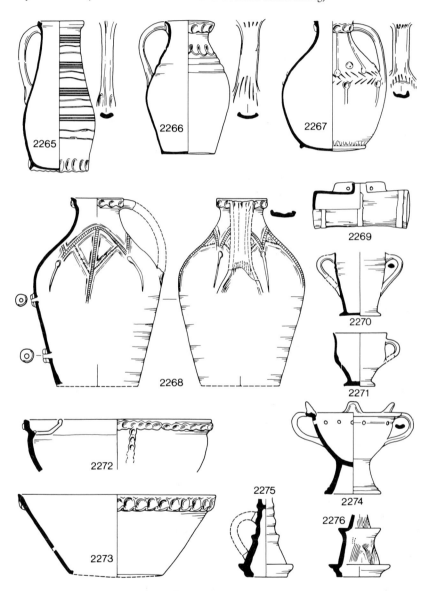

d. *Chew Valley Lake* (Rahtz and Greenfield 1977)

Series of sites south of Bristol produced south Somerset wares, including highly decorated jugs in the medieval tradition but dated to 16th–17th century.

Fig. 290   SOMERSET

South Somerset: 2277–90, South Somerset wares, possibly Donyatt or Wrangway products, from Exeter. 2277–85, early–mid 16th cent.; 2286–90, *c.* 1600. (After Allan 1984)

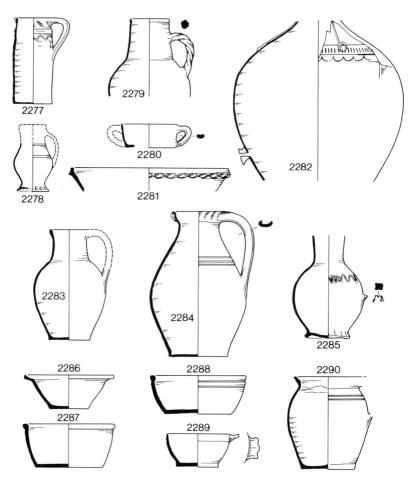

4. Devon

a. *Exeter* (Allan 1984): Figs. 291–2

(i) *Production sites*

Goldsmith Street – site within city walls; pits with wasters. Some aspects of the forms are strongly reminiscent of Dutch types. Lay Subsidy Rolls of 1524–5 list immigrants from Holland, Friesland and Zealand, and whilst no specific references to potters occur, the possibility of immigrant craftsmen cannot be discounted.

Valiant Soldier – small Type 2a kiln similar to that at Donyatt Site 3, excavated on

Fig. 291 SOMERSET
South Somerset: 2298–2305, South Somerset wares from Exeter, early 16th cent.
(After Allan 1984)
       DEVON
Exeter: 2291, Fabric 40, mid 14th–mid 15th cent. 2292–5, Fabric 43, early 15th cent.
(After Allan 1984)
Okehampton: 2296, Fabric 1, late 15th–early 16th cent. 2297, Fabric 7, late 15th–
early 16th cent. (After Allan and Perry 1982)

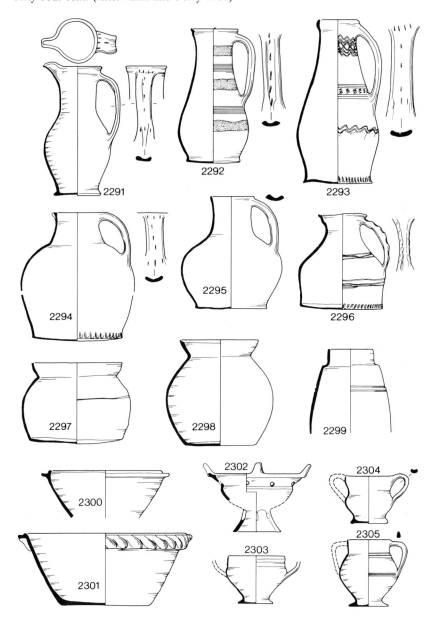

Fig. 292   DEVON
Exeter: 2306–19, Goldsmith Street kiln products, early 16th cent. (After Allan 1984)

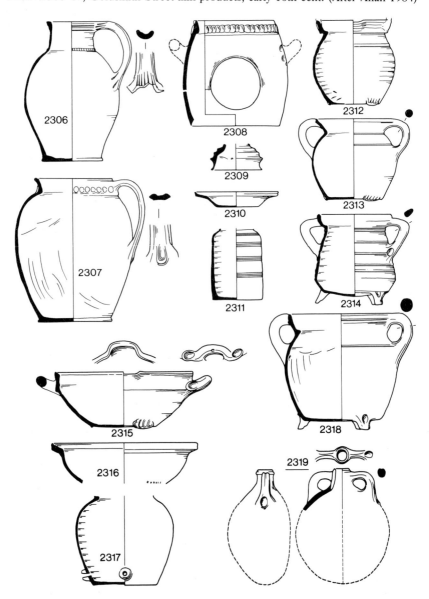

road to south outside city walls. Oven only 1m in diameter; one flue partly revetted by clay-bonded roof tiles, possibly forming part of flue arch.

(ii) *Pottery*

Goldsmith Street – forms include jugs, side-handled bowls, plates, chafing dishes, bowls, pipkins (with and without feet), cisterns, flasks, bottles, dripping pans and cups. Some features, such as handles and flat bases together with cistern and cup forms, closer to south-west traditions than to Dutch. Wasters show marked intermingling of both Dutch and English traits. Dated to early 16th century by analogy with continental wares.

Valiant Soldier – site very unusual in that floor tiles formed nearly 80 percent of products; tile kilns usually rectangular and of much larger capacity. Ridge tiles formed *c.* 11 percent of products; remainder comprising poor quality wheel-thrown cooking pots, jugs, lids and bowls; some glazed, some unglazed. Site probably of short duration; dated to early 16th century on basis of stratigraphy and associated finds.

Other sites – Horizon J: Fabrics 40 and 43 continue as dominant types with jugs as main form. Cooking pots, lobed cups and shallow bowls minor elements. Dated to 1350–1450.

Horizon K: Fabric 40 replaced by South Somerset wares. Cooking pots present but rare; also two-handled cups, chafing dishes, cisterns, costrels, jugs. Dated to *c.* 1450–1500.

Post-medieval: local coarse sandy wares and South Somerset wares dominate assemblages until 1650. Donyatt likely to be important contributor but possibly other sources. Local coarse wares are quartz-tempered with some iron-ore and occasional chert; pancheons, white-slipped jugs, shallow dishes, pipkins similar to Low Countries forms, bottles, chamber pots and storage jars.

b. Bideford and Barnstaple (Grant 1983)

(i) *Production sites*
At Bideford earliest known potter is Thomas Chope, died 1607, though production probably began much earlier. 17th century potteries located in The Strand and Rope Walk, very close to river Torridge. In Barnstaple no kilns known before 17th century, though production probably began in 16th century. Early potters known to be located close to river Taw on Litchdon Street, but they moved in early 17th century to the river Yeo frontage where one potter, Peter Takell, may also have made clay tobacco pipes.

(ii) *Pottery*
North Devon wares – three main fabrics: gravel-free with crushed shell; gravel-free without shell; gravel-tempered wares, sometimes micaceous but with abundant quartz. Wide range of forms, all wheel-thrown, including dishes, jugs, bowls, tripod skillets, porringers, chafing dishes, chamber pots, tankards, saucers, tall jars, crocks, cups, baking pans, cisterns, handled cooking pots. Closely dated at Exeter, Polsloe Priory and Okehampton Castle; North Devon wares in production by 1500–40.

c. Okehampton Castle (Allan and Perry 1982): Fig. 291

Fabric 1, hand-made cooking pots, continues as main North Devon-East Cornish type into 15th century. North Devon gravel-tempered wares appear before 1540, forming up to 89 percent of pottery in late 16th century. At this time there seems to be a heavy emphasis on jars, the forms of which continue into the 17th–18th century. Bowls and pans, previously rare to non-existent, achieve steadily greater significance during 16th-17th century.

Fabric 7, coarse fabric with sandstone grits, typologically similar to but petrologically distinct from Fabric 1; hand-made cooking pots. Late medieval.

d. Plymouth (Allan forthcoming)

Best sequences from Woolster Street. Pottery dominated by late medieval micaceous coarse wares with metamorphic inclusions; reduced and oxidized forms known, including some glazed wares. Limited range of forms including cisterns, rectangular and circular pans, a cucurbit. In 16th century North Devon types completely displace local products at Plymouth. South Somerset types, abundant in 16th century Exeter, do not become established in Plymouth until 17th century.

5. Cornwall

a. St Germans (Douch 1969): Fig. 293

(i) Production site

Documentary references: a Richard Crocker selling crests in 1462–3; potter William Prynne died in 1595; and Thomas Rowe, a 'clomer' or potter, was paying rent in 1596. Continuing series of references to potters throughout the 17th and early 18th century, many names similar to those at Lostwithiel. Type 2a kilns excavated at St Germans, a creek on Tamar estuary.

(ii) Pottery

Hard quartz sand-tempered fabrics with varying micaceous surface appearance, reduced and oxidized wares. Forms include wheel-thrown vessels, and hand-made ones with some coils showing in fractures but signs of wheel-finishing on rims; cooking pots, bowls, frying pans, lids, pipkins and cisterns, some with two bung-holes.

b. Lostwithiel (Miles T.J. 1976; 1979)

(i) Production site

References to the purchase of crests in 1454, and a long string of references in 17th–18th centuries. Wasters discovered in parish of Lanlivery in streets close to river Fowey waterfront.

(ii) Pottery

Fabrics and forms virtually the same as at St Germans but more micaceous.

c. Constantine (Douch 1969)

Production site

Potters at Gweek referred to in 1544 Lay Subsidy Roll and subsequently in parish registers.

d. St Stephens in Brannel (Douch 1969a)

Production site

Possible connections between the Grubbe family, some of whom were potters at St Stephens, with Mawgan in Meneage, Lostwithiel and St Germans.

Fig. 293 CORNWALL
St Germans: 2320–23, St Germans-type ware from Plymouth, 15th cent. or later.
2324, St Germans ware. (After Pearson 1979; unpublished vessel in Truro
Museum.)

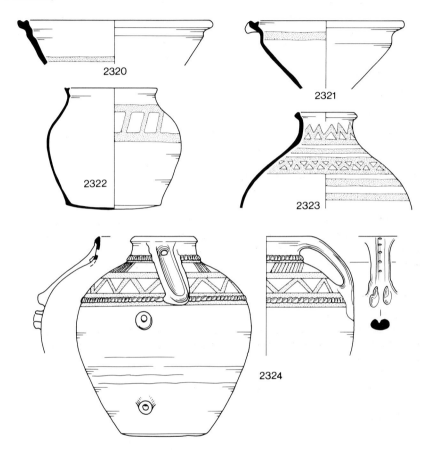

West Midlands (Fig. 294)

1. Herefordshire

a. *Deerfold Forest* (Thomas 1982)

Production sites

Many kilns attested from written and archaeological sources from early 17th
century in Deerfold Forest; amongst products are blackwares such as multi-handled
cups or tygs, tankards, bottles, jars and tripod skillets.

Fig. 294   West Midlands, location map
1 Norton Priory, 2 Chester, 3 Burslem, 4 Stoke on Trent, 5 Nuneaton, 6 Coventry,
7 Warwick, 8 Hanley Castle, 9 Malvern Hills, 10 Worcester, 11 Deerfold Forest, 12
Hereford, 13 Stroat.

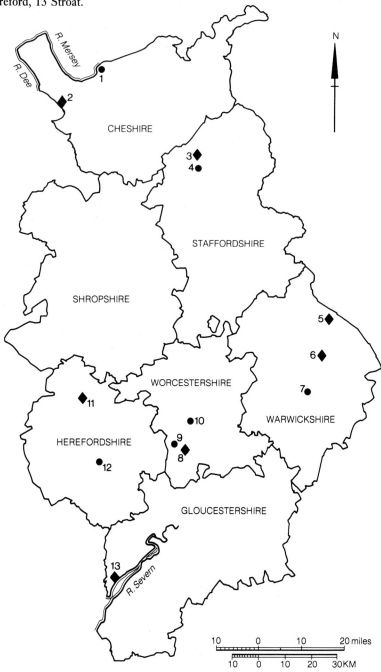

b. Hereford (Vince 1977; 1985b; forthcoming): Fig. 296

Group A wares (A7b) – quartz-tempered with some white mica. Wheel-thrown forms; jugs form up to 95%, including globular and baluster shapes and smaller vessels of drinking jug type. Decoration – applied strips, some white-slipped lines, occasional rouletting and anthropomorphic motifs. Minor forms include cooking pots, dishes and an aquamanile; one example of a hand-made baking tray with low walls and internal glaze. Several possible sources, including Weobley and Hereford. Dates stratigraphically-based, from 13th century, peaking in the later 14th and declining in the 15th century.

Fabric A7c – fine fabric with occasional quartz and white mica; wheel-thrown cups with three handles and flaring rims, and possible salts. Dated to mid-16th century.

Fabric A7d – fine fabric with occasional quartz inclusions; wheel-thrown internally-glazed jars, bowls and cylindrical tygs/cups with wheel-turned grooves. At least eight production centres known in Gloucestershire, Gwent, Powys and Herefordshire, but petrological analysis little help in distinguishing wares. Mainly 17th century, but sherds occasionally occur in levels dated to 16th century.

Group B wares (Malvernian – B4) – chief inclusion is quartz but igneous rocks and sandstone fragments also occur; oxidized but colours variable, becoming red or red-yellow with a brown slip in 17th century. Hollow wares – wheel-thrown, including various jug forms, tripod pipkins and skillets, large jars, cisterns, cooking pots, bowls, pancheons, chafing dishes, lobed cups, multi-handled cups and three-handled conical cups/tygs. Flat wares – hand-made, possibly slab-constructed, oval baking trays with low walls and the ends pulled into spouts; internal glaze and external surfaces sooted. Major pit group at Berrington Street contained 70 percent jars, 19 percent bowls with very small quantities of other forms.

Dated on stratigraphic grounds; begins in late 14th century, peaking in the 16th century, when the Malvernian B4 type constitutes the major source of earthenwares for about 80km around Malvern Chase. In 17th century B4 declines and products of Malvern Chase potteries gradually replaced in Hereford by Herefordshire wares, notably Fabric A7d.

2. Worcestershire

a. Malvern Chase-Hanley Castle (Vince 1977): Figs. 295–6

Production sites

Documentary references for substantial pottery production at Hanley, also known as Potters Hanley in the 16th century. Many of these refer to licences to take wood and dig clay on the Chase. One landowner, writing at the end of the 16th century, was alarmed at the increase in the number of potters and the consequent destruction of the woods.

b. Worcester (Morris 1980a): Fig. 296

Late 14th–15th century: local production declines quickly but Malvern region continues to supply town with glazed vessels. New forms include tripod pipkins, bowls, two-handled cups and cisterns.

16th to mid 17th century: main new forms are straight-sided tankards and cups of Cistercian ware type, both appearing in the 16th century, probably from Hanley Castle.

Fig. 295   HEREFORDSHIRE/WORCESTERSHIRE
Malvern Chase area: 2325–6, 2331–2, Malvernian B4 fabric from Hereford, late
medieval–16th cent. 2327–30, 2333, 2339–40, 2343, Malvern Chase ware from
Worcester, late 14th–17th cent. 2341, Malvernian ware from Hereford, 16th–17th
cent. 2334–7, 2342, Herefordshire ware from Worcester, late 15th–17th cent. 2338,
Fabric A7c from Hereford, mid 16th cent. (After Morris 1980a; Vince 1985b)

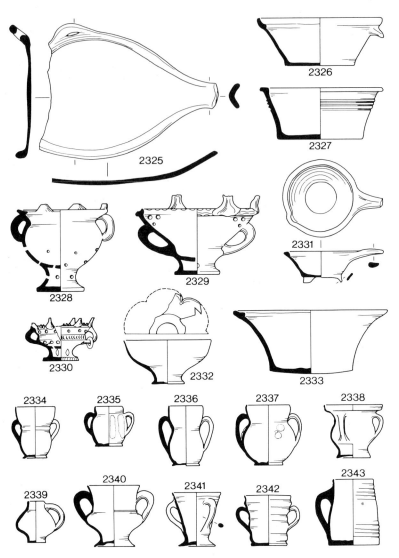

Fig. 296 HEREFORDSHIRE/WORCESTERSHIRE
Malvern Chase area: 2344–5, 2350, Malvern Chase ware from Worcester. 2344–5,
14th–16th cent. 2346–8, 2352, Malvern Chase ware from Hereford and Worcester,
15th–17th cent. 2355–7, Malvernian B4 fabric from Hereford and Worcester, 14th–
15th cent. (After Morris 1980a; Vince 1985b)
Hereford: 2351, 2353, Ware A7b, 14th–15th cent. (After Vince 1985b)
Worcester: 2349, 2354, Midland Yellow ware, 17th cent. (After Morris 1980a)

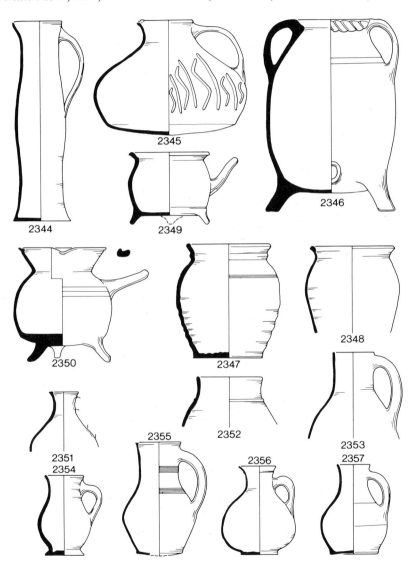

3. Gloucestershire

a. *Stroat* (Vince forthcoming)

Production site

Kilns known to have been operating from at least 1599; products include internally-glazed conical bowls (see Chepstow).

4. Staffordshire

a. *Stoke on Trent* (Brears 1971; Greaves 1976)

Production site

Despite later prominence of Staffordshire industries, evidence for production before the mid-17th century has not been recognized archaeologically. Excavations at Burslem produced range of Midland Purple and Midland Yellow hollow and flat wares, as well as some 'iron glazed wares', all believed to be in production before 1620. Dating evidence is tenuous, and amounts of material recovered, including cups/tygs, shallow dishes and jars, appears to have been very small.

Documentary sources refer to potters Thomas Adams I and II and William Adams from before 1563 to 1629 in Burslem.

5. Cheshire

a. *Chester* (Rutter J.A. 1977b and pers. comm.): Fig. 297

(i) *Production site*

Small number of Cistercian wares from Newgate, Eastgate and Foregate Street include badly flawed vessels, possibly wasters.

(ii) *Pottery*

The possible wasters include drinking vessels, some decorated with floral designs in strips and dots of white clay under a clear glaze on highly-fired red bodies.

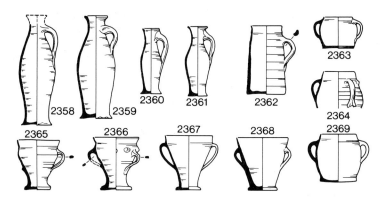

Fig. 297 CHESHIRE
Chester: 2358–61, hard gritty fabrics of unknown source, late 14th cent. (After Rutter J.A. 1977b)
Norton Priory: 2362–9, Fabrics 28–9, mid 16th cent. (After Greene and Noake 1977)

b. Norton Priory (Greene and Noake 1977): Fig. 297

Deposits associated with the Dissolution and the subsequent conversion of the Priory into a Tudor mansion; large quantity of Cistercian ware drinking vessels, comprising two fine hard slightly sandy fabrics with dark glazes (Fabrics 28–9). Cup forms differ from the Yorkshire types; sources uncertain but location in Cheshire possible. Cistercian wares start early in the 16th century; stratified below Dissolution deposits.

6. Warwickshire

a. Warwick (Mytum n.d.)

(i) Production site

Kilns located at Shire Hall; waster dumps present. Clay source likely to be Keuper Marls with Keuper Sandstones as source of filler. Site located in backlands but within the medieval walled area.

(ii) Pottery

Hard smooth sandy wares. Forms include glazed and unglazed cooking pots, jugs, pipkins, dripping pans and decorated roof tiles. Dated typologically to 14th–15th century.

b. Nuneaton (Mayes and Scott 1984; M. Stokes pers. comm.): see Fig. 60 Nos. 5, 6

(i) Production sites

Documentary references to potters between 15th and 17th centuries. There are fifteen 4-flued kilns and nine 5-flued kilns; some are in stratigraphic relationships with 3-flued Type 3 kilns at Sites 1 and 2. Coal may have been used in firing though it seems unlikely that it was the sole fuel used. Some kilns were associated with drains and gullies.

(ii) Pottery

Most fabrics have little or no discernable tempering material and the colour range is pink, red and brown. Fabric F is white-firing; D is also known as Midland Purple and E is Cistercian ware. Forms associated with the 4- and 5-flued kilns are similar and include jugs, cisterns, varying sizes of bowl, cooking pots, curfews, mortars, lids, pipkins, skillets, bottles, lamps, lobed cups and tiles. Cistercian wares and saggars associated with both types of kiln, though saggars may not have been used in the earliest phases of Cistercian ware production. Rare forms include so-called chicken-feeders and a ceramic marble. Thermoluminescence date of 1375 ± 11 for feature 20, but this not associated with any other structure. Pottery otherwise dated largely typologically at production site.

c. Coventry (Redknap 1985)

(i) Production sites

Potter Row mentioned in 1410–11, but this may refer to the sellers of metal wares and does not necessarily indicate production. Tile production attested at Stoke (Potters Green) between the 14th-16th century. Two Coventry potters in the 15th century were members of the important Guild of Holy Trinity.

(ii) *Pottery*

Excavations at Charterhouse (founded 1385) produced undecorated red wares with quartz and some sandstone tempering, and smooth mostly oxidized surfaces. Wheel-thrown forms include medium and large bowls, jugs and chafing dishes.

Wales (Fig. 298)

1. Monmouthshire

a. Trefaldu, Cwmcarvan (Thomas H.O. 1980)

Production site

Wasters and sandstone 'bats' with cup/tyg bases adhering and possible saggars. Homogeneous grey-brown fabrics; forms are tygs, posset pots, flasks, pancheons and storage jars of Cistercian ware type. Date suggested as post-1550.

b. Monmouth (Evans 1980)

(i) *Production site*

Within area enclosed by medieval defences, wasters and kiln furniture found, including hollow kiln props and sandstone 'bats' with runs of glaze.

(ii) *Pottery*

Fine orange to brick-red fabric, some examples vitrified; forms include Cistercian ware cups, jugs, jars and bowls. Dated to later 16th or early 17th century.

c. Dixton (Clarke *et al.* 1984)

Production site

Wasters, burnt clay, sandstone 'bats' with glaze runs and saggars. Cistercian ware cups and tygs, some with applied floral motifs in a white clay, jugs, jars, plates and bowls.

Other kilns of similar date and producing similar forms also attested elsewhere in valley of the Monnow and its tributaries.

d. Abergavenny (Lewis 1980b; Scott-Tucker 1984)

Production site

Cistercian ware wasters of three-handled cups, suggesting production centre in vicinity.

e. Chepstow (Vince forthcoming)

Fabric Hd: hard oxidized fabric with quartz, mica and sandstone inclusions, very similar to 12th-13th century Ha wares. Forms are internally-glazed conical bowls; source – kilns at Stroat, Gloucestershire, known to have been operating from at least 1599.

Fabric He: hard oxidized fabric with few inclusions; forms include wheel-thrown glazed jugs, two-handled cups and other Cistercian ware types. Possible source in general region of Monmouth or Herefordshire, where there are a number of kilns producing Cistercian-type and other blackwares. Dated to early 16th century, as they occur in pre-Dissolution deposits.

Fig. 298 Wales: location map
1 Buckley, 2 Montgomery, 3 Whole House, Talgarth, 4 Abergavenny, 5 Dixton, 6 Monmouth, 7 Trefaldu, 8 Chepstow, 9 Ewenny, 10 Newport.

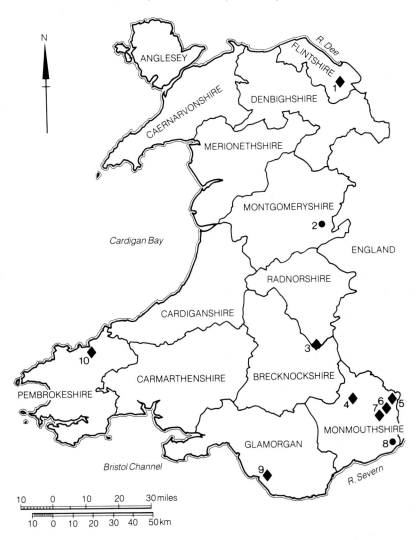

2. Glamorgan

a. *Ewenny* (Lewis 1982; Talbot 1968)

Production site

Major post-medieval pottery at which documentary references to personal names and some place-names suggest an origin at least as early as 1427.

3. Pembrokeshire

a. *Newport* (Talbot 1968)

(i) *Production site*
Type 1b kiln excavated.
(ii) *Pottery*
Hard sandy fabrics, largely oxidized; forms – cooking pots, bowls and jugs; dated to later medieval period.

4. Flintshire

a. *Ewloe, Buckley* (Harrison and Davey 1977)

Production site
Major post-medieval pottery production well known in area. Fieldwork has produced sherds in five main groups, all potentially local and possibly 15th century. Main inclusion is quartz occurring in different quantities; fine white, grey-white and red-pink fabrics and coarse red and grey wares. Forms include cooking pots, bowls, storage jars, skillets, jugs, a costrel and roof furniture.

5. Radnorshire

a. *Whole House, Talgarth* (Lewis 1980a)

(i) *Production site*
Three blackened areas and part of stone-built kiln structure excavated. Sandstone slabs cemented with glaze and with tyg bases adhering.
(ii) *Pottery*
Fine hard red or brown to grey fabrics with no obvious inclusions. Forms include cups/tygs, posset pots, plates, dishes, jars and bowls. Dated to 17th century on presence of slip-trailed decoration, but could begin earlier. In same tradition as Monmouthshire and Herefordshire Cistercian-blackware potteries.

6. Montgomeryshire

a. *Montgomery Castle* (Knight 1982 and pers. comm.)

Ceramic sequence continues to 1649; good groups associated with major rebuilding in 1535–40. Pottery is largely non-local, being imported from Malverns and possibly Staffordshire.

Bibliography

Adams, L., 1977. *Medieval Pottery from Broadgate East, Lincoln, 1973*.

Adams, L., 1978. 'Appliqué face-jug from Motherby Hill, Lincoln', *Lincolnshire Hist. Archaeol.*, *13*: 87–8.

Adams, W.Y. 1979. 'On the argument from ceramics to history: a challenge based on evidence from medieval Nubia', *Current Anthropology*, *20*: 727–44.

Addis, L., 1976. 'The pottery', in D. Austin, 'Fieldwork and excavation at Hart, Co. Durham, 1965–75', *Archaeol. Aeliana*, *4* (5th ser.): 100–24.

Addis, L., 1980. 'Pottery', in P.A.G. Clack, 'Rescue excavations in Co. Durham 1976–1978', *Trans. Architect. Archaeol. Soc. Durham Northumberland*, *5*: 62–7.

Addyman, P.V., 1965. 'Late Saxon settlements in the St Neots area, I', *Proc. Cambridge Antiq. Soc.*, *58*: 38–73.

Addyman, P.V., 1969. 'Late Saxon settlements in the St Neots area, II', *Proc. Cambridge Antiq. Soc.*, *62*: 59–93.

Addyman, P.V., 1973. 'Late Saxon settlements in the St Neots area, III', *Proc. Cambridge Antiq. Soc.*, *64*: 45–99.

Addyman, P.V. and Biddle, M., 1965. 'Medieval Cambridge: recent finds and excavations', *Proc. Cambridge Antiq. Soc.*, *58*: 74–137.

Addyman, P.V. and Marjoram, J., 1972. 'An eighteenth century mansion, a fishpond and post medieval finds from St Neots, Huntingdonshire', *Post-Medieval Archaeol.*, *6*: 69–106.

Addyman, P.V., Hopkins, B.G. and Norton G.T., 1972. 'A Saxo-Norman pottery-kiln producing stamped wares at Michelmersh, Hants', *Medieval Archaeol.*, *16*: 127–30.

Ainsworth, C., 1967. 'A tile and pottery kiln at Binsted, Sussex', *Medieval Archaeol.*, *11*: 316–17.

Aldsworth, F.G. and Down, A., 1976. 'Medieval potteries at East Lavington', *Sussex Archaeol. Collect.*, *114*: 333.

Algar, D.J., Light, A. and Treharne, P., 1979. *The Verwood and District Potteries*.

Allan, J.P., 1978. 'The pottery', in D. Austin, 'Excavations in Okehampton Park, Devon 1976–8', *Proc. Devon Archaeol. Soc.*, *36*: 191–239.

Allan, J.P., 1984. *Medieval and Post Medieval Finds From Exeter 1971–1980*.

Allan, J.P., forthcoming. 'The pottery', in C. Gaskell Brown (ed.), *Plymouth Excavations, The Medieval Waterfront. Finds from Woolster Street, 1963–69*.

Allan, J.P. and Perry, I., 1982. 'Pottery and tiles', in R.A. Higham, J.P. Allan and S.R. Blaylock, 'Excavations at Okehampton Castle, Devon. Part 2 – the bailey', *Proc. Devon Archaeol. Soc.*, *40*: 19–151.

Amis, P., 1968. 'Some domestic vessels of southern Britain: a social and technical analysis', *J. Ceramic Hist.*, *2*.

Annable, F.K., 1958–60. 'A possible medieval pottery site at Lyneham', *Wiltshire Archaeol. Natur. Hist. Mag.*, *57*: 403–4.

Armstrong, P., 1977. 'Excavations in Sewer Lane, Hull, 1974', *E. Riding Archaeol.*, *3*.

Armstrong, P., 1980. 'Excavations in Scale Lane/Lowgate 1974', *E. Riding Archaeol.*, *6*, 1–93.

Arnold, D., 1985. *Ceramic Theory and Cultural Process.*

Ashworth, H., 1983. 'Evidence for a medieval pottery industry at Potter Row, Great Missenden, Buckinghamshire', *Rec. Buckinghamshire.*, *25*: 153–9.

Atkin, M., Ayres, B. and Jennings, S., 1983. 'Thetford-type ware production in Norwich', *E. Anglian Archaeol.*, *17*: 61–104.

Attenborough, F.L., 1922. *The Laws of the Earliest English Kings.*

Austin, T. (ed.), 1888. *Two Fifteenth Century Cookery Books.*

Baker, D. and E., Hassall, J. and Simco, A., 1979. 'Excavations in Bedford 1967–1977', *Bedfordshire Archaeol. J.*, *13*: 1–309.

Baker, O., 1921. *Black Jacks and Leather Bottells.*

Balfet, H., 1966. 'Ethnographical observations in North Africa and archaeological interpretation', in F.R. Matson (ed.), *Ceramics and Man*: 161–77.

Balfet, H., 1984. 'Methods of formation and the shape of pottery', in S. van der Leeuw and A. Pritchard (eds.), *The Many Dimensions of Pottery*: 171–97.

Balkwill, C.J., 1980. 'Archaeology in Suffolk, 1977', *Proc. Suffolk Inst. Archaeol. Hist.*, *34*: 147–50.

Barker, P.A., 1970. *The Medieval Pottery of Shropshire from the Conquest to 1400.*

Barker, P. and Higham, R., 1982. *Hen Domen, Montgomery, A Timber Castle on the English Welsh Border*: vol. 1.

Barley, M.W., 1964. 'The medieval borough of Torksey, 1960–62', *Antiq. J.*, *44*: 165–87.

Barley, M.W., 1981. 'The medieval borough of Torksey, excavations 1963–8', *Antiq. J.*, *61*: 264–91.

Barrett, K., 1985. 'Medieval pottery, 1977', in D.H. Evans and D.H. Heslop, 'Two medieval sites in Yarm', *Yorkshire Archaeol. J.*, *57*: 61–8.

Bartlett, K.S., 1971. 'Excavations at Potovens, near Wakefield, 1968', *Post-Medieval Archaeol.*, *5:* 1–34.

Barton, K.J., 1960. 'Excavations at Back Hall, Bristol, 1958', *Trans. Bristol Gloucestershire Archaeol. Soc.*, *79*: 251–86.

Barton, K.J., 1963. 'The medieval pottery kiln at Ham Green, Bristol', *Trans. Bristol Gloucestershire Archaeol. Soc.*, *82:* 95–126.

Barton, K.J., 1967a. 'A note on the distribution of Ham Green pottery', *Trans. Bristol Gloucestershire Archaeol. Soc.*, *86:* 201–2.

Barton, K.J., 1967b. 'Three groups of medieval jugs and their wider significance', *Proc. Hampshire Fld. Club Archaeol. Soc.*, *24:* 62–72.

Barton, K.J., 1968. 'Medieval pottery from the city of Worcester', *Trans. Worcestershire Archaeol. Soc.*, *1* (3rd ser.): 29–54.

Barton, K.J., 1974. 'The post Roman wares, late Saxon to 16th century', in Down 1974: 85–91.

Barton, K.J., 1979. *Medieval Sussex Pottery.*

Barton, K.J. and Brears, P.C.D., 1976. 'A medieval pottery kiln at Bentley, Hampshire', *Proc. Hampshire Fld. Club Archaeol. Soc.*, *32*: 71–5.

Barton, K.J. and Holden, E.W., 1967. 'Excavations at Michelham Priory', *Sussex Archaeol. Collect.*, *105:* 1–12.

Barton, K.J. and Holden, E.W., 1977. 'Excavations at Bramber Castle, Sussex, 1966–7', *Archaeol. J., 134:* 11–79.

Batey, C., Morris, C.D. and Rackham, D.J., 1984. 'Freswick Castle, Caithness: report on rescue excavations carried out in 1979', *Glasgow Archaeol.* J., *11:* 83–118.

Bavoux, A., 1983. *Potiers et Poteries.*

Bellamy, B., 1983. 'Medieval pottery kilns at Stanion', *Northamptonshire Archaeol., 18:* 153–61.

Bellamy, C.V. and Le Patourel, H.E.J., 1970. 'Four medieval pottery kilns on Woodhouse Farm, Winksley, near Ripon, West Riding of Yorkshire', *Medieval Archaeol., 14:* 104–25.

Bemrose, G.J.V., 1956–7. 'A medieval pottery kiln at Sneyd Green', *Trans. N. Staffordshire Fld. Club, 91:* 86.

Bennett, P. and Macpherson-Grant, N., 1980. 'Tyler Hill 1979 (N.G.R. TR142624)', in P. Bennett et al., 'Four minor sites excavated by the Canterbury Archaeological Trust, 1978–1979', *Archaeol. Cantiana., 96:* 293–7.

Benson, D.G., James, H.J. and Jones S., 1978. 'A medieval pottery group from Gwbert, Dyfed', *Medieval and Later Pottery in Wales, 1:* 26–39.

Beresford, G., 1971. 'Tresmorn, St Gennys', *Cornish Archaeol., 10:* 55–73.

Beresford, G., 1974. 'The medieval manor of Penhallom, Jacobstow, Cornwall', *Medieval Archaeol., 18:* 90–145.

Beresford, G., 1975. *The Medieval Clay-Land Village: Excavations at Goltho and Barton Blount.*

Beresford, G., 1977. 'Excavation of a moated site at Wintringham in Huntingdonshire', *Archaeol. J., 134:* 194–286.

Beresford, G., 1979. 'Three deserted medieval settlements on Dartmoor: a report on the late E. Marie Minter's excavations', *Medieval Archaeol., 23:* 98–158.

Beresford, M.W. and Hurst, J.G., 1974. *Deserted Medieval Villages.*

Biddle, M., 1961. 'Nonsuch Palace 1959–60: an interim report', *Surrey Archaeol. Collect. 58:* 1–20.

Biddle, M., 1961–2. 'The deserted medieval village of Seacourt, Berkshire', *Oxoniensia, 26–7:* 70–201.

Biddle, M., 1964. 'The excavation of a motte and bailey castle at Therfield, Hertfordshire', *J. Brit. Archaeol. Ass., 27* (3rd ser.): 53–92.

Biddle, M., 1976a. 'Towns', in D.M. Wilson (ed.), *The Archaeology of Anglo-Saxon England:* 99–150.

Biddle, M., 1976b. *Winchester in the Early Middle ages, an Edition and Discussion of the Winton Domesday.*

Biddle, M. and Barclay, K., 1974. 'Winchester ware', in Evison *et al.* 1974: 137–65.

Biddle, M., Barfield, L. and Millard, A., 1959. 'The excavation of the Manor of the More, Rickmansworth, Hertfordshire', *Archaeol. J., 116:* 136–99.

Blake, H., 1978. 'Medieval pottery: technical innovation or economic change?', in H. Blake, T.W. Potter and D.B. Whitehouse (eds.), *Papers in Italian Archaeology I,* Brit. Archaeol. Rep. (Int. Ser.) 41 (ii): 435–72.

Blake, H., 1980. 'Technology, supply or demand?', *Medieval Ceram., 4:* 3–12.

Blake, H. and Davey P. 1983. *Guidelines for the Processing and Publication of Medieval Pottery from Excavations.* Dept of Environment Occ. Paper no. 5.

Blanchard, I.S.W., 1981. 'Lead mining and smelting in medieval England and Wales', in D.W. Crossley (ed.), *Medieval Industry*: 72–84.

Boserup, E., 1981. *Population and Technology*.

Bown, L., 1985. 'The pottery', in D.M. O'Sullivan, 'An excavation in Holy Island village, 1977', *Archaeol. Aeliana, 13* (5th ser.): 47–80.

Bown, L., forthcoming. 'Edlingham Castle: pottery report'.

Brears, P.C.D., 1967. 'Excavations at Potovens, near Wakefield', *Post-Medieval Archaeol., 1*: 3–43.

Brears, P.C.D., 1968. *A Catalogue of English Country Pottery Housed in the Yorkshire Museum, York*.

Brears, P.C.D., 1971. *The English Country Pottery*.

Brears, P.C.D., 1983. 'The post-medieval pottery', in P. Mayes and L.A.S. Butler, *Sandal Castle Excavations 1964–1973*: 215–24.

Brewster, T.C.M., 1952. *Two Medieval Habitation Sites in the Vale of Pickering*, Studies in Yorkshire Archaeology, No. 1.

Brewster, T.C.M., 1958. 'Staxton ware – an interim report', *Yorkshire Archaeol. J., 39*: 445–6.

Bridbury, A.R., 1977. 'The Black Death', *Econ. Hist. Rev., 30* (2nd ser.) 393–410.

Brooke, S., 1948–51. 'A late medieval pottery site near Yearsley', *Yorkshire Archaeol. J., 37*: 435–8.

Brooks, C.M., 1978–80. 'Medieval pottery from the kiln site at Colstoun, E. Lothian', *Proc. Soc. Antiq. Scot., 110*: 364–403.

Brooks, C.M., 1987. *Medieval and Later Pottery from Aldwark and Other Sites*, Archaeology of York 16/3.

Brooks, C.M., forthcoming. 'The pottery', in H.E.J. Le Patourel and M.R. McCarthy, 'Excavations at Hinton Hall, Haddenham, Cambridgeshire, 1969', *Proc. Cambridge Antiq. Soc.*

Brooks, C.M. and Haggarty, G., 1976–7. 'Notes on Scottish medieval kiln furniture from Rattray, Aberdeenshire', *Proc. Soc. Antiq. Scot., 108*: 379–82.

Brooks, C.M. and Mainman, A.J., 1984. 'Torksey ware viewed from the north', in P.V. Addyman and V. Black (eds.), *Archaeological Papers from York*: 63–70.

Brooks, C.M., Haggarty, G.R. and Thoms, L.M., n.d. 'West High Street, Linlithgow, 1973. The pottery', unpublished report.

Brooks, R.L., 1982. 'Events in the archaeological context and archaeological explanation', *Curr. Anthropol., 23*: 67–75.

Brown, D.H., 1986. 'The pottery', in J. Oxley (ed.), *Excavations at Southampton Castle*: 85–103.

Bruce-Mitford, R.L.S., 1939. 'The archaeology of the site of the Bodleian Extension in Broad Street, Oxford', *Oxoniensia, 4*: 89–146.

Bryant, G.F., 1970. 'Two experimental Romano-British kiln firings at Barton on Humber, Lincolnshire', *J. Scunthorpe Mus. Soc., 3*: 1–16.

Bryant, G.F., 1977. 'Experimental kiln firings at Barton on Humber, South Humberside 1971', *Medieval Archaeol., 21*: 106–23.

Bryant, G.F. and Steane, J.M., 1969. 'Excavations at the deserted medieval settlement at Lyveden', *J. Northampton Mus., 5*.

Bryant, G.F. and Steane, J.M., 1971. 'Excavations at the deserted medieval settlement at Lyveden. A third interim report', *J. Northampton Mus., 9*.

Buckland, P.C, Dolby. M.J., Hayfield, C. and Magilton, J.R., 1979. *The Medieval Pottery Industry at Hallgate, Doncaster*, Archaeology of Doncaster 2/1.

Bushnell, G.H.S. and Hurst, J.G., 1952. 'Some further examples of Sgraffito ware from Cambridge', *Proc. Cambridge Antiq. Soc., 46:* 21–6.

Butler, L.A.S., 1969. 'Faxton', *Curr. Archaeol., 16:* 144–7.

Caldwell, D.H. and Dean V.E., 1981. 'The post medieval pottery industry at Throsk, Stirlingshire', *Scot. Pottery Hist. Rev., 6:* 21–7.

Caldwell, D.H. and Dean, V.E., 1986. 'Post-medieval pots and potters at Throsk in Stirlingshire', *Rev. Scot. Culture, 2:* 105–12.

Cane, C. and J. and Carver, M.O.H., 1983. 'Saxon and medieval Stafford, new results and theories 1983', *W. Midlands Archaeol., 26:* 49–65.

Carrington, P., 1977. 'Chester: Castle Esplanade Hoard Pot', in P.J. Davey (ed.), *Medieval Pottery from Excavations in the North West:* 12–15.

Carter, A., 1971. 'Nottingham town wall: Park Row excavations, 1968', *Trans. Thoroton Soc. Nottinghamshire, 85:* 33–40.

Carver, M.O.H., 1974. 'Excavations in New Elvet, Durham city, 1961–1973', *Archaeol. Aeliana, 2* (5th ser.): 91–148.

Carver, M.O.H., 1979. 'Three Saxo-Norman tenements in Durham city', *Medieval Archaeol., 23:* 1–80.

Carver, M.O.H., 1980. 'A medieval kiln found in Diglis in 1860: and documentary evidence for potting and tiling in medieval Worcester', in M.O.H. Carver (ed.), 'Medieval Worcester: an archaeological framework', *Trans. Worcestershire Archaeol. Soc., 7* (3rd ser.): 255–62.

Carver, M.O.H., 1983. *Two Town Houses in Medieval Shrewsbury.*

Chapman, H., Coppack, G. and Drewett, P., 1975. *Excavations at the Bishop's Palace, Lincoln, 1968–72.*

Chatwin, P.B., 1955. 'Brandon Castle, Warwickshire', *Trans. Birmingham Warwickshire Archaeol. Soc., 73:* 63–83.

Cherry, J., 1985. 'Sex, magic and Dr Gerald Dunning', *Medieval Ceram., 9:* 5–20.

Cherry, J. and P.J., 1984. 'Medieval pottery kiln at Muckleground, Waberthwaite', *Trans. Cumberland Westmorland Antiq. Archaeol. Soc., 84:* 267.

Childe, V.G., 1954. 'Rotary motion', in C. Singer, E.J. Holmyard and A.R. Hall (eds.), *A History of Technology*, vol. I: 186–215.

Clarke, D.L., 1968. *Analytical Archaeology.*

Clarke, D.L., 1970. *Beaker Pottery of Great Britain and Ireland.*

Clarke, H., 1970. 'Excavations on a kiln site at Grimston, Pott Row, Norfolk', *Norfolk Archaeol., 35;* 79–95.

Clarke, H. and Carter, A., 1977. *Excavations in King's Lynn 1963–70.*

Clarke, K.C., 1984. 'Appendix IV: analysis of two samples from site 18 F106', in Mayes and Scott 1984: 194–5.

Clarke, R.R., 1953–7. 'Archaeological discoveries in Norfolk, 1949–54', *Norfolk Archaeol., 31:* 395–416.

Clarke, S. and Jackson R. and P., 1984. 'Pottery from a post medieval kiln at Dixton, Gwent', *Medieval and Later Pottery in Wales, 7:* 9–24.

Coates, B.E., 1965. 'The origin and distribution of markets and fairs in medieval Derbyshire', *Derbyshire Archaeol. J., 85:* 92–111.

Cockayne, O., 1864–6. *Leechdoms, Wortcunning, and Starcraft of Early England.* 3 vols., Rolls Ser.

Cole, G.H. and Timby, J.R., 1982. 'Excavations at Park Row, Farnham, Surrey: a medieval pottery kiln', *Surrey Archaeol. Collect., 73:* 101–14.

Coleman-Smith, R.J. and Pearson, T., forthcoming. *Excavations in the Donyatt Potteries, Somerset.*

Collis, J., *et al.* 1978. *Winchester Excavations 1949–60,* vol. II.

Colvin, H.K., 1963. *The History of the Kings Works, Vol. I: The Middle Ages.*

Cook, A.M., Mynard, D.C. and Rigold, S.E., 1969. 'Excavations at Dover Castle, principally in the Inner Bailey', *J. Brit. Archaeol. Ass., 32* (3rd ser.): 54–104.

Coppack, G., 1968. 'A medieval well and associated pottery from Keighton, Nottinghamshire', *Trans. Thoroton Soc. Nottinghamshire, 72:* 51–8.

Coppack, G., 1971. 'The deserted medieval village of Keighton', *Trans. Thoroton Soc. Nottinghamshire, 85:* 41–58.

Coppack, G., 1972. 'Medieval and post medieval pottery', in R.A. Hall and G. Coppack, 'Excavations at Full Street, Derby, 1972', *Derbyshire Archaeol. J., 92:* 44–76.

Coppack, G., 1973. 'The excavation of a Roman and medieval site at Flaxengate, Lincoln', *Lincolnshire Hist. Archaeol., 8:* 73–114.

Coppack, G., 1976. 'The pottery', in P. Drewett, 'The excavation of the Great Hall at Bolingbroke Castle, Lincolnshire, 1973', *Post-Medieval Archaeol., 10:* 6–24.

Coppack, G., 1978. 'A thirteenth century pottery kiln at Nottingham', *Trans. Thoroton Soc. Nottinghamshire., 82:* 21–5.

Coppack, G., 1980a. 'Medieval and post-medieval pottery', in P.M. Christie and J.G. Coad, 'Excavations at Denny Abbey', *Archaeol. J., 137:* 223–52.

Coppack, G., 1980b. *The Medieval Pottery of Lincoln, Nottingham and Derby,* unpublished PhD thesis, University of Nottingham.

Couchman, C.R., 1979. 'Work of Essex County Council Archaeological Section, 1978', *Essex Archaeol. Hist., 11:* 32–77.

Cox, E., 1984. 'Petrological examination of the ceramic material from pits BY and AQ', in Tabraham 1984: 386–95.

Cracknell, S. and Jones, M., forthcoming. 'Medieval kiln debris from School Road, Alcester', *Trans. Birmingham Warwickshire Archaeol. Soc.*

Craster, O.E., 1967. 'Skenfrith Castle: when was it built?', *Archaeol. Cambrensis, 116:* 133–58.

Crowdy, A., 1986. 'The pottery', in P. Dixon, *Excavations in the Fishing Town of Eyemouth, 1982–4.*

Cruden, S., 1951–2. 'Scottish medieval pottery: the Bothwell Castle collection', *Proc. Soc. Antiq. Scot., 86:* 140–70.

Cruden, S., 1952–3. 'Scottish medieval pottery: the Melrose Abbey collection', *Proc. Soc. Antiq. Scot., 87:* 161–74.

Cruden, S., 1955–6. 'Scottish medieval pottery', *Proc. Soc. Antiq. Scot., 89:* 67–82.

Crummy, P., 1981. *Aspects of Anglo-Saxon and Norman Colchester.*

Cunliffe, B., 1970. 'The Saxon culture-sequence at Portchester castle', *Antiq. J., 50:* 67–85.

Cunliffe, B., 1976. *Excavations at Portchester Castle, Vol. II: Saxon.*

Cunliffe, B., 1977. *Excavations at Portchester Castle, Vol. III: Medieval, the Outer Bailey and its Defences.*

Cunliffe, B., 1985. *Excavations at Portchester Castle, Vol. IV: Medieval, The Inner Bailey.*

Cunningham, C.M., 1982a. 'Medieval and post-medieval pottery', in P.J. Drury, 'Aspects of the origins and development of Colchester Castle', *Archaeol. J., 139:* 358–80.

Cunningham, C.M., 1982b. 'The medieval pottery', in S.R. Bassett, *Saffron Walden: Excavations and Research 1972–80.*

Cunningham, C.M., 1984. 'Summary of the pottery produced in the kilns', in P. Crummy, *Excavations at Lion Walk, Balkerne Lane, and Middleborough, Colchester, Essex:* 186–9.

Cunningham, C.M. and Drury, P.J., 1985. *Post medieval sites and their pottery: Moulsham Street, Chelmsford.*

Cunningham, C.M. and Farmer, P.G. and N.C., 1983. 'A horse and rider aquamanile from Harwich and the significance of Scarborough ware in Essex', *Essex Archaeol. Hist., 15:* 54–67.

Curle, A.O., 1939. 'A Viking settlement at Freswick, Caithness', *Proc. Soc. Antiq. Scot., 73:* 71–110.

Dallas, C., 1980. 'The pottery', in R. Willcox, 'Castle Acre Priory excavations, 1972–76', *Norfolk Archaeol., 37:* 251–64.

Davey, N., 1939–41. 'Pottery kilns at East Runton, Norfolk', *Norfolk Archaeol., 27:* 308–14.

Davey, P.J., 1978. *Prescot Action Area: An Archaeological View,* University of Liverpool.

Davey, P.J. and Hodges, R. (eds.), 1983. *Ceramics and Trade.*

Davies, S.M., 1983. 'Excavations at Christchurch, Dorset 1981–83', *Proc. Dorset Natur. Hist. Archaeol. Soc., 105:* 21–56.

Davis, N. (ed.), 1971. *Paston Letters and Papers of the Fifteenth Century: Part 1.*

Davison, B.K., 1967. 'The late Saxon town of Thetford: an interim report on the 1964–6 excavations', *Medieval Archaeol., 11:* 189–208.

Davison, B.K., 1972. 'Castle Neroche: an abandoned Norman fortress in South Somerset', *Somerset Archaeol. Natur. Hist., 116:* 16–58.

Dawson, D., and Kent, O., 1984. 'Methods of kiln reconstruction', *Bull. Experimental Firing Group, 2:* 13–17.

Dawson, D.P., Jackson, R.G. and Ponsford, M.W., 1972. 'Medieval kiln wasters from St Peters Church, Bristol', *Trans. Bristol Gloucestershire Archaeol. Soc., 91:* 159–67.

Dawson, W.R., 1934. *A Leechbook or Collection of Medical Recipes of the Fifteenth Century.*

deBoer, W.R. and Lathrap, D.W., 1979. 'The making and breaking of Shipibo-Conibo ceramics', in C. Kramer (ed.), *Ethnoarchaeology: Implications of Ethnography for the Archaeologist:* 102–38.

de Boüard, M., 1974. 'Observations on the treatise of Eraclius, *De coloribus et artibus Romanorum*', in Evison *et al.* 1974: 67–76.

Denham, V., 1985. 'The Saxon pottery', in J.H. Williams, M. Shaw and V. Denham, *Middle Saxon Palaces at Northampton:* 46–62.

Dennis, G. and Hinton, P., 1983. 'A medieval kiln group from Bankside, SE 1', *London Archaeol., 4:* 283–7.

Dixon, P., 1981. 'Eshott: medieval kiln and settlement', *Univ. Durham Newcastle Archaeol. Rep., 1981:* 64–6.

Dobson, R.B., and Taylor, J., 1976. *Rymes of Robin Hood.*

Dodds, G. and O'Brien, C., 1984. *Newcastle Quayside Archaeological Project. A medieval pottery kiln: interim report* (unpublished report).

Douch, H.L., 1969. 'Cornish earthenware potters', *J. Roy. Inst. Cornwall, 6 Pt. I* (n. ser.): 33–64.

Down, A., 1974. *Chichester Excavations II.*

Down, A., 1978. *Chichester Excavations III.*

Down, A., 1981. *Chichester Excavations V.*

Down, A. and Rule, M., 1970. *Chichester Excavations I.*

Draper, J., 1976. 'A group of thirteenth century pottery from West Stafford, Dorset', *Proc. Dorset Natural Hist. Archaeol. Soc., 97*: 60–2.

Draper, J. 1981. 'Medieval pottery', in D.W.A. Startin, 'Excavations at South Grove Cottage, Dorchester', *Proc. Dorset Natur. Hist. and Archaeol. Soc., 103*: 62–5.

Draper, J., and Chaplin, C., 1982. *Dorchester Excavations*, vol. I.

Drummond, B.G., forthcoming. 'Pottery from Rievaulx Abbey'.

Drury, P.J., 1981. 'The production of brick and tile in medieval England', in D.W. Crossley (ed.), *Medieval Industry*: 126–42.

Drury, P.J. and Petchey, M.R., 1975. 'Medieval potteries at Mile End and Great Horkesley, near Colchester', *Essex Archaeol. Hist., 7*: 33–60.

Drury, P.J. and Pratt, G.D., 1975. 'A late 13th and early 14th century tile factory at Danbury, Essex', *Medieval Archaeol.,19*: 92–164.

Dudley, D. and Minter, E.M., 1966. 'The excavation of a medieval settlement at Treworld, Lesnewth 1963', *Cornish Archaeol., 5*: 34–58.

Dulley, A.J.F., 1967. 'Excavations at Pevensey, Sussex, 1962–6', *Medieval Archaeol., 11*: 209–32.

Dunbar, J.G. and Hay, G.D., 1960–1. 'Excavations at Lour, Stobo, 1959–60', *Proc. Soc. Antiq. Scot., 94*: 196–210.

Dunning, G.C., 1933. 'Inventory of medieval polychrome ware found in England and Scotland', *Archaeologia, 83*: 126–34.

Dunning, G.C., 1949. 'Report on the medieval pottery', in H.S. Gracie, 'Hut sites on Selsley Common, near Stroud', *Trans. Bristol Gloucestershire Archaeol. Soc., 68*: 30–44.

Dunning, G.C., 1950a. 'Notes on the Trinity College jug', in C.I. Fell and G.H.S. Bushnell, 'Archaeological notes', *Proc. Cambridge Antiq. Soc., 46*: 21–6.

Dunning, G.C., 1950b. 'Pottery from the Abinger motte', in B. Hope-Taylor, 'The excavation of a motte at Abinger in Surrey', *Archaeol. J., 107*: 33–41.

Dunning, G.C., 1956. 'Trade relations between England and the Continent in the late Anglo-Saxon Period', in D.B. Harden (ed.), *Dark Age Britain: Studies Presented to E.T. Leeds*: 218–33.

Dunning, G.C., 1961. 'A medieval pottery inkstand from Byland Abbey', *Medieval Archaeol., 5*: 307.

Dunning, G.C., 1962. 'Saxon and Norman pottery from Colchester castle park', *Antiq. J., 42*: 62–7.

Dunning, G.C., 1964. 'Barrel-shaped and cylindrical costrels on the Continent and in England', in B. Cunliffe, *Winchester Excavations 1949–1960, Vol. I*: 127–40.

Dunning, G.C., 1967. 'Late medieval jugs with lettering', *Medieval Archaeol., 11*: 233–41.

Dunning, G.C., 1968. 'The trade in medieval pottery around the North Sea', in J.G.N. Renaud (ed.), *Rotterdam Papers*: 35–58.

Dunning, G.C., 1969a. 'The typology of the Knighton costrel', in Fenelly 1969: 108–10.

Dunning, G.C., 1969b. 'Medieval church cruets in pottery', *Medieval Archaeol.*, *13*: 147–9.

Dunning, G.C., 1973. 'Appendix', in D.C. Mynard, 'Medieval pottery from Dartford', *Archaeol. Cantiana*, *88*: 195–9.

Dunning, G.C., 1977a. 'The anthropomorphic jug', in Beresford 1977: 253–5.

Dunning, G.C., 1977b. 'Beaumaris', in P.J. Davey (ed.), *Medieval Pottery from Excavations in the North West*: 8–9.

Dunning, G.C., 1977c. 'Curfews', in Cunliffe 1977: 189–92.

Dunning, G.C., Hodges, H.M.W. and Jope, E.M., 1957–8. 'Kirkcudbright Castle, its pottery and ironwork', *Proc. Soc. Antiq. Scot.*, *91*: 117–38.

Dunning, G.C., Hurst, J.G., Myres, J.N.L. and Tischler F., 1959. 'Anglo-Saxon pottery: a symposium', *Medieval Archaeol.*, *3*: 1–78.

Durham, B., 1980. 'Wallingford', C.B.A. Group 9, *Newsletter*, *11*: 140–2.

Dyer, C., 1980. *Lords and Peasants in a Changing Society*.

Dyer, C., 1982. 'The social and economic changes of the later Middle Ages and the pottery of the period', *Medieval Ceram.*, *6*: 33–42.

Earnshaw, J.R. and Watkins, J.G., 1984. *An Excavation at Kirkgate, Bridlington, 1980–81*.

Eddy, M.R. and Priddy, D., 1981. 'Danbury, Eves Corner Kiln', *Essex Archaeol. Hist.* *3*: 42–3.

Edwards, B.J.N., 1977. 'Medieval pottery in Lancashire', in P.J. Davey (ed.), *Medieval Pottery From Excavations in the North West*: 108.

Edwards, R., 1974. 'London potters circa 1570–1710', *J. Ceram. Hist.*, *6*.

Ellis, E., Hellier, R., McRea, C.T., and Thompson, B. and S.D., n.d. *Four medieval pottery kilns at Thirlby, nr. Thirsk, in the North Riding of Yorkshire* (unpublished report).

Ellison, M., 1981. 'The pottery', in B. Harbottle and M. Ellison, 'An excavation in the Castle Ditch, Newcastle upon Tyne, 1974–6', *Archaeol. Aeliana*, *9* (5th ser.): 95–164.

Evans, D.H., 1980. 'Wasters from St. James House, Monmouth, Gwent', *Medieval and Later Pottery in Wales*, *3*: 38–44.

Evans, D.H., 1983. 'Some current problems in defining late medieval pottery in Wales', *Medieval and Later Pottery in Wales*, *6*: 1–22.

Evans, D.H. and Carter, A., 1985. 'Excavations on 31–51 Pottergate (Site 149N)', in M. Atkin, A. Carter and D.H. Evans, 'Excavations in Norwich 1971–1978', *E. Anglian Archaeol.*, *26*: 9–84.

Evans, J. and Elbeih, S.M., 1984. 'Medieval food residues from Exeter', in Allan 1984: 37–9.

Everitt, A., 1967. 'The market towns', in J. Thirsk (ed.), *The Agrarian History of England and Wales*: 467–506.

Evison, V., Hodges, H. and Hurst, J.G. (eds.), 1974. *Medieval Pottery from Excavations: Studies Presented to Gerald Clough Dunning*.

Fairbrother, J., 1984, *Faccombe Netherton: Archaeological and Historical Research*, unpublished MPhil thesis, University of Southampton.

Farley, M.E., 1974. 'Aylesbury – a defended town?', *Rec. Buckinghamshire*, *19*: 429–48.

Farley, M.E., 1976. 'Saxon and medieval Walton, Buckinghamshire: excavations 1973–4', *Rec. Buckinghamshire, 20*: 153–90.

Farley, M.E., 1979. 'Pottery and pottery kilns of the post medieval period at Brill, Buckinghamshire', *Post-Medieval Archaeol., 13*: 127–52.

Farley, M.E., 1982. 'A medieval pottery industry at Boarstall, Buckinghamshire', *Rec. Buckinghamshire, 24*: 107–18.

Farmer, P.G., 1979. *An Introduction to Scarborough Ware and a Re-assessment of Knight Jugs.*

Farmer, P.G. and N.C., 1982. 'The dating of the Scarborough ware pottery industry', *Medieval Ceram., 6*: 66–86.

Fennelly, L.R., 1969. 'A late medieval kiln at Knighton, IOW', *Proc. Hampshire Fld. Club Archaeol. Soc., 26*: 97–110.

Ferguson, R.S. (ed.), 1893. *Testamenta Karleolensis.*

Field, N.H., 1966. 'A thirteenth century kiln at Hermitage, Dorset', *Proc. Dorset Natur. Hist. Archaeol. Soc., 88*: 161–75.

Field, R.K., 1965. 'Worcestershire peasant buildings, household goods and farming equipment in the later Middle Ages', *Medieval Archaeol., 9*: 105–49.

Foster, G.M., 1966. 'The sociology of pottery: questions and hypotheses arising from contemporary Mexican work', in F.R. Matson (ed.), *Ceramics and Man*: 43–61.

Fox, A. and Dunning, G.C., 1957. 'A medieval pottery kiln in Exeter', *Antiq. J., 36*: 43–50.

Francis, M. and Lewis, J.M., 1984. 'Medieval pottery from Kenfig Castle', *Medieval and Later Pottery in Wales, 7*: 1–8.

Freke, D.J., 1975. 'Excavations in Lewes, 1974', *Sussex Archaeol. Collect., 113*: 66–84.

Freke, D.J., 1976. 'Further excavations in Lewes, 1975', *Sussex Archaeol. Collect., 114*: 176–93.

Freke, D.J., 1979. 'The excavation of a 16th-century pottery kiln at Lower Parrock, Hartfield, East Sussex, 1977', *Post-Medieval Archaeol., 13*: 79–125.

Frere, S.S., 1941. 'A medieval pottery at Ashtead', *Surrey Archaeol. Collect., 47*: 58–66.

Frere, S.S., 1954. 'Canterbury excavations, summer, 1946. The Rose Lane sites', *Archaeol. Cantiana, 68*: 101–43.

Gilmour, L.A. *et al.*, forthcoming. *Early Medieval Pottery from Flaxengate*, Archaeology of Lincoln XV11/2.

Goodall, A.R., 1981. 'The medieval bronzesmith and his products', in D.W. Crossley (ed.), *Medieval Industry*: 143–50.

Gooder, E., 1984. 'Clayworking in the Nuneaton area', in Mayes and Scott 1984: 3–18.

Grant, A., 1983. *North Devon Pottery: the Seventeenth Century.*

Greaves, S.J., 1976. 'A post medieval excavation in Woodbank Street, Burslem, Stoke on Trent, Staffs', *City Stoke-on-Trent Mus. Archaeol. Soc. Rep., 10.*

Green, H.J.M. and Curnow, P.E., 1963. 'The Palace of Whitehall and after: Tudor and later discoveries made during the reconstruction of Downing Street and the Treasury'. *Illus. London News*, July 1963: 14–17.

Greene, J.P. and Johnson B., 1978. 'An experimental tile kiln at Norton Priory, Cheshire', *Medieval Ceram., 2*: 31–42.

Greene, J.P. and Noake, B., 1977. 'Norton Priory', in P.J. Davey (ed.), *Medieval Pottery from Excavations in the North West*: 54–9.

Grierson, P., 1959. 'Commerce in the Dark Ages: a critique of the evidence', *Trans. Roy. Hist. Soc.,* 9: 123–40.

Grigg, D., 1980. *Population Growth and Agrarian Change.*

Grove, L.R.A., 1967. 'Maidstone', *Archaeol. Cantiana, 82*: 294–6.

Grove, L.R.A. and Warhurst, A., 1952. 'A thirteenth-century kiln site at Ashford', *Archaeol. Cantiana, 65*: 183–7.

Gryspeerdt, M., 1978. 'The pottery', in J.H. Williams, 'Excavations at Greyfriars, Northampton 1972', *Northamptonshire Archaeol., 13*: 133–47.

Gryspeerdt, M., 1979. 'The pottery', in F. Williams, 'Excavations on Marefair, Northampton 1977', *Northamptonshire Archaeol.,* 14: 57–67.

Gryspeerdt, M., 1981a. ' Early-Middle Saxon pottery in Northampton: a review of the evidence', *Medieval Ceram.,* 5: 27–34.

Gryspeerdt, M., 1981b. 'The pottery', in J.H. Williams and M. Shaw, 'Excavations at Chalk Lane, Northampton, 1975–78', *Northamptonshire Archaeol.,* 16: 108–21.

Haggarty, G.R., 1980. 'The pottery', in G. Ewart, 'Excavations at Stirling Castle 1977–1978', *Post-Medieval Archaeol.,* 14: 36–46.

Haggarty, G.R., 1981. 'Coarsewares', in G.L. Good and C.J. Tabraham, 'Excavations at Threave Castle, Galloway, 1974–78', *Medieval Archaeol.,* 25: 129–31.

Haggarty, G.R., 1984. 'Observations on the ceramic material from phase 1 pits BY and AQ', in Tabraham 1984: 395–7.

Haggarty, G.R., 1985. 'The pottery', in G. Ewart, *Cruggleton Castle. Report of Excavations 1978–1981.*

Haggarty, G.R. and Tabraham, C.J., 1982. 'Excavation of a motte near Roberton, Clydesdale, 1979', *Trans. Dumfriesshire Galloway Natur. Hist. Antiq. Soc.,* 57, 51–64.

Haggarty, G.R. and Thoms, L.M., 1982. 'Report on the pottery', in L.M. Thoms, 'Trial excavation at St Ann's Lane, Perth', *Proc. Soc. Antiq. Scot.,* 112: 440–7.

Haldon, R. and Mellor, M., 1977. 'Late Saxon and medieval pottery', in B. Durham, 'Archaeological excavations in St Aldates, Oxford', *Oxoniensia, 42*: 111–39.

Hall, D., 1982. 'The pottery', in J. Wordsworth and A.R. Gordon, 'Lesmahagow Priory', *Glasgow Archaeol. J.,* 9: microfiche 51/68.

Hall, D.N., 1971. 'A thirteenth century pottery kiln-site at Harrold, Bedfordshire', *Milton Keynes J. Archaeol. Hist.,* 1: 23–32.

Hall, D.N., 1974. 'Paulerspury', *Northamptonshire Archaeol.,* 9: 112.

Hall, R.A., 1984. *The Viking Dig.*

Hamilton, J.R.G., 1956. *Excavations at Jarlshof, Shetland.*

Hampe, R. and Winter, A., 1965. *Bei Töpfern und Zieglern in Süditalien, Sizilien und Griechenland.*

Harrison, B.P. and Williams, D.F., 1979. 'Sherborne Old Castle, Dorset: medieval pottery fabrics', *Proc. Dorset Natur. Hist. Archaeol. Soc.,* 101: 91–102.

Harrison, H.M. and Davey, P.J., 1977. 'Ewloe kiln', in P.J. Davey (ed.), *Medieval Pottery from Excavations in the North West*: 92–9.

Hart, C., 1974. 'Hereward the Wake', *Proc. Cambridge Antiq. Soc.,* 65: 28–40.

Hartley, D. and Elliot, M.N., 1928. *Life and Work of the People of England: the Fourteenth Century.*

Haslam, J., 1975. 'The Saxon pottery and the Tudor pottery groups from the cesspit', in M.J. Hammerson, 'Excavations on the site of Arundel House in the Strand WC2 in 1972', *Trans. London Middlesex Archaeol. Soc.,* 26: 221–42.

Haslam, J., 1978. *Medieval Pottery*.

Hassall, J., 1976. 'Medieval pottery and a possible kiln site at Everton', *Bedfordshire Archaeol. J.*, *11*: 69–75.

Hassall, M. and Rhodes, J., 1974. 'Excavations at the New Market Hall, Gloucester, 1966–7', *Trans. Bristol Gloucestershire Archaeol. Soc.*, *93*: 15–100.

Hayes, R.H., 1978. 'Post-medieval pottery at Grimstone Manor Farm, near Gilling', *Trans. Scarborough Archaeol. Hist. Soc.*, *21*: 1–10.

Hayfield, C., 1980. 'Techniques of pottery manufacture in east Yorkshire and north Lincolnshire', *Medieval Ceram.*, *4*: 29–37.

Hayfield, C., 1984a. 'A late-medieval pottery group from Humberston Abbey, S. Humberside', *Lincolnshire Hist. Archaeol.*, *19*: 107–10.

Hayfield, C., 1984b. 'An early-medieval, splashed-glaze pottery kiln at Market Place, Doncaster', *Yorkshire Archaeol. J.*, *56*: 41–3.

Hayfield, C., 1985. *Humberside Medieval Pottery*, Brit. Archaeol. Rep., 140.

Hayfield, C. and Slater, T., 1984. *The Medieval Town of Hedon. Excavations 1975–76*.

Haynes, J., 1952. 'A thirteenth century kiln site at Potters Marston', *Trans. Leicestershire Archaeol. Hist. Soc.*, *28*: 55–62.

Healey, R.H., 1969. 'Bourne Ware', *Lincolnshire Hist. Archaeol.*, *4*: 108–9.

Healey, R.H., 1974. 'Pottery from Potterhanworth', *Lincolnshire Hist. Archaeol.*, *9*: 30–1, 33.

Healey, R.H., 1975. *Medieval and Sub-Medieval Pottery in Lincolnshire*, unpublished MPhil thesis, University of Nottingham.

Healey, R.H., 1984. 'Toynton All Saints: decorated jugs from the Roses kiln', in N. Field and A. White (eds.), *A Prospect of Lincolnshire*: 73–8.

Hebditch, M.G., 1967–8. 'A Saxo-Norman pottery kiln discovered in Southgate Street, Leicester, 1964', *Trans. Leicestershire Archaeol. Hist. Soc.*, *43*: 4–9.

Henisch, B.A., 1976. *Fast and Feast: Food in Medieval Society*.

Hilton, R.H., 1975. *The English Peasantry in the Later Middle Ages*.

Hilton, R.H., 1985. 'Medieval market towns and simple commodity production', *Past Present, 109*: 3–23.

Hinton, D.A. and Hodges, R.A., 1977. 'Excavations in Wareham, 1974–5', *Proc. Dorset Natur. Hist. Archaeol. Soc.*, *99*: 42–83.

Hinton, M. and Nelson, S., 1980. 'Medieval and later pottery made in Kingston upon Thames', *London Archaeol.*, *3 no.14*: 377–83.

Hodder, I., 1974. 'Some marketing models for Romano-British coarse pottery', *Britannia, 5*: 340–59.

Hodder, I., 1979. 'Pottery distributions: service and tribal areas', in M. Millett (ed.), *Pottery and the Archaeologist*: 7–23.

Hodder, I., 1982. *The Present Past: an Introduction to Anthropology for Archaeologists*.

Hodges, H., 1964. *Artifacts*.

Hodges, H., 1970. *Technology in the Ancient World*.

Hodges, H., 1973. 'Archaeology and the history of medieval technology', in D.E. Strong (ed.), *Archaeological Theory and Practice*: 265–73.

Hodges, H., 1974. 'Medieval potter: artisan or artist', in Evison *et al.* 1974: 33–40.

Hodges, R., 1980. *The Hamwih Pottery: the Local and Imported Wares from Thirty Years Excavations and their European Context*.

Hodges, R., 1982. *Dark Age Economics*.

Holdsworth, J., 1978. *Selected Pottery Groups AD 650–1780*, Archaeology of York 16/1.

Holland, W.F., 1958. *Fifty Years a Potter.*

Holling, F., 1971. 'A preliminary note on the pottery industry of the Hampshire-Surrey borders', *Surrey Archaeol. Collect., 68*: 57–88.

Holling, F., 1974. 'Farnborough: Farnborough Hill Hampshire', *Surrey Archaeol. Collect., 70*: 152–3.

Holling, F., 1977. 'Reflections on Tudor Green', *Post-Medieval Archaeol., 11*: 61–6.

Holling, F., 1984. 'Early post medieval pottery from no. 137 High Street, Guildford', *Surrey Archaeol. Collect., 75*: 295–301.

Holmes, N.M., 1975. 'Excavations within the Tron Kirk, Edinburgh, 1974', *Post-Medieval Archaeol., 9*: 137–63.

Huggins, R.M., 1972. 'Pottery', in P.J. Huggins, 'Monastic grange and outer close excavations, Waltham Abbey, Essex, 1970–1972', *Essex Archaeol. Hist., 4*: 97–110.

Huggins, R.M., 1973. 'Pottery', in P.J. and R.M. Huggins, 'Excavation of monastic forge and Saxo-Norman enclosure, Waltham Abbey, Essex, 1972–73', *Essex Archaeol. Hist., 5*: 155–66.

Huggins, R.M., 1976. 'Pottery', in P.J. Huggins, 'The excavation of an 11th-century Viking hall and 14th-century rooms at Waltham Abbey, Essex, 1969–71', *Medieval Archaeol., 20*: 101–14.

Hughes, R.G., 1957. 'Medieval pottery kiln site: Burley Hill, Duffield', *J. Derbyshire Archaeol. Natur. Hist. Soc., 77*: 57–60.

Hunter, J.R., 1981. 'The medieval glass industry', in D.W. Crossley (ed.), *Medieval Industry*: 143–50.

Hunter, R., 1979. 'St Neots-type ware', in J.H. Williams, *Excavations at St Peters Street, Northampton, 1973–6*: 230–40.

Hurst, D.G., 1968. 'Post-medieval Britain in 1967', *Post-Medieval Archaeol., 2*: 175–94.

Hurst, D.G., 1970. 'Post-medieval Britain in 1969', *Post-Medieval Archaeol., 4*: 174–88.

Hurst, D.G. and J.G., 1967. 'Excavation of two moated sites: Milton, Hampshire and Ashwell, Hertfordshire', *J. Brit. Archaeol. Ass., 30* (3rd ser.): 48–86.

Hurst, J.G., 1957. 'Saxo-Norman pottery in East Anglia: Part II. Thetford ware', *Proc. Cambridge Antiq. Soc., 50*: 29–60.

Hurst, J.G., 1961. 'The kitchen area of Northolt manor, Middlesex', *Medieval Archaeol., 5*: 211–99.

Hurst, J.G., 1962–3. 'White Castle and the dating of medieval pottery', *Medieval Archaeol., 6–7*: 135–55.

Hurst, J.G., 1964a. 'The pottery', in Smedley and Owles 1964: 314–27.

Hurst, J.G., 1964b. 'Tudor green ware', in B. Cunliffe, *Winchester Excavations 1949–60, Vol. I*: 140–2.

Hurst, J.G., 1966. 'Waterbeach: the medieval pottery', in M.D. Cra'ster, 'Waterbeach Abbey', *Proc. Cambridge Antiq. Soc., 59*: 89–93.

Hurst, J.G., 1969. 'The pottery', in R. Cramp, 'Excavations at the Saxon monastic sites of Wearmouth and Jarrow, Co. Durham: an interim report', *Medieval Archaeol., 13*: 59–64.

Hurst, J.G., 1976. 'The Pottery', in D.M. Wilson (ed.), *The Archaeology of Anglo-Saxon England*: 283–348.

Hurst, J.G. and Beresford, M.W., 1974. *Deserted Medieval Villages.*

Hurst, J.G. and D.G., 1964. 'Excavations at the deserted medieval village of Hangleton. Part II', *Sussex Archaeol. Collect., 102*: 94–142.

Hutchinson, G., 1979. 'The bar-lug pottery of Cornwall', *Cornish Archaeol., 18*: 81–103.

Ivens, R.J., 1981. 'Medieval pottery kilns at Brill, Buckinghamshire', *Rec. Buckinghamshire, 23*: 102–6.

Ivens, R.J., 1982. 'Medieval pottery from the 1978 excavations at Temple Farm, Brill', *Rec. Buckinghamshire, 24*: 144–70.

James, H., 1982. 'Medieval pottery from Carmarthen: a fabric type series', *Medieval and Later Pottery in Wales, 5*: 1–8.

Jarrett, M.G. and Edwards, B.J.N., 1964. 'The medieval pottery', in R. Hogg, 'Excavations at Tullie House, Carlisle, 1954–6', *Trans. Cumberland Westmorland Antiq. Archaeol. Soc., 64*: 41–57.

Jenner, A. and Vince, A.G., 1983. 'A dated type series of London medieval pottery: Part 3, Hertfordshire Glazed ware', *Trans. London Middlesex Archaeol. Soc., 34*: 151–70.

Jennings, S., 1981. 'Eighteen centuries of pottery from Norwich', *E. Anglian Archaeol., 13*.

Jewitt, L., 1878. *The Ceramic Art of Great Britain.*

Jones, P., 1984. 'Saxon and medieval pottery', in K.R. Crouch and S.A. Shanks, *Excavations in Staines 1975–6: the Friends Burial Ground Site*: 74–9.

Jope, E.M., 1950. 'Northamptonshire: a late medieval pottery kiln at Potterspury', *Archaeol. News Letter, 2 no. 10*: 156–7.

Jope, E.M., 1952. 'Regional character in West Country medieval pottery', *Trans. Bristol Gloucestershire Archaeol. Soc., 71*: 88–97.

Jope, E.M., 1952–3. 'Late Saxon pits under Oxford Castle Mound: excavations in 1952', *Oxoniensia, 17–18*: 77–111.

Jope, E.M., 1956. 'Ceramics: medieval', in C. Singer, E.J. Holmyard, A.R. Hall and T.I. Williams (eds.), *A History of Technology*, vol. II: 284–310.

Jope, E.M., 1963. 'The regional cultures of medieval Britain', in I.L. Foster and L. Alcock (eds.), *Culture and Environment*: 327–50.

Jope, E.M., 1972. 'Pre-conquest pottery', in C.A. Ralegh Radford, 'Excavations at Cricklade 1948–63', *Wiltshire Archaeol. Natur. Hist. Mag., 67*: 90–4.

Jope, E.M. and Hodges, H.W.M., 1955. 'Medieval pottery from Castle Street', in R. Hogg, 'Excavations in Carlisle, 1953', *Trans. Cumberland Westmorland Antiq. Archaeol. Soc., 55*: 79–107.

Jope, E.M. and Ivens, R.J., 1981. 'Some early products of the Brill Pottery, Buckinghamshire', *Rec. Buckinghamshire, 23*: 32–8.

Jope, E.M., Jope, H.M. and Rigold, S.E., 1950. 'Pottery from a late 12th century well-filling and other medieval finds from St John's College, Oxford, 1947', *Oxoniensia, 15*: 44–62.

Jope, E.M. and Threlfall, R.I., 1958. 'Excavations of a medieval settlement at Beere, North Tawton, Devon', *Medieval Archaeol., 2*: 112–40.

Jope, E.M. and Threlfall, R.I., 1959. 'The twelfth century castle of Ascot Doilly, Oxon', *Antiq. J., 39*: 219–73.

Keen, L., 1977. 'Late Saxon pottery from St Peters Church, Shaftesbury', *Proc. Dorset Natur. Hist. Archaeol. Soc., 99*: 129–30.

Kelly, D.B., 1972. 'An early Tudor kiln at Hareplain, Biddenden', *Archaeol. Cantiana,*

87: 159–76.

Kerr, N.A., n.d. *A Medieval and Post Medieval Pottery Industry: Excavations in Eastgate, Bourne, Lincolnshire. Interim Report*, unpublished report.

Kilmurry, K., 1980. *The Pottery Industry of Stamford, Lincolnshire, AD 850–1250*, Brit. Archaeol. Rep. 84.

Knight, J.K., 1977. 'Pottery production in Wales during the Anglo-Norman Conquest', in P.J. Davey (ed.), *Medieval Pottery from Excavations in the North West*: 113–14.

Knight, J.K., 1982. 'Montgomery Castle: a provisional check list of fabrics', *Medieval and Later Pottery in Wales, 5*: 44–62.

Kraus, D. and H., 1975. *The Hidden World of Misericords*.

Laing, L.R., 1966–7. 'Excavations at Linlithgow Palace, West Lothian, 1966–7', *Proc. Soc. Antiq. Scot., 99*: 111–47.

Laing, L.R., 1968–9. 'Medieval and other material in Linlithgow Palace Museum', *Proc. Soc. Antiq. Scot., 101*: 134–45.

Laing, L.R., 1970–1. 'Medieval pottery in Dundee Museum', *Proc. Soc. Antiq. Scot., 103*: 169–77.

Laing, L.R., 1973. 'Cooking-pots and the origins of the Scottish medieval pottery industry', *Archaeol. J., 130*: 183–216.

Laing, L.R. and Robertson, W.N., 1969–70. 'Notes on Scottish medieval pottery', *Proc. Soc. Antiq. Scot., 102*: 146–54.

Laing, L.R. and Talbot, E.J., 1974. 'Some medieval and post medieval pottery from South West Scotland', *Glasgow Archaeol. J., 3*: 43–50.

Le Patourel, H.E.J., 1959. 'The pottery', in K.M. Richardson, 'Excavations in Hungate, York', *Archaeol. J., 126*: 90–100.

Le Patourel, H.E.J., 1965. 'Appendix B. The pottery', in C.V. Bellamy, 'Pontefract Priory excavations', *Publ. Thoresby Soc., 49*: 106–19.

Le Patourel, H.E.J., 1966a. 'Knaresborough Castle', *Yorkshire Archaeol. J., 41*: 591–607.

Le Patourel, H.E.J., 1966b. 'The pottery', in Mayes and Pirie 1966: 262–9.

Le Patourel, H.E.J., 1967. 'The pottery', in E.J.E. Pirie *et al.*, 'Kirkstall Abbey excavations 1960–1964', *Publ. Thoresby Soc., 51*: 36–50.

Le Patourel, H.E.J., 1968. 'Documentary evidence and the medieval pottery industry', *Medieval Archaeol., 12*: 101–26.

Le Patourel, H.E.J., 1972. 'Medieval pottery', in L.P. Wenham, 'Excavations in Low Petergate, York, 1957–8', *Yorkshire Archaeol. J., 44*: 108–13.

Le Patourel, H.E.J., 1979a. 'Medieval pottery', in D.D. Andrews and G. Milne (eds.), *Wharram: a Study of Settlement on the Yorkshire Wolds, Vol. I: Domestic Settlement, 1: Areas 10 and 6*: 74–107.

Le Patourel, H.E.J., 1979b. 'Pottery as evidence for social and economic change', in P.H. Sawyer (ed.), *English Medieval Settlement*: 86–96.

Le Patourel, H.E.J., 1986. 'Pots and potters: the fifth Gerald Dunning Memorial Lecture', *Medieval Ceram., 10*: 3–16.

Le Patourel, H.E.J. and Wood, P., 1973. 'Excavation at the Archbishop of York's manor house at Otley', *Yorkshire Archaeol. J., 45*: 115–41.

Lewis, J.M., 1964–6. 'Some medieval pottery from Cardiff', *Trans. Cardiff Natur. Soc., 93*: 40–5.

Lewis, J.M., 1968. 'Medieval church cruets in pottery', *Medieval Archaeol., 12*: 147–9.

Lewis, J.M., 1970. 'Early Christian stone from Pen-Y-Fai', *Archaeol. Cambrensis, 119*: 73.

Lewis, J.M., 1978. *Medieval Pottery and Metal-Ware in Wales*.

Lewis, J.M., 1980a. 'Pottery from a post medieval kiln at Whole House, Talgarth, Powys', *Medieval and Later Pottery in Wales, 3*: 48–55.

Lewis, J.M., 1980b. 'The Cistercian ware wasters from Abergavenny, Gwent', *Medieval and Later Pottery in Wales, 3*: 56–8.

Lewis, J.M., 1982. *The Ewenny Potteries*.

Lewis, J.M. and Vyner, B.E., 1979. 'Medieval pottery from Loughor Castle', *Medieval and Later Pottery in Wales, 2*: 1–13.

Linger, S. and Kennett, D.H., 1972. 'Medieval jugs from Bedford', *Bedfordshire Archaeol. J. 7*: 67–72.

Loyn, H.R., 1962. *Anglo-Saxon England and the Norman Conquest*.

Lyne, M. and Jefferies R.S., 1974. 'The Alice Holt medieval potters', *Surrey Archaeol. Collect., 70*: 25–46.

MacAskill, N.L., 1982a. 'Pottery', in J. Wordsworth, 'Excavation of the settlement at 13–21, Castle Street Inverness, 1979', *Proc. Soc. Antiq. Scot., 112*: 355–68.

MacAskill, N.L., 1982b. 'The pottery', in N.A. McGavin, 'Excavations in Kirkwall, 1978', *Proc. Soc. Antiq. Scot., 112*: 405–13.

MacAskill, N.L., 1983. 'The pottery', in J. Wordsworth, 'Excavations in Inverkeithing, 1981', *Proc. Soc. Antiq. Scot., 113*: 535–42.

McCarthy, M.R., 1974. 'The medieval kilns on Nash Hill, Lacock, Wiltshire', *Wiltshire Archaeol. Natur. Hist. Mag., 69*: 97–145.

McCarthy, M.R., 1977. 'The pottery', in P. Everson, 'Excavations in the Vicarage Garden at Brixworth, 1972', *J. Brit. Archaeol. Ass., 130* (3 ser.): 82–92.

McCarthy, M.R., 1979. 'The pottery', in J.H. Williams, *St Peter's Street, Northampton: Excavations 1973–76*: 151–229.

McCarthy, M.R. and Williams, J.H., 1978. 'A Note on Potters Field and Potter Hill, Northampton', *Northamptonshire Archaeol., 13*: 169–171.

McNeil, R., 1983. 'Two twelfth century wich houses in Nantwich, Cheshire', *Medieval Archaeol., 27*: 40–88.

Macpherson-Grant, N., 1978. 'Medieval pottery', in P. Bennett, 'Excavations at 16–21 North Lane, Canterbury', *Archaeol. Cantiana, 94*: 178–90.

Macpherson-Grant, N., 1986. 'Interim note on a twelfth century pottery kiln from Canterbury', *Medieval Ceram., 10*: 49–55.

Macpherson-Grant, N., n.d. *The Evolution of Canterbury Ceramics: Simplified Notes* (unpublished).

Mahany, C., Burchard, A. and Simpson, G., 1982. *Excavations in Stamford, Lincolnshire 1963–1969*.

Mainman, A.J., 1983. *Early and Middle Saxon Kent – a ceramic viewpoint*, unpublished PhD thesis, University of Sheffield.

Manby, T.G., 1965. 'Medieval pottery kilns at Upper Heaton, West Yorkshire', *Archaeol. J., 121*: 70–110.

Marsh, G., 1981. 'London's Samian supply and its relationship to the development of the Gallic Samian industry', in A.C. and A.S. Anderson (eds.), *Roman Pottery Research in Britain and North West Europe: Papers presented to Graham Webster*, Brit. Archaeol. Rep. (Int. Ser.) 123: 173–238.

Marshall, C.J., 1924. 'A medieval pottery kiln discovered at Cheam', *Surrey Archaeol. Collect., 35*: 79–97.

Marshall, C.J., 1941. 'The sites of two more thirteenth century pottery kilns at Cheam', *Surrey Archaeol. Collect., 47,* 99–100.

Martin, E., Plouviez, J. and Ross, H., 1984. 'Archaeology in Suffolk, 1983'. *Proc. Suffolk Inst. Archaeol. Hist., 36*: 43–53.

Martin, E., Plouviez, J. and Ross, H., 1984. 'Archaeology in Suffolk, 1983'., *Proc. Suffolk Inst. Archaeol. Hist., 35*: 321–8.

Mate, M., 1984. 'Agrarian economy after the Black Death: the manors of Canterbury Cathedral Priory 1348–1391', *Econ. Hist. Rev., 37* (2nd ser.): 341–54.

Matthews, L.G. and Green, H.J.M., 1970. 'Post medieval pottery of the Inns of Court', *Post-Medieval Archaeol., 3*: 1–17.

Maxwell, I.S., 1962. 'Yorkshire: the North Riding', in H.C. Darby and I.S. Maxwell (eds.), *The Domesday Geography of Northern England*: 85–163.

Mayes, P., 1968. 'A seventeenth century kiln site at Potterspury, Northamptonshire', *Post-Medieval Archaeol., 2*: 55–82.

Mayes, P. and Hayfield, C., 1980. 'A late-medieval pottery kiln at Holme-upon-Spalding Moor', *E. Riding Archaeol, 6*: 99–111.

Mayes, P., and Pirie, E.J., 1966. 'A Cistercian ware kiln of the early sixteenth century at Potterton, Yorkshire', *Antiq. J., 46*: 255–76.

Mayes, P., and Scott, K., 1984. *Pottery Kilns at Chilvers Coton, Nuneaton.*

Mellor, M., 1976. 'The pottery', in A. Rogerson, 'Excavations on Fullers Hill, Great Yarmouth', *E. Anglian Archaeol., 22*: 169–95.

Mellor, M., 1980a. 'Late Saxon pottery from Oxfordshire: evidence and speculation', *Medieval Ceram., 4*: 17–27.

Mellor, M., 1980b. 'Pottery', in N. Palmer, 'A Beaker burial and medieval tenements in The Hamel, Oxford', *Oxoniensia, 45*: 160–82.

Mellor, M., 1983. 'Swyncombe', *South Midlands Archaeol.,* C.B.A. Group 9: 147.

Mellor, M., 1985a. 'The medieval and post-medieval pottery', in G. Lambrick, 'Further excavations of the Dominican Friary, Oxford', *Oxoniensia, 50*: 172–7.

Mellor, M., 1985b. 'Pottery', in D. Sturdy and J. Munby, 'Early domestic sites in Oxford: excavations in Cornmarket and Queen Street, 1959–62', *Oxoniensia, 50*: 75–6.

Miles, H., 1976. 'Early medieval occupation at Honeyditches, Seaton', *Proc. Devon Archaeol. Soc., 34*: 73–6.

Miles, H., 1977. 'Rhuddlan', in P.J. Davey (ed.), *Medieval Pottery from Excavations in the North West*: 100–2.

Miles, T.J., 1976. 'Late medieval potters' waste from Lostwithiel', *Cornish Archaeol., 15*: 115–17.

Miles, T.J., 1979. 'Late medieval potters' waste from Lostwithiel', *Cornish Archaeol., 18*: 103–4.

Millar, E.G., 1932. *The Luttrell Psalter.*

Milligan, W., 1982. 'Pottery', in J.G. Coad and A.D.F. Streeten, 'Excavations at Castle Acre Castle, Norfolk, 1972–7', *Archaeol. J., 139*: 199–227.

Moore, W.R.G., 1974. 'Yardley Gobion', *Northamptonshire Archaeol., 9*: 112.

Moorhouse, S., 1970. 'Finds from Basing House, Hampshire', *Post-Medieval Archaeol., 4*: 31–91.

Moorhouse, S., 1971a. 'The pottery', in V. Russell and S. Moorhouse, 'Excavations near the Bishop's Palace at Nettleham, 1959', *Lincolnshire Hist. Archaeol., 6*: 22–6.

Moorhouse, S., 1971b. 'A distinctive type of late medieval pottery in the East Midlands', *Proc. Cambridge Antiq. Soc.*, *65*: 46–59.

Moorhouse, S., 1971c. 'Two late and post medieval pottery groups from Farnham Castle, Surrey', *Surrey Archaeol. Collect.*, *68*: 39–55.

Moorhouse, S., 1971d. 'A sixteenth century Tudor Green group from Overton, Hampshire', *Post-Medieval Archaeol.*, *5*: 182–5.

Moorhouse, S., 1971e. 'The kiln superstructures', in K.S. Bartlett, 'Excavations at Potovens, near Wakefield, 1968', *Post-Medieval Archaeol.*, *5*: 13–18.

Moorhouse, S., 1972a. 'Finds from excavations in the refectory at the Dominican Friary, Boston', *Lincolnshire Hist. Archaeol.*, *7*: 21–53.

Moorhouse, S., 1972b. 'Medieval distilling apparatus of glass and pottery', *Medieval Archaeol.*, *16*: 79–121.

Moorhouse, S., 1974a. 'A distinctive type of late medieval pottery in the East Midlands', *Proc. Cambridge Antiq. Soc.*, *65*: 46–59.

Moorhouse, S., 1974b. 'A late medieval domestic rubbish deposit from Broughton, Lincolnshire', *Lincolnshire Hist. Archaeol.*, *9*: 3–16.

Moorhouse, S., 1978. 'Documentary evidence for the uses of medieval pottery: an interim statement', *Medieval Ceram.*, *2*: 3–21.

Moorhouse, S., 1979. 'Tudor Green: some further thoughts', *Medieval Ceram.*, *3*: 53–61.

Moorhouse, S., 1981. 'The medieval pottery industry and its markets', in D.W. Crossley (ed.), *Medieval Industry*: 96–125.

Moorhouse, S., 1982. 'The pottery', in J.R. Hunter, 'Medieval Berwick-upon-Tweed', *Archaeol. Aeliana*, *10* (5th ser.): 99–123.

Moorhouse, S., 1983a. 'Documentary evidence and its potential for understanding the inland movement of medieval pottery', *Medieval Ceram.*, *7*: 45–87.

Moorhouse, S., 1983b. 'The medieval pottery', in P. Mayes and L.A.S. Butler, *Sandal Castle Excavations 1964–1973*: 83–212.

Moorhouse, S., 1983c. 'The Medieval Pottery Research Group', in D.A. Hinton (ed.), *25 Years of Medieval Archaeology*: 102–16.

Moorhouse, S., 1984. 'Late medieval pottery plant-holders from eastern Yorkshire', *Medieval Archaeol.*, *28*: 194–202.

Morris, E., 1980a. 'Medieval and post medieval pottery in Worcester – a type series', in M.O.H. Carver (ed.), 'Medieval Worcester: an archaeological framework', *Trans. Worcestershire Archaeol. Soc.*, *7* (3rd ser.): 221–54.

Morris, E., 1980b. 'The excavation of three medieval craftsmen's tenements at Sidbury, Worcester 1975–6', in M.O.H. Carver (ed.), 'Medieval Worcester: an archaeological framework', *Trans. Worcestershire Archaeol. Soc.*, *7* (3rd ser.): 155–219.

Murray, H.K. and J.C., 1986. *The Medieval Burgh of Rattray. Interim Report for 1985* (unpublished).

Murray, J.C., 1982. 'The pottery', in J.C. Murray (ed.), *Excavations in the Medieval Burgh of Aberdeen, 1981*: 116–76.

Musty, J.W.G., 1973. 'A preliminary account of a medieval pottery industry at Minety, North Wiltshire', *Wiltshire Archaeol. Natur. Hist. Mag.*, *68*: 79–88.

Musty, J.W.G., 1974. 'Medieval pottery kilns', in Evison *et al.* 1974: 41–65.

Musty, J.W.G., 1984. 'Technology and affinities of the pottery kilns', in Mayes and Scott 1984: 26–8.

Musty, J.W.G. and Rahtz, P.A., 1964. 'The suburbs of Old Sarum', *Wiltshire Archaeol. Natur. Hist. Mag., 59*: 130–54.

Musty, J.W.G., Algar, D.J. and Ewence, P.F., 1969. 'The medieval pottery kilns at Laverstock, near Salisbury, Wiltshire', *Archaeologia, 102*: 83–150.

Mynard, D.C., 1969a. 'Description of the pottery', in D.G. and J.G. Hurst, 'Excavations at the deserted medieval village of Wythemail, Northamptonshire', *Medieval Archaeol., 13*: 182–98.

Mynard, D.C., 1969b. 'Excavations at Somerby, Lincs., 1957', *Lincolnshire Hist. Archaeol., 4*: 63–91.

Mynard, D.C., 1969c. 'Pottery', in A.M. Cook, D.C. Mynard and S.E. Rigold, 'Excavations at Dover Castle, principally in the Inner Bailey', *J. Brit. Archaeol. Ass., 32*: 87–101.

Mynard, D.C., 1970. 'Medieval pottery of Potterspury type', *Bull. Northamptonshire Federation Archaeol. Soc.*: 49–55.

Mynard, D., 1984. 'A medieval pottery industry at Olney Hyde', *Rec. Buckinghamshire, 26*: 56–85.

Mynard, D.C. and Barton, K.J., 1969. 'The pottery', in Fennelly 1969: 100–8.

Mynard, D.C., Petchey, M. and Tilson P., 1983. 'A medieval pottery at Church End, Flitwick, Bedfordshire', *Bedfordshire Archaeol. J., 16*: 75–84.

Myres, J.N.L., 1969. *Anglo-Saxon Pottery and the Settlement of England.*

Mytum, H.C., n.d. *Medieval Pottery in Warwick* (unpublished).

Nailor, V., 1984. 'A preliminary note on a Late Saxon ware from Nottingham', *Medieval Ceram., 8*: 59–63.

Nash, M., 1966. *Primitive and Peasant Economic Systems.*

Newton, E.F. and Bibbings, E., 1958. 'Seventeenth century pottery sites at Harlow, Essex', *Trans. Essex Archaeol. Soc., 25*: 358–77.

Noble, J.V., 1966. *The Techniques of Painted Attic Pottery.*

Oetgen, J.M., 1983–4. 'The absorption of foodstuffs by ceramics', *Bull. Experimental Firing Group, 2*: 41–56.

O' Mahoney, C., 1985. 'West Wales fabrics – an interim note', *Medieval and Later Pottery in Wales, 8*: 20–4.

Orton, C., 1977. 'Medieval pottery', in T.R. Blurton and M. Rhodes, 'Excavations at Angel Court, Walbrook, 1974', *Trans. London Middlesex Archaeol. Soc., 28*: 80–6.

Orton, C., 1979. 'The excavation of a late medieval/transitional pottery kiln at Cheam, Surrey', *Surrey Archaeol. Collect., 73*: 49–92.

Orton, C., 1982. 'Pottery evidence for the dating of the revetments', in G. and C. Milne, *Medieval Waterfront Development at Trig Lane, London*: 92–9.

Orton, C., 1985. 'Diffusion or impedance – obstacles to innovation in medieval ceramics', *Medieval Ceram., 9*: 21–34.

Oswald, A., 1962–3. 'Excavation of a thirteenth century wooden building at Weoley castle, Birmingham, 1960–1', *Medieval Archaeol., 6–7*: 109–34.

Owles, E.J., 1970. 'A medieval moated farmstead at Debenham', *Proc. Suffolk Inst. Archaeol. Hist., 31*: 160–71.

Owles, E.J., 1973. 'Archaeology in Suffolk, 1971 and 1972', *Proc. Suffolk Inst. Archaeol. Hist., 32*: 205–14, 282–91.

Owles, E.J., 1976. 'Archaeology in Suffolk, 1975', *Proc. Suffolk Inst. Archaeol. Hist., 33*: 322–8.

Parfitt, J.H., 1976. 'A moated site at Moat Farm, Leigh, Kent', *Archaeol. Cantiana, 92*: 173–201.

Parker, A., 1932. 'Nottingham pottery', *Trans. Thoroton Soc. of Nottinghamshire, 36*: 79–124.

Patterson, H., 1985. 'Medieval pottery, 1980', in D.H. Evans and D.H. Heslop, 'Two medieval sites in Yarm', *Yorkshire Archaeol. J., 57*: 68–72.

Peacock, D.P.S., 1982. *Pottery in the Roman World*.

Pearce, J., 1984. 'Getting a handle on medieval pottery', *London Archaeol., 5*: 17–23.

Pearce, J., Vince, A.G. and Jenner, A., 1985. *A Dated Type Series of London Medieval Pottery. Part 2: London-type Ware*, London Middlesex Archaeol. Soc. Special Paper No. 6.

Pearce, J., Vince, A.G. and White, R., with Cunningham, C.M., 1982. 'A dated type series of London medieval pottery. Part 1: Mill Green ware', *Trans. London Middlesex Archaeol. Soc., 33*: 266–98.

Pearson, T., 1979. 'The British wares', in C. Gaskell Brown (ed.), *Plymouth Excavations: Castle Street, The Pottery*: 11.

Pearson, T., 1982. 'The post-Roman pottery', in P. Leach, *Ilchester Vol. I: Excavations 1974–5*: 169–217.

Pearson, T., 1983. 'An aquamanile from the Raunds excavations in Northamptonshire', *S. Midlands Archaeol.*, C. B. A. Group 9: 28–31.

Pearson, T., 1984. 'Medieval and post medieval ceramics', in P. Leach, *The Archaeology of Taunton*: 142–4 and Microfiche 1–2.

Pearson, Trevor, 1982. 'The dating of Scarborough ware', *Medieval Ceram., 6*: 87–93.

Picolpasso, C., 1934. *The Three Books of the Potter's Art*.

Pike, G., 1965–6. 'A medieval pottery kiln site on the Camley Gardens Estate, Maidenhead', *Berkshire Archaeol. J., 62*: 22–33.

Platt, C. and Coleman-Smith, R., 1975. *Excavations in Medieval Southampton 1953–69*.

Plog, S., 1980. *Stylistic Variation in Prehistoric Ceramics*.

Plot, R., 1686. *The Natural History of Staffordshire*.

Ponsford, M.W., 1971. 'Nottingham Town Wall: Park Row excavations 1967', *Trans. Thoroton Soc. Nottinghamshire, 85*: 5–32.

Ponsford, M.W., 1974. 'Late Saxon pottery from Bristol', in Evison *et al.* 1974: 120–2.

Ponsford, M.W., 1978. 'Excavations at Ham Green', *Bristol Archaeol. Res. Gp., 6*, no.6: 144–6.

Ponsford, M.W., 1979. *Bristol Castle: the Archaeology and History of a Royal Fortress*, unpublished MLitt thesis, University of Bristol.

Ponsford, M.W., 1983. 'North European pottery imported into Bristol 1200–1500', in Davey and Hodges 1983: 219–24.

Poos, L.R., 1985. 'The rural population of Essex in the later Middle Ages', *Econ. Hist. Rev., 38*: 515–30.

Postan, M.M., 1972. *The Medieval Economy and Society*.

Postan, M.M., 1973. *Essays on Medieval Agriculture and General Problems of the Medieval Economy*.

Poulsen, J., 'Excavations on a medieval settlement at Woolcombe Farm, Toller Porcorum 1966–69', *Proc. Dorset Natur. Hist. Archaeol. Soc., 105*: 75–81.

Prendergast, M.D., 1974. 'Limpsfield medieval coarseware: a descriptive analysis', *Surrey Archaeol. Collect.*, *70*: 57–77.

Price, C. and Newman, R., 1985. 'Vale Fabric': a revaluation', *Medieval and Later Pottery in Wales*, *8*: 10–19.

Price, R., 1979. 'Notes concerning medieval Bristol potters', *Rescue Archaeol. in the Bristol Area*, *1*: 57–8.

Rackham, B., 1948. *Medieval English Pottery* (1st edn).

Rackham, B., 1952. 'Farnham pottery of the 16th century', *Surrey Archaeol. Collect.*, *52*: 50–5.

Rackham, B., 1972. *Medieval English Pottery* (2nd edn).

Rackham, O., 1980. *Ancient Woodland: Its History, Vegetation and Uses in England.*

Rackham, O., forthcoming. 'The forest of Neroche and the fuel supply of the Donyatt kilns', in Coleman-Smith and Pearson forthcoming.

Radcliffe, F., 1961–2. 'Excavations at Logic Lane', *Oxoniensia*, *26–7*: 38–69.

Rahtz, P.A., 1959. 'Holworth, medieval village excavations 1958', *Proc. Dorset Natur. Hist. Archaeol. Soc.*, *81*: 127–47.

Rahtz, P.A., 1969a. *Excavations at King John's Hunting Lodge, Writtle, Essex, 1955–57.*

Rahtz, P.A., 1969b. 'Upton, Gloucestershire, 1964–68. Second report', *Trans. Bristol Gloucestershire Archaeol. Soc.*, *88*: 74–126.

Rahtz, P.A., 1974. 'Pottery in Somerset AD 400–1066', in Evison *et al.* 1974: 95–126.

Rahtz, P.A., 1979. *The Saxon and Medieval Palaces at Cheddar*, Brit. Archaeol. Rep. (Brit. Ser.) 65.

Rahtz, P.A., 1982. 'Celtic society in Somerset AD 400–700', *Bull. Board Celtic Stud.*, *30*: 176–200.

Rahtz, P.A. and Greenfield, E., 1977. *Excavations at Chew Valley Lake, Somerset.*

Randall, L.M.C., 1966. *Images in the Margins of Gothic Manuscripts.*

R.C.H.M., 1960. 'Excavations in the West Bailey at Corfe Castle', *Medieval Archaeol.*, *4*: 29–55.

Redknap, M., 1985. 'Twelfth and thirteenth century Coventry wares with special reference to a waster group from the Cannon Park Estate, Coventry', *Medieval Ceram.*, *9*: 65–77.

Renfrew, C., 1975. 'Trade as action at a distance', in J.A. Sabloff and C.C. Lamberg-Karlovsky (eds.), *Ancient Civilisation and Trade*: 3–59.

Renfrew, C., 1977. 'Production and exchange in early State societies, the evidence of pottery', in D.P.S. Peacock (ed.), *Pottery and Early Commerce*: 1–20.

Renfrew, C., 1979. 'Systems collapse as social transformation', in C. Renfrew and K.L. Cooke (eds.), *Transformations, Mathematical Approaches to Culture Change*: 481–506.

Renn, D.F., 1960. 'The keep of Wareham Castle', *Medieval Archaeol.*, *4*: 56–68.

Renn, D.F., 1964. *Potters and Kilns in Medieval Hertfordshire.*

Rhodes, D., 1957. *Clay and Glazes for the Potter.*

Rice, P., 1981. 'Evolution of specialised pottery production: a trial model', *Curr. Anthropol.*, *22*: 219–40.

Rice, P., 1984. 'Change and conservatism in pottery-producing systems', in S. van der Leeuw and A. Pritchard (eds.), *The Many Dimensions of Pottery*: 231–88.

Rieth, A., 1960. *5000 Jahre Töpferscheibe.*

Rigold, S.E., 1962–3. 'The Anglian cathedral of North Elmham', *Medieval Archaeol.,* *6–7*: 67–108.

Rigold, S.E., 1971. 'Eynsford Castle and its excavation', *Archaeol. Cantiana, 86*: 109–71.

Rigold, S.E. and Fleming, A.J., 1973. 'Eynsford Castle: the moat and bridge', *Archaeol. Cantiana, 88*: 87–116.

Rix, M.M. and Dunning, G.C., 1955. 'Excavation of a medieval garderobe in Snargate Street, Dover, in 1945', *Archaeol. Cantiana, 69*: 132–58.

Robertson, A.J., 1925. *Laws of the Kings of England from Edmund to Henry I.*

Robertson, W.N., 1974. 'Report on pottery found at Innerpeffray Church, Perthshire', *Glasgow Archaeol. J., 3*: 19–25.

Rogerson, A. and Adams, N., 1978. 'A Saxo-Norman pottery kiln at Bircham', *E. Anglian Archaeol., 8*: 33–44.

Rogerson, A. and Ashley, S.J., 1985. 'A medieval pottery production site at Blackborough End, Middleton', *Norfolk Archaeol., 39*: 181–9.

Rogerson, A. and Dallas, C., 1984. 'Excavations in Thetford 1948–59 and 1973–80', *E. Anglian Archaeol., 22.*

Rutter, J.A., 1977a. 'Ashton', in P.J. Davey (ed.), *Medieval Pottery from Excavations in the North West*: 70–85.

Rutter, J.A., 1977b. 'Chester, Old Market Hall Pit Group', in P.J. Davey (ed.), *Medieval Pottery from Excavations in the North West*: 18–21.

Rutter, J.A., 1985. 'The pottery', in D.J.P. Mason, *Excavations at Chester, 26–42 Lower Bridge Street 1974–6: the Dark Age and Saxon periods*: 40–55.

Rutter, J.G., 1961. *Medieval Pottery in the Scarborough Museum*, Scarborough Dist. Archaeol. Soc. Res. Rep.3.

Rye, C.G. and Hurst, J.G., 1968. 'Medieval pottery from Great Yarmouth', *Norfolk Archaeol., 34*: 279–92.

Rye, O.S., 1977. 'Pottery manufacturing techniques: X-ray studies', *Archaeometry, 19*: 205–11.

Rye, O.S., 1981. *Pottery Technology: Principles and Reconstruction.*

Salzman, L.F., 1923. *English Industries of the Middle Ages.*

Saraswati, B. and Behura, N.K., 1966. *Pottery Techniques in Peasant India.*

Sawday, D., forthcoming. 'The pottery', in J.E. Mellor and T. Pearce, *Excavations at St Nicholas Circle, Leicester 2: Post Roman Occupation.*

Scott, C. and Blanchard, L.,1983. 'The pottery', in L. Blanchard, 'An excavation at 45, Canal Street, Perth, 1978–9', *Proc. Soc. Antiq. Scot., 113*: 503–10.

Scott, L., 1954. 'Pottery', in C. Singer, E.J. Holmyard and A.R. Hall (eds.), *A History of Technology*, vol. 1: 376–412.

Scott-Tucker, A., 1984. 'Abergavenny – a possible kiln site', *Medieval and Later Pottery in Wales, 7*: 63–4.

Sell, S.H., 1984. 'The medieval incurved dish – a topic for discussion', *Medieval and Later Pottery in Wales, 7*: 53–60.

Sellers, E., 1970. 'Ingatestone – Mill Green, TL 643 022', *Trans. Essex Archaeol. Soc., 2*: 337–8.

Shepard, A.O., 1956. *Ceramics For the Archaeologist.*

Sheppard, D., 1977. 'A medieval pottery kiln at Pinner, Middlesex', *London Archaeol., 3*, no.2: 31–5.

Sheppard, T., 1939. 'Viking and other relics at Crayke, Yorkshire', *Yorkshire Archaeol. J., 34*: 273–81.

Simpson, G., 1982. 'Two medieval pottery kilns', in Mahany *et al.* 1982: 145–75.

Smedley, N. and Owles, E.J., 1964. 'Some Suffolk kilns: IV. Saxon kilns in Cox lane, Ipswich, 1961', *Proc. Suffolk Inst. Archaeol. Hist., 29*: 304–35.

Smedley, N. and Owles, E.J., 1967. 'A sherd of Ipswich ware with face-mask decoration', *Proc. Suffolk Inst. Archaeol. Hist., 31*: 84–7.

Smith, A.E. and Hurst, J.G., 1963. 'Pottery', in E.W. Holden, 'Excavations at the deserted medieval village of Hangleton. Part I', *Sussex Archaeol. Collect., 101*: 112–44.

Smith, G.H., 1979. 'The excavation of the Hospital of St Mary of Ospringe, commonly called Maison Dieu', *Archaeol. Cantiana, 95*: 81–184.

Solon, L.M., 1885. *The Art of the Old English Potter.*

Spillett, P.J., Stebbing, W.P.D. and Dunning, G.C., 1942. 'A pottery kiln site at Tyler Hill, near Canterbury', *Archaeol. Cantiana, 55*: 57–64.

Steane, J.M., 1967. 'Excavations at Lyveden 1967', *J. Northampton Mus., 2.*

Steane, J.M. and Bryant, G.F., 1975. 'Excavations at the deserted medieval settlement at Lyveden, Northants', *J. Northampton Mus., 12.*

Stebbing, N., Rhodes, J. and Mellor, M., 1980. *The Clay Industries of Oxfordshire: Oxfordshire Potteries.*

Sterud, G., 1973. 'A paradigmatic view of prehistory', in C. Renfrew (ed.), *The Explanation of Culture Change: Models in Prehistory*: 3–17.

Stevenson, R.B.K. and Henshall, A.S., 1956–7. 'Probable 13th-century kiln-site at Perth', *Proc. Soc. Antiq. Scot., 90*: 250–2.

Stone, J.F.S. and Charlton, J., 1935. 'Trial excavations in the east suburbs of Old Sarum', *Antiq. J., 15*: 174–90.

Streeten, A.D.F., 1980. 'Potters, kilns and markets in medieval Sussex: a preliminary study', *Sussex Archaeol. Collect., 118*: 105–18.

Streeten, A.D.F., 1981. 'Craft and industry: medieval and later potters in south east England', in H. Howard and E. Morris, *Production and Distribution: a ceramic viewpoint*, Brit. Archaeol. Rep. (Int. Ser.) 120: 323–46.

Streeten, A.D.F., 1982. 'Potters, kilns, and markets in medieval Kent: a preliminary study', in P.E. Leach (ed.), *Archaeology in Kent to AD 1500*: 87–95.

Surtees Society, 1897. *Register of the Freemen of the City of York, Vol. I: 1272–1558*, Publications of the Surtees Society, 96.

Swan, V.G., 1984. *The Pottery Kilns of Roman Britain.*

Swanson, H., 1980. *Craftsmen and Industry in Late Medieval York*, unpublished DPhil thesis, University of York.

Tabraham, C.J., 1984. 'Excavations at Kelso Abbey', *Proc. Soc. Antiq. Scot., 114*: 365–404.

Talbot, E.J., 1968. 'Welsh ceramics: a documentary and archaeological survey', *Post-Medieval Archaeol., 2*: 119–39.

Tatton-Brown, T., and Macpherson-Grant, N., 1983. 'Medieval kilns in the Tyler Hill area', in T. Tatton-Brown *et al.*, 'Recent fieldwork around Canterbury', *Archaeol. Cantiana, 99*: 127–31.

Tait, J., 1936. *The Medieval English Borough.*

Taylor, J., forthcoming. 'The pottery', in M.R. McCarthy, *Excavations at Blackfriars Street, Carlisle 1977–8.*

Tebbutt, C.F., Rudd, G. and Moorhouse, S., 1971. 'Excavation of a moated site at Ellington, Huntingdonshire', *Proc. Cambridge Antiq. Soc., 63*: 31–73.

Tester, P.J., 1956. 'Medieval pottery found in Bexley church', *Archaeol. Cantiana, 70*: 260–1.

Tester, P.J., 1968. 'Medieval pottery', in A.C. Harrison and C. Flight, 'The Roman and medieval defences of Rochester in the light of recent excavations', *Archaeol. Cantiana, 83*: 94–9.

Tester, P.J., 1970. 'Medieval pottery', in A.C. Harrison, 'Excavations in Rochester', *Archaeol. Cantiana, 85*: 108–9.

Tester, P.J., 1972. 'Medieval pottery', in A.C. Harrison, 'Rochester East Gate, 1969', *Archaeol. Cantiana, 87*: 142–50.

Tester, P.J., 1978. 'Medieval pottery', in C. Flight and A.C. Harrison, 'Rochester Castle, 1976', *Archaeol. Cantiana, 94*: 41–2.

Tester, P.J., 1979. 'Medieval jugs', in A.C. Harrison and D. Williams, 'Excavation at Prior's Gate House, Rochester, 1976–7', *Archaeol. Cantiana, 95*: 31–4.

Theophilus, 1979. *On Divers Arts*.

Thirsk, J., 1967. *The Agrarian History of England and Wales*.

Thomas, A.C., 1963. 'Unpublished pottery from Cornish Museums: 2. Gunwalloe pottery, Helston Museums', *Cornish Archaeol., 2*: 60–4.

Thomas, A.C., 1964. 'Minor sites in the Gwithian Area (Iron Age to recent times)', *Cornish Archaeol., 3*: 37–62.

Thomas, A.C., 1968. 'Grass-marked pottery in Cornwall', in J.M. Coles and D.D.A. Simpson (eds.), *Studies in Ancient Europe*: 311–31.

Thomas, H.O., 1980. 'A post medieval kiln-site at Trefaldu, Cwmcarvan, Gwent', *Medieval and Later Pottery in Wales, 3*: 38–44.

Thomas, H.O., 1982. 'The North Herefordshire pottery industry – a common regional tradition', *Medieval and Later Pottery in Wales, 5*: 63–72.

Thomas, L.C. and Musty, J.W.G., 1961. 'A spectroscopic survey of English and Continental medieval glazed pottery', *Nature, 192*: 1143–4.

Thompson, N.P., 1970. 'A medieval pit at Great Somerford', *Wiltshire Archaeol. and Natur. Hist. Mag., 65*: 167–71.

Thoms, L.M., 1975–6. 'Coarse pottery', in J. Schofield, 'Excavations south of Edinburgh High Street, 1972–4', *Proc. Soc. Antiq. Scot., 107*: 190–206.

Thoms, L.M., 1982. 'Trial excavation at St Ann's Lane, Perth', *Proc. Soc. Antiq. Scot., 112*: 437–54.

Thomson, R.G., Barton, K.J. and Jarvis, K., 1983. 'The pottery', in K. Jarvis, *Excavations in Christchurch 1969–80*: 53–68.

Thorn, J., 1979. 'The pottery', in Smith 1979: 154–83.

Trigger, B., 1972. 'Determinants of urban growth in pre-industrial societies', in P. Ucko *et al.* (eds.), *Man, Settlement and Urbanism*: 579–99.

Turner D.J., 1974. 'Medieval pottery kiln at Bushfield Shaw, Earlswood', *Surrey Archaeol. Collect., 70*: 47–55.

Turner, D.J. and Dunbar J.G., 1969–70. 'Breachacha Castle, Coll: excavations and field survey, 1965–8', *Proc. Soc. Antiq. Scot., 102*: 155–87.

van der Leeuw, S., 1975. 'Medieval pottery from Haarlem: a model', in J.G. Renaud (ed.), *Rotterdam Papers II*: 67–87.

van der Leeuw, S., 1976. *Studies in the Technology of Ancient Pottery*.

van der Leeuw, S., 1984. 'Dust to dust: a transformational view of the ceramic cycle', in S. van der Leeuw and A. Pritchard (eds.), *The Many Dimensions of Pottery*: 707–73.

Vidler, L., 1933. 'Medieval pottery and kilns found at Rye', *Sussex Archaeol. Collect.*, *74*: 45–64.

Vidler, L., 1936. 'Medieval pottery, tiles and kilns found at Rye. Final report', *Sussex Archaeol. Collect.*, *77*: 106–18.

Vince, A.G., 1977. 'Medieval and post medieval pottery', in C.J. Bond and A.M. Hunt, 'Recent archaeological work in Pershore', *Vale Evesham Hist. Soc. Res. Pap.*, *6*: 52–62.

Vince, A.G., 1979a. 'The medieval pottery', in B. Cunliffe, *Excavations in Bath 1950–1979*: 27–51.

Vince, A.G., 1979b. 'Appendix 1, the pottery', in C.M. Heighway, A.P. Garrod and A.G. Vince, 'Excavations at 1, Westgate Street, Gloucester 1975', *Medieval Archaeol.*, 23: 159–213.

Vince, A.G., 1981. 'The medieval pottery industry in southern England, 10th to 13th centuries', in H. Howard and E. Morris (eds.), *Production and Distribution; a Ceramic Viewpoint*, Brit. Archaeol. Rep. (Int. Ser.) 120: 309–22.

Vince, A.G., 1982. 'Post Roman pottery', in R.H. Leech and A.D. McWhirr, 'Excavations at St John's Hospital, Cirencester, 1971 and 1976', *Trans. Bristol Gloucestershire Archaeol. Soc.*, *100*: 191–210.

Vince, A.G., 1983. 'Medieval white-slipped jugs', *London Archaeol.*, *4*: 330–6.

Vince, A.G., 1984a. 'Summary of pottery from Ladybellegate Street excavations', in H. Hurst, 'The archaeology of Gloucester Castle: an introduction', *Trans. Bristol Gloucestershire Archaeol. Soc.*, *102*: 114–16.

Vince, A.G., 1984b. 'Late Saxon and medieval pottery in Gloucestershire', in A. Saville (ed.), *Archaeology in Gloucestershire: Essays Dedicated to Helen O'Neill and the Late Elsie Clifford*: 248–75.

Vince, A.G., 1984c. 'The use of petrology in the study of medieval ceramics', *Medieval Ceram.*, *8*: 31–45.

Vince, A.G., 1985a. 'The Saxon and medieval pottery of London: a review', *Medieval Archaeol.*, *29*: 25–93.

Vince, A.G., 1985b. 'The ceramic finds', in R. Shoesmith, *The Archaeology of Hereford*: 34–69.

Vince, A.G., forthcoming. 'The medieval pottery', in R. Shoesmith, *Excavations at Chepstow*.

Vyner, B.E., 1982. 'Vale fabric: a medieval pottery industry in Glamorgan', *Medieval and Later Pottery in Wales*, *5*: 31–43.

Wade, K., 1976. 'Excavations at Langhale, Kirstead', *E. Anglian Archaeol.*, *2*: 101–29.

Wade, K., 1980. 'The pottery', in P. Wade-Martins, 'Excavations in North Elmham Park 1967–72', *E. Anglian Archaeol.*, *9*: 413–78.

Wade-Martins, P., 1983. 'Two post-medieval earthenware pottery groups from Fulmodeston, Norfolk', *E. Anglian Archaeol.*, *19*.

Waterer, J.W., 1956. 'Leather', in C. Singer, E.J. Holmyard, A.R. Hall, and T.I. Williams (eds.), *A History of Technology*, vol. II: 284–310.

Waterman, D., 1953. 'A group of twelfth-century pottery and other finds from Knaresborough Castle', *Antiq. J.*, *33*: 211–13.

Watkins, J.G., forthcoming a. 'The pottery', in P. Armstrong, 'Excavations at Lurk Lane, Beverley', *Archaeol. J.*

Watkins, J.G., forthcoming b. 'The pottery', in P. Armstrong and B.S. Ayers, 'Excavations in High Street and Blackfriargate', *E. Riding Archaeol.*

Watkins, J.G. and Williams, R.A.H., 1983. 'An excavation in Highgate, Beverley, 1977', *E. Riding Archaeol., 7:* 71–84.

Watts, L. and Rahtz, P.A., 1985. *Mary Le Port Bristol: Excavations 1962–3.*

Webster, A., 1975. 'Pottery report', in Steane and Bryant 1975: 60–95.

Webster, G. and Dunning, G.C., 1960. 'A medieval pottery kiln at Audlem, Cheshire', *Medieval Archaeol., 4:* 109–25.

Webster, L.E. and Cherry, J., 1972. 'Medieval Britain in 1971', *Medieval Archaeol., 16:* 147–212.

Webster, L.E. and Cherry, J., 1973. 'Medieval Britain in 1972', *Medieval Archaeol., 17:* 138–88.

Webster, L.E. and Cherry, J., 1974. 'Medieval Britain in 1973', *Medieval Archaeol., 18:* 174–223.

Webster, L.E. and Cherry, J., 1978. 'Medieval Britain in 1977', *Medieval Archaeol., 22:* 142–88.

Webster, P.V. (ed.), 'The pottery', in *Llantrithyd: a Ringwork in South Glamorgan,* Cardiff Archaeol. Soc.: 23–45.

Weijs, L.J., van de Watering, C.J.J. and Slootmans, C.J.F., 1970. *Tussen Hete Vuren: techniek en produkt, familiebetrekkingen en archivalia van de Bergen op Zoomse potmakers.*

West, S.E., 1964. 'Excavations at Cox Lane (1958) and at the town defences, Shire Hall Yard, Ipswich (1959)', *Proc. Suffolk Inst. Archaeol. Hist., 29:* 233–303.

Whinney, R., 1981. 'Jack-o-Tooles Row, Boarhunt – a medieval kiln dump', *Proc. Hampshire Fld Club Archaeol. Soc., 37:* 41–8.

White, A.J., 1976. 'A medieval pottery bottle from Lincoln', *Lincolnshire Hist. Archaeol., 11:* 63.

White, A.J., 1977. 'Silverdale', and 'Kiln sites and documentary evidence in North Lancashire', in P.J. Davey (ed.), *Medieval Pottery from Excavations in the North West:* 108, 121.

White, A.J., 1984. 'Medieval fisheries in the Witham and its tributaries', *Lincolnshire Hist. Archaeol., 19:* 29–35.

White, L., 1962. *Medieval Technology and Social Change.*

Whitehouse, D., 1984. 'Kangan: a traditional pottery in southern Iran', *Medieval Ceram., 8:* 11–26.

Whitwell, J.B., 1966. 'Archaeological notes: Old Bolingbroke', *Lincolnshire Hist. Archaeol., 1:* 49.

Wildgoose, R.H., 1961. 'The defences of the pre-Conquest borough of Nottingham', *Trans. Thoroton Soc. Nottinghamshire, 65:* 19–26.

Williams, D.W., 1983. '16 Bell Street, Reigate', *Surrey Archaeol. Collect., 74:* 47–89.

Williams, D.W., 1984. 'Excavations at 43 High Street, Reigate, 1981', *Surrey Archaeol. Collect., 75:* 111–53.

Williams, J.H., 1974. 'A Saxo-Norman pit group from Northampton', *Northamptonshire Archaeol., 9:* 46–56.

Wilson, C.A., 1973. *Food and Drink in Britain.*

Wilson, D.M., 1985. *The Bayeux Tapestry.*

Wilson, D.M. and Hurst, D.G., 1961. 'Medieval Britain in 1960', *Medieval Archaeol., 5:* 309–39.

Wilson, D.M. and Hurst, D.G., 1962–3. 'Medieval Britain in 1961', *Medieval Archaeol., 6–7:* 306–49.

Wilson, D.M. and Hurst, D.G., 1964. 'Medieval Britain in 1962 and 1963', *Medieval Archaeol.*, *8*: 231–99.

Wilson, D.M. and Hurst, D.G., 1965. 'Medieval Britain in 1964', *Medieval Archaeol.*, *9*: 170–220.

Wilson, D.M. and Hurst, D.G., 1966. 'Medieval Britain in 1965', *Medieval Archaeol.*, *10*: 168–219.

Wilson, D.M. and Hurst, D.G., 1967. 'Medieval Britain in 1966', *Medieval Archaeol.*, *11*: 262–319.

Wilson, D.M. and Hurst, D.G., 1970. 'Medieval Britain in 1969', *Medieval Archaeol.*, *14*: 155–208.

Wilson, D.M. and Hurst, J.G., 1958. 'Medieval Britain in 1957', *Medieval Archaeol.*, *2*: 183–213.

Wilson, D.M. and Hurst, J.G., 1959. 'Medieval Britain in 1958', *Medieval Archaeol.*, *3*: 295–326.

Wilson, D.M. and Hurst, J.G., 1960. 'Medieval Britain in 1959', *Medieval Archaeol.*, *4*: 134–65.

Wilson, D.M. and Moorhouse, S., 1971. 'Medieval Britain in 1970', *Medieval Archaeol.*, *15*: 124–79.

Wilson, M., 1983. 'The pottery', in S.S. Frere and S. Stowe, *Excavations in the St George's Street and Burgate Street Areas*, Archaeology of Canterbury, vol. VII: 192–299.

Woodland, R., 1981. 'The pottery', in J.E. Mellor and T. Pearce, *The Austin Friars, Leicester*: 81–125.

Woodrow, K.J., 1971. 'Cistercian ware from Silcoates School, near Wakefield', *Post-Medieval Archaeol.*, *5*: 185–8.

Woodward, D., 1981. 'Wage rates and living standards in pre-industrial England', *Past Present*, *91*: 28–45.

Woodward, P.J., 1983. 'Wimborne Minster, Dorset – excavations in the town centre 1975–80', *Proc. Dorset Natur. Hist. Archaeol. Soc.*, *105*: 57–74.

Wrathmell, S., 1981. 'A medieval pottery kiln and wasters at Penhow, Gwent', *Medieval and Later Pottery in Wales*, *4*: 1–7.

Wrathmell, S. and S., 1976–7. 'Excavations at the Moat Site, Walsall 1975', *Trans. S. Staffordshire Archaeol. Hist. Soc.*, *18*: 29–46.

Yeoman, P.A., 1983. 'The medieval pottery', in D. Allen and C.H. Dalwood, 'Iron Age occupation, a Middle Saxon cemetery and twelfth to nineteenth century urban occupation: excavations in George Street, Aylesbury, 1981', *Rec. Buckinghamshire*, *25*: 20–9.

Yeoman, P.A., 1984–5. 'An early sixteenth century pottery and tile kiln at Brill, Buckinghamshire', *Bull. Experimental Firing Group*, *3*: 5–9.

Young, D., 1979. 'The Verwood potteries', *Proc. Dorset Natur. Hist. Archaeol. Soc.*, *101*: 103–20.

Youngs, S.M., Clark, J. and Barry, T.B., 1983. 'Medieval Britain and Ireland in 1982', *Medieval Archaeol.*, *27*: 161–229.

Note: Very common pottery forms including bowls, cooking pots, jugs, pans, pancheons, pipkins and pitchers are listed for Part One only. Wares, such as Humber ware, Mill Green ware etc., are not listed.

Index